# International Handbook of Corporate Communication

*by*

William V. Ruch

McFarland & Company, Inc., Publishers
*Jefferson, North Carolina, and London*

To
Carroll G. Parks
of Allentown, Pennsylvania,
who taught me

**British Library Cataloguing-in-Publication data available**

**Library of Congress Cataloguing-in-Publication Data**

Ruch, William V.
  *International handbook of corporate communication.*

  Bibliography: p. 457.
  Includes index.
  1. Communication in management.   2. Communication in
organizations.   I. Title.
HD30.3.R823   1989        658.4'5        88-43481

ISBN 0-89950-386-1 (lib. bdg. : 50# alk. paper) ∞

Printed in the United States of America

*McFarland & Company, Inc., Publishers*
  *Box 611, Jefferson, North Carolina 28640*

# Table of Contents

*List of Figures*   vi
*List of Tables*   viii
*Preface and Acknowledgments* ix
*Introduction*   1

**1. Communication in the Organization**   5
   Introduction   5
   The Information Age   5
   Culture   12
   Communication   19
   Intercultural Communication   29
   Notes   34

**2. North America**   35
   Introduction   35
   The United States   35
   A Survey   47
   Canada   48
   *Case Study: Dofasco, Inc.,*
   *Hamilton, Ontario 53; Case*
   *Study: Inco Limited, Toronto*
   *55; Case Study: Molson Com-*
   *panies, Ltd., Toronto 56*
   Notes   58

**3. Latin America**   59
   Introduction   59
   *Case Study: Cristaleria Peldar,*
   *Medellin, Colombia 67*
   Mexico   69

   **Central America**   77
   Belize   77
   Costa Rica   78
   El Salvador   80
   Guatemala   81
   Honduras   82
   Nicaragua   83
   Panama   84

*The Caribbean Islands*   86
   Barbados   86
   Dominican Republic   87
   Haiti   88
   Jamaica   89
   Trinidad and Tobago   90
*U.S. Territories*   91
   Puerto Rico   91
   Virgin Islands   92
*British Territories*   92
   Bahamas   92
   Bermuda   93
   British Virgin Islands   93
   French Antilles   93
   Netherlands Antilles   94

**South America**   94
   Argentina   95
   Bolivia   96
   Brazil   98
   Chile   100
   Colombia   102
   Ecuador   104
   French Guiana   105
   Guyana   106
   Paraguay   107
   Peru   108
   Suriname   110
   Uruguay   111
   Venezuela   112
   Notes   115

**4. Western Europe**   117

   **EEC Countries**   121
   Belgium   123
   Denmark   127
   *Case Study: Aalborg Portland*
   *131*
   France   133

*Case Study: Renault 139*
Greece     141
*Case Study: J.E. Condellis S.A.
144*
Ireland     145
*Case Study: Cement-Roadstone
Holdings PLC 148; Case Study:
Waterford Glass Group PLC 149*
Italy     149
Luxembourg     153
The Netherlands     154
*Case Study: Akzo 158*
Portugal     159
Spain     161
United Kingdom     168
*Case Study: Cadbury Schweppes
177; Case Study: Burmah Oil
Trading Limited 179; Case
Study: Jaguar 180; Case Study:
Rank Xerox 182; Case Study:
Unilever 183*
West Germany     184
*Case Study: BMW 193; Case
Study: Krupp 194; Case Study:
Viag 195*

**Other European Countries**     196
Austria     196
*Case Study: Austria Tabak 198*
Finland     200
*Case Study: Valmet 202*
Iceland     203
Liechtenstein     205
Norway     205
*Case Study: Norsk Data 208*
Sweden     210
*Case Study: Electrolux 213; Case
Study: Procordia 215*
Switzerland     216
*Case Study: Brown Boveri 218;
Case Study: Ciba-Geigy 219;
Case Study: Nestle Group 220*
Notes     222

**5. The Middle East**     225
Bahrain     243
Iran     246
Iraq     247
Israel     248
*Case Study: Israel Aircraft In-
dustries, Inc. 252*
Jordan     252
*Case Study: Alia—The Royal
Jordanian Airline 256*

Kuwait     256
Lebanon     258
Oman     259
Qatar     261
Saudi Arabia     262
Syria     264
Turkey     266
*Case Study: Rabak 269*
United Arab Emirates     269
Yemen Arab Republic (North
Yemen)     270
People's Democratic Republic of
Yemen (South Yemen)     271
Notes     272

**6. Africa**     273

**Muslim Africa**     280
Algeria     280
Chad     282
Djibouti     283
Egypt     284
The Gambia     287
Guinea     288
Guinea-Bissau     289
Libya     290
Mali     292
Mauritania     293
Morocco     294
Niger     295
Senegal     297
Somalia     298
Sudan     299
Tunisia     300

**The Non-Muslim North**     301
Benin     301
Burkina Faso     303
Ethiopia     304
Ghana     305
Ivory Coast     307
Liberia     308
Nigeria     310
Sierra Leone     312
Togo     313

**The Central Region**     314
Burundi     314
Cameroon     315
Central African Republic     316
Congo     317
Equatorial Guinea     318
Gabon     319

Kenya    320
*Case Study: East African*
*Breweries, Inc. 323*
Rwanda    325
Tanzania    326
Uganda    328

**The Southern Region**    329
Angola    329
Botswana    330
Lesotho    331
Malawi    331
Mozambique    332
Namibia    333
South Africa    334
*Case Study: Barlow Rand*
*Limited 337; Case Study: Sasol*
*Limited 342*
Swaziland    343
Zaire    344
Zambia    346
Zimbabwe    347
*Case Study: African Distillers*
*Limited 348; Case Study: Rio*
*Tinto 350; Case Study: Zim-*
*babwe Alloys Limited 353*
Notes    353

**7. Asia and the Pacific**    355

**Pacific Rim Countries**    357
Hong Kong    357
Indonesia    363
*Case Study: Pertamina 365*
Japan    367
*Case Study: Mazda Motor Cor-*
*poration 377*
Malaysia    379
*Case Study: Malaysian Airline*
*System 382*
The Philippines    382
*Case Study: Atlantic, Gulf and*
*Pacific Company of Manila, Inc.*
*385*
Singapore    387
*Case Study: Far Eastern Lev-*
*ingston Shipbuilding Ltd. 389*

*Case Study: Singapore Airlines*
*390*
South Korea    392
*Case Study: Daewoo Corpora-*
*tion 396*
Taiwan    397
Thailand    400

**Other Asian Countries**    404
Bangladesh    404
Burma    406
India    407
Pakistan    410
Sri Lanka    412

**The Pacific Region**    413
Australia    413
*Case Study: BHP 418; Case*
*Study: CSR Limited 419*
New Zealand    421
*Case Study: Air New Zealand*
*423; Case Study: Cable Price*
*Downer Limited 423*
Notes    424

**8. Survey Results: Comparison**
**and Discussion**    427
Introduction    427
Formal Communication System
430

**9. Communication *Is* the Organi-**
**zation — Worldwide**    445

*Appendix:* General Motors Cor-
poration Communication
Policy    451
*Bibliography*    457
Books    457
Periodicals    464
Newspapers    468
Miscellaneous    470

*Index*    475

# List of Figures

1. Japanese advertising on a Spanish matador's uniform.    2
2. The Information Age has changed office decor and tools.    8
3. Sony Corporation (San Diego) employees in morning exercises.    17
4. Improved communication technology has brought the world's people closer together.    19
5. Formal communication in American corporations.    43
6. Formal communication in Canadian corporations.    54
7. Employee communication program at Molson Companies, Ltd., Toronto, Canada.    57
8. Formal communication in Latin American corporations.    68
9. Communication system at Aalborg Portland Company.    132
10. Excellent facilities like these at L'Oreal help make meetings productive.    139
11. Corporate communication system of Renault Corporation.    141
12. Communication system of J.A. Condellis Company, Athens, Greece.    145
13. Corporate communication system of Cement Roadstone Holdings PLC.    148
14. Corporate communication system of Akzo Corporation.    158
15. Communication system of the United Kingdom Corporation.    175
16. At British Aerospace, a series of seminars has been held between employees and the Chairman (Sir Austin Pearce, standing) to exchange views.    179
17. Works Councils in Hoechst AG, Frankfurt am Main, West Germany.    187
18. Personal contact is important in most European firms, including this German one.    190
19. Communication in the West German corporation.    193
20. Employees of VIAG Aktiengesellschaft, Berlin/Bonn, West Germany, confer in the field.    195
21. Communication system at Austria Tabak.    199
22. Communication system of Norsk Data.    209
23. The Hegira year 1409 compared to the Gregorian year 1988–89.    228
24. The market in Tangier, Morocco.    237
25. Employees at Israel Aircraft Industries work on sophisticated design programs.    250

26. The communication system of Israel Aircraft Industries, Inc. 251
27. In Jordan women have achieved a level of equality with men that is unusual in the Arab world, as proved by this new woman pilot. 254
28. The communication system of Alia—the Royal Jordanian Airline. 255
29. Communication system of Rabak Corporation. 268
30. Communication system of East African Breweries, Ltd., Kenya. 324
31 and 32. Both outings and study are part of the new Barlow Rand Limited People Interaction Enhancement Programme. 338
33. Communication system of Sasol Limited, Johannesburg. 342
34. Communication system of African Distillers Limited, Harare, Zimbabwe. 349
35. Communication system of the Rio Tinto Corporation. 351
36. Communication system of Zimbabwe Alloys Limited. 352
37. Communication system of Pertamina, Jakarta, Indonesia. 366
38. Office arrangements like this at Nihon Chukuko Company, Ltd., of Tokyo allow easy interactions among all employees. 371
39. The communication system of the Japanese corporation. 374
40. Communication in Mazda Motor Corporation, Hiroshima, Japan. 378
41. The communication system of Malaysian Airlines System, Kuala Lumpur, Malaysia. 381
42. The communication system of Atlantic, Gulf and Pacific Company of Manila, Inc. 386
43. The communication system of Daewoo Corporation, Seoul, Korea. 396
44. Communication is no problem for these young Chinese workers. 399
45. A policy of Siam Cement Company, Limited, is to provide training to employees at all levels. 403
46. Communication system of BHP Corporation, Melbourne, Australia. 418
47. Communication system of CSR Limited, Sydney, Australia. 420
48. Communication system of Air New Zealand. 422

# List of Tables

1. The Information Age and Industrial Age Compared.    6
2. Cultural Universals.    13
3. Americans' Views of Themselves and Foreigners' Views of Americans Compared.    37
4. Communication Practices in the Latin American Firm.    68
5. Some Communication Practices in the Belgian Corporation.    126
6. Some Communication Practices in the Danish Corporation.    131
7. Some Communication Practices in the French Corporation.    140
8. Some Communication Practices in the Greek Corporation.    144
9. Some Communication Practices in the Irish Corporation.    147
10. Some Communication Practices in the Italian Corporation.    152
11. Some Communication Practices in the Dutch Corporation.    157
12. Some Communication Practices in the Portuguese Corporation.    161
13. Some Communication Practices in the Spanish Corporation.    167
14. British Business Terms and Their American English Translations.    174
15. Some Communication Practices in the British Corporation.    178
16. Communication in the German Corporation.    192
17. Some Communication Practices in the Austrian Corporation.    198
18. Some Communication Practices in the Finnish Corporation.    203
19. Some Communication Practices in the Norwegian Corporation.    208
20. Some Communication Practices in the Swedish Corporation.    213
21. The Peoples of Islam.    227
22. Differences in U.S. and Middle East Management.    234
23. Some Communication Practices in the Arab Corporation.    242
24. Managerial Gaps Between Developing Countries and the United States.    243
25. Some Communication Practices of the African Firm.    280
26. Some Communication Practices in the Hong Kong Corporation.    362
27. Japanese Management Trends of the 1990s.    370
28. Some Communication Practices in the Japanese Corporation.    376
29. Comparison of Americans and Filipinos.    384
30. Some Communication Practices in the South Korean Corporation.    395
31. Some Communication Practices in the Australian Corporation.    417
32. Survey Results, by Region of the World.    429
33. Communication Channels Used by Foreign Firms.    431

# Preface and
# Acknowledgments

How can you discuss any subject that includes the entire nonsocialist world in a book of this size? You do it by being very specific about the topic being covered, by selecting the best sources, both primary and secondary, and by admitting that what this book hopes to do for the reader is only a beginning of an intensive, extended study of this most important subject.

I have travelled throughout the Soviet Union, Asia and Europe, have "touched down" in Africa and Latin America, and have taught for two years in Japan and for one year in Europe. To the old saying that people are the same everywhere I would add the obvious fact that their cultures are different. Even the simplest interaction between me and a member of any one of these countries contained the seed of misunderstanding. For example, while driving from Italy to Spain in 1984, travelling from the location of one semester's teaching to the next, I stopped at the toll booth just outside of Barcelona. To be sure I was on the right road, I asked the attendant "Madrid?" while pointing ahead of me. "Eh?" he responded, so I repeated with rising inflection, "Madrid?" motioning forward with my hand again. Still he didn't understand. Nobody was waiting behind me, so I pointed on the map the country's capital. "Ah, Ma-da-drid," the man exclaimed, flapping the "r" and smiling in great relief with a touch of embarrassment for me. I had pronounced a word in a way he was not used to because we don't flap our r's in English, and the result was a lack of communication. The effort was worth it, however, because I had not been on the right road to Madrid.

I hope that this book will save you from similar experiences in intercultural communicating in general and in corporate communicating in particular.

My deepest indebtedness for help received in the writing of this book must go to the many business persons from around the world who participated in my study of corporate communication. Many of them, from countries where English is not spoken natively, ignored the presumption of my communicating in my language, not theirs, and responded, also in my language. I acknowledge the years of study it took for them to achieve the second-language fluency that allowed them to do that and appreciate their willingness to use their skills in my behalf. Foreign embassy staffs in this country and the staffs of United States consulates and embassies abroad were unstinting in giving me aid, telephoning my home when they required additional information to be sure they were providing the right data.

I also used the large body of literature on the subject of life and work in foreign countries. The United States government series, *A Country Study/Area Handbook,* constantly being revised and updated, provided much useful background information. Similarly materials of the David M. Kennedy Center for International Studies at Brigham Young University were extremely helpful—"culturegrams" on practically every country in the world and booklets on selected regions and countries. The East-West Center in Honolulu has a wide variety of materials available on the Pacific area. The Hong Kong and Shanghai Bank sent me free of charge its slick, professional "Business Profile Series" which filled in crucial details not found elsewhere. The SRI Business Intelligence Program provides a "Doing Business in" series of booklets covering business and protocol practices in many countries. Numerous publications of Intercultural Press of Yarmouth, Maine, particularly its "Update" series, was of considerable help in this work. The output of several other publishing houses specializing in international communication and business topics was similarly helpful in this study: Gale Research Company of Detroit, Facts on File of New York City, Sage of Beverly Hills, and Inter-Crescent Press of Garden Grove, California. Their specific works are listed in the Bibliography.

Finally, anyone doing a study on this subject must acknowledge with gratitude the insightful work of anthropologist Edward T. Hall, particularly that in his book *Beyond Culture.* It has helped clarify so much of the subject of intercultural communicating for so many of us.

# Introduction

Of all the possible occasions in life when a lack of knowledge handicaps individuals, not knowing how to communicate across cultures in attempting to transact business is surely among the costliest. Consider the consequence, for example, of not knowing that the word "billion" in the United States means thousands of times more than in some other countries, that "yes" in certain countries may actually mean "no," or that the increased "heat" of the American hard sell may actually douse the flame of interest in the minds of some foreigners.

Travelling Americans would hardly think that doing business abroad presents much of a problem; American products are on display almost anywhere that one goes. American television programs with foreign-language dubbing can be seen in almost any foreign country. So what's the problem with regard to exporting American products and services?

Most of the American entry into foreign markets occurred at a time when competition was nearly nonexistent. Abundant evidence exists to prove that that is not the case anymore.

During one vacation period, for instance, the author visited Portugal to experience the culture and to compare it with the Spanish culture. A visit to the Portuguese bullfight near Lisbon one evening showed it to be very different from the Spanish bullfight. In Portugal the matador is on horseback; in Spain he is on foot. In Portugal the bull's horns are covered with a type of canvas and he is not killed. The horse and rider move adroitly and rapidly around the ring, avoiding the pursuing bull by inches, enabling the matador to thrust a spear into the bull's back. The top of the spear comes off and attached to it is a flag that the matador waves triumphantly as the horse prances around the edge of the ring, relishing the crowd's cheers.

About the third time this happened, a red design was discernible on the flag and as the matador passed the audience could see that it was the three-diamond logo of the Mitsubishi Company. Posters on the walls of the bull ring proclaimed that Japanese company sponsors of the event! The Japanese today are sparing nothing in terms of money or imagination to get their message across all around the world. Since then, the picture in Figure 1 appeared in the newspaper; as you can see, it shows a Spanish bull fighter whose uniform displays the name of another Japanese company.

The Rastro in Madrid is reputed to be one of the world's largest flea markets. For block after block merchants set up stands near the city's down-

**Figure 1. Japanese advertising on a Spanish matador's uniform. (AP/Wide World Photos, New York.)**

town area each Sunday. Crowds are so huge that at times one can't even move, and at every second block or so one sees Japanese agricultural products being demonstrated by the Spanish to crowds of interested onlookers. Japanese marketing practices today, like most of their products, are impressive.

One wonders, while living in Europe, why Americans have not kept up in foreign markets and what we need to do to catch up. Such thinking always settles on the same theme: we Americans have to learn to communicate in a way that goes beyond the kind of talking to presold consumers we could depend on in the past. That entails really knowing potential foreign consumers and what they want and how they expect to be addressed — skills American business persons haven't had to worry about before. This book seeks to help Americans learn more about foreign cultures and the preferred communication practices within those cultures, particularly in their organizations.

Sources of information used in this study were (1) a survey of the Fortune International 500 companies as well as selected companies from third-world nations which were poorly represented on or excluded from the Fortune list, (2) an intensive literature search, (3) letters to foreign embassies and consulates in Washington and New York City, (4) letters to American consulates in foreign countries asking for help and direction, (5) visits to a few embassies and consulates in New York City and (6) the author's own worldwide travel experience.

The decision was made at the beginning of this study to cover only the world outside the communist or socialist countries. When the author visited the Luch watch factory in Minsk during a tour some years ago in the Soviet Union, the only communicating going on was the use of posters. The plant had two huge posters on the walls, one listing those workers who had made quota and the other listing those who didn't. The message was clear: if you are on the wrong one, you had better work harder. When asked what would happen to a worker who refused to at least try or who didn't come to work at all, our Russian guide thought for a long minute as though the suggestion were preposterous and then said, "The police would get involved."

Although Soviet leader Mikhail Gorbachev's *glasnost* campaign is showing signs of changing the attitudes implicit in the above — workers are starting to be paid by output rather than by time present — the country has a long, long way to go to reach the point where the proper communication techniques make a difference. So communist countries are omitted from this book, with the single exception of Nicaragua. Discussing Latin America without Nicaragua would have been like talking about the Seven Dwarfs without "Sleepy"; you would then have had only six dwarfs.

The scope of this book is unavoidably broader than just communication. It is impossible to discuss business communication in foreign countries without also discussing their business organizations, which in turn requires a knowledge of the cultures in which the organizations operate. So this book discusses as much of the culture of a country as needed to introduce it adequately to the reader and proceeds then to organizations and corporate communication in this sequence: the land, the people, a brief history, the economy and organizational communication.

It became apparent during the work that two regions of the world are so similar as to allow greater regionalizing of discussion than was possible in the rest. Latin America and the Middle East, therefore, are discussed extensively as regions and less thoroughly as individual countries. In other areas, countries were necessarily considered on more of an individual basis.

The reader is expected to use the information provided to interpret conditions in any particular country. For instance, the percentage of workers engaged in agriculture as opposed to industry or services provides some indication of the stage of development of a country's economy — Agricultural, Industrial or Information Age, primarily. In a country with a very low literacy rate and a mostly nonfunctioning telephone system, visiting foreign business persons have little alternative but to communicate personally with large groups of workers.

A study of communication programs will show management's attitude toward employee communication. A downward system that is better-developed than the upward system — and in some countries the differences are startling — provides insights into management's communication attitude.

The content of this book should be viewed as a start in the long process of learning about foreign countries and cultures to the point where business persons can function in them in the same successful and competent manner as they do in their own.

# 1. Communication in the Organization

## Introduction

Using a felt-tip pen to draw additional boxes and arrows on pre-prepared transparencies, a speaker at the 1987 International Conference of the Association for Business Communication explained in meticulous detail how thinking about corporate communication has changed in the decade that she has been teaching the subject. With the concurrence of her business-college colleagues in a large, prestigious, midwestern university, she now presents communication as another function of management, along with planning, organizing, staffing, directing and controlling. As the author discussed with her afterwards, however, her analysis seemed more descriptive of what we need than what we have in many organizations and still the approach is too narrow. In this Information Age our thinking about communication in organizations must be that communication *is* the organization, communication *is* management.

Imagine any organization without communication, if you can. The definition of "organization" presupposes communication: An organization is people working together to achieve some agreed-upon objectives. How could you agree upon the objectives much less work together to achieve them without communicating? The whole world is beginning to understand what the Japanese have known for a long time: the most important element of any organization is not the physical plant nor the technology nor the product nor the profit but the personnel, and dealing with personnel requires communication. Extend the organization across national borders, cultures and languages, and the importance of communication competency increases exponentially.

This chapter discusses some subjects important for creating successful worldwide communication programs: the Information Age, culture, communication and intercultural communication.

## The Information Age

Following a long industrial era, the world is experiencing the rapid growth of the Information Age as the third great transformation in our planetary pattern of living. Our ancestors learned to grow their own food around 8000 B.C.,

## Table 1. The Information Age and Industrial Age Compared

| *Industrial Age* | *Information Age* |
|---|---|
| **SOCIETY** | |
| Total of human knowledge doubles every ten years | Total of human knowledge doubles every year |
| Based on mechanization | Based on computerization |
| Separate national economic structures | Unified worldwide economic structure |
| Developing countries play only marginal role in worldwide economic activity | Developing countries participate in worldwide economic structure by taking over basic industries |
| Data bases numerous and scattered | Worldwide data base provides best, most current information available |
| Information shared worldwide by delayed transmission | Instantaneously shared information worldwide by satellites |
| **CORPORATIONS** | |
| Control based on supervision | Control based on feedback |
| Value increased by labor | Value increased by knowledge |
| Foundation for work is profit | Foundation for work is systematic acquisition of information |
| Information acquired as needed | Information central to operation |
| Communication based on "need to know" | Communication is basic function |
| **MANAGEMENT AND EMPLOYEES** | |
| Manager a decision maker | Manager an information processor |
| Production workers predominate | "Knowledge workers" predominate |
| Emphasis on total organization | Emphasis on small groups and individuals |
| Requires people who obey orders | Requires resourceful and individualistic people who accept responsibility and are capable of using all their skills |
| Education for definite period of 12 or 16 years | Lifelong education |

initiating the Agricultural Age which has evolved to its present state in which only 3 percent of all American workers are in agriculture. With the invention of the steam engine in the eighteenth century, the Industrial Age began in England and swept across Europe and the rest of the world. Now the Industrial Age is on the downturn of its 300-year cycle, by the end of which only a predicted 3 percent — instead of the present 30 percent — of all American workers will be engaged in manufacturing.

The Information Age was in place in America by 1956, when white-collar workers outnumbered blue-collar workers for the first time: more workers were dealing with information than were producing goods. In the following year, Russia launched Sputnik, pushing the new Information Age to worldwide dimensions. Life in the fully developed Information Age will be almost totally different; Table 1 lists some of the differences. The rate of change is increasing, and so is the magnitude of those changes.

Broad social changes that the Information Age is bringing include accelerated accumulation of knowledge — to the point where it will be doubling every year by 1995. Around 1950, total knowledge worldwide was said by some to be doubling every ten years; around 1970 it was every five years.

Based on computerization instead of mechanization, the Information Age is also changing the worldwide economy from separate domestic markets to a worldwide, integrated market in which developing countries participate fully. That trend is facilitated by a similar merging of individual data bases into one international data base that will provide the latest information on any subject.

Information Age corporations differ from their predecessors in many respects. Managers maintain control through feedback instead of supervision. Value is based on the accumulation of information rather than profit, and that information becomes central to the Information Age corporation rather than being gathered as required. Communication in such an organization would naturally be a basic function instead of an extra something based on employees' "need to know."

Managers in Information Age corporations will serve as information processors more than decision makers, and employees as knowledge workers instead of production workers. These corporations will require individualistic people who accept responsibility readily and apply all of their skills. The office for many employees will be portable computers with frequent contact to a highly automated headquarters building virtually devoid of secretaries or middle managers; already the office has changed as illustrated by Figure 2. Dealing with constant change will require an open, flexible mind that is opportunity-oriented. Employees who merely obey orders will be left behind in favor of those who pursue education lifelong to meet the continuing challenges of an evolving environment.

The satellite permits top executives to think globally, allowing clear telephone conversations with almost anyone anywhere. Ironically and unfortunately, because of the colonial past, corporate executives in developing countries in Latin America and Africa often can hear associates in foreign countries as though they were just across the street, but they hear those across the street

**Figure 2. The Information Age has changed office decor and tools. (Xerox Corporation, Stamford, Conn.)**

as though they were in another hemisphere. Facsimile equipment permits business people to transmit not only messages but also drawings worldwide.

By the next century, electronic media in a corporation's centralized communication system will connect offices and plants worldwide, allowing fast, flexible and cheap transferral of messages. Cordless telephones will become powerful computer phones able to do immediate translations of foreign language conversations into English and vice versa. Without an up-to-date communication system, companies will lose business.

Future organizations will be concerned about "information impacts" to the same extent that present organizations worry about environmental and social impacts. Corporations will be viewed as information producers in addition to economic producers. The result will be more competition to control information, more demand for open accounting and more pressure for truth in advertising and lending.

## Worldwide Economy

The most important aspect of the Information Age for the country and the world is the new worldwide economy. The world's 169 or so countries are locked in a closed system of economic interdependence with most of them having at least one asset that some other country lacks. No nation is totally self-reliant.[1] Already the facts are startling. Some 80 percent of American industry faces international competition with roughly a third of corporate profits coming from international business.[2] About 93,000 United States firms engage in international trade, and 25 percent of them maintain offices abroad.[3] Among the largest United States companies, some derive over 35 percent of their revenues from international trade.[4] Every billion dollars' worth of exports create 25,000 new jobs, our reason for taking the international marketplace seriously; nevertheless, at the present time, exports account for only 1.5 percent of the American gross national product.[5] It is clear that cross-cultural awareness is no longer optional.[6] We must study how business manners, methods and motivation differ from one region to another, one country to another.

International interdependency is best illustrated by events such as the formation of OPEC and the subsequent worldwide oil crisis. The "greenhouse" effect, depletion of the ozone layer, and air and ocean pollution are worldwide problems, as is the growing worldwide AIDS epidemic. No longer can a country contain its national crises, such as the Chernobyl disaster, within its borders; instead, each nation is obligated to protect international interests. The Soviet information service, in withholding information about the nuclear catastrophe, failed the world, particularly the country's own neighbors, miserably. Our few, faltering attempts to explore outer space also emphasize the point that earth's inhabitants are or should be unified. For further proof, examine trade and investment patterns of the major developed countries for their international quality.

In Europe, GEC (Britain) and Philips (the Netherlands) are merging their medical technology divisions; SGS (Italy) and Thomson (France) are merging their chip operations; Bertlesmann (Germany) and C$^{ie}$ Luxembourgeoise de Télédiffusion (Luxembourg) have entered a joint venture in European television.[7]

This new interdependence necessitates fundamental changes in the way we all do business. As one writer has said, it no longer makes sense to say *"Your end of the boat is sinking,"* because we are all in the same boat.[8] When the New York stock market declined sharply in 1987, similar drops occurred in Toronto, London, Tokyo, Hong Kong, Seoul and Melbourne.

As the realization grows that all human lives are intertwined, Americans are recognizing also that we communicate poorly across cultures and that the survival of our economic system depends on our learning to do so quickly and well. Extracting crucial information from customer companies and even foreign subsidiaries requires skill and a strategy adapted to each country. The barriers of language and cultural differences must be factored into these strategies by managers who take a global perspective, often for the first time.

For Americans, this new competition represents a drastic change of status from secure economic superiority to insecure competitive equality. In the past, American technology in many fields had no competition, so foreign buyers had no choice but to "buy American." International business expertise was unimportant to American business persons whose products sold themselves, usually after negotiations willingly conducted in English. That is no longer the case, and it is not a change that Americans are adapting to easily. "Today, most businesses feel the pinch of international competition directly—either from foreigners invading their home market or from the need to expand internationally. Quality management based on real knowledge and skills is now considered essential just to stay in the competitive game, let alone succeed."[9] The Japanese are already speaking about a world in which the United States is the world food supplier, the Far East the world supplier of hardware and software, and Europe the cultural museum of the world.[10]

Information Age managers must be much more culturally sensitive than their predecessors with a much greater understanding of communication as it takes place in their own work setting as well as between cultures. According to a Canadian study, the essential qualities of an international manager are two-way communication, empathy, respect, personal knowledge orientation, openness, role integration, tolerance for ambiguity and persistence.[11] It's interesting that the first item on the list is two-way communication and most of the others relate to communication.

Global strategic planning requires the kind of international management information system that few American companies now have. Today's global manager is "cosmopolitan, effective as an intercultural communicator and negotiator, creates cultural synergy, and leads cultural change, especially, at work, in organizations and on project teams."[12] Most modern American managers still require a great deal of training to arrive at a point where they will be successful in international markets. The Business Council for International Understanding has estimated that persons dealing in international markets who go abroad without cross-cultural preparation have a failure rate of from 33 to 66 percent compared to only 2 percent for those with such training.[13]

An excellent description of the demands being put on international managers and how they might handle them was provided by Robert T. Moran in his column "Cross-Cultural Contact" in the British publication *International Management*. He quotes Yo Miyoshi, president of H.B. Fuller Japan Company in Tokyo, as saying that dealing in international markets is like handling two swords at the same time: "When I discuss something with the head office in the United States, I try to be Western. But when I deal with my people in the company here, I am Oriental or Japanese." Moran then presents this list of words which, he says, could be used to describe an international manager and asks the reader to circle those which describe himself or herself:

> assertive, energetic, decisive, ambitious, confident, aggressive, quick, competitive, impatient, impulsive, quick-tempered, intelligent, excitable, informal, versatile, persuasive, imaginative, original, witty, colorful, calm, easygoing, good-natured, tactful, unemotional, good listener, inhibited, shy, absent-minded, cautious, methodical, timid, lazy, procrastinator, like responsibility, resourceful, individualist, broad interests, limited interests, good team-worker, like to work alone, sociable, cooperative, quiet, easily distracted, serious, idealistic, ethnocentric, cynical, conscientious, flexible, mature, dependable, honest, sincere, reliable, loyal, adaptable, curious

Using the right qualities skillfully is using one sword, says Moran, and he suggests that next the reader reexamine the list and mark the words that he or she feels foreign associates would look for in him or her. The differences between the two lists are the two swords. The second sword is the one we are expected to carry by foreigners.[14] Doing business abroad requires a style shift that is based on knowledge of foreign business practices which allows us to compete anywhere anytime.

To date, American business persons have tried to use the same sword abroad that we use at home. We have approached customers, colleagues and employees with an ignorance that would be unthinkable, even impossible, at home. We have tried to transact business with foreigners without understanding who they are, what they want, how they view the world, how their corporations work. For example, imposing the American-style merit system abroad may be an intolerable affront to a respected, established seniority system. American self-reliance and independence tend to offend the sensibilities of foreigners who stress family and community responsibility and whose friends, family, tribe or employer are valued as social insurance. A Kenyan woman, discussing why her country has the world's highest population-growth rate and will probably continue to have into the future, explained that women want children as a source of happiness in their marriages and that parents have an average of eight children as old-age insurance. Socially, having children indicates responsible citizenship. Imagine the challenge of introducing population control measures in that culture!

The literature contains innumerable examples of failed attempts to transact business abroad with only one sword — using the same techniques abroad that work domestically. Americans still expect others to speak English when we are in their countries and to behave as we do, giving the clear impression that we consider ourselves superior to them. One multinational company tried to sell baby food in Africa by using on the jar its regular label showing a baby. The local population interpreted that to mean the jar contained ground-up babies.[15]

A telephone company tried to "go Latin" in a commercial by employing Puerto Ricans in which the wife said to her husband: "Run downstairs and phone Mary and tell her we'll be a little late." The commercial contained two major cultural flaws: Latin wives seldom dare order their husbands around and almost no Latin would feel it necessary to phone to warn of tardiness since it is more or less expected.[16]

A British supervisor of a bridge-building project in Nigeria was shocked when his workers refused to continue the project after he had asked them to choose their own team leader. Although he knew that his workers were from different tribes, he didn't realize that the rivalry was so great as to bring the work to a halt.[17]

American managers, so adept at using one sword, must develop the kind of ambidexterity that Miyoshi recommends, and they must do it quickly.

# Culture

Americans believe that learning to do business worldwide begins with studying organizations in other countries and how they work, but systems theory says that understanding what goes on inside the firms requires understanding what is happening outside them. The culture and economy within which a firm operates strongly influence corporate practices so that managers in different cultures make different assumptions about management and the organization. These assumptions shape different value systems and translate into corresponding managerial and organizational practices which reinforce the original assumptions.[18] Learning to communicate internationally, therefore, begins with studying other cultures in the world.

"Culture" is defined as collective programming of the mind. Every culture provides the individual with a sense of identity, regulation of behavior, understanding of one's place in the scheme of things, and the opportunity to transmit this knowledge to subsequent generations. Culture is predominantly in our minds, not something external to human beings with an existence of its own. Culture is the sum of everything we have learned as part of our environments. We carry "mental programs" which develop in the family and are reinforced in schools and churches as well as through informal groups such as peers. In growing up, we learn the values, attitudes and assumptions about life that our culture teaches. Culture teaches what behavior is approved and disapproved, which needs are emphasized, what we believe and how we behave. Every person alive is the product of culture.

Cultural universals are aspects of life that all cultures address, many of them listed on Table 2. Milton Rokeach in *The Nature of Human Values* writes that "all men everywhere possess the same values to different degrees" and that "the antecedents of human values can be traced to culture, society and its institutions and personality."[19] How different cultures respond to those are cultural variations.

Anthropologists say that cultures differ because various people have had to deal with diverse circumstances to meet their human needs: different climates, different resources and different terrain. For example, people in some cultures refrain from putting mouth on mouth, at least in public, and the female breast — an organ for providing food for the nursing infant — has no sexual significance. In Japan, the back of a woman's neck is considered the most alluring part of her anatomy. Also in Japan, swimmers don't enter the

## Table 2. Cultural Universals

| | | |
|---|---|---|
| Age grading | Food taboos | Music |
| Athletic sports | Funeral rites | Mythology |
| Bodily adornment | Games | Numerals |
| Calendar | Gestures | Obstetrics |
| Cleanliness training | Gift giving | Penal sanctions |
| Community organization | Government | Personal names |
| Cooking | Greetings | Population policy |
| Cooperative labor | Hairstyles | Postnatal care |
| Cosmology | Hospitality | Pregnancy usages |
| Courtship | Housing hygiene | Property rights |
| Dancing | Incest taboos | Propitiation of super- |
| Decorative art | Inheritance rules | natural beings |
| Divination | Joking | Puberty customs |
| Division of labor | Kingroups | Religious rituals |
| Dream interpretation | Kinship nomenclature | Residence rules |
| Education | Language | Sexual restrictions |
| Eschatology | Law | Soul concepts |
| Ethics | Luck superstitions | Status differentiation |
| Ethnobotany | Magic | Surgery |
| Etiquette | Marriage | Tool making |
| Faith healing | Mealtimes | Trade |
| Family | Medicine | Visiting |
| Feasting | Modesty concerning | Weaning |
| Fire making | natural functions | Weather control |
| Folklore | Mourning | |

*(Source: George P. Murdock, "The Common Denominator of Cultures,"* The Science of Man in the World Crises, *ed. Ralph Linton [New York: Columbia University Press, 1945], pp. 123–42.)*

water without first doing their exercises; news reports often attribute drownings to the victims' failure to do their exercises.

As this is being written, a conflict is growing between the large Hindu Indian population and other residents of Jersey City, New Jersey. Both blacks and whites complain to television reporters that the Indians don't maintain an acceptable level of cleanliness. "There are roaches and mice all over those houses," one of them said. Indians interviewed protest that the animosity stems from jealousy others feel about the Indians' business success which has followed diligence and hard work. As for the roaches and mice, they explain that, as Hindus, they don't believe in killing any of God's creatures.

All human beings share the same physiological needs which furnish a basis for culture. Everyone requires food, water, sex gratification, rest, sleep, and freedom from danger and pain. Motivational theorist Abraham Maslow said that humans satisfy their needs in a definite order: physiological, security, social, self-esteem and esteem of others, and self-actualization. People in all cultures find their own ways to satisfy these needs. Those living at the survival level value the gathering of food and seeking adequate clothing and shelter; the Kalahari Bushmen of Africa, for example, search all day for food. Those pursuing a higher level value money, job titles, and law and order. This theory is helpful for understanding the reward preferences employees have in different countries.

In one study, managers from 14 countries were asked to rank five needs: security, social, esteem, autonomy and self-actualization. In every country, needs for self-actualization were ranked most important. The French, Japanese and U.S. managers felt strongest about it, but the differences among all of the countries were negligible. Managers thus put the highest priority on opportunities for growth, realizing their potential and worthwhile accomplishment. Needs for autonomy were ranked second by most but third by some managers. Swedish, German and Japanese managers felt strongest about these needs; Danish and Norwegian managers attached slightly less than average importance to autonomy needs.

Ranked third were security needs; however, respondents disagreed more in their views than with the previous two items. Managers in Spain and Germany regarded security needs as more important than in other countries; French and American managers gave them the least importance. Social needs ranked fourth for most countries, though they were third for the United States and Japan and fifth for Germany and Italy. German managers ranked social needs especially low both in relation to the other needs and to the other countries. Finally, esteem needs were ranked last in all countries except Italy, where they were second in importance after self-actualization, and Germany, where they were fourth. The Danish managers gave them an especially low rating.

The importance of the findings lies in the similarity of the results across countries and cultures. Spanish managers are not much different from German or English or Japanese managers in the ratings they give needs. The similarities were greatest with the two needs that were ranked highest by most countries: self-actualization and autonomy. The study indicates that managers in different countries, at least with regard to these needs, are relatively unaffected by their cultural environment.

The results can be grouped by countries: (1) Nordic-European (West Germany, Denmark, Sweden and Norway); (2) Latin-European (Spain, France, Belgium and Italy); (3) Anglo-American (United States and United Kingdom); (4) developing (Argentina, Chile and India); and (5) Japanese. The results included the fact that developing-country managers had a higher deficiency of fulfilling all needs than did all other groups. Anglo-American managers ranked social needs higher than managers from other developed countries, but felt the least deficiency in the fulfillment of this need. Both the Latin-European and developing managers showed considerably more dissatisfaction in social need fulfillment than the other areas, thus indicating a greater opportunity for using status, social esteem and prestige as employee motivators in those countries.

Considering all of the needs together, managers in the northern European countries, especially the Scandinavian countries, are more satisfied than those in the southern European countries, especially Spain and Italy. Almost a perfect correlation exists, in fact, between the overall degree of satisfaction and the median latitude of European countries. Why and what is the reason that

Japan's profile is so unusual in that they give almost equal importance to all five needs? The answer seems to lie in social-cultural factors, especially in the role of the manager in occupational status hierarchies and the role of business in the daily affairs of each country.[20]

One source lists these areas in which people differ:

1. Physical attributes—physical size, eye, hair and skin color.
2. Material attributes—income, wealth, tools, economic development.
3. Demographic attributes—sex, race, age, social organization.
4. Systems of beliefs—religions, ideologies, sense of relations between humans, nature, and the universe.
5. Aesthetic attributes—arts, music, folklore, fashion, dress, architecture.
6. Language—written and spoken language, nonverbal expression.
7. Institutions—political, economic, legal, defense and education functions.[21]

Although culture influences everything in society, we examine here those aspects that will be discussed later in this book with regard to individual countries: beliefs, attitudes and behaviors; thinking and learning; interpersonal relationships; sense of self and space; time consciousness; dress and appearance; and food and eating habits.

## Beliefs, Attitudes and Behavior

Although belief systems vary, all people seem to have a concern for the supernatural that is evident in their religious practices. Western culture has been influenced by Judeo-Christian traditions, while Eastern cultures seem to have been dominated by Buddhism, Hinduism and Islam.

Attitudes derive from beliefs, and from attitudes are established norms of behavior, ranging from the work ethic to the pursuit of pure pleasure, from absolute obedience to total permissiveness for children, from unquestioning submission of wives to women's liberation.

## Thinking and Learning

Cultures emphasize one aspect of personal development over another. Some, like the United States, prefer abstract thinking and conceptualization; others, like Japan, prefer rote memory and learning.

## Interpersonal Relationships

Cultures establish interpersonal relationships by age, sex, status, wealth, power and wisdom. The family represents the most common unit of expression. Some cultures accept only monogamous marriage relationships; others allow polygamy or polyandry. The head of the house may be the male or female, a relationship that extends to the community. The elderly are honored in some cultures and ignored in others. Women wear veils in some cultures; in others, females and males are recognized as equal. Several languages of India include different terms for elder brother-in-law and younger brother-in-law — a reflection of a hierarchical society.[22]

## Sense of Self and Space

Self-expression differs by culture. Some cultures promote submissive behavior, independence and individuality, much distance between individuals, and structure and formality. Other cultures prefer macho behavior, group cooperation, closeness between individuals, and fluidity and changeability. Most cultures include a healthy mix of characteristics from each group.

## Time Consciousness

Sense of time differs so that some cultures, like Germany, are exacting and others, like Italy, are more relaxed. In some cultures age or status determines promptness; in other countries, subordinates are expected to be on time at staff meetings, but the boss may be late.

## Dress and Appearance

Dress and appearance include outward garments and adornments as well as body decorations. Some tribes still decorate their faces for battle, while in other cultures most women and an increasing number of men use cosmetics to improve their appearance.

## Food and Eating Habits

Selecting, preparing, presenting and eating food all often differ by culture. The dog, for instance, is a pet in some countries and the center of a sumptuous meal in others. The beef that Americans love is forbidden to Hindus; the forbidden food to Muslims and Jews is pork, eaten extensively by the Chinese and others. Feeding habits range from using hands and chopsticks to full sets of cutlery. Even when cultures use the same utensil, they may do it differently; one can still distinguish a European from an American by which hand holds the fork.

## Culture and Organizations

As microcultures within the larger context of a national macroculture, organizations reflect the culture that surrounds them, forming shared tradi-

**Figure 3. Sony Corporation (San Diego) employees in morning exercises. (Union-Tribune Publishing Co.)**

tions, behavioral norms and value systems. Personnel of organizations tend to share similar backgrounds, both social and educational. Even departments or divisions of the same organization may develop their own personalities, recruiting new members through social networks based on common social and educational background, common values, even political or kinship links.

Other business management practices influenced by culture include attitudes toward work and achievement and decision-making patterns. The Japanese believe employees benefit by beginning their work day with exercises, a custom they have brought to the United States as the photograph in Figure 3 of Sony employees in San Diego shows.

*Attitudes Toward Work and Achievement.* Culture influences the way people view work of all levels of the organization. Job-related cultural variations include attitudes toward work, dominant types of work, division of work and work practices like promotions and rewards. In some cultures everyone is expected to produce through worthwhile activity; others encourage cultural pursuits in music and the arts or sports. Distinctions exist between white-collar and blue-collar jobs and between paper-shuffling and machine-handling jobs.

Geert Hofstede of the Institute for Research on Intercultural Cooperation, the Netherlands, studied the scope of differences in national work-related value systems, using four dimensions:

1. Power Distance—the extent to which the members of a society accept that power in institutions and organizations is distributed unequally.
2. Uncertainty Avoidance—the degree to which the members of a society feel uncomfortable with uncertainty and ambiguity, which leads them to support beliefs promising certainty and to maintain institutions protecting conformity.
3. Individualism—a preference for a loosely knit social framework in

society in which individuals are supposed to take care of themselves and their immediate families only; as opposed to collectivism, which stands for a preference for a tightly knit social framework in which individuals can expect their relatives, clan or other in-group to look after them, in exchange for unquestioning loyalty.

4. Masculinity — a preference for achievement, heroism, assertiveness and material success; as opposed to femininity, which stands for a preference for relationships, modesty, caring for the weak and the quality of life. In a masculine society, even the women prefer assertiveness; in a feminine society, even the men prefer modesty.

Different combinations of Power Distance and Uncertainty Avoidance lead to different models in people's minds of what an organization should be. Hofstede argues that large Power Distance plus strong Uncertainty Avoidance leads to people viewing an organization as "a pyramid of people," that is, a hierarchical bureaucracy (typical of France and other Latin and Mediterranean countries); small Power Distance plus strong Uncertainty Avoidance leads to viewing it as a "well-oiled machine," that is, an impersonal bureaucracy (typical for Germany and other Central-European countries); small Power Distance plus weak Uncertainty Avoidance leads to viewing it as a "village market," that is, an economy that might be termed an "ad-hocracy" (typical of Great Britain and other Anglo and Nordic countries); and large Power Distance plus weak Uncertainty Avoidance leads to viewing the organization as a family (typical of India and other Asian and African countries). Hofstede makes similar observations regarding the other dimensions, individualism and masculinity.

Implicit models, Hofstede concludes, do not depend on nationality alone. They are affected also by the purpose and values of the organization. Members of the same organization tend to share the same implicit model. Persons from other cultures joining it may initially hold the wrong model and be ineffective until they adapt to the others. In cultural matters, the boss has to adapt to the subordinates to be effective. He or she can try to educate the others, but educating against cultures is an uphill battle.[23]

When people from different cultures transact business, each responds according to individual conditioning. When we ignore or misunderstand different conditioning patterns, problems result. Culture influences virtually every aspect of the management process.

Cultural attitudes toward wealth affect the types and numbers of persons who become entrepreneurs and managers as well as workers' responses to incentives. In some societies a worker stays on the job until he or she earns a certain amount of money and then leaves until those earnings are depleted.

*Decision-making Patterns.* These may be distributed among workers or reserved by top managers for themselves. Workers in some societies prefer an authoritarian approach; the democratic-participative style that requires their input makes these workers uncomfortable. The result is a preference for the centralized over the decentralized approach. In some cultures everyone who can contribute relevant information to a decision is expected to do so; in others, a senior executive may be the accepted decision-maker. Expressing disagreement with decisions differs by culture. Some cultures value politeness over

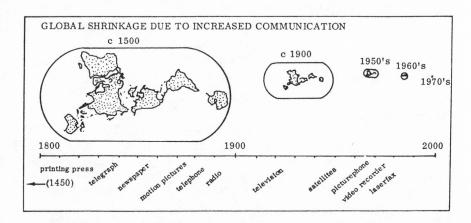

*(Source: John McHale,* The Future of the Future *[New York: George Braziller, 1969], p. 269.)*

**Figure 4. Improved communication technology has brought the world's people closer together.**

blunt truth. Trying to improve the quality of decision-making may be construed as a personal attack. Subordinates disagreeing with a boss risk offending or insulting him or her by saying so. Subordinates are expected to support superiors' decisions or be silent.

# Communication

Communication—the transference of thought between people—is at the heart of all organizational operations at home and abroad. Thanks to modern technology, it is now possible to communicate collectively with more people in the world simultaneously than even existed in the entire world a few centuries ago. Figure 4 shows how increased communication capabilities have caused the globe to shrink.

Communication is so closely linked to culture that virtually all human social interaction is culturally linked. All cultures use the same basic communication skills: how to pay attention, how to ask questions, how to use body language, how to reflect feelings, how to focus on a problem, how to provide feedback, and so on.[24] Confusion arises when these skills differ in practice. Misunderstanding the communicating habits of those in other cultures causes costly inefficiencies for a corporation. It's impossible to estimate the value to a company of teaching a manager as much as possible about communication methods used in his or her own culture as well as about those in other cultures.

First to describe the value of communication in organizations was Chester I. Barnard, then president of New Jersey Bell Telephone Company. In *The*

*Functions of the Executive,* published in 1938, he connected organizational structure and scope to communication techniques, saying that communication should occupy a central place in organizational life.[25] It has taken managers all this time to begin to understand what Barnard was saying. A full comprehension begins with examining the communication process in general.

## Shannon-Weaver Model

Claude Shannon and Warren Weaver demonstrated the communication process in *The Mathematical Theory of Communication,* published in 1948. Shannon worked for Bell Laboratories, and the two were trying to describe how information is passed electronically through telephone wires. Among the technical telecommunications problems they faced was that of determining the minimum quantity of signals required to transmit a message as well as the maximum volume of information that could be passed over a given number of circuits. They said the elements of the communication process were these:

**source — — transmitter — — channel — — receiver — — destination**

They also included the element of noise, which is anything that interferes with the communication process at any stage along the way.

You can describe any communication process using this model. For example, in this paragraph, the author's brain (source) is encoding ideas into words and typing the words into a word processor (transmitter) for eventual printing in your book (channel) to you (receiver) for decoding by your brain (destination). To the extent you receive the message as sent and respond, in new understanding, we have communicated. Noise, of course, is anything which interferes with the process at any point along the way, causing distortion of the message: a printing error, a coffee stain on the page or a disturbance outside your room as you try to read.

## Behavioral Model

Experts in the behavioral sciences — psychology, sociology, and anthropology — simplified that model somewhat to this:

**source — — channel — — destination**

The behavioral scientists removed the transmitter and receiver, which are, after all, part of the source and destination, respectively, in human communication. They also omitted noise, though it is an ever-present possibility in communicating, and added the important element of feedback that the destination provides the source as a method for measuring actual performance against expected performance. Without feedback, the source has little idea whether attempted communication has succeeded or failed and is not able to adjust efforts accordingly.

Using the behavioral model, we can more easily represent any communication process. When you talk on the telephone to a client, for example, you are the source, the telephone system is the channel, the client the destination, and any response to your comments feedback. When your client speaks on a different subject, the situation is reversed with you being the destination this time. Communication is an ongoing, two-way process, not a static, one-way matter as the models might suggest.

## Contextual Model

Going a step further, communication experts began to consider in the contextual model the whole environment in which communication occurs. This model is basically the same as the behavioral model except that it takes into consideration the contexts in which the message is sent and received— sometimes the same context. Aspects of the environment taken into consideration in this model are the climate for communicating, the experience of the parties, their communication skills, emotions, status, sense of security, mental abilities and habits. For the source, the purpose of the communication is important; for the destination, the reaction is important. Breakdowns in communication occur when people fail to differentiate between various environments. Communicating that is quite acceptable in an advertising agency, for example, might be out of place in an accounting firm. Comments made at a disco in tones loud enough to be heard would attract unwanted attention in a church or library.

Every communication situation has its own symbols, rules, roles and purpose. The symbols include both the language through which we express our thoughts and the objects or signs that have meaning for us—the dollar sign, for instance, or nonverbal messages like the two-finger "V for victory" gesture. Rules also cover both verbal and nonverbal communication, varying with the situation. They differ between casual conversations and formal speech-making, between a hurriedly scribbled note and a formal report. The same applies to nonverbal communication. In a crowded elevator, where it is necessary to stand closer to strangers than Americans like, we are uncomfortable and stare upwards at the floor indicator. Any conversation between strangers in that elevator is limited to impersonal subjects like the weather. Communicators' roles determine how people interact; transactions are as equals or as superior-inferior. If the roles are ignored, disordered communication results. The same is true if we ignore any of the many elements of the contextual model.

We can apply these communication models to communicating that takes place all around us all of the time. Such exchanges occur on four levels: intrapersonal, interpersonal, group and organizational.

## Intrapersonal Communication

Many tasks tend to be solitary, requiring much self-communication, called intrapersonal communication, during which an individual processes information by observation, problem-solving, listening, thinking, dreaming, and so on. These are times when attitudes are shaped. The nature of such intrapersonal communicating influences all other communication and, indeed, determines whether any other communication occurs.

Employees' perceptions and understanding spring directly from intrapersonal communicating. If employees see their work as important, if its function in the organization is understood, if others are seen as contributing to their work, then attempts at communicating are usually successful. Intrapersonal communication influences how and when and whether employees communicate with others.

## Interpersonal Communication

Interpersonal communication takes place between two or more people on a personal level. Individuals exchange thoughts to establish relationships and control one another through interpersonal communication. Factors that come into play are the persons' expectations, intentions, and other emotional thoughts and feelings.

Communication for American employees has often been less than interpersonal; it has come from the top of the chain of command down to employees with little means for employees to respond. Workers have received instructions from management through such downward communication and performed their work as directed.

We are just now beginning to learn, through the use of such upward-communication techniques as quality circles, however, that employees have much to offer their organizations. Some of the responsibility for communicating with these new methods is placed on the employee who must establish relationships with others for sending and receiving information.

Also important in interpersonal communication is the realization that the benefits of any single communication exchange must outweigh the costs for each individual, according to exchange theory. That is:

$$\text{Value of Interpersonal Communication Exchange} = f(\text{Benefits} - \text{Costs})$$

For communication to begin and continue, each party must sense that the benefits exceed the costs and that the value of the exchange is nearly equal for both parties. If one party seems to be at a disadvantage, the other party must emphasize whatever benefits accrue to the organization that will include that other party.

Reducing costs of exchanges may mean decreasing the frequency or length of meetings or increasing the pleasure or value to both participants. Other benefits of interpersonal communication include acquiring knowledge, maintaining a relationship, keeping a communication channel open, solving a problem, enjoying a conversation, and venting strong feelings. All of these can seem to offset the costs to the participants which include taking time from other tasks, expending energy, being bored, becoming angry, exposing belief and conviction to contradiction, and revealing poor communication skills.[26]

## Group Communication

Almost all activity in organizations takes place in groups, formal and informal. "Group" is defined as two or more persons who are interdependent and interact for the purpose of achieving a common goal or objective. Group activity enables employees to accomplish faster and more efficiently together what they could not do alone.

Communication in groups enables members to achieve the group's task — make decisions, solve problems, get the job done — or to maintain themselves as a group by developing morale and helping individual members grow and improve. Communication roles develop within groups according to who communicates with whom. In fact, group membership is defined according to communication. A person is a group member if more than half of his or her communications are with others in the group. If half or fewer of an individual's communications are within the group, then multiple-group membership is possible.

## Organizational Communication

Everyone except organizational theorists has largely overlooked the central role of communication in organizational life. As one writer said in reference to culture, if birds and fish were suddenly endowed with scientific inquiry, they would probably overlook the air and water. So it is with humans and communication, particularly in organizations.

Communication varies according to structure and management factors. An organization's structure can be tall — meaning many levels between the top and bottom — or flat. Management factors include location of decision-making authority (centralized or decentralized) as well as style (authoritarian or democratic) and corporate climate.

*Structure.* With a tall structure, closer coordination and control are possible because each manager works with fewer people; employees tend to be more boss-oriented in this structure. Communication lines up and down the chain of command are longer, however, providing more possibilities for misinterpretation and filtering.

The flat structure allows shorter, simpler communication connections, but managers have so many more persons to direct that they can't spend much time with any one group member. Because they are freer of hierarchical controls, employees prefer this structure. It benefits employees who have initiative and who spend less time trying to please the boss.

*Management Decision-Making.* The location of decision-making power in an organization, whether centralized solely in top management or decentralized further down the management chart, determines much about communicating patterns. With centralization, specialists in the same field work together and communicate easily with one another, producing efficient internal communications, and increasing personal satisfaction among those experts. Centralization also gives top management greater control over the organization with economies of scale advantages. This system, however, presents a greater need to communicate among all organizational units just when communication between units is most difficult because of their differing goals.

When decision-making is decentralized — meaning decision-making power is pushed down the chain of command as far as it can go — communication within autonomous units improves for several reasons: (1) Members share a perception of common goals and are thus more motivated to communicate with one another to achieve them. (2) Over a period of time, members develop a communication shorthand from their long, close associations which facilitates understanding between them. (3) Members have more opportunity for informal interactions and for more rapid and frequent communications. (4) Members of single units have less reason to deliberately filter out information, and even if they did, such distortion would be more easily detectable. In communication, then, as in other respects, the decentralized system is more efficient. In general, managers must decide what information they need and how they are going to use it in decision-making. This process, of course, is the same across cultures. How it is done varies by culture and even by organization within the same culture.

*Management Style.* Communication in a company also depends on whether its management style is authoritarian or democratic. The authoritarian leader allows subordinates little freedom for action; leaders who follow democratic or human relations principles place greater emphasis on employee initiative, responsibility and authority.

Many executives instead choose to operate on the basis of the systems approach, which sees the organization as made up of interacting organisms (departments) tied together by a sophisticated system of information exchange. Yet another style is being called the "contingency" approach which treats each situation according to the demands of the moment — authoritarian, human relations, systems, or a combination of them.

The result of following one or another of these management styles is an attitude that either welcomes or discourages communication. Everyone in the organization soon learns what that attitude is and responds accordingly by sharing willingly their information and ideas or by withholding them to the detriment of the entire organization. A company experiencing communication difficulties may need to review and revise its management style. Poor communication is at best a provision for lower achievement and at worst for complete failure.

Good communication means open, free-flowing message sending and receiving among employees. In investigating this subject, Chris Argyris found that companies that do not encourage open communication elicit from employees defensiveness and the concealment of important facts needed for effective decision-making. Argyris also concluded that lack of openness in communicating reduced employee commitment to organizational goals.[27]

*Corporate Climate.* The spirit of an organization, the quality of feeling responsible for the relationships between individuals in an organization is called corporate climate which determines volume and type of communication.

Both physical and psychological factors describe corporate climate, but the latter predominate. Executives tend to pay much more attention to physical surroundings than to the more ethereal aspects of the organization: attitude, opportunity, confidence, and comfort. Clear communication requires the right balance, and if effective communication increases the company's sense of success, poor communication diminishes it. A negative corporate-communication climate fosters mistrust or disrespect, power games, duplication of checkpoints, secretiveness or loquacity, and overt sabotage of transmission.

A climate of trust encourages open communication, which in turn produces better performance and higher profitability. Open communication frees employees to share feelings and intentions with other employees of any level on matters pertinent to their jobs and the company. Many factors come into play in creating this climate of trust so conducive to open communicating. Probably the most important factor is the attitude of the chief executive officer.

## Communication Conflict

Inevitably in organizations of humans, conflicts occur in communicating. Although it is a broad subject, briefly presented here are the kinds of conflict that can occur on each of the four levels of communication — intrapersonal, interpersonal, group and organizational — and a few solutions to such conflicts.

*Intrapersonal Conflict.* This takes the form of frustration when one's ambitions to achieve something are thwarted or when an individual experiences indecision between goals.

*Interpersonal Conflict.* This may be between two individuals or between an individual and a group. It may be from competition for a promotion, for instance, or for choice assignments. Such conflict causes stress to individuals involved and problems to the organization.

*Group Conflict.* This occurs within a group or between two or more groups and may relate to work being done or associations between group members. Interdepartmental competition for limited resources is a common example of group conflict. A certain amount of this sort of conflict has been shown to be beneficial to an organization, but either too little or too much of it is dysfunctional.

*Organizational Conflict.* Conflict within one organization or between organizations is also, of course, dysfunctional if carried to extremes. As with group conflict, however, just enough conflict helps the organization — one of the reasons a competitive economic system works so well.

## Controlling Conflict

Managing conflict in an organization is a skill, an essential one if an organization is to survive. Methods for controlling conflict include these:

- Avoidance — withdrawal to avoid conflict, one of the most common but least effective responses to conflict.
- Dominance — by one party over the others.
- Bargaining — either *distributive,* in which limited resources are allocated, or *integrative,* in which needs of parties are combined into a single solution.
- Alterations — changes in the human or structural variables.
- Cooperative Problem Solving — attainment of common interests of all parties.
- Third-Party Methods — calling in a supervisor or executive, or possibly a mediator or arbitrator.[28]

Communication conflict will never be eliminated in a competitive society like ours that grows more complex as our social and business concerns extend worldwide. A certain amount has even been proved in research studies to be beneficial to an organization. Conflict needs to be monitored very closely, however, and controlled when it starts to get out of control.

## *Nonverbal Communication*

Nonverbal communications include all intentional and unintentional messages sent without the use of words; they are responsible for conveying much of our attitudes and feelings. It is easy to see how an unfamiliarity with messages conveyed nonverbally would lead to difficulty.

Understanding nonverbal communication is important for two reasons. The major part of any oral message is transmitted nonverbally: Theorists estimate that 93 percent of the emotional content of a verbal message sent orally is transmitted via nonverbal communication (researchers further divide the 93 percent into 38 percent vocal feeling and 55 percent facial feeling).[29] Disguising the true message nonverbally is difficult; the real message often gets through. We have to conclude after a discussion of nonverbal communication that it is impossible not to communicate. A message — the nonverbal one — always comes across.

Nonverbal forms of communication serve several purposes: repeating, contradicting, substituting, complementing, accenting and regulating. Nonverbal messages repeat when they restate the verbal message. Someone holding up two fingers in telling you it is two o'clock is repeating nonverbally. We also nonverbally contradict our verbal message. When a parent tells a child he administers spankings because the child is loved, the nonverbal message seems painfully contradictory.

Sometimes nonverbal communication substitutes for verbal messages. Two fingers held up in a peace sign stand for a potentially lengthy verbal defense of peace. Some nonverbal methods complement verbal messages. A shrug of the shoulders is complementary to saying you don't know. So is nodding the head front and back while saying "yes" and shaking it side to side while saying "no." We accent a verbal message nonverbally when we bang on a table and say it louder. That's a double nonverbal message to supplement words.

Nonverbal messages often regulate verbal messages by indicating that you want to interrupt another speaker or that you've finished your thought.

To demonstrate dominance over employees, some managers elevate themselves — on a platform of some kind — over that person. This causes "talking down" to the individual.

Touching can be an endorsement or an interrupt signal. Everyone knows that a firm handshake indicates confidence. Did you know, though, that when a person turns your hand over so his or her palm is directly on top of yours, he or she is attempting a type of physical dominance? Offering your hand with palm up shows a willingness to accept a subordinate role. Moving closer is viewed as acceptance by the person moving.

A discussion of nonverbal communication is easily divided into these categories: proxemics, kinesics, oculesics, paralanguage, physical characteristics and artifacts.

*Proxemics.* Using space in communication, called proxemics, includes your environment: where you live, how you decorate your home or apartment, what kind of car you drive, and so on. These all communicate about you. The same living quarters take on entirely different qualities depending on who occupies them. The same person communicates different messages while driving a red Porsche than while driving a tan Volkswagen.

Proxemics also refers to positioning oneself with respect to objects and other persons. Even more than most nonverbal cues, space and spacing are very different in various cultures. In Italy and certain Arab countries, for instance, residents are not offended when others invade what Americans consider their intimate zone. When they do that to American visitors, the latter tend to back up which usually causes confusion in the minds of their hosts.

Control of personal space also communicates. Whether an office is private or shared, whether it has a wooden door or one with a glass in it, whether the glass is clear or frosted, all communicate.

To improve productivity, some designers of office buildings advocate the "open landscape system," widely used in Germany and Japan. In it there are no enclosed offices; the appearance of private offices is achieved by use of panels, partitions, furniture, and accessories. There are no floor-to-ceiling separations of any kind.

Steelcase, Inc., of Grand Rapids, Michigan, has designed its new $75 million research center to encourage "group decision-making triggered by spontaneous encounters." The new Corporate Development Center is

> designed to foster communication among all levels of the organization, putting in practice the theory that spontaneous interaction is the best catalyst for creativeness.... To encourage that kind of spontaneity, there are few barriers in the building; escalators are used instead of elevators; and four entrances to the building feed into a central meeting place or "town square" in the atrium.

Using what designers have dubbed the "cave and commons" approach, each employee will have his or her own private space, or "cave." But in the middle of a circle of caves will be the group's commons area, also dubbed "interaction nodes," for group meetings. Each of these areas will be equipped with a coffee and soft drink bar — and a marker board for when the conversation turns to product ideas. . . .

Executives will be in the directors' cluster, a ring of private offices in the middle of the building. For the "lone rangers," there will be small offices without telephones or other potential distractions. . . .

"At most companies, the process of developing a product is usually linear, like a relay race where the person does his part and passes it on to the next person," [Wayne D.] Veneklasen [organizational environmental psychologist] said. "We're taking the rugby team approach. The designers, the engineers, the manufacturing people, the marketing people and the corporate communications people will pass the ball back and forth, but all going in the same direction at the same time."[30]

*Kinesics.* All of one's body movements communicate, including all gestures and body postures. We call this kinesics. Ray Birdwhistell in *Kinesics and Context* has said that the human face is capable of over 250,000 different expressions.[31] We inherit certain basic physical reactions that communicate hate, fear, love, amusement, sadness, and other basic emotions. Research has shown that individuals from all cultures turn up the corners of the mouth when happy and turn them down when sad. We all lift the eyebrows, wrinkle the forehead, and use a variety of other facial expressions in common. But our culture teaches us precisely how and when to use these facial expressions and exactly how we interpret them.

*Oculesics.* This refers to the use of eye contact in communicating. Eye contact regulates the flow of conversation, indicating to others that it is all right to talk and experience emotions among human beings. A teacher uses this to signal to students the time to answer a question — and by looking at certain students, to indicate who is expected to answer. By opening the eyelids, by squinting, and by other movements of the skin and eyes, we can transmit almost any message.

*Paralanguage.* Aspects of the voice, other than the words spoken, all communicate. These include pitch, rhythm, rate, resonance and other forms of vocalization such as laughing, sighing, coughing and sneezing. These we call paralanguage because they describe uttered communication but do not refer to the words.

Another important form of nonverbal communication is the use of silence. In many cultures silence is used very effectively in the course of conversations; Americans, on the other hand, rush to fill silence, talking when they should wait patiently. This hinders communication, preventing users of silence to get their message across to Americans and causing Americans to miss much of the message.

*Physical Characteristics.* A person's size, shape, general attractiveness, hair and skin color, and how he or she presents all of these are great communicators. If you have ever grown a moustache or beard, dyed your hair an entirely different color, gained or lost a lot of weight, or changed some other physical feature so that others noticed, you know how easily physical characteristics communicate.

*Artifacts.* Closely allied to physical characteristics are all of those artifacts with which you adorn your body: clothing, jewelry, makeup, perfume, eyeglasses, and so on. Both clothing and appearance help others establish status, credibility and persuasiveness. The color of artifacts also communicates. Black in most Western countries has historically been associated with death; in parts of the Far East and in Latin America, however, white has the same connotation.

# Intercultural Communication

"I've a feeling we're not in Kansas anymore," Dorothy says to her little dog, Toto, when she first sees the Land of Oz. Her sense of bewilderment is matched by that of modern business people who go abroad for the first time in behalf of their companies, especially when they are not prepared.

One realizes very quickly that communication across cultural boundaries is difficult because it goes much deeper than language; ways of thinking and manner of living also relate to communication. Differences in customs, behavior and values result in problems that can be managed only through effective cross-cultural communication and interaction. As one international executive stated: "Like banana skins, solutions to communications problems can in some contexts be protective, in others catastrophic."[32]

The concept of intercultural communication recognizes what is involved in one's image of self and role and of personal needs, values, standards and expectations that are all culturally conditioned.[33] When people from different cultures do business, each responds to the relationship according to his or her own psychological conditioning. People in all cultures are socially conditioned as children. Persons of dissimilar backgrounds usually require more time than those of the same culture to become familiar with each other, to be willing to speak openly, to share sufficiently in common ideas and to understand one another. One writer stated it well: "The person of substance abroad is someone who 'carries his scenery with him,' meaning someone who enables others to see his background, to see him in context, to understand him."[34]

Intercultural communicating is not just a matter of one's understanding foreigners and what they say and don't say. To be successful, a business person must influence them. This requires the opposite action as well: them understanding him or her. To influence people of another culture, one must have the rare ability to imagine oneself as one of their tribe. In competitive international industrial sales situations, for example, it is often this ability, more than concrete product advantages, price or quality, that in the end determines who gets the business.

To a large degree international business depends on communication and languages are the principal means of communication. Every time a language barrier must be crossed, the potential for communication problems arises. Communication between persons of different cultures is particularly difficult because the unseen, even unconscious, assumptions, meanings and images that underlie understanding are so different.

Dimensions of importance to intercultural competence can be identified:

1. The capacity to be flexible.
2. The capacity to be nonjudgmental.
3. Tolerance for ambiguity.
4. The capacity to communicate respect.
5. The capacity to personalize one's knowledge and perceptions.
6. The capacity to display empathy.
7. The capacity for turn taking.[35]

The increased possibility for error in intercultural communication, however, means that more of the message content must be made explicit than would be necessary between members of the same culture. Even though written communication is more time consuming and, some think, more tedious, it is recommended across cultures more than oral communication, which has a greater chance of being misunderstood. A word not understood means a message is lost. Nuances are also lost; tones of voice misinterpreted; expression in a person's eyes misconstrued. Except for the nonverbal cues, the problems are magnified when one attempts to communicate only by telephone or radio instead of in person.

In spite of all the communication equipment and data preparation of a big company, recent research indicates that managers still pay far more attention to face-to-face communication than to written reports. If a manager allows cultural barriers to make him or her unreceptive to information from some members of the staff, his or her ability to make correct decisions may be severely impaired.

As Edward Hall has argued in his book *Beyond Culture,* cultures differ in the relative importance they place on words for conveying information. Some cultures, including those of the United States, England and northern European countries, give words great importance. Those who have grown up in these cultures feel unsure unless feelings or ideas are expressed in words; our contacts are likely to be very elaborate and specific. We believe that ideas should be evaluated on their own merit—in their own words, that is—and not on the basis of who said the words, where, or when. In Hall's terms, we give relatively little attention to the context of communication and very much attention to the words. He calls these low-context cultures. High-context cultures take the entire context of a communication exchange into consideration when interpreting a message, including where and when the message was sent by whom and under what circumstances.[36]

Hall has also distinguished between cultures in their use of time: "monochronic" (M-time) and "polychronic" (P-time). M-time cultures value taking care of "one thing at a time" so that time is lineal and segmented. Though time may not be money, M-time cultures treat it that way. M-time people like exact scheduling of appointments and are distracted and distressed by interruptions.

In contrast, P-time cultures are characterized by many events happening at once, and with a much "looser" notion of what is "on time" or "late." Interruptions are routine, delays to be expected. Human activities are not expected to proceed like clockwork.[37]

## *Barriers to Intercultural Communication*

Misunderstanding of communication habits in other cultures causes major inefficiencies, especially in multinational companies. Multiculturism adds to the complexity of international firms by increasing the number of perspectives, approaches and business methods. If an export manager sent out by his or her company cannot communicate on the business and social level with the foreign customer and has no respect for the different ways of conducting business and behaving socially, the customer may well choose another partner. Teaching managers to use communication skills effectively in their own culture makes it much easier for them to master communication difficulties with other cultures. Intercultural communication is hampered by five major barriers: verbal systems, nonverbal systems, ethnocentrism, lack of empathy and differences in perception.

*Verbal Systems.* Language is important in any culture because it is the embodiment of a culture, reflecting the lifestyle and philosophy of a group of people. More than a method of communicating, language is a framework for thinking. Language therefore affects the way we communicate in two ways: our ability to encode or formulate our thoughts systematically, and our ability to express these thoughts clearly. We require an adequate number of words to express meanings accurately and the ability to spell and pronounce the words correctly as well as use grammar and punctuation properly. Then we are able to share with others our thoughts, feelings and attitudes and to influence the thoughts, feelings and attitudes of those with whom we communicate.

Benjamin L. Whorf discussed the impact of language on thought. He said that language is a shaper of ideas as well as a reproducing instrument for voicing ideas. "Listen to a man's language," Whorf said, "and you will hear his history and his culture."[38] People take on the world view of their language community. Different people, therefore, differ not only on the use of words but also on what those words say.

Language as a built-in communication barrier across cultures can be overcome by becoming adept at foreign languages. More than a vehicle of communication, a foreign language teaches a new mode of thinking and a different pattern of communication. One is thus better able to understand those in the foreign culture, how they think and why they behave as they do. Unfortunately, nine out of ten Americans cannot speak, read or effectively communicate in any other language except English.[39] Fewer than 8 percent of colleges and universities in the United States require knowledge of a foreign language for entrance, and fewer than 5 percent of America's prospective teachers take any courses in international subjects as part of their professional training.[40] If learning a foreign language is impossible, at least we should be aware of communication breakdowns because of language differences and make allowances for them in terms of time, energy and patience.

International business depends on communication and languages are the principal means of communicating. Every time a language barrier must be crossed, there is a potential for communication problems:

1. Failure to understand the culture and therefore the meanings of words, even when one does know the language.
2. Using words improperly because they have multiple meanings in one language but not similar multiple meanings in other languages.
3. Using figures of speech improperly—metaphors, similes, analogies, and so on.[41]

Even primitive societies have complex languages that reflect their environment, making it difficult to translate directly from one language to another. Eskimos have more than 25 words for "snow" but no word for "war." Native Central and South American Indians had no word for guilt, making life difficult for the first missionaries. Arabs have over 6,000 words to describe camels, their parts and equipment.[42] American English has from 700,000 to 800,000 words, about a third of them scientific and technological. In Spanish no word exists for everyone who works in a business organization. Instead there is a word *empleados,* which refers to white-collar workers, and another word *obreros,* which refers to laborers. A clock "runs" in English but "walks" in Spanish.

A new approach to language study is the idea of the beat of a language, which is said to buttress the meaning of what is said and helps organize conversation. When speakers and listeners come from different cultures or from different language backgrounds in the same culture, they often have widely differing rhythmic expectations. A foreigner, for instance, may stress words other than key ones for which a native speaker listens, throwing off the timing and turn-taking in conversations.[43]

Americans have depended on the world to use English so that we have made very little effort to learn foreign languages. This has created communication barriers, particularly in countries where few people understand and communicate in English and in those that take pride in their own language and expect visitors to use that. Americans tend to believe that because an individual speaks English, he or she thinks like Americans, which, of course, is usually not true. When we learn a person has studied in a United States university, we assume he or she knows of our superiority and the worth of our products. That also may not be the case.

The results have been costly for American industry. In cooperative ventures with foreign countries, business is generally conducted in English and the flow of technology has been one-way—from the United States to other countries, primarily Japan. A broad range of products, from electronics to the semiconductor, have been the subject of cooperative agreements with the Japanese only to have them take over the market.

Ask any American which language is best for conducting business internationally and inevitably the answer will be English. Ask a Japanese the same question and the answer will be *"okya ku-sama no kotoba,"* meaning "my customer's language."[44]

*Nonverbal Systems.* While the use of body language is universal, its manifestation differs by culture. Nonverbal communication can become a source of miscommunication when persons from different cultures are unfamiliar with each other's nonverbal signals. A popular signal in one culture, like the American A-OK sign, can be obscene in other cultures.

*Ethnocentrism.* Contributing to intercultural communication difficulties is ethnocentrism, the view that one's own culture is the right one and others are strange and inferior. It is an inevitable outgrowth of the whole system of creating and perpetuating culture. If members of a society didn't feel ethnocentric, they would stop doing what they are doing and the culture would die. Carried to an extreme, however, ethnocentrism causes breakdowns in communication between members of different cultures. Negative effects of ethnocentrism are diminished if we understand how culture works, including how all cultures solve universal problems. We soon realize that no society could survive without these patterns of thinking, feeling and acting which are reasonably systematic and coherent. Ricks relates this story:

> In a wave of ethnocentrism after the purchase of a Spanish company by a U.S. manufacturer, the new owners changed the firm's previous prestigious Spanish name to that of the U.S. parent, flew the "stars and stripes" from the company flagpole, and widely announced the sophisticated and superb technology being introduced. The acts were ones of near chauvinism, heavily suggesting that those who had managed the company prior to takeover by the Americans were incompetent. In a special interview with a prominent U.S. business publication, the new management elaborated on its revamping of the whole Spanish company, boasting that its efforts had succeeded in rejuvenating the floundering Spanish operation. The article found its way back to the Spanish public via wire and greatly angered the Spanish who were associated with the company. In fact, the blunder of treading on Spanish pride was so extensive that it resulted in a general slowdown of work (since strikes were then officially banned), the Spanish press released an extremely damaging attack, local authorities made the conduct of the company's business very difficult, and clients steered away.[45]

*Lack of Empathy.* Empathy is an ability to put oneself in the shoes of another person. Many people lack this ability with persons even within the same culture. When the problem exists across cultures, the negative results are magnified. To influence businessmen of another culture, you must have the rare ability to project yourself as one of their tribe. In competitive international industrial sales situations, it is often this projection, more than concrete product advantages, price, or quality that in the end determines who gets the business.

*Differences in Perception.* Perception is the understanding of the world one has developed as the result of past experiences. Even within one's own culture, differences in perception occur. One researcher has reported that vision alone confronts us with 7,500,000 distinguishable colors and that hearing is estimated to provide approximately 340,000 discriminable tones.[46] When experiences have been in different cultures, it is not surprising that the parties involved will suffer from communication barriers.

# Notes

1. Marvin Cetron, *The Future of American Business,* p. 155.
2. L. Copeland and L. Griggs, *Going International,* p. xv.
3. Ibid., pp. xix–xx.
4. Philip R. Harris and Robert T. Moran, *Managing Cultural Differences,* p. 25.
5. Diana Kurylko, "U.S. Firms Urged to Sell Overseas," p. A14.
6. Neil Chesanow, *The World Class Executive,* p. 18.
7. John Templeton, "Hands Across Europe," p. 64.
8. Wilbur Schramm, "Cross-Cultural Communication: Suggestions for the Building of Bridges," in *New Perspectives in International Communication,* Jim Richstad, ed., p. 16.
9. Michael Johnson, "The Soaring Demand for Global Training," p. 47.
10. W. Dekker, "Changes of Course in a Multinational," p. 5.
11. Jean Phillips-Martinsson, *Swedes as Others See Them,* p. 104.
12. Harris and Moran, p. 8.
13. Ibid., p. 3.
14. Robert T. Moran, "Cross-Cultural Contact," p. 58.
15. Nancy J. Adler, *International Dimensions of Organizational Behavior,* p. 79.
16. David A. Ricks, *Big Business Blunders,* p. 70.
17. Molefi Kete Asante, et al., *Handbook of Intercultural Communication,* p. 449.
18. Andre Laurent, "The Cross-Cultural Puzzle of International Human Relations," p. 97.
19. M. Rokeach, *The Nature of Human Values,* New York: Free Press, 1973, p. 3, as cited in Beatrice K. Reynolds, "A Cross-Cultural Study of Values of Germans and Americans," p. 270.
20. Mason Haire, Edwin E. Ghiselli and Lyman E. Porter, *Managerial Thinking: An International Study,* pp. 32–3, 170–81.
21. R. Hal Mason and Robert S. Spich, *Management: An International Perspective,* p. 52.
22. F. Chothia, *Other Cultures/Other Ways,* pp. 12–3.
23. Geert Hofstede, "National Culture in Four Dimensions," pp. 46–74.
24. David Clutterbuck, "Breaking Through the Cultural Barrier," p. 42.
25. Chester Barnard, *The Functions of the Executive,* p. 91.
26. Jeremiah Sullivan, *Handbook of Accounting Communication,* p. 300.
27. Thomas J. Housel and Warren E. Davis, "The Reduction of Upward Communication Distortion," p. 53.
28. Patricia Hayes Bradley and John E. Baird, Jr., *Communication for Business and the Professions,* pp. 274–6.
29. Albert Mehrabian, *Silent Messages,* p. 44.
30. Lisa Perlman, "From Desks to Office Dynamics," p. B6.
31. Ray Birdwhistell, *Kinesics and Context,* p. 42.
32. Dimitris N. Chorafas, *The Communication Barriers in International Management,* 20.
33. Harris and Moran, p. 9.
34. Copeland and Griggs, p. 16.
35. Louise F. Luce and Elise C. Smith, *Toward Internationalism,* p. 40.
36. Edward T. Hall, *Beyond Culture,* pp. 88–112.
37. Ibid., pp. 14–21.
38. Schramm in Richstad, p. 15.
39. Connie Lauerman, "Most Americans Flunk Foreign Language Test," p. C3.
40. Copeland and Griggs, p. xxii.
41. Richard N. Robinson, *International Business Management,* pp. 302–3.
42. Chothia, p. 13.
43. Carole Douglas, "The Beat Goes On," pp. 37–9, 42.
44. Philip R. Harris, *New Worlds, New Ways, New Management,* p. 332.
45. "The Spanish-American Business Wars," *Worldwide P & I Planning* (May–June 1971), pp. 30–40, as cited in Ricks et al., *International Business Blunders,* pp. 43–4.
46. Frank A. Geldard, *The Human Senses,* New York: Wiley, 1953, p. 53, as cited in Stewart, *American Cultural Patterns,* p. 15.

# 2. North America

## Introduction

This chapter discusses North America only partially. The North American geographic unit includes Canada and the United States, along with Mexico and Central America to the Isthmus of Panama, as well as the West Indies and the island of Greenland (under Danish control). Culturally, socially and economically, however, Mexico, Central America and the West Indies belong to Latin America, the subject of the next chapter. This chapter, therefore, discusses only the United States and Canada.

## ———————— The United States ————————

*Official Name:* The United States of America; *Government:* federal republic; *Subdivisions:* 50 states and the District of Columbia (*plus* possessions such as Puerto Rico, the Virgin Islands, Guam, etc.); *Population:* 243,084,000 (July 1987); *Density:* 65.3 per square mile; *Currency:* dollar; *Language:* English; *Literacy:* 99 percent.

### The Land

The land mass that extends almost from the Arctic to Cape Horn was named "America" after the sixteenth century Italian explorer Amerigo Vespucci. Inhabitants of the United States have appropriated (some, especially Latin cultures, might say misappropriated) the right to the title of "Americans," a term used in that context in this book.

The United States is almost as diverse as its people. From fruitful coastal areas, the land extends over vast plains and deserts to rugged mountain ranges. It includes the contiguous 48 states and the District of Columbia plus Alaska in the northwestern tip of the hemisphere; Hawaii, west of the mainland; and the territories, notably, of Puerto Rico and the Virgin Islands.

Since the end of World War II, the United States has administered 11 trust territories in the South Pacific, but it has been gradually relinquishing responsibility for them in favor of independence. Between 1975 and 1980, accords were negotiated with the native islanders to establish the commonwealths of the northern Marianas, the Republic of Palau, the Marshall Islands and the Federated States of Micronesia.

## A Brief History

The United States was built some 200 years ago by European immigrants mainly, and, in the South, black slaves. It has never experienced feudalism or isolation. After a revolution, the United States won independence from Great Britain and expanded from east to west, eventually reaching the Pacific Ocean. The country is today the fourth largest in the world both in size, after the U.S.S.R., Canada and China, and in population, after China, India and the Soviet Union.

## The People

Inhabited almost entirely by immigrants from older nations and their descendants, America has been called the "melting pot" of diverse cultures. The home of the aboriginal Indian tribes, the country was settled by small groups of British, French, Dutch and Swedes. Later successive waves brought in Scotch-Irish, German, Irish, Scandinavians, Eastern Europeans, Middle-Easterners, Spaniards and Portuguese. French and Spanish colonizers in the South and West were absorbed and to the west eventually came Asian immigrants. About 11 percent of the population is made up of descendants of slaves from Africa. Recent waves of immigrants have come from Indochina, Cuba and Haiti. Ethnic divisions in 1980 were these: 83.1 percent white, 11.6 percent black, 6.45 Hispanic, 0.62 American Indian, Eskimo and Aleut, 0.36 Chinese, 0.34 Filipino, 0.31 Japanese, 0.16 Korean, 0.12 Vietnamese and 0.16 other Asian.[1] The result is a diverse yet homogenous American society. America's speech is as varied as its people, climate and geography. American English includes as many as 18 dialects. Spanish is rising in importance as more Hispanics immigrate.

The Spanish refer to people in the United States as "Norte Americanos" to distinguish them from South Americans who, of course, are much closer to their Spanish motherland. Additionally, persons in the United States identify themselves with a number of adjectives that change radically when viewed from foreign lands. Table 3 shows the differences.

*Informal, Friendly, Casual.* Americans believe themselves to be the easiest people to know and like because they dislike ceremony and are warm, casual, open, informal and friendly. They think the best of everyone, giving anyone the benefit of the doubt, and are practically uninsultable. Foreigners, on the other hand, see them as undisciplined and overly personal and familiar before a proper personal relationship has developed.

*Egalitarian.* They believe in equality among people, which eliminates the need for elaborate forms of social address; they ignore the importance of rank and feel uncomfortable in formal clothes at formal occasions. Even though social classes exist, it is easy to move from one to another. United States

### Table 3. Americans' Views of Themselves and Foreigners' Views of Americans Compared

| *American Description* | *Foreigners' View* |
| --- | --- |
| Informal, Friendly, Casual | Undisciplined, Too Personal, Familiar |
| Egalitarian | Insensitive to Status |
| Direct, Aggressive | Blunt, Rude, Oppressive |
| Efficient | Obsessed with Time, Opportunistic |
| Goal and Achievement Oriented | Promising More Than Can Be Delivered |
| Profit-oriented | Materialistic |
| Resourceful, Ingenious | Interested in Deals over People, Work-oriented |
| Individualistic, Progressive | Self-Absorbed, Equating the "New" with Best |
| Dynamic, Finding Identity in Work | Driven |
| Enthusiastic, Preferring the Hard-sell | Deceptive, Fearsome |
| Open | Weak, Untrustworthy |

managers express the belief that all people are created equal more strongly than managers of any other nationality.

Americans are not averse to manual labor, no matter what their social status. They shine their own shoes, wash their own cars, mow their own lawns, paint their own houses and so on, if they feel like it. Although they may have reasons for not doing some of these, fear of losing social status is not among them as it is in other countries.

To others, they are impersonal, forward and familiar. They come on too strong and too fast for most foreigners; they are seen as driven, intimidating a large number of them. Foreign business persons see Americans making appointments, entering offices uninvited, taking seats, and getting right to the point.

*Direct, Aggressive.* Americans are willing to put anything into words anytime because in their culture, the most successful people express everything verbally as quickly, concisely and convincingly as possible. They consider it acceptably polite to be direct in conversation and social relations.

This way of doing business in America is often considered rude and repugnant by foreigners who interpret directness, for example, as too demanding. An open person in some cultures is seen as weak and untrustworthy, incapable of exercising restraint. Expecting direct replies to questions, Western managers are confused by their absence. Asians, on the other hand, are mystified by our inability to grasp the subtle signals transmitted regarding the progress of negotiations.

*Efficient, Intelligent, Imaginative.* Americans value promptness; they live by schedules. Time is money; punctuality and efficiency are emphasized; tardiness indicates indifference and inefficiency; Americans spend time transacting business to make a profit. Everything must have a measurable purpose. Americans believe in personal initiative, but they are also group people, trained from childhood to be "one of the gang," to cooperate, to merge easily into various organizations. Most of them belong to a number of groups concurrently: religious, civic, athletic, recreational or professional. Western democracies and their educational systems tend to foster group feelings, ranking the good of the community higher than personal values.

Foreigners describe Americans as slaves to the clock — obsessed, harried and jittery. In other cultures, time is seen as an unlimited resource to be used not to create efficient production but to be enjoyed while a task is being done. Delays, postponements and cancellations are viewed with less alarm than they are in the United States. Time in these countries is best spent in creating a pleasant interpersonal atmosphere.

*Goal and Achievement Oriented.* Americans work best by schedules. We race to beat deadlines which we feel heighten the importance of a task, creating a sense of urgency to get the work done. A Western manager faced with a problem will attempt to solve it as quickly as possible. Practically every American parent reads to practically every American child the story of *The Little Engine That Could,* a lesson in overcoming adversity in life; and practically every child gets the message that by trying harder and harder he or she can accomplish anything, even the impossible. We CAN influence the future; we ARE masters of our own destiny; hard work WILL be rewarded. Because of the well-known Puritan work ethic, Americans take pride in the work they do, conduct business at social functions and take work home with them.

Elsewhere deadlines may produce the opposite results. Arabs view deadlines as insulting. In Ethiopia, prestige is attached to anything which takes a long time to complete.

*Profit-oriented.* In the American culture it is deemed admirable to succeed in business and accumulate wealth; person-to-person competition is considered healthy and constructive. Americans expend much effort to improve socially and economically, and they treat the wealthy and successful with great respect. In conducting business, they are intelligent, resourceful, imaginative, ingenious, inventive and progressive.

Foreigners view this attitude as single-minded and materialistic, valuing self over ethical standards and some of the intangibles of life such as honor and dignity. Money is often secondary to family life and sometimes to friendship as well.

*Resourceful, Ingenious.* The American manager willingly accepts impersonal relations in his or her business dealings. In most American corporations, the buyer and seller are strangers and don't need to know each other to talk shop. Getting acquainted is nice but it takes time. The right person and offer can result in a deal.

Foreigners place more importance in establishing a personal relationship with a client prior to conducting business to find out who they are dealing with before negotiations begin. Americans are seen as emphasizing the deal over people. For example: in 1985, there were large air disasters near Tokyo and near Dallas. The Japanese airline company accepted responsibility, apologized, negotiated and settled claims. The Americans scrambled for legal advice, solicited attorney offers and ended up with multiple law suits.[2]

In many cultures, the person making an offer and the manner in which it is made supersede the offer itself. Individual initiative is governed by role and status and may even be discouraged through a prolonged development period. Credit for initiative funnels upward and frequently the young, creative individual is ignored until he or she ripens into middle age. When one has achieved senior status, he or she may exercise initiative as part of the job. In the meantime, the individual is rewarded for obedience and unobtrusiveness.

*Individualistic, Progressive.* Hofstede found Americans to be one of the world's most individualistic peoples.[3] It's a quality that gives them a great measure of pride because they attribute to it much of their success.

Cooperation rather than competition, however, is the mode of conduct preferred in many parts of the world, including Japan. Foreigners decry the Americans' reliance on paperwork and their lack of knowledge of the outside world. Americans, they say, are too self-absorbed, naive internationally, the most ethnocentric of all business persons, and mistaken in equating everything "new" with best. Americans, they say, also have the highest attrition rate among managers of any country in the world.

*Enthusiastic, Preferring the Hard Sell.* Americans throw their whole unbridled personalities into living and working; it is best to "be themselves," they feel. Out of that originality have come some of the most progressive ideas that have helped shape the world for decades.

More reserved, conservative peoples often find this approach frightening and somewhat deceptive. The true self, they say, is buried deeper than the brash personality an American displays, and they detect sharp differences between the open, enthusiastic person and the hidden feelings.

*Dynamic, Finding Identity in Work.* Americans describe their own manner of doing business as dynamic; they have a dollars-and-cents orientation; they are goal and achievement oriented; they talk shop anytime in a style that is enthusiastic, aggressive and hard-sell. They apply pressure for making decisions quickly. All aspects of American life are affected by the predominance of *doing*. Work gives Americans identity. They often define themselves and others by the work they do; the first question they ask new acquaintances is what they do for a living.

A recent study of work patterns by the United States Bureau of Labor Statistics found that most Americans do not want a shorter work week. Nearly two-thirds of those questioned wanted no change—except for longer hours. People are working longer hours and liking it. When work was studied in relation to other activities, it ranked third after child care and socializing but ahead of reading, sports, spectator events, crafts, television, cooking, repairs, organizations, shopping and cleaning.[4] A conclusion of the study was that work is so popular because it allows people to interact with other people and these interpersonal relationships on the job are very important. Characteristics of the job ranked very highly. People said they received satisfaction from the nature of the job, and it is higher for jobs that are also challenging.

Elsewhere identity often stems from religion, family and community. Others see Americans as "workaholics." In many other cultures, work is seen as something that must be done out of necessity. It is not an all-consuming drive and certainly not appreciated for its own sake. In some countries, in fact, hard work for men is considered unmanly.

Foreigners feel Americans often promise more than they can deliver in order to clinch a deal. A Royal Bank of Canada publication once expressed Canadians' views toward their neighbors, among which were that Americans are:

> much given to travel, colourful clothing, gadgets, handheld foods, and striking metaphoric variations of the English language. They prefer first and second names, and, in conversation, they seem to use "yours" in every sentence or two.... They belong to clubs and lodges named after animals. They talk to strangers on street corners and at lunch counters. As they themselves would put it, they're "friendly as hell."

*Open.* Although the desire to save face exists in the United States, it is not so strong as in some other countries. Americans may feel a little guilty or inadequate when a mistake is pointed out to them; an Asian, Arab or South American may feel deep shame and humiliation. What Americans see as a little constructive criticism, others may take as a devastating blow to pride and dignity. They consider it weak and untrustworthy to embarrass others by open criticism.

Americans' view of space also differs from that of other nations. To us space indicates status. More important people have more space. Window offices are high-status in the United States. In other countries they may be the opposite; in Japan, for example, the expression "sitting near the window" indicates employees who are ready for retirement.[5] Others, like Arabs, Latins and some Asians want to get much closer than Americans like in interpersonal relations.

In *The Hidden Dimension,* Edward T. Hall describes the space requirements of the American culture. We all operate within a space bubble, he asserts, that is about arm's length around us — up to 18 inches. If anyone comes within that zone, he or she had better have good reason for doing so — like to tell us a secret. That Hall calls our intimate zone. Space from there to four feet he calls our personal zone, the space for interpersonal communicating without discomfort; most business transactions occur in this zone. Up to ten feet is our social zone, the area in which we do most of our socializing, and beyond ten feet is our public zone in which, for example, we do our public speaking.[6]

## The Economy

The growth of the American economy after World War II was remarkable; in 1940 the gross national product of the country amounted to about $100 billion. By the 1960s, it had reached $850 billion, more than 40 percent of the output of the rest of the noncommunist world.

The United States is today number one in the world in gross national product (source: *Statistical Abstracts of the U.S.,* 1988), gold reserves (millions of ounces of gold held; source: International Monetary Fund) and imports and second in exports. The country's industrial/agricultural/technological lead in the world market is awesome but under challenge. In 1945, the United States commanded a 40 percent share of the global economy; by 1990, that share is expected to be about 18 percent. As the economy weakens, middle managers are being pared in a process called "downsizing," and those that survive are finding their responsibilities expanded and their functions changed.

A 1988 report of the MIT Commission on Industrial Productivity listed these causes for problems in the American economy:

- Excessive attention to activities and investments that are profitable in the short run.
- Parochial attitudes that led American businesses to pay insufficient attention to foreign competitors.
- A lack of cooperation within firms, among competing firms and between firms and their suppliers.
- Weaknesses in human resource management which views workers as a cost factor rather than as an evolving resource that has to be educated and motivated.
- Failure to apply technology to make simple, reliable, high-quality products.

Corporate structures are changing to accommodate broader information gathering and to let data flow from shop floor to executive suite without the editing, monitoring and second-guessing that have been the middle manager's function.[7] Companies are now saying, "We'll take care of you as long as we're winning." Workers are responding by lowering loyalty to their organizations.[8]

The proportion of people employed in America has increased from 40 percent of the population in 1970 to 46 percent today. The overall labor force has grown by nearly 28 percent since 1973, to more than 115 million, as the baby boom has swelled the number of working-age people. Two-thirds of the 33 million new workers are women, who now account for 44 percent of all employees.[9]

## Organizational Communication

Communication is important in all human activity. According to David Berlo, the average American spends about 70 percent of waking hours communicating verbally—listening, speaking, reading, and writing, in that order. Each person spends about 11 hours every day performing verbal communication behaviors.[10] Much of that time is spent on the job where communication is intensified and expanded.

In doing business with American firms, one can expect prompt responses to letters with usually a receptive attitude to business relations. The Information Age is changing how business is conducted from that point on. If you send materials on fax machines for example, for the sake of speed, you may be asked to also send by mail the original copy for record-keeping purposes. If you telephone an American office, your number may be shown on a screen, enabling the receiver to answer or not as he or she wishes, to let you leave a message or to send the call to another person for handling.

Because Americans view time as money, they try to use it productively and compartmentalize it into efficient intervals of activity on their daily calendars. So being punctual for appointments is considered important. In many ways Americans rank matters of time — earlier is better than later, first is better than last, faster better than slower, and so on.

Usually the location of a meeting is important. The higher up an office is in a building, the higher the status of the individual with whom one has the appointment. Top floors are often reserved for the top manager and his staff. Visitors asked to wait in a public or general waiting room more than likely have a meeting with a middle manager. Upper management usually has private areas where visitors may wait in considerable comfort.

A visitor will be kept waiting only briefly, if at all; a long wait communicates disrespect or lack of interest, or an extreme disparity in status. The American greeting ceremony is brief and uncomplicated. Hands may be shaken or not; and if a handshake is offered, a firm grip should be returned. The visitor should present a business card during the early stages of the visit. After a few pleasantries, the people at the meeting will get straight down to the purpose of the meeting and will complete the time in the allotted time — 20 minutes, 40 minutes or an hour. During conversations, it is proper to look into the face and eyes of the other individual, a sign of honesty and straightforwardness. Most American business firms are decentralized so that decision-making authority is widely dispersed. Those with whom you are meeting may or may not have the right to make final decisions on business matters.

In other cultures, meetings begin with a process of getting acquainted which may take hours, days or even weeks during which the objectives of the meeting are not mentioned. Arabs consider the drinking of coffee and chatting as "doing something"; Americans view that as "doing nothing." During these apparently aimless conversations, progress is being made toward establishing credibility and rapport which are fundamental to doing business in those cultures.

Every American business organization has two systems of communication, formal and informal. The formal system, shown on Figure 5, follows the chain of command. Authority is delegated from one level of the organization to another according to strict codes which include communication procedures. It is erroneous, however, to equate the chain of command with the communication system, as some do, because it is just one of numerous influences on corporate communication, including important social and procedural factors.

The informal system is found in social relationships of employees. Management neither requires nor controls it. An informal communication system generally arises in a corporation as a dynamic, variable force running across organizational lines and rapidly changing course. Employees refer to this communication network as the grapevine and to messages it carries as rumors, though research has shown it carries more than that.

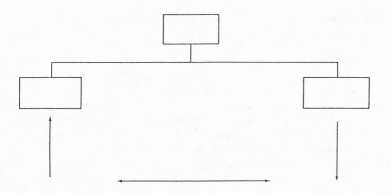

*Upward*

Written:
  memorandum
  report
  suggestion system
  question box
  company newspaper/magazine

Personal:
  meeting
  manager's meal
  plant panel
  telephone hotline
  interview
  open-door policy
  grievance procedure
  employee counselor
  rumor-control center

*Downward*

Print:
  annual report
  annual report to employees
  company newspaper/magazine
  newsletter
  bulletin board
  orientation manual
  letters to employees' homes
  pay envelope inserts
  manual/handbook
  mailgram

Electronic:
  telephone messages
  closed-circuit television
  teleconferencing
  film
  videotape
  electronic mail

*Horizontal*

personal contact
memorandum
meetings/conferences

**Figure 5. Formal communication in American corporations.**

*The Formal System.* Usually based on a written policy like that of General Motors Corporation in the Appendix, the formal communication system in American corporations is described by the directional flow of information through channels: downward, upward, and horizontal. Information is defined as knowledge that contains an element of surprise. If it didn't, why would anyone want it? A channel is the means through which the message travels from the source to the destination.

Also part of the formal corporate communication system are messages into the organization in the form of reports, letters, telephone calls, and visits to the company by outsiders, and messages out of the company through reports, letters, telephone calls, and visits outside by employees.

Most corporations base their formal communication systems on a corporate communication policy that expresses objectives management wants to achieve through its communication program and contains guidelines for decision-making about communication issues. Writing such a communication policy down creates proactive rather than reactive methods of management; that is, methods that emphasize planning and preparation rather than reaction to events as they unfold. A written policy also increases employee participation in communication programs. Many companies, however, choose not to put the communication policy into writing, with the result that each manager is free to create a policy for himself or herself. Most written communication policy statements include a need for regular, open, two-way communication; list some subjects that should and should not be covered; and state who is responsible for carrying out the program — sometimes a corporate communications manager and sometimes all individual managers and supervisors of the company.

Channels of communication take different forms based on the organization and the country in which it is located. The communication program in the American business organization is best equipped for downward communication and is designed for speed and efficiency.

Superiors communicate with subordinates through downward channels, the most studied form of communication in American business organizations. Channels for communicating downward are usually numerous and opportunities for using them unlimited, to inform employees about the organization and direct them in work tasks. Those at the top have the status for initiating communication as well as a greater need to do so, and they are certainly less inhibited about taking such action. Communicating well is part of a manager's directing function, in which he or she tries to ensure that subordinates contribute as much as possible to the organization's success. Such emphasis must cover every level in an organization and every group within it, including the union. Only then can there be free expression by all who are in a position to contribute to organizational efficiency. The most important piece of business communication, the annual report, is included here because most companies use it to communicate with employees along with other important publics. Relaying orders, policies and plans is at the heart of managerial communication.

The day is past in the United States, however, when those are the only purposes for sending information down the organizational chart. Sophisticated, better educated employees are demanding to know more about the company, its future and its position versus the competition. Other subjects that interest them are facts about new products, fringe benefit programs, sales successes, work of other departments and divisions, status of company products, business trends, competition, and the company's stand on union issues.

Old methods of "talking to" employees through print media primarily have become inadequate. More and more companies are using audiovisual techniques to do the same job quicker and cheaper. Both the oldest and newest techniques — and some feel the most exciting methods — of communicating down the management line are electronic. The growth of the telephone has paralleled that of the corporation, at least in the United States. And modern methods of film making and teleconferencing are rapidly revolutionizing corporate communication today.

A problem with downward media is their one-way nature. Most American companies would benefit from greater attention to upward communication as a balance to downward communication. Upward communication is the transmission of information from subordinate to superior, not necessarily one's immediate supervisor. Informal oral reporting of job performance to a supervisor is the most common form of upward communication. Communicating up the line helps employees relieve job pressures and frustrations, enhances employees' sense of participating in the business, and suggests better methods of downward communication. A good system of upward communication requires these elements: a permissive atmosphere for communicating, a purposeful effort by management that encourages communication, and channels available for upward communicating.

A 1988 survey by Louis Harris and Associates determined that American office workers "want to work under management that lets them help make decisions, that encourages free exchange of information and that is honest and ethical."[11] Most respondents said they did not presently work for such a management team. A companion study of management showed that top executives are increasingly aware of employees' desires for more participation and openness, but many of them appeared to underestimate the priority that workers give to those noneconomic aspects of the job.

Upward communication is effective to the extent that downward communication is successful. When downward communication remains consistent and forthright, upward communicating grows easier and stronger. Little helpful upward communication takes place unless downward messages set the tone and establish the kind of permissive atmosphere for communicating in which subordinates have access to higher management and superiors are receptive to communications from lower levels of the organizational chart.

Upward communication is the response that completes the circuit begun by downward communication. The destination takes the source's message and completes the circuit by responding. A circuit broken by poor upward flow of information reduces for management the stimulation of employee interest and participation, valuable employee ideas, understanding of how downward communication has been accepted, and more information for better planning and decision-making. Even more urgent than the right atmosphere, though, is a conscientious effort by managers to encourage upward communication. Managers who cannot get subordinates to communicate freely remain ignorant of subjects they should know.

Finally, for proper communicating up the line, channels must exist for upward communication; messages sent upward must be heeded; and skills of all involved in upward communication must be sharpened to eliminate distortion and speed transmission. Upward communication should include highlights of employees' work; achievements, progress, and future job plans; information on unsolved problems; suggestions for improvements in employees' own jobs or in the company as a whole; and employee attitudes and opinions about the company. That managers would prefer to ignore any of those today is unimaginable, but many do.

Peter Drucker has suggested that a requirement of the information-based corporation—and in the Information Age, all corporations are that—is that everyone takes information responsibility. Each employee should ask questions like these: Who in this corporation depends on me for what information? On whom, in turn, do I depend? Each list, Drucker states, will include both superiors and subordinates, but the most important names on it will be those of colleagues, people with whom one's primary relationship is coordination and whose communication is horizontal.[12]

Usually for the purpose of coordinating work between lateral units in the organization, horizontal communication has very few channels: personal contact, memos and meetings. Even though more communicating goes on between employees on the same level of the organization than between those on different levels (through vertical communication), horizontal communication is the least studied form of corporate communication. That's unfortunate because improvements are needed for communicating laterally in American companies. To encourage horizontal communication, a manager must treat subordinates impartially, demanding no special recognition for himself or herself, and must keep information flowing circularly through his department and vertically to higher as well as lower sources.

Often lateral communication is a tedious process in which a person wishing to transmit a message to another person on the same level of the management chart, but to one who reports to a different supervisor, must give the message to his or her own superior who then relays it to the individual on his or her supervisory level on the management chart (to whom the destination-individual reports) who in turn sends it down to that person.

For those who report to the same superior, the process of communicating laterally is easier. It simply involves the superior's getting employees together in meetings and conferences periodically to allow them to discuss their work.

The importance of horizontal communication varies with management style. In an authoritarian system, information becomes the protected property of select groups for use in controlling people at lower levels; little communication moves between lateral groups. The division executive, for example, knows about his or her department heads and their respective areas, but each of them knows little or nothing about one another's areas. That leaves the division executive in a powerful position to manipulate and control his or her subordinates at will.

*The Informal System.* In addition to the formal communication system, the American corporation has an informal system, often called the grapevine (a term traceable to the Civil War custom of hanging telegraph wires loosely from tree to tree like a grapevine. Messages were often garbled and false information was attributed to the grapevine).

We say the grapevine supplements the formal system; however, studies show that more than half and sometimes as much as 85 percent of information circulating in an organization is being transmitted on the grapevine. Because informal channels are predicated on social relationships, the grapevine transmits information faster than formal channels do.

Research has also shown that information on the grapevine moves in clusters. That is, one person tells three or four others, only some of whom pass it along. That grouping is called a cluster; the whole framework is called a cluster chain. By the time information reaches the fourth cluster, it is only about 5 percent complete. Overall, however, information passed along the informal network of communication is from 75 to 95 percent accurate.[13] The grapevine is particularly effective in coordinating horizontal activities.

Managers can use the grapevine to "feed" information to employees by identifying employees who serve as transmitters of grapevine information. They can use it also to identify employee sentiments on any given subject.

Though the grapevine serves as an important channel of much communication, according to surveys, it also contains many rumors and much gossip. In 1984 *Fortune* magazine estimated that a minimum of 33 million fresh rumors a day circulate in American industry.[14] That number is probably greater today. Rumors are the elements in the grapevine that inject inaccuracies, the part managers need to bring under control.

Rumors proliferate during periods of stress in a company — a strike or threatened strike; negotiations on a merger, invited or not; change of any sort. Many companies have found it useful during such periods to set up a rumor control center where any employee can take any rumor and have it confirmed or denied on the spot.

# A Survey

For information on how corporations around the world communicate internally, the author conducted a survey. Questionnaires were mailed to 475 companies from the Fortune International 500 list (whose addresses were available) in December 1986 and January 1987 and to 100 companies of third-world countries with poor or no representation on that list.

The questionnaire was intended to compare the organizational communication systems in foreign corporations with that of the United States described above. A sample questionnaire appears in Chapter 8. The first two questions in the survey asked whether the receiver's company uses a communication policy and whether it is written down. Respondents were then provided a list of the most-used channels of upward communication in the American corporation and asked to check off those that they also use and to add others that they use frequently. The same procedure was followed for downward and horizontal communication. Finally, inquiries were made about channels that may be unique to the company, the importance in the company of the grapevine, the importance of nonverbal communication in the firm and suggested methods of improving the company's system of communicating. The results of the survey appear in full and are described thoroughly in Chapter 8. The survey results also form the basis for discussions of organizational communication programs in countries discussed throughout the book.

# Canada

*Official Name:* Canada; *Capital:* Ottowa; *Government:* federal state recognizing Elizabeth II as sovereign; *Subdivisions:* 10 provinces and 2 territories; *Population:* 25,857,943 (July 1987); *Density:* 5 per square mile; *Currency:* dollar; *Official Languages:* English and French; *Literacy:* 99 percent.

## The Land

The largest country in the Western Hemisphere and second largest in the world next to the Soviet Union, Canada occupies the northern half of the North American continent along with Alaska and Greenland. Within its area are six time zones.

Canada includes ten provinces and the two territories of the Yukon and the Northwest Territories, both of which are located in the northernmost parts of the country. New Brunswick, Prince Edward Island and Nova Scotia are collectively referred to as the Maritime Provinces. With Newfoundland included, they are the Atlantic Provinces.

Canada encompasses many contrasts in topography, climate, vegetation and resources; the country has been called a "geographical improbability." Much of the land is mountainous and rocky or is under an Arctic climate. The developed portion represents less than a third of the total land area.

Canada has no equivalent of the United States' South or Midwest. Between the east and west lie nearly 1,000 miles of the core of an eroded mountain chain called the Canadian Shield (a vast, U-shaped, rocky expanse that surrounds the Hudson Bay). It covers 46 percent of the country's land area and 80 percent of the Province of Quebec and includes 470,000 square miles of rocky coniferous forest and some of the oldest rock in the world. There are prairies and Rocky Mountains in the west and forest and tundra in the north.

The Canadian Maritime Provinces and New England form a natural unit. The narrow belt of heavy population running from Montreal through Toronto to include the peninsula that is southern Ontario is geographically a part of the American Midwest. Toronto and Montreal, however, are not Canada's Chicago; rather they are sociologically more like New York. Winnipeg—what Canadians call the West—is the natural geographic extension of North Dakota, Montana and Idaho. Beyond the Rockies is Canada's Pacific coast, a natural extension of the American Pacific Northwest, whose residents relate more closely to the southern neighbors in Washington and Oregon than they do to residents of Ontario and Quebec.

Canada avoided having a "wild West" because civilization in the form of the Royal Canadian Mounted Police ("Mounties"), the railway agent, the bank manager, the missionary and Hudson's Bay Company usually arrived before or along with the settlers. Thus there have always been less violence and greater respect for authority in Canada than in the United States.

## The People

One of the least densely populated countries in the world, Canada is only twenty-eighth among nations in terms of population. Canada is experiencing decreased fertility, increased divorce, smaller families, a growing number of aged, and an increasing number of households. Though still a small proportion of total Canadian families, one-parent families are increasing faster than husband-wife families.

Most of the population lives within 200 miles of Canada's southern border. Their ancestry is English and French, with some German, Dutch and Irish. French Canadians are dominant in Quebec but also live throughout the Maritimes; New Brunswick is 40 percent French-speaking. The English presence in the Atlantic Provinces is principally in the industrial centers.

Canada is the most difficult country in the world for which to discern a distinct national character, primarily because it is divided into two different linguistic and cultural traditions — English and French — that remain exclusive of each other. About 28 percent of the population is French, with the majority concentrated in the Province of Quebec. Quebec is actively encouraging the French language and culture in that province by laws emphasizing, and in most cases requiring, the French language in government, business and the professions. Businesses operating in Quebec may be subject to provincial legislation requiring the use of French in certain circumstances, such as operations and advertising. Generally the French-speaking people are more outgoing and open than those of British descent. Canadian people are generally more reserved than Americans.

With large-scale immigration in the twentieth century, this dualism became pluralism. Strong European ethnic affiliations are maintained by various groups of Canadians, a system deeply embedded in Canadian values. Their position in the British Commonwealth has perhaps decreased a push for a distinctive Canadian ethnicity, a new nation with dominant cultural goals such as life, liberty and the pursuit of happiness or equality and opportunity. National identity is superseded by a strong regional identification; however, overriding national concerns are peace, good government and order.

The family is the center of Canadian society; homes are often passed on from generation to generation. Canadians are generally not as mobile as are residents of the United States and ties among relatives are strong. The family unit is the center of society. The average size of a Canadian family is 3.5 persons.

Somewhat nationalistic, Canadians today resent the arrogance of the United States, particularly regarding a perceived insensitivity to Canadians' feelings. A favorite saying is "Big and strong and never wrong." Former Prime Minister Pierre Trudeau, in a well-known remark, compared the United States–Canada relationship to an elephant in bed with a mouse. "Even a friendly nuzzling can sometimes lead to frightening consequence."[15] Canadians focus on their differences with residents of the United States, even though they find it difficult to describe those differences. Canadians resent the Americans' habit of emphasizing the similarities and expressing the view that they are "just like us." One writer explained the attitude this way:

> The basic experience of Canadian history has been that of sharing the northern part of the continent with the other, larger America. Everywhere in the twentieth century, man is becoming American, or, to put it another way, is moving in some way towards a condition of high industrialization, affluence and leisure, instant communication, an urban man-made environment, and a mingling of cultures and traditions in a mobile, classless global society. There is no country in the world, except the United States, which has gone further in this direction than Canada; none that has done so in such an American way; and none that is so experienced in the art of living with, emulating and differing with the United States.[16]

Many members of the Canadian elite fear that the natural progression of this growing similarity is that the American culture will so dominate the Canadian culture that Canada will eventually join America politically. Many worry that Canadian resources are increasingly owned and operated by Americans for their own profit; that when the chips are down, United States branch offices will become the instruments of American foreign policy.

## A Brief History

Jacques Cartier, sailing into the Gulf of St. Lawrence, claimed his newly discovered land, now Quebec, for the king of France on July 24, 1534. Cabot discovered Newfoundland for the British as early as 1497, but it was not until 1583 that formal claim to Newfoundland was made by Sir Humphrey Gilbert for Queen Elizabeth I. These earliest explorers found native peoples — Indians and Eskimos — living in the area.

The North American rivalry between the French and English began early and was a reflection of the great European conflicts between France and England. In the early seventeenth century, large numbers of French explorers seeking riches found them in the lucrative fur trade which led to the establishment of French colonies in the area surrounding the Gulf of St. Lawrence and the St. Lawrence River and its tributaries. Soon English traders arrived to establish trading posts along the shore of Hudson Bay.

Canada was united as a separate nation on July 1, 1867, by the British North American Act. Only recently, however, has the House of Parliament in the United Kingdom voted to amend it so that the Canadian constitution could be brought home (that is, so the nation would not suffer the indignity of being founded on a piece of British legislation). By the end of the first quarter of the twentieth century, Canada's independence, actually achieved in earlier years, had been formally confirmed, with all aspects of Canada's administration controlled by popularly elected government. However, Canada remains an active member of the Commonwealth.

The variations between Canada and the United States stem from the founding event which gave birth to both: the American Revolution. Residents of the colonies loyal to the Crown — "Tories" to Americans and "United Empire Loyalists" to Canadians — went to Canada. The British forces ultimately defeated the French, and control of the upper half of the North American continent passed into British hands in 1763 at the end of the Seven Years' War. For Canadians to have a "United Empire Loyalist" in their ancestry is as prestigious as it is for Americans to have a *Mayflower* passenger in theirs.

After World War II, Canadians saw the increasing link with the United States as a symbol of their growing independence from the United Kingdom. Today Canada retains formal ties with Britain; but, as a result of the revised constitution of 1982, it is completely independent in both internal and foreign affairs. In the summer of 1987, Prime Minister Brian Mulroney and the premiers of all 10 provinces signed an accord making Quebec a full constitutional partner by recognizing its distinct French culture.[17]

Canada's political system is British by origin, even though it has been influenced by political practices in the United States. Canadians place a greater emphasis on order than do residents of the United States, who treasure liberty above all else. Canada's first constitution set up objectives of "peace, order and good government" (not "life, liberty and the pursuit of happiness").

## The Economy

Canada and the United States conduct the world's largest bilateral trade and are each other's best trading partners. Almost 80 percent of Canadian exports are absorbed by the United States market and an estimated two million Canadian jobs are directly dependent upon continued access to this market. The two-way volume of trade between Canada and the United States — $236 billion (U.S.) in goods and $56 billion in services in 1986 — is the largest between any two nations in the world. Most of this trade is relatively tariff-free and unrestricted, partly as a result of the last General Agreement on Tariffs and Trade (GATT) round of multilateral trade negotiations, but also because of the integrated nature of the two economies. Much of this integration arises from the strong intra-corporate ties between the two countries. Roughly 50 percent of total two-way trade occurs between related firms, that is, between parent companies and their subsidiaries located in the other country.[18] These two countries also share the world's largest undefended border and are partners in the North American Aerospace Defense Command (NORAD).

The Canadian economy is only about 10 percent that of the American economy. To the United States, Canada is just one of many trading partners. To Canada, the United States is an omnipresent colossus. It takes the bulk of Canadian exports and provides the bulk of Canadian imports and is an enormous presence in all dimensions.

Because of strong cultural ties to Europe, particularly France and England, European styles prevail. Canada differs from America and resembles Britain in recruiting business and political elite from among those without a professional or technical education. "Canadian managers tend to be less well educated than their counterparts in any other industrialized country with the possible exception of Britain."[19] Entrance to the economic elite is easiest from the upper classes in Canada, much more so than in the United States. "The U.S. elite is more open, recruiting from a much broader class base than is the case in Canada. Sixty-one percent of the Canadian top executives are of upper-class origin compared to 36 percent of the Americans."[20] Canada is still a more elitist or deferential society than the United States, although it is less so than two decades ago.

Canada is the world's second largest producer of gold, the third largest producer of silver, fourth in uranium and fifth in copper and iron ore. It also produces a great amount of barley, oats and wheat.

The labor force in Canada as a percentage of the total population is very high at nearly 60 percent, partly because of the large number of immigrants coming in at ages between 20 and 45 to swell the work force. It is also due to a great increase in the number of women going to work, now more than 50 percent higher than in the mid-1960s. From a management standpoint, workers are very punctual, but the fun-loving French Canadians are more easy-going and less time conscious.

Labor relations are less settled than in the United States or Britain and as a result there are more strikes. The Canadian government has tried to overcome this through a sensible Labour Code which provides that both employees and employers may organize for collective bargaining; that unions may be certified as sole bargaining agents if they have a majority of the unionized work force; that unions and employers must bargain in good faith; that no strike may be called until after a cooling-off period; and that arbitration must be resorted to and respected in the case of a deadlock in negotiations. Fair employment practices, prohibiting discrimination because of race, religion, or national origin, are enforced, and work standards, especially with respect to hours, are maintained.

## Organizational Communication

Canadian English more closely resembles that spoken in the United States than that in the United Kingdom, though a few British usages remain: "vitamin" with "vit" pronounced to rhyme with "bit," "aluminium" with four syllables and a changed accent (on the third syllable), "controversy" with the accent on the second syllable, "schedule" as if there were no "c," "been" pronounced like "bean," "again" pronounced like "a-gane," "lieutenant" pronounced like "leftenant," "out" and "house" pronounced like "ute" and "whose," and "eh?" tacked on to end of sentences.

The common assumption that more formality is needed in Canadian business relations is not really true. As in America, the telephone call is the preferred method of making an appointment and one may do so with an executive's secretary who controls his or her schedule. Because many people are conservative, they may be suspicious of new ideas or a "slick salesman" approach. Canadians are very down-to-earth people who appreciate this quality in others.

Gestures in Canada are the same as in the United States. The handshake is common. Canadian men like to leave two buttons rather than one unbuttoned at the top of their shirts. Women in Quebec tend to look a bit more European than other women in the country. Topics to avoid are Canada's political or economic separateness from the United States. Belittling Canada will cause a visitor to lose credibility very rapidly.

Also as in the United States, the luncheon is an appropriate forum for business. In Canada, one has a greater chance than in the United States of being invited to a business associate's home or even to a weekend place.

Business communications are direct and to the point; the expectation is for clarity and thoroughness in information exchange. Be conservative in presentation and behavior and, more important, be familiar with Canada's geography, political system and current events. The formal communication system of a typical Canadian company is shown on Figure 6.

## CASE STUDY: DOFASCO, INC., HAMILTON, ONTARIO

*History.* Dofasco, Inc., largest producer of flat rolled steel in Canada, began as a steel foundry in 1912, with 150 employees who produced 80 tons of castings per day from one open-hearth furnace. The company became a fully integrated steelmaker in 1951 with the commissioning of the first blast furnace. In 1954, the first heat was tapped from the first basic oxygen furnace in North America, followed in 1955 by the operation of the first continuous galvanizing line in Canada. Today the plant is Canada's second largest steelmaker with an annual capacity of more than four million tons produced by 11,300 employees.

*Management.* From the beginning, management at Dofasco was designed to reflect two basic priorities: people and process. The idea was this: "it's good business to create an environment of trust in which such labels as 'employee/employer' and 'blue collar/white collar' are not enshrined." It was designed as a form of employee relations from which technical excellence, quality and productivity — the process side of the equation — would be a natural outcome. Dofasco's management approach has been to try to create the right environment. Dofasco people have created the right results.

*Communication.* Communication is so important to the Dofasco approach, it cannot be left to chance, or good intentions. It's built into the day-to-day operations of the company at every level. But beyond that, are more formalized communications pipelines — their publications.

*News 'n' Views,* the monthly employee newspaper is designed to keep employees as well as those in the government and business worlds abreast of company developments that affect the company. It also contains news of promotions, recreation programs, births, deaths, retirements and even a

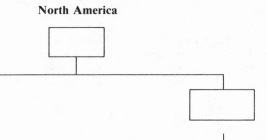

*Upward*                                        *Downard*

Written:                        Print:
  memo                            annual report
  report                           newspaper/magazine
  suggestion system                bulletin board
                                   orientation manual
Personal:                         letters
  meeting                          handbook
  interview
  open-door policy               Electronic:
                                   telephone
Formal:                           videotape
  performance
  evaluation                     Personal:
                                   meetings
                                   special events

*Horizontal*

personal contact
memorandum
meeting
teams or task forces

**Figure 6. Formal communication in Canadian corporations.**

classified ad section. An interesting and unusual feature of this newspaper is a "Sending Thanks" column through which employees may extend appreciation to anyone they wish for favors rendered.

The Dofasco *Illustrated News* is a four-color magazine that appears eight times annually. This publication covers stories of general interest to Canadians, not related to either Dofasco or the steel industry, as well as stories on promotions and plant activities. *Illustrated News* goes out to all employees, shareholders and a wide variety of other readers, including public servants and politicians from all levels of government, libraries across Canada and the media.

*Steel Quarter,* which appears four times annually, is aimed at customers and those in media who cover the steel industry. It contains stories on new products and services, economic projections and supply bulletins.

Besides these publications, Dofasco communicates with its employees in a host of other ways. Bulletin boards throughout the office and plant provide an immediate vehicle for swift communications requirements. The company also uses the annual report and orientation manual to communicate with employees. A *Management Newsletter* is sent out monthly by the president to keep supervisors apprised of current company developments. An active publicity program ensures that the media are kept abreast of company positions and activities. Various letters are inserted into pay envelopes and an employee handbook is constantly updated.

Various forms of electronic communications are used for day-to-day business, including telephones and teleconferencing as well as film, videotape and other visual assists for oral presentations and training.

If an employee has a question or concern and is not satisfied with the answer from his or her immediate supervisor, there is a clearly stated right to take the problem to the next supervisory level . . . and the next. If still not satisfied, the employee has open-door access to senior management, including the president. Decisions can be modified or reversed at any level. The system aims at providing a fair and sympathetic hearing, but not necessarily the answer the employee is looking for.

The suggestion program gives employees an opportunity to share directly in the company's performance. Awards are based on the revenue or savings that the idea will generate. The company's top award is $30,000, on which the tax is paid. Since the program began in 1936, about 100,000 ideas have been submitted. Last year alone, 1,800 suggestions were implemented with awards totalling $286,000. It's a program from which both the company and employees benefit directly.

In addition, the company holds special events for employees each year which serve as means of communication. The Christmas party each year is attended by 33,000 employees and their families; the Quarter Century Club dinners recognize the completion of various apprenticeship and supervisory training courses; and special dinners and golf tournaments are held for the Dofasco ladies and other groups.

The company's Recreation Park, established on 100 acres in Hamilton, includes an all-weather track, soccer/football field, five baseball diamonds, a double-pad ice skating arena, tennis courts, a (golf) driving range, and a miniature golf layout. The various recreational programs that employees and their families participate in are a form of communicating and encouraging teamwork among employees.

## CASE STUDY: INCO LIMITED, TORONTO

*Management.* Inco Limited is the noncommunist world's leading producer of nickel and a substantial producer of copper, precious metals and cobalt. It is also the world's largest supplier of wrought and mechanically alloyed nickel alloys as well as a leading manufacturer of blades, discs, rings and other frazed and precious-machined components made from special alloy materials.

*Communication.* The company places great emphasis on maintaining open lines of communication with employees and working cooperatively with other unions. In its own words, this is how the company feels about communication:

The company will communicate with its employees its policies, plans and activities in order to reflect in a clear and timely manner its performance, current status and future interest. In order to accomplish this, each organizational unit will maintain a climate and relationship in which the understanding, respect and cooperation of employees is obtained.

Effective employee communications is the open exchange of information which utilizes the following principles and systems:

1. Management at each location will be responsible for continuous improvements to employee communications programs.

2. The use of face-to-face meetings and presentations will be maximized.

3. Corporate public affairs will disseminate to unit locations corporate messages/articles/information on performance, strategies and policies of the corporation for appropriate communication by the unit.

4. The procedures and programs in place will be monitored on a regular basis to ensure consistent and effective application of the policy.

To ensure consistent and effective application of the policy, all employee communications procedures and programs will be reviewed on a regular basis by a corporate employee communications review committee.

The committee will consist of the corporate vice presidents of industrial relations and employee benefits, human resources, and public affairs; their delegates and other senior management representatives. It will be chaired by the vice president, public affairs. The formation of similar committees is encouraged at each major company location.

## CASE STUDY: MOLSON COMPANIES, LTD., TORONTO

*History.* In 1786, John Molson founded a brewery in Montreal, now the oldest brewery in North America. The company today is a diversified Canadian corporation, employing 11,000 individuals in Canada and 35 other countries around the world.

Its current management system is decentralized. The company states of its philosophy: "As one of the oldest companies in Canada, we feel a responsibility to behave fairly, ethically and having regard for the wider consequences of our actions."

*Communication.* A Molson Companies employee publication, *Corp/Us,* described a system of "Lunching with the President." Employees lunch with the president every five or six weeks. The president is quoted as saying:

I see a lunch as another low key, relaxed opportunity for enhancing communication between the CEO and Corporate staff. What I would like to do as the host of the luncheons is informally bring people together who might not otherwise have the opportunity to sit down with each other to exchange

### Staff Luncheons

*Social element included to bring all
employees together
*Update employees on broad com-
pany issues, policies, results, etc.
*Some two-way communication
through questions/answers

### Corp/Us

*Formally covers business topics
*Updating TMCL "social" news
*Generally one-way communication

### Supervisors

*Formal and informal relationship to
discuss and address employee and
departmental issues, policies, etc.
*Two-way communication

### Announcements

*Specific items about people, results,
acquisitions, etc.
*One-way communication
*Bulletin boards

### J.P.R. Luncheon

*Get to know other employees better
*Exchange stories, ideas, suggestions
*Ask questions
*Two-way communication

### Peers

*Informal social network among
friends and co-workers who often
have common interests
*Two-way exchange of ideas and
opinions
*Many opportunities: pub, cafeteria,
Christmas party, special events,
children's party

**Figure 7. Employee communication program at Molson Companies, Ltd., Toronto, Canada.**

ideas and impressions about the Company and issues which confront us. In addition, as host, I guess I have the prerogative of serving one of my own interests, which is to get to know people a little more on a personal level. We did this sort of thing when I was in Brewing and I had positive response to the many dialogues we had.

A reporter responded: "But don't we already have a number of other vehicles for communication purposes?" The president replied:

Yes, there are a number of vehicles for communication with various groups of employees throughout the Corporation, and there are a number of vehicles that are used to communicate with employees at the Corporate Office. I think this informal luncheon series fills in the gap or completes the circle to ensure that we have complete, full, two-way communication at all levels. It might be best illustrated by a diagram [presented here as Figure 7].

Who's included in the luncheon and how are employees selected?

All permanent employees at the Corporate Office are on the invitation list. We want to make the selection as random as possible, and, in fact, names will literally be pulled out of a hat — or should I say envelope. However, to ensure that we have a good cross section of staff the process is designed to have people from different functions at each lunch.

I think it's important to bear in mind, however, that each person is included as a TMCL employee, and is not coming to the luncheon in an official capacity or position within the Company. The reason for the mixture is to ensure that a broad cross section of points of view be brought to the table.

# Notes

1. *Handbook of the Nations,* p. 256.
2. Philip R. Harris and Robert T. Moran, *Managing Cultural Differences,* p. 4.
3. Nancy J. Adler and Mariann Jelinek, "Is 'Organizational Culture' Culture Bound?" p. 79.
4. Carol Kleiman, "Thank God It's Friday!" p. 19.
5. L. Copeland and L. Griggs, *Going International,* p. 16.
6. Edward T. Hall, *The Hidden Dimension,* pp. 116–25.
7. "A New Era for Management," p. 50.
8. Thomas F. O'Boyle, "US Workers' Loyalty to Companies Wanes as Disillusion Mounts," p. 10.
9. Aaron Bernstein, "Warning: The Standard of Living Is Slipping," p. 49.
10. David Berlo, *The Process of Communication,* p. 1.
11. Michael R. Kagay, "Workers Want Their Employers to Listen to Them, Survey Shows," p. A25.
12. Peter Drucker, "The Coming of the New Organization," p. 49.
13. Keith Davis, *Human Behavior at Work,* p. 335.
14. Matt Miller, "Psssst ... Have You Heard the Latest?" p. 2.
15. "Foreigners Give the US Mixed Reviews," p. A12.
16. Richard G. Lipsey, "Canada and the United States," in Charles F. Doran and John H. Sigler, eds., *Canada and the US,* pp. 90–3.
17. "Canadian Premiers Sign Quebec into Fold," p. 2.
18. "The Economy," p. 1.
19. Seymour Martin Lipset, "Canada and the United States," in Doran and Sigler, p. 146.
20. Ibid.

# 3. Latin America

## Introduction

Latin America includes Mexico, 7 Central American countries and 12 South American countries plus numerous Caribbean islands. In Central America, all but Belize are primarily Spanish in culture. Nine of the 12 South American countries have a Spanish cultural base along with an ancient Indian heritage; one nation each has Portuguese, French and Dutch cultural inputs; all but Suriname share the Roman Catholic tradition. Only three Caribbean islands have a Spanish background.

Spanish America (i.e., not including Brazil) encompasses these 16 countries and three Caribbean islands: Argentina, Bolivia, Chile, Colombia, Costa Rica, Cuba, Ecuador, El Salvador, Guatemala, Honduras, Mexico, Nicaragua, Panama, Paraguay, Peru, Puerto Rico, Santo Domingo, Uruguay and Venezuela. Spain's heritage — feudal, dogmatic, hierarchical — still strongly influences the entire region.

## The Land

Covering over a seventh of the world's land surface, Latin America contains nearly every possible climate and landscape, even though three-quarters of its territory lies within the equatorial belt. More than half of Latin America is heavily forested, mountainous or arid. The Amazon River trunk of the world's largest river system is here, as is Mt. Aconcagua on the border of Chile and Argentina, the Western Hemisphere's highest point at 22,834 feet and just one of several peaks over 20,000 feet in the Andes, the world's largest mountain chain. Only 4 percent of the land has been cultivated. Geographically all of South America lies east of Florida.

## The People

Latin America has more than 340 million inhabitants, about half of them residing in Mexico and Brazil. A larger percentage of the population here is younger than in the United States. Most of the people have settled within 200 miles of the coast so that nearly all of the largest cities, with the notable exceptions of Mexico City and Bogota, are located on or near the coast.

The Aztecs and Incas, two of the most famous ancient civilizations, controlled large areas when Columbus landed in the Bahamas on October 12, 1492. The first Spanish colony, Santo Domingo, preceded colonization in the United States by more than a century.

The ancestors of most Latin Americans were born in Spain, Portugal and the Americas; however, immigrants have come from almost everywhere. A large number of Germans have settled in southern Brazil, Uruguay, Argentina and southern Chile, areas that resemble their homeland. Roughly half of Argentinians are of Italian descent. Southern Brazil includes the largest concentration of Asians in the Western World. The Caribbean, northern South America and Brazil have a large percentage of blacks, the descendants of Africans transported by European colonists to replace the Indians as slaves. Frequent intermarriage among races and nationalities has produced these distinct groups: *mestizos,* those of European and Indian ancestry; *mulattoes,* of mixed European and African descent; and *zambos,* of mixed Indian and Black heritage. People of European ancestry generally assume the most prestigious roles in Latin American society.

The spiritual unity of Latin America is *la raza,* the race. A Latin's concerns, in this order, are himself, family, personal friends, political party and country. Reaching a Latin individual requires relating everything in that order.

Spanish domination of Spanish America began in 1519; Portuguese domination of Brazil started in 1500. "The aims of the Conquest were economic, religious and political; or more colloquially, gold, souls and subjects."[1] Achieving that depended on controlling the indigenous population. "By 1650, six-sevenths of the Indian population — over ten million people — had been wiped out."[2] The Indians had suffered exploitation, biological collapse, deculturation and defeat.

The term "Indian" in Latin America today is used more in a socioeconomic and cultural than an ethnic sense. Indians are people who are mostly tribal, living in rural areas and employing ancient types of land cultivation that produce hardly enough to feed themselves; people who lack ambition or hope of improving their economic condition through better use of their land; people who lack time perspective in their economic behavior so that they fail to save against future contingencies.[3]

Basic differences exist between North Americans and Latin Americans. In the United States and many other countries, for example, the ideal of equality stresses similarities among people. Latin Americans look for the difference and uniqueness of individuals. Latin Americans also tend to assert themselves, to be inner-centered, to defend their identity when challenged and to respond to strength and aggression rather than persuasion and logic. Transcending everything is *personalismo* — concern for oneself. Getting work done in Latin organizations requires an intimate, personal relationship with the people doing the work plus a feeling of kinship.

Reserved, thoughtful ability does not appeal to them most in leadership; charisma, virility and strength speak far louder. Their sense of personal honor may make them seem touchy, sometimes over-sensitive to criticism or insult, needing considerable supportive praise. Latin Americans tend to trust only themselves, appearing at first to be skeptical, uncooperative and competitive. If others do not follow their lead, they may react arrogantly or express hurt feelings because their personal integrity is injured when their dignity is challenged. Often their family pride is damaged as well.

Another important aspect of Latin American life is *machismo* (literally "maleness"), the composite of virility, zest for action, competitiveness and the will to conquer which is revealed less in words than in actions like carrying pistols or keeping mistresses. His having *machismo* means that a man exhibits forcefulness and self confidence, visible courage and leadership with a flourish. Sexual prowess is included which is why birth control measures have always been resisted in Latin America. *Machismo* translates into business life through authoritarianism, an orientation with which Americans are likely to be uncomfortable. *Machismo* also limits women to subordinate roles in Latin organizations.

Fatalistic attitudes have been said to determine all Latin attitudes and modes of behavior. Fatalism inspires either heroic defiance or passive resignation. The first dictates that individuals must strive to live best and then die with *dignidad*. The tendency is strong, however, to "let chance guide destiny," and many seek to strike it rich by speculation, manipulation and gambling. As a result, many business managers are less interested in stable growth than they should be.

The single most important institution in Latin American life is the family whose relationships extend beyond blood and marriage by such institutions as *compadrazgo* (godfatherhood). Latin Americans use both the mother's and father's name, a source of pride to them and a factor in structuring the whole society. Family names identify lineage, economic, social and political position, and religion. Emphasis is placed on family connections in conducting both private and public enterprises.[4] These family relationships continue into adulthood, reinforcing the rigid character formation of the child which is strengthened further in the schools and churches.

The greatest problem in Latin America, particularly Central America, today is population growth, among the highest in the world. "A rapidly growing population is a fundamental source of the region's turmoil, intimately linked to the problems of health, housing, education, nutrition and land use."[5] According to the Latin American Demographic Center, a branch of the United Nations, in 1987 the population of the five Central American democracies exceeded 27 million, more than double the figure of 25 years earlier. The figure is projected to 40 million by the turn of the century, despite civil wars, mass migrations and a slightly declining birth rate.[6]

## A Brief History

Latin American history is fairly uniform. In the fifteenth and sixteenth centuries, European invaders, mostly Spanish conquistadores but also Portuguese conquerors, arrived and with surprising speed overpowered the native Indians. They quickly formed colonies for their homelands and stayed for 300 years. In fewer than 60 years — from 1492 to 1550 — the estimated 30,000 conquerors, colonizers and evangelizers explored vast territories, vanquished great empires, founded cities that still exist today as well as others that have since disappeared, and ineradicably spread the Roman Catholic faith and the Spanish and Portuguese languages and cultures.

As late as 1700, the Spanish American empire was richer, more powerful and more successful than the British colonies in North America. When the British were still trying to build their colonies, cities like Mexico City and Lima and a score of others were already thriving. By the end of the eighteenth century no city in North America could compare with many growing metropolises in Spanish America.

What happened later is well known. There was no Declaration of Independence among the Latin American states, no effort to unify them under a single constitution, no Manifest Destiny. Many other qualities of life in North America that made the difference were lacking as well. Basic attitudes toward work, for example, are quite different in the two cultures. To the British and other northern European settlers, manual labor was acceptable; to the Spanish colonists to the south, it was demeaning. Relationships within the family also differed. In the British colonies, wives were treated more as equals by their husbands, and the women pitched in and did their share of the farming. In Spanish households to the south, husbands dominated wives so as to obviate even the possibility of such cooperation. The Spanish believed that life follows a preordained course and all human action is ordained by God; the Northern Europeans believed the individual can influence the future. The Latins thought they should adapt to the physical environment rather than try to alter it; the Northern Europeans tried to change and improve the environment. The Latins said that hard work is only one prerequisite of success along with wisdom, luck and time; the Northern Europeans advanced the Puritan ethic: hard work accomplishes objectives.

Hidalgo and Morelos, two Catholic priests, led the early Mexican rebellions against Spain which culminated in 1821 in an empire consisting of Mexico and Central America. After two years, the Central American provinces separated and created the Central American Federation which broke apart in 1838 into the five present-day countries of Guatemala, Honduras, El Salvador, Nicaragua and Costa Rica. These have often historically been referred to as the five democracies of Central America. Belize is not included because, as British Honduras, it was not under Spanish rule. Panama is similarly excluded because it aligned itself with Colombia instead of joining the Federation.

South America ended Spanish rule at the battle of Ayacucho, Peru, in 1824. The new independent nations were basically the same as today's except that Panama, Colombia, Venezuela, and Ecuador were united as the Republic of Gran Colombia from 1819 until 1830, and Panama remained part of Colombia until 1903.

The Latin American social structure remained highly polarized until the early 1900s, with a small group of professionals squeezed between a few elite and the masses. The lower classes were identified mainly by manual labor, occupation, dress and degree of Spanish literacy; upper classes were distinguished by family membership in the landed and merchant aristocracy, including leadership of church, state and military.[7] Since World War II, many factors have contributed to the rapid growth of the middle class: immigration, industrialization, education and state-sponsored development programs. Latin American countries today, including those which share an Iberian background, differ from one another in outlook, temperament, political organization and management development.

## The Economy

For nearly 30 years beginning in 1950, Latin America boasted some of the highest economic growth rates in the world. Most Central American economies, for example, grew at a rate higher than that of the industrialized nations. Latin America was taking off economically.[8] Suddenly it all stopped and it is easy to understand why.

The growing economy did not alter the inequitable distribution of income and resources. The socioeconomic structure of the area repressed any attempts to broaden economic participation. The upper classes took most of the profits, leaving very little for anyone else. The oligarchy, which had controlled the coffee economy since 1950, expanded its control to other agricultural areas like sugar and cotton and to industry. A repressive security system enforced the interests of the few over the many. Finally, foreign corporations and banks directed industrialization in the region, using the national elite as junior partners.[9]

The result of the loss of prosperity has been an equal loss of interest in the region by foreign investors.

> A 1984 survey by the Council of the Americas, an association of major companies with Latin American affiliates, found that more than 35 percent of subsidiaries surveyed had cut back or closed their operations during the preceding year, and 40 percent more had not increased them. More than half the affiliates remitted no earnings to their U.S. parents from 1982 to 1984. From a peak of $38.8 billion in 1980, total U.S. investment fell to $32.7 billion in 1982 and to $29 billion in 1985. Now, barely 12 percent of all U.S. foreign investment is in Latin America, the smallest proportion since American companies began investing abroad.[10]

Today some United States companies have total world sales greater than the gross national products of certain Latin American countries. A few countries depend mainly on the production of a single crop or resource: tin in Bolivia, copper in Chile, beef in Uruguay, bananas in Honduras and oil in Venezuela.

On the other hand, Latin American economies have proven in the past to be very resilient. That was the message of a recent talk by David Rockefeller, former chairman of the board of Chase Manhattan Bank and in 1988 president of the Americas Society:

> Between 1980 and 1984, Brazil moved from a trade deficit of $2.8 billion to a surplus of more than $13 billion. Between 1981 and 1985, Mexico moved from a trade deficit of $4 billion to a surplus of nearly $14 billion.

These nations face serious problems again, but there is reason to believe that with patient cooperation among all interested parties these difficulties will not persist forever. Mexico already is recovering impressively. It also is significant that the interest payments of non-oil-exporting Latin American debtors as a percentage of their export earnings actually declined from 47 percent in 1982 to 34 percent in 1986.[11]

Latin America today is poorer than it was in the early 1980s. Per capita income dropped 14 percent in the first half of the eighties, so we would expect to find everyone a little worse off. If the cost of adjustment had been distributed evenly, that would be the case; however, the most disadvantaged have borne the brunt of the burden. The deterioration in the social situation throughout the region as a result has been proven in numerous studies and is now generally recognized.[12]

Complicating the situation further is the fact that many Latin Americans have an aversion for tasks that they consider menial. The work one does is directly related to the social class one is in, so many Latins prefer prestigious professions like law or medicine, believing that dealing with money is somehow demeaning. These aristocratic values have created an imbalance between manpower needs and supply. Seventy percent of Latin American workers have no industrial skills at all. The remaining 30 percent constitute an over supply of professional workers.[13]

The area today suffers from an acute shortage of managers. In Latin America, the line between white-collar and blue-collar workers is sharply drawn. In Spanish a white-collar is an *empleado* and a blue-collar worker is an *obrero*. The terms may also be used to distinguish manual from nonmanual workers, salaried from wage earners, office workers from factory workers, and union from nonunion members. In Latin America, the Spanish terms have greater significance than any of their English counterparts, however, because they represent the basic dividing line in the hierarchy both of a corporation and in society at large. In most traditional Latin firms, the words represent two stratification hierarchies. Since one has little chance of crossing the line between them, it is easiest for outsiders to think of the differences within each group as class differences and the differences between the two groups as caste differences.[14] In Latin America, *empleados* and *obreros* are different kinds of people. To some the difference is one of degree that could be overcome in moving from one position to the other; to others the condition is natural and fixed or at least should be.

If this stratification system is the most basic distinction among employees in Latin firms, the most characteristic feature of the management system is centralized decision-making. Decisions are made by the top managers who often are also the owners. In Latin America, management is a person, not a position or function.

A natural outcome of this management system is bypassing, the tendency for employees all along the chain of command to go straight to the decision-maker (the owner/manager) with any problems they may have instead of going through the chain of command. This violates the basic management tenet of unity of command which says information and authority should flow in a step-by-step process from top to bottom of the organizational chart.

To a certain extent bypassing grows out of the *patron* system that has long existed in Latin America. The *patron* relationship was originally a reciprocal one tying members of various social strata together in terms of reciprocal but unequal obligations. The owner of each *hacienda* or ranch is *patron* to his workers, owing them wages, housing, tools and maybe even a small plot of land as well as intangibles like protection from the law in times of trouble. The *patron* is expected to take a personal interest in each one of his workers and their families. In return, they owe him work and loyalty. Similarly, the owner-manager or *caudillo* (leader) of a corporation is master of his domain; he possesses great power and exercises total authority, believing that his employees want a strong man who can give orders. This same *caudillo,* however, will jump instantly when a more powerful person beckons.

Basic differences exist between methods of doing business in Latin America and North America. North Americans believe the best-qualified person should receive an available position; Latin Americans base appointments on family, friendship and other considerations. Those not performing well are terminated in North America; in Latin America such action would bring a great loss of prestige so it is done only rarely. Decisions in North America are made by persons in the best position to do so; in Latin America decisions are made by the person in authority and to question decisions indicates a lack of confidence in the leader's wisdom and judgment.

As owners or representatives of family interests, Latin managers are rarely guided by purely objective criteria as managers should be; instead they abide by family contacts and influences. This situation is beginning to change as experience teaches owners that ineffective past practice must be replaced by a more systematic method of selecting and training leaders. Generally speaking, Latin American managers are improving in education and are striving to do their best in a government-created commercial climate that at best is encouraging and at worst dismal.[15]

## Organizational Communication

Latin America is a very hierarchical society; status differences and authority are strongly emphasized. Respect is expressed in both tone of voice and manner, denoting grades of inferiority and superiority. Superior-subordinate relationships do not permit a Latin employee to approach a foreman or manager directly to discuss a problem. It is exceedingly difficult for Latin American people to express their differences face-to-face, especially with an authoritarian boss. Workers seek a third party—the government, sometimes— to solve their problems. To encourage upward communication within the Latin American firm, therefore, managers must not only provide employees channels of communication, as elsewhere, but they must also encourage employees to use them.

The most important communication problem in Latin American firms is bypassing, discussed in the previous section. On the one hand bypassing allows employees access to information when they need it; on the other hand, it interferes with proper management functions. With a properly operating formal communication system in place, employees would have no need to bypass their immediate supervisors in search of information or decisions.

As with so many other aspects of their lives, differences in communicating exist between Latin American countries and their northern neighbors. North Americans believe that information should be shared with anyone who needs it in the organization and that each person is expected to express opinions freely, even when they oppose others' views. Latin Americans prefer to withhold information to gain or maintain power, giving deference to persons in power or authority and offering opinions only when they agree with their superiors' thinking.

Anyone doing business in Latin American firms for the first time will find that one can make appointments by letter or by phone, but conducting business must be in person. Trying to do business in any other way is considered too impersonal by Latin Americans. The telephone is to them inappropriate for long business discussions; they usually use the telephone to ask simple questions that require easy answers or to arrange personal meetings. Letters received from Spanish firms are quite formal, respectful and complimentary; even in business they tend to be flowery. When communicating by mail or telex, answer a Latin's letter in the same language in which it was written—even when you know the recipient is fluent in English. If a Latin prefers to communicate in English, he will do so from the start.

The visitor will also find that Latin American business practices are conservative and formal. Business cards are usually exchanged, preferably printed in both Spanish and English on opposite sides and properly presented Spanish-side up. They should be retained as a valuable source of information for later use. Latin Americans shake hands on meeting and departing, usually with a loose grip that lasts about twice as long as the North American is used to. It is absolutely the minimum symbol of good manners and respect. If there are several people in the room, shake hands with each one. The *abrazo* or embrace is common among those who know each other well. One should not be too familiar and informal with strangers, however. Coffee will be offered and should not be refused, a sign of rejection to a Latin American. The nonbusiness conversation over coffee allows both parties to get to know one another better.

Don't call others by their first names until invited to do so. Take time to comment about the weather briefly. Discussion about families is not safe unless the Latin American brings up the subject. After a brief period of sizing up through informal discussion, the Latin American will decide when he knows the visitor well enough to do business. The approach will then be direct and to the point; however, the visitor may feel uncomfortable at the host's behavior. Discussion will be at a distance of four to eight inches, far closer than is common in the United States, but backing away is considered rude. The custom in the United States is a minimum of 18 inches for such discussions; closer than that makes an individual uncomfortable. A professor at a Puerto Rican university reported that her students feel North Americans are unfriendly because we are always backing away during conversations.

More important for the North American, touching is an important part of communication in Latin American countries. This may include shoulder, arm or chest tapping, lapel fingering and arm squeezing or poking. It's a sign of sincerity, a way of emphasizing their points, making sure you are listening and being personal. To show any sign of annoyance indicates rejection and insincerity to the Latin American.

It is extremely important to sell yourself, not your company, with Latin Americans because they can see you; the company is an unseen entity. It's the individual who counts in Latin America. The visitor may also learn that the host does not have the authority to make decisions on the business matters under discussion, that instead he explains that the matter will have to go to the top man for a final decision.

The host will do everything possible to avoid a confrontation with the visitor, even to the point of saying "yes" but meaning "no." The visitor is being turned down when the host says, "I can agree to that, but wait to hear from us on it before you proceed." In group discussions, everyone will discuss a point from every possible angle, testing the air, to allow those with minority views to back down and thereby save face.

During a meeting, the host may receive a phone call, excuse himself without explanation and leave. You may be told by the substitute representative, one with lesser authority, that a family matter called your original host away.

Nonverbal signs have different meanings in Latin America than elsewhere. The American "OK" sign, with thumb and index finger forming a circle, is obscene in Latin America and should not be used. Placing the index finger by the eyes means "be careful." Maintaining eye contact while conversing indicates interest and sincerity.

Table 4 summarizes some characteristics of Latin American organizational communication practices, and Figure 8 shows the Latin American organizational communication system.

## CASE STUDY: CRISTALERIA PELDAR, MEDELLIN, COLOMBIA

*History.* Cristaleria Peldar is the largest glass producer in Colombia. Products include glass containers, clear and bronze flat glass, rolled glass, mirrors and glasses and tumblers. Peldar has three manufacturing plants, realized 1986 sales of approximately $75 million (U.S.) and employs around 2,200 persons.

Peldar has a decentralized organization with three principal profit centers, each headed by a general manager. The company is in the midst of a program to modernize plants and equipment and to improve quality in all product lines. The company's objective is to be "The Best at What We Do."

*Communication.* Cristaleria Peldar does not have a formal, written policy concerning internal communication between management and employees nor among employees, but it does have a tradition of formal and informal communication that serves all levels of the organization.

### Table 4. Some Communication Practices in the Latin American Firm

Latin Americans:

1. Prefer face-to-face communication.
2. Are conservative and formal.
3. Expect to receive business cards, preferably printed in both English and Spanish (and to receive them Spanish-side up).
4. Shake hands loosely and twice as long as North Americans do.
5. Require a "sizing up" period.
6. Are direct and to the point in discussions.
7. Sometimes conduct business at a distance of 4 to 8 inches.
8. Touch others frequently during conversations.
9. Reserve decision-making for top managers.
10. Often say "yes" when they mean "no."
11. Avoid confrontations at any cost.
12. Often withhold information from others as a source of power.
13. Place family concerns above business matters.
14. Are high-context communicators.
15. Use time polychronically.

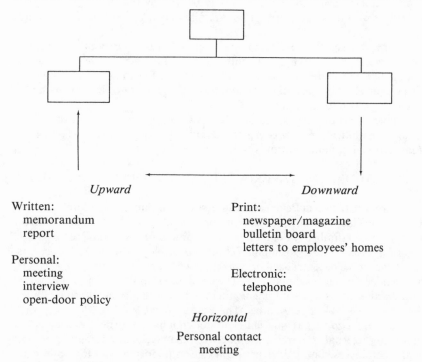

| *Upward* | | *Downward* |
|---|---|---|
| Written: | | Print: |
| memorandum | | newspaper/magazine |
| report | | bulletin board |
| | | letters to employees' homes |
| Personal: | | |
| meeting | | Electronic: |
| interview | | telephone |
| open-door policy | | |

*Horizontal*

Personal contact
meeting

**Figure 8. Formal communication in Latin American corporations.**

Modes of communication used by the company include the annual report, monthly letters from the president, plant newspapers and safety bulletins, and bulletin boards. Most formal, day-to-day communications with hourly people are handled through the use of the plant bulletin boards. Electronic modes of communication include primarily the telephone and secondarily videotape.

In addition to verbal communication, a great deal of information is channeled through the Colombian Manufacturers' Association. This includes information identified as from Peldar as well as anonymous surveys. The primary audience for this information is not the employee group. The company sometimes provides the same information through the more appropriate channels. Gilberto E. Restreto V., president of Peldar Corporation, stated this about his company:

> In understanding communications with hourly workers, it is important to understand something of the social situation in Colombia. Formal communications with labor are through the Communist-oriented union whose stated objective is to destroy the social institutions that exist in the country. Although the union speaks for the employees in its monthly and weekly newsletters and in contract negotiations, everyone is not in agreement with all of the stated objectives of the union. Written communications from the employees to management are exclusively controlled by the union, although an open-door policy per se does exist. There is considerable verbal communication directly with the workers and a grievance procedure does exist. Salaried employees, though, are informed through memorandums, reports, newspaper and an open-door policy for personal meetings.

Perhaps because of general education levels (in Colombia, education is mandatory through the fourth grade), the company tends to have some unique forms of communication. The most notable would be the safety magazine in the format of a comic book with colorful pictures and few written words.

# Mexico

*Official Name:* United Mexican States; *Capital:* Mexico City; *Government:* federal republic; *Subdivisions:* 31 states and 1 federal district; *Population:* 81,860,566 (July 1986); *Density:* 104.7 per square mile; *Currency:* peso; *Official Language:* Spanish; *Literacy:* 88.1 percent.

## The Land

The word "Mexico" (pronounced *May*-hee-co) derives from the language of the ancient Aztecs. About three times the size of Texas or one-quarter as large as the United States, Mexico is the fourteenth largest country in the world and the third in Latin America (after Brazil and Argentina).

The Third World and First World confront one another along the 1500-mile border that Mexico shares with the United States. No border on earth separates two more widely divergent standards of living between two nations.

It is the border crossed in both directions by more people than any other international border in the world.

Mexico is separated from the United States, on the east, or Texan end, by
the Rio Bravo (known in the U.S. as the Rio Grande) and on the western end
by the artificial frontiers of 1848 and 1853. To the south it is separated from
the republic of Guatemala by the Suchiate River, and from Belize by an agreed
frontier based on the Rio Hondo. To the east, Mexico has a 1,708-mile
coastline on the Gulf of Mexico; to the west, its Pacific Ocean coast extends
for 4,441 miles and into that ocean projects for more than 500 miles the
desolate peninsula of Baja California. In addition there are a number of small
islands off the coast; although economically important, these make up an insignificant proportion of the national territory.

Northern Mexico is a low desert plain; the large central plateau is flanked
by the Sierra Madre Oriental on the east and Sierra Madre Occidental on the
west. Mexico is one of the most mountainous countries of the world, a
characteristic that caused Hernan Cortes, the sixteenth-century conqueror of
Mexico, to compare the country's topography to a crumpled piece of paper.
Only about 10 percent of the land area of Mexico is suitable for cultivation.
Jungles and swamp line the Gulf Coast.

## The People

The world's largest Spanish-speaking country, Mexico has the eleventh
largest population in the world. It has about half the population of Brazil, the
most populous state in Latin America, and well over twice the population of
Argentina, the country with the third-largest population. The great majority
of Mexicans are *mestizos* (mixed Spanish and Indian blood), 30 percent are
pure Indian and nine percent are of European ancestry. Some 97 percent are
Catholics. The average Mexican family has 4.9 persons. Mexican family unity
is very important; family responsibilities often supersede all other responsibilities. The father is the undisputed family leader, but the mother is in charge
of running the household. The family typically includes many relations and
particularly brothers and sisters who remain in close contact into adulthood.
About 60 percent of the people live in urban areas.

About 55 percent of Mexico's inhabitants are estimated to be under the age
of 15, a fact essential to an understanding of this country. The number of
young persons moving into their economically active ages during the next few
years, for example, will exceed those persons leaving the labor force by a factor
of two or three.

There is large disparity between the upper classes and lower classes. About
40 percent of the nation's income goes to the richest 10 percent. In the United
States it goes to the richest 26 percent.

Most Mexicans take pride in being different. People view age, sex, role and
rank in distinctly different ways. American culture downplays such factors;
Mexicans use them to guide their actions toward others. A person who "pulls
rank" or demands his way because of age is not necessarily resisted in Mexico.

Mexicans view the outside world with caution, even suspicion; they operate under a set of predispositions about foreigners. They feel a cultural affinity to the Spanish and French. The Germans are blunt but efficient and reliable. The Japanese are somewhat incomprehensible and mysterious, but their business success is admirable. North Americans are aggressive and direct but necessary for conducting business.

Hints of condescension from North Americans or comparison with the United States are resented. "Poor Mexico," lamented that nation's last prerevolutionary president, Porfirio Diaz, "so far from God, and so near the United States."[16] The images that residents of the two countries have of themselves and each other began not in the "New World" but in Europe. England and Spain were world adversaries with differing language, customs and religion. English settlers accepted hard physical labor; the Spaniards disdained it. Religious differences were also divisive. The English passed down from generation to generation stories and rumors about the Inquisition, a lust for gold and Spanish cruelty to the Indians.

For historical, cultural and economic reasons, Mexico sees itself intimately linked to all Latin American countries. Significantly, however, unlike most Latin American countries, Mexico identifies far more with its Indian than its Spanish past. Though proud of their Spanish past, Mexicans seem uncomfortable with Cortes and his treatment of the Indians. Cortes' palaces have been preserved, but no statues have been erected to him in this nation filled with monuments to the country's revolutionary leaders. The last two Aztec emperors, Moctezuma and Cuauhtemoc are national heroes. Since the Revolution of 1910, the theme of *la raza* has aided in the unification of Mexico by bringing the Indian into the mainstream of the culture. There are 200 different tribes and ethnic groups to which have been added small groups of Africans and Europeans. The intermingling of the races is so varied that Mexico maintains no ethnic statistics.

A male-oriented society, Mexico has an active public life that revolves around the cafe and the market square where male members of different families meet to exchange conversation. Mexicans generally tie responsibility to fate. To tell a Mexican that he or she is personally responsible for some failure is deeply offensive.

## A Brief History

The land that is now Mexico was populated for centuries by hundreds of warring tribes in which class lines were rigid; today about 150 different languages are spoken in Mexico. The Mayans and Aztecs were two great ancient civilizations in this area. Mexico City was the capital of the Aztecs from the fourteenth to the sixteenth centuries; it is the oldest continuously inhabited urban settlement in the Americas.

This long line of advanced civilizations ended with the arrival of the Spanish, a band of about 400 armed soldiers who landed in 1519 from 11 ships under Cortes' command. They were stunned by the grandeur of the lake-encircled capital of the Aztecs—a shining metropolis of some 300,000 people, larger than any city in Europe. The Spanish conquered the Aztecs with surprising ease, enslaved them and put them to work building European-style cities. This was only 25 years after the Spanish had driven the Moors out of their country following centuries of Arabic rule; one can still see Arabic influences that the Spanish brought to Mexico with them—the blue tiles, the ornate arches, the wrought-iron work.

For over 300 years Mexico was a tightly controlled Spanish colony whose farm and mineral exports provided the largest single source of income for the Spanish Crown. The drive for independence began on September 16, 1810; independence was gained 11 years later.

Mexico lost the territory of Central America in 1824. The territory of Texas seceded from Mexico in 1836 and joined the United States, leading to a war between the two countries. After the Mexican War (1846–48) Mexico was forced in the Treaty of Guadalupe to cede half of its territory—Arizona, New Mexico, Nevada, and California, plus parts of Utah and Colorado—to the United States. Prior to the War, Mexico was by far the largest single political unit in the world. In 1861, French troops invaded and occupied Mexico City and named as emperor Austria Archduke Maximillian. When they withdrew, however, the Mexicans overthrew Maximillian.

After almost a century of rule by Mexican dictators, *mestizos* began to exert their power in the revolution of 1910. The revolution sought to carry out land reform, labor rights, and national control of resources. Over a million lives were lost before the violence was ended by the establishment of a new social covenant, the 1917 Constitution.

Mexican affairs since 1940 have been marked by economic progress and political stability. The Constitution of 1917 is in force today. It is now an authoritarian system governed by a president who cannot be reelected.

## The Economy

Mexico's economy is divided this way: services, 31.4 percent; agriculture, forestry, hunting, fishing, 26 percent; commerce 13.9; manufacturing 12.8; construction 9.5; transportation 4.8; mining and quarrying 1.3; electricity 0.3; unemployed, 10 percent; and underemployed, 40 percent. About 90 percent of production workers in establishments of over 25 workers are organized in unions. They are plant or work-site unions. Few craft unions exist, but plant unions tend to join national federations.

Mexico is the fifth largest trading partner of the United States; almost 70 percent of all Mexican imports originate in the United States. Among these are products from about 800 *maquiladora* (in bond) plants just across the border. *Maquiladora* operations enjoy nearly total freedom from the requirements of partial domestic ownership, technology transfer and local purchase of materials and equipment. Cheaper labor costs and minimal foreign investment have proven attractive to American businesses in labor-intensive industries.

Mexico's productive capacity is now the ninth largest in the world, excluding the Communist countries. Its natural resources are diverse and abundant; its hydrocarbon reserves are the fourth largest in the world; it is one of the main producers of metallic and nonmetallic minerals; it is the world's second largest producer of silver. Mexico's agriculture is diversified and its industry bigger than that of some developed countries, such as Sweden, Belgium, Denmark, Norway and Spain, and developing countries such as South Korea and India. At least 80 Mexican companies operate abroad, three-fourths of them in Central America.

Because of the petroleum industry, the economic situation has improved over the past 50 years. Recently, however, Mexico has been in an extremely difficult economic situation with the worldwide oil glut, high inflation, unemployment and an $80 billion foreign debt (second largest in the world). Mining and petroleum production are the most important industries.

The structure of the firm is different in Mexico from most Latin American countries. The old elite has lost a large measure of its property and power. A large middle class has grown among small landowners who today are supporting industrial expansion and financial development.

Everything in Mexico is arranged hierarchically. In one recent study of the degree to which people in 39 societies accepted this kind of power structure, Mexico ranked second. Many businesses are run by corporate family structures. The leader of an organization in Mexico is viewed like a father in the traditional Mexican family. Authority resides in the top man, who is also probably the owner, instead of being spread throughout a managerial team, for no such team exists. Mexican employees prefer an authoritarian boss who patronizes his workers rather than one who shares the responsibility of decision making. The "boss" in Mexico plays a high-profile role, even in large corporations, appearing before employees at business and recreational events and keeping informed of employees' personal lives and problems.

The result is a stability in organizational structure, a general absence of the *empleado-obrero* barrier, and little tension regarding the foreman role. But despite an increased division of labor, power remains at the top. Any authority delegated is on the basis of *confianza* (trust), not competence. Credibility is demonstrated more through position and "connections" than personal achievement. Often things get done through these unofficial channels. Even top-level managers lack authority of their own. One described the situation this way: "If the men who give the orders were not the owners, they could not give the orders." The owner is the ultimate and often the only source of authority in the firm; hired management is there to carry out his directives. Thus a distinct separation exists between the owner of a firm and his employee underlings.

The centralization of authority creates problems of responsibility down the chain of command; superiors complain that their subordinates are unwilling to accept responsibility. In owner-manager firms, this complaint is directed at middle-level executive management; centralization at the middle-level means the complaint is usually directed at the foreman. If attempts to involve subordinate participation in making decisions are interpreted as showing ignorance or weakness, the Mexican worker may decide his own course of action without informing his supervisor.

Because of this highly centralized decision-making system, the Mexican firm is unable to use staff properly. The difference between line and staff is not well understood. Modern management techniques such as the matrix system are not usable either in this environment of one-man rule where responsibility is delegated upward. Mexican employees have difficulty understanding concepts of the American business organization like the board of directors, group vice presidents, or stockholders. Instead they look to an individual, depending on personal relationships to define roles. Another difference between Mexican and American business practices is the fact that a labor law in Mexico gives workers job protection, after a 30-day trial period, to the extent that they are regarded as permanent employees. Mexicans tend to lack social cohesion; groups splinter easily; people find it hard to work together for long periods in any kind of enterprise. Few of them function well on committees; they are not fundamentally "team" people.

Where a choice is to be made between family obligation and obeying some rule or abstract principle, the Mexicans choose the former, Americans the latter. One should not press some influential man on business matters if one suspects he has counter-pressures from the family.

Mexican managers tend to be young — men in their late 30s and early 40s. Farther down the ladder are managers in their late 20s and early 30s who run an entire division or branch. Unlike other Latin American countries, Mexico has a broad based education system that provides trainable employees who are able to assume responsibility early. Also, Mexicans are very hard working. It is not unusual for the same individual to have a business breakfast at 7:30 a.m. and another meeting at 8 p.m.

## Organizational Communication

Despite problems of centralization and an unwillingness to accept responsibility at the bottom, vertical communication does not seem to have many problems, unlike horizontal communication which is often quite problematical. Although natural divisions between different departments exist in all organizations, whatever the cultural tradition, authority patterns in Mexican enterprises make the separation between corporate divisions particularly acute, creating problems of horizontal communication. Workers trust a superior sooner than a fellow worker in another department; a foreman or department head interacts more easily with his subordinates or his own superior than a foreman from another part of the plant. More than one line of authority usually exists, and communication is more open and cooperation more frequent within any one line than between them. Organizational hierarchies in Mexico thus seem to be determined by relations of vertical trust and horizontal mistrust. Organizations seem to function better when people at any one level are not asked to cooperate with one another, but instead communicate directly with the boss. Line of trust and communication also tended to parallel natural divisions of labor, the breach between technical and administrative parts of a firm being the strongest. This is especially true when the factory and the offices were geographically separated.

Another critical effect of the centralization of authority is bypassing, discussed previously. Organizational control depends on an order from the top filtering through all successive levels until it reaches its intended recipient. Bypassing destroys such control. Through bypassing, owners/managers, especially in smaller firms, can communicate directly with anyone at any level. On lower levels, department heads welcome bypassing of the foreman in favor of direct relations with workers as part of empire-building schemes.

In Mexican communication, "context" plays an important role. Who says something, when, where and how it is said, unspoken trust — these matters are extremely important in Mexico and should not be ignored in an effort to understand the words that are exchanged.

Latins' respect for status must be expressed verbally — and frequently. One manager said that an employee given an incorrect directive would carry it out anyway because he had been told to do so. Conversely, if someone knew how to do something which was expected of him, he would not do it unless explicitly told to do so. Clear job descriptions that would establish amounts of authority go unprepared with the result that a continual power struggle is waged at all levels.

Employees also deceive by saying something is finished when in fact work on it has not even begun. Business persons may promise to have an item ready at a specified time, knowing it will not be ready. Either person to the agreement may die before the due date; the customer may renege on the contract; the customer may forget the exact due date or not insist on timely delivery; a miracle might happen and the item may be ready on time. When a visitor asks for information that a Mexican doesn't have, the Mexican does his best to say something that will please the visitor. Mexican subordinates also withhold negative information, even if important, and present only positive information, a problem called the filter effect — they filter out the bad news and only transmit the good.

The environment in which business is transacted also communicates. American managers like to have their own private office, a source of status and prestige. Mexicans tend to be located in the same huge office. In American offices, desks are likely to be distributed around a wall allowing use of the center of the room for transit, or perhaps for group meetings, or for files that everyone uses. In Mexico the key man may be placed in the center of the room in order to control activities as is often true in France and elsewhere.

Mexicans' concept of time is more relaxed than that of North Americans. Individuals in Mexico are more important than schedules. If a visitor stops in unexpectedly, most Mexicans will agree to talk, regardless of how long it takes — a sign of the polychronic use of time.

Personal relationships are essential to business and are best established through representatives in Mexico, because much business goes through unofficial channels and one's connections. Business is usually conducted face to face; far less is done by telephone than in other countries. Telephones offend the Mexican desire for personal contacts.

It is important for the American or northern European to make and confirm appointments and to turn up on time for them. Vagueness about time keeping is a characteristic reserved for other nations. One does not apologize for being late until one is half an hour overdue for an appointment, unless the time has been specified as *hora ingles* (English time), in which case punctuality is intended.

Whether the foreigner is early or late for an appointment, he or she will probably have to wait a while before seeing his or her host. The waiting period may be a message: a long wait may be a signal that the status of the foreigner is viewed as inferior. It may also indicate a lack of interest. More than likely, however, the host is simply busy. Experienced travelers report that seeing the local executive usually takes 30 minutes, but may require as much as an hour.

After two business persons have agreed to meet, secretaries typically handle the follow-up. Regularly, secretaries will communicate—usually by phone—about two weeks ahead of the appointment in order to reconfirm the arrangement. Then, if the foreigner has representation in Mexico, his agent will check again about one week in advance.

Business contacts are often made during the two- or three-hour lunch break. These are social meetings for the most part, with business being conducted in the last few minutes.

Mexican business dress is conservative. Suits in subdued colors are correct; ties are appropriate at all times. Shirt colors can vary, but a white shirt is proper in the evening or for a call on a senior manager. Shake hands when arriving, each time you meet someone, and when leaving. Exchange business cards immediately; often, however, the receptionist or a secretary has accomplished this before the meeting.

The first name is not used unless you know a person very well and are on friendly terms. The opening conversation should establish a personal relationship before transacting business, establishing cordial associations. Mexicans typically inquire about each other's health and family before talking business; such questions among strangers, however, are possible only after they know each other socially. Many North Americans see Mexican speech as excessively emotional and overly dramatic. Americans like to be practical, efficient and clear when they speak, not wasting time with small talk, which is associated with a lack of seriousness of purpose. Most Mexicans (indeed most Latins) are generous in spoken gratitude and praise. They are careful to give abundant credit; they like awards and honors; they are lavish with supportive messages and telegrams; they leave no one out lest feelings be hurt. In expressing anger, on the other hand, Latins usually blow up in a voluble rage with many sweeping gestures. The overall atmosphere will be formal, courteous, perhaps even ritualistic. Small talk should extend no more than 10 or 15 minutes. The host expects the visitor to gradually move the conversation toward business talk.

Mexicans stand and sit close to one another and touch each other. The warm embrace (the *abrazo*) is a typical greeting between two Mexican businessmen well acquainted with each other. Attempts to avoid such gestures are considered rejections. They are intended as signs of warm interaction. Americans tend to use the neck and head for emphasis; Mexican movement, like Latin American movement generally, involves much more of the trunk. Americans when seated tend to slump more, which may be interpreted in Mexico as a lack of alertness or lack of interest in the people nearby. The use of the hands in self expression is generally more extensive in Mexico than in the United States. "No" can be indicated by moving the hand left to right with the index finger extended, palm outward. The "thumbs up" gesture is also used for approval, as in the United States. A common way to beckon people is with the "psst-psst" sound, which is not considered impolite.

# CENTRAL AMERICA

Although the 1,150-mile-long, 50- to 250-mile-wide stretch of land between the two huge continents in the Western Hemisphere is called Central America, it is really part of North America. Not everyone agrees, however, precisely which countries are included in "Central America." Some people include all seven countries in the area between Mexico and Colombia— Guatemala, Belize, Honduras, Nicaragua, El Salvador, Costa Rica and Panama.

Others suggest that only five countries are included in Central America— Guatemala, Honduras, Nicaragua, El Salvador and Costa Rica. These five republics together proclaimed their independence from Spain in 1821 and they initially attempted a united Central American Federation. Although the Federation was unsuccessful, the five have joined in other cooperative ventures over the years, including the Central American peace plan in the late eighties.

Belize and Panama are the other two. As British Honduras, Belize was for a long time a colony, achieving independence only in 1981. Its principal language is English, not the Spanish that is spoken in the other countries; its ties are closer to the Caribbean islands that have a similar British colonial background. Panama chose not to join the Central American Federation in 1821, aligning itself instead with Colombia. With the help of the United States who wanted to build the Canal, Panama won its independence from Colombia in 1903. It has remained aloof from regional organizations.

## Belize

*Official Name:* Belize; *Capital:* Belmopan; *Government:* parliamentary democracy; *Subdivisions:* 6 districts; *Population:* 168,204 (July 1987); *Density:* 18.3 per square mile; *Currency:* dollar; *Official Language:* English; *Literacy:* 91.2 percent.

*The Land.* In the Mayan language, "Belize" is said to mean "muddy waters." Formerly British Honduras, Belize is slightly larger than Massachusetts. In the north and west is Mexico and in the south and west is Guatemala. Its greatest length, north to south is 174 miles and its greatest width is 68 miles. Forests occupy some 65 percent of the area.

Its coastlands on the Caribbean Sea along the eastern shore of Central America just below the Yucatan peninsula are low and swampy with many salt and fresh water lagoons and some sandy beaches. Inland are low mountains. The most fertile area of the country is in the northern foothills of the Maya Mountains. Agricultural pursuits include growing citrus fruit and sugar cane as well as cattle raising.

*The People.* The most sparsely populated territory in Central America, Belize has a population that is richly diverse. About half are of African or partly African ancestry; some 17 percent are Indians, mostly Mayans; around 10 percent are black Caribs, descendants of the Caribs deported from St. Vincent in 1797; and another 10 percent are of European ancestry (most of them Mennonites). Half of Belizeans are Roman Catholic; the other half belong to Protestant churches: Anglican, Seventh Day Adventist, Methodist, Baptist, Jehovah's Witnesses and Mennonite.

*A Brief History.* For centuries the Mayan civilization flourished in the area that is now Belize, although it mysteriously moved to Yucatan long before European contact started in 1502 when Columbus sailed along the coast. The first settlers were Englishmen and their black slaves from Jamaica who came about 1640 to cut logwood, then the source of textile dyes. Although the British made no claim to the territory, they tried to protect the wood-cutters through treaties with Spain.

British Honduras became a colony in 1862 and was made self-governing in 1964. The country's name was changed in 1973, and Belize became independent on September 21, 1981. British troops were sent to Belize in 1975 and 1977 to protect against attack by Guatemala, which claims the territory. Guatemalans even include Belize in their maps of Guatemala.

*The Economy.* The economy is divided this way: agriculture, 30 percent; services 16, government 15.4, commerce 11.2, manufacturing 10.3; and the unemployed, 14 percent. There is a chronic shortage of skilled labor and all types of technical personnel. About 15 percent of the labor force is unionized.

Forestry was the only economic activity until well into the twentieth century. Sugar has become the principal export in recent years with expanding production of citrus, beef, bananas and tropical fruit. The smallscale domestic industry is limited by the relatively high cost of labor and a small domestic market. Initial developments in industry were agriculture-related (fertilizers, feed milling, sugar cane milling, citrus fruit extraction and flour milling). Major industries in Belize today are sugar refining, clothing, timber and forest products, furniture, rum, soap, beverages and cigarettes.

# Costa Rica

*Official Name:* Republic of Costa Rica; *Capital:* San Jose; *Government:* democratic republic; *Subdivisions:* 7 provinces; *Population:* 2,811,652 (July 1987); *Density:* 127.6 per square mile; *Currency:* colon; *Official Language:* none, but Spanish is the national language, spoken by more residents; *Literacy:* 93 percent.

*The Land.* About the size of West Virginia, Costa Rica is the second smallest of the Central American states, after El Salvador. A mountainous country, Costa Rica lies between Nicaragua in the south, with which it shares a 186-mile border, and Panama in the north, with a 226-mile border. It has both Pacific and Atlantic coasts, the distance from ocean to ocean varying from 75 to 175 miles. It has heavy tropical forests, cultivated lowlands and sandy beaches.

*The People.* Although only Panama has fewer inhabitants than Costa Rica, the population is remarkable because about 96 percent of them are white (mostly of Spanish origin, but also German, Dutch and Swiss origin) or mestizo. The 2 percent who are black live mostly on the Atlantic coast. Indigenous Indians now number about 200,000, some 20 percent fewer than were there when the area was first settled in 1522. There are also small Indian and Chinese populations. A social class system exists, with most people being extremely rich or poor. The Costa Ricans are the most pro–North American of all Latin Americans.

Costa Rica is the only Latin American country with no army, navy or air force and with no revolutions. Its peaceful nature has been attributed to the many family farmers who settled the region, rather than the fortune hunters who could not find sufficient gold and silver to warrant staking out claims here. It is also a country with more teachers than policemen. Some 96 percent are Roman Catholic. Relationships with individuals are considered more important than adherence to schedules. The literacy rate is high, at about 93 percent.

*A Brief History.* Columbus discovered Costa Rica during his voyage of 1502. Its name, meaning "rich coast" derives from rumors of rich gold reserves; however, a lack of valuable minerals caused the small colony to be ignored by Spain. As a result the first colonists were peaceful homesteaders and cattle ranchers, a fact responsible, many believe, for the peaceful nature of Costa Rica today.

With the rest of Central America, Costa Rica declared its independence in 1821. For a short time, it was a state in the Central American Federation but withdrew in 1838 to become completely independent.

Costa Rica has one of the most stable and democratic governments in Latin America. It also has the highest literacy rate and standard of living in Latin America. The country abolished the army in 1949, although it maintains an efficient Civil Guard.

*The Economy.* The labor force is divided this way: 27 percent are employed in agriculture, 34 percent in commerce and industry, 21 percent in services and government, and 8 percent in other areas. About 10 percent are unemployed. Some 15 percent of the labor force is unionized.

Costa Rica was the first country in Central America to grow coffee, which was introduced from Cuba in 1808. Major industries today include food processing, textiles and clothing, construction materials, shoes, furniture, chemicals and fertilizer. Many businessmen take lunch at home, followed by a siesta.

*Organizational Communication.* Punctuality is not as important in Costa

Rica as it is in North America. The people are aware of North American attitudes toward time, however, and may expect their Northern guests to be punctual, even if the Costa Ricans are not. Eye to eye contact is not always expected in conversation.

## El Salvador

*Official Name:* Republic of El Salvador; *Capital:* San Salvador; *Government:* republic; *Subdivisions:* 14 departments; *Population:* 5,260,478 (July 1987); *Density:* 400 per square mile; *Currency:* colon; *Official Language:* Spanish; *Literacy:* 65 percent.

*The Land.* El Salvador, a name meaning "the savior," is distinctive among Central American republics for two reasons: it is the smallest and the only one without an Atlantic seacoast. In fact, El Salvador is the smallest mainland nation in the Western Hemisphere. About the size of Massachusetts, the country is separated by mountains into three regions: a southern coastal belt, central valleys and plateaus, and northern mountains. Its border with Honduras in the north and east is 208 miles and with Guatemala in the west is 126 miles. El Salvador's soils are rich and easily accessible from its 189-mile Pacific coast. It is one of the few Latin American countries having its whole national territory settled.

*The People.* The Pipil Indians in El Salvador had an advanced civilization related to that of the Aztecs. Spanish settlers intermarried with the Indians so that 92 percent of today's population represents a fusion of the two people. Other ethnic groups are Indian, 6 percent, and white, 2 percent. El Salvador is the most densely populated country on the American mainland.

Three basic classes exist in El Salvador: upper, with 15 percent of the population; middle, 25 percent; and lower, 60 percent, including 19 percent in absolute poverty. Only 4 percent of the country's income goes to the poorest 20 percent of the people.

Salvadorans maintain very close family ties, respecting and caring for their elderly. The father is the head of the family, which averages over five people.

Salvadorans are a sports-loving people who have excellent success in many sports. The country is the center of sports events in Central America; every town has its athletic fields and gymnasiums.

A handshake is the customary greeting, but sometimes a slight nod of the head is also used. First names are used only among close acquaintances. Friends stand close together when conversing; an arm around the shoulders of another is a common way to show friendship. It is particularly important in this country to show respect to the elderly.

Elaborate hand or head gestures when expressing feelings are considered poor manners. Neither is it appropriate to point one's feet or fingers at anyone. Only close friends are beckoned with a hand wave.

*A Brief History.* In 1525 Pedro de Alvarado conquered El Salvador for Spain, creating a colonial rule that lasted until 1821 when the country joined the Mexican empire before becoming part of the Central American Federation in 1823. In 1841, El Salvador became an independent republic.

*The Economy.* The work force is divided this way: agriculture, 40 percent; manufacturing, 16 percent; commerce 16; government 13; financial services 9; and transportation, 6 percent. The country has a large pool of unskilled laborers and a shortage of skilled laborers. About 8 percent of the labor force is unionized.

Once the most highly industrialized country in Latin America, El Salvador has been battered by political violence. A small clique of 14 families owns virtually everything in the country.

Although it is the smallest and most crowded nation in Central America, El Salvador leads the area in yield per acre of coffee and cotton. Coffee accounts for half of El Salvador's exports; the country is the ninth largest producer of coffee in the world. Others are cotton, sugar and rice. The government has fostered a rapid industrial growth by constructing a hydroelectric dam, a geothermal electricity-generated plant, public housing and highways. The most dynamic sectors of the economy are chemicals and textiles; another important industry is food processing. El Salvador is a member of the Central American Common Market.

# Guatemala

*Official Name:* Republic of Guatemala; *Capital:* Guatemala City; *Government:* republic; Subdivisions: 22 departments and Guatemala City; *Population:* 8,622,387 (July 1987); *Density:* 199 per square mile; *Currency:* quetzal; *Official Language:* Spanish; *Literacy:* 48 percent.

*The Land.* To the north of the Central American isthmus, Guatemala is the northernmost and most populous of the five Central American republics. Its border with Mexico in the north and west is 575 miles long; with Belize in the northeast it is 162 miles long; with Honduras in the east it is 154 miles long; and with El Salvador in the east it is 104 miles long. Guatemala also claims the entire territory of Belize.

About the size of Ohio, Guatemala has a 53-mile coastline on the Caribbean and a 200-mile coast on the Pacific Ocean. Most of the country is mountainous with a fertile coastal plain. A number of volcanoes are intermittently active and earthquakes are frequent. Over half of the country is rich forest which is particularly dense in the northwest.

*The People.* Guatemala is the only country in Central America that is largely Indian in language and culture. The Mayan Indian empire flourished for over a thousand years in what is today Guatemala and about half of the people in Guatemala are descendants of Mayans. The rest are largely a mixture of Spanish and Indian descent. Most people are Roman Catholic and speak Spanish as well as one of 23 Indian languages.

Distinct differences exist between city and rural dwellers. Cities are generally influenced by European and American trends, while small towns and villages change very little in their beliefs and standards.

The extended family, the basis of society, exerts a major influence on an individual's life and decisions. As head of the family, the father leads all conversations and decision making. Approximately 65 percent of the births are what North Americans might call illegitimate; this is due to the high rate of common-law marriages.

Facial and body movements are more pronounced here than in the United States, but most common American finger gestures should be avoided here; the open hand is used extensively in gesturing. Punctuality is not strictly observed; individuals are considered far more important than schedules. When speaking, eye contact and an occasional smile are important.

*A Brief History.* The Mayan empire flourished in the territory that is now Guatemala for over a thousand years until it began to decline in the 1100s. From 1524 until 1821, Spain ruled all of Central America. In the 1700s, Antigua, Guatemala's original capital, was one of the greatest cities of the New World; it was destroyed by an earthquake in 1773.

In 1821, Mexico annexed Guatemala, making it a member of the Central American Federation from 1823 until 1838, when it achieved independence. Since that time, Guatemala has largely been under the control of military dictatorships. A reform government lasted from 1945 until 1951. A variety of political leaders in recent decades campaigned against terrorism and dissent and ultimately established a republican form of government with an elected president.

*The Economy.* The work force is divided this way: agricultural, 57 percent; manufacturing, 14 percent; services 13; commerce 7; construction 4; transport 3; utilities 0.8; mining 0.4; and unemployed and underemployed, 40 percent. About 10 percent of the work force is unionized. The Mayan Indians, who make up more than half the population, remain outside the money economy.

Food processing factories and cosmetics and tire plants in Guatemala City have been built to supplement coffee and bananas, the country's old economic standbys. Other industries include textiles, construction materials, tires and pharmaceuticals.

# Honduras

*Official Name:* Republic of Honduras; *Capital:* Tegucigalpa; *Government:* constitutional republic; *Subdivisions:* 18 departments; *Population:* 4,823,818 (July 1987); *Density:* 101 per square mile; *Currency:* lempira; *Official Language:* Spanish; *Literacy:* 56 percent.

*The Land.* Columbus named Honduras, using the Spanish name for "depths," which signifies the deep waters off the country's north coast. Slightly larger than Tennessee, Honduras shares borders of 154 miles with Guatemala,

573 miles with Nicaragua, and 208 miles with El Salvador. It also has coastline on the Caribbean of 367 miles and the Gulf of Fonseca of 46 miles. The coastal plain along the Caribbean is wet and tropical. Two mountain ranges dissect the country; parts of the eastern area can only be reached by air or by coastal boat. Honduras' Olancho Forest Reserve is the largest pine forest in Latin America.

*The People.* This second-largest country in Central America has the second smallest population, most of them farm laborers, largely impoverished and illiterate. The population is 90 percent mestizo, 7 percent Indian, 2 percent black, and 1 percent white. About 97 percent of all residents are Roman Catholic. While the father is respected as the head of the household, the mother often has the greatest responsibility and influence in the everyday life of the family.

*A Brief History.* A center of Mayan civilization for centuries, Honduras was discovered by Columbus in 1502. The Spanish and Indians battled until the Indians were conquered in late 1530. Honduras was a part of Guatemala until 1821 when the Central American provinces declared their independence from Spain. They were annexed briefly by Mexico, but broke away and joined the Central American Federation from 1823 to 1838 when independence was declared. Rival parties have since fought for dominance. The government has been controlled by the military since 1972.

Today its own people call Honduras "the land of the 70s: 70 percent illiterate, 70 percent rural, 70 percent illegitimate." In nearly a century and a half of independence, Honduras has had 136 revolutions and only two constitutionally elected presidents who served full terms.

*The Economy.* The labor force is divided this way: agriculture, 62 percent; services, 20 percent; manufacturing 9; construction 3; other areas 6; unemployed, 25 percent; and underemployed, 25 percent. Some 40 percent of the work force is unionized.

Honduras is the least developed country in Central America; it has only about 400 miles of paved roads. Its economy is structured on agriculture. Honduras is the second-largest banana-exporting country in the world. It also exports coffee and tobacco. Silver, lead and zinc are mined for export, and frozen food is gaining in importance.

# Nicaragua

*Official Name:* Republic of Nicaragua; *Capital:* Managua; *Government:* Sandinista dictatorship; *Subdivisions:* 16 departments and 1 national district; *Population:* 3,319,059 (July 1987); *Density:* 65 per square mile; *Currency:* cordoba; *Official Language:* Spanish; *Literacy:* 66 percent.

*The Land.* The largest country in Central America, Nicaragua is about the size of Iowa. It shares a 573-mile border with Honduras in the north and a 186-mile border with Costa Rica in the south and has coasts on the Caribbean of 297 miles and on the Pacific of 215 miles. The land is 50 percent forest;

7 percent arable land; 7 percent prairie and pasture; and 36 percent urban, waste or other.

Most residents live in the fertile volcanic belt in the middle of Lake Nicaragua, Lake Managua and the Pacific Ocean. Tropical rain forests and swampland cover the east with pine forests on the low hills and mountains of the interior. The country has three navigable rivers.

*The People.* The Nicaraguan culture follows the lines of its Ibero-European ancestry with its Spanish influence prevailing. About 86 percent of Nicaraguans describe themselves as "ladino" (a cultural and ethnic term indicative of Hispanization). The ethnic and cultural blending of Europeans and Indians is more or less complete. Some 69 percent of the people are mestizos of mixed Spanish and Indian descent; about 17 percent are white; 9 percent are black; and 5 percent are Indian. On the Caribbean coast live descendants of blacks and of Europeans who came to Nicaragua in the nineteenth century.

Nicaraguans are a gregarious people who defend their honor vigorously. Personal criticism is taken seriously. The family serves as the foundation for society. The concept of *machismo* is prevalent. Approximately 95 percent of the population belong to the Roman Catholic Church; missionaries of any other denomination are not allowed in the country.

*A Brief History.* Twenty years after Columbus discovered Nicaragua in 1502, the colonial period began with the arrival of the Spanish conquistadores. The country was ruled by Guatemala until 1821 when it declared independence. Part of the United Provinces of Central America, Nicaragua became self-governing in 1838. Revolutions kept Nicaragua turbulent for almost a century following the country's independence. Then in 1936, Anastasio Somoza took control. Somoza helped develop Nicaragua while amassing a $60 million personal fortune. The Sandinistas ousted Somoza on July 19, 1979.

*The Economy.* The 49 percent of Nicaragua's population engaged in economic activities — the lowest rate in the world — support the remaining 51 percent of the population. The labor force is divided this way: services, 45 percent; agriculture 42, industry 13; and unemployed, 25 percent. About 35 percent of the labor force is unionized.

Nicaragua's resources are primarily agricultural. Some estimates indicate that some 70 percent of the nation's territory is usable for agriculture or livestock. About 46 percent of the working population is engaged in providing services; 41 percent is in agriculture; and 13 percent is in industry. The industrialized sector is still small, but it grew rapidly following the formation of the Central American Common Market. Cotton is the most important export commodity. Gold, silver and gypsum are mined and subsistence farming still predominates.

## Panama

*Official Name:* Republic of Panama; *Capital:* Panama City; *Government:* partial democracy; *Subdivisions:* 9 provinces and 1 intendancy; *Population:* 2,274,833 (July 1987); *Density:* 75 per square mile; *Cur-*

*rency:* balboa; *Official Languages:* Spanish and English; *Literacy:* 84 percent.

*The Land.* "Panama" is an Indian word meaning "an abundance of fish." Panama is half as large as Florida. It's a narrow isthmus, 480 miles long and varying in width from 37 to 110 miles, connecting North and South America. The land is 24 percent agricultural; 20 percent exploitable forest; and 56 percent forest, urban or waste.

Panama includes the U.S. territory (until 1999) of the Canal Zone, the narrow strip of land that bisects the country along the canal. The Panama Canal Zone extends for five miles on each side of the canal that crosses at about the middle of the country. The country is bordered for 226 miles by Costa Rica in the north and for 165 miles by Colombia in the south. It has coasts on the Caribbean Sea, the Pacific Ocean and the Gulf of Panama.

The central part of the country is mountainous, with hills sloping to the coastal plains and beaches. A rain forest is on the eastern side. Most people live in the coastal lowlands.

*The People.* Panama's population is the smallest in Latin America. The culture, customs and language of the Panamanians are predominantly Caribbean Spanish. Ethnic groups include 70 percent mestizo (called Panamenos), 14 percent West Indian, 10 percent white and 6 percent Indian. Some 94 percent of the population is Roman Catholic. The percentage of divorced people is the highest in the world.

Panamanians put great emphasis on individuality. They consider all people to be of worth regardless of their social status and believe all people should be treated with dignity.

*A Brief History.* Spanish explorers first visited eastern Panama in 1501. In 1513, Balboa was the first European to cross the isthmus to the Pacific. The Spanish ruled for 300 years, during which time Panama served as a shipping base for South American treasures bound for the New World.

Panama became a province of Colombia when Colombia, Venezuela and Ecuador formed the Republic of Gran Colombia in 1821. Panama declared independence from Colombia in 1903, the same year that a treaty between Panama and the United States leased use of a zone 10 miles wide from the Atlantic to the Pacific. Canal construction lasted from 1907 to 1914. In 1977, the United States and Panama agreed to a new treaty that will return control of the Canal Zone and the country to Panama in 1999.

*The Economy.* The labor force is divided this way: commerce, finance and services, 45 percent; agriculture, hunting and fishing, 29 percent; manufacturing and mining 10; construction 5; transportation and communication 5; Canal Zone operations 4; utilities 1.2; and unemployed, 20 percent. The country has an oversupply of unskilled laborers and a scarcity of skilled ones. About 17 percent of the labor force is unionized.

Panama is most famous as a crossroads of world trade; its economy is based mainly on trade brought by an accident of geography. Its major source of income — 14 percent — is derived from the operation of the Canal. Unlike other countries in Central America with primarily agrarian economies,

Panama is a service economy. It is also mostly an urban society, with over half
of its residents living in Panama City and Colon, the cities located at either end
of the Canal.

This country produces bananas and cocoa; about half of the country are
farmers. Industries include oil refining, food processing, forestry and mining.
Panama has large deposits of copper and some gold.

# The Caribbean Islands

From Florida to Venezuela, a 2000-mile-long crescent of islands splits the
Atlantic to cradle the Caribbean Sea. The northern tier, that closest to the
United States, is known as the Greater Antilles: Cuba, the Caymans, Jamaica,
Haiti, the Dominican Republic and Puerto Rico. The British colony of the
Turks and Caicos, directly west of Florida and north of the Greater Antilles,
lies entirely in the Atlantic Ocean; however, because of its proximity and
similar tropical environment, it is generally included in discussions of the
Caribbean.

The islands of the southern and eastern Caribbean are called the Lesser
Antilles; they are greater in number but smaller in size. The eastern Caribbean
islands begin with the Virgin Islands and curve to the south to Grenada in two
groups: the Leewards (the United States and British Virgin Islands, Anguilla,
St. Maarten, St. Bart, Saba, St. Eustatius, Montserrat and Guadeloupe) and
the Windwards (Dominica, Martinique, St. Lucia, Barbados, St. Vincent and
the Grenadines and Grenada).

The southern Caribbean islands lie off the coast of Venezuela also in two
groups: Netherlands Antilles — Aruba, Bonaire and Curacao — on the west, and
Trinidad and Tobago (a two-island nation) on the east.

Before Columbus sighted the New World, the lands of the Caribbean
region were populated by Indian tribes — by the peaceful Arawak or Tainos or
by the fierce Caribs, from whom the sea takes its name. Within a century of
Columbus's voyages, the Indian population had almost vanished because of
war, disease and enslavement.

Among these islands, only Cuba, Puerto Rico and Santo Domingo share
a common Spanish heritage. Some of the other larger ones are important and
will be discussed in this section as well. Because of its communist government,
Cuba is omitted.

# Barbados

*Official Name:* Barbados; *Capital:* Bridgetown; *Government:* constitutional monarchy (and British Commonwealth member); *Subdivisions:* 11
parishes and city of Bridgetown; *Population:* 323,839 (July 1987); *Density:* 1,526 per square mile; *Currency:* dollar; *Official Language:* English;
*Literacy:* 99 percent.

*The Land.* The word "Barbados" is said to be Spanish; a logical transition from "los barbados," meaning "the bearded ones," it probably refers to the beardlike hanging roots of the banyan trees which covered the island. The most easterly and the most densely populated of the Caribbean islands, Barbados has been British since its settlement in 1627. About three times the size of Washington, D.C., Barbados is the second smallest country in the Western Hemisphere. The island's terrain is flat, rising to a ridge in the center; its total coastline stretches 63 miles.

*The People.* Barbados ranks fourth in the world in population density; virtually the whole island is inhabited. The ethnic mix includes 92 percent African, 3.8 percent mulattoes, and 0.4 percent East Indian. Religions represented include 70 percent Anglican as well as small groups of Roman Catholic, Methodist and Moravian.

*A Brief History.* British sailors landed on this uninhabited island in 1624 or 1625. Arawak Indians were believed to have lived here; it is thought they were destroyed by the Carib Indians, who then abandoned the island. Since it lies outside of the gentle curve of the Caribbean Islands, Barbados was spared the interest that pirates and explorers showed in its neighbors. The first British settlers came in 1627 or 1628 and the island remained under British control until independence was achieved in 1966. The island has had an elected legislature since 1639, and has been fully self-governing since 1961. The government today is a Constitutional Monarchy; it is a member of the British Commonwealth.

*The Economy.* The labor force is divided this way: services and government, 37 percent; commerce, 22 percent; manufacturing and construction 22; transportation, storage, communications and financial institutions 9; agriculture 8; and utilities, 2 percent. Some 32 percent of the labor force is unionized.

The sugar industry was the main commercial interest in the early years, and slaves were brought from Africa to work the plantations until slavery was abolished in the British Empire in 1833. More recently tourism and light industry have become important; nevertheless, the majority of the 169 present-day establishments are engaged in some form of sugar processing.

# Dominican Republic

*Official Name:* Dominican Republic; *Capital:* Santo Domingo; *Government:* parliamentary democracy; *Subdivisions:* 26 provinces and the National District; *Population:* 6,960,743 (July 1987); *Density:* 331 per square mile; *Currency:* peso; *Official Language:* Spanish; *Literacy:* 68 percent.

*The Land.* About twice the size of New Hampshire, the Dominican Republic occupies the eastern two-thirds of the island of Hispaniola which it shares with Haiti in the Caribbean Sea between Puerto Rico and Cuba. Its border with Haiti is 193 miles long; its coastline is 1,000 miles long. A coastal plain rises to four mountain chains that traverse the island; these are the highest mountains in the Caribbean. About 45 percent of the land is forest; 20 percent is built up or waste; 17 percent is meadow and pasture; and 14 percent is cultivated.

*The People.* Most residents (73 percent) of the Dominican Republic are of mixed ethnic origin. Of the rest, 16 percent are white and 11 percent are black. About 95 percent of the people are Roman Catholic.

Cultural backgrounds in the Dominican Republic and Haiti are divided. The Dominican Republic has a Spanish cultural orientation, in contrast to which Haiti has a black African orientation.

*History.* The Carib and Arawak Indians were the island's first inhabitants. Columbus claimed the island for Spain in 1492. Its capital, Santo Domingo, founded in 1493, was the first permanent European settlement in the Western Hemisphere and has the oldest cathedral and oldest university in the Western Hemisphere. Spain continued to rule the island until 1697 when they were forced to cede the western third to France. In 1795, the rest of the island came under French rule.

The Haitians conquered Santo Domingo in 1801; the Dominicans helped the French resist the Haitians. In 1804, the Dominicans revolted against French rule and proclaimed the republic independent, but the country was again ruled by the Spanish and by the Haitians before it was again proclaimed a republic in 1844. In 1861, the Dominicans voluntarily returned to the Spanish Empire until 1865 when independence was restored.

In 1905 the United States began administration of Dominican customs and later established a military government that ruled until 1924, and again intervened in 1965, four years after the dictator, Trujillo, was assassinated. Democratic elections have since been reinstated.

*The Economy.* The work force is divided this way: agriculture, 45 percent; industry, 34 percent; and services, 16 percent. Most people in the Dominican Republic are small landowners. Some 12.5 percent of the labor force is unionized. Sugar accounts for half the country's exports. Major industries include tourism, sugar processing, nickel mining, gold mining, textiles and cement.

# Haiti

*Official Name:* Republic of Haiti; *Capital:* Port-au-Prince; *Government:* republic; *Subdivisions:* 5 departments; *Population:* 6,187,115 (July 1987); *Density:* 614 per square mile; *Currency:* gourde; *Official Language:* French; *Literacy:* 23 percent.

*The Land.* The native Arawak Indians called this island "Hayti," "the mountainous country," because mountains cover about four-fifths of the land. About the size of Maryland, Haiti occupies the western third of the island of Hispaniola, which it shares with the Dominican Republic. The border separating the two countries is 224 miles long; Haiti's coastline is 646 miles long. Four mountain chains traverse the island; the coastal plain is hot and humid. Some 44 percent of the land is unproductive; 31 percent is cultivated; 18 percent is rough pasture; and 7 percent is forest.

*The People.* Haiti is one of the world's most densely populated lands. Some 95 percent of the people are of black African descent — from Senegal, the Sudan, the Gold Coast and Dahomey — and 5 percent are mulattoes.

Roman Catholicism is the religion of the majority of residents, with about 10 percent adhering to Protestantism and another 10 percent to other beliefs. Many Haitians practice voodoo, a type of animism with African roots. Although French is the official language, it is spoken by only 10 percent of inhabitants; most of them speak Creole, a blend of French, Spanish, English and Dutch, with a distinct basis in African dialects and tongues.

French and African customs blend with some Indian and Spanish influence to create a unique cultural heritage. Haiti has the lowest literacy rate and life expectancy in the hemisphere.

*A Brief History.* The Spanish, who arrived after Columbus claimed the island for Spain in 1492, killed most of the native Arawak Indians and concentrated their settlements on the eastern side of the island. The western side became a base for French and English buccaneers.

In 1697, Spain ceded the western half of the island to France; French colonists imported many slaves from Africa to develop the vast sugar plantations. Intolerable conditions of slavery and brutality led to fierce slave rebellions in the late eighteenth century. Most of the white population was murdered; the white survivors emigrated. Thus today 95 percent of the population is black. Haiti became independent in 1804, establishing the only black republic in the New World.

*The Economy.* The labor force is divided this way: agriculture, 66 percent; services, 25 percent; and industry, 9 percent. There is a scarcity of skilled laborers and overabundance of unskilled laborers. Less than 1 percent of the work force is unionized.

Most Haitians do subsistence farming or work in assembly plants which make clothing, sporting goods and electronic equipment. Others work on coffee or sugar plantations or in mining bauxite.

## Jamaica

*Official Name:* Jamaica; *Capital:* Kingston; *Government:* independent state within British Commonwealth; *Subdivisions:* 12 parishes and the Kingston–St. Andrew area; *Population:* 2,455,536 (July 1987); *Density:* 549 per square mile; *Currency:* dollar; *Official Languages:* English, Creole; *Literacy:* 76 percent.

*The Land.* Natives called this island "Xamayco," meaning "a land of wood and water." About 90 miles from Cuba and 600 miles from the southeast coast of Florida, Jamaica is the third largest island in the Caribbean. Mountains cover 80 percent of its surface; the island includes coastal plains divided by the Blue Mountain range in the east and hills and limestone plateaus in the central and western areas of the interior.

*The People.* About 91.4 percent of Jamaicans are of African origin; about 3.4 are East Indians and Afro-East Indian; 3.2 are white; 1.2 are Chinese and

Afro-Chinese; and 0.9 percent are members of other groups. Although the inhabitants have adopted the British culture of their former rulers, black racial consciousness is a social and political force in the island. The Anglican Church is the largest on the island but there are also groups that follow the Baptist, Roman Catholic, and Methodist churches and small groups of Muslims, Hindus and Jews.

*A Brief History.* Discovered by Columbus in 1494, Jamaica was colonized by Columbus's son Diego as a kind of private fief under the Spanish crown during the early sixteenth century. In 1655, British forces occupied the island, and in 1670 Great Britain gained full possession through the Treaty of Madrid. Africans were imported to work as slaves in the plantations; when slavery was abolished in 1807, East Indians and Chinese were imported to replace them.

Independence in 1962 from Britain left Jamaica with a real two-party system and a democratic constitution.

*The Economy.* The labor force is divided this way: agriculture, 32 percent; industry and commerce 28; services 27; government 13; and unemployed, 30 percent. There is a shortage of technical and managerial personnel.

Jamaica's economy is based on plantation agriculture, primarily sugar and bananas. The discovery of bauxite in the 1950s and subsequent establishment of the bauxite-alumina industries became dominant factors in the island's economic growth. During the 1960s, tourism and local manufacturing industries were emphasized. New enterprises such as the production of bauxite and women's clothing have been attracted by Jamaica's favorable tax laws and the availability of literate, low-cost labor. Present industries include bauxite, garments, processed foods, sugar, rum, molasses, cement, metal, paper, chemical products and tourism.

# Trinidad and Tobago

*Official Name:* Republic of Trinidad and Tobago; *Capital:* Port-of-Spain; *Government:* parliamentary democracy; *Subdivisions:* 8 counties; *Population:* 1,250,839 (July 1987); *Density:* 565 per square mile; *Currency:* dollar; *Official Language:* English; *Literacy:* 89 percent.

*The Land.* Trinidad and Tobago are the southernmost islands of the Lesser Antilles chain in the Caribbean. About the size of Delaware, the island-country includes 16 smaller islands.

Trinidad is separated from Venezuela by seven miles of the Gulf of Paria. The island is 89 miles long and 38 miles wide and is divided by three relatively low east-to-west mountain ranges. Between the Northern and Central ranges is flat, well-watered land; between the Central and Southern ranges are rolling hills. Tropical forests cover about half of the island; swamps are found along part of the east and west coasts.

Port-au-Spain, the principal commercial center in the eastern Caribbean, is located on the major sea and air lanes between South America and the United States and Europe.

Lying 19 miles northeast of Trinidad, Tobago has long stretches of scenic and almost-deserted beaches. This island is 26 miles long and 7 miles wide. A ridge of volcanic origin lies along the center of the island.

*The People.* About 43 percent of the population is African; 40 East Indian; 14 mixed; 2 white; and 1 percent Chinese and other.

The Roman Catholic faith is the religion of 32.9 percent of the inhabitants; 24.4 percent are Hindus; 14.7 are Anglicans; and 5.8 percent are Muslims.

*A Brief History.* Trinidad was discovered by Columbus in 1498 on his third voyage to the Western Hemisphere. The island was inhabited by several Arawak tribes which were destroyed by the European settlers. The Spanish began to colonize Trinidad in 1592. The island was captured by the British in 1797 and ceded finally to Great Britain in 1802. Indentured servants were brought in from India in the nineteenth and twentieth centuries to replace the African slaves when slavery was abolished in 1833. The East Indians still dominate the country's agriculture, although many have moved into business and the professions.

Tobago has probably changed hands more often than any other West Indian island; the Dutch, French and British captured it from each other before it was finally ceded to Great Britain in 1814.

Trinidad and Tobago merged in 1888 to form a single colony. They obtained full independence and joined the British Commonwealth of Nations in 1962.

*The Economy.* The labor force is divided this way: construction and utilities, 18.1 percent; manufacturing, mining and quarrying 14.8; agriculture 10.9; other services 47.9; and unemployed, 15.4 percent. About 40 percent of the work force is unionized.

Oil production on Trinidad gives it one of the highest per capita incomes in the hemisphere. Tobago, 30 air miles away, relies on tourism and the raising of cacao and sugar to maintain its relative prosperity.

Petroleum has made Trinidad and Tobago one of the most prosperous countries of the Caribbean. Residents enjoy the third highest standard of living in the Western Hemisphere, surpassed only by the United States and Canada. More than 600 establishments produce or assemble over 400 categories of goods.

# U.S. Territories

## Puerto Rico

Puerto Rico is a United States commonwealth which had been liberated from Spain in 1898. Its economy is one of the fastest growing in the world.

About the size of Delaware and Rhode Island combined, Puerto Rico is the smallest of the islands in the Greater Antilles group—the largest is Hispaniola. The island, 100 miles long and 30 miles wide, includes a variety of mountains, deserts, rain forests, coastal plains and beaches. The coastal plains are densely populated because three-fourths of the island is mountainous, leaving little land for cultivation.

Columbus claimed the island for Spain in 1493, on his second voyage to the New World. Spanish settlers, who first colonized the island in 1508, imported black slaves to work on the sugarcane, coffee and tobacco plantations. The Spanish also annihilated the men but not the women of the original Taino Indians in the sixteenth century. Slavery was abolished in 1873.

In 1897, Spain granted self-government to Puerto Ricans. The following year, United States troops invaded the island during the Spanish-American War, and Spain ceded the island to the United States. In 1917, Puerto Rico became a territory of the United States and its people, United States citizens. The first elected governor took office in 1948. Puerto Rico became a commonwealth with its own constitution in 1952.

Spanish rule and American affiliation have meant a culture still in transition and people who still experience an identity crisis. Leading modern industries are oil refining, manufacturing, food processing, agriculture and tourism.

## Virgin Islands

These islands were bought from Denmark in 1917. They remained backward until the 1950s when cheap airline fares made them easily accessible to American tourists.

# British Territories

## Bahamas

The word "Bahamas" may be derived from the Spanish phrase *baja mar* or "shallow sea." Some 700 islands, only 20 of them inhabited, make up the Bahamas, which lie in the western Atlantic Ocean. Flat, long, coral islands which cumulatively are about the size of Connecticut, the Bahamas extend from about 60 miles off the coast of southeast Florida in a 750-mile arc down to the northern edge of the Caribbean. Some 29 percent of the land is forest; 1 percent is cultivated; and 70 percent is built on, wasteland and other.

Christopher Columbus discovered the Bahamas in 1492. English and Bermudan religious refugees established the first European settlement in 1647. It became a British crown colony in 1717.

About 85 percent of Bahamans are blacks whose ancestors arrived here when it was a staging area for the slave trade or were brought here by the thousands by British loyalists who fled the Revolutionary War.

Religions followed are Baptist, 29 percent; Anglican 23; and Roman Catholic, 22 percent. A small number of residents follow other Protestant denominations and the Greek Orthodox faith. There are also a few Jews.

About 30 percent of the Bahamas labor force works for the government; 25 percent works in hotels and restaurants; 10 percent in business services, and 6 percent in agriculture. About 25 percent of the labor force is unionized.

Tourism is the mainstay of the economy, accounting for about 75 percent of the GNP and employing two-thirds of the work force. Other industries are banking, tourism, cement, oil refining and transshipment, lumber, rum, aragonite, pharmaceuticals and steel pipe.

## Bermuda

One of Britain's oldest colonies, Bermuda is now virtually self-governing. About the size of Washington, D.C., Bermuda is an archipelago of about 360 small coral hilly islands, including 7 main islands, lying about 650 miles east of North Carolina. The main islands, clustered together and connected by bridges are considered a geographic unit and are referred to as the Island of Bermuda, about 24 miles long and less than a mile wide on average. About 60 percent of it is forest; 21 percent built on, waste land or other; 11 leased for air and naval bases; and 8 percent arable.

Bermuda was discovered in 1503 by Spanish explorer Juan de Bermudez, who did not try to land because of the treacherous reef surrounding the islands. In 1609, some British colonists were shipwrecked and stranded on the islands for ten months. Their reports aroused interest in the area and in 1612 King James extended the Charter of the Virginia Company to include them. Later that year, about 60 British colonists arrived and founded St. George, the oldest continuously English-speaking settlement in the Western Hemisphere.

About 61 percent of the population is black; 39 percent is white or other. Religions followed are 37 percent Anglican, 21 other Protestant, 14 Roman Catholic, and 28 percent other.

Bermuda has no heavy industry and only a few light manufacturing industries, a small, poorly equipped fishing industry and limited agricultural output. The labor force is divided this way: 25 percent clerical, 22 services, 21 laborers, 13 professional and technical, 10 administrative and managerial, 7 sales, and 2 percent agriculture and fishing.

## British Virgin Islands

These more than 60 islands have been British since 1628. They include Tortola, Beef Island, Virgin Gordo, Anegada, Jost Van Dyke and Peter Island.

# French Antilles

France owned many Caribbean islands in the 18th century, but it lost most of them to the British in 1782. Today aside from a section of St. Martin, it owns only these two, known as the French Antilles: Guadeloupe and Martinique.

Settled by the French in 1635, Guadeloupe is composed of two main islands: Basse-Terre (or Guadeloupe proper) and Grande Terre. They are about twice the size of New York City. Primarily agricultural, the islands export sugar and bananas. Ethnic groups are black and mulatto, 90 percent;

white, 5 percent; and East Indian, Lebanese and Chinese, less than 5 percent. Martinique is a 426-square-mile island that is mainly agricultural also, exporting bananas, sugar and rum. Ethnic groups represented are African and African-Caucasian-Indian mix, 90 percent; Caucasian, 5 percent; and East Indian, Lebanese and Chinese, less than 5 percent. About 95 percent are Roman Catholic; the rest, Hindu and African or animist. The land divides this way: 31 percent crop, 29 forest, 24 waste or built on, and 16 percent pasture.

## Netherlands Antilles

Two groups of islands make up the Netherlands Antilles. One is the Leeward Islands, including Aruba, Bonaire and Curacao. They are 15 to 38 miles off the northwestern coast of Venezuela. The other, the Dutch Windwards, including St. Eustatius, Saba and the southern part of the island the French call St. Martin and the Dutch call Sint Maarten. They are 220 miles east of Puerto Rico.

Spanish explorers landed in Curacao in 1499. In 1527, Spain took possession of Curacao, Bonaire and Aruba. In 1634 the three islands passed to the Netherlands where they have remained except for two short periods during the Napoleonic Wars when the British ruled.

Although the Windward Islands changed hands frequently during the seventeenth and eighteenth centuries, all three have been under Dutch rule since the beginning of the nineteenth century. In 1954 the Netherlands Antilles became an autonomous part of the Dutch kingdom.

The economic well being of the islands depends on the operations of two huge oil refineries. They import crude oil from Venezuela and the Middle East and ship petroleum products mainly to North America. Other industries include tourism, offshore investing and banking.

*Aruba.* The chief business of Aruba is refining and shipping oil imported from Venezuela. It is located 42 miles west of Curacao, 15 miles from Venezuela.

*Bonaire.* Slightly larger than Aruba, Bonaire lacks refineries and so is not nearly so prosperous. Its 7,000 people raise some livestock. It is located 25 miles east of Curacao.

*Curacao.* In Dutch hands since 1816, Curacao has a booming oil business and a growing tourist trade. It is a low, hilly island of volcanic origin with little natural vegetation.

*Sint Maarten.* The southern half of the island is Dutch; the northern half, French. This small island grows and ships livestock and welcomes tourists.

*Sint Eustatius.* This is a relatively underdeveloped island on which are found several small plantations.

*Saba.* An extinct volcano rises dramatically to almost 3,000 feet on this island. Vegetation is lush.

# SOUTH AMERICA

South America includes 12 countries; nine of them Latin peoples who, along with their Indian heritage, have a Spanish cultural base; and one nation each has a Portuguese, French or Dutch cultural base. All but Suriname share the Roman Catholic tradition. Geographically all of South America lies east of Florida.

This continent is far richer in resources than is generally known. The Amazon, whose drainage basin covers an area about the size of the United States, excluding Alaska, is the center of a great fanshaped system of rivers and streams providing 2,300 miles of navigable waterways. Only 4 percent of the land has been cultivated; the continent has only 17 persons per square mile. The potential for progress and development is present; what is lacking is the social, intellectual and political framework on which to build.

# Argentina

*Official Name:* Argentine Republic; *Capital:* Buenos Aires; *Government:* constitutional democracy; *Subdivisions:* 22 provinces, 1 district and 1 territory (Tierra del Fuego); *Population:* 31,144,775 (July 1987); *Density:* 27.1 per square mile; *Currency:* austral; *Official Language:* Spanish; *Literacy:* 94 percent.

*The Land.* Considered the melting pot of South America, Argentina is nearly twice as large as Alaska. It is the eighth largest country in the world and is the second largest country in South America (after Brazil). The country is separated from Chile in the west by 3,298 miles of the Andes and borders Bolivia for 461 miles and Paraguay for 1,056 miles in the north and Brazil for 703 miles and Uruguay for 308 miles and the South Atlantic Ocean in the east. It is noted for its vast plains, called the Pampas, which contain some of the best cattle country in the world. Farther south, on the often cold and windy grasslands of Patagonia, sheep ranches and recently developed oil wells predominate. A large plain rises from the Atlantic to the towering Andes mountains in the west, along the Chilean border. The northeast includes the swampy Chaco and the great rivers of the Plata system, known as the "Argentine Mesopotamia."

*The People.* In the century from 1857 to 1954, over four million immigrants came to Argentina, the peak being reached in the first decade of this century when about 1,100,000 new people arrived. Over 80 percent of the people are of Spanish or Italian descent. Because of the low density of population, the government encourages immigration from Europe. The people are 84 percent white and 16 percent mestizo, Indian and other. Their religions include 90 percent Roman Catholic, 2 percent Protestant, 2 percent Jewish and 6 percent other.

Argentinians are cosmopolitan, progressive, gregarious and independent. Intense opinions and attitudes regarding government, politics, taxes and police are common. Failure is more accepted here than in the United States. The official and predominant religion is Roman Catholicism but the Constitution grants complete freedom of worship. There are no color, racial, religious or minority group problems.

The roles of men and women are well defined. Marriages are generally stable and cohesive. Families tend to be small, averaging 3.8 people. Deference is given to the father, but he also considers the opinions of the rest of the family. The elderly are respected and generally cared for by the family.

*A Brief History.* Discovered by Spanish conquistadores in 1536 and first colonized by Spain, Argentina has since attracted immigrants from all over Europe. Many people of British, German or Italian descent live here. In 1810, Spanish rule was replaced by a revolutionary junta. Argentina declared its independence in 1816; since then it has been anything but serene politically, often being ruled by demagogues. Juan Peron became president in 1946 and under his dictatorship, the economy declined. He was exiled, but he later returned and was elected president. His wife became vice-president. She succeeded him when he died, the first woman to head a national government in the Western Hemisphere. She was placed under house arrest in 1976 following a bloodless coup. Argentina has been under the rule of a military junta since then. It fought a losing war with Great Britain in 1982 over control of the Falkland Islands (called the Malvinas by Argentina) in the south Atlantic.

*The Economy.* The labor force is divided this way: agriculture, 15.9 percent; manufacturing 24.3; commerce 13.2; transportation and communication 11.5; finance and banking 7.7; utilities 4.4; construction 3.6; mining 2.7; services and other 16.7; and unemployed, 6.3 percent. About 33 percent of the work force is unionized.

Industry, manufacturing and oil production are the most important economic activities in Argentina, but livestock and agricultural products (especially beef and wheat) are still the most important exports. Argentina is among the top 15 trading nations in the world, ranking fourth in wool and hide production and fifth in cattle and horse production. The country is also a major producer of soybeans, wheat and corn.

Other industries include food processing, motor vehicles, consumer durables, textiles, metallurgy and chemicals. One of the wealthiest countries in Latin America with impressive natural resources, Argentina has suffered from political instability since the 1950s.

*Organizational Communication.* Argentinians are certainly more formal than most of their continental neighbors. Punctuality is preferred but not always realized. In conversation, one should speak in a relaxed manner, maintain eye contact, and avoid using excessive gestures. House numbers are placed after street names in addressing envelopes and the postal code is placed before the name of the city.

# Bolivia

*Official Name:* Republic of Bolivia; *Capital:* La Paz; *Government:* parliamentary democracy; *Subdivisions:* 9 departments; *Population:* 6,309,642 (July 1987); *Density:* 16 per square mile; *Currency:* peso; *Official Language:* Spanish; *Literacy:* 75 percent.

*The Land.* The country was named for the South American liberator, Simon Bolivar. Landlocked near the center of the South American continent in the Andes, Bolivia is bordered for 1,942 miles by Brazil in the north and east, for 470 miles by Paraguay on the southeast, for 461 miles by Argentina on the south, for 535 miles by Chile on the southwest and for 651 miles by Peru on the northwest. The fifth largest country in South America, Bolivia is rich in minerals, including tin of which it is the world's third-largest producer. Three times larger than California, the country stretches 1,000 miles from north to south and 800 miles east to west. Three quarters of the country consists of fertile, tropical lowlands producing rubber and Brazil nuts. Lake Titicaca, the highest navigable body of water in the world, is in Bolivia.

*The People.* Ethnic background of the population is 55 percent Indian, 5 to 15 percent European, and 25 to 30 percent mestizo. The Indians belong to the Quechua, Aymara and Guarani tribes whose culture has blended with the Spanish to form a rich heritage. Bolivians take pride in the pre–Columbian Indian ruins and the masterpieces of Hispanic art created by Spanish and Indian artists.

For four centuries, the rigid social structure reserved education for only the elite minority. Illiteracy, however, is declining rapidly as a result of the high priority given to education by the national government. About 95 percent of the people are Roman Catholic.

*A Brief History.* Once part of the Inca empire, the Bolivian region was conquered by Spain in 1525. Bolivia was one of the first colonies to rebel, but its war for independence, which began in 1809, did not end until 1825. After losing her seacoast to Chile in the War of the Pacific (1879–83), Bolivia has negotiated with surrounding countries to try to obtain a land corridor to the Pacific Ocean. In 1976, Argentina granted Bolivia a free-port zone at Rosario on the Parana River. In 1952 a revolution nationalized the tin mines and brought comprehensive social reforms, but the country is not yet politically stable.

*The Economy.* The economy is divided this way: agriculture, 50 percent; service and utilities 26; manufacturing 10; mining 4; and other areas, 10 percent. Although the poorest, least developed nation in South America with one of the lowest income levels in Latin America, Bolivia's literacy and standard of living are increasing as the government places priority on improving educational facilities and opportunities. Despite the fact that Bolivia has immense natural resources, two-thirds of the people, mostly Indians, live in poverty on the barren high plateau where the Incas once nursed the soil to fertility. It is also one of the least urbanized countries in Latin America.

Main crops include potatoes, rice, corn, sugar cane, yucca and bananas. Although mining employs only 3 percent of the people, tin, zinc, silver and other minerals provide the majority of the national income. Bolivia is the world's largest producer of bismuth and is the second largest producer of tin and antimony.

Bolivia has virtually no heavy industry. Its industries include food processing and beverages, 35 percent; textiles and leather 32; furniture 10; chemicals 9; and tobacco, 8 percent.

*Organizational Communication.* Bolivians often use their hands, eyes and facial expressions in communicating. The absence of eye contact is considered very insulting.

# Brazil

*Official Name:* Federative Republic of Brazil; *Capital:* Brasilia; *Government:* federal republic; *Subdivisions:* 22 states, 4 territories, and 1 federal district; *Population:* 147,094,739 (July 1987); *Density:* 42 per square mile; *Currency:* cruzado; *Official Language:* Portuguese; *Literacy:* 76 percent.

*The Land.* Occupying almost half of the South American continent, Brazil is the fifth largest country in the world (after the Soviet Union, Canada, China and the United States). The widest points north to south and east to west are about the same: 2,700 miles. The Atlantic coastline is 4,500 miles long.

Bordered by every South American country except Chile and Ecuador, the country is a sprawling mixture of vast forests and huge cities. About three-fifths of its area is tropical rain forest, largest in the world, in the Amazon Basin. Other terrain is semiarid scrubland, rugged hills and mountains, rolling plains and a coastal strip. The land is 60 percent forest, 23 percent built on, waste and other, 13 percent pasture and 4 percent cultivated.

Brazilians divide their country between the rural and less-developed north and the urban and industrialized south and between coastal and inland areas. The majority of people live along the coast.

*The People.* About half of the people are of European origin; 40 percent are of mixed European, African or Indian ancestry; and the rest are of other origins. More than 90 percent of the population lives on 10 percent of the land—a 200-mile-wide zone along the South Atlantic. Though the basic stock of Brazil is Portuguese and most Brazilians consider themselves white, the African and Indian influence in the country's racial makeup is significant. Many Germans, Italians and Japanese have settled in the southern states of Brazil. Most people live on the east coast, especially in the larger cities of the southeast. A strong African influence, the legacy of slaves brought to Brazil, exists in the northeast. Some 89 percent of the inhabitants are Roman Catholic.

Brazil is different and proudly independent from the rest of South America. Brazil is the only country in Latin America in which Portuguese, not Spanish, is the national language. About half of the population is under 20 years of age. Brazilians are friendly, warm people and show affection easily. They are good conversationalists. They have a good sense of humor and are fond of gadgets and practical jokes. Brazilians are traditionally casual about time and work, although industrialization is changing this. Brazil is a very free and relaxed country—people are not very formal. In 1977 the Brazilian congress legalized divorce in what is the world's largest Roman Catholic country.

*A Brief History.* Brazil was discovered by the Portuguese in 1500 and ruled as a colony until 1808 when the Portuguese royal family, having fled Napoleonic armies, established the seat of government first in Salvador and then in Rio de Janeiro. Brazil became a kingdom under Dom Joao VI who returned to Portugal in 1821, leaving his son, Dom Pedro I, as regent. With the people's support, Dom Pedro I declared Brazil's independence in September 1822 and became emperor. The second emperor, Dom Pedro II, ruled from 1831 until 1889 when a federal republic was established. Independence was achieved peacefully. Since the last Brazilian emperor in 1889, the country has had a fairly stable government, with leadership changes seldom resulting in violence. Since 1964 the republic has been dominated by military leaders.

*The Economy.* The work force is divided among services, 40 percent; agriculture, 35 percent; and industry, 25 percent.

Families are very strong and their obligations affect many areas of business. The country is self-sufficient in most foodstuffs and consumer goods. Farmers constitute more than half of the working force even though less than 5 percent of the land is cultivated. The agricultural output is nonetheless highly diversified: Brazil supplies nearly half of the world's coffee, is one of the world's largest producers of cocoa beans, and includes sugar, cotton, oranges and tobacco among its range of exports. Brazil is also rich in minerals, containing for example an estimated 14 percent of the world's total reserves of iron ore. The automobile manufacturing industry produces nearly half a million new cars each year. Its iron and steel industry is the largest in Latin America.

The Brazilian man demonstrates his strength but through aggressive pursuit and courteous respect. He must be the aggressor in all senses including taking the initiative in a business deal. Less competition for jobs exists in Brazil, where many jobs are gained through friends and family connections, and people are frequently judged on personal standards rather than abstract qualities. Brazilians are suspicious of ambition and may regard the ambitious person as one who tries to keep others down for his own benefit. The means to an end are important to Brazilians who seem often to pursue goals different from those of residents of the United States who value directness. Brazilians, because of the value placed on human relations and comfortable interaction, often approach a subject or a problem indirectly, working toward a solution by degrees.

Sao Paulo is the largest and most modern industrial complex in Latin America. According to one Sao Paulo executive search consultant, it was only after the car industry started in Brazil in the mid–1950s that there was such a thing as business administration. "It wasn't until much later, around 1968, that management acquired any kind of sophistication." They realized, for example, that promoting a son-in-law to a position of responsibility was no answer to a management problem.[17]

The typical Brazilian executive graduates from engineering school, takes some courses in management and then acquires some exposure to advanced management techniques in an American- or European-based multinational. Next he joins a Brazilian firm and rises rapidly; if he fails to rise, he tries elsewhere.

*Organizational Communication.* It is rare for business to be conducted by telephone or letter. Foreign business persons should conduct business in person as much as possible, and try to maintain a continuous working relationship. In business matters, the Brazilian works on an interpersonal level. If he likes you, he will do business with you, but even then he will not let business get in the way of his leisure. Visitors should be relaxed and refrain from trying to get down to business immediately. Brazilians like to bargain. Proceedings will be formal, but presentations should be made with enthusiasm. Invitations that tell you to come "American" or "airport" time mean to be on time; otherwise, it is best to be a little late so as not to embarrass your hosts by arriving before they are ready.

Brazilians overcome time unpredictability by scheduling meetings in their offices so that they can continue to work while waiting for someone. Brazilians also deal with several persons simultaneously instead of individually in separate appointments. Brazilian business people, particularly public officials, are accustomed to dealing with several people and several issues at once, and to do so does not mean one issue or one person is less important and not worthy of individual attention. It is simply doing business Brazilian style.

The Brazilian often adds emphasis to a statement, particularly when referring to something done rapidly or under pressure by snapping the fingers with a whip of the hand. To indicate "I don't know," the tips of the fingers are brushed forward under the chin. To express great liking or appreciation of something, one takes the lobe of his ear between the thumb and forefinger. To put this expression in the superlative, he will make the same gesture, reaching behind the head to the opposite ear.

Brazilians feel that Americans have substituted words for actions, that an American must articulate what the Brazilian can demonstrate. Brazilians look at one another more than do North Americans. During conversation, eye contact is maintained between both speaker and listener to a degree that Americans often consider a stare.

# Chile

*Official Name:* Republic of Chile; *Capital:* Santiago; *Government:* republic; *Subdivisions:* 12 regions and 1 metropolitan district; *Population:* 12,448,008 (July 1987); *Density:* 41.8 per square mile; *Currency:* peso; *Language:* Spanish; *Literacy:* 89 percent.

*The Land.* The word "Chile" is derived from the Aymara Indian word meaning "where the land ends." Chile stretches 2,653 miles along the southwestern coast of South America, wedged between the Pacific Ocean and the Andes Mountains, but averages only 110 miles in width. It borders Peru on the north and Bolivia and Argentina on the east.

Chile's geography includes high mountains, one of the driest deserts in the world, pampas and rain forests. Northern Chile is desert and contains great mineral wealth, primarily copper and nitrates. A fertile central valley, about 600 miles long and 45 miles wide, is the center of Chile's agriculture and industry and the home of 90 percent of the population. Southern Chile is rich in forests and grazing lands and has a string of volcanos and lakes. The southern extreme is an archipelago with Cape Horn at its tip. Earthquakes are common. Some 47 percent of the land is barren mountain, desert or urban; 29 percent is forest; 15 percent is permanent pasture or meadow; 7 percent is other arable land; and 2 percent is cultivated.

*The People.* Few Latin American countries have a more homogeneous population. This may result from the geographical and cultural isolation of the country's early history. Some 95 percent of the citizens are European or European-Indian; 3 percent are Indian; and 2 percent are other. Most Chileans are mestizos. German, Irish, English, Italian, Yugoslav, French and Arab immigrants have left a strong imprint on Chilean culture. Over 300,000 Indians live in the south-central area, mostly descendants of the Araucanians. German, Italian, Quechua and Araucan are spoken by a small percentage of the population. About 89 percent of residents are Roman Catholic; the rest are Protestant.

Chile is not a tropical Latin country with steaming tropical jungles, palm trees, sombreros or burros. No "manana" feelings exist. Most businessmen are of German, English, Spanish or Italian descent and behave accordingly. Race is not a divisive factor in politics or society. It is one of the most urbanized nations in Latin America with over 83.36 percent of the population living in urban areas.

*A Brief History.* Ferdinand Magellan first sighted Chilean shores in 1520 after navigating around the southern tip of the continent. Spanish settlement began in 1541 and colonization continued until independence was granted in 1818 after a seven-year war against the Spanish forces.

Historically, Chile has been one of the few Latin American countries where the government has been chosen by free elections and where human rights are respected. By and large the military respects fair play and honest elections; only once since 1891 has the nation veered from constitutionalism (but this was in 1973). Chile also has a free press and intelligent economic planning. But wealth (derived from the mining of copper and other minerals) is concentrated in a few hands. The infant mortality rate is one of the world's highest. Living costs are exorbitant. Peonage is common and inflation is rampant.

One result is that Chile has a strong and voluble Communist Party. However, a left-wing Christian party bested the Communists in late 1964 and began leading Chile in a search for democratic solutions to its problems. Following decades of political reform and material progress, a Marxist regime took office in 1970 with the election of Salvador Allende. Allende established diplomatic relations with communist states, expropriated many banks and vital industries, and nationalized foreign-owned businesses. A coup d'etat, led by Agusto Pinochet, resulted in Allende's assassination in 1973 and a military government was instituted.

*The Economy.* The labor force is divided this way: services, 38.6 percent; industry and commerce 31.3; agriculture, forestry and fishing 15.9; mining 8.7; construction 4.4; and unemployed, 13.9 percent. About 12 percent of the work force is unionized.

Chile is the world's third largest producer of copper and also is a major producer of silver. Because Chile has lagged in developing improved farming methods and manufacturing industries, it must import much of its food and consumer products. Principal crops are wheat, rice, oats, rye, and fruits. Large forests provide hard and soft woods. Coastal waters produce shellfish, abalone, lobster, tuna, swordfish and sardines.

Article 130 of the Labor Code requires that the work day of white collar workers be divided into two equal halves, with at least two hours in between for lunch — probably a holdover from the traditional *siesta* period. The workers like to go home for lunch and if they live some distance from the factory, they need considerable time to get there. As a result of this provision, the work day in Chile for the white-collar worker is much longer than it is for the American counterpart.

Article 91 of the Labor Code states that "No enterprise may initiate, renew or paralyze its activities or effect important changes without first having given notice according to the formalities provided for in the regulations, to the corresponding inspector of labor."

Each employer must draw up and submit to the Direccion General del Trabajo for approval two so-called Internal Regulations, one dealing with manual workers, the other with white collar workers. In the case of the manual workers, the Internal Regulations must include the following items:

1. The hours at which work begins and ends, and the hours of each shift, if the work is done in that way.
2. The rest periods.
3. The wage scale.
4. The minimum wage in case there is one fixed for the particular industry.
5. The place, day and hour of wage payment.
6. The obligations and prohibitions to which the workers are subject.
7. The fines applicable for violations of the Regulation.
8. Rules concerning order, hygiene and security.
9. Designation of persons to whom grievances or requests for better conditions are to be submitted.
10. Any special rules concerning particular parts of the plant with regard to the age and sex of the workers.
11. The means of fulfillment of the laws concerning social security, obligatory military service, identification card and in the case of minors, the fulfillment of school attendance obligation.[18]

Such a thorough policy gives us an idea of the way business is conducted in Chile as well as the nature of Chilean society.

An executive of Indus Lever, the Unilever subsidiary in Santiago, reports that the quality of Chilean management is quite high. "Chileans are anxious to learn, the universities have good quality graduates and our own factory management is extremely good."[19]

# Colombia

*Official Name:* Republic of Colombia; *Capital:* Bogota; *Government:* parliamentary democracy; *Subdivisions:* 22 departments; *Population:* 30,660,504 (July 1987); *Density:* 66.6 per square mile; *Currency:* peso; *Language:* Spanish; *Literacy:* 80 percent.

*The Land.* Colombia was named after Columbus who during his first trip to the Caribbean landed at certain points of the present Colombian territory. It is located in the northwest corner of South America. Three times as large as the state of Montana, Colombia is the only South American nation with both Atlantic and Pacific ports. Its Pacific coastline is 900 miles and its Caribbean coastline is 1,100 miles long. Colombia includes divergent geographical areas: low, flat coastal plains on the Caribbean coast, a mountainous west-central region crossed by three parallel ranges of the Andes, the eastern plains, and tropical jungle in the south.

*The People.* Ethnically, Colombians are 58 percent mestizo, 18 white, 14 mulatto, 4 black, 1 Indian and 3 percent *zambos* (mixed black and Indian). About 95 percent are Roman Catholic.

Colombians who live on the coast share the ethnic composition of the Caribbean peoples, with particularly strong black influence. Elsewhere the people are a combination of Indian — mostly Quimbaya, Chibcha and Chiriqui — and Hispanic cultures. The very exclusive upper class wields the most influence in economic and political affairs; the larger middle class enjoys some modern conveniences.

Colombia is one of the most Spanish of all South American countries, although persons of pure Spanish blood constitute only 20 percent of the population. Spanish values dominate Colombian society and the ideal for all non-white groups is to adopt all possible Spanish traits. An estimated 60 Indian tribes are scattered throughout the country.

Colombia is notable for its people's predilection for spending their evenings in intellectual talk. Bogota, the capital, has 11 universities, a number of museums and five daily newspapers.

*A Brief History.* Permanent colonization of Colombia began after 1514 when the region was part of New Granada, which included portions of present-day Panama, Venezuela and Ecuador. The country won its freedom in the revolt of the Spanish American colonies from 1810 to 1824. Simon Bolivar established the Republic of Gran Colombia in 1819 from which Venezuela and Ecuador withdrew in 1829–1830. The remaining territory was called New Granada, which was changed to the Republic of Colombia in 1886. Panama declared itself independent in 1903 when Colombia refused to lease territory to the United States to build the Panama Canal.

Colombia was politically stable until the assassination of the Liberal idol Jorge Gaitan in 1948 provoked a 12-day riot. Continuing violence has resulted in the death of 200,000 people in 15 years. To abate the violence, the rival Liberal and Conservative parties finally agreed to share political power equally, alternating the presidency every four years. Colombian democracy does not really function; the strangely chosen government is feeble.

*The Economy.* The work force is divided this way: services, 53 percent; agriculture 26; industry 21; and unemployed, 14 percent. About 8 percent of the labor force is unionized.

Colombia is second only to Brazil in coffee production. Livestock raising is also an important activity. Colombia has a wealth of natural resources. Most consumer goods are imported, while exports are mostly agricultural products—coffee, bananas, cotton and sugar. It is an important petroleum producer, contains 60 percent of South America's coal reserves, and is a major world source of emeralds. Government-owned oil refineries and hydroelectric plants are speeding industrialization.

Major industries include textiles and garments, chemicals, metal products, cement, cardboard containers, plastic resins and manufacturers, beverages and tourism. Most industrial establishments are small scale family-owned enterprises. About 65 percent are sole proprietorships and 23 percent partnerships.

*Organizational Communication.* The article "A Tale of Pluck," appearing in 1981 in the British publication *International Management,* described communication as it occurs in one Colombian company: Pollos Vencedor, Ltd., is a chicken processing company, founded in 1973, that operates as a cooperative. All employees who have worked for the company more than six months become members of the cooperative assembly. The employees appoint annually four committees that oversee every aspect of company life: management, production, finance and education.

The elections, that take over a week, are seen as a recharging of employees' participative batteries. They start with a four-hour presentation at each of the six main corporate units, at which each of the four committees outlines what it has done over the previous year and what it believes should be done in the future.

In the next few days, there are two-hour meetings in which all the cooperative's members split into small groups to discuss the reports in detail. The unit members then elect the members of the four committees for their part of the company.

Finally, everyone meets in Bogota for the annual general meeting. The opinions and ideas hammered out in unit meetings are aired and pieced together to achieve a consensus on the company's direction for the next year, and a 14-person general executive council is elected. This body then selects the managing director and most members of the four corporate-level committees.

The committees operate by consensus and act as a conduit of ideas from other employees. They have provided numerous money-saving suggestions.[20]

--------------------------  **Ecuador**  --------------------------

*Official Name:* Republic of Ecuador; *Capital:* Quito; *Government:* republic; *Subdivisions:* 20 provinces; *Population:* 9,954,609 (July 1987); *Density:* 90.4 per square mile; *Currency:* sucre; *Language:* Spanish; *Literacy:* 62 percent.

*The Land.* "A rich country inhabited by a poor people" is what ex–President Galo Plaza calls Ecuador. The equator ("ecuador" in Spanish) passes through the country. Located in the northwest corner of the South American continent and straddling the equator, Ecuador is about the size of Nevada. It shares a border of 334 miles with Colombia and 818 miles with Peru. Two parallel Andes ranges traverse the country, running nearly north and south, with jungle and elevated plains between the eastern and western ranges. The Amazon River originates in the Andes Mountains in Ecuador.

The Galapagos islands, on the equator 650 miles west, belong to Ecuador. The 60 volcanic islands were declared a national park to protect the unique wildlife, especially 15 species of giant tortoises, considered to be the oldest living creatures on earth, with a life span of 200 years, and weighing up to 500 pounds.

*The People.* Ecuador's people include communities of pure Indian descent and other descendants of the Spanish conquerors and black slaves. Ethnic groups are these: 25 percent are Indian; 55 mestizo; 10 percent Spanish; and 10 percent are African.

Ecuadorians feel it important to have a clean, nicely furnished house, but that is less important than keeping up the outside. Personal appearance is very important to Ecuadorians and even the poor will spend money on good clothes so that they can be well-dressed in public.

*A Brief History.* The Incas ruled the territory that is now Ecuador until the Spanish conquest in 1534. Spanish colonists introduced new crops and domestic animals and brought Christianity to the Indians, but native culture declined as the Spanish enslaved the Indians. Ecuador won independence in 1822. It became part of Bolivar's Gran Colombia. When the confederation was dissolved in 1830, Ecuador declared itself a republic.

From 1830 to 1948 Ecuador was ruled by 62 different presidents, dictators and military juntas. The instability continues today. In almost a century and a half of independence Ecuador had 17 constitutions. The Indians who dwell in poverty in the chill highlands, and who constitute half of Ecuador's population, are a prime source of instability.

*The Economy.* The labor force is divided this way: agriculture, 52 percent; manufacturing 13; commerce 7; construction 4; public administration 4; and other services, 16 percent. Less than 15 percent of the labor force is unionized.

The economy of this small country depends on exports of sugar, bananas, coffee and cacao—commodities whose prices fluctuate nervously. Its economy has boomed as it has become an important oil-producing nation. New discoveries of natural gas, gold and silver are also being exploited. Forestry and fishing are other major industries. About 49 percent of the country's work force is in agriculture; 11 percent is in industry; 17 percent is in services; and 11 percent is in sales.

The country has 500 corporations and 100 factories. There is very little heavy industry. The four largest manufacturing subsectors are food processing, textiles, machinery and chemicals.

# French Guiana

*Official Name:* Department of French Guiana; *Capital:* Cayenne; *Government:* overseas department and region of France; *Subdivisions:*

2 arrondissements and 19 communes; *Population:* 92,038 (July 1987); *Density:* 8.6 per square mile; *Currency:* franc; *Language:* French; *Literacy:* 73 percent.

*The Land.* The country is slightly smaller than Maine. Its terrain is low-lying coastal plains and tropical forest rising to hills.

*The People.* The population is 66 percent African and Afro-European, and 12 percent East Asian, Chinese and Amerindian.

*A Brief History.* France colonized Guiana in 1635. Between 1852 and 1947, French convicts were sent to Devil's Island, Guiana's penal colony. In 1946, the territory became an overseas department of France and has representation in the French parliament. This former penal colony has been in a continuous decline for years.

*The Economy.* The labor force is divided this way: services, government and commerce, 60.6 percent; industry 21.2; agriculture 18.2; and unemployed, 10 percent. About 7 percent of the labor force is unionized. Some 90 percent of the land is forest; 10 percent is waste, built on, inland water or other. Its exports, particularly of sugar, are used to pay for imports. France built a spare research center at Kourou, a site of a former prison camp, and recent French investments have developed paper manufacturing industries. Bananas, pineapples, sugarcane, fruits and vegetables are principal agricultural products. Gold is exported, but large deposits of bauxite have not yet been exploited. Major industries include construction, shrimp processing, forestry products, rum and gold mining.

# Guyana

*Official Name:* Cooperative Republic of Guyana; *Capital:* Georgetown; *Government:* republic within the British Commonwealth; *Subdivisions:* 6 governmental districts; *Population:* 765,844 (July 1987); *Density:* 300 per square mile; *Currency:* dollar; *Language:* English; *Literacy:* 85 percent.

*The Land.* About the size of Kansas, Guyana is covered by thick, uninhabited tropical forest, the upper reaches of the Amazon Jungle. It also includes a coastal plain and a grass-covered savannah and lies partly below sea level and must be protected by dikes. Located in the northeast region of South America, Guyana shares a 751-mile border with Brazil, a 404-mile border with Venezuela and a 451-mile border with Suriname.

The land is divided this way: 66 percent is forest; 22 is water, urban or waste; 8 is savannah; 3 is pasture; and 1 percent is cropland.

*The People.* The population of Guyana is 51 percent East Indian, 43 percent black and mixed, 4 percent Amerindian and 2 percent European and Chinese. They adhere to religion in these proportions: 57 percent Christian, 33 percent Hindu, 9 percent Muslim and 1 percent other. Ninety percent of the population lives on 4 percent of the land along its narrow coastline. Vast areas of the interior are virtually uninhabited.

East Indians have been allowed to retain their cultural, religious and linguistic traditions. Their cultural isolation was reinforced by the compulsory education law of 1871 which exempted them from attending Christian schools.

*A Brief History.* Guyana was settled by the Dutch in the sixteenth century, but the area was ceded to Britain in 1814. Following the abolition of slavery in 1834, indentured workers were brought primarily from India but also from Portugal and China. The British stopped the practice in 1917. Conflicts between East Indians and blacks delayed the granting of independence by Britain until 1966. Guyana became a republic in 1970. It is the only Marxist socialist country on the South American continent.

*The Economy.* The work force is divided this way: industry and commerce, 44.5 percent; agriculture 33.8; services 21.7; and public sector, 60 to 80 percent. About 34 percent of the work force is unionized.

Much of Guyana is unexplored. The government owns and operates most of the industry. Mining and processing of bauxite is a principal source of revenue. Other exports include sugar, alumina, rice, gold, diamonds and shrimp.

There are only 81 units in manufacturing that employ over 5 workers. The government nationalized the Booker Sugar Estates in 1976 and became the largest employer in the country. Processing of raw sugar is the country's largest industry. Major industries include bauxite mining, sugar and rice milling, timber, fishing (shrimp), textiles and gold mining.

# Paraguay

*Official Name:* Republic of Paraguay; *Capital:* Asuncion; *Government:* modified democracy; *Subdivisions:* 20 departments; *Population:* 4,251,924 (July 1987); *Density:* 22.9 per square mile; *Currency:* guarani; *Language:* Spanish; *Literacy:* 81 percent.

*The Land.* Paraguay is about the size of California. The arid, sparsely settled Chaco Boreal lies to the west; the east is a heavily populated, subtropical plateau region. Landlocked in the heart of South America, Paraguay is bordered by Argentina for 1,056 miles, by Brazil for 832 miles and by Bolivia for 470 miles. The Paraguay River divides the country into two parts: Eastern Paraguay — gently rolling country with wooded hills, tropical forests and fertile grasslands — and Western Paraguay, called the *Chaco* — low, marshy plains covered with dense scrub forests. The Parana and Paraguay rivers provide a direct outlet to the sea.

About 52 percent of the land is forest; 24 percent is meadow and pasture; 22 percent is urban, waste or other; and 2 percent is crop.

*The People.* Ethnically, socially and culturally, Paraguay probably has the most homogeneous population in South America. About 95 percent of them are of mixed Spanish and Guarani Indian descent. Italians, Germans,

Japanese, Brazilians and Argentines constitute small minorities. It is one of the few countries where Indians assimilated the Spanish rather than vice versa and where the resulting fusion shows more Indian than Spanish characteristics. Much of the population is rural, living in the countryside or in small settlements. Spanish is the official language, but Guarani is spoken by most Paraguayans. Around 98 percent are Roman Catholics and 1 percent are Mennonites.

*A Brief History.* First claimed as a Spanish possession in 1524, Paraguay gained its independence from Spain peaceably in 1811. Dictators ruled from 1814. Only some 30,000 males survived the disastrous war of the Triple Alliance in which Brazil, Argentina and Uruguay allied themselves against Paraguay in a five-year struggle. By 1970 when the war ended, Paraguay had lost 55,000 square miles of territory and over 300,000 people. The Chaco War with Bolivia in the 1930s cost another 20,000 lives. In 1954, General Alfredo Stroessner seized power and established himself as dictator. Since then, thousands have emigrated. He was overthrown by a close military associate in early 1989.

*The Economy.* The labor force is divided this way: agriculture, 44 percent; industry and commerce 34; services 18; government 4; and unemployed, 25 percent. About 5 percent of the work force is unionized.

Paraguay is one of the poorest countries in South America. Since it has no important mineral resources, the economy is based on agriculture, cattle raising and forestry.

About 44 percent of the labor force works in agriculture; 34 percent works in industry and commerce; 18 percent provides services; and 4 percent works in government.

Paraguayan businessmen are courteous and friendly, but business decisions are not made quickly due to a shortage of second-level management. All decisions have to be made at the top.

Paraguay's limited industrial base is confined to processing of agricultural products and small scale manufacture of consumer goods such as textiles. The only medium industry is a new steel mill near Asuncion. Other industries are meat packing, textiles and sugar refining.

*Organizational Communication.* Proper behavior in Paraguay is important. Desks, tables and floors are not considered proper places to sit. Erect posture while sitting in chairs is very important.

Nonverbal communication is unique in some ways. In Paraguay, tilting the head backwards means "I forgot." Blinking one eye while raising the other eyebrow has romantic connotations. Brushing the fingers forward under the chin means "I don't know."

# Peru

*Official Name:* Republic of Peru; *Capital:* Lima; *Government:* republic; *Subdivisions:* 23 departments and 1 constitutional province; *Population:*

20,739,218 (July 1987); *Density:* 39.7 per square mile; *Currency:* sol; *Languages:* Spanish and Quechua; *Literacy:* 80 percent.

*The Land.* Located in western South America, Peru is the third largest country on the South American continent and the fourth largest Latin American country. It is more than three times the size of California. However, nature has not treated this country kindly; it is divided into three major parts: the narrow, accessible coastal desert, where most of the cities and industries are situated; the unyielding Andes, where subsistence farming is carried on by poor Indians; and the virtually inaccessible eastern lowland jungle.

Peru shares a border of 950 miles with Ecuador, of 936 miles with Colombia, of 1,754 miles with Brazil, of 651 miles with Bolivia and of 105 miles with Chile. Its Pacific coastline stretches over 1,913 miles. Some 55 percent of the land is forest; 14 is meadow and pasture; 2 is crop; and 29 percent is urban, waste and other.

*The People.* Ethnic groups include Indian, 45 percent; mestizo 37, whites 15, and black, Japanese, Chinese and other, 3 percent. The relationship between the Hispanic and Indian cultures determines much of the nation's cultural expression.

Peruvians are very strong-willed and nationalistic. They have a good sense of humor and are accommodating and eager to please.

*A Brief History.* When Pizarro reached Peru, the Inca Empire extended from the area of northern Ecuador to central Chile. Francisco Pizarro conquered the empire in 1532 with fewer than 200 men and Peru became the richest and most powerful Spanish colony in the New World. The Spanish introduced a money economy, concepts of private property and socioeconomic values based on ownership and control, all of them in conflict with the socialistic system of the Incas. Three years after independence was declared in 1821, Simon Bolivar's forces, under the command of General Antonio Jose de Sucre, along with armies from Chile and Argentina, defeated the Spanish troops at Ayacucho in 1824, and freedom from Spain was secured.

Peru was defeated by Chile in the War of the Pacific (1879–83) and lost three of its southern provinces. One of them was later restored. In the twentieth century, Peruvian governments have alternated between constitutional civilian and military regimes. The military has governed since 1968.

*The Economy.* The labor force is divided this way: government and other services, 44 percent; agriculture 38; industry 18; unemployed 10.9; and underemployed, 57.4 percent. About 40 percent of salaried workers are unionized.

A small minority of the population garners the bulk of the nation's income; the bottom half averages an annual per capita income of $50. A third of the people do not speak Spanish, the language of the upper class.

Peru has a wealth of agricultural, mineral and forest resources, but only recently has it developed the industries to capitalize on them. In 1977 the Trans-Andean pipeline began delivering oil to the coast and the opening of two huge copper mines has nearly doubled Peru's copper output. Agriculture, the basic economic activity of Peru, occupies half of the population. Cotton and sugar are exported. Peru is the world's largest producer of guano, a fertilizer made from the dung of birds which feed on offshore fish. Major industries include food processing, textiles, steel, motor vehicle assembly, chemicals, pulp and paper, machinery and transportation equipment, rubber and construction.

Management education in Peru has bloomed in the past 20 years, nurturing a first generation of highly qualified managers. Of 32 Peruvian universities, 22 have management programs, 22 have accounting programs and 26 have economics programs. However, a shortage of managers with an acceptable level of education still exists. Peruvian managers must obey the industrial community law, which mandates that companies must distribute 27 percent of their earnings to the workers every year—15 percent in cash and the rest in shares. The law also provides for worker representation on boards of directors, despite the low educational level of many Peruvian workers. Some companies admit that they hold two separate board meetings, one "real" one among company executives and one that is attended by worker representatives.[21]

Visitors to Peru should be on time for meetings even when natives are not.

# Suriname

*Official Name:* Republic of Suriname; *Capital:* Paramaribo; *Government:* military dictatorship; *Subdivisions:* 9 districts; *Population:* 388,636 (July 1987); *Density:* 5.2 per square mile; *Currency:* guilder; *Language:* Dutch; *Literacy:* 65 percent.

*The Land.* Located on the north-central coast of South America and separated from neighboring Guyana and French Guiana by large rivers, Suriname is slightly larger than Georgia and is the smallest independent nation on the South American continent. Its border with French Guiana is 290 miles, with Brazil 368 miles and with Guyana 451 miles.

*The People.* The residents are ethnically divided this way: 37 percent Hindustani, 31 Creole, 15.3 Javanese, 10.3 Bush Negro, 2.6 Amerindian, 1.7 Chinese, 1 European and 1.1 percent other. The residents are 27.4 percent Hindu; 19.6 Muslim; 22.8 Roman Catholic; and 25.2 percent Protestant; about 5 percent follow other or indigenous beliefs.

*A Brief History.* Christopher Columbus first sighted the land in 1498 but it was unattractive because of lack of gold. The first large-scale colonization efforts were made by the English governor of Barbados, who became the region's first governor. In 1667, the Dutch received Suriname from the English in exchange for New Netherlands (now New York). The area fell to England again during the Napoleonic Wars; a series of agreements among England, France and the Netherlands divided the territory, which is sometimes referred to as "the Guianas," into three parts. Suriname later became Dutch territory.

*The Economy.* The labor force is divided this way: agriculture, 29 percent; industry and commerce 15; government 42; and unemployed, 14 percent. About 50 percent of the labor force is unionized. Bauxite deposits, assistance from the Netherlands and hard-working immigrants have made this into the most prosperous spot in the Guianas. The country is 76 percent forest; 16 percent built on, waste or other; and 8 percent unused. Major industries include bauxite mining, alumina and aluminum products, lumbering and food processing.

---

# Uruguay

---

*Official Name:* Oriental Republic of Uruguay; *Capital:* Montevideo; *Government:* republic; *Subdivisions:* 19 departments; *Population:* 2,964,052 (July 1987); *Density:* 45.6 per square mile; *Currency:* peso; *Language:* Spanish; *Literacy:* 94.3 percent.

*The Land.* This is a peaceful, democratic, cattle-and-sheep-raising state long known as the "Switzerland of America." The second smallest country in South America, Uruguay is about the size of the State of Washington. The country is mostly a rolling lowland plain covered with prairie which is excellent for stock raising and agriculture. It lies between Brazil in the northeast with which it shares a 623-mile border and Argentina in the west on the Atlantic Coast with which it shares a 308-mile border. With a coastline of more than 200 miles along the rio de la Plata and Atlantic Ocean, the country has many attractive beaches and several resort towns. Except for a mountainous area in the north, the land is level, with many natural waterways and extensive beaches that attract tourists. Stockraising is therefore the economy's traditional base. Uruguay is about the size of Missouri; it is the only South American country with no large uninhabited areas.

About 84 percent of the land is agricultural and 16 percent is forest, urban or other.

*The People.* Ethnic groups of Uruguayans are white, 88 percent; mestizo, 8 percent; and black, 4 percent. About 66 percent are Roman Catholic; 2 percent are Protestant; 2 percent are Jewish; and 30 percent are nonprofessing or other.

Uruguayans share a Spanish linguistic and cultural background. Nearly half of them live in Montevideo—the commercial, cultural and political center of the nation. Uruguayans are energetic, living for the most part in a modern, urban society similar to that of the largest cities of Europe or the United States. Literate and educated to a higher level than any other Latin American people, Uruguayans have contributed significantly to literature and the dramatic arts.

*A Brief History.* The first European settlers were the Spanish, who established a colony at Soriano in 1624. Spanish rule ended with the war of independence (1810–14). In 1820, Portuguese troops from Brazil occupied the country. A group of patriots known as the "Thirty-three Immortals" declared Uruguay an independent republic in 1825 and the country threw off Portuguese rule. In 1828, Uruguay was established as an independent nation.

The socialism launched by President Jose Batlle y Ordonez in the 1910s simply ran away with itself; the country today is deeply in debt. The government bureaucracy is vast in size.

Democratic government was predominant until 1973, when Juan M. Bordaberry dissolved the legislature and imposed government controls on the press and industry. He was ousted by a military coup in 1976 and a military government has ruled since that time.

*The Economy.* The labor force is divided this way: government, 25 percent, manufacturing 19, agriculture 11, commerce 12, utilities, construction, transportation and communication 12, other services 21, and unemployed, 11 percent.

Uruguay's greatest natural resource is its rich agricultural land which is used mainly for livestock production. There are few mineral resources; all petroleum must be imported. Workers labor six hours a day, enjoy 44 legal holidays a year and retire with full pensions at 55. As a result, Uruguay's productivity is declining.

Major industries in the country include food, beverages and tobacco, clothing and footwear, metal products, textiles, wood products, and chemicals.

*Organizational Communication.* Generally meetings begin later than scheduled, and late arrivers are not criticized. Meetings are, however, expected to be well organized and formal.

# Venezuela

*Official Name:* Republic of Venezuela; *Capital:* Caracas; *Government:* republic; *Subdivisions:* 20 states, 2 federal territories, 1 federal district and a federal dependency; *Population:* 18,291,134 (July 1987); *Density:* 45.7 per square mile; *Currency:* bolivar; *Language:* Spanish; *Literacy:* 85.6 percent.

*The Land.* Venezuela is the northernmost country in South America, equal in size to Texas and Oklahoma combined. The northwest peaks of the Andes Mountains gradually descend to the central plains and the high plateaus and rolling plains of the south and east; its Caribbean coastline is 1,750 miles long. The country is green, moist and productive, watered by the 1600-mile Orinoco River and over 1000 other rivers.

About 21 percent of the land is forest; 18 is pasture; 4 is cropland; and 57 percent is urban, waste or other.

*The People.* Some 68 percent of the people are mestizo; 20 percent are white; 10 percent are black and 2 percent are pure Indian. The blacks are descendants of African slaves originally imported by Spanish colonists. Rising prosperity in this century has attracted many Europeans who constitute about 10 percent of the population. Nearly 53 percent of the population is under 18 years of age. Nearly 96 percent of them are Roman Catholic; the remainder are Protestant.

Venezuela is the most urban and the richest of the countries of Latin America. Venezuelans tend to be less religious than other Latins; family continues to be a dominant factor in business life. Venezuela is also one of the least densely populated countries in the Western Hemisphere.

*A Brief History.* After Columbus discovered the Orinoco River in 1498 during his third voyage, colonization by Spain began. The Spanish named the land Venezuela or little Venice, because the houses built on stilts reminded them of Venice, Italy.

Although independence was declared in 1811, Venezuela remained under Spanish domination until 1821, when Simon Bolivar made Venezuela part of the Republic of Gran Colombia. Venezuela withdrew and became independent in 1830. Bolivar freed not only Venezuela but also four other South American countries.

Venezuela has been ruled largely by dictators since her independence. In 1958, democratic processes were restored; the current government is stable and prosperous.

*The Economy.* The labor force is divided this way: services, 56 percent, industry 28, agriculture 16, and unemployed, 10.5 percent. Some 32 percent of the labor force is unionized.

Venezuela is the most prosperous country in Latin America. Oil and iron account for 99 percent of the country's exports. Oil, of which Venezuela is the world's leading exporter, earns the country roughly 20 percent of its national income and helps to give Venezuela the highest per capita income in South America. But the country faces increasing competition from other oil producers. Venezuela has the world's largest petroleum refineries. Revenues are badly distributed, however. One out of seven Venezuelans is illiterate and half of them live on a bare subsistence level. Recent governments have tried to help by accelerating land reform, improving educational facilities and developing the mineral resources of eastern Venezuela. Venezuela is one of the top producers of electrical power in Latin America. Other mineral resources are iron, gold and diamonds, manganese, bauxite, copper, coal and salt.

Industry in Venezuela is in transition, from small, labor-intensive units engaged in the production of intermediate and consumer goods to large enterprises producing heavy and capital goods. This strategy is called *Sembrado el Petroleo* (sowing back petroleum) which means plowing back oil revenues into industrial development and diversification in order to replace oil as a source of revenue when the reserves are exhausted.

The average Venezuelan businessman is sophisticated, well educated, busy and used to overseas visitors. He expects promptness and prefers that business move along quickly. He appreciates the longest possible advance notice of appointments which should be made in the afternoons and not for lunch. Venezuelan businessmen prefer to go home to lunch and a siesta at midday.

Venezuela does, however, have a shortage of skilled technicians, mainly because the mark of success in this society is to get an education and a white shirt and sit in an air-conditioned office. Here, as in other Latin countries, delegation is upwards, meaning that lower echelon managers negotiate and then make recommendations to their superiors.

Business is complicated by the fact that Venezuela is a small country where everybody knows everybody else. One manager said that he has 25 first cousins and untold second cousins but he keeps in touch with all of them in case he needs help. An accountant from the United States, now a citizen of this country, described how the country has improved in the 28 years he has lived there: "When I got here 28 years ago, many towns did not have any kind of state school. The streets were of dirt. People did not dress well. Children had distended bellies. Now there are state schools and clinics for everybody. The streets are paved. The people are well dressed and the children are healthy looking."[22] Better management methods might have had something to do with those improvements but so did oil.

A Venezuelan manager said in a speech: "Future economic growth in Venezuela will depend not so much on the amount of oil produced and exported, or even the price we can charge for the oil. It will depend on our capacity to improve the quality of management."[23]

*Organizational Communication.* A business approach should be direct and to the point. The normal tone in business is fairly conservative and formal. Men wear their jackets in most places and always wear ties. Juniors hold doors for seniors; they show visible respect for those ahead of them either in age or rank, being careful not to precede them through doorways, interrupt, argue or take over a conversation. Courtesies are important and not superseded by camaraderie. People tend not to like doing business by phone. They make appointments on the telephone, but prefer to do actual business face to face (and at 4 to 8 inches) as much as possible.

Calling cards are essential in conducting business internationally, especially where names are difficult for both sides to understand and spell. If you receive a letter in Spanish it is expected that you will reply in Spanish. Venezuelans and most South Americans are proud and highly sensitive people, quick to feel slights and discourtesies, as well as quick to respond warmly to friendship.

Most Latins feel their individuality is violated by any lines at all; they do not like to be held down by "group conformity." They are filled with *personalismo* and *dignidad*. Many of them think that Europeans act like sheep and appear too subdued as they wait meekly in lines; Europeans and North Americans on the other hand, think them pushy and aggressive.

Normal business procedure in Venezuela is to discuss a question at length first, from a number of different views. Direct confrontations are avoided to the fullest extent so that no one loses face, by having to yield a point. Everyone first tests the air and comes to understand everyone else's position. This enables the minority to back down gently and inconspicuously, changing course, or modifying their stand as the picture clarifies. Direct negatives should always be avoided.

With practice business people in Venezuela develop the art of saying "yes" when they mean "no" but getting the idea across just the same. They never tell a person that they are too busy to see him. They send the word "yes, but some other day," or "later if possible." Latins say "we understand that ten yesses mean one no." They develop their ability to recognize when a "yes" really means "no — but I'm too polite to confront you so bluntly."

One of Venezuelans' major complaints about North Americans lies in the realm of perceived impersonality. We write memos, talk on the intercom or phone, but stay tucked away in our offices, out of sight and out of personal touch far more than most Latins do. In Venezuela actual presence, face to face contact, handshakes, shared cups of coffee are all important in the business day.

# Notes

1. Stanley Davis, "Managerial Resource Development in Mexico," in Robert R. Rehder, *Latin American Management,* p. 135.
2. Ibid.
3. Albert Lauterbach, *Enterprise in Latin America,* p. 3.
4. Rehder, p. 16.
5. Larry Rohter, "Central American Plight," p. 1.
6. Ibid.
7. Rehder, p. 14.
8. Tom Barry and Deb Preusch, *The Central American Fact Book,* p. 127.
9. Ibid., p. 128.
10. Mark Levinson, "Yanqui Come Back!" p. 24.
11. David Rockefeller, "Let's Not Write Off Latin America," p. 15.
12. Vikto E. Tokman, "Adjustment and Employment in Latin America," p. 533.
13. Philip R. Harris and Robert T. Moran, *Managing Cultural Differences,* p. 377.
14. Stanley M. Davis, "Managerial Resource Development in Mexico," in Rehder, *Latin American Management,* pp. 143-5.
15. Roy Hill, "The Ripening of Latin American Management," p. 26.
16. John C. Condon, *Good Neighbors,* p. xv.
17. Hill, pp. 24-5.
18. Robert J. Alexander, *Labor Relations in Argentina, Brazil and Chile,* pp. 348-9.
19. Hill, p. 26.
20. David Clutterbuck, "A Tale of Great Pluck," pp. 28-9.
21. Hill, p. 26.
22. Ibid.
23. Ibid.

# 4. Western Europe

## The Land

Occupying an eighth of the earth's land mass, Europe is the second smallest continent (after Australia), yet contains more than a fifth of the world's population, a people who have produced unlimited cultural and economic activity reaching all around the globe. Europe extends from the Ural Mountains in Russia to Iceland in the Atlantic, from the northlands of Scandinavia to the Mediterranean Sea. Western Europe is bounded on the north by the North Sea, on the west by the Bay of Biscay, on the south by the Mediterranean and on the east by the dividing line between the two Germanys.

## The People

The peoples of Western Europe are a highly diverse group of nations, each with its own customs and culture. See the descriptions of the individual countries for these.

One quality Western European countries share is population decline; births have fallen to a level below that necessary to replace present numbers. West Germany's population declines by 3,000 a week; one result is that army service has been extended from 15 to 18 months to meet commitments to Western allies. Sweden, Denmark and Norway are already staggering under increased welfare and pension costs for the growing retirement community while fewer young people are available to be taxed. Italy's sudden decrease in fertility is throwing its social services and educational systems out of balance.[1] By contrast Africa's population doubles every 21 years.

"During 1987," said Philippe Bourcier de Carbon of the French National Institute for Demographic Studies, "as many children will be born in Turkey and Egypt as in all 12 countries of the European Common Market."[2] In 100 years, the number of Europeans will be half what it is today, reported West German demographer Rolf Benkert in a Council of Europe study.[3]

Among the reasons for the declining population are: (1) young people who cannot afford to or do not want to have big families, (2) fewer marriages, and (3) women who are having children later, if at all, and (4) an increasing trend toward stopping at two children. One result will be increased pressure for immigration to Europe from the more crowded third-world nations of Africa, Asia and the Middle East.

# A Brief History

Given Europe's natural resources and its people's spirit, it is not surprising that as a world power it dispatched culture, armies and entrepreneurs worldwide. World War II left the continent in near total ruin with entire cities wasted, including its vast industrial complex, but Europe is now entering one of the most prosperous times in its history.

# The Economy

Europe has impressive reserves of minerals and raw materials. The continent is the world's leading producer of coal, iron and lignite and produces two-thirds of the world's mercury and scores of other industrial raw materials. Its farmland yields a rich output; its navigable waterways supply transportation as well as sources of power and irrigation.

Industry is flourishing today despite the ravages of numerous local wars and two world wars. In 1900 Western Europe accounted for about nine-tenths of the world's industrial output; by the early 1950s it was producing only three-fourths that of the United States alone and a little more than a quarter of the world's output. On the other hand European hydroelectric output has increased more than 200 percent since 1938, and automobile production over the same period leaped by more than 300 percent while the output of steel and iron soared proportionately.

# Organizational Communication

Unlike Americans, Europeans dislike telephone conversations prior to a personal meeting. Europeans are often shocked when Americans telephone from a hotel without advance warning and try to transact business. Although Europeans usually won't conduct business over the phone with people they have not met face-to-face, they do use the telephone to arrange future meetings. If something takes more than a few minutes to say, it should be said in person in Europe. After a personal meeting has taken place, however, telephone negotiations are acceptable.

Europeans also dislike being called at any hour of the day or night which to them is an invasion of privacy. Even when you have been given someone's home telephone number, it is best not to call a European after normal working hours or on weekends, and never at home unless you are old friends. Business should be limited to business hours, and these vary across the continent. In Northern Europe, the morning—around 10:00 or 11:00—is probably the best time to telephone. In Southern Europe, where business people may go home for a siesta from noon until three, around four in the afternoon is best.

Likewise, attitude toward schedules varies across the continent. Europeans may keep you waiting from a few minutes to over an hour in an outer office; nevertheless, you are expected to arrive on time. Sit and wait—without showing frustration or doing busy work — as evidence that you respect the opportunity of a meeting. Be exactly on time North of the Alps — not a minute too early; wait outside or in the lobby if you must, watching the time. Being late is also frowned upon by Northern Europeans.

Most Europeans shake hands both on arrival and departure with a light grip, not a firm one. In Latin Europe, handshakes last about twice as long as Americans are accustomed to, five to seven strokes. Pulling the hand away too soon creates an impression of rejection. As in many other areas of life, the French shake hands in their own special way: one brisk definitive stroke. When you meet a group, shake hands with the oldest or most senior person first, and go down the line. The highest ranking person does the extending; the person of lesser status does the receiving. Europeans often reshake hands whenever they are apart for more than a few minutes. When leaving a colleague at the office to go to lunch, they shake hands both on departure and return.

In Europe some form of informal exchange nearly always precedes serious business talk. Even Germanic peoples, who prefer to get right down to business, usually talk for a few minutes about your industry, how your firm fits into it, and how you fit into the firm. Then they explain how things are in Europe. This short exchange of information soon winds down so that the matter at hand can be addressed.

In both oral and written communication, use European nomenclature and honorific titles whenever possible — especially in the United Kingdom where spelling often varies from that in America.

On being admitted to a Latin office, you'll be invited to an informal lounge area for something to drink, usually coffee or tea. If you refuse it, politeness prevents your host from drinking and without drinks, you have no excuse to discuss subjects other than business, allowing you to get to know each other.

Speak slowly and softly, and don't come on too strong. Europeans feel Americans overwhelm them with intense, psychic energy. They respond best to calm logic, preferring situations where emotions are kept under control — including salesmanship and facial expressions that reveal anger, aggression, frustration, incredulity, amazement, arrogance and superiority.

Be ready to exchange business cards with yours in both English and the language of your host and presented with his language up. Latin Europeans may use two last names on business cards and in correspondence. If a colleague's name is Jose Ramirez Garcia, Ramirez is the father's name, Garcia the mother's. The mother's name is not used in conversation. Jose Ramirez Garcia becomes Jose Ramirez in speech; Garcia is dropped. When writing, though, you may refer to him as Mr. Ramirez Garcia (although simply Mr. Ramirez is still correct). If a European has an academic title printed on his business card, use it as given. Fritz Brenner, Economist, is "Economist Brenner."

North of the Alps, executives may have two titles on their cards — a company director and an economist, for instance. Titles that are earned and denote academic distinction are more prestigious than conferred titles indicating corporate status. You can use either the academic title alone or both titles with the academic one first. Thus Brenner becomes "Economist Director Brenner."

Americans believe the system gets out of hand, however, when a person is credited with as many titles as he has gathered. "In the case of Friedrich von Hayek, who was a local Nobel laureate," reports an American visitor to Austria, "four doctorates preceded his name."[4] Northern Europeans also admire longevity so that if your firm is old, you should have its founding date printed on your cards.[5]

Advanced education is greatly admired, particularly among northern Europeans; it carries social as well as professional prestige. If you have an M.B.A. or a Ph.D. relating to your business field, have it printed on your cards to help establish your credibility.

Your wardrobe for Europe should be natural in fiber — cotton, wool, silk, and so on — not synthetic. Dark gray, dark blue and black are the colors European decision makers wear to work. In Latin Europe, white shirts and black lace-up shoes are preferred for office attire and required for evening wear.

Collateral materials presented to business people of Central and Northern Europe should be professionally prepared with a design that is complete, concise, clean and clear, but always conservative. North of the Alps one's approach should be direct, factual, detailed and thorough — almost academic in approach — but concise. Objectivity will do more than adjectives to convince Germanic, Nordic and British peoples. Europeans are often suspicious of business proposals that require the hard sell rather than being allowed to stand on their own merits. Written proposals and statistical reports achieve more than flashy literature. Northern Europeans advertise to their own customers this way, but they prefer not to be sold this way themselves. Illustrations should be professional graphic aids. Any illustration that doesn't contribute to the story should be omitted.

For an organized, meticulous appearance, use extra devices like index tabs or different colored paper for different sections to subdivide lengthy documents. It impresses Northern Europeans who are highly organized and meticulous themselves. Latins prefer livelier, more colorful documents with flashy features to spruce up the story. But Latin business people know quality and expect to see it in your collateral materials. If you will be preparing materials in Europe, be prepared for the standard stationery size of 8¼ × 11⅝ inches.

Make the benefits of your proposition apparent in your presentation without drawing conclusions. In Europe, presentations are intended to clarify, not sell. The American method of guiding a client step by step through a maze of detail will fail. The European prefers to have a path cleared through the maze so that he can decide whether to take the path.

In Southern Europe's major commercial centers, like Milan, the same presentation guidelines apply. Farther south, oral presentations must be slower, since English is less widely spoken or understood, with a pause after each main point and a repetition of the same point in different ways. In Portugal, Spain, southern France, southern Italy, and Greece, be patient but never be condescending, something Latins are acutely sensitive to.

Throughout Europe be conscious of American idioms — bottom line, no way, leading edge, ASAP, FYI, need it yesterday, and so on. Even Europe's best second-language English speakers—Germans, Dutch and Scandinavians—have mastered textbook (usually British) English, not idiomatic American English, and British English often differs from American English, discussed further in the part of this chapter on the United Kingdom.

Europeans may also have different concepts of space both from each other and from Americans. Latin Europeans usually stand or sit closely together in conversations, often only several inches away. Americans are comfortable conversing at about arm's length and feel their personal space has been invaded by the Latin need to be close. The American tendency to back off implies to a Latin insincerity and rejection. Latins also touch other people while they talk much more than Americans are used to which also makes Americans uncomfortable. North of the Alps and in Britain, people don't gesture much with their hands.

In France and Mediterranean Europe, executives may not have separate offices. Their desks are in the middle of an open departmental area, enabling the person in charge to keep an eye on subordinates—a sign of power. The walled office that is a status symbol in the United States isolates and thus confines managerial authority in Latin Europe.

Europeans are beginning to use electronic media of communications like teleconferencing. More and more managers are using electronic mailboxes, storing up messages and voices until the most appropriate time for the manager to tap and use them.

# EEC COUNTRIES

The European Economic Community (EEC) may be defined as an organization set up by a group of Western European countries with the aim of achieving eventual political union through a gradual process of practical economic integration. It was established with six members (Germany, France, Italy, Belgium, Luxembourg and the Netherlands) in 1958. By July 1, 1968, a year and a half ahead of schedule, there was free trade within the community both in industrial goods and most forms of produce. The six countries had eliminated intracommunity tariffs and established a common tariff on goods imported from nonmember countries.

In 1961, Britain, Denmark, Ireland and Norway applied to join, but were rebuffed in 1963 when President Charles de Gaulle of France exercised on Britain the veto that all existing members possess over the admission of new members. A similar bid by all four in 1967 was again rejected by de Gaulle in 1969. When de Gaulle retired, they tried again in 1969. In 1973 Britain, Denmark and Ireland joined the EEC. In 1981 Greece became the tenth member and in 1986, Spain and Portugal were admitted. The Community is striving to remove hundreds of trade barriers between the 12 members by the end of 1992 to create open, unencumbered economic activity similar to that in the United States. The result will be the largest consumer market in the world.

Expectations are that the southern countries in the Community will begin to lead its development. "The center of gravity of Europe has moved south,"

says Portuguese Premier Anibal Cavaco Silva, whose Social Democrats won
a landslide victory in the 1987 elections. "The southern nations will now
become the motor of the European Community."[6]

"The European Community would like to turn the south of Europe into
a developed area resembling the northern countries," says Antonio La Pergola,
Italy's Sicilian-born, Harvard-educated minister for European Community
relations. "This could create a Sun Belt like in the United States in this
area."[7]

The structure of the EEC was compared by one member country's representative as similar to what would have occurred in the United States had the
North not won the Civil War. The result would have been strong state governments and a weak federal government. That, he said, is descriptive of the EEC
today.

An EEC document, titled "Workers' Rights in Industry," said this about
communication and information:

...the European Commission believes that information and consultation
should be a permanent feature of industrial life. The competitiveness of
companies need not be affected: on the contrary, improved labour relations
can bring increased productivity and a sharper competitive edge. A proposal
made in 1980 and modified in July 1983, following the opinion of the European Parliament and the Economic and Social Committee, calls for the information and consultation of workers in companies where decisions are
taken at a higher level than that to which workers' representatives have access. The companies involved are those with a number of subsidiaries or factories, whether in the same country as the parent firm or in a number of
countries. The directive would therefore apply to multinational companies,
even if their head office is not in the Community. The draft proposal calls
for:

• The presentation to workers' representatives of a general but detailed
rundown of the structure of the company, its economic and financial situation, its employment and investment prospects, at least once a year, and on
each occasion that this information goes to creditors and shareholders. The
workers can approach the head office directly if management of a subsidiary
fails to give this information;

• Workers' representatives at all relevant subsidiaries must be given prior
information on the motives and impact of any proposal which could have
serious implications for the workforce (a closure, a move, a reduction or
significant alteration in activities, cooperation agreements with other firms,
a major change in organization, working methods, or manufacturing techniques, as a result, perhaps, of the introduction of new technology, as well
as any proposals which might affect health or safety). Before a final decision
can be made (or implemented, if secrecy is needed to prevent the plan from
being compromised or ruined) the workers must be given 30 days in which
to give their opinion and hold consultations on steps to be taken to protect
the workforce. The draft directive is aimed at firms employing at least 1,000
people within the Community. Member States could limit its application to
subsidiaries with a recognized structure of worker representatives. Infor-

mation for the workers would, in principle, be passed on from the head office through local management.[8]

# Belgium

*Official Name:* Kingdom of Belgium; *Capital:* Brussels; *Government:* constitutional monarchy; *Subdivisions:* 9 provinces; *Population:* 9,873,066 (July 1987); *Density:* 840.3 per square mile; *Currency:* franc; *Official Languages:* Dutch (Flemish) and French; *Literacy:* 98 percent.

*The Land.* This country's name goes back to a Celtic tribe, the Belgae, whom Julius Caesar described in his commentaries as the most courageous tribe in all of Gaul.

Slightly larger than Maryland, Belgium is one of the smallest countries in Europe. Its location at the crossroads of Europe on the North Sea, its inland port of Antwerp, and its network of canals, rivers and railroads help to make it one of the Continent's major importers and exporters. The stretch from its two farthest points is 175 miles. The country lies within 100 miles of London, Paris, the Ruhr Valley and most of the Netherlands.

Belgium, which lies in the shape of a triangle, shares a 280-mile border with the Netherlands, a 380-mile border with France to the south, a 200-mile border with West Germany and Luxembourg on the east, and a 40-mile coastline on the North Sea. England is about 54 miles away across the English Channel. Its terrain varies from coastal plains in the northwest, through gently rolling countryside in the center, to the Ardennes Mountains in the southeast. Like the Netherlands, Belgium has a system of dikes and seawalls along the coast to prevent tidal flooding. Belgium consists of two parts which are physically very different: the great plain in the north and the Ardennes Mountains in the south. The Ardennes is a heavily wooded plateau located in southeast Belgium and continuing into France.

About 28 percent of the land is cultivated; 24 percent is meadow and pasture; 20 percent is forest and 28 percent is waste, urban and other.

*The People.* Belgians are Indo-European descendants of the Gauls and Franks. They comprise cultural elements of Celtic, Roman, German, French, Dutch, Spanish and Austrian origin. In the north are the Flemings, a Catholic people akin to the Dutch, and in the south are the Walloons who are French and Protestant. The Flemings now account for 60 percent of the total population, live in the most densely populated part and are richer than the Walloons. But this was not always so and the Flemish Movement, begun in the mid-nineteenth century, only achieved equality with the French-speakers in the 1960s. Both languages are now official and equal and most places have two place names.

About 56 percent of the residents speak Flemish (Dutch) while 32 percent speak French and 1 percent speak German. About 75 percent of those residents are Roman Catholic; the rest are Protestant and other.

There are strong tensions between the Flemish-speaking Roman Catholics of the north and the large anticlerical French-speaking people of the south. Flemish is to Dutch as American English is to British English. The ratio of Flemings (Flemish-speakers) and Walloons (French-speakers) is about five to four. Language usage remains a powerful issue in contemporary Belgium. Under the revised constitution of 1981, and after long battles in the areas of government affairs, education, etc., separate cultural councils within the parliament were set up for each of the Dutch and French linguistic areas, as well as a bilingual area for Brussels, the capital.

The French-speaking Walloons have a reputation for being spontaneous, quick-witted and often caustic or skeptical as well as stubborn and headstrong. They are intensely proud of their language and rich cultural heritage, especially in painting and architecture.

The work ethic and an appreciation for culture and refinement are prominent ideals in Belgian life. The business world in Belgium and businessmen as individuals enjoy considerably more prestige, relative to government circles, than is the case in Britain, though not America. Belgians tend to be individuals with strong regional and family ties. External conformity has traditionally been the passport to full inner freedom; however, Belgians are somewhat contemptuous of authority from centuries of foreign rulers. The rights of the individual are more important than obligations to society; tax evasion has become an art. Belgians are highly independent, making their living mostly as farmers and small shopkeepers.

*A Brief History.* The Belgae were a Celtic people who settled much of what is now Belgium and Holland many centuries ago. A manufacturing nation since the Middle Ages, when its textile mills were Europe's most important, Belgium is today one of the most heavily industrialized countries on the Continent.

The linguistic line in Belgium today roughly reflects the ancient boundary between the Roman Empire in the south and the territory dominated by the Germanic Franks in the north. In the Middle Ages, the area produced some of the wealthiest trading cities in the world and developed high cultural achievements. Belgium was originally composed of a number of duchies and counties, the names of which continue to be used for the provinces that now lie in the Netherlands and Belgium. Some of the dukes and counts owed allegiance to the King of France; others to the Holy Roman Emperor. Gradually they freed themselves and by inheritance and war they were united in the fifteenth century under the Dukes of Burgundy. Succession eventually passed to the King of Spain. During Philip II's reign, a religious war, following the development of Protestantism in the Netherlands, led to the independence of the northern provinces. The southern provinces remained under the King of Spain and then passed to the Austrian House of Hapsburg. During the reign of Napoleon, the Belgian provinces were treated as part of France. By the peace treaty of 1815, they were united with the northern provinces under the King of the Netherlands. In 1830, the Belgians revolted and gained their independence, electing their first monarch, Leopold I, on July 21, 1831.

Subsequently, Belgium came under Burgundian, Spanish and Austrian control before becoming independent. The town of Waterloo where Napoleon was defeated by the British in 1815 is just a few miles south of Brussels. In the nineteenth century it had a colony in Africa — the Belgian Congo (Zaire). Though supported by Great Britain, Belgium was overrun by German armies in both 1914 and 1940. After World War II, Belgium became a founding member of NATO, and Brussels now serves as headquarters for NATO and the EEC.

*The Economy.* The labor force is divided this way: services, 58 percent; industry 37; agriculture 5; and unemployed, 13.6 percent. About 70 percent of the labor force is unionized, making it one of the most highly unionized countries in the world.

Belgium was one of the first countries in the world to become heavily industrialized because of its large coal reserves and to a lesser extent iron ore deposits. It first introduced railways to the European continent. The economy of Belgium is highly industrialized and one of the strongest in the world. About 75 percent of its trade is within the European Common Market. Belgium is the world's third largest producer of wool and cigars, the fifth largest producer of beer, sixth in cigarettes and tenth in meat. Belgian steel, the principal export, is world famous and accounts for 32 percent of the country's GNP. Other industries include engineering and metal products, food and beverage processing, chemicals, textiles, petroleum, diamond cutting, fishing, chemicals, wood products, leather goods. Linen and fine lace are the main textile products.

The city of Antwerp, the world's third largest seaport, is the industrial center of Belgium. Exports include steel, textiles and industrial machinery. Its coal deposits are among the world's richest; it is also a major manufacturer of steel and of petrochemicals. Although Belgium is also an important agricultural producer, it must import food for its basically urban population. The country produces 80 percent of its own food supplies and ships abroad billions of francs' worth of dairy products, sugar, chocolate, processed cereals, canned fruit and luxury products. One of every 11 jobs in the country is provided by the 904 American companies doing business in Belgium.

Historically, the Walloons and Flemings engaged in different occupations that often affected their economic well-being and accentuated their differences. Flemings were small farmers and merchants and tended to be conservative. Walloons were pioneers of industry and political life and were generally more receptive to changing social philosophies. In recent years, however, light industries have moved into Flemish Belgium while traditional industries in the south have languished.

Brussels and Antwerp have been gaining in importance as the administrative center of the European Common Market and NATO activities. Brussels is now the commercial and economic hub of Western Europe.

*Organizational Communication.* Visitors should secure an appointment before calling on businesses in Belgium, and the Belgians will select the time and place. Business cards are widely used, and in a multiple language country like Belgium, it is a good idea to have them printed in each language — Dutch, French and German.

The Belgians shake hands in a manner that is quick with light pressure. The firm, pumping American-style handshake is considered unrefined. A man

**Table 5. Some Communication Practices in the Belgian Corporation**

The Belgians:

1. Require an appointment before business calls.

2. Choose the time and place of a meeting.

3. Expect business cards to be in Dutch, French and German.

4. Shake hands quickly, with light pressure each time they meet and leave.

5. Are willing to discuss business over meals.

6. Expect punctuality and get right down to business.

7. Are formal and efficient.

8. Must establish trust before they will do business.

9. Allow information to flow through liaisons.

10. Transact business via mail, telex or telephone.

11. Use first names only after friendship has developed.

12. Take cultural cues from the French, Germans or Dutch.

13. Depending on cultural orientation, have either a high-context (German and Dutch) or low-context (French) culture.

14. For the most part, use time monochronically.

should wait for a woman to extend her hand. Shake hands each time you meet someone and each time you leave, including each morning and at the end of every day, and do not forget anyone. Introduce yourself to anyone in the office whom you don't know. During meals keep both hands on the table. You may discuss business during a meal, but wait for the Belgian to initiate work-related conversation.

Be punctual and come straight to the point of your business, but don't be casual or neglect formalities. Belgians are shrewd business persons and tough negotiators. Be prepared with facts and figures. Proceedings will be formal and efficient. Often, however, the first meeting will achieve only an acquaintanceship. Belgians must trust you and have confidence in your company to do business with you.

As in most of Europe, typically casual American attitudes may be regarded in Belgium as rudeness and a sign of poor breeding. Never talk to another with your hands in your pockets or anything in the mouth. Everyone should maintain good posture and never put feet on tables or chairs. Most Belgians do not use first names until a friendship has been formed.

Close liaison should be maintained with distributors and customers to exchange information and ideas. Mail, telegraphic and telephone communication are usually sufficient, but periodic personal visits help keep distributors apprised of new developments and resolve problems quickly and efficiently.

In Brussels you are dealing with the Belgian French who take their cultural cues from France, but they are easier going in transacting business. Attempting to speak French here is appreciated, unlike in France. Belgian French are also more polite, less argumentative, less critical and less philosophical about business principles than the French. Because their country is smaller with fewer natural resources, the Belgians are more pragmatic and more open to compromise than the French. Because the country is a constitutional monarchy rather than socialist, the mountain of red tape that entangles you in France does not exist in Belgium.[9]

Table 5 lists some communication practices in the Belgian firm.

# Denmark

*Official Name:* Kingdom of Denmark; *Capital:* Copenhagen; *Government:* constitutional monarchy; *Subdivisions:* 14 counties; *Population:* 5,121,766 (July 1987); *Density:* 312.8 per square mile; *Currency:* krone; *Official Language:* Danish; *Literacy:* 99 percent.

*The Land.* "Denmark" means "the field of the Danes." Almost twice the size of New Jersey, Denmark is the southernmost, the flattest and the smallest of the Scandinavian countries. Located strategically at the mouth of the Baltic Sea, Denmark consists of the peninsula of Jutland and 406 neighboring islands (97 of them inhabited), including the Faroe Islands (located in the North Sea between Norway and Iceland), and Bornholm, an island in the Baltic Sea. The straits between the islands connect the Baltic and North Seas. Only Jutland connects it to the European mainland, its border there being with West Germany. A less-prosperous part of Denmark is the ice-covered Atlantic island of Greenland, considered a Danish colony. The largest island in the world (not counting the continent of Australia), about 84 percent of Greenland lies under a permanent ice cap. Denmark is 64 percent arable land, 11 percent forest, 8 meadow and pasture, and 17 percent other.

*The People.* The Danes, a homogeneous Gothic-Germanic people, have inhabited Denmark since prehistoric times. Danish people are informal and very friendly, but they place a high value on being polite. Of all the Scandinavians, the Danes are also the most adaptable. Other Scandinavians describe the Danes as smooth, polished and worldly creatures as well as friendly, gregarious and in tune with their social environment. In business dealings, the Danes are often called ruthless.

Almost a third of the population lives in Greater Copenhagen, which accounts for 45 percent of retail sales. Copenhagen is on Zealand, the largest island, which is linked to Funen, the next largest island, which in turn is linked to the mainland by bridge.

The family is close-knit and quite stable. A distinguishing aspect of the Danish culture is the importance given the individual—a concept taught and honored in Danish homes. About 97 percent of the population is Evangelical Lutheran; 2 percent belong to other Protestant denominations and the Roman Catholic church; and 1 percent are other.

The Danish people are avid readers. They are addicted to newspapers and are one of the leading book-buying nations in the world. The country ranks first in number of books borrowed from public libraries. Denmark is one of the few countries outside the United States that commemorates the American Independence Day in honor of the good relations between the two countries.

*A Brief History.* Denmark's royal family (the House of Glucksborg) represents the oldest continuous monarchy in the world. It is descended from the House of Oldenburg which was established on the Danish throne in 1448 when Christian I became king. A liberal constitution was adopted in 1849 under King Frederik VII when Denmark became a constitutional monarchy governed by a bicameral parliament. In 1953 it was replaced by a single-chamber parliament.

Despite many wars and invasions because of its location, Denmark is very stable. Denmark was a country of great power during the days of the Vikings (A.D. 790–1030). These seagoing warriors conquered parts of England and Normandy, invaded the Mediterranean and visited the coasts of North America. They forged Denmark into the most powerful European empire of their era. The country remained neutral during World War I, but even though it had a nonaggression pact with Hitler, it was invaded at the beginning of World War II and occupied by Nazi Germany from 1940 until it was liberated by the British in 1945.

*The Economy.* The work force is divided this way: government, 33.2 percent; manufacturing 20.7, commerce 13.2, banking and business services 7.5, transportation 7.2, construction 5.9, agriculture, forestry and fishing, 2.0 percent, and unemployed, 10.3 percent. About 65 percent of the labor force is unionized.

Denmark's standard of living is one of the highest in the world and is the third highest in Europe. Within Denmark's borders lie some of the most fertile soil of the European plain. Agriculture still accounts for 30 percent of Danish exports; 86 percent of Denmark's farmland is cultivated. The country has a shortage of natural resources, but has long been renowned for its high-quality agricultural produce. Some 70 percent of the total land area is devoted to agriculture, the foundation of Danish wealth, even though it contributes only about 5.5 percent of GDP.

Denmark is now highly industrialized, even though it almost totally lacks raw materials, except salt and newly discovered North Sea oil and gas. What the Danes lack in raw materials they must make up for in highly skilled labor and high quality production. Denmark is the world's largest exporter of insulin for diabetics and of industrial enzymes. Profits derived from the export sale of cattle, pigs, dairy products, fruit, grains and potatoes, processed and marketed through a highly developed system of farmers' cooperatives, are the bulwark of the economy. Denmark is today the world's second largest producer of beer and third largest producer of meat. With the income from such exports, mineral-poor Denmark has been able to purchase raw materials for its industries (shipbuilding, chemicals and machinery) and to supply its citizens a stable government and a great variety of social services. Products for which the country is known are diesel engines, electrical equipment, dairy machines, refrigerating plants and cement-making machinery. Local workshops produce excellent porcelain, silverware and furniture.

Denmark is a leading shipbuilding country, constructing all types of vessels from supertankers and icebreakers to whale-catchers, car ferries and coasters, trawlers, motorboats and sail dinghies. Specialized products which are exported in quantity are winches, cranes, containers, pumps, ventilators, navigational instruments and generators. Danish marine diesel motors are known the world over and made on license in 35 countries. The world's first ocean-going motor ship was built in Denmark.

A highly advanced refrigeration industry has formed, stimulated by Denmark's extensive export of foodstuffs. Refrigerated cool-storage chains have been developed so that these foods can be transported from one end of the world to the other.

The metal processing sector is Denmark's dominant industrial sector and employs about 40 percent of the industrial labor force.

It is also natural that a country with a long agricultural tradition should have an extensive production and export of agricultural machinery including combine harvesters, hay pressers, forage harvesters, ploughs, harrows and cultivators, seed drills, fertilizer spreaders, silos, milking machines and many others.

Consultation between management and labor is carried on by means of joint industrial committees. One-third of the members of executive boards of large limited companies must be workers' representatives.

The workers' participation movement in Denmark has grown through a series of Co-operation Agreements — 1947, 1964, 1970 and 1984 — and the 1981 Agreement on New Technology. Communication plays an important role in the Agreements and program of workers' participation. The 1947 Agreement had as a declared aim the promotion of efficiency and job satisfaction and toward that end provided for the establishment in enterprises employing at least 25 persons of joint labor-management "cooperation committees." "This phase of the development of industrial democracy can be said to have helped in establishing the useful habit of regular exchanges of information on matters concerning conditions of work and day-to-day production."[10]

If the 1947 Agreement emphasized information, the 1964 one focussed on dialogue, and the cooperation committees discussed issues touching on the economy, employment, production and efficiency, ensuring that the rationale behind management decisions was better understood by the work force. The 1970 highlighted "co-influence," a term applied to the right of workers to be heard or consulted before management implemented its decisions.

The Labor Agreement and the Agreement on Technology stated this about what employees need to know about technology:

It is important for the employees to be clear about:

What is going to happen.

Who might be affected or might serve on committees being informed and educated on what and why.

How the plans can be carried out without unnecessary resistance or difficulties and how further information and education will take place and how the commitment to progress will be insured.

When the planned changes ought to be instituted and followed up.[11]

The "Cooperation Agreement of June 9, 1986" between the Danish Employers' Confederation and the Danish Federation of Trade Unions has this to say about information:

> Communication between management and employees is essential to cooperation within an enterprise. Information shall be directed to individual employees as well as groups of employees. It shall be given sufficiently early to allow employees to put forward their viewpoints, ideas and proposals for consideration before any decision is made. Employees shall receive such information as is required to permit them to contribute to structuring their work.
>
> Information conveyed shall contain management's assessment of the consequences of any changes contemplated and shall be formulated in plain language. All information shall be adapted to the groups of employees for which it is intended. Both management and employees shall take an active part in the mutual exchange of information.[12]

The Agreement continues for two pages to discuss the importance of information and communication to the smooth operation of their organizations.

The Cooperation Agreement also contains these 12 pointers:

1. The employees receive current information from management on the economic position and future prospects of the company as well as plans for introduction of new technology or changes in existing technology.
2. Management informs the proper committee before introducing new technology or changing existing technology.
3. The information should be organized clearly and easily understood.
4. Management presents the technical, economical, personnel, and environmental consequences of the technological change.
5. Management gives up-to-date news of essential changes in the established plans.
6. The proper committee discusses the above-mentioned problems and consequences.
7. The committee is the decision maker regarding education, retraining and job transfers, including information dissemination/education as needed.
8. The committee has influence on major reorganizations (management gives the committee opportunities to exchange opinions and suggestions that thereafter become part of the basis for management decisions).
9. The committee may consult with experts from within the organization (if anyone desires it) or from outside the organization (if everyone agrees). The collaboration committee is, however, always permitted to give advice, guidance and counsel toward the advancement of cooperation on technology problems.
10. The committee is responsible for dissemination of information to all employees.
11. The committee shall work for pleasant and peaceful working conditions in the company in the area of technology.
12. The committee deals with the above-mentioned matters systematically and sets up the system to do it. (Why? Who? How? When?)[13]

Danish industry is overwhelmingly privately owned. The state does not engage in industrial production and is seldom willing to subsidize lameduck industries. Also, only about one-twelfth of Denmark's industries are foreign-owned. Firms in Denmark are of small and medium size, with an average of 60 employees. Almost half employ fewer than 20. Industry in Denmark is also geographically dispersed. There is no one concentrated industrial region. One sharp difference of opinion which exists between employers and trade unions is the latters' wish to introduce what they call "economic democracy." There are already forms of employee participation in the firms' decision-making, but this does not extend to sharing profits.

*Organizational Communication.* Denmark, like Sweden and Finland, has a very informal business culture. Danish business persons are traditionally said to be the best salespersons among the Scandinavian nations. They are outward-looking and like foreigners. Nearly all Danish firms will conduct correspondence in English.

Punctuality is very important for all appointments. In all of Scandinavia, one can see guests waiting outside their hosts' homes the few minutes that they allocated for early arrival so that they can arrive punctually at the door.[14] Foreign visitors who have business appointments will not have to wait long, but arriving late communicates that they are uninterested or discourteous.

Handshaking is customarily with a firm grip and with eyes meeting for its duration. It is also customary to exchange business cards. Usually only close friends use first names.

Table 6 lists some communication practices of the Danish firm.

### Table 6. Some Communication Practices in the Danish Corporation

The Danes:
1. Conduct business informally and in English.

2. Expect punctuality.

3. Shake hands with a firm grip and eye contact for its duration.

4. Exchange business cards.

5. Use first names only with close friends.

6. Have a low-context culture.

7. Use time monochronically.

### CASE STUDY: AALBORG PORTLAND

Aktieselskabet Aalborg Portland-Cement-Fabrik was founded in 1899 on the initiative of the Aalborg merchant, Consul Hans Holm, who together with the founders of F.L. Smidth & Company, F.L. Smidth, Poul Larsen and Alexander Foss, all engineers, raised the initial capital to the cement plant Rordal near Aalborg. The Rordal plant was already the largest cement factory in Denmark.

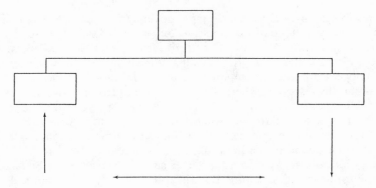

*Upward*

Written:
  memorandum
  report
  newspaper/magazine

Personal:
  meeting
  interview
  open-door policy
  grievance procedure

*Downward*

Print:
  annual report
  annual report to employees
  newspaper/magazine
  bulletin board
  orientation manual
  letters
  pay envelope inserts
  safety manual
  organization and work manual and
    manual on handling of chemicals

Electronic:
  telephone
  film
  videotape

*Horizontal*

personal contact
memorandum
meeting

**Figure 9. Communication system at Aalborg Portland Company.**

By the 1970s Denmark's cement consumption had reached 2.6 million tons and the Aalborg company was producing it at four plants: the Rordal and the Denmark plants at Aalborg, the Dania plant at Mariarger and the Karlstrup plant near Koge. The Company today manufactures and sells a number of special cements, most importantly white cement, for export to 80 countries. To do so the company has its own harbor, its own silo stations throughout the country and its own trucks and tankers to ensure efficient delivery of its products.

The communication system of Aalborg is covered in its objectives:

    We aim at encouraging the inspiration and imagination of our employees and at guaranteeing them meaningful assignments by reducing routine work as much as possible. Ideas, proposals, and criticism from one or more of the employees must be treated objectively from a positive point of view.

The company's work rule manual also discusses communication with employees. The communication system is shown in Figure 9. In addition, the company uses interviews and meetings, a well organized system of cooperation and a computer-based training system that includes safety. All new employees participate in a 40-hour orientation course of the company and industry. Company magazines are *3-Kanten,* an Aalborg Portland magazine, and *FLS-Orienteering,* a group magazine for all employees of the FLS-group of which Aalborg Portland is a part.

By law one-third of the members of the company's board of directors are elected among the employees, which in Aalborg Portland's case are four directors. The company's union representation system is well developed as is its joint co-operation-committee system.

For communication with one another, Aalborg Portland employees have different organizations and events such as sports organizations within the company and the company magazine.

# France

*Official Name:* French Republic; *Capital:* Paris; *Government:* republic; *Subdivisions:* 22 regions; *Population:* 55,596,030 (July 1987); *Density:* 261.9 per square mile; *Currency:* franc; *Official Language:* French; *Literacy:* 99 percent.

*The Land.* Slightly smaller than Texas, France is the largest country in Western Europe and the second largest (next to the U.S.S.R.) in all of Europe and lies near the geographical center of Western Europe. The country is shaped roughly like a hexagon with three sides bordering on land and three sides on water. A mere 650 miles separate the Belgian border in the north from the Mediterranean or the city of Strasbourg on the Rhine River from the western tip of Brittany. It is bordered on the north by Belgium and the North Sea, on the northeast by Luxembourg and West Germany, in the east by Switzerland and Italy, in the south by the Mediterranean Sea, in the southwest by Andorra and Spain, in the west by the Bay of Biscay and the Atlantic Ocean, and in the northwest by the English Channel. It has greatly varied topography; two-thirds is flat plains or gently rolling hills; the rest is mountainous. The topography includes the Pyrenees Mountains in the south, a high central plateau, valleys and Alpine Mountains up to 15,000-foot Mt. Blanc in the southeast, and the low, coastal plains in the north and west. French sovereignty also encompasses the island of Corsica as well as 10 overseas departments or territories.

The land is 34 percent cultivated, 24 percent meadow and pasture, 27 percent forested and 15 percent waste, urban and other.

*The People.* The French are a mixture of Nordic, Alpine, Mediterranean and North African Arab peoples. Between the two world wars, nearly 3 million immigrants, mostly of Slavic origin, came to France. In recent years, great numbers have come from North Africa, particularly French expatriates and Algerian refugees. In 1980, the Bonnet Law set stringent requirements for entry into France, strictly limiting immigration and encouraging immigrant workers to return to their country of origin.

Characteristics displayed by the French are those commonly associated with the Latin temperament. They are demonstrative, voluble, animated and frequently happy, enlivening conversations with gestures and mimicry. The men tend to be conservative in dress, even dowdy, while with women there is a sharp division corresponding to social categories. One trait the French themselves would probably agree they have in common is an innate distrust of human nature which is commonly described as cynicism. But fortunately the Frenchman's cynicism does not prevent him from being one of the most tolerant persons in the world.

The motto of the French Republic is "Liberty, Equality and Fraternity," values which they believe should transcend everything else. Paradoxically, social classes remain very important in this country: aristocracy, upper bourgeoisie, upper-middle bourgeoisie, middle, lower-middle and lower (blue-collar workers, peasants). It is difficult for a French person to move between these classes.

The French are generally conservative in dress and manner, very individualistic and hesitant to join organized activities, which explains why their trade unions often splinter. The French admire intelligence, logic and clear thought and the ability to express oneself in an articulate, precise and elegant manner. To foreigners they may seem abrupt, intolerant, obnoxious — or totally captivating. The author is undecided after a week spent in Paris. Having driven into that beautiful city at around 5 p.m. on a Friday afternoon, this traveller's introduction to French life was a city-wide traffic jam where the lesson learned was that French drivers stopped in traffic on a hot summer day are the same as any place else — angry. After checking into L'Hotel Campanile on Boulevard du General-de-Gaulle, the tired traveller went touring. The hotel was located on a busy one-way street near a bridge, reachable from the direction of center city only by making two right-hand turns onto narrow alleyways, the second of which led onto the parking lot. Guided so by fractured French, the taxi-cab driver returning the traveller to the hotel became suddenly suspicious after slowing down near the hotel and not seeing anyone and sped off toward the street. "No, no, no," the traveller insisted and he stopped to discharge him.

On the following day, the traveller lunched in a small restaurant near the Eiffel Tower. After finishing, he picked up the check and headed toward the cash register to pay it. The waiter, who was supposed to have been paid, thought the traveller was leaving without paying and growled, redfaced and angry, while making change. The French are the least hospitable hosts in all Europe and possibly throughout the world. About 90 percent of the population are Roman Catholic; 2 percent are Protestant; 1 percent are Jewish; 1 percent are Muslim; and 6 percent are unaffiliated.

The French believe that success is judged by educational level, the reputation of one's family, and financial status. They are very patriotic, and proud of their culture.

In old buildings the custom is to ride up but walk down. This is because elevators in older buildings tend to be small; the "up-people" take precedence.

*A Brief History.* For nearly five centuries, the Romans dominated France (Gaul). The Gauls adopted the Roman ways of life, including their customs, language and laws. France was unified under a national spirit on Christmas Day, 800, when Charlemagne, king of the Franks, was crowned by the pope in Rome as Holy Roman Emperor. The Franks (who gave the country its name) ruled over France as well as most of Western Europe.

In the Hundred Years War with England (1337–1453) France was devastated and her people starved. At the Battle of Orleans, Joan of Arc inspired the French army to rout the English, leading to ultimate French victory.

During the reign of Louis XIV (1643–1715), France was the preeminent power in Europe. France remained an absolute monarchy until the French Revolution, which began in 1789. The chaos that followed the revolution resulted in the rise of a young artillery officer, Napoleon Bonaparte, who as dictator undertook to spread the ideal of liberty to the world through conquest. Napoleon conquered nearly the entire European continent.

Until the early 19th century, France was the most powerful state in Europe, but the coming of the Industrial Revolution wrested the power from them. Inadequate supplies of coal and iron ore put France at a considerable disadvantage to countries like England and Germany, which possessed large deposits of both.

France was a major battleground for both World Wars. The Fourth Republic of modern France lasted from 1946 until the constitution establishing the Fifth Republic was approved by referendum in 1958 and General Charles de Gaulle became president. He was followed by Georges Pompidou and then Valery Giscard d'Estaing. In 1981 Francois Mitterrand, a socialist, was elected president; he was re-elected in 1988.

*The Economy.* The labor force is divided this way: services, 60.8 percent; industry 24, agriculture 7.6, other areas 7.6, and unemployed, 10.6 percent. About 20 percent of the labor force is unionized.

France is the predominant agricultural nation of the EEC, though only 7.6 percent of the work force is employed in agriculture. It is the world's third largest producer of wine, milk and butter and the fourth largest producer of cheese, barley and wool.

France is a great industrial and commercial nation. About 61.2 percent of the work force is employed in services and 21.7 percent work in industry. Industry is based largely on coal, iron and steel. Other industries include textiles and a variety of luxury goods. France is the world's fourth largest producer of cars. The French automotive, aviation and nuclear industries are very advanced. About 20 percent of the work force is unionized.

The French view business organizations very differently than Americans do:

U.S. managers and most northern Europeans tend to define organization in terms of functions – who does what, why, how important is it to the success of the organization and how it interrelates with other parts of the whole organization.

This contrasts with what (Professor Andre) Laurent (of INSEAD/ CEDEP, the International business school at Fontainbleau in France) calls the "social approach" of countries such as France and Italy, where organization is defined more in terms of social status and authority.

The functional approach requires that superior-subordinate relationships are viewed in impersonal and highly specific terms. Since authority, under this approach, has a rational basis, it can best be challenged on rational grounds. Emotive, or personal, grounds are considered inadequate.

The social approach, in contrast, stresses the personal and general superiority of one individual in an organization over another. Authority is more concerned with power than with achieving specific objectives. Hierarchy is perceived as a hierarchy of persons rather than of status. Since authority is founded on a non-rational basis, it cannot be challenged on rational grounds, says Laurent.

Laurent asked 772 managers whether they agreed that obtaining power is more motivating to managers than achieving objectives. Sixty-three percent of the Italian managers agreed, as did 56 percent of the French managers, but only 26 percent of the Dutch and 25 percent of the Danish managers did.[15]

The French are not personally oriented toward competition, a term that to them refers to intense athletic activity. When foreigners who do feel competitive interact with the French, it is difficult not to appear aggressive, antagonistic and power-mad. Feeling threatened, the French either overreact emotionally or withdraw.

The daily French newspaper *France-Soir* asked "Are the French Lazy?" and answered the question in the negative but added perhaps they're a little sleepy. Francois Dalle's recent government report on how to create more jobs is quoted by the newspaper as saying that French workers spend too much time thinking of their annual minimum five-week vacation or the next three-day weekend, all of which handicap competitiveness.

Toward improving competitiveness, a 1971 law established statutory requirements for continuing education in companies with ten or more employees. In 1984 this law was amended to include all companies; however, only companies with ten or more employees are required to spend 1.1 percent of the preceding year's payroll on training and development or pay an equivalent amount in additional tax. Each year, management must submit its plan for professional training to the *comite d'entreprise* (works council) in companies with more than 50 employees or to *delegues du personnel* (personnel representatives) in companies with less than 50 employees for approval. Training programs can be conducted either by company personnel or outside firms recognized by the Labor Department or by the Department of Professional and Vocational Education.

French industrial organization presents a unique difficulty to the foreign visitor: finding the appropriate contact within the French organization's hierarchy. Normal structure appears to link a specific responsibility to a specific individual — by name — rather than to a function or title. This practice seems to be a result of the French appreciation of individuality and the expectation of results from a person rather than from team effort. As a consequence, top managers tend to juggle titles, responsibilities and official status to the detriment of clear channels and an identifiable power structure.

France is extraordinarily bureaucratic; paperwork and procedures complicate business efforts. The government is the top employer, with a staggering number of civil servants. The state keeps tight control of parts of its commercial activity, although this has begun to change as the government has sold some of these companies to private owners; among them are Paribas, Saint-Gobain, Societe Generale and the largest television station in the country. France has also recently lowered taxes and made it easier for companies to lay off workers.

Decision-making in France is centralized, reserved for upper to top management. The gap between top and bottom management levels is large. The owner or top manager of a smaller concern also embraces the concept of centralization of power. Decision-making power rests in one individual who literally directs all change. A visitor must, consequently, expect a considerable amount of his or her waiting to be for lower-level bureaucrats to gauge the position of upper-level decision makers. State-owned organizations validate this pattern of stressing behavior, not results.

French workers are protected by an impressive bulk of social legislation designed to ensure the fullest possible co-operation between management and labor and guarantee the rights of workers. Any firm, for example, which employs more than ten persons must have a number of "delegates" representing and elected by the employees to protect their claims and complaints to the management, which is obliged to receive them at least once a month and pay them for fifteen hours monthly devoted to staff affairs. Industrial firms with more than 50 employees and commercial firms with more than 500 must have a *comite d'entreprise* (personnel-management committee) presided over by the owner or general manager and consisting of representatives elected by the employees for two years. The role of the committee is to run the various social amenities such as canteens and recreation facilities, but especially to ensure the association of the workers with the management of the firm who are bound to consult the committee on technical, financial and commercial matters.

A growing trend in France is use of quality circles. Some 25,000 quality circles have been formed since 1980, as many as in all the rest of Europe. They are found mainly in large companies in heavy industry and electronics, but increasingly also in smaller companies in service industries and now in the administrative sector and even in government. Over 2,500 companies have established quality circles.[16]

*Organizational Communication.* As in most European countries, the visitor in France is expected to establish a relationship prior to conducting business. Invitations are seldom issued formally, but formal, written invitations will receive a written, formal response. A simple telephoned or verbal invitation will be ignored, overlooked or rejected. A drop-in will be kept waiting or asked to return later when an appointment has been made. As one writer has stated, the French are more distant than formal in their business relationships.

The French have not acknowledged the full scope of using the telephone. They prefer letters of inquiry to questions by phone—better yet, they would like you to come around in person with a note.

Some notable differences exist between the United States and France in letter-writing style. Following common European style, the French show the date with the day preceding the month. The French also type the city of the sender of the letter in front of the date. In the inside address, the zip code precedes the name of the city, by French postal regulation.[17] Flowery endings to formal letters are very much practiced still, even if the letter itself is less amiable. The most universal—equivalent to both "yours faithfully" and "yours sincerely"—is *Veuillez agreer, Monsieur, l'expression de mes sentiments distingues.* French business letters, particularly letters of job application, may also be handwritten and they are often analyzed by the receiver.

The French expect the visitor to arrive on time, but then will have him or her wait. The French view time as a tactical weapon in negotiations. Having to wait is normal. The party who waits gets the message that his or her issue is not a burning interest.

Appearance in general is an important consideration in France. For the visitor, a suit is *de rigueur,* but it need not be in totally subdued patterns or colors.

The usual French way of shaking hands is a loose grip and a single, quick shake; the firm, pumping American-style handshake is considered impolite. At the first meeting, a handshake is in order if the French host offers. If several individuals are involved, the visitor should first greet the man most senior in status. Meetings often take place in the finest of facilities, like those in Figure 10.

It is a good idea to include academic credentials on business cards. Frenchmen do not appreciate foreigners' attempts to speak their language; college French will not suffice in the business world. If you are not fluent, they will ask you to get an interpreter.

Small talk is brief, conversations turning quickly to business. The highly private life of a Frenchman is guarded, and any discussion of family, marital status or place of residence will be received unkindly.

The French enjoy conflict and debate; it will be difficult to convince them of anything immediately. They will interrupt communications with countless arguments, voicing disagreements only remotely connected to the topic at hand. The foreigner must persist, relying on his logic and his strong points and should be meticulously coherent, informative, and well organized. Presentations should be factual, rational, reasonable and formal. Soft sell succeeds where extravaganzas and emotional spectaculars will not.

Body language is low key. It is correct to look a Frenchman in the eye during negotiations. Typically the French will use their entire faces to lend additional expression to what is being said or heard. Arm waving or lively handtalk is not a part of normal business communication. The hand gesture that means

**Figure 10. Excellent facilities like these at L'Oreal help make meetings productive. (L'Oreal, Clichy, France.)**

"okay" to Americans means zero to the French. The French sign for "okay" is thumbs up.

In general, Frenchmen stand close together while talking to each other; however, the case in business is different. A reserved distance is maintained between negotiators. Old friends or small merchants may narrow the gap, but a visitor should respect the privacy of space. Physical touching – "moving in" on the French – is not acceptable.

Begin with the premise that any request will probably receive a negative response. Just as the Japanese often say "yes" when they mean "no," the French say "no" when they mean "yes," because they want to be in control. They also like to be polite, so that the visitor should accept any courteous gesture. If the host motions the visitor through the door first, he or she should go. "After you" games are self-defeating.

French business persons disdain business lunches as an invasion of privacy and an affront to their gastronomic fastidiousness. To discuss business at lunch with a Frenchman is to lose him as a client, benefactor, friend or associate.

Table 7 lists some communication practices in the French firm.

## CASE STUDY: RENAULT

Louis Renault built his first car in 1898, about the same time as Ford, Peugeot and Daimler. By 1910, the company was among the most important

**Table 7. Some Communication Practices in the French Corporation**

The French:

1. Prefer personal visits to letters but letters to the telephone.

2. Write letters in a different way than Americans do.

3. Expect to establish personal relationships prior to conducting business.

4. Respond to formal, written invitations but ignore oral ones.

5. Expect punctuality but then make visitors wait.

6. Shake hands loosely with one, quick shake.

7. Are impressed with academic credentials on business cards.

8. Include brief small talk before getting down to business.

9. Maintain eye contact when conversing.

10. Dislike personal questions.

11. Tie responsibility to a person rather than a position.

12. Often say "no" when they mean "yes."

13. Enjoy conflict and debate.

14. Expect presentations to be factual, professional and complete.

15. Use body language sparingly.

16. Maintain a reserved distance from others.

17. Use quality circles more than any other European country.

18. Have a disdain for the business lunch.

19. Have a high-context culture.

20. Use time polychronically.

car makers in the world and was extending into other areas such as trucks and engines. In 1945, Renault was nationalized; the company chairman is nominated by the government. However, Renault is organized and managed as a private company. Renault is the sixth largest car manufacturer in the world, producing two million vehicles per year. The company makes an effort to avoid excessive administration or centralization of control.

These are Renault's stated goals: to stay among the main car manufacturers in the world, to remain an international company, to become more profit-minded, and to emphasize quality and service for the public. Figure 11 shows Renault's corporate communication system.

In answering the question of how the company would improve its corporate communication if it could, a company spokesperson said: "It would be interesting to simplify the relations between managers and employees: it is a problem of attitude, but also of training."

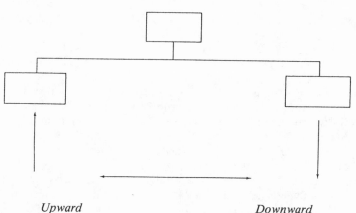

Upward

Written:
  memorandum
  report
  suggestion system

Personal:
  meeting
  interview
  open-door policy

Downward

Print:
  annual report
  newspaper/magazine
  bulletin board
  letters
  posters/billboards

Electronic:
  telephone
  film
  videotape
  electronic mail

*Horizontal*

personal contact
memorandum
meeting

**Figure 11. Corporate communication system of Renault Corporation.**

# Greece

*Official Name:* Hellenic Republic; *Capital:* Athens; *Government:* presidential parliamentary republic; *Subdivisions:* 51 prefectures; *Population:* 9,987,785 (July 1987); *Density:* 198.3 per square mile; *Currency:* drachma; *Official Language:* Greek; *Literacy:* 95 percent.

*The Land.* Located in southeastern Europe on the southern tip of the Balkan Peninsula, Greece is about the size of North Carolina and geologically has been one of the least-favored lands on earth. It is a stony, mountainous peninsula surrounded by Yugoslavia and Bulgaria in the north, by Turkey in the northeast, by the Aegean Sea in the east, by the Mediterranean Sea in the south, by the Ionian Sea on the west and southwest and by Albania in the northwest. The country includes more than 1,400 islands—only 170 of them inhabited, of which Crete is the largest. About 80 percent of the land is mountainous or hilly; much is dry and rocky. Only its narrow valleys are fertile, the omnipresent hills suitable only for herding sheep. Only about 30 percent of the land is arable.

The country is 40 percent meadow and pasture, 29 percent arable and permanent crop land, 20 percent forest, and 11 percent waste, urban and other. The country consists of a large mainland with the Peleponnesus connected to the mainland by the Isthmus of Corinth, and more than 1,400 islands, the best known of which are Crete and Rhodes. It has 9,300 miles of coastline and a land boundary of 725 miles.

*The People.* The victims of a grudging nature, the Greeks have also suffered at the hands of man. They have been invaded, conquered and controlled by the neighboring powers for most of the past two millennia: by the Romans, by the Byzantine Empire, by the Ottoman Empire and more recently by the Italian and German armies in World War II.

Approximately 98 percent of the people are Greek. The only numerically significant minority is the Turks, who constitue about 1 percent of the population.

Ancient Greeks believed a stranger might be a god in disguise, and were therefore warm to all strangers. The tradition of hospitality has continued to the present. A friend of mine touring Greece with a backpack found the Greeks among the most considerate people in Europe. If he was in his sleeping bag, for example, those passing would become very quiet as they passed so as not to disturb him. Greek society retains the traditional values of family, education, the individual and honor. Individualism in Greece is prized; self-esteem is paramount. They are a mobile people; there are three million people of Greek heritage living in the United States alone. Greek society is upwardly mobile. Education is highly esteemed not only because it transmits culture and knowledge but also because it contributes to social and cultural mobility.

Greeks are invariably named after saints, each having a special day in the Orthodox calendar, and celebrate these days rather than their birthdays. The family unit is very strong in Greece. It is very important that no member bring shame or dishonor to the family. Most Greeks care for their aged parents. The elderly are respected, addressed by courteous titles, served first, and have much authority. Children are treated with firm discipline.

Greek business people are astute bargainers. Success in business dealings depends on a combination of patience and quick judgment. Greeks are warm and cordial in their personal relationships and business is usually conducted over a cup of coffee.

*A Brief History.* Often called the cradle of Western civilization, Greece has a rich history as the place and the people that in the ten centuries before Christ created perhaps the noblest and most intellectually creative civilization ever seen. The Greeks invented democracy and almost the entire substructure of ideas and concepts that underlie Western civilization.

Athens was the center of a then-vast overseas empire. Ancient Greece was the place of much of man's first studies of government; the basic concepts of justice, liberty and law were developed greatly in ancient Greece. Greece has given the world a great heritage of poetry, drama, government, architecture, sculpture, science and philosophy and established many of the foundations of modern civilization. It is no exaggeration to say that Greece has influenced every modern Western nation.

But then, as if punishing themselves for what their own ethical system taught was the worst of sins, intellectual pride, the Greeks went a long way toward destroying their civilization in the Peloponnesian Wars. After the death of Alexander the Great in 323 B.C., the empire began to decline, and by 146 B.C. had become a part of the Roman Empire. Later it was the principal administrator of the Byzantine empire, which lasted through the fifteenth century. The winning of the modern nation's independence from Turkey in 1821 by no means brought tranquillity, but since the trials of World War II and a subsequent four years of civil war, the Greeks have built an increasingly prosperous society.

*The Economy.* The labor force is divided this way: services, 43 percent; agriculture 27, manufacturing and mining 20, construction 7, and unemployed, 8.3 percent. About half of the labor force is self-employed and 90 percent of Greek firms have fewer than ten workers. From 10 to 15 percent of the work force is unionized.

Greece's economy is mostly agricultural with some industry. Despite the fact that Greece has the most ancient civilization in Europe, a history which includes factories that go back more than 2,500 years, the Greeks now resist industrialization. Its merchant fleet is the world's seventh largest; modern agriculture is making the ancient land more productive; industries such as textiles, chemicals and mining are growing and tourism is on the rise.

Greece does not have raw materials to transform it into a manufacturing country. Local factories produce olive oil, wine, thread, cigarettes, chemicals and refined petroleum. Also produced are textiles, tobacco, food processing, cement and shipbuilding.

Greeks as a whole prefer to do business in the office. The Greek normally goes home for lunch and follows it with a siesta. He attaches great importance to punctuality in office hours.

More perhaps than in most European countries, the key to doing successful business in Greece is the ability to play it by ear, as indeed the Greeks themselves do. As one successful Greek businessman remarked, there are plenty of regulations but no rules.

The Greeks see delegation of duties to subordinates as devious because it happens outside the conference room where it goes unseen. In Greece, delegation means to some sacrificing personal power and authority. On the other hand, Greek workers expect to be told precisely what to do with little room for exercising their own initiative.

*Organizational Communication.* Like other Mediterranean peoples, the Greeks dislike directness. To state bluntly the purpose of a visit shows poor technique. Instead one should state the general principles of a proposal with tactful indirection. The specifics of the transaction should emerge in lengthy

## Table 8. Some Communication Practices in the Greek Corporation

The Greeks:

  1. May not keep appointments promptly.

  2. Expect the exchange of business cards.

  3. Do not allocate a specific duration time for meetings.

  4. Dislike directness.

  5. Say "no" with a slight upward nod of the head and "yes" by tilting the head to either side.

  6. Sometimes smile when angry or upset.

  7. Expect, as employees, to be told exactly what to do.

  8. Expect, as managers, full discussion of a subject to avoid appearing to hide something.

  9. Have a high-context culture.

  10. Use time polychronically.

dialogue moving from general overview to specific details. Meetings in Greece can thus last a long time.

They may not be prompt in keeping appointments and consider it foolish to prescribe a specific length of time for a meeting. The exchange of business cards is an essential formality and a valuable one; English names are as difficult for Greeks to master as theirs are for English speakers.

A slight upward nod of the head means "no" not "yes." Tilting the head to either side, therefore, means "yes." A Greek may smile not only when happy but sometimes when angry or upset.

A manager being sent to Greece needs to be a good leader, able to give orders clearly, because in general Greek workers expect to be told precisely what to do. Everything must be discussed openly to avoid the appearance of trying to hide something.

Table 8 lists some communication practices in the Greek firm.

### CASE STUDY: J.E. CONDELLIS S.A.

The company was established as a Ford agent on the Island of Lesvos in 1919. The founder, John Condellis, had just returned after ten years of work as an immigrant in America. The small company expanded throughout Greece and moved its headquarters to Athens. It distributed agricultural equipment, industrial and earthmoving equipment, Alfa Romea cars, Iveco trucks and Kubota and Yanmar Tractors. The company presently employs 700 workers.

The company's communication system is as shown on Figure 12. If it could, the company would improve its communication system by calling more formal meetings, encouraging more informal/social meetings for bringing employees closer more frequently and introducing more modern electronic communication methods.

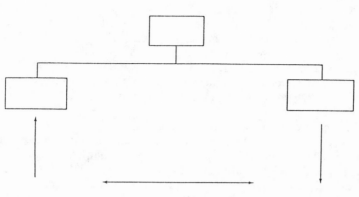

*Upward*

Written:
  memorandum
  report

Personal:
  meeting
  interview
  open-door policy

*Downward*

Print:
  annual report
  bulletin board
  letters

Electronic:
  telephone
  teleconference
  electronic mail

Personal:
  personal contact

*Horizontal*

personal contact
memorandum
meeting

**Figure 12. Communication system of J.A. Condellis Company, Athens, Greece.**

# Ireland

*Official Name:* Ireland, Eire (Gaelic); *Capital:* Dublin; *Government:* parliamentary republic; *Subdivisions:* 26 counties; *Population:* 3,534,553 (July 1987); *Density:* 129 per square mile; *Currency:* pound; *Official Languages:* Irish Gaelic, English; *Literacy:* 99 percent.

*The Land.* Somewhat larger than West Virginia, Ireland occupies most of the island it shares with Northern Ireland off the west coast of England and Scotland and the northwest coast of Europe. It is separated from Great Britain by the Irish Sea. North to south its greatest length is 302 miles; east to west its greatest width is 171 miles. It consists mainly of an undulating plain almost completely surrounded by coastal highlands. It is bordered on the north by the North Channel, which separates it from Scotland, on the northeast by

Northern Ireland, on the southeast and east by the Irish Sea and St. George's Channel which separates it from England and Wales, and on the west, north and south by the Atlantic Ocean. No part of the island is more than 70 miles from the sea. Ireland has rugged mountains and hilly coastlines with lush valleys and plains in the interior basin. About 51 percent of the land is meadow and pasture; 27 percent, waste or urban; 17 arable; 3 forest; and 2 percent is inland water.

*The People.* The population consists of mainly Irish (Celts) with an Anglo-Irish minority. This is a land that the British essayist G.K. Chesterton once characterized as one where all the wars are merry and all the songs are sad.

Irish people generally are not concerned with material goods and status as much as in the U.S. Tradition is very important and the Catholic Church is a firm tradition in Ireland. About 94 percent of the residents belong to that church. Another 4 percent are Anglican; the final 2 percent follow other beliefs or none at all. The Irish are lighthearted, easygoing, good-humored and cheerful. They are quick-witted people and have the ability to laugh at themselves. They have the outlook that everything will work out in the end.

Close family ties are maintained, and relatives generally live near each other. Family reunions are held for birthdays, weddings, religious festivals, and so on. Thirty percent of the population is under 14 years of age, one of Europe's youngest populations. Today, Ireland has only half as many people as it had in 1845.

*A Brief History.* From the eighth century to the eleventh century, Norse Vikings established seaports in Ireland. In the twelfth century, Pope Adrian IV granted overlordship of the island to King Henry II of England who forced Irish nobles to recognize his overlordship in 1171. The Act of Union, creating the United Kingdom of Great Britain and Ireland, was promulgated in 1801. Ireland spent seven and a half centuries under frequently repressive British rule, a fact reflected in the present-day division of the island into two separate political entities: the independent republic of Ireland (Eire) and the six counties that constitute Northern Ireland, a part of the United Kingdom. Foreign domination did not help Ireland.

In the 1840s, blight struck the potato crops that were the basic diet of its people. A million and a half Irishmen died; another million emigrated. Political conflict in following decades brought alternating rebellions and constitutional agitation for independence, which climaxed in 1921 with the signing of the Anglo-Irish Treaty establishing the Irish Free State as a British dominion and allowed six northern counties to remain in the United Kingdom as Northern Ireland. In 1949, Ireland declared itself a republic and withdrew from the British Commonwealth. Talks with Britain over Northern Ireland are continuing.

*The Economy.* The labor force is divided this way: manufacturing and construction, 27.5 percent; services 20.4; agriculture, forestry and fishing, 16.4; government 6.6, transportation 6.2, other areas 22.9, and unemployed, 17.4 percent. About 36 percent of the labor force is unionized.

The crop disaster of the 1840s also caused a revolution in Irish farming; nowadays utilizing its legendary grand grass, Ireland specializes in dairying and the raising of cattle, horses and sheep. Since attaining independence, the Irish have succeeded in establishing considerable light industry; exports of such goods as paper, machinery and textiles are on the rise. It has a large quantity of zinc ores, as well as copper, sulphur, baryte, gypsum and dolomite. Its only valuable energy source is peat or turf bogs. It lacks sizable coal deposits, and it is only beginning to extract natural gas.

Since the 1950s a minor industrial revolution has occurred in Ireland. Over 160 new Irish and foreign-based plants have created thousands of new jobs and are turning out products that range from transistor radios and pianos to heavy cranes and oil heaters. Ireland's economic ties with Great Britain are as firm today as they ever were, a truth the Irish are reluctant to accept.

Ireland joined the EEC in 1973 and as an agricultural economy has benefitted from membership; all of the Republic qualifies for EEC regional aid. Major industries are beverages, chemicals, clothing, food processing, footwear, metal and engineering products, textiles and tobacco.

*Organizational Communication.* Irish people are hospitable and sociable and it is common for visiting business people to be invited out in the evening. The business lunch is used a good deal, tending to be a social occasion with business introduced at the end of the meal. The Irish reputation for unpunctuality has some foundation but it is not generally true of business people.

Business cards are not used much, partly because of the relatively close personal contact between people in a small country, but it is an accepted practice for visitors from outside the country to present business cards to provide a future contact address.

The Irish business tends to mix business with pleasure and much negotiating is done over food and drink in dining rooms and pubs. Gerald Malmed, publisher of *Sapphire* magazine, is enthusiastic about Irish business methods. "A handshake in a pub," says Malmed, "is better than any contract I've ever seen."

Table 9 lists some communication practices in the Irish firm.

**Table 9. Some Communication Practices in the Irish Corporation**

The Irish:

1. Are hospitable and sociable.

2. Often invite business visitors out in the evening.

3. Use the business lunch a good deal.

4. Are usually punctual in business matters but not social affairs.

5. Do not use business cards much.

6. Have a low-context culture.

7. Use time monochronically.

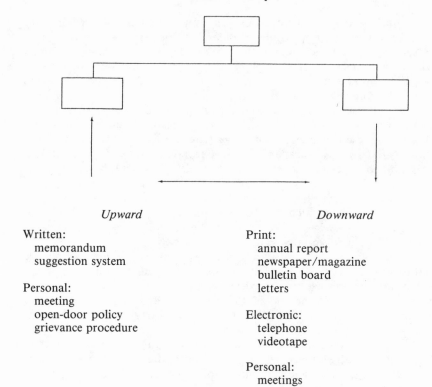

*Upward*

Written:
  memorandum
  suggestion system

Personal:
  meeting
  open-door policy
  grievance procedure

*Downward*

Print:
  annual report
  newspaper/magazine
  bulletin board
  letters

Electronic:
  telephone
  videotape

Personal:
  meetings

*Horizontal*

personal contact
meeting

**Figure 13. Corporate communication system of Cement Roadstone Holdings PLC.**

CASE STUDY: CEMENT-ROADSTONE HOLDINGS PLC

The company, with headquarters in Dublin, is Ireland's largest manufacturer and supplier of a wide range of materials to the construction industry and operates internationally in similar or related fields. In Ireland, the Group owns almost two billion tons of strategically placed stone, sand and gravel reserves, operates from 61 locations and is the sole cement producer in the Republic, with all its current operating capacity using the fuel-efficient dry process and fully equipped for either coal or oil-burning. Other products include asphalt, tarmacadam, readymix concrete, concrete blocks, prestressed concrete flooring, rooftiles, agricultural and chemical limestone, pressure, sewerage and drainage pipes, insulating and packaging products and magnesia. The company has branches in Northern Ireland, Britain, the Netherlands and the United States and employs 7,236 people.

"Communicatons in C-RH are not formalized to any great extent," reports

Seamus O'Carroll, General Manager, Planning. "The operating companies have a high degree of management independence and have developed their own management styles within the Group. Each company has developed its own communication methods. As most of the individual companies have less than 800 employees, the emphasis is on less formal face-to-face communications; bulletin boards are probably the most formal method in most companies." The corporate communication system is shown in Figure 13.

### CASE STUDY: WATERFORD GLASS GROUP PLC

Waterford is the world's preeminent manufacturer and marketer of premium-quality crystal. Under new management in the mid–1980s, the company experienced revitalization that resulted in an improved financial position and significantly higher earnings. Approximately 50 percent of Waterford's sales are in the American market and another 30 percent to Americans traveling abroad. In 1986, the company acquired Wedgewood, a producer of fine china/dinnerware.

The company's communication policy states this: It is our policy to maintain and develop within the company an effective and homogeneous communication system able to stimulate interfunctional relationships as well as those between the company and personnel. The system is based on timely, clear and true information in order to build up a climate of productivity, efficiency, motivation and discussion. The company hopes to achieve this by ensuring spread of information, developing two-way communication attitudes and participating in the more general company communication process.

---

# Italy

---

*Official Name:* Italian Republic; *Capital:* Rome; *Government:* republic; *Subdivisions:* 20 regions; *Population:* 57,350,850 (July 1987); *Density:* 504.7 per square mile; *Currency:* lira; *Official Language:* Italian; *Literacy:* 93 percent.

*The Land.* Flanked by the Tyrrhenian and Adriatic Seas, the mountainous boot-shaped peninsula of Italy sweeps 730 miles into the Mediterranean from the southern coast of Europe, giving the country 5,280 miles of coastline. It includes the large islands of Sardinia, Sicily, Pantelleria and the Eolian (Lipari) group. The peninsula is 43 miles from Albania and Sicily is 90 miles from the African mainland. Slightly larger than Arizona, Italy is mostly mountainous. The Alps lie along its northern border, and the Apennines form an infertile spine down most of the peninsula. In the north is the Po River basin, with some of Italy's richest farmland and most of its heavy industry. The southern part of the peninsula as well as the islands of Sicily and Sardinia are also rocky and mountainous with agricultural areas subject to severe droughts. The mountains that separate Italy from the rest of Europe have not served as a barrier to outside contacts as have the Pyrenees or the English Channel, partly because Italy never controlled the mountains to prevent incursions from the north.

About half of the land is cultivated. Another 21 percent is forest; 17 percent is meadow and pasture; 9 percent is waste or urban; and 3 percent is un-used but potentially productive.

Within peninsular Italy there are two tiny independent states, the Vatican City in Rome and the Republic of San Marino, the oldest state in Europe, situated about 15 miles inland from Rimini on the Adriatic coast.

*The People.* Linguistically and religiously, the Italians are homogeneous, but culturally, economically and politically they are diverse. Italian culture flourished in the Renaissance during the 14th century.

*A Brief History.* The Greeks settled southern Italy and Sicily during the eighth century B.C. establishing colonies of city-states. In the third century B.C., the Romans conquered Italy and established a great empire from Rome. Julius Caesar reigned during the first century B.C., and it was his conquest of France (Gaul) that made Rome supreme over much of the civilized world. Italy later dissolved into a collection of bickering petty kingdoms and papal states after the disappearance of Roman authority in the fifth century A.D. There was a period of some 500 years of obscurity under barbarian invaders. The country re-emerged after the tenth century with the rise of the Communes in opposition to monarchical institutions and the dawning of the Renaissance. This was followed by periods under Spanish, French and Austrian domination.

The unity of Italy was proclaimed in 1861 under the House of Savoy and its sovereignty was extended to something more than the present territory by 1918. Actual unification came under King Victor Emmanuel II of Sardinia in 1870. Unity did not bring stability. In 1922, after years of economic unrest, Benito Mussolini became premier of Italy and, as its dictator, set Italy upon the fateful road of fascism, empire and alliance with Nazi Germany.

After defeat in World War II the country was an economic and political shambles. Abolishing the monarchy and establishing a republic, Italy began to rebuild with American aid. Italy joined the European Common Market as a charter member in 1958 for numerous reasons, but primarily the move was motivated by a paucity of raw materials, power and capital investment. Italy was a relatively poor, weak country. The policy of expansionism pursued be-tween the wars had failed and now it was time to try another course: joining their destiny to that of greater Europe.

*The Economy.* The labor force is divided this way: services, 48.6 percent; industry 30.5, agriculture 10.5, and unemployed, 10.8 percent. From 40 to 45 percent of the labor force is unionized.

Throughout history, Italy's position on the main routes between Europe, Africa and the Near and Far East has given it great political, economic and strategic importance. By the 1950s, Italy was in the midst of an amazing economic expansion, known not only for its traditional exports of fruits, wines and cheeses but for sleek autos, well-designed machinery, efficient electronics products and high-fashion clothes. Most of these products came from the bustling cities of Milan, Turin and Genoa in the northern Po Valley, where the hydroelectric power from the Alps and the valley's complex of rivers was used to overcome Italy's critical shortage of coal and other industrial fuels. The Po Valley is also Italy's agricultural heartland. Central Italy contains the historic cities of Rome, Florence and Pisa, which help attract more than 27 million visitors each year. In spite of massive public-works projects, the south, with its barren soil and overpopulation, remains an economically depressed section.

Most industries are small-scale, though state ownership via large holding companies is important in numerous industries, including heavy engineering, chemicals and telecommunications. Italian management tends to be highly autocratic when dealing with employees.

The author's experiences with Italian workmanship were not always positive. A pair of slacks that had been altered was returned with numerous strands of thread along the seam. When a car had to be tuned up at a Ford dealership prior to driving to Spain, it didn't accelerate properly afterwards. An embarrassed mechanic at the garage discovered that he had not reconnected one of the hoses in the engine.

Italy ranks fourth in the world in the production of cement and fifth in car production. It is a major steel and iron producer. Tourism is a very important source of revenue. Italy is visited by more people each year than any other country in the world except Spain.

Major industries are automobiles, chemicals, engineering, food processing, footwear, machinery, petroleum refining, textiles and tourism.

The Italians are experiencing a remarkable economic boom thanks to their adaptability and enterprise. Once ridiculed as a nation of incurable romantics, and poorest of the seven most industrialized nations in the world, Italy may soon surpass Britain among the top five. Today 76 percent of Italian households have a car, compared with Britain's 58 percent, while 81 percent have dishwashers against 77 percent in Britain.

In the article "The Italians: the Best Europeans?" in the British-published *International Management,* is this:

"Among Europeans, the Italians have the greatest ability for adaptation," believes Jean-Pierre Salzmann, a Swiss who is director of public relations and alumni affairs for the Fontainebleau-based INSEAD business school. "There are cliches about other nationalities — that the Germans are stiff, the Dutch stubborn, and the French and British condescending — but this has never been the case with the Italians, who have a gift for making the most of the environment in which they work."

Italians agree with him. "Our people have a genius in the art of survival, of finding the pragmatic, even cynical solution," says Claudio Belli, president of Hay International, a London-based management consultancy. "And this does not only mean surviving at home, but anywhere. We had to migrate to make a living — from the poor south of Italy to the richer north and from the north to foreign countries — so we have a heritage of not being afraid."[18]

The article speculates that perhaps Italy's success internationally can be explained by the relatively underdeveloped national consciousness. "Until 1870, Italy was not even a nation, but a patchwork of weak states, many of them dominated by powerful and quarrelsome neighbours, and united only by common cultural roots and a constant mingling of their citizens."

*Organizational Communication.* Prior appointments are absolutely necessary for all business dealings. Write in Italian all correspondence re-

**Table 10. Some Communication Practices in the Italian Corporation**

The Italians:

1. Expect prior appointments for conducting business.
2. Prefer to receive correspondence and collateral materials in Italian.
3. Expect punctuality—in the North more than in the South.
4. Shake hands when arriving and leaving.
5. Expect to exchange business cards.
6. Get down to business after a few minutes of general discussion.
7. Dislike being made to lose face.
8. Have begun to use the business luncheon.
9. Have a high-context culture.
10. Use time polychronically.

questing a meeting. If the reply is in English, you may correspond in that language. All collateral material should be printed in Italian.

Northern Italian business executives, more so than those in the south, respect and expect punctuality. Business cards are now obligatory; they spell out even minor posts held by the proud presenter. A conservative business suit with a vest is the most appropriate attire. Hand shaking is appropriate when arriving and leaving. Get down to business after a few minutes of general conversation. Don't talk business at a social event nor joke at a purely business meeting. Most important of all, don't do anything to cause an Italian to lose face, *baella figura*. Italians dislike being placed in a position where they publicly lose face over a deal.

Upper-level executives have begun to entertain and conduct business over lunch. Foreign visitors are seldom invited to Italians' homes, mainly because few wives speak English.

Table 10 lists some communication practices in the Italian corporation.

Esso Italiano is one company in this country with a written communication policy:

> It is our policy to maintain and develop within the Company an effective and homogeneous communication system able to stimulate interfunctional relationships as well as those between the Company and personnel. The system is based on timely, clear and true information in order to build up a climate of productivity, efficiency, motivation and discussion.

Everyone participates in the corporate communication program with slightly different responsibilities for the Employee Relations Department who is in charge of implementing it and those in the various functions of the company:

> Employee Relations: Formulate proposals for strategies and general programs. Find out most appropriate tools and channels. Assist other functions.

Functions: Ensure speed of information. Develop two-way communication attitude. Participate in the more general Company communication process.

# Luxembourg

*Official Name:* Grand Duchy of Luxembourg; *Capital:* Luxembourg; *Government:* constitutional monarchy; *Subdivisions:* 3 districts; *Population:* 366,127 (July 1987); *Density:* 374 per square mile; *Currency:* franc; *Official Languages:* Luxembourgish, German, French; *Literacy:* 100 percent.

*The Land.* The name of this country is derived from the German for "little fortress." The Grand Duchy of Luxembourg is a tiny, landlocked country bordered on the south by France, on the east by the Federal Republic of Germany, and on the west and north by Belgium. With about 1000 square miles, it is slightly smaller than Rhode Island. From north to south, Luxembourg is 51 miles and from east to west 35 miles.

The lowlands rise gradually from the iron-mining basin in the southwest to the rugged Ardennes Plateau in the north. About 43.9 percent of the land is arable; 33 percent, mostly in the north, is forest; 27 percent is meadow and pasture; and 15 percent is water or urban.

*The People.* Residents of this country follow a unique way of life, expressing independence and national solidarity while espousing a pragmatic international outlook. The nearly 60,000 foreigners among them include workers in the mining and steel industries and employees of foreign firms and international organizations.

The ethnic background of the people is a Celtic base with a French and German blend. About 97 percent of the people are Roman Catholic and 3 percent are Protestant and Jewish.

For centuries these people have kept their individuality despite the many invasions and occupations that have characterized their history. Some Luxembourgers paint the national motto on the front of their house: "We want to remain what we are."

Letzeburghesch, a mixture of German and French, is the spoken language; German is the written language of most newspapers and of commercial life, and French is the written language of the administrators.

*A Brief History.* Under Charlemagne, this area was part of the Frankish empire. In A.D. 963, Siegfried, Count of the Ardennes, established the Luxembourg dynasty by having a castle built on a rocky promontory, the size of the present city of Luxembourg. Several towns grew up around the castle and in turn were surrounded by heavy fortifications, until the entire area became a single, mighty, impregnable, hilltop fortress with 450 acres behind walls (thus the country's name) called the "Gibraltar of the North." In 1308 the Count of Luxembourg became Holy Roman Emperor Henry VII. A large and major power in the Middle Ages, Luxembourg was divided and seized by its neighbors time and again over the centuries beginning in 1443; not until 1867 did the European nations grant it independence in the Treaty of London.

Luxembourg and Belgium form the Belgo-Luxembourg Economic Union (BLEU) and the fact that there is no customs clearance between the two and that trade statistics are generally unified often causes misunderstandings about the status of Luxembourg. To confuse matters more, the southeasternmost region of Belgium is also known as "Luxembourg."

*The Economy.* The labor force is divided this way: services, 48.9 percent; industry 24.7, government 13.2, construction 8.8, agriculture 4.4, and unemployed, 1.5 percent.

Today it is small but prosperous; its land is intensively farmed and large deposits of iron ore help to make Luxembourg Europe's seventh largest steel producer. About 42 percent of its people work in industry. Major industries include food processing, iron and steel, chemicals, metal products, tires and banking.

Luxembourg is home to the Secretariat of the European Parliament, the Palace of the European Court of Justice, the European Investment Bank and other facilities of the EEC that include a 22-story office tower and an ultramodern conference center. The European Council of Ministers holds its April, June and October sessions here.

*Organizational Communication.* Titles are used only in official correspondence or when writing to doctors of medicine. Business titles should be in French.

Luxembourg businessmen are inclined to do business in the office, rather than over extensive meals. You will need business cards.

--------------------- **The Netherlands** ---------------------

> *Official Name:* Kingdom of the Netherlands; *Capital:* Amsterdam; *Government:* constitutional monarchy; *Subdivisions:* 11 provinces; *Population:* 14,641,554 (July 1987); *Density:* 925 per square mile; *Currency:* guilder; *Official Language:* Dutch; *Literacy:* 99 percent.

*The Land.* The Netherlands derives its name from its unusually low or "nether" geographic location; more than a quarter of its total land is below sea-level. Much of the country is built on land reclaimed from the sea by various advanced draining techniques. It is bordered on the east by West Germany, on the south by Belgium and on the west and north by the North Sea.

The country is about the size of Massachusetts and Connecticut combined. The country is crisscrossed by three large rivers and numerous canals. The Netherlands has always reclaimed land from the North Sea with sturdy systems of dikes, ditches and pumping stations. Old windmills which used to pump water out of the land still dot the Dutch landscape, but water is now pumped by modern, electrically powered stations.

About 70 percent of the land is cultivated; 8 percent is forest; 8 percent is inland water; 5 percent is waste, and 9 percent is other.

*The People.* The Netherlands is the most densely populated country in

Europe. Religion influences Dutch history, society, institutions and attitudes. About 40 percent of the Dutch are Roman Catholic; 31 percent are Protestant and 24 percent are unaffiliated. Although church and state are separate, a few historical ties remain — the royal couple belong to the Dutch Reformed Church. The Dutch have strong families, which are moderate in size. Of the extensive building of dikes to reclaim land from the sea, the Dutch have a saying: "God made the earth, but the Dutch made Holland."

*A Brief History.* After 80 years of intermittent war with Spain, the Dutch finally won their independence. In the following years, they built a vast overseas empire, becoming for a time the world's leading maritime and commercial power. In 1794, French revolutionary forces under the command of Napoleon invaded the Netherlands and set up the Republic of Batavia. The Congress of Vienna liberated the country from France in 1815 and reestablished the United Kingdom of the Netherlands, which included present-day Belgium. Belgium seceded in 1830.

Once a major seafaring nation, the Netherlands now has scattered territories in South America (Suriname) and the Antilles. The word "Holland," frequently informally used as the name of the whole country, is in fact precisely correct only in designating two western provinces, North Holland and South Holland.

*The Economy.* The work force is divided this way: services, 50.1 percent; manufacturing and construction 27.8, government 16.1, agriculture 6, and unemployed, 14.4 percent. Some 29 percent of the labor force is unionized.

An astonishing range of industrial and agricultural products makes the Netherlands one of the world's busiest trading centers. A modern, efficient industrial complex was built out of the rubble of World War II. The country produces, among other things, steel, ships, textiles, chemicals and such diverse goods as chinaware and electrical appliances. Holland's agricultural output is equally prodigious, with exports of dairy products, vegetables and grains, as well as the famous tulip and other flower bulbs. As a result, Holland's main port, Rotterdam, moves more goods than any other world seaport. It handles more than 100 million tons each year, regularly surpassing the port of New York.

Major industries are chemicals, construction, engineering, electronics, food processing, metal work, mining, petroleum refining, ship-building, and textiles.

*Organizational Communication.* Make appointments with Dutch business persons well in advance of the desired meeting date, because they travel a great deal. Dutch firms are conscientious about confirmations and correspondence in general. Firms of any consequence usually reply by telex. In correspondence, Dutch businessmen generally use their academic or hereditary titles.

Dutch business people like to entertain and be entertained. From Anglo-American influences the Dutch have taken certain business customs, like the business luncheon. Most Dutchmen are punctual for meetings and intolerant of those who are not.

A handshake is an appropriate greeting for men, women and children. Continued eye contact and facial expressions are important. It is not customary to touch another person except when shaking hands; pointing to the forehead with the finger is considered an insult. The Dutch admire longevity, so if your company is an old one, have its founding date printed on your business card.

The Dutch are pragmatic and down-to-earth, so presentations must be factual and full of figures. Track record is what counts, not boasts or plans. In negotiating, the Dutch do not like haggling.

Table 11 lists some communication practices in the Dutch corporation.

In a booklet called *Communications: A Strategic Service,* Philips International B.V. proves they have confronted the challenges of the Information Age. Resisting a desire to reproduce the whole document, the author includes instead only these excerpts:

> Efficient business communications provide a company with a strategic edge over its competition.
>
> This has always been so, but communications have become faster and more effective. Timely knowledge of technological and economic developments around the world has become of prime importance. This is especially true for Philips, which is active in more than 60 countries and employs some 350,000 people. Strategic decisions and methodology of working are influenced by technological, economical and political events worldwide. The company with the capability to anticipate and react to these developments by using flexible communication facilities remains ahead of its competition.
>
> Philips has production spread over more than 400 factories, research and development spread around the world and marketing organisations responsible for sales of over 60,000 million guilders per year. The amount of information interchanged within Philips is large and of vital importance to the efficient operation of the organization and the quality of its products and services. This all requires an efficient corporate communications network which is reliable and, above all, secure. Timely interchange of information between the various Philips partners can reduce costs substantially. Its multinational character can be used to advantage, with communications bridging frontiers and time zones. Effective business communication is a corporate asset. A strategic weapon. And its importance is increasing rapidly.
>
> A communication network should be designed and implemented in the most effective manner. It must also be operated as a cost-viable service towards the end user. To do this, it requires a well-planned infrastructure. Users need to be aware of what is available and to use the resources effectively. But it also needs to be serviced and kept up to date with the latest state-of-the-art equipment if it is to remain effective.
>
> Communications cost Philips in excess of a thousand million guilders a year and require the attention from top management at corporate and national level appropriate to such a valuable asset. National Organisations paying the appropriate attention have already benefitted from their investment with improved services.

## Table 11. Some Communication Practices in the Dutch Corporation

The Dutch:

1. Require appointments well in advance of expected meeting dates.

2. Are conscientious about replying to correspondence.

3. Use academic titles in correspondence.

4. Prefer to use the telex over letters.

5. Expect punctuality.

6. Shake hands as a greeting.

7. Do not touch each other during conversations.

8. Expect presentations to be factual and documented.

9. Like to entertain and be entertained.

10. Like the business lunch.

11. Have a low-context culture.

12. Use time monochronically.

### INTERNATIONAL COMMUNICATIONS

Philips is a worldwide company and therefore requires efficient and reliable international communications 24-hours a day, seven days a week, in order to operate efficiently. Daily messages and data are exchanged between continents as part of the normal business. Our business knows no frontiers.

*Corporate Communications*

Due to technological and economic developments, there is a trend towards integration of communication services. Philips has therefore taken the decision to create one department to be responsible for these services — Corporate Communications.

The aims of Corporate Communications are to influence, guide and control the national, extent, build-up, management and exploitation of business communications media and services throughout the International structure of Philips. And to ensure that this is achieved in the most efficient and cost-effective manner, since savings of a fraction of a percent on the budget can represent millions of guilders.

The Corporate Communications Department therefore manages and operates international communications within the Company in the areas of voice, mail, message, computer data and images. Policy is decided by the Communications Board, comprising members of the Board of Management, Corporate Building Design, Plant Engineering and Communications, Corporate Communications, Corporate ISA and Corporate TEO.

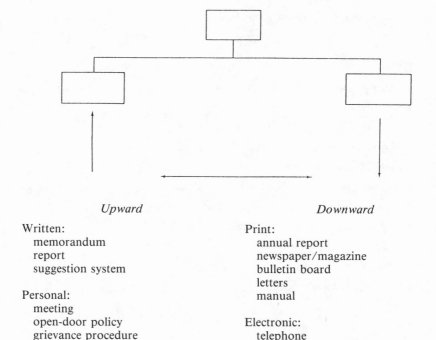

Upward                                  Downward

Written:
  memorandum
  report
  suggestion system

Personal:
  meeting
  open-door policy
  grievance procedure

Print:
  annual report
  newspaper/magazine
  bulletin board
  letters
  manual

Electronic:
  telephone
  videotape

Horizontal

personal contact
memorandum
meeting

**Figure 14. Corporate communication system of Akzo Corporation.**

The remainder of the Philips booklet discusses parts of the program: National Communications Managers, Mail, Telephony, Messaging, Computer Data Communications and The Future. It is impossible not to feel by the time one has finished reading this extraordinarily professional document that one company has confronted the future and everything is well under control.

CASE STUDY: AKZO

Akzo is an international group of industrial enterprises with the headquarters in Arnhem, The Netherlands. The company produces and sells manmade fibers, salt, heavy and specialty chemicals, coatings, pharmaceuticals, plastics, technical and consumer products, and provides consultation services in engineering, organization and automation. Akzo employs about 66,000 people in more than 220 locations in nearly 50 countries. The seven divisions of the company operate almost autonomously in a highly decentralized system. A company document explains employee involvement in the decision-making process: "The employees are able to influence decisions to a certain extent because in the framework of the organizational set-up room has been created for the contribution of their own ideas and opinions in the decision-making process. Akzo aims at open and objective communication on its policy and its actions and stimulates consultation between management and employees."[19] Figure 14 shows the Akzo corporate communication system.

# Portugal

*Official Name:* Portuguese Republic; *Capital:* Lisbon; *Government:* republic; *Subdivisions:* 18 districts and 2 autonomous regions; *Population:* 10,314,727 (July 1987); *Density:* 295.4 per square mile; *Currency:* escudo; *Official Language:* Portuguese; *Literacy:* 80 percent.

*The Land.* The westernmost country in continental Europe, Portugal is located on the western edge of the Iberian peninsula. It is bordered by Spain in the north and east and by the Atlantic Ocean in the south and west. The Portuguese Republic includes the mainland, the Azores and Madeira Islands (600–850 miles off the Atlantic coast) and Macao (a small colony on the southern coast of China). The total land area is about the size of Indiana.

Portugal is a rugged land with fine harbors. Portugal is the least urbanized country in all of Europe. Around 70 percent of the population still live rurally.

About 49 percent of the land is arable; 31 percent is forest; 6 percent is meadow and pasture, and 14 percent is waste, urban, inland water and other.

*The People.* Portugal is the third most ethnically homogeneous country in the world (the first two are Korea and Japan); 99 percent of the people are of Mediterranean stock.

The Portuguese are a highly individualistic people, but they are also tolerant, friendly, polite and patient, and form a relatively cohesive society. The core of Portuguese life, the family, is strengthened by a clan spirit that extends to aunts, uncles and cousins. Less than 1 percent of the people are divorced, one of the lowest percentages in the world.

Historically classes were very distinct, with a large poor lower class and a small, powerful upper class. In recent years, the middle class has grown, while the upper class has almost disappeared.

*A Brief History.* After a period of Roman domination, this area was ruled by the Visigoths until they were defeated by the Moors. Portugal was ruled by the Moors from A.D. 700 to 1100. In 1143, it became independent under King Afonso Henriques. In the fourteenth and fifteenth centuries, Portuguese explorers gave Portugal a huge overseas empire. Spain and France both ruled Portugal for a time before the monarchy was overthrown in 1910 and a republic was established. Portugal had been a dictatorship since 1932, when Dr. Antonio de Oliveira Salazar took control of the country. He was succeeded by a series of revolving-door governments until Premier Anibal Cavaco Silva's Social Democrats won a landslide victory in the 1987 election, which has stabilized the government. Portugal finally entered the European Economic Community on January 1, 1986, following years of tedious negotiations.

*The Economy.* The labor force is divided this way: services, 45 percent; industry 34, agriculture 21, and unemployed, 11.1 percent. About 55 percent of the labor force is unionized.

The poorest country in Europe, Portugal is also one of the most beautiful. Its exports consist of such products as olive oil, cork and port wine. Agriculture is generally underdeveloped. Important products include grains, potatoes, olives and grapes for wine. Portugal is the world's fourth largest wine producer. Most of Portugal's industry deals with the preparation of export products: mainly cork, wine and cotton textiles. Also footwear, wood pulp, paper, metalworking, oil refining, chemicals and fish canning are important. Recently advancements have been made in the development of hydroelectric power and the construction of factories to facilitate nitrate and fertilizer production.

Delegation of authority is not common; therefore, it is always necessary to go directly to the top man—be he the company president or the government minister—to get a decision. Modern business techniques are relatively new in Portugal.

Major industries are cement, chemicals, cork processing, electronics, fertilizers, food processing, glassware, paper and paper products, ship building and repair, textiles and wine.

*Organizational Communication.* The Portuguese are formal in both social and business situations. They are too polite to risk offending others by saying "no" directly, so one has to accept their vague promises and postponed decisions which often constitute their refusal of a proposal.

Correspondence requesting meetings should be translated into Portuguese. If a business person plans to do business with smaller companies, it is best to hire interpreters since few employees are likely to know English.

As in all of Latin Europe, attitudes about time are relaxed here. The punctual visitor should not be surprised or upset if the host is up to 30 minutes late or even more. Ask for a business card only from senior managers, but always present a business card when calling. When handing over the card bend over the top left-hand corner in the Continental tradition to indicate that the card has been delivered personally.

Shake hands when meeting someone and shake hands with everyone in groups. Don't shake hands with friends, however. Men also embrace and slap one another on the back; women kiss on both cheeks. Use first names only when invited to do so.

For business, even in hot weather, men should wear suits and ties; however, when Portuguese businessmen remove their jackets, you may do the same. Women should wear dresses and heels.

The Portuguese are rather reserved with their gestures. A visitor should avoid being overly physical. A sincere smile is always welcome.

Anyone doing business in Portugal must have great amounts of patience

**Table 12. Some Communication Practices in the Portuguese Corporation**

The Portuguese:

1. Are formal in business and social situations.

2. Don't say "no" directly for fear of offending others.

3. Expect to receive correspondence and collateral materials in Portuguese.

4. Are relaxed about time.

5. Use business cards only among senior managers.

6. Shake hands when meeting someone.

7. Use first names only when invited to.

8. Expect to see a suit and tie on a man even in hot weather.

9. Use gestures sparingly.

10. Are a high-context culture.

11. Use time polychronically.

and perseverance. Relaxed attitudes combined with one of the most burdensome bureaucracies in Europe will frustrate a business person accustomed to the more streamlined systems of northern Europe or the United States. When a person signs his or her name for even the most insignificant transaction, for example, he or she must often have his or her name "recognized" by a public notary. To do so requires endless hours in line to sign the name and even at times to be fingerprinted.

Table 12 lists some communication practices in the Portuguese firm.

## Spain

*Official Name:* Spanish State; *Capital:* Madrid; *Government:* constitutional monarchy; *Subdivisions:* 50 provinces; *Population:* 39,000,804 (July 1987); *Density:* 205.3 per square mile; *Currency:* peseta; *Official Language:* Spanish; *Literacy:* 96 percent.

*The Land.* The second largest country in Western Europe, Spain has a total land area slightly smaller than the states of Utah and Nevada combined. It is situated at the southwestern corner of the continent and with Portugal forms the peninsula called Iberia by Greek geographers and Lusitania by the Romans who left impressive architectural and engineering works in the region. With its high mountains, Spain has the second highest average altitude in Europe, exceeded only by Switzerland. The country is surrounded by the Bay of Biscay, France and Andorra in the north, the Mediterranean Sea in the east and south, Gibraltar and the Strait of Gibraltar in the south, the Gulf of Cadiz in the southwest, and Portugal and the Atlantic Ocean in the west.

Spain's territories include the Balearic Islands (off the coast of Spain), the

Canary Islands (off the west coast of Africa) and Ceuta and Melilla, two cities on the Mediterranean coast of Morocco.

About 41 percent of the land is arable and crop; 27 percent is meadow and pasture; 22 percent is forest; and 10 percent is urban and other.

*The People.* The Spanish people are a homogeneous composite of Mediterranean and Nordic descent. About 99 percent of the residents are Roman Catholic; the remaining 1 percent follow other religions.

Spain has a varied, colorful, exciting and slightly mystifying culture, which is described perfectly by the Spanish word *ambiente* (atmosphere). Spain is both ancient and modern, reactionary and revolutionary, religious and anticlerical, ascetic and materialistic, centralist and fragmented provincial. The Spanish are generally friendly, helpful and individualistic. They enjoy talking as well as giving advice to others, and believe that it is their duty to correct "errors" as they see them in others. Along with this spirit of individualism comes a strong sense of personal pride. Spanish people feel it is important to project the appearance of affluence and social position.

Perhaps because of their afternoon siesta, usually from 12 noon to 2 p.m. and even later, the Spanish eat a late dinner and retire very late at night. Life in the apartment house in which the author lived never settled down until well after midnight — usually just in time to be interrupted by the noisy nightly garbage pickup.

Each Spaniard knows that he is special and unique. For that reason, every trait which he possesses is of inestimable value, particularly in his own opinion. Spanish *individualismo* comes across to Americans as an overwhelming self-confidence. Successfully dealing with the Spanish means keeping in mind this pride in individuality, never offending a person's honor by causing embarrassment in any way. *"¡Viva yo!"* the Spanish say, meaning "Hurray for me."

Any project with which he is involved is sure to be a failure unless the Spaniard decides to cooperate. His time is worth more to him than pesetas, and he is far more proud of his family than any material possession. His employer is lucky to have him, and if he is your friend, all the better for you! Individualism is important in business associations, at church, at home, in official government circles, at the theater, post office or anywhere else two Spaniards might be conversing.

The family is very important in Spain. Only half of 1 percent of the population is divorced, giving it the fourth lowest divorce rate in the world. The father is usually the undisputed head of the home.

The Moorish, or Arab, influence is evident in the Spanish language — about 20 percent of the words are derived from Arabic — and in several fine buildings, such as the Alhambra in Granada.

*Espana es diferente, inclusiva de ella misma,* "Spain is different, even from itself."[20] The Spaniards are very regional in their outlook, first declaring themselves as coming from a region and only then from a nation. The business visitor encounters three major, different, regional attitudes. They are centered on Madrid, Barcelona and the northern industrial and port city of Bilbao. Inhabitants of these three areas have one thing in common: they look down on the other citizens of Spain.

Madrid is the center of over 80 of Spain's largest 100 concerns. Castilians are eloquent, sophisticated, and somewhat imperious. Madrilenos are conscious of being at the core of national life.

The Catalans clustered around Barcelona are aggressively independent. Their government represents fierce regionalism. Catalonia has sufficient power to demand concessions from Madrid. When the author passed through Barcelona on the way to teach in Madrid, the Catalans were eager to teach about their culture. Taxi drivers, hotel clerks and shop keepers were eager to discuss differences among themselves and other groups of Spaniards.

The Catalans' ardent push for autonomy is not a separatist movement, but a drive to seek cultural identity and recognition. Politically Catalans lean left despite their relative affluence. As individuals they tend to reflect the same temperament as their neighbors in French Provence. They take to flights of fancy, are passionate, and as businessmen work tremendously hard. New ideas appeal to the Catalan, who is an individualist, a libertarian, and always ready to be an iconoclast.

The separatist struggles of the Basques are well known, and their very language is emblematic of this drive: It stands alone, has no known linguistic relative. Basques are industrious—some people call them the lumberjacks of Spain. As businessmen, they are good organizers; they are also introspective, quiet and discreet, lacking the ebullience of their southern neighbors. Like the Catalans, the Basques were eager to talk with the author about their plight, but with a tinge of bitterness and determination that was not present in Barcelona. In the northern resort city of San Sebastian, revolutionary slogans appeared on the walls, the army maintained a very cautious presence and a tankful of watchful soldiers guarded the city hall. The atmosphere of a city under siege was very apparent in sharp contrast to the carefree abandon of the vacationers at the city's beaches.

*A Brief History.* A site of Greek colonies and later a part of the Roman Empire, Spain was largely conquered and controlled by the Moors from the eighth to the fifteenth centuries. Then the monarchs of Aragon and Castile, Ferdinand and Isabella, married, united their kingdoms and expelled the Moors.

In 1492, Isabella and Ferdinand dispatched Christopher Columbus westward, a move that eventually gave Spain control over major portions of South and Central America. During the sixteenth and seventeenth centuries, Spain was the largest and most powerful empire in the world. The gold that flowed in from those vast realms made Spain rich but brought it into violent and sustained conflict with other expanding countries. In 1588 a British fleet destroyed the Spanish Armada off English shores after which Spain began the long decline into the poverty that has characterized the country in recent centuries.

After a cruel Civil War in the 1930s, General Francisco Franco assumed complete control of the country. When he died, Juan Carlos of Borbon was crowned king in 1976, and he adroitly established a constitutional monarchy. He relinquished his power in 1978 and gave control of the government to an elected parliament. On January 1, 1986, Spain joined the European Economic

Community, entering a promising, new era in its history. Today the country continues to manage a double transition — from dictatorship to democracy and from underdevelopment to industrialization. Jose Antonio Martinez Soler, former foreign editor and business editor of the Madrid daily, *El Pais,* has said, "A new generation, born in the 1950s without electricity and running water, is maturing in the 1980s with computers and satellites. In 30 years, Spain has gone straight from the third world into the first. We are now closer to Europe than to Morocco. Africa no longer begins at the Pyrenees. In foreign policy, we are finally aligned with our neighbors of the European Community and reconciled, at last, with Jewish Sephardic ancestors expelled in 1492. Last year, Spain established diplomatic relations with Israel, without, however, renouncing fraternal Arab ties."[21]

*The Economy.* The work force is divided this way: services, 52 percent; industry 24.4, agriculture 16.1, construction 7.5, and unemployed, 21.5 percent. About 25 percent of the work force is unionized.

Spain is one of the poorest countries in Western Europe. Industry is very important in the north and northeast. Spain is a major producer of both automobiles and nuclear energy. Other important industries include textiles, footwear, food and beverage processing, metal manufacturing and chemicals. Agriculture and mining are also an important part of Spain's economy and provide much of the nation's exports. In good crop years, Spain is virtually self-sufficient in food products. Spain is one of the largest producers of wine in the world. It is also a major producer of barley and eggs, and has one of the largest fish catches in the world. Tourism is an important part of the Spanish economy; more tourists visit Spain each year than any other country in the world.

The Spanish claim that control of their country rests in the hands of 200 families. To know a member of one of these families is to have an introduction into the system. Eight large, family-owned banks dominate the economy. Members of influential banks' boards of directors sit on similar bodies of all important industrial concerns. The five biggest banks control more than 50 of Spain's 200 largest private enterprises. The "big eight" can call the shots in over 40 percent of Spain's industry.

Spain's King Juan Carlos has given a challenge to his managerial elite by stating: "A modern and free society needs everyone's participation in making decisions."

The present trend toward liberalization is indeed beginning to shift the center of power to the younger generation and the professional manager. This momentum, however, is not a torrent. Traditional power sites resist this nudging and most Spaniards still laconically claim that all business decisions are made on the Calle Alcala, the banking street of Madrid.

In fact, decision making in Spain is greatly centralized. Lower management levels are psychologically preconditioned to seek patronage and to court approval from above; hence they lack both training and practice in decision making. The traditional elite reinforces its control with ownership of facilities. Its natural reluctance to pass the fate of its fortunes to others is easy to understand.

Spain's centralist outlook can be traced historically to the Castilian monarchy, whose hegemony the Catholic church supported. It is no surprise that Franco in turn favored the few, the monopolies, the cartels. A tightly knit power structure facilitates control.

Now the Spanish church is drifting away from its close liaison with government circles. However, the church not only controls many enterprises directly, but also retains some of its influence over decision makers of the old school.

Some criteria that affect decisions to a considerable extent are beyond the control of any visiting businessman. The Spanish top man must weigh personal considerations involving family, loyalty, friendship, and patronage and its resulting reciprocity. These considerations may well supplant any material or technical advantage the foreigner can offer. Since many decisions made on this basis lack logical or rational support, the power elite exercises its prerogative in an overt, often arbitrary manner. This behavior tends to perpetuate existing patterns. Thus it can be said that Spanish managers are empire, not organization, builders.

Decision making in public bodies is still done with considerable anxiety. Bureaucrats have historically acted as implementors of official policy, and maintenance of their positions has depended on sensing every zephyr from above. Going against the grain meant a serious reprimand at best, a loss of job at worst. Scandals were frequent and frequently hushed up; efficiency was not even a minor objective.

In Spanish there is no word to refer to everyone who works in a business organization. Instead there is the word *empleados,* which refers to white-collar workers, and another word, *obreros,* which refers to laborers. This differentiation reflects the substantial class difference attributed to each group.

Major industries are chemicals, engineering, fishing, footwear, furniture, mining, ship building, steel, textiles and transport equipment.

*Organizational Communication.* In initial letters to Spanish companies, it is best to write in English. Translated letters may not be flowery enough for the recipients and risk offending them.[22] Correspondence should all be formal, even after you think you know your Spanish business contacts well. As stated, the Spanish use as their last name their family surname followed by the mother's maiden name. In correspondence, use both but face-to-face use only the surname.

The best way to deal with the Spanish is through a local contact. Because the Spanish value personal relationships, the Spanish representative will help accomplish what you could never do alone.

Proper attire for men, even in warm weather, is a suit and tie. Women should wear dresses or blouses and skirts.

Most Spaniards are unpunctual but they expect the foreign visitor to be on time. The Spanish have a very casual attitude toward time so that arriving late for an appointment is not serious. Even when on time, however, you may be kept waiting. The importance of a visitor's case or the stature of his or her introduction will determine the length of the wait prior to an appointment. A 15-minute delay should cause no concern. Waiting time beyond half an hour might be a bad omen. The Spanish host may not have returned from an urgent visit or may still be preoccupied with other business or a meal. An amusing difference in phrasing between English and Spanish is that a clock "runs" in English but it "walks" in Spanish.

The first thing to do after shaking hands is present a business card which should be printed in both English and Spanish and given Spanish side up. Senior Spanish managers are generally so conservative as to appear cold and austere—and some of them are. Most, however, are warm and friendly once you get to know them. It is a favorable sign if the host moves from behind his desk and joins the visitor in a separate seating arrangement, should one be available. Conversations that take place across a desk are distinct signs of distance.

Opening conversation should center on nonbusiness issues. In a manner similar to the Arabs, the Spanish follow a procedure that requires initial establishment of personal rapport. A visitor must be *simpatico* if he desires fruitful future interaction. You may never get to the subject of business during the initial meeting.

Progress will be slow. Frequent interruptions such as a phone call or an essential word to another person will occur and are entirely normal. To a great extent, pragmatism controls the overall business environment in that the constantly changing immediate situation determines behavior.

The Spanish like to negotiate in person. Other forms of communication are considered dehumanized. Business discussions are between people, not between functions or representatives of organizations. An assumption underlying person-to-person contact is that once a friendship is established, the negotiating partner will feel obligated to give a preferential price and product that can be relied upon. An American working in Barcelona placed an order with a local supplier over the telephone, but the goods never arrived. A Spanish associate advised him to meet the supplier personally to become acquainted. Though he thought this a waste of time, the American did it and then everything was fine. Once a working relationship has been established, as here, you can usually transact short business deals on the telephone.

In his presentation, the foreigner should emphasize stability. This orientation plays to the Spaniard's perception of time which includes a view of the present as tenuous and insecure.

The visitor's manner need not be subdued. Spaniards relish superlatives, anything larger than life. To this end, body language is employed ebulliently. Hands are equal to mouths when making a case. Like the Arabs, the Spanish enjoy bargaining and they are shrewdly manipulative.

The visitor should also take care to present his or her offer clearly and forcefully. If the Spanish negotiator fails to comprehend, he may be afraid to seek clarification. This threat to his honor may become a roadblock to further negotiations. Even when considerations demonstrate Spanish advantage, the negotiator may let proceedings fail.

Historically, dress has denoted social status. Though standards of business dress have loosened up, good business dress is recommended at all times. Spanish etiquette is changing, but the older executives, the upper management levels and the social elite maintain high standards of dress.

## Table 13. Some Communication Practices in the Spanish Corporation

The Spanish:

1. Expect correspondence to be formal.

2. Use father's name followed by mother's maiden name in written communication but only father's name in oral communication.

3. Do business best through a Spanish representative of foreigners.

4. Expect to see a suit and tie on men even in hot weather.

5. Are casual about time.

6. Shake hands and exchange business cards.

7. Are conservative in doing business.

8. Expect small talk prior to getting down to business to be sure that visitors are *simpatico.*

9. Prefer communications to be in person.

10. Relish superlatives in communication and use gestures generously.

11. Relate better to an atmosphere of modesty than ostentation.

12. Prefer to do business when visitors are well connected.

13. Make good use of the informal system of communication.

14. Have a high-context culture.

15. Use time polychronically.

Spaniards who know each other and are of similar class or status touch each other during conversation as a sign of intimacy and friendship. Such rapport takes some time, but it should not be avoided. It is a favorable sign and means that barriers are lowered. Higher-status and upper-class Spaniards bridge the social gap with a physical gesture. While conversing they often hold their lower-level partner by the arm or by the shoulder as a sign of reassurance. Physical attributes of success or material affluence should be toned down in Spain. They are likely to generate envy, which will hinder progress. An atmosphere of modesty should prevail over one of ostentation. Sophistication is admired. In this respect, a European outlook sets the standard.

The Spanish word for a well-connected man is *enchufado,* which derives from *enchufe,* electric plug. An *enchufado* can introduce people, cause the current to flow, and generate action.[23] Without a strong recommendation, the foreign visitor will languish in waiting rooms and converse with the powerless — and his mission will atrophy. The Spanish cultivate untold marginal relationships in order to be able to drop the right name, at the right time, in the right place.

In the absence of any responses from Spanish companies to the survey conducted as part of this study, the author interviewed Josep Bertran, Director of Industrial Products and Investments at the Spanish Embassy in New York. He had had two years of experience in the Commercial Department of a

Spanish company employing 300 people in Barcelona. He made these points regarding communication in the Spanish firm:

- There is no established way of communicating among employees.
- Employees communicate by stopping at each other's desks and while discussing different topics, they would also talk about their personal situation within the company.
- The lack of communication created much misunderstanding among employees regarding management's opinions and views toward them.
- Due to lack of communication, people identified less with the company and failed to see it as their own company.
- Communication is very important when the company is facing difficulties since this gives rise to rumors regarding dismissal and fear on the part of employees for no apparent reason.

Undoubtedly, Spain's entry into the European Economic Community might wind up changing all of that since, as discussed, they issue guidelines to member countries on how employees should receive information.

Table 13 lists some communication practices of the Spanish firm.

# ——————————— United Kingdom ———————————

*Official Name:* United Kingdom of Great Britain and Northern Ireland; *Capital:* London; *Government:* constitutional monarchy; *Subdivisions:* 6 metropolitan counties, 48 nonmetropolitan counties; 9 regions; 3 island areas and 26 local government districts; *Population:* 56,845,195 (July 1987); *Density:* 598.5 per square mile; *Official Languages:* English, Welsh, Scottish form of Gaelic; *Literacy:* 99 percent.

*The Land.* Great Britain refers to England, Scotland and Wales; the United Kingdom includes Northern Ireland as well. It forms part of the British Isles, a group of islands situated on the continental shelf off the northwest coast of Europe.

Great Britain is about the size of Oregon. From Northern Scotland to the Channel, the country has a maximum length of 600 miles and, at its widest point from east to west, a width of 300 miles. At no point in Britain are you farther than 75 miles from the sea or tidal waters. At its closest point, England is about 22 miles from France and about 75 miles from Northern Ireland.

Behind England's chalky cliffs in the south and southeast lie rolling plains. There are hilly districts in the west, southwest and north. The Cheviot Hills divide England from Scotland.

Scotland is roughly one-eighth the size of England and its capital, Edinburgh, is about 400 miles north of London. Scotland's "uplands" in the south consist of rolling hills and wooded slopes; the control "lowlands" are mostly farm country. Scotland has some 2,300 miles of broken coastline facing the cold Atlantic on the west and the North Sea on the east. Some 800 islands lie off these shores, many of them in two northeast groups: the Orkneys and the Shetlands. The other major group forms the large Western Islands which comprise the Inner and Outer Hebrides.

Wales is generally mountainous except along the coast where much of the farming is done.

*The People.* Nearly 68 percent of the people live in cities with more than a third in nine urban areas. Living in crowded conditions has made an impact on the psychology of the British. It accounts in part for the British reserve, the desire for privacy which is demonstrated by the gates and fences around their homes, drawn curtains and closed office doors.

The English have long been a markedly homogeneous people, descendants of groups that settled in the country before the end of the twelfth century: Angles, Saxons, Celts, Romans, Norse, Vikings and Normans. Through the ages, the Scots, Welsh and Irish have maintained their own identities. This is most evident in their speech and their varied characteristics.

There are currently about five times as many Scots living outside Scotland as inside.

*A Brief History.* After the decline of the Roman Empire, of which this country had been a part, various Germanic invaders — Angles, Saxons and Jutes — occupied Britain. They in turn were invaded by marauding Danes until 1066 when William the Conqueror, a Norman duke, led the last successful attack on Britain. Subsequent British sovereigns attempted to add to the empire by unifying Wales, Ireland, Scotland and parts of France under the British Crown. Britain established itself as a major naval power by defeating the Spanish Armada in 1588 and remained the world's greatest power from the mid-eighteenth century until the end of World War II.

England added Wales and Ireland by the end of the thirteenth century and then Scotland in 1603 under James I of England who was also James VI of Scotland. The term "United Kingdom" came into use in 1808 when the parliament of Ireland was joined to that of Great Britain. In 1922, Southern Ireland (now the Republic of Ireland) became independent, the six counties of Northern Ireland, often referred to as Ulster, remaining part of the United Kingdom.

During the eighteenth and nineteenth centuries as a result of the Industrial Revolution, Britain emerged as the first great industrial nation, creating in the country a vast middle class. The development was accompanied by extensive colonial settlement and expansion overseas, reaching its peak as the British Empire, in the latter half of the nineteenth century. It wasn't until after World War I that British expansionism ended. During the twentieth century, Britain has granted independence to the majority of former overseas possessions, now member nations of the Commonwealth.

Hard hit by World War II, in which its empire was weakened, its financial resources virtually exhausted, and its traditional leadership in world trade lost to the United States, this island country is now trying to adjust to the new world order. Explanations of why the country in which the Industrial Revolution began is entering the Information Age with difficulty are many. A *Frontline* program on the Public Broadcasting System, "Will There Always Be an England?" was one of these. In it Sir Geoffrey Chandler, introduced as a director of industry, said this:

> A hundred and thirty years ago, Britain was at the pinnacle of her industrial pre-eminence. Britain led the world, Britain was the workshop of the world.

And we had no competition. The difference today is that we have acute competition and we have not faced that competition effectively. We have grown, our competitors have grown much faster. And in about a hundred years and it's now measurable, we have gone from the top of the industrial tree virtually to the bottom in terms of standard of living.[24]

In the same program, Ian Wrigglesworth, Member of Parliament, S.D.P., said:
We're down now, to the same level as about Puerto Rico. I mean Italy's overtaken us, we're in the third category of nations. And very shortly we're going to be about the poorest country in Europe. West Germany has a national income per head of population of twice the size of Great Britain. France has overtaken us, Belgium, Holland. Every other country in Europe. Apart from Spain and Greece, recently come into the European, Portugal, recently come into the European community. And they are rapidly catching up on us and in a few years time they will have overtaken us as well.[25]

A recent surge in the British economy is proving these predictions of doom premature. Focussing on the past and seeking answers to why the sharp decline in the country's economy result in a listing like this one:

1. Failure to modernize capital equipment as a result of a short-term focus.
2. Poor technical innovation procedures.
3. Outmoded financial structures that direct savings into investments.
4. Anti-industrial culture and class system that misdirects talent into public sector administration, urban studies and universities.
5. Underinvestment in human capital. France and West Germany had 64 percent and 68 percent, respectively, of youth in full-time vocational education and apprenticeships compared to only 24 percent in Britain.
6. Poor management of strategic change.[26]

The first four relate to the whole nation; the final two to British organizations.

The British Commonwealth today is a free association of 49 sovereign and independent states. For 18 nations the Queen is the actual Head of State; others appoint their own Heads of State but recognize the Queen as the symbol of the Commonwealth connection. The Commonwealth's 1.2 billion people (more than a quarter of the world's population) occupy a fifth of the world's land surface and make up a third of the world's nations.

*The Economy.* The work force is divided this way: services, 49.8 percent; manufacturing and construction 24.5; government 13, self-employed 9.8, agriculture 1.1, and unemployed, 11.4 percent. Some 42 percent of the work force is unionized.

Still one of the most highly industrialized nations in the world, Britain is a leading producer of coal, iron and steel and of heavy machinery, automobiles, aircraft and textiles. Despite the fact that Britain has granted independence to more than 20 states encompassing 700 million people since the war, it is still a major political force in the world. Nevertheless, this industrial structure has begun to show cracks and, worse, an increasing inability to compete successfully abroad. Toward correcting this situation, the government has privatized British Telecom, Rolls-Royce and other companies valued at a total of more than $10 billion and has begun to deregulate financial markets.

Class lines are very apparent on the job. Many daily patterns in business-worker relationships clearly demonstrate these class lines; they still do in many plants. Factories often have a number of separate lunch rooms — or different eating hours — for various levels of employees. Clubs, neighborhoods, vacation spots and holiday programs define class lines more clearly than do pay checks.

In a C-SPAN interview on June 1, 1988, Michael Jackson, of KABC radio, and a British native, explained how the British class system affects attitudes. "If several American workers saw someone pass in a Ferrari, they would think, 'Someday I'll have one of those.' In the same situation, British workers would think, 'Someday we'll get him out of there.'"

Decision making in Great Britain generally remains the prerogative of highly placed management. A stubborn absence of genuine communications, combined with a lack of trust in middle managers, has concentrated key activities near the top. The manager may appoint committees to decide certain matters with the help of some trusted staff advisors.

British labor also has a say in decision making. Its primary channel for input is the government. This application of power has apparently not, so far, been particularly effective in charting the course of a company. Rather, union decision making is primarily restricted to the plant level: the job site and the work environment. Voluntarism — part of a social philosophy that encourages the pursuit of self interests — is a hallmark of industrial relations in Britain today. There are few limitations on the right to strike. Strikes are often unexpected and more disruptive than they are in the United States. Some experts point to labor strife along with industrial stagnation and bad management as the causes of Britain's industrial problems.[27]

A graduate of the European School of Management Studies, a three-year course for applicants from EEC countries who spend a year each in Paris, at Oxford and in Berlin, said that he noticed the British participants feel it is bad to take things too seriously. He described the arrival in Brussels of a British engineering manager who was tendering for a contract in Zambia. He came to see the Zambian manager but: "He had got the address wrong, the date wrong, the phone number wrong. He thought all this perfectly normal, and so in a way did I. But I couldn't imagine it from a French or German businessman, though I suppose the French would be ten minutes late."[28] Graduates of the School list two reasons for this British attitude: The British economic system survived World War II relatively intact, which prevented the rebuilding of the industrial infrastructure (which because of the war had become necessary in other European countries) but also prevented a development of any sense of urgency among the population. And, work is less important in the English social system compared with other European countries. Heinz Luchterhand, a 1981 graduate, said that in England, "you've been to the right school, the right university, you belong to the right clubs, you live in the right area. Nobody can take these things away from you. In Germany, if you lose your job, your whole status goes with it."[29]

Another factor is that in Britain, higher education is devoted to the cultivation of social, intellectual, even moral character. In other European countries, higher education is career-oriented. "In this sense, the managerial revolution never happened in Britain — no management class developed and no management education to go with it. This helps to explain why our industrial relations are still cast in an 'owners versus workers' mould."[30] While the British identify with their equals, other managers around the world identify with their companies.

Major industries are chemicals, consumer goods, electrical engineering, food processing, iron and steel, motor vehicles and transport equipment, petroleum refining, and textiles.

A visitor should reach and involve potential decision makers even during early negotiation stages. They will not only channel information to the top, but will also provide a flow of feedback during the discussions. All the while, the foreigner should provide information that aids analysis, an important part of British decision making.

*Organizational Communication.* With the British, appearances are important — as are form and manners. The British are a little less direct in communications for fear of offending others. You hear the use of "please" and "thank you" more in Britain than in the United States too, an effort to avoid appearing rude.

The British approach business matters in a reserved fashion even internationally. Decrying the fact that Cap Gemini Sogeti, the largest independent professional computer software and service supplier in Europe in 1986, is virtually unknown in the United States, the general manager of the company said, "It's not in our culture to say 'Here we are!'"[31]

The British usually have separate offices for the majority of their executives. And the office proper has long functioned as a status symbol.

Space is a matter of privacy, of distance. Moving close to the Briton during business talks is incorrect because it violates neutral space. Closeness is not even a typical practice in familiar situations. Physical touching to emphasize a point or to underline a feeling will very likely perplex the Briton. Britons normally keep their office doors closed, as a polite insurance of privacy.

After being shown in and introduced by your British host's secretary, a firm handshake is appropriate. First names are not used until a personal relationship has been established. Wait until you are invited to sit down before you do. After a discussion of the weather, the traffic or the weekend soccer matches, it is time to pay attention to matters at hand — the British are interested in your proposal. However, it is wise to avoid the "hard sell." Provide facts and details at the same time as you explain the practical implications; this will help your host develop a feeling of trust in you. Don't prolong the meeting; after you have covered your material and have arranged for a subsequent meeting or follow up, it is up to you as the visitor to end the meeting. Unless your English host is pressed for time, he would consider it extremely rude to dismiss a visitor. Your host will walk you to the door; again, a firm handshake is appropriate.

Striped ties in Britain usually represent regiments or schools and wearing one when you are not entitled to it is unforgivable. The English complain also that American shirt pockets are always full of pencils, pens, plastic rulers and cigarettes. In Britain this is considered unsightly.

The business dinner is more common in Britain than the British lunch, and spouses are frequently invited. A good way to strengthen ties with British hosts is to send a follow-up letter of appreciation for hospitality and cooperation as soon as possible after a meeting.

When dealing with the Scots, get to the point quickly. They are direct, frank, straightforward people who work with facts. Painfully honest, they will quickly and abruptly cease dealing with anyone who is not. Before bringing up a subject for discussion, make sure that you know your facts and are fully prepared to discuss the subject with confidence.

Scots are reserved. On the whole they tend to be suspicious of foreigners whom they call "incomers." The typical Scot will not go out of his way to establish a personal relationship with the foreign visitor.

Necessity has made the Scots excellent negotiators; they will not disclose everything, nor will they expect you to. However, they will not cover up with false statements — and they expect the same of you. New ideas are scrutinized over a considerable period of time; new products or ideas are not easily sold, especially those that cost money. Budgets are closely worked out and stringently kept, both personally and in business.

Business cards are helpful as the Scots find our accents difficult to understand and many of our names hard to "catch" or pronounce. The Scots take to first names more readily than many English do, but you should still wait for them to give the sign.

The Welsh also center their patriotism locally.

Sir Winston Churchill's comment (quoting George Bernard Shaw) during World War II that America and the United Kingdom were two countries divided by a common language is a factor in business relationships. Language differences between British and American English are shown in Table 14. To "table it" in American would mean put it aside, but in Britain would mean discuss it immediately. Don't assume the British are just like us because we share the same language and heritage. Points of view between our countries differ considerably. The communication systems of America and the United Kingdom are remarkably similar; Figure 15 shows the British system.

A survey conducted by a London-based public relations agency showed that companies in the two countries are similar in another way: both are using written communication policies as a basis for corporate communications programs. Of the 145 firms responding in the 1980 survey, 40 percent use the policies. This was double the figure reported in a similar 1976 survey. A dozen years ago, only 2 percent of firms reported using communication policies.[32] The change indicates a new serious approach to communicating with employees by British corporations.

One such company is Wilkie & Paul, Ltd., which holds regular briefings and consultative council meetings to communicate with all of its 300 employees. Managing Director R.B. Paul says of the program: "people feel that this company is trying to give them all of the things that they think they ought to have."[33]

## Table 14. British Business Terms and Their American English Translations

| British English | American English |
|---|---|
| Annual General Meeting | Annual Meeting of Shareholders |
| assurance | insurance |
| bagman | traveling salesman |
| bean-feast | company picnic |
| billion | trillion |
| bill of quantity | cost estimate |
| bonus issue (bonus share) | stock dividend |
| chartered accountant | certified public accountant |
| clerk of the works | maintenance man |
| Commissioner of Oaths | notary public |
| deposit account | savings account |
| doorstep salesman | door-to-door salesman |
| engage | employ |
| fully found | all expenses paid |
| ganger | gang foreman |
| gearing | leverage |
| hammer | declare insolvent |
| haulage contractor | trucking company |
| headed paper | letterhead |
| hoarding | billboard |
| land agent | real estate broker |
| limited company | corporation |
| mains | electric power source |
| navvy | construction worker |
| milliard | billion |
| notice board | bulletin board |
| nude contract | void contract |
| odd-man | odd job man |
| on the strength | on the payroll |
| on the telephone | to have a telephone |
| over the odds | above market value |
| paper knife | letter opener |
| pension cover | pension benefits |
| post-free | postpaid |
| relief | deduction, exemption |
| scheme of arrangement | reorganization plan |
| soft goods | textiles |
| superannuation scheme | pension plan |
| take a decision | make a decision |
| tally plan | installment plan |
| threshold agreement | union cost-of-living contract |
| trunk call | long-distance call |
| wage restraint | wage control |
| wages sheet | payroll |
| works | factory |
| work to rule | work by the book |
| work to time | watch the clock |

*(Source: Norman W. Schur,* British English: A to Zed *[New York: Facts on File Publications, 1987].)*

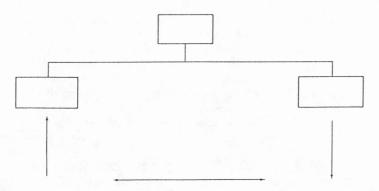

|  | Upward |  | Downward |
|---|---|---|---|

**Upward**

Written:
  memorandum
  report
  suggestion system
  newspaper/magazine

Personal:
  meeting
  interview
  open-door policy
  grievance procedure
  quality circle meetings
  skip-level conferences
  trade union activities

Electronic:
  telephone

**Downward**

Print:
  annual report
  annual report to employees
  newspaper/magazine
  bulletin board
  letters
  pay envelope inserts
  manual
  handbook

Electronic:
  telephone
  videotape
  electronic mail

Personal:
  conferences
  personal contact
  team briefings

*Horizontal*

Personal:
  personal contact
  meetings
  social activities
  sporting events

Written:
  memorandum

Electronic:
  telephone
  telex
  telefax

**Figure 15. Communication system of the United Kingdom Corporation.**

The line of communication begins on the first Monday of each month, at a meeting Paul holds with his five directors who oversee the works, marketing, technical, financial and personnel areas. The session, which lasts for an hour or more, covers topics ranging from new orders booked to such longer-term concerns as the need to convert to the metric system over the next year.

The product of this session is a typewritten document of a few pages, known as the brief, and generally summarizing each of the items discussed by Paul and his team. Some items, however, are eliminated from the brief because they are of a confidential nature. For example, a brief prepared earlier this year omitted mention of an impending visit by foreign businessmen to discuss possible collaboration on a project. Paul was afraid the news would arouse unwarranted speculation.

The brief is distributed to the five top managers who discuss its contents with their assistants. Such discussions are repeated at lower levels during the next two days.[34]

The London-based Standard Telephone and Cable (STC) annual report includes a note illustrating the emphasis on consultation with employees:

The Company has, for many years, been firmly committed to securing the full cooperation and involvement of its employees in the success of the business.

This is achieved by direct communication and consultation with all employees and with representatives, where appropriate, at the locations in which they work. The methods include face-to-face briefing and discussion groups, employee information meetings and consultative committees. The Company newspaper, the *SCT News,* and locations newspapers all enjoy an independent editorial policy.

An important factor is the provision, on a continuing basis, of economic and financial information concerning the Company which is of interest to employees.[35]

An item in ARC's industrial relations manual, entitled *Communication and Consultation,* states

Managers are required to communicate with all employees under their control. . . . The manner in which this is done will depend on the nature of the subject, but information should be disseminated in a form easily understood by subordinates. [Later the same document explains] Communication is a two way process and in addition to communicating with subordinates, manager must ensure that relevant information is passed to their supervisors through the management system.[36]

British Petroleum, under the heading "Communication of Information and Consultation," says this in a document entitled *Employee Involvement Arrangements in BP Companies Operating in the UK:*

Employees are provided with information and are given the opportunity to express their views on issues immediately related to their own activities at the workplace. Such issues typically include: the setting of work objectives and standards, the organization of work, work methods and ways of improving efficiency, working environment, personnel procedures and pension schemes, progress towards objectives, safety requirements and accident prevention, training and skill improvement.

Employees are kept informed, on a regular basis, of the organisation, the general objectives and performance of their employing company. They are informed of the economic/business circumstances in which the managers of the company take their decisions. They are told of decisions made elsewhere in the Group which may have consequences for their work practices or employment. They are informed of these decisions as early as possible. The reasons for the decisions are explained to them and they have the opportunity to comment and put forward suggestions for handling implementation and consequences.

The scope for communicating information and seeking the views of employees before decisions are taken may be restricted by the need to preserve confidentiality and to safeguard commercial or other sensitivities; to avoid damaging delays to the business; to avoid substantial injury to the Group and to respect prohibitions imposed by law.[37]

That company's annual report for 1984 described the *Management Brief,* published with the authority of the Chairman and intended to provide "'top-down' information which managers can use to supplement information on local activities in regular face-to-face communication briefings and discussions."[38] Among topics published in three issues of *Briefs* are "The Challenge of Information Technology," "BP's Case for Stable Oil Prices," "Acid Rain," and "Lead in Gasoline: The Position in Europe."

In *Corporate Communication for Managers,* Peter Jackson who has worked in the field for 30 years in Britain observes that many firms in his country are trying to match in their corporate communication programs the success of the unions. "Uninformed managers lack contacts, information and commitment to company objectives," Jackson notes. Then he adds:

They have seen that growth of information for unions and other participative structures has often meant that those working for them know more than they do about what's happening in the company.

One of my jobs for a large UK group was to produce the annual report for employees. It went out, in all its multi-coloured glory, with sparkling prose and all-human-life-is-there pictures. The staff sat back and congratulated themselves. A month later we launched a survey to see how the report had been received.

At one large factory all the employees ticked the box labelled "not seen" so we asked some more questions. Investigation revealed that the pack of 500 reports was still sitting behind the telephone shelf in reception because the managers were not concerned enough to arrange for them to be distributed.[39]

Table 15 lists some communication practices of the British firm. British Aerospace, for one, establishes communication between the Chairman, Sir Austin Pearce, and managers through seminars, shown in Figure 16. Information presented is expected to "cascade" down through the organization.

## CASE STUDY: CADBURY SCHWEPPES

The Cadbury Schweppes international group of companies is dedicated to the complementary markets of confectionary and beverages. The Group has developed a unique understanding of consumer needs in this buoyant leisure food and drink category and an expertise in their shared distribution channels.

## Table 15. Some Communication Practices
## in the British Corporation

The British:

1. Shake hands firmly.

2. Use first names only after a friendship has developed.

3. Address business at meetings only after a little small talk.

4. Dislike the "hard sell."

5. Consider appearance — including form and manner — important.

6. Are somewhat indirect in communicating for fear of offending others.

7. Use space as a matter of privacy and distance.

8. Are perplexed by touching during conversations.

9. Prefer the business dinner over the business lunch.

10. Use many terms differently than their American business associates.

11. Are learning to use the written communication policy.

12. Depend on oral communication more than do Americans.

13. Have communication systems very similar to those of Americans and Canadians.

14. Have a low-context culture.

15. Use time monochronically.

The Cadbury Schweppes Group comprises nearly 50 subsidiary and associated companies in 21 countries. It has an extensive network of soft drink bottling franchises in Europe, America, Africa and Australia. Group products are exported to over 100 countries.

Over 28,000 people are employed by Cadbury Schweppes around the world, 13,000 of whom are in the UK. Another 3,000 are in Australia and 4,000 in Africa, Asia and New Zealand.

A brochure called "The Character of the Company," written by Sir Adrian Cadbury, Chairman of the Company, includes this about communication:

> The principle of openness should apply in all our dealings inside and outside the Company. It follows that we should keep everyone in the business as well informed as possible within the legal limits of confidentiality. It also implies a readiness to listen. I believe in an open style of management and in involving people in the decisions which affect them, because it is right to do so and because it helps to bring individual and Company aims closer together. The responsibility for decisions rests on those appointed to take them, but if they are arrived at openly, the decisions are likely to be better and the commitment to them greater. Openness and trust are the basis of good working relationships on which the effectiveness of the organisation depends. They imply an acceptance of the mutual balance of rights and duties between individuals and the Company.

**Figure 16. At British Aerospace, a series of seminars has been held between employees and the Chairman (Sir Austin Pearce, standing) to exchange views. (British Aerospace Public Ltd. Co., London.)**

## CASE STUDY: BURMAH OIL TRADING LIMITED

Burmah Oil today is a financially strong, compact Group, concentrating on the manufacture and marketing of lubricants and specialty chemicals and a major gas shipment project. The Group has operations in over 30 countries, and employs some 10,000 people, 3,900 of them in the UK. This comment in the company's 1985 annual report concerns communication:

Depending on the characteristics of each unit, UK operating companies employ a number of different methods and practices to promote effective involvement of employees, all of which are aimed at improving communication on business issues relevant to employees' interests.

All employees have the opportunity for informal discussions with management on relevant work matters. Works councils and consultative committees cover a wide range of business matters and other topics of concern to employees. In addition there are formal negotiations and consultations with recognised trade unions. . . . Following the announcement of the group's financial results, the chairman and other executive directors address meetings of senior management from the UK and overseas, who are responsible for onward briefing. In addition, several employee reports are published, either on their own or as supplements to employee newspapers, and copies of the group's annual report and accounts are made available to employees. Some companies organise special briefings on current performance and future objectives to coincide with pay negotiations or when reorganisations are planned. Overall, increasing efforts are being made to improve employee awareness and interest in the performance of the company.

A letter from the Head of Public Affairs of Burmah Oil also states:

Within Burmah we have a policy of decentralisation, leaving it to our divisions and their operating units to determine and develop communications policies and practices that best suit their own circumstances. However, we do try corporately, by example, to promote effective communications worldwide, e.g., each year we make a video that is used by each of our operating units for their own briefing purposes.

## CASE STUDY: JAGUAR

The origins of Jaguar can be traced to 1922 when Sir William Lyons organized a partnership called the Swallow Sidecar Company to produce motorcycle sidecars. Over the years the business expanded into automobile production and evolved into a publicly owned company known as Jaguar Cars Limited. In 1960 Jaguar Cars Limited acquired the Daimler Company Limited, a rival manufacturer of luxury automobiles.

Jaguar Cars Limited merged with the British Motor Corporation Limited in 1966 in a move designed to establish a bigger and stronger unit in the motor industry. The resulting company, British Motor Holdings Limited, itself merged in 1968 with the Leyland Motor Corporation Limited, to form British Leyland Motor Corporation Limited.

The British government acquired substantially all of the outstanding shares of British Leyland Motor Corporation Limited in 1975 as a result of that company's large and continuing operating losses, and thereafter provided much of the funding required. Such shareholdings were placed in a new holding company, BL Public Limited Company.

A speech by Sir John Egan, chairman of the company, discusses the part communication played in reviving Jaguar after some difficult years:

The first thing we did was tell everyone in the company what we were trying to achieve and get them all going in the same direction. We then placed the responsibility for action on the 150 fault codes where they could best be analysed and solved. Having made that decision and formulated an operating strategy, we sought a simple catch-phrase aptly to sum up our objectives. "In pursuit of perfection" was chosen although at the time it looked as if it was going to be a long chase! The "Pursuit of perfection" campaign started in mid 1980, let me outline it briefly.

First, multi-disciplinary task forces were set up with the 150 faults divided between those management groups — incidentally, the board of directors was given the job of dealing with the worst 12 faults. The task forces' objectives were quite straightforward — diagnose the fault, find and test the cure and rapidly implement a solution.... As I explained earlier, we took the view at an early stage that all the workforce should be involved in this recovery programme.

Consequently, video programmes were produced to describe the company's performance in general, the quality programme's immediate objectives and the specific requirements for various groups of workers.

It was abundantly clear from the outset that emphasizing quality as the number one priority of the company met with the full approval of the workforce. It was also absolutely clear to us that we could make good cars purely and simply because everybody was utterly determined to play his part. The company was going to win because the employees wanted to win.

We then introduced the first of our quality circles, primarily because we wanted more problem-solving capability but also we sought grass roots quality monitoring.... We now have over 60 quality circles in operation. We would like to have more but we are having to re-organise our management structure to cope with the enormous enthusiasm and request for change required from those active trouble-shooting groups. Our ultimate objective is to have all our employees involved in quality circles....

Quality, timing, productivity and product improvement are the four key areas that we have had to tackle since 1980. They have been underpinned by an increasing commitment to two management philosophies one internal and one external. Inside the company we have given special attention to the twin but related subjects of training and communication....

Every week management in Jaguar are fully briefed on the performance of the company and this information cascades down to supervisor and foreman level. On Mondays we actually take a 15 minute break from production so that our first level managers can brief the entire workforce on what is happening in the company — this can range from how many cars we built the previous week to details about VIP's visiting the factory and who therefore will be seen on the shopfloor — we even give out the results of our racing programmes in Europe and the US — and that is always eagerly received!

Every three or four months the workforce in groups of 200 to 300 is invited to attend a series of video programmes prepared within the company. These tell of our progress and highlight those areas where difficulties or inefficiencies still exist.

A senior director is always present at these events and the interchange of views have ranged from the highly political to valuable identification of problem areas and suggestions for resolution of the problems.

These formal face-to-face sessions are reinforced by the usual media of employee publications/notice boards, etc., but we have also introduced or reinstated a number of other activities which might not seem central to car manufacturing, including: • Family nights at which the employees were invited to bring their relatives and friends to witness the progress the company was making and to hear of our future plans and projects. • Open days where employees and families can visit our factories and see their place of work.

• Company organised events for all the employees' families such as bonfire night celebrations, mini-marathons and pantomime visits for the children. . . .

It is a simple philosophy. We believe that everyone working for Jaguar must be kept fully informed of its progress. This is the means we have adopted to encourage them to understand their place in a team working towards success and prosperity.

## CASE STUDY: RANK XEROX

Rank Xerox is a leading supplier of office equipment in over 80 countries in the Eastern Hemisphere. Five factories in Europe and four factories in Japan produce the widest range of copiers and duplicators in the industry. Company goals regarding internal communications are:

To establish systems of keeping company employees throughout the organisation informed on corporate activities, issues and actions that affect the operating unit and its people. It is for decision by the operating unit whether the responsibility for this activity lies with the corporate affairs or personnel function.

Rank Xerox includes employees among its most important groups for corporate communicating, with purposes stated this way:

• The Company wants to be known by both existing employees and the public as a good employer with enlightened staff policies; excellent career development opportunities both within individual countries and internationally; and as offering an attractive working atmosphere.

• The Company wishes to create an employee team spirit at all levels. This includes fostering among its employees internationally an awareness both of their interdependence and of the extent of their interdependence. It means the evolution of common interests and a common identity.

• The Company recognises all its employees as partners in an enterprise for their mutual prosperity, and wants them to view themselves as such. Rank Xerox believes that good human relationships are essential in achieving this prosperity and that good relationships depend on good communication.

*Employee Communications*

The purpose is to promote effective communication of relevant information to employees of Rank Xerox Companies in accordance with natural needs for information and in a standard manner consistent with Company policy.

The subject matter of employee communications should include the following aspects, although the list cannot be comprehensive and meet the requirements of every situation.

*Employee Contract.* The information which companies are legally obliged to communicate to each employee or through works councils or staff associations, e.g., such matters as pay rates, working hours, holidays, grievance procedure, etc.

*Personnel Policies.* Information on Company intent toward employees in general, including, for example, pension schemes, social clubs, management development programmes, social leave policy, etc.

*Company Procedures.* Aspects of internal administration such as how to claim expenses, how to recruit a replacement, how to obtain new stationery, etc.

*Centralised Information Points.* Copies of all the above written information can be helpfully stored at one central point, e.g., Department Secretary, in the Library, etc. This helps an employee to know where to seek information which he needs.

## CASE STUDY: UNILEVER

The Unilever group of companies provides a wide range of products and services in some 75 countries, employing about 300,000 people. In most of these countries the products are manufactured locally. Unilever has existed for more than 50 years as a group, but can trace its roots back much further than that. The company:

- is an Anglo-Dutch business formed in 1930.
- comprises two parent companies with identical boards.
- has a three-man chief executive known as the Special Committee.
- is one of the world's largest producers of consumer goods.
- is known for its branded foods and drinks, detergents and personal products.
- concentrates also on other core activities like specialty chemicals, plantations and UAC International.
- makes 60 percent of its sales in Europe and 20 percent in North America.
- spends about 250 million pounds annually on research and development.

In a brochure titled "Unilever's Responsibilities as an International Business," the company states this about communication:

Our employees understandably want to be better informed about, and more involved in, the progress of the company in which they work. How this is expressed in practice varies from one country to another. In a number of countries, including the Netherlands, there is legislation on co-determination, and a great variety of decisions are taken in close consultation between the company management and the employee-representative bodies concerned. Other countries, like Britain, are still at the stage where companies are experimental with joint consultation. This situation is not surprising since it reflects the often very different ways in which industrial relations have evolved in each country. Because of this, there is no generally applicable procedure. We believe our operating companies in each country are best placed to judge how to respond constructively. In countries where there are no laws in this respect we expect our companies to respond actively to their employees who want to know more about decisions affecting them and to have their views taken into account.

# West Germany

*Official Name:* Federal Republic of Germany; *Capital:* Bonn; *Government:* federal republic; *Subdivisions:* 10 states; *Population:* 60,989,419 (July 1987); *Density:* 642.8 per square mile; *Currency:* Deutsch Mark; *Official Language:* German; *Literacy:* 99 percent.

*The Land.* West Germany is slightly smaller than the state of Oregon. The country occupies a central position in northern Europe and has borders with Denmark to the north, the German Democratic Republic (East Germany) and Czechoslovakia to the east, Austria and Switzerland to the south, and France, Luxembourg, Belgium and the Netherlands to the west. It also has coastlines on the North Sea to the northwest and the Baltic to the north. There are four geographical zones: the wide lowlands in the north, the central uplands, the wide valley and gorge of the Rhine River in the south and west, and the mountains and plateaus of the south. Some 54 percent of West Germany's land remains either in pasture or crop land; another 29 percent is forest. The industrialized areas are highly concentrated. Beyond them are medieval cities, vineyards, broad river valleys and old-world towns dominated by fortressed castles.

About 33 percent of the land is cultivated; 29 percent is forest; 23 percent is meadow and pasture; 13 percent is waste or urban; and 2 percent is inland water.

*The People.* Germany is 97 percent homogeneous. There are nearly 4,000,000 foreigners (mostly Turks, Yugoslavians, Italians, Danes and Greeks) in the country.

Discipline, cleanliness, efficiency and a strong sense of duty are among the outstanding characteristics for which Germans are known. Germans pride themselves on their ability to manage a densely populated land and a burgeoning economy effectively. Germans are generally a conservative and hardworking people with a tendency toward formality and reserve. They share a common heritage which combines Teutonic strands (like the Scandinavians) with Latin and Slavic elements. West Germany shares its border with ten nations and there is a consequent intermixing with other cultures.

About 45 percent of the people are Roman Catholic; 44 percent Protestant; and 11 percent other.

In "A Cross-cultural Study of Values of Germans and Americans," Beatrice K. Reynolds of the University of Houston, Victoria, found differences between the two peoples in authoritarianism, individualism and concepts of self and society. Germans combine individualism with loyalty to the widest culturally defined group—the state. Germans take pride in self-control and have a self-concept that is related to "rational striving" with which the sociocentric virtues of loyalty, kindness and honesty relate positively. They are aware of their obligation to the state and make sacrifices accordingly. Americans are more egocentric in pursuing personal interests, feeling an obligation to self and an unconscious need for achievement. Americans believe that each person working for his or her own good will mean the greatest good for the largest number.[40]

*A Brief History.* German history is at first that of the Germanic tribes such as the Angles, Saxons, Alemans and Franks. The banks of the Rhine were a battleground for these warlike tribes until they were politically united under Charlemagne around A.D. 800. Otto I, Saxon king of Germans, is credited with the creation of the Holy Roman Empire in 962.

After 1250 the powerful unity of the Empire began to decrease, while the power of territorial princes increased. Germany was the center of the Reformation, initiated by Martin Luther in 1517.

Germany did not become a nation-state until 1871. Prior to that it was divided for much of its history into a patchwork of small states and principalities under the Holy Roman Empire. After the unification engineered by the Prussian leader Otto von Bismarck, Germany became a powerful, modern, industrialized, military state, but was politically and socially less developed.

Germany lived through the devastation of the two world wars. Two decades after World War II, however, West Germany is the most prosperous nation in Europe. It is also a partner in the Western alliance. Formed out of the American, British and French zones of occupation in 1949, the Federal Republic signed a "peace contract" with the United States, Britain and France in 1952. It attained full sovereignty in 1955, the same year it became a member of the North Atlantic Treaty Organization and pledged itself (on French insistence) never to manufacture nuclear arms.

*The Economy.* The labor force is divided this way: industry, 41.6 percent; services and other, 34.7 percent; trade and transport, 18.2 percent; agriculture, 5.4 percent; and unemployed, 9 percent. About 34 percent of the labor force is unionized.

Although the economy has experienced some problems in recent years, West Germany is still one of the world's wealthiest industrial powers. It is rich in three resources: coal, potash and salt—needed for the pharmaceutical industry. West Germany makes fertilizers, dyes, synthetic fibers, plastics and industrial chemicals. It has giant iron and steel works in the Ruhr. Close by are plants for making steel products like machinery, fine tools, cutlery. The country has major producers of cameras, clocks and watches. It ranks fourth in the world in steel manufacturing and third in the automotive industry. Textiles manufactured are cotton, woolens, silks and linen goods. It engages in making sugar, beer and wine, leather goods, paper, aluminum, cars and toys.

Along 3,000 miles of highways roar 10 million Volkswagens, Porsches, Opels and Mercedeses. Across the country rise modern factories turning out an endless tide of products each year: 2.9 million cars, buses and trucks, 6.4 million radio and television sets, 37 million metric tons of steel.

The two common forms of German corporations are the *Gesellschaft mit beschränkter Haftung,* or GmbH, a limited-liability, joint-stock private company whose stock is not quoted publicly, and the *Aktiengesellschaft,* or AG, a full public company with limited liability and quoted shares. Shareholders of the latter meet annually in a *Hauptversammlung* where they elect the *Aufsichtsrat,* or Supervisory Board, which appoints the *Vorstand,* or Executive Board, the company's decision-making body. The *Vorstand* usually has a chairman and deputy chairman and its members also have departmental responsibility. The smaller GmbH companies usually have a single chief executive, titled *der Geschaftsfuhrer,* to whom departmental managers report.

German management is unique in many ways. In 1952, the *Betriebsverfassungsgesetz* was passed, establishing a *Betriebsrat,* or Works Council, for all organizations with more than five employees. Such councils existed in the 1920s and came into existence spontaneously after World War II. Figure 17 shows how the Works Council is positioned in Hoechst AG. Laws passed in 1972 and 1976 gave the Work Councils the right of *Mitbestimmungsrecht,* or codetermination, in regard to the appointment of workers to new positions, internal transfers of workers, transfers between different wage groups, filling newly created internal posts, dismissals, setting the start and finish of the work day, deciding when breaks should be taken, fixing canteen prices, preventing and investigating industrial accidents and holiday arrangements.[41] In large companies with 500 or more employees, one-third of the directors must be representatives of the employees, except in large coal and steel industries where half the supervisory board must be employees.

The result of this arrangement is a surprisingly cordial relationship between management and labor:

> There is no solid working class in Germany. Leaders of industry tend to meet any reasonable demands of the workers more than halfway, and strikes stand opposed to that general social prestige which is more important than money. The result is something that never ceases to astonish the Americans, English, and French: that the numerically large and seemingly powerful German unions, with their 6 million members, do not play a decisive role in the republic's political and economic life.[42]

Another result is enhanced communications. "In a crisis," explains Ferdinance Turek, a worker director at Siemens, "co-determination has proven efficient because the workers understand more about what is going on." Says worker director Ferdinand Nieswandt, chairman of Krupp's supervisory board: "Worker directors pass information down to the works councils. There's a permanent flow of information from top to bottom and back. As a result there is a better relationship between workers and management."[43]

Secrecy also has a significant role in German business and its general aura is pervasive. Top management's ostensible justification for this condition is that lower levels should not be bothered with bigger issues. They might disturb the *Arbeitsfrieden* — the peaceful work environment. Probably closer to the truth, information represents power and power is the name of the German decision-making game. The consequence for the foreigner is that obtaining information is difficult. This difficulty leads to longer negotiations, since necessary data will be released only bit by bit.

Germans form ad hoc groups in order to solve problems. This concept is sometimes called matrix management. The overall German orientation is technical and factual. From the beginning, the visitor should stress concrete, tangible concepts. Germans in business downplay imagination; expansive presentations tend to be written off as fantasy. Orderly, logical presentations, on the contrary, deserve respect. Explanations delivered with a dogmatic air carry the cachet of truth; authorities, real or imagined, are right.

# Works Constitution of Hoechst AG

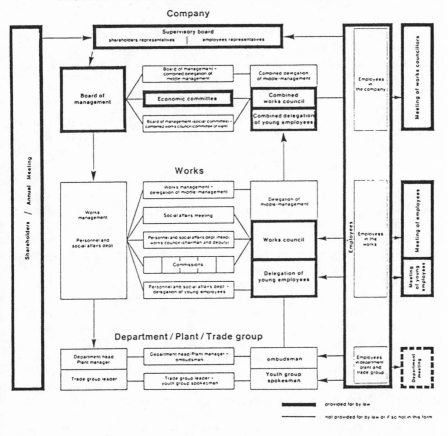

**Figure 17. Works Councils in Hoechst AG, Frankfurt am Main, West Germany.**

Over 40 percent of German managers have had an engineering-oriented education. Another 20 percent come from the field of theoretical economics. Most of them have been trained in the fundamentals of industrial administration. Typical German executives are not professionally mobile. Over 80 percent of them have had only one or two employers in their lifetimes. This constancy makes for company loyalty and a well-trained managerial cadre. A deep sense of duty and obedience is pervasive, particularly in middle management.

Recent attitude surveys try again and again to demonstrate a fading of the work ethic. Self-enhancement and self-indulgence are presented as the values of the new Germans. Perhaps the young man outside the system or the man at the lathe or the press feels the system is secure and that he can slow down or even slack off. German management, however, remains as devoted and hard driving as ever. These men unstintingly do their duties. They identify with their workplace and their self-esteem derives in part from work performance.

The decision-making process and the locus of power are German in design, structure and purpose. Power flows from the top down, but carefully and slowly from one organizational level to the next.

German management theory has been dominated by technical concerns. Sociology, or the human side of the enterprise, has played a minor role. As a result, German organization is hierarchically oriented, and wide vertical participation in decision making is not practiced. Participative management and even decision making decentralization receive considerable lip service, but neither is thoroughly implemented.

German society is paternalistic. The father is at least the titular head of the family. This structure extends to the workplace where boss-as-father is the typical pattern. The workers themselves charge the man in power with making decisions and taking responsibility.

In a small or medium-size company, or in a family-controlled company, decision making is typically centralized at the top. Often one individual makes judgments on virtually all issues. Larger corporations must pass major policy decisions through their boards of directors.

Major industries are chemicals, clothing, electrical engineering, electronics, food processing, iron and steel, mechanical engineering, mining, motor vehicles and transport equipment and textiles.

Cash-rich German firms are today taking over American firms because of the weak dollar and as a way to enter the American market. Siemens, the electronics company that has several branches in New Jersey, recently took over Tel-Plus Communications, a Florida-based distributor of office telephone equipment. American Hoechst Corporation of Bridgewater, New Jersey, bought Celanese Corporation, making its Frankfurt-based parent the world's largest chemical producer. Tengelmann Group, the German supermarket chain, is majority owner of The Great Atlantic and Pacific Tea Company of Montvale, New Jersey, which operates A&P food stores.

> In Germany, we think international [Dr. Klaus E. Goehrmann, chairman of the Hannover Trade Fair Authority in West Germany said]. We have to because 35 percent of our gross national product is exports. We all look at this amazing U.S. market with good infrastructure and good distribution. Why should you then sell in Nigeria? That is why the effort to gain shares or position in the U.S. market will be even more dramatic in the next few years.[44]

The country has adopted a new *Drang nach Osten* (drive to the East) policy, part of which is a $2.1 billion credit line seven banks have granted to the Soviet Union since the Intermediate Nuclear Forces (INF) Treaty was signed in 1988.

*Organizational Communication.* In Germany a quality a business person must try to acquire and apply in any cultural environment is *Fingerspitzengefuhl,* meaning literally, "sensitivity in the tips of your fingers."

In Germany 6/7/88 means the sixth of July in 1988 — not the seventh of June. This system, used throughout Europe, is quite logical in writing the day, month and year. A new international standard has been approved, but is not widely used, with the sequence of first year, then month, then day.

Germans have discussed effective letter writing since the eighteenth century when they created *Briefsteller,* books of sample letters for all occasions to encourage people to write good business letters.[45]

In both social and business relationships, Germans are more formal than Americans. Most German executives will not see a visitor unless he has arranged a firm date well ahead of time. An inborn sense of order and an aversion to surprises justify this position. Appointments are best set up by mail, although a telex or a phone call may be suitable once contact has been established.

An initial letter sent to a German company might receive a confusing response with two signatures, no typed names below them and no names in the letterhead. What do you do to reply? The letter also has a reference number in the upper right-hand corner, and using that, you can write the company and ask the names of the gentlemen who signed the letter. The names are obscured to highlight the name of the company.

The custom of putting dual signatures on German correspondence is indicative of German management practice. Frequently the signature on the right belongs to a functional specialist; that on the left, to a person with authority. Both signers represent their company first and foremost, and the personalization implied by spelling out their names would be improper. Another explanation for dual signatures might be that the foreigner's subject has touched areas of overlapping responsibility in the German firm, and both departments involved have recorded a reply. Finally, two signatures may be the result of company rules specifying that one of the individuals may act only in conjunction with, or supported by, another member of the enterprise.

In West Germany, you may gauge the importance of the people you meet by the initials preceding their names on business cards and in correspondence. A *ppa (pro procura)* or *Prokurist* has registered signing authority; he's a key decision maker, with broad powers to negotiate for management. An *i.V.* or *in Vollmacht* (in full power), can also negotiate, but his decision making authority is limited. If your first contact is with an *i.A., im Auftrag,* meaning "signing for another," he's not a decision maker, even though he may represent his firm in initial face-to-face meetings.

Appointments should be sought with persons at the highest possible level. In small or medium size concerns — which constitute 75 percent of all German business — that would be the head of the firm.

If the visitor is punctual, he probably will not wait long. A delay in the secretary's anteroom would be brief. In the meantime, this room may offer some clue as to the status of the person being visited. The secretary whose office has an outside window and is decorated with fine wood furniture probably works for a high-level executive.

A peculiar mannerism should be mentioned regarding encounters with Germans in a group. It is appropriate to greet collectively people who have congregated for some apparently common purpose. Germans entering the breakfast room in a hotel, for example, say a general *guten Morgen.* Similar encounters — walking into a small shop or a waiting room — might best be accompanied with a *guten Tag.*

**Figure 18. Personal contact is important in most European firms, including this German one. (Zahnradfabrik Friedrichshafen, Friedrichshafen, West Germany.)**

A vigorous handshake is proper and required when meeting a German. A recent survey in a major German industrial concern revealed that the average employee spent 20 minutes of his working day shaking hands. Conform to this established practice with a firm handshake. When you shake hands, the older person or one with highest position holds his hand out first. If several Germans are present, the visitor must shake hands with all of them. The most senior man will extend his hand first. The typical introduction during this greeting includes the surname only. Since the German admires longevity, if your company is an old one, have its founding date printed on your business cards. Personal contact, like that in Figure 18, is important in German corporations.

The German concept of "business secrecy" is also important. A meeting usually begins after the office door has been closed. When the meeting starts, a little small talk is certainly in order. Topics such as sports, cars, apolitical current events, or comments about the city are proper.

Privacy is highly respected in Germany. That is why doors are closed and why personal topics are best omitted from opening conversations. In German organizations, if you can be seen outside the occupant's office door, you are felt to have entered the office by entering the person's field of vision, which is rather rude before being formally invited inside. Humor or funny occurrences are best avoided. Germans have their own sense of humor and understanding it takes time.

Germans are not initially outgoing. They do not attempt to build bridges between people. By no means, however, should aloofness be confused with ineptitude: German business acumen is high. To them formality merely enhances communications. The overall atmosphere of the first meeting, therefore, will be formal, distant, somber and *feierlich*. Germans find such spiritual solemnity appropriate for business dealings. Things have a definite order and as long as this solemnity seems to please the Germans, it would be improper to disrupt it.

Germans also dislike disarray, a deviation from the expected. Their sense of *Ordnung* encompasses status, time, plan, appearance and behavior. In the latter instance, it is tied to discipline. Things must not just "be" in order, they must "look" as though they are in order.

Perhaps the key rule for the visitor is restraint. The initial presentation must be a soft sell. It is entirely out of order to begin with an open-throttled pitch outlining superior goods or services. In fact, the Germans may take offense at this approach, since they are justly proud of their own achievements.

All materials presented to Germans should be precise. Printing errors, overprints or hand-written corrections are amateurish. The local businessman is a professional; inattention to detail creates an unfavorable impression.

The initial negotiating phase will come to a conclusion after a relatively short period of time. It is up to the visitor to note when it is time to leave.

There appears to be no correct moment for offering a business card. In social circumstances, it is offered when meeting a stranger. In business, the card may be attached to printed material or more commonly, exchanged just prior to leaving a meeting. The visitor should always take the initiative in this gesture.

Before leaving a meeting, one should shake hands with all members present. The top man should be offered the first goodbye.

Demeanor is very important during negotiations. Voice control and speech methods are significant. German meetings are at times dominated by a man with a *Besehlstimme,* a commanding tone. His purpose is to project authority and self-confidence. A visitor should not attempt parade ground tactics, but his delivery should be firm and command confidence. Nothing could be worse than sounding hesitant, doubtful or uninformed.

Hands should be used with calculated dignity. They should never be jammed into pockets, nor serve as lively instruments to emphasize points in conversation. The entire game plan is to appear calm under pressure.

All agreements will ultimately be executed in writing. Whereas elsewhere it may be customary to leave some items to trade practice, or even to hold some contractual clauses open while working things out, German agreements are completely "nailed down." There is no leeway for ambiguity and virtually nothing is left to interpretation.

German business people have become more and more conservative in both attitude and dress. The message is clear: seriousness of purpose goes hand-in-hand with serious attire.

**Table 16. Some Communication Practices in the German Corporation**

The Germans:

1. Expect appointments to be made well in advance of meeting dates.

2. Consider mail the best method for communicating, although telex and the telephone can be used when a relationship is established.

3. Strive for *Fingerspitzengefuhl* for *Arbeitsfrieden*.

4. Write letters in a different way from Americans.

5. Begin meetings punctually, thanks usually to one with a *Besehlstimme*.

6. Are formal in both social and business relations.

7. Shake hands vigorously.

8. Address almost immediately the reason for the meeting.

9. Tolerate no disorder in status, time, place, appearance or behavior.

10. Consider demeanor during discussions very important.

11. Prize privacy highly.

12. Expect presentations to be precise in every detail.

13. Favor "soft sell" over "hard sell."

14. Will hold you to a contract if you lead them to believe that one exists.

15. Expect visitors to take the initiative in exchanging business cards — at any time during meetings.

16. Prefer visitors who appear calm under pressure.

17. Expect all agreements to be put in writing.

18. Admire longevity in companies.

19. Have a low-context culture.

20. Use time monochronically.

The German office worker closes his door in order to avoid distraction. He does his work privately and interaction with other people is not part of a desirable routine. The visitor to West Germany must respect the inviolability of the office. Before entering any closed door, therefore, he should observe common courtesies by knocking and waiting for the invitation to enter or for the occupant to open the door.

The protocol of left and right sides is important. For instance, it is proper for a junior executive to walk on the left side of the senior manager. A gentleman always walks on the lady's left. Seating at table follows the same placement.

Moderation and modesty in personal behavior will leave a good impression. One must not be too ebullient, too friendly, too nonchalant or too pushy.

Under both German and Swiss law, if you induce a party to believe a

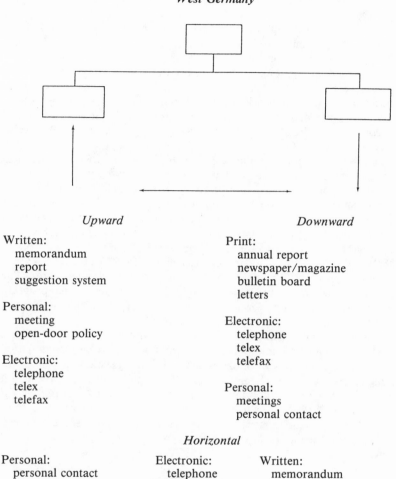

*Upward*

Written:
  memorandum
  report
  suggestion system

Personal:
  meeting
  open-door policy

Electronic:
  telephone
  telex
  telefax

*Downward*

Print:
  annual report
  newspaper/magazine
  bulletin board
  letters

Electronic:
  telephone
  telex
  telefax

Personal:
  meetings
  personal contact

*Horizontal*

Personal:
  personal contact
  meeting

Electronic:
  telephone
  telex
  telefax

Written:
  memorandum

**Figure 19. Communication in the West German corporation.**

contract will be concluded and the contract does not materialize, you may be liable for damages.

Table 16 lists some communication practices of the German firm, and Figure 19 shows the corporate communication system of the German firm.

## CASE STUDY: BMW

The history of BMW is characterized by three waves. Each time BMW was forced to make a new start in its development. This happened the first time at the end of World War I, shortly after the company had been established. The production of aircraft engines was forbidden in Germany—and aircraft engines were BMW's only product line.

The bottom of the second wave came at the end of World War II: BMW, an arms company at the time, was first closed down; then its facilities were dismantled. This seemed to be the end of the road. With the German currency reform, however, the company made a new start. But just a dozen years later the BMW story appeared to be over once and for all: The Board of Management recommended the sale of the company. Why, then, did BMW survive even this critical phase?

Among other things, the history of BMW is a story of technical innovation—a story often linked with just a few names and a chain of technical successes that became the basis for BMW's sporty reputation.

The BMW symbol presents this image clearly and convincingly: the ancient symbol of the wheel and cross, of continuous motion and the target. Even back in 1920—when BMW was still next to nothing—this symbol was used in a collage by Hannah Hoch to represent the world of mobility.

BMW publishes a company newspaper founded in 1973—a monthly given to every employee—and includes an issue that covers the annual report. The annual report is also made available to employees. A quarterly video program is available, especially made for staff information purposes. The latest video program lasts two hours and costs $6 per cassette.

As usual in German companies there are staff meetings held several times a year where management and union representatives report on the company, production, sales, business outlook, and so on. A suggestion scheme is encouraging employees to suggest useful ideas that mainly affect the production details of cars. A bonus for good ideas may add up to DM 100 (more than US $50). A specialty of BMW is called *Learnstatt,* a system of employee meetings somewhat similar to quality circles. This system was invented some ten years ago, and in the meantime has become a good example to improve staff relations.

## CASE STUDY: KRUPP

Fried. Krupp of Essen manufactures technologically demanding materials, complex machinery, systems and installations; it also provides engineering, commercial and other services. Company structure provides for unified direction under the parent company Fried. Krupp GmbH, which has delegated to the subsidiary companies the responsibility and authority for business operations, thereby combining the flexibility of a market- and operations-oriented, decentralized management with the advantages and the strengths of a large company.

Management informs the employees in timely and complete fashion about events and developments that are significant with respect to their work. Management informs them also about basic facts concerning the company, thereby promoting work morale and company loyalty. Management encourages employees to seek on their own accessible information as necessary in the performance of their work. The employees in timely fashion inform

**Figure 20. Employees of VIAG Aktiengesellschaft, Berlin/Bonn, West Germany, confer in the field. (VIAG.)**

management about work results and about events that are significant with respect to work progress or that deviate from the normal course of events.

## CASE STUDY: VIAG

VIAG AG, a holding company, was founded in 1923 to unite diverse industrial firms under centralized, efficient management. Today, VIAG is one of Germany's 50 largest corporations with worldwide sales of more than DM 12 billion. The Group includes more than 100 firms in Germany and abroad, with over 30,000 employees involved in marketing and manufacturing operations in Europe, Australia, Canada and the United States. The VIAG group is decentralized and its management style reflects this principle. In practice, this means a high degree of independence and responsibility for performance. VIAG's corporate philosophy is to concentrate on carefully directed diversification and risk-spreading in three main sectors, each with a secure future: Energy, Aluminum and Chemicals.

Regarding communication, the Company views information exchange as an essential prerequisite for smooth and efficient cooperation, preventing bad decisions, misunderstandings and interpersonal tension. One instance of such an exchange of information is shown in Figure 20. Management must accordingly inform employees in a timely and comprehensive fashion, and with emphasis on company context, about everything that is necessary for the performance of work tasks. In return, all employees are to inform their supervisors and others as may be called for about significant developments and events in their area of responsibility. Implementation takes several forms: (1) The managing committee makes sure that employees are being informed about important events and developments in the company. (2) Information that is important to all employees is announced in the company magazine, in special notices, memoranda or company meetings. (3) Core areas and sectors keep each other informed about changes in their areas of work. (4) Management informs the employees in individual and group discussions and may open up other communications channels to them (technical literature, other departments, seminars, etc.). (5) The employees are to exercise personal initiative in obtaining necessary information.

# OTHER EUROPEAN COUNTRIES

## Austria

*Official Name:* Republic of Austria; *Capital:* Vienna; *Government:* republic; *Subdivisions:* 9 states; *Population:* 7,569,283 (July 1987); *Density:* 231.7 per square mile; *Currency:* schilling; *Official Language:* German; *Literacy:* 98 percent.

*The Land.* Austria (Osterreich) means "Eastern Empire" and in A.D. 788 it referred to the eastern reaches of Charlemagne's conquests. Landlocked and a little smaller than Maine, Austria is a tiny country of magnificent scenery which clings to the sides of three mountain ranges of Alps that cross the country from west to east. The country stretches from the Federal Republic of Germany to sunny Italy, from the Iron Curtain to Switzerland. The Danube runs through the northeast.

Austria borders more countries than does any other Western European country but West Germany: West Germany and Czechoslovakia lie to the north, Hungary to the east, Yugoslavia to the southeast, Italy to the south and Switzerland and Liechtenstein to the west.

About 38 percent of the land is forest; 26 percent is meadow and pasture; 20 percent is cultivated; 15 percent is waste or urban; and 1 percent is inland water.

*The People.* The Austrians are famous for their *Gemutlichkeit,* a relaxed and happy approach to life. A good natured sense of frustration and a bittersweet attitude toward reality are peculiar national traits.

On Christmas Eve, 1984, the author drove from Italy into Austria, hoping to reach Vienna. A driving snowstorm cut the trip off at Graz, however, where refuge was found in a hotel. Everything else was closed excepting a restaurant or two, and the Christmas Spirit was everywhere. People stopped this camera-carrying American on the street to wish the best of the season. One television program after another featured musicians from around the country, many of them oom-pa-pa bands, playing Christmas carols, particularly "Silent Night" which was written by an Austrian priest.

Some 99.4 percent of all Austrians are of Germanic descent, but there are also tiny Croatian (0.3 percent) and Slovene (0.2 percent) minorities and 0.1 percent of other groups. About 88 percent of the population are Roman Catholic; 6 percent are Protestant; and 6 percent are other.

*A Brief History.* Austria was part of both the Roman Empire and Charlemagne Empire. Taking control in the thirteenth century, the royal Hapsburg family ruled Austria for 600 years. The Hapsburgs built up the country through judicious marriages rather than war and were instrumental in pushing the Turks out of Europe after the eighteenth century. Austria's power peaked in the early nineteenth century after it helped defeat Napoleon, but the Hapsburg empire declined because of growing nationalism.

In 1914, the assassination of Archduke Francis Ferdinand, heir to the Hapsburg throne, triggered World War I and led to the eventual demise of the Austro-Hungarian Empire in 1918. Until then, Austria did a brisk business within its own territory of the Empire which stretched into present-day Hungary, Czechoslovakia, Poland, Romania, Italy and Yugoslavia. After World War I the empire collapsed and the Treaty of Versailles set up the vastly reduced first Austrian republic (1918–38) which struggled for acceptance and survival, but was eventually swallowed up into Hitler's Germany and suffered with it through World War II. After 1945, Austria was divided into four areas, each governed by one of the four powers (United States, Great Britain, France and the Soviet Union). Ten years later, it was reborn as an independent and neutral democratic republic.

*The Economy.* The labor force is divided this way: services, 57.6 percent; industry and crafts, 41.1 percent; agriculture and forestry, 1.4 percent; unemployed, 4.8 percent. Some 67 percent of the labor force is unionized.

Left out of the EEC, Austria promptly joined another group called the European Free Trade Association (EFTA) with Great Britain, Denmark, Norway, Sweden and Portugal.

Austrians work oil fields; mine iron, magnesium, copper and zinc; process steel; farm; and tend their forests. But their number one business is to cater to the thousands of tourists who flock in winter and summer. Since World War II, Austria's economic base has been transformed from agriculture to industry. The visiting business person may be bewildered by the forest of red tape and paperwork in which he becomes entangled.

By law, firms with a staff of more than five must have elected workers' representatives; firms with 20 or more must have elected workers' councils. These groups participate in the setting of personnel policy, management decisions and working conditions. Disputes over division of work, transfers, dismissals, and other matters are settled by the joint decision of employers and workers' councils. Workers receive two bonuses each equal to one month's pay—one in June and the other in December.

Major industries are ceramics, chemicals, electronics, food and beverages, iron and steel, mechanical engineering, metal goods, paper manufacturing and processing, petroleum and textiles. Not a single privately owned large multi-

**Table 17. Some Communication Practices in the Austrian Corporation**

The Austrians:

1. Are formal in social and business affairs.

2. Prefer punctuality.

3. Exchange business cards.

4. Shake hands on arrival and departure.

5. Don't use first names at first.

6. Like the business lunch.

7. Have a low-context culture.

8. Use time monochronically.

national has emerged among them. Amid the worldwide revolution in computers, electronics and biotechnology, Austria still excels mainly in tourism.

*Organizational Communication.* Austrians tend to be formal in both social and business dealings, though not so formal as the Germans. Austrian business persons are always punctual and it is considered ill-mannered to arrive more than five minutes late for any appointment. It is a good idea to bring a good supply of business cards; the Austrians are outdone only by the Japanese in their exchange of these cards. Shake hands on arrival and departure, but don't call people by their first names. Use of titles is normal when addressing a business associate. Business decisions are made by top executives. The business luncheon is now very well accepted. Table 17 lists some communication practices in the Austrian corporation.

## CASE STUDY: AUSTRIA TABAK

Founded in 1784 as the Austrian Tobacco Monopoly, the company survived all of the upheavals in national history described above and changed its name between the world wars. In 1949, the government decided that Austria Tabakwerke should remain a joint stock company with the Republic of Austria as the sole shareholder. Following the State Treaty of 1955, the company had to start fresh by modernizing its machinery and automating its processes, calling for reductions in the work force. Because the number of workers was reduced from 4,223 in 1960 to 1,578 in 1982, the company avoided the structural crises of many large companies in the beginning of the 1980s.

Austria Tabak has long thrown off its mantle of officialdom: the bowing and scraping demanded by the dignitaries of the old Tobacco Monopoly have given way to managerial thinking of a modern corporation. Although it is a monopoly, the company is run as if it had to compete against stiff competition. The company has no written communication policy; however, it follows a long and successful practice of working and communication with workers. Informal communication is particularly important in the company due to the political situation—a monopoly operating in a country with two main political parties.

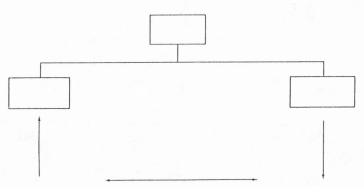

|               | Upward | Downward |               |
|---------------|--------|----------|---------------|

<table>
<tr><td>Upward</td><td>Downward</td></tr>
</table>

| Upward | Downward |
|--------|----------|
| Written:<br>  memorandum<br>  report<br>  suggestion system<br><br>Personal:<br>  meeting<br>  interview<br>  open-door policy<br>  grievance procedure<br><br>Electronic:<br>  telephone<br>  telex | Print:<br>  annual report<br>  newspaper/magazine<br>  bulletin board<br>  letters<br><br>Electronic:<br>  telephone<br>  film<br>  videotape<br>  electronic mail<br><br>Personal:<br>  meetings<br>  seminars<br>  training sessions |

*Horizontal*

| Personal: | Written: | Electronic: |
|-----------|----------|-------------|
|   personal contact<br>  meeting<br>  trade union activities<br>  employees' council |   memorandum<br>  letters |   telephone<br>  telex |

**Figure 21. Communication system at Austria Tabak.**

Most employees — some third- and fourth-generation workers — stay with the company mostly until retirement so that the turnover rate is very low compared to other companies. The company sponsors informal activities such as use of a company-owned dwelling, sports activities, company's holiday welfare facilities, social events, etc. The communication system of Austria Tabak is shown on Figure 21.

————————————— **Finland** —————————————

*Official Name:* Republic of Finland; *Capital:* Helsinki; *Government:* republic; *Subdivisions:* 12 provinces; *Population:* 4,939,880 (July 1987); *Density:* 37.7 per square mile; *Currency:* markka; *Official Languages:* Finnish, Swedish; *Literacy:* 99 percent.

*The Land.* Finland is the northernmost country in Europe, reaching to within 1,370 miles of the North Pole. About the size of New Mexico, Finland ranks fifth in size among European countries and stretches 700 miles from the Gulf of Finland in the south to north of the Arctic Circle. The distance across Finland from the Gulf of Bothnia to the Russo-Finnish border is only 335 miles at the widest point.

Some 57 percent of its area is forest, 9 percent lakes and rivers, and 8 percent cultivated land. Finland has about 65,000 lakes. Standing between the East and West blocs, and lying partially above the Arctic Circle and partially in the North Temperate Zone, Finland represents a human triumph in a severe political and physical environment. The land frontier with Sweden to the west is 364 miles long; with Norway to the north it is 445 miles long; and with the Soviet Union to the east it is 703 miles long.

The country can be divided into three geographical areas: the low fertile plains of south and southwestern Finland; the lake district of central Finland with 55,000 lakes; and north and northeastern Finland with barren mountains and extensive forests. Only about 9 percent of the land is arable.

Finland can be described as civilization in the rough. Its modern, clean, beautifully designed cities are surrounded by some of the most scenic virgin countryside in the world, a patchwork of dense forests and many lakes. About 58 percent of the land is forest; 34 percent is other; and 8 percent is arable.

*The People.* Finland is one of the most sparsely populated countries in Europe. A large majority of the people are Finns, though a significant Swedish minority exists as do very small minorities of native Lapps as well as Tatars and Gypsies. Due to the extreme northern location of Finland, more than half of the population lives in the southern part of the country.

Finns enjoy nature. They maintain high ideals of loyalty and reliability, and promises and agreements are taken seriously. Finns are much more reserved in showing emotion than Americans. They are very proud of Finland. The sauna is a Finnish institution; there are more than half a million of them in Finland.

About 97 percent of the Finns are Evangelical Lutheran; 1.2 percent are Greek Orthodox; and 1.8 percent are other.

The Finnish language is closer to Hungarian than to any other language; it bears no relationship to the Scandinavian languages. Finland is often not included in discussions about the Scandinavian countries.

*A Brief History.* About 2000 years ago, a group of people from Russia and Estonia migrated to the area now called Finland. By the A.D. 700s, they had taken the country from the native Lapps. Finland was conquered in 1155 by Sweden and it was for centuries the scene of Swedish-Russian wars. In 1809 the

Russians gained control of the country and Finland became a self-governing entity inside the autocratic Russian empire. It broke away from Russia in 1917 but unfortunately continued to be involved in power struggles. Finland adopted a republican constitution in 1919. It fought and lost a 1939–40 war to keep the Russians from using Finnish territory to build defenses against Germany. In 1941, to recover its lost territory, it joined Nazi Germany in a second war on Russia and lost again. Finland paid the Soviet Union a huge indemnity, ceding a tenth of its land to Russia. Since then, Finland has pursued a policy of cooperation with the Soviet Union as well as friendship with the West.

*The Economy.* The work force is divided this way: services, 27.9 percent; mining and manufacturing 24.5, commerce 20.9, agriculture, forestry and fishing 11.5, transportation and communication 7.6, construction 7.3, and unemployed, 6.2 percent. About 80 percent of the labor force is unionized.

The country's extensive forests are the backbone of the national economy. Thus lumbering and wood-working rank first. They produce plywood, pulp, cellulose, paper, veneer, wallboard, furniture and lumber. Other industrial products include metals, textiles, leather, processed foods, ceramics and glass. Finland has sizable copper reserves; the Outokumpu mine is said to be among Europe's largest.

In almost every firm in Finland, only the top men, at most the top three, count. They see everyone, they travel everywhere, they do all the entertaining — you must see them.

The Finnish businessman's favorite rendezvous is lunch. He has a healthy appetite, prefers to eat fairly quickly and then settle down to business with coffee and brandy. The man who issued the invitation picks up the bill.

Major industries include chemicals, electronics, engineering, food processing, furniture, metals, paper and paper products and textiles.

*Organizational Communication.* Finnish businessmen are generally conservative and formal. Make appointments well in advance and be punctual for all meetings. It is customary to shake hands with men and women when introduced and people may use both hands, but further physical contact is avoided. It is not appropriate to use first names unless invited to do so. Business cards are exchanged, and it is necessary because Finnish names are hard to remember. When conversing, look the other person in the eye.

A sauna bath is often part of the routine hospitality extended to visiting businessmen. One company that uses the sauna as part of its regular communication program is Oy Wilh. Schauman Ab in which get-togethers between management and workers are frequently held in one of the company's saunas.

In the warm, informal atmosphere both sides are more open to frank discussion. The trappings of rank tend to disappear when no one has any clothes on. . . . Schauman's sauna meetings are just one of a variety of informal and formal discussions the wood and engineering company has developed to improve internal communications between management and workers over the past 15 years. All the meetings are organized by a company committee, composed of both management and workers and called appropriately the "cooperation committee."

Most of the company saunas hold about 20 people and a member of the co-operation committee usually sits in to help discussions along. "It's a bit like sensitivity training," explains Major T.U. Wind, head of the personnel department. "We run a little to get warm before we go into the sauna. We drink some beer and eat bread." In the sauna, he continues, "there is no difference between boss and worker. The atmosphere between the two sides is cleansed, and the discussion gets a lot better than before.

"In one factory a conflict between the boss and the workers had gone on for years. They had a gripe session in the sauna for an hour and a half. After this the work climate was much better."

Less urgent needs for two-way communications are catered for by panel discussions and "socio-ethical conferences." In panel discussions a team of experts and the audience together discuss broad questions such as "Should the state take over this company?" Airing such issues helps workers and management comprehend each other's attitudes and ways of thinking, maintains Wind.

The socio-ethical conferences feature guest speakers, often from abroad, and some local religious leaders, whose role originally was to stimulate discussion.

In addition to all these types of meeting, the company has a highly developed participation structure, which is also organized by the co-operation committee. Management and workers regularly take part in sub-committee discussions about housing, information, training, suggestions and welfare.[46]

Table 18 lists some communication practices in the Finnish firm.

## CASE STUDY: VALMET

The Valmet Corporation is a Finnish metal and engineering company with annual sales in excess of 7 billion Finnmarks (US $1.4 billion). Total group personnel is 18,000, out of whom 4,000 work for the company's foreign subsidiaries. Valmet is a state-owned company, its origins dating back to defense manufacturing during Finland's early independence.

A letter to the author from Hakan Nordquist, Vice President, Public Affairs, revealed that Valmet expresses communication policies through several statements, the most important ones being the president's general policies on corporate management; the Public Affairs Department's strategic communication objectives, which form the basis of annual activities and budgets; and the general personnel policies on internal information. Basically all of these speak on behalf of open, two-way communication. The Public Affairs Department uses skillful and well-timed communications as a source of corporate competitive advantage.

Downward communication methods are used in different mixes depending on the corporate unit. There is a wide variety of printed information but verbal communication and meetings with personnel representatives form a significant method as well. Typically leadership in Finland is very personalized and not too formal. They also use electronic means for communicating, including a computer network.

**Table 18. Some Communication Practices in the Finnish Corporation**

The Finns:

1. Are conscientious and formal.
2. Prefer that appointments be made well in advance.
3. Prefer punctuality.
4. Shake hands and sometimes use both hands.
5. Avoid touching during conversations.
6. Dislike using first names until asked to do so.
7. Exchange business cards.
8. Sometimes conduct meetings in a sauna.
9. Have a low-context culture.
10. Use time monochronically.

In addition to all of the usual means of upward communication, employees enjoy a fairly advanced form of employee participation in the Valmet organization. They have a corporation-wide cooperation committee together with management and also a right to nominate representatives to Valmet's Supervisory Board. This method is not common in Finland, although it is in Sweden. In Finland it exists in government-owned companies only.

Informal communication patterns are also very important. The contacts between top management and shop stewards are usually close on the personal level and marked by mutual respect. Informal communication is very important in settling matters of industrial dispute.

Finnish legislation provides for a certain extent of labor participation in preparing decision making in industry. There are rules to follow and employees are always consulted in matters that concern them before final decisions are made by corporate bodies. It is illegal to act otherwise. The Finnish laws on participation are, however, less stringent than those in Sweden.

## Iceland

*Official Name:* Republic of Iceland; *Capital:* Reykjavik; *Government:* republic; *Subdivisions:* 23 counties; *Population:* 244,676 (July 1987); *Density:* 6 per square mile; *Currency:* kronur; *Official Language:* Icelandic; *Literacy:* 99.9 percent.

*The Land.* Slightly smaller in area than Kentucky, Iceland lies in the northcentral Atlantic Ocean about midway between Canada and Europe. It is 2,600 miles from New York, 520 miles from Scotland and about 650 miles from Norway. Almost 80 percent uninhabited, much of Iceland is covered with glaciers, hot geyser sprays or lava. Iceland is one of the most volcanically active countries in the world, averaging one eruption every five years. Earthquakes are also common. The English word "geyser" is Icelandic. About 22 percent of the land is meadow and pasture.

*The People.* Most people are of Norwegian descent, with some mixture of Celtic blood from those who came from Ireland and the Scottish islands. Iceland has an intense interest in education, as is typical of Scandinavian countries, and has one of the highest literacy rates in the world.

Women do not change their names after marriage. Their last name is the possessive form of their father's first name, followed by *dottir*. A man's last name is the possessive of his father's first name, followed by son. Although names in the telephone directory are alphabetized by the "Christian," or first, name it is important to know both first and last names to locate someone.

Icelanders boast of a classless society with virtually no crime. They judge others, they say, on the basis of their ability rather than their station in life. About 95 percent are Evangelical Lutherans, 3 percent are other Protestant and Roman Catholic groups, and 2 percent have no affiliation.

*A Brief History.* The first people believed to have settled in Iceland were Irish monks who came in the eighth century A.D. They left, however, with the arrival of pagan Norsemen in the ninth century. Later immigrants from Sweden and the British Isles arrived. In 930, the Icelanders founded the Althing, their supreme general assembly, the oldest parliament in the world. It is Europe's westernmost country. In 982, an Icelander, Eric the Red, discovered Greenland, and in the year 1000, his son, Leif Ericson discovered North America. Christianity was adopted in the year 1000. Dominated by Norway from 1264 to 1380 and then under Danish control or domination until World War II, Iceland retains close ties with Scandinavia.

*The Economy.* The work force is divided this way: commerce, finance and services, 55.4 percent; agriculture 11.3, fish processing 8, fishing 5, other manufacturing 20.3, and unemployed, 0.9 percent. Some 60 percent of the labor force is unionized. Icelanders live mostly on the coastal shores. Fishing is the major industry; cod, herring and such fishing by products as cod-liver oil account for more than 80 percent of the country's exports. Iceland has one natural resource in abundance: hydroelectric power. Native minerals include diatomite, pumice and calcium carbonate. The most important manufacturing industry is freezing and canning of fish products. Sheepskins and woolen products are also exported. Primary aluminum provides 15 percent of the foreign exchange earnings.

Icelandic firms are small and more often than not the manager is also the owner. Major industries include fish processing, aluminum smelting, diatomite production and hydroelectricity.

*Organizational Communication.* The natives are generally not very punctual but expect others to be. A handshake is the usual form of greeting. Most business persons use business cards. All Icelanders are called by their first name which applies to those with titles also.

# Liechtenstein

*Official Name:* Principality of Liechtenstein; *Capital:* Vaduz; *Government:* hereditary constitutional monarchy; *Subdivisions:* 11 communes; *Population:* 27,074 (July 1987); *Density:* 416 per square mile; *Currency:* Swiss franc; *Official Language:* German; *Literacy:* 100 percent.

*The Land.* Liechtenstein is located in central Europe between Switzerland and Austria in the Alps. A third of the country lies in the upper Rhine Valley. The rest is mountainous.

*The People.* The people of Liechtenstein are homogeneous, stemming from a Germanic tribe — the Alemanni. Liechtenstein is ruled by a 15-member Landtag and a hereditary prince of the House of Liechtenstein. It has no army and only 18 policemen and lives largely by providing a tax shelter for foreign firms.

Some 95 percent of the people are Alemannic; 5 percent are Italian and other. About 82.7 percent are Roman Catholic, 7.1 percent are Protestant, and 10.2 percent are other.

*A Brief History.* Inhabited since the Neolithic Age by Celts, Romans and the Alemanni, the area became a direct fief of the Holy Roman Empire in 1396. The Imperial Principality of Liechtenstein was established in 1719, when the princely House of Liechtenstein, to maintain a seat in the Imperial Diet of the Holy Roman Empire, purchased the territory and gave its name to the region. Liechtenstein became a sovereign nation in 1866. Its ports were administered by Austria until 1920. The country established a customs and monetary union with Switzerland in 1923, a country which has also administered its postal service since 1921. The country remained neutral in both world wars.

*The Economy.* The labor force is divided this way: industry, trade and building, 54.4 percent; services, 41.6 percent; agriculture, fishing, forestry and horticulture, 4 percent. There is no unemployment.

Major industries include electronics, metal manufacturing, textiles, ceramics, pharmaceuticals and food products.

The country has progressed in only three decades from mainly an agricultural economy to a highly industrialized one, producing a wide range of specialized articles.

# Norway

*Official Name:* Kingdom of Norway; *Capital:* Oslo; *Government:* constitutional monarchy; *Subdivisions:* 19 counties; *Population:* 4,178,545 (July 1987); *Density:* 33.6 per square mile; *Currency:* krone; *Official Languages:* Norwegian, Lappish; *Literacy:* 99 percent.

*The Land.* The Norwegian name Norge means "the northern way." Norway's geography has had a profound impact on its inhabitants. On the one side, an almost endless coastline opens Norway's doors to the world; on the other side, rugged mountains isolate its people. With deep waterways called fjords slicing far into its mountainous countryside, Norway has more than 2,000 miles of probably the most jagged coastline in the world on the western part of the Scandinavian peninsula and its length is about 1,100 miles. Neighboring countries are Sweden in the east, Finland and the Soviet Union in the northeast, Denmark in the south (across the Skagerak) and Scotland in the southwest (across the North Sea), and the Norwegian Sea is in the west. Slightly larger than New Mexico, Norway occupies 40 percent of the Scandinavian Peninsula. Almost two-thirds of the land is covered by mountains. About 7 percent of its area consists of 50,000 islands of which 2,000 are inhabited. Only about 3 percent of the land is arable farmland.

*The People.* Germanic and Scandinavian in origin, the population is predominantly Norwegian, with a small indigenous Lapp minority in the north. Norway limits immigration but with the discovery of oil in the North Sea, foreign immigrant workers have become more common.

Tolerance, human kindness and independence are important Norwegian ideals. Neighbors even in larger cities get along very well. Punctuality is very important. The family is very important; husbands and wives consider each other equals. The standard of living in Norway is one of the highest in Europe and poverty is virtually nonexistent.

About 94 percent are Evangelical Lutheran; 4 percent are in other Protestant churches and the Roman Catholic Church; 2 percent are other. Norway is first in the world in the number of books printed per capita.

*A Brief History.* Harold the Fairhaired became the first supreme ruler of unified Norway in A.D. 872. Between 800 and 1000, the Vikings of Norway raided and occupied parts of Europe. Christianity was introduced in 1030. The country was united with Denmark from 1381 to 1814 and then with Sweden from 1814 to 1905. When the Swedish union was dissolved, a Danish prince, Haakon VII, was installed as King of Norway. Nazi Germany attacked Norway on April 9, 1940, and held it until liberation on May 8, 1945.

*The Economy.* The labor force is divided this way: services, 30.9 percent; mining and manufacturing 19.9, commerce 16.7, transportation 8.8, construction 7.6, agriculture, forestry and fishing, 7.2, banking and financial services 5.7, and unemployed, 2.3 percent. Some 66 percent of the labor force is unionized. Norwegian men and women have the world's shortest working week, with just 24.9 hours and 30.6 hours respectively, according to the International Labor Organization.

Norway has long been a nation of the sea and ships. It has the fourth-largest merchant fleet in the world; fishing is a major industry. Less than 4 percent of the land is cultivated, but there is considerable dairying, and vast forests give rise to lumbering and pulp and paper making. Water and mountains provide the country with another blessing: cheap power. The harnessed mountain streams and rivers make Norway the most hydroelectrified country in the world in proportion to population. Norway is a leading aluminum producer. Its coastal region has rich titanium deposits. Other important products include fertilizers, iron ore, paints, metals, ships, machinery, cement, furniture and textiles.

Norway's industry is highly decentralized. Major industries are aluminum smelting, chemicals, electrical machinery, food manufactures, metal products, nonmetallic mineral products, paper and paper products, petroleum and natural gas production, printing and publishing, shipbuilding and transport equipment.

*Organizational Communication.* Arrange appointments at least a week ahead of a meeting. The Norwegian business person is punctual for appointments and expects callers to arrive on time. Business cards are normally exchanged. Norwegian business persons do less business out of their offices than do their British and American counterparts, and most of them dislike business lunches as unnecessarily time consuming. It is common to address men by their last names only (that is, without the "Mr.").

Norwegian companies are active in implementing innovative management programs, particularly when they also involve communications.

Norske Shell AS of Oslo takes attitude surveys of its employees every six months. Fifteen months' preparation went into the development of the survey. Both employees and managers were consulted about the questions that should be asked. The survey is designed to prompt follow-up action. Such was the case when the survey showed that employee attitudes were becoming more negative about the company's annual practice of having each superior sit down with subordinates to assess past performance and future performance. In the survey employees were asked to comment on the statement "The last staff appraisal interview has proved of benefit to my work." The negative results shocked managers who thought they were putting a lot of effort into the interviews. Training sessions in appraisal interviewing were provided.

The question on appraisal interviewing is one of 26 standard statements on the survey questionnaire. They are grouped under eight areas: remuneration, personal development, participation, communications, job satisfaction, work conditions, efficiency and environment. As a tool for management, the surveys have proven their worth. A managing director reports that "They have become an essential tool in our feedback process. We discuss them regularly at our top management meetings."[47]

Another organization trying to do something about communication is the Norwegian Shipowners' Association. One of the more successful experiments has been conducted at Fearnley & Eger, the seventh largest Norwegian company in terms of tonnage. Problems uncovered at this and other companies were that managers said employees never offered ideas for improving the work and employees complained that managers never listened.

In a week-long training session, managers undergo sensitivity-type training to make them more aware of their communication problems and better able to deal with them. To transfer the learning to the workplace, trainers spend three weeks in individual companies, helping managers use the techniques in their work settings with the stated intention of fostering more open communicating. Managers who have completed the training are then appointed "environment worker," to keep the pressure on top management to maintain open communication.

Johan Aamodt, a psychologist in the Norwegian Centre for Organiza-

**Table 19. Some Communication Practices in the Norwegian Corporation**

The Norwegians:

1. Prefer at least a week's notice of meetings.
2. Expect punctuality.
3. Exchange business cards.
4. Dislike the business lunch.
5. Prefer to conduct business in their offices.
6. Address other men by their last name only.
7. Have a low-context culture.
8. Use time monochronically.

tional Learning, suggests following these rules for establishing an atmosphere for open communications to thrive:

1. Accept conflict.
2. Be willing to experiment and learn.
3. Accept oneself and others as they are.
4. Be prepared to ignore position and title.
5. Develop two-way trust with the company leaders.
6. Give no cause for anxiety about the consequences of open behavior.
7. Try to reach an honest understanding of others' points of view.
8. Be sensitive to your own and others' "signals," such as the way things are said, gestures and facial expressions.
9. Be willing to listen to others.
10. Accept deviation in opinion and behavior.
11. Be willing to take risks.
12. Give no cause to fear consequences on the professional level (such as threats to career arising from open behavior).
13. Give security against the misuse of any weak points revealed.
14. Work towards a clear, open environment.[48]

Table 19 lists some communication practices of the Norwegian firm.

## CASE STUDY: NORSK DATA

The company is in the information-technology industry which designs, develops, manufactures, sells and services a compatible line of general purpose minicomputers. Sales and customer support are handled by wholly owned subsidiaries in 11 countries through 62 offices. Norsk Data computers are used for business data processing and for high-speed scientific and technical applications. The business applications include time sharing and transaction processing as well as office support, which covers word processing and information retrieval. Norsk Data is also an end-user oriented supplier of integrated information systems where hardware, software and networking products together with supporting services aim at making people perform better.

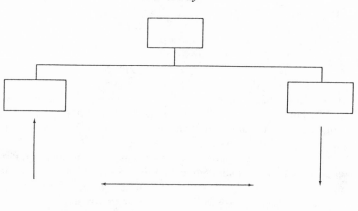

<table>
<tr><td>*Upward*</td><td>*Downward*</td></tr>
</table>

*Upward*

Written:
  memorandum

Personal:
  meeting
  interview
  open-door policy

*Downward*

Print:
  annual report
  newspaper/magazine
  letters/memos
  handbook

Electronic:
  telephone
  videotape
  electronic mail

*Horizontal*

personal contact
meeting
small pause groups at coffee/lunch time

**Figure 22. Communication system of Norsk Data.**

The communication system of Norsk Data is shown on Figure 22. Although the company does not use orientation manuals, one of its pamphlets, called "The ND Spirit," serves somewhat the same purpose. Using a drawn figure that Americans might compare to Caspar the Ghost, but with the ND logo drawn on its "chest," the pamphlet introduces newcomers to the company in a series of drawings and captions:

    *Welcome to Norsk Data. As a member of the ND team, you have the opportunity to become a contributor to the company's success. The way you do this is up to you. However, we will explain a little bit about our style—our "Spirit"—and help you feel at home more quickly. By capitalizing on this style, you can reap both personal and professional rewards.

    *Norsk Data comprises people from all over the world; with varied backgrounds, priorities and contributions to make. Underneath the differences, however, there are some values binding us together. To varying degrees, ND people:

are cooperating individualists,
have a strong personal need to make a contribution,
have a rich dose of initiative,
are willing to take on responsibility, and
are honest to themselves and others.

*These people have made Norsk Data a very special place to be. We are a tightly knit team, relying on strong personal commitment and contribution. Your contribution and behavior make an impact. ND is only a sum of the people who work here.

*You now have the opportunity to use all the pent-up imagination and creativity! Go out and find important, interesting things to do. Invite frank discussion with your colleagues, and find out if the things that you think are important are consistent with the group's goals.

The booklet continues in a similar vein for 15 additional pages, resulting in the best introduction to a company this writer has ever seen.

# Sweden

*Official Name:* Kingdom of Sweden; *Capital:* Stockholm; *Government:* constitutional monarchy; *Subdivisions:* 24 counties; *Population:* 8,383,026 (July 1987); *Density:* 48.7 per square mile; *Currency:* kronor; *Official Language:* Swedish; *Literacy:* 98 percent.

*The Land.* Sweden occupies the eastern half of the Scandinavian Peninsula, the northern tip extending into the Arctic Circle. Rugged mountains and forest in the north, rolling hills in the south and many lakes and rivers make up the country's landscape. Slightly larger than California, Sweden is bounded by Finland in the north and northeast, by the Gulf of Bothnia in the east, by the Baltic Sea in the southeast, by Oresund, Kaltegat and Skagarrak in the southwest and by Norway in the west. It is separated from Denmark and the European continent by the narrow Baltic Straits. The average width of the land is 250 miles; the country extends a thousand miles from north to south, with 90 percent of the people living in the southern part of the country.

Vast forests that cover 61 percent of the land and enormous hydroelectric-power resources are the country's two main assets. Sweden's top products are metal objects ranging from small tools and fine instruments, aircraft, automobiles, and heavy machinery. Close behind are wood products such as cellulose, lumber and paper. Iron smelting plants and foundries also operate in central Sweden. The Swedish glass industry is famous for its artistry.

Seven percent of the land is arable; 2 percent is meadow and pasture; and 36 percent is other.

*The People.* Sweden has a homogeneous white population about 88 percent of which are Swedes. About 12 percent of the people are foreign born or first-generation immigrants, including Finns, Yugoslavs, Danes, Norwegians and Greeks. The Lapps, a small indigenous ethnic minority, live in northern Sweden.

Illiteracy is virtually unknown in Sweden. The Swedish government spends more money per pupil than any other country in the world. According to the Book of World Rankings, the Swedes are the most happy people in the world. Some 33 percent are extremely happy and 33 percent are content with their standard of living. This is twice as many as the average Common Market country, where the least contented are the French with only 7 percent very satisfied and as much as 47 discontented as opposed to the Swedes' 15 percent discontented. Only 1 percent of all Swedes think their lives are really miserable, which is the lowest rate in Europe. This may be why Sweden enjoys the highest life expectancy in the world. It also has one of the lowest birth rates.

Swedes are at the top of the list when it comes to drinking coffee and juice, eating frozen foods and buying newspapers; second in consuming paper products; and third in reading books and owning telephones. Only six countries have more divorces and legal abortions than Sweden and spend more money equipping their soldiers.

About 93.5 percent of the people are Evangelical Lutheran; 1 percent is Roman Catholic; 5.5 percent are other.

*A Brief History.* In the A.D. 800s, Rurik, the semilegendary chieftain of the Swedes, is said to have founded Russia. By the 900s, Swedish influence extended to the Black Sea. Warfare against Norsemen and Danes continued for centuries. Scandinavia was united in 1397 under the queen of Denmark. Sweden became an independent country in 1523 with Gustaf I as ruler. Napoleon's brilliant marshal Jean Baptiste Jules Bernadotte succeeded Karl XIII and founded the present Swedish dynasty in 1818. The last war in Swedish history was fought in 1814 and Norway became part of Sweden until 1905. During the Thirty Years War, Sweden led the Protestant side and in the reign of Charles XII, they all but conquered the whole of northern Europe, including Russia. After the Napoleonic Wars ended in 1815, Sweden turned its energies in other directions, building what is today a thriving economy.

*The Economy.* The labor force is divided this way: services, 32.8 percent; government 30, mining and manufacturing 22, construction 5.9, agriculture, forestry and fishing 5, electricity, gas and waterworks 0.9, and unemployed, 2.8 percent. About 90 percent of the work force is unionized.

Sweden has based its economy on lumber, hydroelectric power and a high-grade steel. Sweden is also producer of merchant ships and fine glassware and its fishing fleets are world-renowned. The country's success has been remarkable. From one of the poorest countries in the early nineteenth century, Sweden has reached the front ranks of the industrialized ones. Economist Paul Samuelson has said this:

> Sweden, which early in the 19th century was one of the poorest countries of Europe, did, by virtue of steady productivity growth and luck in staying out of all wars, reach the front ranks of world affluence. The Swedish miracle was, seemingly, a double miracle.

> There was the one miracle of an egalitarian society: fair shares all around; redistributive graduated tax system; cradle-to-grave social securities in the way of pensions and health services; trade unions that looked out especially

for their lower-skilled members. And all this with the scrupulous maintenance of personal civil liberties; religious freedom; uncensored press; multiple-party democracy and so forth.

More miraculous, experienced observers felt, was the co-existence of this welfare-state egalitarianism with maintained progress in productivity at an impressive rate.[49]

It is always best when dealing with a Swedish company to talk with the top man who is also likely to be the decision maker. Both Sweden and Norway have a problem motivating their managers because once they reach a certain level, they settle in and don't try to advance. The rewards for a higher effort are perceived to be worth less than the effort to win them.[50]

Major industries include cement, chemicals, electronics, iron and steel, machinery, motor vehicles, paper and paper products and ship building.

*Organizational Communication.* Swedes rarely reply to letters. The telephone is seen as quicker and more economical. Use the telephone or telex to make an appointment and then be punctual for it. Be punctual, prepared, direct, technically correct and formal. Don't be overly friendly, as you will seem insincere or pushy. Avoid physical contact, such as pats on the back. Be sober, not flamboyant. Do not waste time. Don't talk or laugh loudly in public places. As in other European countries you should shake hands and present your business card at the start of a meeting. Business lunches and dinners are popular in Sweden.

The upper classes in Sweden address each other in the third person — not using "you." You don't need to change your style in conversations, however, including maintaining eye contact throughout.

Despite their protestations to the contrary, Swedes are the most formal of the Scandinavians; in social interchange they are the most conservative. They get right down to business with no small talk and hardly any gestures. In their struggle to be efficient and productive, they ignore personal and public relations. Some contacts say they are even stiff. Swedish business persons and Sweden in general tend to be somewhat reserved and formal until they have taken a few drinks. These are among the qualities that have transformed Sweden from one of Europe's poorest to one of the most affluent.

Swedish business persons consider it efficient to prepare agendas in advance and to stick to them in meetings, an approach that people from other cultures feel is inefficient and dishonest because it leaves no room for creativity and initiative.[51]

In international business, foreign business persons complain that Swedish representatives are too young. In countries in which wisdom is thought to come with age, this can be a handicap; they were insulted by having to deal with someone they felt was too young to make decisions.

Compliments are vociferously denied by Swedes. Intrusion into one's personal affairs will offend. When the Swede feels his business behavior is appropriately cautious, it may be misinterpreted by others as "indecisiveness." Many Latins consider the Swede "uncommunicative" due to his relatively silent behavior. The Swedes, on the other hand, often consider Latins to be bad

**Table 20. Some Communication Practices in the Swedish Corporation**

The Swedes:

1. Are formal and conservative in business and social affairs.
2. Prefer the telephone or telex communication to writing letters.
3. Expect punctuality.
4. Shake hands and exchange business cards.
5. Get right down to business with no small talk.
6. Use few gestures.
7. Like business lunches and dinners.
8. Address each other in the third person — in the upper classes.
9. Like to maintain eye contact while conversing.
10. Deny compliments vociferously.
11. Expect totally professional presentations.
12. Have a low-context culture.
13. Use time monochronically.

communicators because of their verbal capacity and apparent lack of listening ability.[52]

Table 20 lists some communication practices of the Swedish firm.

## CASE STUDY: ELECTROLUX

This is one of those companies that is so a part of everyone's life that we all think of it as American. But the headquarters for the 400 subsidiaries in 40 countries is in Stockholm. As a decentralized company, it includes a variety of communication philosophies and uses a broad spectrum of communication techniques. With that in mind, a member of the Public Affairs Department described how at least part of the company communicates.

Generally it can be said that an important part of our corporate image is a flexible and non-bureaucratic structure. Thus the contacts between management and staff often are very informal. The Group has no written-down communication policy. The only policy we have is to keep the communication as open and informal as possible. Often it is simpler to choose the telephone than a written memorandum.

For communicating with employees, there are, of course, several channels:

*Electrolux-Rapport* is a magazine that appears 8 times a year for the Scandinavian staff. It contains articles and interviews from our Scandinavian units. This magazine is a very important place to strengthen the interest among the staff for our group projects for quality, training and cost reduction.

\*For our executives we have our management magazine, *Executive.* It has an international approach and is distributed in all countries where we have subsidiaries.

\*For quick news, like for example organizational changes, company acquisitions and new managers, there is a "Newsletter." It has two editions — a Swedish and an English — and appears every second week "globally."

\*The last five years, the Group has made very much effort to build up its global computer-net, for communication via electronic mail. Our target is to equip all employees with their own PC.

\*In connection with publishing of consolidated results, AGM, half-yearly results, company acquisitions, etc., the Group President and CEO always give further details to the subsidiary Presidents in a "President's Letter" that is of a more confidential character. This type of information is always distributed via telex or telefax to the rest of the staff in the subsidiaries as well (i.e., consolidated results, AGM, half-yearly results and company acquisitions).

On the other hand, i.e., when employees want to get in touch with their managers or even the Group Management, the characteristic of this Group is "the open-door policy." It is always possible for any employee to make a call or visit managers, without having to speak "through" a secretary.

We also want the staff to feel that the house magazines are open to them. Suggestion boxes are also a means of communication.

An article in *Magazine X,* a publication for Electrolux executives, presented in interview-style format an article about the President, Anders Scharp, and how he maintains contact with his people during his extensive travels.

Personally, I spend around half of my working hours travelling. It is essential to see things with your own eyes. The problems a subsidiary company manager might be experiencing can be more easily discussed with him on the spot.

Another way of maintaining good contacts at management level is through conferences. This year we have already had what we call national conferences in Italy and Great Britain. Later this autumn, there'll be one in France. Next year, it will be the turn of Germany, Switzerland and the U.S. Then the time will have come round for a new top management conference, like the one held in Nice last year.

Other contact channels include "Magazine X," our international top management magazine, and my President's Letter which I send five or six times a year to around 250 top managers. Otherwise, I write very few letters and memoranda. I receive an enormous amount of mail though. But I never have a chance to read more than a couple of pages in office hours, anything longer than that has to be saved for evenings and weekends.

When I am at Head Office, I spend a good deal of my time on the phone. It is important that people in Electrolux can contact me whenever they like. Of course, there are limits to the level of detail I can take an interest in, but this normally becomes clear quite quickly.[53]

## CASE STUDY: PROCORDIA

The Statsforetag Group was founded in 1969 by the Swedish Government to centralize State ownership of certain state-run companies. The Group had heavy losses during the years 1976–1982. The problem was accentuated in 1981 and 1982 as the financial resources had been fully consumed. On December 31, 1982, Statsforetag was restructured. The reconstruction provided a more reasonable balance between equity, earning capacity and expected capital balance between equity, earning capacity and expected capital requirements. The reconstruction was effected formally by the State's taking over the shares of some companies, at their book value. The sale meant that substantial assets were replaced.

Since 1984 the Group has been further restructured in order to reach a concentrated and balanced structure. The profit for 1984 was 533,000,000 Swedish kronor and in 1985, 733,000,000. The Group expected to reach a profit exceeding K800,000,000 for 1986. In January 1985 Statsforetag changed its name to Procordia.

### Procordia Communication Policy

Every employee of the Group must be given an opportunity to become involved and to participate in the processes which shape Procordia.

To enable everyone — in their job and with their knowledge and experience — to contribute to this work, it is necessary for our business objectives and philosophies to be communicated, i.e., to be made clear and to enjoy support at all levels internally. The purpose of such communications is to enable all Procordia employees in different ways to follow the continuous internal dialogue on the aims and methods of our operations, in order that they can then manifest their responsibility at work.

Creating such conditions is part of managerial responsibility within the Group.

In order to achieve the "right" communications climate, it is necessary for every corporate group and company within Procordia to think through the plan for both internal and external communications.

This work must be decentralized and can be carried out in many ways, but it has to be consistent with the business and communications objectives that apply to the Group and the respective company.

In this way, together we open a "circulatory system" for the communications required for the overall task of bringing about change — a give and take that may be crucial to how effectively we succeed in implementing our process of renewal.

A number of conditions must characterize communication at Procordia:
*Communications are a business responsibility for every manager and executive within the Procordia Group, a powerful tool in the operative management of our businesses.
*Communications are an administrative instrument for applying the "seven S's."

*Every executive must thus assess his or her communications resources.
*Procordia needs a strong, clear, obviously positive image.
*Key concepts are efficiency, decisiveness, dynamism and optimism.
*This image is shaped through active, businesslike actions which are effectively communicated.
*The responsibility for creating the desired image rests with both the Parent Company and with each company in the Group.
*This image is established and reinforced by an interplay and a division of responsibility between central and local levels.
*This applies both to internal and external work.
*In each company in the Group, there should be a communications plan adapted to that company.
*These plans must include objectives, target groups, activities, timetable and budgets.
*The guiding principles must be to present one's message with simplicity and clarity and to do so aggressively and with a sense of commitment.
*Communications work must not be allowed to "run out of steam."
*All employees can, and should, participate in this task.

We define "communications" here as the collection, interpretation and crafting of information/advertising/PR and the transfer of this information/advertising/PR as part of a dialogue with recipients. This is both an internal and an external process for each Procordia company.

# Switzerland

*Official Name:* Swiss Confederation; *Capital:* Bern; *Government:* federal republic; *Subdivisions:* 23 cantons; *Population:* 6,572,739 (July 1987); *Density:* 401.6 per square mile; *Currency:* franc; *Official Languages:* German, French, Italian and Romansch; *Literacy:* 99 percent.

*The Land.* Switzerland is situated in the center of Western Europe. One of Europe's smallest countries, Switzerland is about twice the size of New Jersey. Landlocked, it is bounded mostly by natural frontiers. It is bordered by the Federal Republic of Germany to the north, Austria and Liechtenstein to the east, France to the west and Italy to the south. Switzerland controls some of the major routes of communications between these countries, particularly the passes and tunnels through the Alps.

The Alps cover three-fifths of Switzerland's area and are its most outstanding geographic feature. Forests, rivers and lakes and valleys create a varied landscape.

*The People.* About 69 percent of the people are of German descent, 19 French, 10 Italian, and 1 percent Romansch.

The Swiss are a sober, honest, thrifty people with a spirit of self-reliance and a certain aloofness and formality. They have been accused of being too complacent, conservative and traditional, of discouraging intellectual adventure and creativity. The Swiss oppose pretension and display and believe that industry, diligence and thrift are qualities to which mankind should aspire.

It was in Luzerne, Switzerland, where a hotel clerk assured the author that a fully packed station wagon would be completely safe parked on the street all night since the hotel parking lot was full. It was. In the other 13 European countries visited, the message was more a warning to park in a local underground garage if the hotel didn't have its own.

German, French, Italian and Romansch (a language derived from spoken Latin) are the four official national languages and four different overlapping cultural influences characterize the country.

*A Brief History.* Switzerland was born when the people of the three mountain states of Uri, Schwyz (from which the country takes its name) and Unterwalden signed the Perpetual Covenant of 1291. This was a solemn pledge of mutual support and defense against the encroachments of the House of Hapsburg on the rights which the emperor of the Holy Roman Empire had earlier granted to some of them as guardians of the passes of the Alps.

The Swiss resisted assaults by the Austrians and Italians. Defeat at Marignano inflicted damaging losses, however, and led to a reversal of Swiss attitude in international affairs and led to the policy of neutrality it has followed since. The Treaty of Westphalia which ended the Thirty Years War in 1649 recognized Swiss independence.

In 1798 Switzerland was invaded by the armies of the French Revolution and became a battlefield of the European powers. Napoleon restored the confederation in 1803. By the final act of the Congress of Vienna in 1815, the Swiss Confederation was recognized and the country's independence and neutrality guaranteed. Switzerland remained neutral in both world wars.

*The Economy.* The labor force is divided this way: services, 42 percent; industry and crafts 39, government 11, agriculture and forestry 7, other areas, 1 percent; and unemployed, 0.9 percent. About 20 percent of the labor force is unionized.

High in the Alps, Switzerland is a nation poor in natural resources but prosperous from unlimited water power, the superb skills of its people and the beauty of mountains that attract more than six million tourists a year. The Swiss turn out a variety of products: watches, precision machinery, textiles, chocolates and chemicals. The country is home to some of the world's leading banking concerns. Tourism, industry and crafts represent the greatest portion of the national income. Organizations are paternalistic and decision making is centralized.

*Organizational Communication.* Envelopes should be written to the company instead of an individual so that they will be opened if the person is away or has left the company's employ. Address the letter itself to the individual. Be punctual for an appointment and present your business card both to the receptionist and the person you are meeting.

Attire should prefer the formal over the exotic. Generally people are formal and business proceeds in an orderly, planned fashion. Don't use first names. A handshake is customary when first meeting someone and when leaving. The Swiss admire longevity, so that if your company is an old one, have its founding date printed on your business card.

## CASE STUDY: BROWN BOVERI

With 98,000 employees in 60 countries and worldwide sales of some 14 billion Swiss francs, Brown Boveri (BBC) is among the leading companies in electrical and electronic engineering and the manufacture of turbomachinery. BBC supplies products and installations for the generation and distribution of electricity and its utilization in industry and for transportation, environmental protection and building services. The parent company of the Group in Baden, Switzerland, is the headquarters of the Corporate Managing Board and operates as a holding company and an industrial enterprise.

### BBC Rules of Communication

*Public Interest*
We recognize that what our private enterprise does and what happens within it are of public interest. We recognise that the duty of politicians and the information media is to represent the public interest and to help form public opinion, and also that our obligation is to assist them in this.
*Work Force*
Communication within the environment includes — and with the highest priority — communications with our own workforce. These people are the company and at the same time are part of the public. The employees of the company comprise an information source of great credibility. With all information, therefore, the workforce comes first.
*Decisions within the Company*
All decisions within the company must take into account their influence on public opinion. Whenever possible we have to act in a way which secures a favorable public attitude towards the company.
*Credibility*
Our statements in the context of communication must be true to the facts and fair. If necessary, the reality of the enterprise must be improved, not merely glossed over by the statement. But it can happen that in the interest of business not everything can be said. Under all circumstances the criterion must be to retain credibility.
*Politics*
BBC does not stand apart from politics. Our activity calls for close communication with governments and administrations. In all contacts, national legislation must be strictly observed, and our economic importance must not be misused.

BBC welcomes the involvement of employees in political office, but has no influence on their conduct in political matters. In the event of a conflict of interests, restraint is expected. Political activity in the company is not allowed.

## CASE STUDY: CIBA-GEIGY

With just under 80,000 employees, 20,000 of them in Switzerland, Ciba-Geigy is the second largest Swiss company in terms of sales. Worldwide, too, with affiliates in 60 countries, it ranks among the giants of the *Fortune* and other lists. Ciba-Geigy was created in 1970 by the merger of two concerns, each of which had its own long and distinct tradition. Both companies had a common geographical location — the Swiss city of Basle — and both had taken the decision to embark on the manufacture of synthetic dyestuffs, and thereby enter the world of industrial chemistry, in the same year, 1859.

### Principles of Information Policy

1. *Link with Corporate Principles.* Our information policy is based on the Corporate Principles and the Principles of Leadership and Teamwork. It aims actively and continuously to build up and foster reciprocal understanding and trust between the company and its employees, its investors, and the general public.

2. *Information as a Basic Need.* We recognize the desire to be informed and to communicate as a basic human need.

3. *Congruence of Corporate and Information Policy.* Corporate and information policy are indivisible. Corporate policy is manifested primarily in the company's activities and its conduct. It is the task of information policy to reflect both, making them easily comprehensible and illuminating the context in which they take place. Because corporate and information policy are indivisible, every important decision should include provisions for disseminating information about it.

4. *Open Door Policy.* We are fundamentally committed to an open door policy and, as far as reasonably possible, take into consideration the various target audiences' information desires. We strive to publish information that is timely, objective, candid and clear. We are aware that only information which admits the company's problems is credible.

5. *Internal Information.* We distinguish between internal and external information. Internal information, destined for employees, is vital to the functioning of a multi-layered social structure such as our company embodies. Informed employees are better employees.

Internal information is primarily the responsibility of immediate supervisors, as outlined in the Principles of Leadership and Teamwork. For information which must be directly and rapidly conveyed to a large number of recipients, central channels such as the circulars and periodicals issued by the Public Relations Service are available.

6. *External Information.* The flow of external information between our company and its investors and the public at large serves to underpin corporate operations, documenting our economic and sociopolitical importance. For the implementation of such information the Public Relations Service of the parent company is at the disposal of the Executive Committee

(KL), Divisions and Groups, Central Functions and Staff Units, Regional Services and, in cooperation with local information officers, the Group companies for both advice and execution. In the parent company all contacts between the firm and the public media are routed through the Public Relations Service.

7. *Coordination of Internal and External Information.* Internal and external information are coordinated. The basic rule is to inform our employees first, then outside parties. We are aware of the essential role that employees play in diffusing the company image: "Public relations begin at home."

8. *Ensuring Accuracy of Information.* In preparing information for publication the competent authority to deal with the subject matter involved must be consulted.

9. *Limits of Information.* In certain instances the vital interests of the company may make confidentiality necessary. The right to information is governed by the overall interests of the business. Information may furthermore be withheld:
  — when received on a confidential basis from outside parties or when its disclosure could be detrimental to the interests of outside parties with whom we are bound by contract;
  — when it is of a personal nature, unless the person concerned expressly authorizes its release.
Wherever possible the inquiring party will be given an explanation of why the requested information cannot be supplied.

10. *Revision.* These Information Policy Principles shall be reviewed at least every three years in the light of social and political developments.

## CASE STUDY: NESTLE GROUP

Since the end of World War II, the company has grown significantly. Its turnover increased by a factor of 16 in terms of constant Swiss francs. Four periods of growth include: a period of rapid internal growth from 1946 to the end of the 1950s, external expansion from 1960 to 1974, a difficult confrontation with a greatly changed environment from 1975 to 1980, and vigorous strengthening of the Group's resources from 1981 to the present. The communication has a clearly delineated communication program, all of it presented in its *Guidelines to Public Relations and Information,* which includes the following:

> The choice of the means of communication among the various possibilities listed below depends on several factors:
>   — the target group to be reached;
>   — the type of message to be conveyed;
>   — the urgency of the communication.

> *Meetings.* This medium has the advantage of providing direct contact between the transmitter and the receiver of the information. If the group of

receivers is not too large (generally up to 30 to 40 people), a dialogue (questions and answers) can also be established. This is the only way of ensuring the message has actually been understood by the receivers.

Information meetings need to be prepared carefully and in detail. The following, in particular, should be determined:

a. the target group and its interest;
b. the message to be conveyed;
c. the subject-matter to be discussed;
d. the choice of speakers and panel;
e. the visual aids to be used;
f. the choice and arrangement of the room;
g. any documents to be distributed at the end of the meeting.

This method of communication is particularly suitable for internal information. To ensure that there is a dialogue, preferences should be given to the "cascade" system of meetings, e.g.:

a. Market head informs senior staff;
b. Division heads inform staff;
c. Senior staff inform employees.

If the importance of the message warrants it or if there is a crisis situation, the market head himself should personally communicate with all levels of the company.

*Company Magazine/Newspaper.* This is a publication for personnel which comes out regularly. It should serve as a vehicle for management to pass on information about the company's business and its views on the various subjects it considers important.

It should give news of the various departments that make up the company and of its personnel. The contents normally include:

a. an editorial from management,
b. a report on the company's progress,
c. special events (new equipment, new products, advertising campaigns, etc.) in the life of the company,
d. social events (club activities, new employees, transfers, marriages, births, etc.).

*Initiation Document.* This should include: letter of welcome, staff regulations, working hours, company restaurant (directions for use), social insurance, social benefits and facilities provided by the company.

*Fact Sheet.* A document of this kind, intended for all of the company's target groups, is both a brochure and a management report in miniature. It is published annually and contains the company's key figures for the preceding year. It can contain photographs and illustrations, but can also be printed in a very simple form in one color.

*Newsletters.* This should take a simple form (offset printing) with the contents being more important than the way they are presented. The comments —generally covering the company's business and activities—should correspond to the message it is intended to convey and to the specific interests of the target groups.

# Notes

1. Mort Rosenblum, "European Population in Decline," p. A10.
2. Ibid.
3. Ibid.
4. Diana Burgwyn, "Dr. Dr. Dr. Dr., May I Call You Freddie?" p. 43.
5. Neil Chesanow, *The World Class Executive,* p. 80.
6. Dennis Redmont, "Southern Stars Are Rising in European Constellation," p. D5.
7. Ibid.
8. "Workers' Rights in Industry," pp. 7 and 8.
9. Chesanow, p. 90.
10. Poul Roos, "Workers' Participation and Personnel Policy in Denmark," p. 704.
11. "Teknologi, ledelse og samarbejde," p. 24.
12. Ibid., pp. 22-5.
13. Ibid., pp. 27-8.
14. "Doing Business in Scandinavia," p. 5.
15. Roy Hill, "Once a Frenchman Always a Frenchman," p. 45.
16. Linda Bernier, "French Quality Circles Multiply," p. 30.
17. Iris I. Varner, "Comparison of American and French Business Communication," p. 2.
18. Leigh Bruce, "The Italians," p. 25.
19. "An Outline of the Akzo Organization," p. 6.
20. "Doing Business in Spain," p. 25.
21. Jose Antonio Martinez Soler, "Spain Is Learning to Cope with Democracy and Progress," p. 3.
22. Nancy L. Braganti and Elizabeth Devine, *The Travellers' Guide to European Customs and Manners,* p. 222.
23. "Doing Business in Spain," p. 17.
24. "Will There Always Be an England?" p. 3.
25. Ibid.
26. Paul R. Sparrow and Andrew M. Pettigrew, "Britain's Training Programs," pp. 111-2.
27. Steve Lohr, "The Best of Times in British Business," p. 1.
28. Peter Wilby, "Hard Work?" p. 64.
29. Ibid.
30. Ibid.
31. Peter C. Jackson, *Corporate Communication for Managers,* p. 16.
32. "The Rush to Communicate," p. 43.
33. "Taking Time to Communicate," pp. 35-6.
34. Ibid.
35. 1984 Annual Report, Standard Telephone and Cable, London, p. 10.
36. "Industrial Relations Manual," ARC, p. 32.
37. "Communication of Information and Consultation," BP Corporation, p. 2.
38. "The Communication of Information," BP Corporation, p. 1.
39. Jackson, p. 28.
40. Beatrice K. Reynolds, "A Cross-Cultural Study of Values of Germans and Americans," pp. 269-70.
41. Peter Lawrence, *Managers and Management in West Germany,* pp. 31, 34, 45-6.
42. Rudolf Walter Leonhardt, *This Germany,* p. 91.
43. David Clutterbuck, "How Effective Are Worker Directors?" p. 16.
44. Joseph R. Perone, "German Trade Fair Welcomes U.S. Firms," p. 7.
45. Iris I. Varner, "A Comparison of American and German Business Communication," p. 15.
46. David Clutterbuck, "Spanning the Communications Gap," pp. 18-9.
47. Jules R. Arbose, "A Question of Attitudes," p. 43.
48. Peter Chambers, "Encouraging an Open Corporate Atmosphere," p. 52.

49. Paul A. Samuelson, "The Failure of the 'Swedish Miracle': Toting Up the Victories — and Problems," p. A5.

50. Gavin Kennedy, *Doing Business Abroad,* p. 186.

51. Jean Phillips-Martinsson, *Swedes As Others See Them,* p. 43.

52. Ibid., p. 10.

53. Anders Scharp, "Being Top Dog," p. 11.

# 5. The Middle East

## The Land

Although the term "Middle East" has been traced to 1900, it may have been used in Britain's India Office since the mid-nineteenth century. American naval historian A.T. Mahan used the term in 1902 to describe the region around the Gulf that, from Europe, was neither "near" nor "far" east.

In World War II both the British and the Allied headquarters in Cairo were known as H.Q. Middle East, covering large parts of northern and eastern Africa as well as Iran, Turkey, and all the Arab states east of the Suez Canal. More recently, the region has become known as the source of more than a quarter of the world's oil production as well as the possessor of more than 60 percent of the world's known oil reserves.

Most of the states of the Middle East are in Asia; however they have strong ties with the Euro-Mediterranean world or the Afro-Indian Ocean world or both. All are Islamic but Cyprus, Israel and Lebanon; all are Arab but Cyprus, Iran, Israel and Turkey.

A few miles of water at the Strait of Gibraltar separate Europe and Africa in the west. The narrow Turkish Straits separate Europe and Asia in the east. Only the Suez Canal prevents Africa and Asia from being joined at the Isthmus of Suez. As the land connection between three continents, therefore, the Middle East has historically been an economic and cultural intermediary between the world's nations.

The transit function of the Middle East is evident in the population distribution of the Eurasia-Africa world island. Population density is highest in western Europe and from the Indian subcontinent to the Far East. The Middle East straddles the land, sea, and air routes between them. Travel is facilitated in the region by the Atlantic and Indian oceans with five additional bodies of water: the Mediterranean, Red, Caspian, and Black seas and the Gulf.

## The People

The Middle East is sparsely populated because of an arid climate and lack of rainfall. The total 1984 population was about 5.6 percent of the world population in a region occupying just over 10 percent of the earth's surface.

Turkey, Egypt and Iran possess the largest populations, ranking globally 18th, 19th and 24th, respectively, and together possess 52 percent of the region's population.

Peoples living in this region have become so racially mixed that it is no longer useful to racially identify groups. The Arabs are probably as mixed racially as the inhabitants of Western Europe. Although 18 states of the Middle East and North Africa are officially Arab, cultural distribution patterns within the region are complex. Some Arab states have non–Arab minorities, and Arab minorities live outside the recognized Arab states.

The Middle East takes pride in its role as the birthplace and core region of Islam. To understand their religion is to begin to understand the Arabs' world. Today there are almost 200 million Arabs but nearly a billion Moslems in the world,[1] – a fifth of the world's population. "Muslim Arabs have never quite acknowledged, have never fully incorporated into their thinking and especially their feeling, either that a non–Muslim is really a complete Arab, or that a non–Arab is really a complete Muslim."[2] Table 21 shows the worldwide distribution of this religion. The religion's focal point is the pilgrim city of Mecca, which the faithful are supposed to visit once during their lifetime in what is called the *hajj*, which is made by two million Muslims each year. Before modern transport, the lands closest to Mecca yielded the greatest number of pilgrims, and unity was most keenly felt at the center.

Making the *hajj* at least once in a lifetime is just one of the five Pillars of Faith, rules stated in the Koran which a Muslim is expected to follow. The others are: professing faith by repeating the Moslem creed; praying five times a day; giving alms to the poor; and fasting during daytime hours of Ramadan, the holy month.

In the Middle East and North Africa, where most Arabs live, they number nearly 120 million people, most of whom are Muslim. An Arab is a person who speaks Arabic and thinks of himself as an Arab. A Muslim, however, is not necessarily an Arab. He practices Islam, the world's largest form of worship. Islam is practiced in some 90 countries. About 90 percent of Middle-Eastern peoples are Muslim.

Islam is less a religion in the Western sense than it is a way of life and a reason for human existence. Its adherents don't worship for an hour or two once a week. Proper practice is daily and day-long. Islam influences most areas of Arab life: business hours, personal conduct, politics, social relations, the treatment of women by men, the contents of national constitutions, and the structure of the legal systems.

Although Islam unites the Middle Esat and North Africa, it also divides it between the Sunni and Shi'i branches. About 90 percent of Muslims are Sunnis. The schism in Islam dates almost from its beginning in the seventh century, originating in a dispute over who would succeed the Prophet Muhammad as Caliph (Successor) of Islam. Sunnis believed the Caliph should be selected on the basis of community consensus; Shi'is believed that the succession should be hereditary, beginning with Ali, Muhammad's son-in-law and the first Imam. Sunnis regard Ali as their fourth Caliph.

Colonel Richard Norton, United States government advisor on Islam,

## Table 21. The Peoples of Islam

*Population*

| Country | Total (000's) | Moslem (000's) | Percent Moslem |
|---|---|---|---|
| Indonesia | 165,000 | 140,250 | 85% |
| Pakistan | 95,000 | 92,150 | 97 |
| Bangladesh | 101,500 | 90,335 | 89 |
| India | 750,000 | 90,000 | 12 |
| Soviet Union | 277,000 | 49,860 | 18 |
| Egypt | 48,000 | 43,680 | 91 |
| Iran | 43,000 | 42,140 | 98 |
| Nigeria | 89,000 | 40,050 | 45 |
| Morocco | 23,000 | 22,770 | 99 |
| Algeria | 22,200 | 21,798 | 99 |
| Sudan | 21,700 | 15,624 | 72 |
| Afghanistan | 15,500 | 15,345 | 99 |
| China | 1,042,000 | 15,000 | 1.4 |
| Iraq | 15,000 | 14,250 | 95 |
| Ethiopia | 36,000 | 12,600 | 35 |
| Syria | 10,200 | 8,976 | 88 |
| Saudi Arabia | 9,000 | 8,910 | 99 |
| Malaysia | 15,700 | 7,693 | 49 |
| Tunisia | 7,100 | 7,029 | 99 |

*(Source: American Institute for Islamic Affairs, as published in Karen Elliott House, "Mosque and State: Rising Islamic Fervor Challenges the West and Every Moslem Ruler,"* Wall Street Journal, *August 7, 1987, p. 4.)*

explained the differences between these two sects and Christianity by saying that Christianity celebrates the birth and resurrection of Christ, two joyous occasions, and the Sunni celebrate the birth of Muhammad, another joyous occasion. The Shi'i, however, observe the death of the first Imam with parades in which young men strike their heads with hands and objects until the blood flows.[3]

The Sunni-Shi'i difference, however, should not be overstated. All Moslems of any sect believe in and practice the Five Pillars of Islam; nevertheless, the schism has created fierce local rivalries from time to time and explains some of the political complexity of the Middle East, especially where geographical proximity of the two groups is most marked.

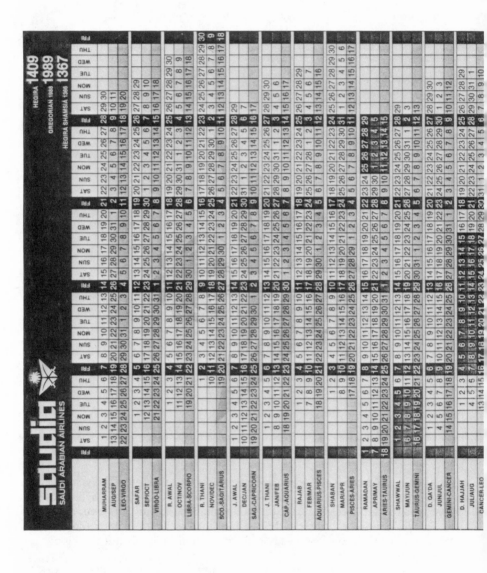

Queuing or standing in line in the Middle East is unknown. Space is public and whoever gets to the oasis or into the taxi first wins. Arabs in national costumes dress similarly, but differences in national attire do exist from one country to the next. Arabs recognize immediately a countryman or an Arab neighbor, for whom they often harbor intense dislike.

Muhammad lived as a prophet for 23 years — 13 in Mecca and 10 in Medina. Arabs' calendar begin with the flight of Muhammad from Mecca to Medina in A.D. 662, called the Hegira. Arabic calendars use the acronym A.H. (Anno Hegirae — "Year of the Hegira") instead of the Christian A.D. (Anno Domini). The Hegira calendar year runs on a 30-year cycle, 19 years with 354 days and 11 years with 355 days. Therefore one Hegira year straddles two Gregorian calendar years.

Since the Hegira calendar is based on lunar rather than solar cycles like the Gregorian calendar, only 29½ days make up an Arab month, and an Arab year is shorter than a Western year by eleven days. This may affect the dates on which annual holidays occur. For example, the holy month of Ramadan takes place about 11 days earlier each ensuing year.

Arab calendars are often printed with Gregorian as well as Hegira dates in parallel columns. Most Arab correspondence — particularly govern-ment letters and telexes — will bear the Hegira, not the Gregorian date, i.e., Oc-tober 18, 1988 to October 6, 1989 corresponds to the year 1409 A.H.

Arab loyalties assume this order of importance: the nuclear family — fast becoming the rule in urban centers, where housing is in short supply, although extended-family ties remain close; the extended family — which may be elaborate, including second cousins of in-laws; Muslim Arab friends; the Arab Islamic community as a whole; their country; and non–Arab Muslims.[4]

Personal status in the Middle East, as in Latin America and Latin Europe, depends on family position and on social contacts. An individual is closely tied to the family and dominated by the father. Group activities are also dominated by social standing, and members of the group show greater allegiance to their superior than the group. One result is that group cooperation is usually lack-ing. Group leaders have to possess overpowering personalities to unify members and accomplish anything.

Generosity matters in the Arab world more than in most other regions; a charge of stinginess here is a serious insult. To ancient Bedouins, from whom modern Arabs take many cultural cues, hospitality strengthened group ties, vital to security in a tenuous nomadic existence in the harsh desert. Today, Arab hospitality is still a two-way street — a show of mutual respect, reci-procity, and delicately balanced obligations between host and guest who will then, in a future situation, become guest and host.

Not only is an Arab obligated by cultural values to give a guest — even a stranger — food and protection, but to refuse such generosity is an insult, a re-jection of bonding to the group with which his host is aligned. When you are offered something by an Arab colleague — coffee, tea, nuts or dates or an invita-

*Opposite:* **Figure 23. The Hegira year 1409 compared to the Gregorian year 1988-1989. (Courtesy of Saudia, Saudia Arabian Airlines.)**

tion to dinner — in the office or out, politeness dictates that you accept it. Whether you want it is irrelevant. It's the symbolic meaning of an offer and its acceptance that matters, not the content of the offer or your desire for it.

Though their numbers are waning, the Bedouins were the first Muslims who spread the faith among Middle Eastern peoples and remain the role model for much of the modern Arab world. The Prophet Muhammad encouraged the Bedouins to spread the faith to neighboring countries, and in less than a decade, they spread Arab Muslim rule over the entire Fertile Crescent.[5] Although some 90 percent of today's Arabs are sedentary rather than being perpetual wanderers in the desert, they exhibit many of the traits of those early Bedouins.

The Arab concept of time is not the minutely divisible concept that is the norm in the United States. Arabs don't view nature or human events as being controllable by man through advance planning, clock watching, and discipline. Such matters are determined by Allah alone, whose will is unknowable and unforeseeable. Arabs traditionally view time as a continuous flow of events in which past, present and future blur together rather than receive separate and well-defined attention. An American expatriate in Riyadh recalled inviting a Saudi couple to his home for dinner on a Wednesday evening two weeks hence. The couple appeared at his front door on the proper day — but a week early. From the American's point of view this was a mix-up. From the Saudis' point of view it was not. By Arab standards of temporal flexibility, they were "on time." In business, unfortunately, it usually works the other way around. Arabs are more apt to be late than early — yet still, as they see it, on time.

If unanticipated events prevent an Arab from doing something he would have liked to do on time — like meeting deadlines on agreed-upon dates — it's the immutable will of Allah. Therefore, it's inevitable, beyond human control. One frequently hears the word *insha allah* — "If God is willing" — in Arab conversation, even English conversation. It implies uncertainty: God may or may not be willing to have your deadlines met. By and large, Westerners believe that the will is human, not divine; God's will has nothing to do with meeting deadlines and is an unacceptable excuse. Arabs believe just the opposite: God determines what gets done, despite an individual's sincerest intentions.

Unlike Americans, Arabs neither see time as money nor place business above family, friends or religion. Unforeseeable events such as family emergencies or previously overlooked religious observances are covered by the *insha allah* in every conversation involving any kind of commitment. Americans can only keep scheduling flexible.

Show an Arab tangible signs of respect to cement a trust relationship. The more an Arab trusts you, the more he'll try to listen to American "reason" in speeding up delays. Otherwise, Allah's will may slow things down.

Don't intrude in an Arab's private life: home, family, particularly their women. Family honor is among the most important of Arab values. The greatest threat to it is the loss of chastity of a female member out of wedlock or a married female relative caught in an extramarital affair.

Women are disfavored economically and educationally in most Arab countries. Traditional social and religious values limit women to the roles of homemakers and mothers. An Arab protects his women with the highest sense of honor. In fact, the word *ird* for honor and the words "wife" and "sister" are used synonymously. A man's honor is his wife and sister and their conduct. A woman who violates her honor is still executed in some Muslim countries. The natural results of such a system are a strong feeling of jealousy about one's women and the felt need to protect them to the extreme as manifested.

For one thing, modern Arabs extend great hospitality to any and all visitors, a reminder of a time when survival in the desert depended on such mutual gestures. For another, Arab nations are very competitive with one another, to the point of complete animosity. This derives from the spirit of the *ghazwa* or raid that was common between desert tribes. Another quality of present-day Arabs that derives from Bedouin life is pride. The Bedouins always felt proud of who they were and what they did, a quality enhanced by the Muslim religion that instilled in them an even greater sense of superiority. Still another Bedouin characteristic that survives is the well-known Arab desire for revenge for any wrong committed against them. Blood vengeance was common in the desert as a social safeguard. Anyone who commits murder will have nobody to protect him. Blood for blood was the rule then and remains the rule in Arab, or Muslim, international relations.

When visitors met with a ruler or his representative, they were considered guests and kept for seven days with no mention of the purpose of the visit. Traces of this custom remain. Whatever his pace, the Arab feels it is "normal" and that the American is out of step by rushing in and out of a country where he or she hopes to do profitable business. This upsets the Arab and presents difficulties in places where all the key government and business figures are busy.

# A Brief History

The Christian West has long viewed Islam with suspicion and fear. For more than a thousand years, Islam threatened Christianity both as a religious institution and as an ideology to the point of conquering the Iberian peninsula in the eighth century and occupying it for seven hundred years. "Eventually," *Time* magazine explained, "the West dispelled the Moslems, but not the memory of a thousand years of dread."[6] The Western response has been expressed in antagonistic and unfavorable writings about Islam and the Moslems, including the Arabs, ascribing to them acts of barbarity of which they were innocent. The price paid for this longstanding hostility between the two sides is an inability to communicate.[7]

Contact between the Arabs and the West began when the European powers, particularly France and Great Britain, established colonies, called League of Nations mandates or protectorates. In 1917, the Zionists persuaded the British government to promise them help in the establishment of a Jewish homeland in Palestine. When Sherif Hussain of Mecca gathered his Arab followers and declared war on Ottoman Turkey, the aim was that the Asian Arabs would achieve their independence after victory. Known as the Balfour Declaration, this promise followed by two years an agreement the British had made with the Arabs, their allies in the war against the Ottoman Empire, that

the Arabs would be autonomous in their countries. The Arabs attained no independence and suffered a divided homeland. The Arab homeland was dismembered into numerous kingdoms and republics under foreign domination.
The resulting geographic mismatch between state and nation has created a permanent obstacle to national integration in some Middle East states. They remain culturally diverse and thus suffer a weak sense of national community.

Arab-Western relations have since suffered a crisis of confidence. To compound the difficulties, a joint Congressional resolution, also signed by President Harding in 1922, affirmed the Balfour Declaration with one significant exception: Christians in Palestine were mentioned by name whereas the majority
of the population, the Moslem Arabs, were relegated to the category of "other
non–Jewish communities." The West has also enraged the Arabs by a policy
of balance of power between Israel's two and a half million people and the
Arab world's over 130 million inhabitants (a figure that does not, of course, include non–Arab Muslims, another 620 million people). Denied the ordinary
channels of communication with the West, Arabs (and Muslims) have frequently resorted to demonstrations, riots and violent attacks against Western
embassies, consulates and information and cultural centers abroad.

Several factors combined to cause this situation: the burden of a historical
and long-enduring antagonism between Islam and Christianity; the Arabs' vic-
timization by colonial rule; the fact that the Arabs belong to the Third-World
region when their pride dwells on their past; a reluctance to side with the West
in its battle against the Soviet and Chinese blocs; and the Western support in
the creation of the state of Israel in the midst of the Arab homeland.

# The Economy

As a whole the countries of the Middle East belong to the Third World.
They are still generally at an early stage of industrialization and heavily dependent on the export of primary products and the import of food, consumer
goods, equipment and technology.

The high-income oil exporters are among the richest countries in the
world, measured by gross national product (GNP) per capita, with the United
Arab Emirates, Qatar and Kuwait ranking first, second and third, respectively,
in the world. Arabs in these countries are aware of this asset's fungibility. They
are frequently heard to say: "My father rode on a camel; I ride in a Cadillac;
my son will ride on a camel." At the other end of the economic scale, the two
Yemens have among the world's lowest GNP per capita.

Three countries — Israel, Syria and Turkey — do not conform with the
typical Third-World economy, in that one fifth or more of their gross domestic
products are derived from manufacturing industry. By contrast, the manufacturing sector in the two Yemens is extremely poorly developed. In fact, these
states are among the 31 states classified by the United Nations as the world's
least developed countries.

Agriculture is the main occupation of a large majority of the inhabitants;
and a further proportion of the people is employed in processing the products

of agriculture, as cotton and tobacco packers, fruit driers, or canners of fruit, vegetables and olive oil.

In medieval times Middle Eastern industrial products had a high reputation. Steelwork, silverware, pottery, leather, and above all, textiles found their way into many parts of Europe. At the present time, however, the scale of Middle Eastern industries is small; lack of fuel (particularly of coal and hydroelectric power), scarcity of mineral ores and some other raw materials, and the poverty of local markets are limiting factors. Over the last few years, however, oil has increasingly been used as prime fuel.

In recent years, significant industrial development has occurred in Egypt, Turkey, Israel and Iran, with some industry on a smaller scale in Iraq, Lebanon and Syria. Textiles — chiefly cotton, but also silk, wool and mohair — are important, together with the transformation of agricultural products (sugar, tobacco, fruit processing and distilling) and the making of cement and bricks, for which there is a considerable local demand.

The Prophet Muhammad was a merchant. To the Arab, conducting business is not only respectable, it is a pleasure. Table 22 compares the Arab business system to that of the United States. "The Arab executive is viewed as a person who is at the helm of an organization which, in turn, is perceived as a business-oriented social system embedded in the larger systems of community and society."[8] Emissaries must be prepared to deal with both private and public employees. The power of the government is pervasive, and virtually all foreign trade transactions require government approval or an official license.

Decision-making power in Arab nations is highly centralized. Control rests in a commercial elite. Thereafter, authority may exist at the next lower level, but functions, titles and actual power do not correspond. In business, top managers often are members of ruling families. Yet it is difficult, even for Arabs, to find the real power in family concerns.

The decision maker leans on personal impressions supplemented by facts. Secrecy is a way of life. Financial statements are unavailable. Decisions may be kept secret until the decision maker feels totally comfortable with them.

An Englishman who has worked in the Middle East compared his experience there with what he knew of Western practices:

> "Compared with Europe," he says, "managers working in the Middle East operate in a much less claustrophobic society. There is a far more positive attitude here toward getting things done, and for that reason alone I've put no personal limitation on the time I spend here. In Europe, there always seem to be 199 reasons why you can't do this or that."
>
> [Philip] Forrest [managing director of Port Khalid], has had virtually a free hand in developing Port Khalid's facilities.... "Sure, we operate in a very competitive environment," he says. "But ports in other parts of the world are submerged in a sea of bureaucracy, labour strife, political restraint or inflexible management. We don't have any of that here. This means I can concentrate on developing opportunities rather than just dealing with problems."[9]

Expatriate executives, the British writer points out, are used to an exception-oriented type of management, where you agree on objectives with your

## Table 22. Differences in U.S. and Middle East Management

| Managerial Function | Middle East | United States |
|---|---|---|
| Organization | Highly bureaucratic, over-centralized, with a significant degree of paternalism | Relatively decentralized, delegation of authority, greater use of staff specialists, much less paternalism |
| Planning and managerial decision making | A high degree of fatalism, with decisions based on intuition; relative static approach; unwillingness to take risks inherent in managerial decisions | Systematized and integrated planning systems; decisions based on rational thinking and scientific method; relatively aggressive approach to decision making |
| Managerial control | Responsibilities are vague, lack of comprehensive or integrated control | A high degree of cost control; systematized, computerized and efficiency-oriented control systems |
| Staffing | Nepotistic, with many key positions filled by members of the family, close personal friends and individuals from the "right social origin" | Upward mobility, with personal training and management development programs, recruitment and advancement on the basis of merit |
| Direction, leadership, motivation | Autocratic, paternalistic seniority system; motivation largely economic; lack of worker participation in management | Much greater use of participative management and emphasis on individualism; high economic rewards and greater emphasis on intrinsic job satisfaction related to performance and challenging work |
| Communication | Social, professional and family influence are ever-present factors; the chain of command must be followed rigidly; people relate to each other tightly and specifically; friendships are intense and binding | Stress is on equality and a minimization of differences, people relate to each other loosely and generally; friendships are not intense or binding |

*(Source: Dr. M.K. Badawy, Cleveland State University, as presented in Jules Arbose, "The Middle East Mirage,"* International Management, *April 1979, p. 23.)*

superior, and he interferes only when you fail to achieve those objectives. Still, in a typical Arab firm, the owner remains very much in control, invariably taking an active, day-to-day part in running the business. "He insists on making even minor decisions, or on having an input into matters that the Westerner feels are so insignificant that the owner shouldn't even know about them. The

Saudis have a saying, 'You tie your donkey where the boss tells you.'"[10] The system does have positive aspects:

> There are no shareholders or management committees to whom you can appeal to reverse a decision.... But this also means that you do not have to go through tiers and tiers of a management hierarchy to get a decision.
>
> If you want money for a project, the owner will tell you "yes" or "no" almost immediately to your face. There's a great dynamism about this, because once he agrees, he'll back you to the hilt. His concern is not "how" but "when." This is why you achieve things at such a phenomenal rate out here compared with Europe.[11]

The Arab business system, however, exhibits a lack of industrial discipline in such things as aversion to systems and procedures, lack of organization (especially delegation), and a nonprofessional attitude toward business.[12] The younger generation of managers is trying to change that system. An illustration is the Saudi's House of Fouad with 32-year-old Abdulla Fouad, Jr., disagreeing with his father's point of view. The 58-year-old sheikh says:

> My son agrees with me that we must make profits and guard our reputation. But I am unsure what redecorating an office and putting in fancy furniture has to do with either. He tells me that the modern way to run a business is to have a larger central organization. To me, the measure of a good organization is not the number of people it employs but the amount of profit that it makes.

The younger man replies:

> My father likes to tell me jokingly, "I am making the money, and you are spending it." He feels that our reputation for honesty and good service is more important than having modern offices. I tell him that modern offices are part of the corporate image that we project and that we can have them without sacrificing any of the things that he believes in.

The younger man believes the paramount needs of the family business are a modern management structure and the development of systems to motivate their multinational workforces and draw synergy from their disparate operating units.

> For a long time I have felt the need for a corporate body that allows us to take a consistent approach to the management of our group's resources. This is absolutely vital to secure our future. If we are to hire and keep good people, then we must establish a feeling of corporate loyalty.

His father remains convinced of his simpler answer to higher profits:

> For me it is not necessary to have vice-presidents to do my job. I may be uneducated, but while my son is educated, he does lack my experience. So, maybe, if it improves his profits, it is a good thing for him to have vice-presidents and try new management ideas.

The younger Fouad is chipping away at the long-established method of managing in which the owner — his father — makes all the decisions.[13]

Arabs usually work a five- or a five-and-a-half-day week. The Arab weekend is Thursday and Friday, not Saturday and Sunday. Friday is the Muslim day of rest. The half-day of work, where it applies, is Thursday morning, a bad time to make appointments.

It is a serious mistake to classify all Arabs under a single identity. A Kuwaiti is a Kuwaiti and a Bahraini is not a lesser cousin of the Saudis. If a Gulf state national perceives that a visitor is just coming through on his way to Riyadh, he may take offense and contact may be lost.

Summer months are far from ideal times for conducting business. Ramadan, the holy month, often curtails business activity. Its fast certainly has a tendency to shorten tempers. *Hajji,* the pilgrimage period, is also not an optimal time for business transactions.

Work abruptly ceases for devout Muslims at prayer times. If you're in a restaurant, bank or other public place at such times, leave the premises. The prayer ritual usually takes from 15 to 30 minutes, possibly longer if an individual goes to a mosque to worship. But many religious Arabs excuse themselves from meetings and pray privately in their offices.

The Arabic culture, typical of an agrarian or nonindustrialized society, is slow-paced. Business transactions, heavily laced with complex social amenities, normally take longer to complete than an American is used to. The Arabs dislike deadlines which make them feel threatened and cornered. It is highly unusual for a deal to be consummated in two meetings.

The Arabs are known for their prompt-paying habits and readiness to measure up to their word. In return, they expect the foreign businessman to be above board in dealings with them and to deliver on promises.

Markets full of frenetically active people are a ubiquitous feature of the Arab world, even though in big cities such as Cairo or Baghdad they are no longer the centerpiece of urban life. Indeed, such "Arab" markets are to be found with local variations throughout most of Asia and Africa and in parts of Latin America.[14] They are a feature of the so-called Third World; Figure 24 shows the Tangier market. They resemble in many ways European markets as they existed before the Industrial Revolution. These markets are different in terms of scale (small versus large stores); they are also part of a whole way of life which is intensely personal, competitive, and open to public participation. They serve as the arena for much of the political and religious life of the city. Mosques and religious shrines are part of the market landscape, permitting visitors and merchants alike to stop and pray during the day.

"Picturesque, yes, but what an inefficient system. . . . The bargaining is so difficult, far too personal as a steady diet."[15] Americans express discomfort at what they feel is the Arab hard sell. One rug merchant in Tangier followed the author from the third floor of his building down to the ground level and out into the street in an attempt to sell a rug. Young merchants carrying their merchandise hawk to foreigners on the street and won't be put off. One has to hurry away for relief. Haggling is such an important part of business practices that prices are highly inflated to allow it. An elderly man knitting winter hats at a small shop in the Tangier Kasbah allowed the author to purchase two of them and silently reduced the price from the one he had quoted in the absence of haggling over price. Americans prefer to be left to themselves when making most purchases. To the Moroccan merchant and his customers, however, offering personal advice on a product is part of the business.

Merchants depend upon and compete with each other. If the customer

**Figure 24. The market in Tangier, Morocco.**

wants something he doesn't have, the merchant may go to one of his fellow merchants to find the style or size required. The other merchant will expect similar favors another day — or may share in the profits. Merchants stand together in matters of taxation and import duties, in concern for the physical condition of the market, in all matters of common interest. In Marrakech, those selling the same kind of goods belong to an organization with a recognized head who can speak for the group and who will arbitrate disputes between members of the organization. All these markets offer goods of foreign manufacture, in greater or lesser quantities.

# Organizational Communication

Communication is important to Arabs and Muslims. When the author visited the great mosque in Cordoba, the guide took the tour group of mostly Americans to the spot in the mosque where the kneeling worshipper can view all of the numerous doorways to the mosque and kept repeating "They had this great communication with the outside, this great communication with nature." Used to worshipping out of doors, usually in the desert, the Muslims retained that connection in their mosques.

The dominant languages in the Middle East are Arabic, Turkish and

Persian. Arabic is a Semitic language that spread out from the Arabian peninsula with successive waves of conquerors and replaced existing languages in all
but a few areas south of the Taurus and Zagros mountains. Kurdish is spoken
in sections of Iraq and Syria and a variety of African tribal languages are
spoken in southern Sudan. Altogether, about 57 percent of the region's inhabitants speak Arabic.

Arabic is among the world's most widely spoken languages, the mother
tongue of nearly 120 million people in the Middle East and North Africa. It is
written and read from right to left in a 28-character script with the same
ancestry as the Roman alphabet. It is rhythmic and musical and full of color,
variety and nuance of sound, but the language also encourages hyperbole and
elaborate verbal rhetoric spoken with great flourish. How something is said
may matter as much or more than its actual content. The Arabic language
allows Muslims to express their feelings with great gradation of emotion.

Not only is the language read from right to left, but pictorial sequences
are also viewed from right to left. One United States marketer of laundry
detergent, unaware of this, designed ads for Arab countries showing a series
of three illustrations as Americans view them — with soiled clothes on the left,
the product in the middle and clean clothes on the right. To the Arabs, the
detergent seemed to take clean clothes and make them dirty.

The letter, cable or telex approach will probably yield no results and the
business person will have to make a trip, perhaps with the purpose of selecting
an agent. Since business in the Middle East is often conducted on a very personal basis (especially in the more paternalistic governments) these contacts
can be valuable. But they create problems because the wrong contact in the
Middle East can be an extreme handicap.

The appropriate way to secure an appointment is to request one via letter,
preferably giving a choice of two or three dates at least six weeks in advance
of the proposed meeting to allow for slow mail delivery. Telex communications
are not recommended because relatively few organizations have terminals.
When a good relationship has been established, you may make a telephone appointment, although days can be spent trying to use the system of overloaded
circuits. Telephone messages also tend to get lost.

No actual written confirmation will return. The prospective visitor can
only hope that his local contact is seeking weekly confirmations, some of them
in person. The agent must apply constant mild pressure to achieve success. As
a broad rule, although with many exceptions, a humorous Bedouin saying applies: "We didn't work when we were poor. Why work now that we are rich?"[16]
The general population still resists regular, systematic work habits.

Requests for appointments should include a statement identifying the purpose of your visit. The appointment seeker's information should excite interest.
Otherwise, no meeting will take place. The Arabs are overwhelmed with proposals, and only well-connected people or people offering something respectable and pertinent will gain access to them. Wear good quality, well tailored
clothes, though women's clothes should not be form-fitting.

Early appointments may be meaningless, because any man of stature tends
to arrive about an hour late to his office. Even established appointments suffer

from competition, both scheduled and unscheduled. Hours, perhaps even days, may constitute a normal waiting period. The typical Arab deals first with relatives, then with countrymen, then with foreigners. The Arab is not intentionally putting the visitor off; other priorities exist in his mind and in his culture.

Arabs are conscious of rank and expect others to observe their protocols. Shake hands with the most important person in an office first — the one sitting in the middle of the room surrounded by other guests who pay him obvious obeisance. Regardless of your sex, it is the duty of the guest to extend a hand to the host and then to greet and shake hands with each guest in turn, even though the guests may have nothing to do with business and you may not know who they are.

The English side of your business card should contain a phonetic transliteration of your company name and your name. Otherwise, many Arabs whose English is imperfect may have trouble pronouncing it. Present your card promptly after shaking hands, Arabic side up. During your meeting, your host will keep the card before him and refer to it often. You may or may not receive a card in return. If not, ask for one. It will generally be translated on the reverse side into English. Arab business cards may contain unlisted telephone numbers and addresses that you might need and are difficult to find by indirect means.

Meetings invariably take longer than novices predict, less gets done at each, and subsequent meetings can be hard to schedule. Keep your return date open. You may shake hands with an Arab several times in one day each time you're apart for a while and remeet. Maintain eye contact, a sign of sincerity. Exchange greetings as you shake hands, and continue shaking until the greetings are finished, which may take several minutes. Arabs seldom communicate concisely. A simple "hello" would be too abrupt in the flowery Arabic style of expression; it lacks warmth and sincerity. The Arab handshake is limp and loose. The actual shaking is light, with only a slight up and down movement, never a pump.

Information received from Arab sources may be colored by unbusinesslike factors. The Arab may, for example, harbor the remnants of a family feud, not like the other party personally, or simply have listened to gossip about him.

Typical Arab conversations are at close range to exclude others. Closeness cannot be avoided; it is a sign that you are being heard. Conversational distance, particularly if there is no desk or table, may shrink to 10 or fewer inches. Physical closeness also involves touching. To make a point or express a feeling, Arabs tap the other person gently, even resting the hand on the arm or hand of the other party, an assurance of attention and improved communication. Anything flagrant such as backslapping must be avoided. Public touching doesn't bother Arabs a bit. They bump and jostle others on the street and pat and squeeze others during conversations. They may also appear out of nowhere to take a taxi for which you've been waiting. Such behavior is natural, not rude, to Arabs.

Some Arabs well-versed in American ways won't feel insulted if you pass a document to them with your left hand or expose the soles of your shoes, because they realize no insult is intended, having spent years being handed documents with left hands and seeing shoe soles exposed in the United States, Europe and other parts of the world.

Also be prepared for what you're likely to find on your first meeting in an Arab office: the ultimate in polychronic time usage. Americans prefer to discuss classified company business in private and are stunned to find their Arab host surrounded by friends, relatives, and professional associates, none of whom seem ready to leave. The Koran says all are equal in Allah's eyes, and by extension, guests of the same host are viewed as equal, without deserving to special privileges. Everyone rises when a new guest enters the room, waits for him to shake hands with and greet the host and others in the room. Rising is a sign of respect based on tribal and familial closeness and the inviolability of friendship and hospitality.

The procedure is proof of the Arab's cultural bias that personal relationships are the essence of any business deal. The gathering consists of friends, relatives, agents, power brokers, and other callers. Basically, all those present are waiting their turns to talk to the person in whose office they are gathered. The selection of who is interviewed, and when, is entirely up to the host, and is based on cultural priorities, courtesies and desires. All the while, subdued conversation takes place between individual visitors and the host, among guests, and with servants who offer various liquid refreshments. The office occupant will also take any number of phone calls. The result may be, at best, a long wait; at worst, no interview at all — rather, an invitation to return the next day.

Even after the visitor is called to the host's desk, which may be in the middle of the room or in one of the corners, interruptions may be frequent. Constant greetings may occur, messengers may be received and sent, mail may require attention, or a special visitor may be given conversational attention. The overall objective for the Arab is to discover if he would like to work with someone. This discovery takes time, a great deal of personal interplay, and almost always information gathered through agents, friends or relatives. The Arab wants a complete and confident impression of the person first; his issues second.

What actually happens during a particular meeting will depend to some extent on who initiated it. If it was your Arab host, you will naturally have a high level of attention. If you are trying to sell something, however, your host may have little idea of what you are describing. When the product or service is not something he is actively seeking and when the business is being done on a cash basis, this vagueness may be compounded by considerable caution. A further complicating factor is the Arab reluctance to say "no," so that the business persons will have to learn to distinguish real interest from politeness.

It is prudent to advise the Arab of the agenda and of discussion points well in advance of personal visits. Here again, a local contact is invaluable. Business relations for the Arab start from a base of distrust. Taking advantage of an Arab will cause him to lose face, and he will refuse further dealings and so will his many friends.

The establishment of trust is essential and that obviously precludes hard selling. The opening proposals of the foreign firm might best be loose and open-ended. Fast or pushy business persons are suspect because they give the impression of trying to mislead or to misrepresent. Overt forthrightness which might accompany time-pressed negotiations is taken as a sign of poor understanding of local customs, lack of finesse or amateurishness. The foreigner's busy schedule does not concern the Arabs. Business matters cannot be completed with correspondence. Paperwork is not an accepted part of hard negotiations.

The visitor will be offered a refreshment as a sign of hospitality, usually a glass of sweet tea or a hot cup of unsweetened coffee. Arabs today also offer carbonated soft drinks. The guest should accept the offer, even if his or her taste or nerves are offended. Refills are automatic, two or three cups are the norm. Thereafter, a gentle side-to-side shaking of the cup will prevent refills.

Initial conversation is usually small talk, much of it personal, with the intent of being courteous. Arabs speak with assertiveness and exaggeration. This linguistic pattern is so ingrained in the Arab people's thinking and behavior that an Arab speaker is constantly afraid that the listener may think that he means the opposite if he does not exaggerate and emphasize his point. Arabs exaggerate in all their language communication, poetry or prose, classical or colloquial, romantic or political. Besides these grammatical types of over-assertion are the numerous stylistic and rhetorical devices to achieve even further exaggeration. Fantastic metaphors and similes are used in abundance, and long arrays of adjectives to modify the same word are quite frequent.

Conversation may not address the business purpose of the meetings for two or three visits. The minimum time for social talk is generally 30–45 minutes. Modern Arabs, particularly those who deal frequently with Western visitors, may prefer to get directly down to business. The foreigner should follow the host's lead. Periods of silence are normal. The Koran advises that God gave man two ears and one tongue so he could listen twice as much as he could talk. The visitor must distinguish purposeful silence from an end to the interview.

During discussions, Arabs maintain eye contact, studying the pupils to judge reactions to various subjects better. The American approach is to maintain eye contact intermittently, looking away frequently.

A meeting frequently concludes with another offer of coffee. Leave-taking should be after coffee has been served and consumed, an indication that further meetings should be arranged.

Once established, a good working relationship will withstand considerable stress. It should be noted that this relationship (to the Arab) is with a person, not with an organization. Once a particular Western representative begins a particular project, it is best for him to stay with it, since a personal reservoir of trust and good will is not transferable to someone else in the same organizations. In the meantime, an agent can keep in touch with ministries and is aware of information on upcoming contracts. He can offer a sound presentation of his principal's product or service, and he can keep abreast of the competition in the area. Traditional agreements with, and among, Arabs usually involve no more than the word and the handshake of the participants.

**Table 23. Some Communication Practices in the Arab Corporation**

The Arabs:

1. Begin from a base of distrust.

2. Prefer face-to-face channels.

3. Keep appointments irregularly, believing interferences to be the will of Allah.

4. Keep visitors waiting for hours or days when they do keep appointments.

5. Are offended by angry reactions.

6. Sometimes conduct business at a distance of 10 inches or less.

7. Touch others frequently.

8. Prefer oral and aural communication.

9. Offer refreshments that should not be refused.

10. Place loyalties in this order: nuclear family
                                    extended family
                                    Muslim-Arab friends
                                    Muslim-Arab community
                                    country
                                    Non-Arab Muslims

11. Are a high-context culture.

12. Use time polychronically.

Except for Iraq, where Western dress has become the norm, Arabs, particularly in Gulf countries, wear national costumes in the office, the local equivalent of a pinstripe suit. Such three-piece outfits include a long loose robe called a *dishdasha* or *thobe* and a headpiece, a white cloth *kaffiya* banded by a black *egal* to secure it.

In an Arab community, "face" counts for a great deal, so if you wish to end an association gracefully, you will have to work out an arrangement that does not leave your man in the "abandoned wife" category. From that position, he will have little choice but to downgrade you. In the Middle East, very little falls into the "no-fault" category, not even what you normally think of as straightforward business decisions.

The vastness of external space is reflected in large offices — signs of prestigious individuals. It also serves as a reminder of the desert, where meetings, naturally, were infrequent.

Arabs may not relate to products they are unable to physically touch and those include a set of neatly bound pages. Product samples, demonstration equipment, and working models that turn abstract items into something that can be seen, handled, and admired will have greater impact.

Other than members of royal families, ministers and high-ranking military officers, Arabs aren't fond of titles. Gulf Arabs in particular disdain pretention and display, titles included.

### Table 24. Managerial Gaps Between
### Developing Countries and the United States

| *Organizational Characteristic* | *Developing Countries of the Middle East* | *The United States* |
|---|---|---|
| Organization: | | |
| orientation | The individual | The system |
| structure | Functional | Program and matrix |
| authority | Centralized | Decentralized |
| management | Owners | Managers |
| accountability | Informal | Formal |
| performance indicators | Adherence to procedures | Results |
| Decision Making: | | |
| nature | Incremental | Strategic |
| participants | Government/public sector | Private sector |
| information base | Weak and spotty | Strong and well balanced |
| psychology | Emotional/personal | Rational/corporate |
| Communication: | | |
| direction | Downward | Multi-directional |
| frequency | Infrequent | Frequent |
| urgency | Urgent | Routine |
| primary purpose | Orders | Information |
| orientation | Reactive | Interactive |
| channels | Obscured/hidden | Open/clear |

*(Source: Adapted from Erdener Kaynak,* International Business in the Middle East, *p. 45.)*

Arabs prefer oral and aural communication. Also, the messages conveyed by another person's smells are many, and kissing the cheek allows them the chance to smell the other person. In some Middle Eastern countries, a groom's representatives call on a prospective bride to smell her for evidence of lingering anger or discontent.

Another unusual aspect about communicating with Arabs is that if you admire something they are wearing or that they have in their homes, they may give it to you, so it's best to withhold even the sincerest compliments.

Table 23 lists some communication practices of the Arab firm and Table 24 compares the communication system and other aspects of American and Middle Eastern businesses.

# Bahrain

*Official Name:* State of Bahrain; *Capital:* Manama; *Government:* constitutional monarchy; *Subdivisions:* none; *Population:* 464,102 (July 1987); *Density:* 1,629 per square mile; *Currency:* dinar; *Official Language:* Arabic; *Literacy:* 46 percent.

*The Land.* Translated loosely from Arabic, the word "Bahrain" means "two seas." Bahrain is an archipelago in the Persian Gulf midway between the tip of the Qatar peninsula and mainland Saudi Arabia. It is 20 miles from the eastern province of Saudi Arabia in the west and 18 miles from the Qatar peninsula to the southwest. In 1986, a $1 billion Saudi-financed causeway opened to traffic between Saudi Arabia and Bahrain.

Bahrain is about the size of New York City and contains 33 islands, the largest of which is also called Bahrain. It has a plentiful fresh water supply from springs and artesian wells. The islands are sandy and low-lying. Farmland and pasture make up about 11 percent of the country. The climate is hot and humid most of the year, with temperatures regularly reaching near 106° F and relative humidity of 70 to 80 percent. The 4 winter months are generally mild and pleasant.

The main island is pear-shaped and runs from north to south. It is about 10 miles across at its widest point in the north of the island and about 30 miles long. Total length of its coastline is 78 miles. It is mostly desert but has some gardens and groves near the northern coasts watered by springs fed by underground sources originating on the mainland. Toward the interior the land rises gradually toward a central range of hills. Most of the smaller islands are flat and sandy. The other islands, 30 in number and lying closeby, are much smaller; only four of them are inhabited. Off the northeast corner and joined to the main island by a two-lane causeway 1.5 miles long is the island of Muharraq.

*The People.* Bahrain is the most densely populated Gulf state. About 90 percent of the population are Arabs. Economic expansion and the absence of taxation have attracted many people from such countries as India, Iran, Pakistan, South Korea, the United Kingdom and the United States. In 1980, an estimated 37 percent of the population was foreign. Most Bahraini nationals are of Arab origin, although perhaps one-fifth are of Iranian descent. About 81 percent of the population is urban; 58 percent of them live in two principal cities: Manama and Al Muharraq.

About 63 percent of the population is Bahraini; 13 percent are Asian; 10 Arabs; 3 Iranian; and 6 percent other. All of the residents are Muslim, 70 percent Shi'a and 30 percent Sunni.

The country's first written constitution, made public in June 1973, proclaims Bahrain to be an Islamic state. Bahrain's culture is not distinct from that found in other Arab states bordering on the Gulf.

The participation of Bahraini women in the workforce remains greater than in any other state of the Arabian Peninsula. In 1981 they constituted 13.3 percent of the labor force, up from 3.8 percent in 1971. Bahraini women predominated in such occupations as teaching, but in the early 1980s, they began to enter banking, finance, engineering, the civil service, commerce and administration. The government encouraged the active participation of women in the labor force by enacting one of the most pro-female labor laws in the world. Women were guaranteed 45 days of full-pay maternity leave plus 15 days at half pay. Nursing periods were provided in addition to coffee breaks. The law forbidding discrimination against working mothers was stringently enforced.

Bahrain is the most socially advanced Gulf state, enjoying the oldest public education system in the Arabian Peninsula. Primary education for boys was introduced in 1919, and separate facilities for girls and various secondary programs were subsequently added. Still in 1984 the estimated illiteracy rate was about 45 percent.

Bahraini women have traditionally constituted a separate society in accord with Islamic heritage. The integration of male and female societies began with development of a modern economy and women have increasingly taken on roles previously reserved for men.

The country today is an independent sovereign state ruled by the Al Khalifa family.

*A Brief History.* Throughout its long history, Bahrain has shared the history of the Arabian Peninsula. Bahrain was a flourishing trading center as early as 2000 B.C. It was occupied by Arabs in the seventh century A.D. and it served as a Portuguese base from 1521 to 1602. From 1602 it came intermittently under the control of Persia (Iran), but the Persians were expelled in 1783. British influence increased in the nineteenth century and to counter claims by Iran and Turkey, Bahrain came under British protection in 1861. Full independence was achieved in 1970 when Bahrain became a member of the Arab League and the United Nations.

*The Economy.* Bahrain is a free-market economy with the private sector dominant. The labor force is divided this way: industry and commerce, 85 percent; agriculture, 5 percent; services, 5 percent; and government, 3 percent. There are no trade unions in Bahrain. Major industries are aluminum smelting, fishing, petroleum and natural gas production.

Petroleum and natural gas are the only significant natural resources. Bahrain was one of the first Arab Gulf states to discover oil, was the first with a refinery and will probably be the region's first post-petroleum economy in 15 or 20 years. Today the economy is 80 percent based on oil.

Oil in Bahrain was first discovered in commercial quantities in 1932 and first exported in 1934. Prior to the discovery of oil, the pearl industry was the mainstream of the economy. Bahrain was the first Gulf emirate to receive substantial revenue surpluses from oil. Known reserves, however, will run out about 1995. As a result, the government has been diversifying, encouraging the development of banking, trade, commerce, shipping and manufacturing in attempts to make Bahrain the Singapore of the Middle East.

Natural gas for domestic industry is plentiful. The major industrial facility is an aluminum smelter opened in 1972, which processes bauxite imported from Australia and exports aluminum to East Asian countries mainly. The aluminum smelter is the biggest non-oil related industrial project in the Gulf. Agriculture and fishing employ about 6.5 percent of the work force.

# Iran

*Official Name:* Islamic Republic of Iran; *Capital:* Tehran; *Government:* theocratic republic; *Subdivisions:* 23 provinces; *Population:* 50,407,763 (July 1987); *Density:* 67 per square mile; *Currency:* rial; *Official Language:* Persian (Farsi); *Literacy:* 48 percent.

*The Land.* About the size of the states of Alaska and of Washington combined, Iran is located in southwestern Asia between the Persian Gulf and the Caspian Sea. Its borders are as follows: 1,081 miles with the Soviet Union to the north, 528 miles with Afghanistan in the east, 516 miles with Pakistan in the southwest, 795 miles with Iraq in the west and 292 miles with Turkey in the northwest. It is a mountainous plateau, mainly, with a desert in the east and a narrow coastal plain in the south.

Scarcity and inaccessibility of water, irregular terrain and climatic extremes have restricted habitation generally to the western and most northern parts of the country. About 70 percent of the land is virtually uninhabited. About 51 percent of the land is desert, waste or urban; 30 percent is arable; 11 percent is forest; and 8 percent is migratory grazing and other.

*The People.* Iran is one of the few countries possessing both a large population and huge oil reserves. About two-thirds of the people are Aryan; they migrated from Central Asia. Some 63 percent of the people are Persian; 18 percent are Turkish; 13 percent are other Iranian; 3 percent are Kurdish; 3 percent are Arab and other Semitic, and 1 percent are other; 93 percent are Shiite Moslem and 5 percent are Sunni Moslem. About 2 percent belong to the Zoroastrian, Jewish, Christian or Bahai faiths.

Society is divided into urban, market-town, village and tribal groups. The urban society reflects the upper, middle and lower classes.

People are identified mainly according to language. Except for the Kurds of the Zagros Mountains, nearly all of the people of Iran follow the Shiite sect of Islam. About 80 percent speak Persian (Iranian). About a third of the people live in cities. Since the Islamic Revolution of 1979, the government has been encouraging people to return to farms. Tribal life has been a traditional part of Iranian society; nomadic and seminomadic groups form 17 percent of the population.

*A Brief History.* Formerly a feudal state ruled by an all-powerful Shah, Iran became a constitutional monarchy in 1906. But in 1921 a new dynasty led by Reza Shah Pahlavi took and centralized power in the monarchy. In 1978, domestic turmoil swept the country as a result of religious and political opposition to the reigning Shah, Reza Pahlavi, who fled the country in January 1979 as control of the government was assumed by Ayatollah Khomeini and his followers. This government has encouraged return to traditional Islamic values while paradoxically it has indiscriminately arrested and executed its enemies. Economic disorder and continued crisis have reigned, including the seizure of the United States embassy compound and its occupants in November 1979. From 1980 into 1988 Iran waged an undeclared war with its neighbor Iraq. Shiite Islam has been the state religion of Iran since A.D. 1500 and is strongly identified with Iranian nationalism. Approximately one-tenth of the world's Moslems are Shiite and Iran is the most populous Shiite Moslem country.

*The Economy.* The work force is divided this way: agriculture, 33 percent; manufacturing, 21 percent; and unemployed, about 35 percent.

Energy production is the most important economic activity in Iran. It is a major producer of oil and natural gas. Iran's war with Iraq has damaged its oil production and has caused a decline in exports both of which had previously been adversely affected by the Islamic Revolution. Agriculture continues to be the chief industry in Iran. Its principal crops are grains, rice, tobacco, cotton, fruit, oil seeds and sugar. The Iranians are renowned for their production of fine Persian carpets, delicate miniature paintings and intricate silver work.

Major industries include building materials, cement, chemicals, food processing, metallurgical products, petrochemicals, tanning and textiles.

*Organizational Communication.* The present government with its anti–Western attitudes shuns much contact with foreigners, particularly Americans. However, that will change and when it does, foreign business persons will need to understand Iran in the same way they do any other country. Iranian businessmen are courteous and friendly, extremely hospitable and more formal than businessmen in other parts of the Middle East.

# Iraq

*Official Name:* Republic of Iraq; *Capital:* Baghdad; *Government:* republic; *Subdivisions:* 18 provinces; *Population:* 16,970,948 (July 1987); *Density:* 93 per square mile; *Currency:* dinar; *Official Language:* Arabic; *Literacy:* 69 percent.

*The Land.* Roughly the size of California, Iraq is a large Arab republic located in the fertile crescent of southwestern Asia. It was once known as Mesopotamia. It is an almost landlocked country with a narrow outlet to the Persian Gulf. The country is bounded to the east by Iran, to the north by Turkey, to the west by Syria and Jordan and to the south by Saudi Arabia and Kuwait. The Tigris River flows through the country for 1,150 miles; the Euphrates River flows through it for 1,460 miles. The country slopes from mountains 10,000 feet above sea level along the border with Iran and Turkey to reedy marshes in the southeast.

About 68 percent of the land is desert, waste and urban; 18 percent is cultivated; 10 percent is seasonal and grazing; and 4 percent is forest and wood. The country is divided into four major regions: desert in the west and southwest; rolling upland between upper Euphrates and Tigris rivers; highlands in the north and northwest; and alluvial plain in the central and southeast sections.

Iraq also produces natural gas and other minerals. Farmland covers 12 percent of the land, pasture another 9 percent and woodland 3½ percent. Agriculture is still a major industry. The chief food crops are wheat, barley, rice, fruits and vegetables. Dates and cotton are the chief cash crops. Sheep and goats are reared mainly in the north, while cattle are kept in the south to supply milk and serve as draft animals.

*The People.* About 95 percent of the people are Muslims. Ethnically about 75 percent of the people are Arab; 15 to 20 percent are Kurdish (in the northeast); and five to ten percent are Persian, Turkish, Assyrian and other. Some 95 percent of all residents are Muslim (55 percent Shi'a and 40 percent Sunni) and 5 percent are Christian and other.

*A Brief History.* The Tigris-Euphrates lowlands were the center for several early civilizations including those of the Sumerians, Babylonians, Assyrians and Chaldeans. Islam was introduced in A.D. 634–641. Iraq was a backward part of the Ottoman Empire from 1638 until World War I whereupon it became a British-mandated territory. In 1920 Iraq was created as a monarchy, with Faisal I becoming king. The country was ruled first under a British mandate but full independence was achieved in 1932. In 1948 troops from Iraq were involved in the Arab-Israeli war and they also participated in later wars.

In 1958 the monarchy was overthrown and Iraq came under military rule. The 1960s were marred by fighting in the northeast with Kurdish nationals who wanted to establish a separate state with Kurds in Iran, Turkey and the U.S.S.R.

*The Economy.* The labor force is divided this way: agriculture, 44 percent; services, 31 percent; and industry, 26 percent. About 11 percent of the labor force is unionized.

Agriculture is the main source of employment and, next to oil, the most important sector. The principal crops are wheat, barley, rice, dates, cotton, maize and millet. But the economy depends almost totally on oil. In 1973, the oil industry was nationalized. Most of its oil is piped to ports on the Mediterranean. Iraq is using its oil revenues in a massive program of industrialization. The latest developments in the manufacturing sector have been in the production of pharmaceuticals, electrical goods, telephone cables and plastics.

The 1980–1988 war with Iran cost about $1 billion a month, and has greatly altered the nature of Iraq's economy.

——————————————— **Israel** ———————————————

*Official Name:* State of Israel; *Capital:* Jerusalem; *Government:* republic; *Subdivisions:* 6 districts; *Population:* 4,222,118 (July 1987); *Density:* 547.8 per square mile; *Currency:* shekel; *Official Language:* Hebrew; *Literacy:* 87 percent.

*The Land.* Nearly the size of Massachusetts, the country has four principal areas. The coastal plain—fertile, humid and thickly populated—stretches along the Mediterranean; the central hills include the Hills of Galilee in the north, with the highest elevation in the country, and the Negev Hills in the south; the Jordan Rift Valley has its lowest point at the Dead Sea; and the Negev Desert accounts for about half the country's area. Irrigation makes Israel's land arable year round.

Israel is divided into 40 percent pasture and meadow; 29 percent unsurveyed, but mostly desert; 20 cultivated; 4 forest; 4 desert, waste or urban; and 3 percent inland water.

*The People.* Nearly 90 percent of the people live in the cities, the fourth highest degree of urbanization in the world. Excluding the occupied areas, 85 percent of the people are Jews. The other 15 percent breaks down as follows: 77 percent Muslim; 14 percent Christian; and 9 percent Druze and other. Also, nearly a million Arabs live in Judea and Samaria (West Bank), administered by Israel since the war of 1967.

Fifty-five percent were born in Israel; 25 percent were born in Europe and the Western Hemisphere; 20 percent were born in Asia and Africa. The two main ethnic groups are the Ashkenazim, those from Central and Eastern Europe, and the Sephardim, Oriental Jews who came from the Near East and Mediterranean Basin. These now account for 60 percent of the population.

Israel has nearly the greatest cultural diversity found anywhere because its people have come literally from the four corners of the world. The population is drawn from 100 countries on five continents. The result is a rich diversity of culture and artistic creativity. Almost half of all Israelis were born in some other land. As the Zionist settlers of the pre-independence period were mainly Europeans, their culture has been fixed in a dominant position. An attempt has been made to Europeanize the later waves of immigration from Persian, Afghan, Kurdish, Yemeni, Iraqi or North African backgrounds. Because these Oriental Jews now outnumber the Europeans, they have begun to assert their own cultural values.

Israel is a land of informality. Titles are less important in Israel than they are in the United States. Army officers and enlisted men call each other by their first names, even nicknames. The society is a changing one that exhibits contrasts of old meeting new. On the streets Talmudic students with long earlocks wear long black coats side by side with stylish women and men in blue jeans.

Families are important in Jewish culture. They tend to be small, with the father the patriarch who exercises considerable influence in the home.

*A Brief History.* In the seventh century A.D., Palestine was conquered by the Muslims. The Ottoman Turks conquered the area in 1517, and ruled for 400 years until the beginning of World War I. In the 1890s Zionism, an international movement, was founded by Theodor Herzl to restore Palestine to the Jews. After World War I, the area came under British control. Finally in 1947 the United Nations agreed to divide Palestine into two independent states, one Jewish and one Arab. On May 14, 1948, Israel was proclaimed independent and the British withdrew.

On the same day, Egypt, Iraq, Jordan, Lebanon, Syria and Saudi Arabia attacked the newly created Israeli state. Since that time four other wars have broken out between Israel and its surrounding Arab neighbors. In 1956, with the help of Britain and France, Israel invaded Egypt's Sinai region, but was soon forced to withdraw. In a six-day war in 1967, Israeli forces fought against Jordanian, Egyptian and Syrian forces, capturing Jerusalem, the Sinai peninsula, the West Bank of the Jordan, the Gaza strip and the Golan Heights. In 1973, Egyptian and Syrian armies launched an attack on Israel, necessitating

**Figure 25. Employees at Israel Aircraft Industries work on sophisticated design programs. (Israel Aircraft Industries, Ltd., Tel Aviv.)**

the deployment of United Nations peacekeeping troops in the area. In 1979, a peace treaty between Israel's former Prime Minister Menachem Begin and Egypt's President Anwar Sadar was signed and Israel began withdrawing from the Sinai and the Gaza strip. A fourth war erupted when Israeli troops crossed into Lebanon in the summer of 1982 and entered Beirut as part of a crusade against the Palestine Liberation Organization. United Nations troops were brought in and a cease-fire was negotiated.

*The Economy.* The labor force is divided this way: public services, 29.5 percent; industry, mining and manufacturing 22.8, commerce 12.8, finance and business 9.5, transport, storage and communications 6.8, construction and public works 6.5, agriculture, forestry and fishing 5.5, personal and other services 5.8, electricity and water, 1 percent; and unemployed, about 6.7 percent. About 90 percent of the work force is unionized.

A major limitation on Israel's economy has been its lack of natural resources; however, the country is rich in skilled labor. Good deposits of potash and phosphate are being exploited, while several chemicals are being extracted from the water of the Dead Sea. Major industries include food processing, textiles, chemicals, metal products, electronic equipment, machinery, diamond cutting and polishing and defense. Its agriculture is efficient and modern. Main products include cereals, fruits, vegetables, poultry and dairy products.

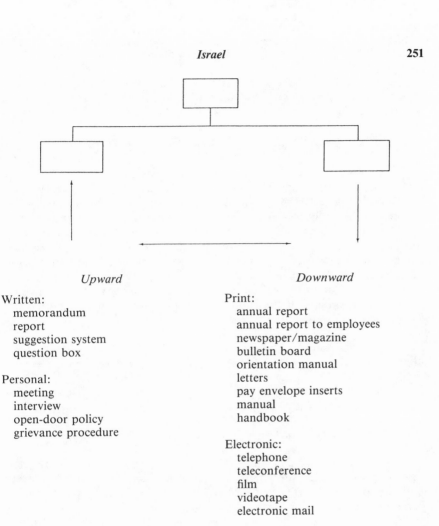

**Figure 26. The communication system of Israel Aircraft Industries, Inc.**

The most important industrial export, at least 40 percent of the total, consists of armaments, including guided missiles, an assortment of guns, and fighter air-craft. The best customers are Latin American dictatorships and South Africa.

Business is strongly affected by religious laws. This is a theocratic society with no separation between church and state. Businesses are closed on Friday afternoons and Saturday.

Major industries include aircraft, chemicals, clothing, electronics, food processing, metals and machinery, petrochemicals and textiles.

*Organizational Communication.* Business in Israel does tend to be conducted in an informal atmosphere. Israelis will not hesitate to express an opinion and will welcome frank, open discussion. You must sell hard in Israel; the soft sell will go unnoticed.

### CASE STUDY: ISRAEL AIRCRAFT INDUSTRIES, INC.

Israel Aircraft Industries, Inc. (IAI), began modestly as an overhaul facility 33 years ago, and today it is Israel's largest industry with 22,000 employees, like those in Figure 25, manufacturing over 300 products for sale in over 60 countries. They engage in research, design, development, integration, test, manufacture, support and service of land, sea, air systems and equipment as well as space technologies and military and civil aircraft, missiles, systems and components. Like Israel, IAI has been forged in the crucible of war; consequently, the products manufactured at five IAI divisions are part of an integrated chain built on knowledge gained through Israel's battle experience and in full cooperation with the country's defense forces. The communication system of IAI is presented in Figure 26.

# ——————————  Jordan  ——————————

*Official Name:* Hashemite Kingdom of Jordan; *Capital:* Amman; *Government:* constitutional monarchy; *Subdivisions:* 5 governorates; *Population:* 2,761,695 (July 1987); *Density:* 92.6 per square mile; *Currency:* dinar; *Official Language:* Arabic; *Literacy:* 71 percent.

*The Land.* The Jordan valley is part of the huge Rift Valley system that extends southward to the Red Sea and eastern Africa. The country is mostly arid, uninhabited desert except for the fertile Jordan River Valley. Close to 8 percent of the land is part of the Great Syrian Desert. The northern end of the valley is just above sea level, but the shoreline of the Dead Sea is 393 meters below sea level, the lowest point on earth. Neighboring countries are Syria in the north, Iraq in the east, Saudi Arabia in the southeast and Israel in the west. The port of Aqaba in the far south gives Jordan a narrow (15-mile wide) outlet to the Red Sea.

Jordan consists of a tilted plateau region in the northwestern corner of the great Arabian plateau. In the west, the edge of the plateau is abruptly marked by the major rift valley, known as El Ghor, of the Dead Sea lowlands. The Jordan River flows through the territory for 97 miles; it empties into the Dead Sea.

Part of the so-called fertile crescent, Jordan is a country of rocky deserts, mountains and rolling plains. About 88 percent is desert or waste. Its borders include 221 miles with Syria, 91 miles with Iraq, 462 miles with Saudi Arabia, and 298 miles with Israel. The latter is a ceasefire line that has never been accepted by Jordan.

About 88 percent of the land is desert, waste or urban; 11 percent is agriculture and 1 percent is forest.

*The People.* The majority of residents are of Mediterranean descent. There is also a small minority of Circassian Russians. About 90 percent of the people are Arabs and the vast majority are Muslim, adherents of the Sunni branch. There is a Christian minority. Most of the people live along the Jordan River. About 4 percent of the population are Bedouin (nomads).

About half of the population are refugees from territories that presently constitute Israel. Nomads have always moved freely across the Syrian, Iraqi and Saudi Arabian borders. Longstanding hostility exists between the Bedouins and non–Bedouins.

The population is 95 percent homogeneous. The Arabic language and Islam are the unifying forces in the country.

The modern culture of Jordan differs little from that in Syria and parts of Lebanon, although the eastern and southern parts of the country are more like Saudi Arabia. In towns and cities, Western styles and habits are being imitated more and more, but there is popular resistance to this in some areas. In the Middle East, lines between various age and social groups are still strong. Older people are honored and respected. Young men or women will generally not smoke, drink or use slang in the presence of their elders and will try to assist them in any way possible.

The family is unquestionably the most important unit in Jordanian society. The extended family shares a close relationship. Cousins are often as close as brothers and sisters are in the West. To be able to help any member of the family is considered a great honor. Older members of the family are revered.

*A Brief History.* Previously occupied by the Romans, the area that is now Jordan became part of the Islamic Empire in A.D. 636 and remained so until 1099 when it was captured by the Crusaders. The Mamelukes of Egypt expelled the Crusaders in 1187, and were themselves ousted by the Ottoman Turks in 1516, beginning a rule which lasted 400 years.

In 1916, Hashemite Sherif Hussain of the Hijaz led an Arab revolt to form a united Arab independent state and introduce progressive social and economic programs. However, the area was split into British and French mandated territories following the defeat of the Turkish Empire in 1918. Palestine came under the British mandate while in 1921 Hussain's son, Abdullah, assumed the throne of Transjordan, which was established as a separate state.

Over the years the British gradually ceded power to local Arab officials and in 1946, Transjordan became independent as the state of Jordan, still with a strong British orientation. The mandate was ended after World War II. In 1948 Jordanian and other Arab armies entered Palestine to help the Palestinian Arabs, believing that they should govern Palestine after Britain's withdrawal. When the war ended, the West Bank became part of Jordan and Palestinian refugees flooded into Jordan and Palestinian guerrilla bases were established. In 1951, Abdullah was assassinated. His son Talal ruled briefly but was deposed by government officials. In 1952 Talal's 17-year-old son Hussein became the new Jordanian monarch. After a series of aircraft hijacks and an attempted assassination of King Hussein, the Jordanian army sought to expel the Palestinian guerrillas and a civil war ensued in 1970–71. In 1973 King Hussein

**Figure 27. In Jordan women have achieved a level of equality with men that is unusual in the Arab world, as proved by this new woman pilot. (Royal Jordanian Airlines, Amman.)**

declared a general amnesty for Palestinians and, in 1974, an Arab Summit Conference in Rabat declared the Palestinian Liberation Organization (PLO) to be the sole legal representative of the Palestinian people. In 1988, King Hussein ceded Jordan's claim to the West Bank to the PLO.

Hussein's rule has been punctuated by regional wars and occasional internal unrest. These problems stem in large part from the refugee status of the Palestinian population who left their homes when Israel was declared an independent state in 1948. The Arab-Israeli conflict has long since changed from a local to a regional one as the surrounding Arab states took up the Palestinian cause.

*The Economy.* The labor force is divided this way: agriculture, 20 percent; industry, 20 percent; and trade and services, 60 percent. About 10 percent of the work force is unionized.

Agriculture is a major sector of the Jordanian economy. However, only 11 percent of Jordan's total land is arable. Cultivation is of a subsistence type. Principal crops are wheat, barley, lentils, citrus fruits and vegetables. Jordan has been experiencing an economic boom due mainly to the export of skilled labor such as technicians, teachers, and business management personnel to the Persian Gulf and Saudi Arabia. Amman has become a business center, particularly after the ongoing civil war in Lebanon forced companies to relocate from Beirut.

Jordan is short of natural resources; in fact, it is one of the least endowed countries in the world in natural resources. The industrial sector is small, and its growth is limited. Jordan has had to rely heavily on foreign aid, which in recent years has been coming increasingly from oil-rich Arab governments. Another source of revenues is the large remittances by Jordanian workers abroad.

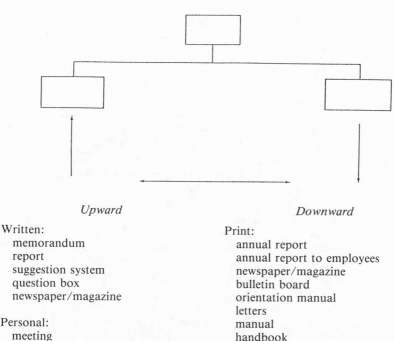

|                        |                          |
| ---------------------- | ------------------------ |
| *Upward*               | *Downward*               |
| Written:               | Print:                   |
|   memorandum |   annual report |
|   report     |   annual report to employees |
|   suggestion system |   newspaper/magazine |
|   question box |   bulletin board |
|   newspaper/magazine |   orientation manual |
|                        |   letters      |
| Personal:              |   manual       |
|   meeting    |   handbook     |
|   interview  |                          |
|   open-door policy | Electronic:         |
|   grievance procedure |   telephone |
|                        |   teleconference |
|                        |   film         |
|                        |   videotape    |

*Horizontal*

personal contact
memorandum
meeting

**Figure 28. The communication system of Alia—the Royal Jordanian Airline.**

Five heavy industries account for the bulk of income from this sector: phosphates, cement, textiles, chemicals and oil refining. Other major industries include beverages, cigarettes, plastics, soap, tanning and vegetable oils. Of the 4,842 industrial units, only 48 employ more than 200 workers.

The country's leading resource is phosphates, but Jordan also has other minerals, like potash and shale oil, and some as yet unexploited. They also raise goats, sheep and cattle. Manufacturing is increasing. Products exported are cigarettes, fruits and vegetables, phosphates, fertilizers, olive oil and soap. Mining is of phosphates and marble. Tourism is important.

In the workplace, employers look after employee interests and are considered responsible for a wider area of concerns than in the West. In many cases, the employer is regarded more like an uncle than a boss.

## CASE STUDY: ALIA – THE ROYAL JORDANIAN AIRLINE

Royal Jordanian Airline was established in 1963 and has developed into a multipurpose aviation conglomerate contributing to the social and economic development of its own country while becoming an international enterprise. It now serves 42 destinations in four continents with 100 active sales offices and representatives throughout the world. It has about 5,000 employees with about 300 members in its cockpit crew, including one woman as shown in Figure 27. The communication system of the company is shown in Figure 28.

Ali Ghandour, chairman and chief executive officer of the airline is calling for regional cooperation of the airline industry:

> Since the U.S. deregulated its aviation industry in 1978, the winds of change have reached all parts of the world. Protectionism is out and it's going to stay out. After 1992, Europe will become one region and one market in aviation, in which no individual country will negotiate separately. The developing countries, particularly in the Middle East, cannot negotiate alone either. We'll be run over if we try.... Royal Jordanian has become more professional and better known. Our new image is a key factor in the first-quarter [of 1988] growth of 24% in traffic and revenues.[17]

# Kuwait

*Official Name:* State of Kuwait; *Capital:* Kuwait; *Government:* constitutional monarchy; *Subdivisions:* 3 governorates; *Population:* 1,863,615 (July 1987); *Density:* 275.6 per square mile; *Currency:* dinar; *Official Language:* Arabic; *Literacy:* 70 percent.

*The Land.* "Kuwait" means "little fort," a diminutive form of the Iraqi Arabic word *kout.* Mohammed bin Ariaar, the sheikh of the Banu Khalid tribe, controlled the area between Basra (Iraq) and the country of Qatar to the south around the 1690s. He established a fort and gave Kuwait its name. Sheikh Sabah I established the state of Kuwait in 1756.

Located in the northeastern corner of the Arabian Peninsula, Kuwait is about the size of New Jersey, an area, rectangular in shape, of flat desert interspersed with low-lying hills at the head of the Persian Gulf. There are only a few natural oases and no supply of fresh water for the city of Kuwait which gives its name to the state. It shares a border of 101 miles with Saudi Arabia in the south and 160 miles with Iraq in the north. Its coastline, excluding the islands, is 132 miles long. The terrain is almost flat desert. The highest land is in the south and west. The land is arid; there are no permanent streams. Kuwait also includes over 625 square miles of islands, only one of which is inhabited.

*The People.* Some 39 percent of the residents are Kuwaitis; 39 percent are other Arab; 9 percent are South Asian; 4 percent are Iranian; and 9 percent are other. About 85 percent of residents are Muslim and 15 percent are Christian, Hindu, Parsi and other.

In addition to the ruling Al Sabah Dynasty which traces its descent from the eighteenth century members of the Anayzah confederation, about 180 other prominent families, called *asilin,* also claim social prominence because of their descent from noble tribes. These families use the prefix *al* before their names.

There are two classes of Kuwaiti citizenship. "Kuwaiti origin" means the family was in Kuwait before 1921. "Naturalized citizen" indicates the family settled in Kuwait after 1921.

Each neighborhood in Kuwait has a mosque, and Muslims are called to prayer five times a day. The Islamic holy day is Friday, thus the "weekend" is Thursday and Friday. Traditionally days begin at sunset rather than midnight. "Monday night," then, is the evening before Monday.

The Islamic value system plus Kuwait's desert history form the basis of the culture. Islam influences the society's view of home life, family roles and respect for another's property. History has promoted hospitality and generosity, both in personal and business relations.

Kuwaiti law emphasizes the importance of family. Kuwaiti law allows a man up to four wives, but generally for the purpose of producing children.

*A Brief History.* In historic times Kuwait was oriented more towards the nomadic culture of the Arabian peninsula rather than the farming cultures to the north. Arabs founded the port of Kuwait at the beginning of the eighteenth century and Kuwait flourished after the accession of the present ruling family of al-Sabah in 1756. In 1899 a treaty made Britain responsible for Kuwait's foreign affairs against the Ottoman Empire. At the outbreak of World War I, Britain declared Kuwait a protectorate. The Sabah family, which had first discovered the country, retained internal authority over the town which was still an uninviting lonely little trading center. This treaty remained in force until 1961 when Kuwait became fully independent. Today the Sabah clan, which has ruled unrivaled since the eighteenth century, shares power with an increasingly vocal Parliament.

*The Economy.* The labor force is divided this way: services, 45 percent; construction 20, trade 12, manufacturing 8.6, finance and real estate 2.6, agriculture 1.9, power and water 1.7, and mining and quarrying, 1.4 percent.

From 150 to 200 Kuwaiti families who have been in business for generations control the country. The firms operated by these families handle a wide variety of industrial and consumer products.

Only about 30 years ago Kuwaitis made their living by simple means: fishing, grazing herds of goats and camels, building small ships or diving for pearls. Then oil was discovered, and today oil is the basis of the whole economy. It has been responsible for bringing in many foreign workers, including 80,000 Iranians and 350,000 Palestinians. The Kuwaitis are a 40 percent minority in their own country.

The Kuwait Oil Company, owned jointly by American and British companies, first began drilling for oil in 1936, but production was not started until after World War II. Large-scale oil production began in 1946; it has become one of the world's richest nations. The chief resources are oil and natural gas. Kuwait has some of the world's largest oil reserves; in fact they are the second largest in the world. Unlike other oil-rich nations of the Gulf, Kuwait has invested heavily in the West — about $80 billion. Less than 0.1 percent of the land is farmed and only 7.5 percent is pasture. Vegetables and dates are grown, but Kuwait imports most of its food. Sheep, goats and cattle are raised.

Major industries are building materials, cement, chemical fertilizers, fishing and petroleum. Industrial development is limited by the relative absence of raw materials, high labor costs, lack of technical manpower and a small domestic market.

Decisions about business life are made with consideration for one's family, friends, the Islamic community and the country — in that order. Outsiders, regardless of rank, importance or financial potential, fall outside those priorities.

Business dealings require a highly personalized touch. There must be frequent trips to meet with agents and customers face to face. It is better to have a resident representative on the spot. Those trying to do business by correspondence will rarely succeed.

*Organizational Communication.* Praise to full measure whatever you admire that is not personal. Do not praise personal possessions. Eye contact is important.

Arabs give each conversation their undivided attention. When two peers are talking, they focus completely on each other, not allowing their eyes to wander. Each person is of the utmost importance to the other for that period of contact. Wandering eyes, as well as wandering minds, are considered extremely discourteous.

# Lebanon

*Official Name:* Republic of Lebanon; *Capital:* Beirut; *Government:* republic; *Subdivisions:* 4 provinces; *Population:* 3,320,522 (July 1987); *Density:* 665 per square mile; *Currency:* pound; *Official Language:* Arabic; *Literacy:* 75 percent.

*The Land.* Lebanon, territorially the smallest land nation of southwest Asia, is located at the eastern end of the Mediterranean Sea. It has four geographical zones: a narrow coastal plain; a coastal mountain range called the Lebanon Mountains; a narrow central valley called the Biq Valley, actually a plateau, about 75 miles long and five to eight miles wide; and an interior mountain range, called the Anti-Lebanon Mountains, bordering on Syria. Behind the coastal plain are the Lebanon Mountains and east of the mountains is a narrow plateau containing the fertile Bekaa valley and the headwaters of the Orontes River. Lebanon is slightly smaller than the state of Connecticut. Sixty percent of the land is desert, 10 percent forest, and only 27 percent is arable. Neighboring countries are Syria in the north and east and Israel in the south.

With superb mountain scenery, Lebanon is perhaps the most attractive region in the Middle East. About 64 percent of the country is desert, waste or urban; 27 percent is agriculture; and 9 percent is forest.

*The People.* Some 57 percent of the people today are Muslims or Druse while 42 percent are Christians and 1 percent are other. Conflict between religious groups is deepseated. Arabs make up 90 percent of the population and there are Armenian, Kurdish, Assyrian, Jewish, Greek and Turkish minorities. Lebanon also contains Palestinian refugees.

About 93 percent of residents are Arab; 6 percent are Armenian; 1 percent are other. Some 57 percent of those residents are Muslim and Druze; 42 percent are Christian; and 1 percent are other.

*A Brief History.* A small part of modern Lebanon, called Mount Lebanon, was a Maronite enclave in the vast Ottoman Empire. This area and all of Syria became a French protectorate when the French and British drove the Ottomans out of the area during World War I. Lebanon became a republic in 1926, but French troops did not withdraw from the country until 1946. The country was set up to ensure the Christians a slight majority of power. The president was to always be a Maronite, while the prime minister was to be a Sunni Muslim. Since the Muslim birthrate is higher, it is generally assumed that the Muslims now form a majority. This fact, along with social disparities between the two, has led to a great deal of internal tension and strife, culminating in the civil wars of 1958 and from 1975 to present. Palestinian refugees have settled in Lebanon and have sided with the Muslims. In 1982, Israel invaded Lebanon and occupied the entire area south of Beirut.

*The Economy.* The labor force is divided this way: industry, commerce and services, 79 percent; agriculture, 11 percent; and government, 10 percent. About 10 percent of the work force is unionized.

Once a center of international commerce and banking, as well as a tourist haven, Lebanon has seen its economy ruined by civil war. Lebanon has few resources, but in normal times it is prosperous with valuable entrepôt and tourist trades. Its business people are energetic entrepreneurs who have made Lebanon an international financial center. Farmland makes up some 34 percent of the country and forests 7 percent.

The economy is based on trading in which trade, banking and tourism generate two-thirds of the national income. The civil war which has waged in the country for years has disrupted most of this activity.

Most industrial enterprises tend to be small. Over 81.1 percent employ fewer than five workers and only 1.9 percent employ more than 25. The industrial sector has suffered most from the civil war.

# Oman

*Official Name:* Sultanate of Oman; *Capital:* Muscat; *Government:* monarchy; *Subdivisions:* 1 province, 2 governorates and numerous districts; *Population:* 1,226,923 (July 1987); *Density:* 8.3 per square mile; *Currency:* rial; *Official Language:* Arabic; *Literacy:* 20 percent.

*The Land.* Located in the eastern part of the Arabian Peninsula facing the Gulf of Oman and Arabian Sea, Oman has a 420-mile border with Saudi Arabia on the west and a 255-mile border with the United Arab Emirates on the north and west, both of which are still undefined, and a 179-mile border on the southwest with South Yemen which is in dispute. About the size of Kansas, Oman is the second largest country in the Arabian Peninsula.

The country has a 1,156-mile coastline on the Gulf of Oman and the Indian Ocean. The territory also includes the top of the strategically important Musandam Peninsula, separated by the United Arab Emirates from the rest of Oman. This peninsula overlooks the Strait of Hormuz, passageway for about 17 percent of the world's daily oil production.

Northern Oman contains a fertile coastal plain which lies northwest of Muscat. Behind the plain is a rugged highland region. Central Oman consists of a barren plateau that merges into the "Empty Quarter" of Saudi Arabia. In the south is a fertile region.

*The People.* About 90 percent of the population is of Arab origin. There are also some descendants of black African slaves and immigrant workers from India, Iran, Pakistan and South Korea. The population is 95 percent rural; no town has more than 100,000 residents.

Foreigners comprise about 20 percent of the population and 80 percent of the nonagricultural work force. At least 200,000 expatriates live in Oman, most of whom (180,000) are guest workers from India, Pakistan, Bangladesh and Sri Lanka as well as from Egypt, Jordan and the Philippines.

Since 1970, the government has placed much emphasis on education. By 1985, some 225,000 students, both male and female, were enrolled in 597 schools. The goal is manpower development, considered a vital factor in the country's economic and social progress.

*A Brief History.* Oman was called the Sultanate of Muscat and Oman until 1970. In ancient times, Oman was a major Indian Ocean trading center. In the seventh century, Oman became one of the first areas to embrace Islam, during the lifetime of the Prophet Muhammad. Portugal ruled the area from 1508 to 1648, when they were turned out by Imam Nasir bin Murshid. Oman's power steadily increased and by 1730 it had taken all the Portuguese settlements in East Africa, including Zanzibar, which it held until the second half of the nineteenth century. It had become the most powerful state in Arabia on the East African coast. But civil wars in Oman led to Iranian intervention. The Iranians were finally expelled in 1749 by Ahmad bin Said, founding the Al-Busaid dynasty which still rules Oman. Except for that brief period of Persian rule, Oman has remained independent since 1650. In 1980 Oman negotiated a defense alliance with the United States.

*The Economy.* The labor force is divided this way: agriculture, 73 percent, and industry, 13 percent. The low level of industrial activity is due to the small size of the domestic market and a lack of trained Omani manpower.

The Oman economy is dominated by oil which was discovered in 1964 with production beginning in 1967. Until then agricultural and fishing were the traditional way of life. Revenues are being used to diversify the economy. Natural gas is being exploited and copper, chromite and other minerals mined.

Agriculture and fishing are also being expanded. Farming is limited to lands around oases but dates and other fruits, vegetables and some cereals are grown.

Major industries include cement, construction materials, food processing, furniture and petroleum.

## Qatar

*Official Name:* State of Qatar; *Capital:* Doha; *Government:* monarchy; *Subdivisions:* none; *Population:* 315,741 (July 1987); *Density:* 61.9 per square mile; *Currency:* riyal; *Official Language:* Arabic; *Literacy:* 40 percent.

*The Land.* Qatar occupies the Qatar peninsula, which juts northward into the Persian Gulf from the eastern Saudi Arabian mainland and includes some small islands in the Persian Gulf. Its terrain is mainly flat and barren, covered with loose sand and gravel and relieved only in the western regions by low ridges. Vegetation is scarce.

Smaller than Connecticut, the Qatar peninsula is about 100 miles long and a minimum of 50 miles wide. It shares a 42-mile border with Saudi Arabia and a 28-mile border with the United Arab Emirates. Its Persian Gulf coastline is 235 miles long. Apart from some hills in the northwest, most of Qatar is flat, barren, stony and sandy desert, with sand dunes and salt marshes in the south. It has a limited supply of underground water which is not suitable for drinking or agriculture.

*The People.* Qatar is one of the world's most urbanized countries; nearly 80 percent of the residents live in the capital Doha. Only about a quarter of the total population is indigenous Qataris; the rest are immigrant workers, including small communities from Europe, the United States and the Far East.

About 40 percent of the population are Arab; 18 percent are Pakistani; 18 percent are Indian; and 10 percent are Iranian. Bedouin tribes roam the interior with herds of camels, sheep and goats, but this way of life is dying out as the government encourages the herders to settle. Some 95 percent of them are Muslim. Over 77 percent of the population lives in the capital city of Doha.

*A Brief History.* The period of dominance over Qatar by the Khalifa family in Bahrain persisted until 1868 when, at the request of the Qatari nobles, the British conducted negotiations for the territory of the Bahraini claim except for the payment of tribute. The tribute ended with the occupation of Qatar by the Ottoman Turks in 1872. Between 1872 and World War I, Qatar was nominally under the control of the Ottoman Empire. In 1916 a treaty made Qatar a British protected state. This treaty remained in force until 1971 when Qatar became fully independent. It then joined the Arab League and the United Nations. HH Shaikh Kalifa bin Hamad Al-Thani, whose family has ruled Qatar since 1868, became Emir in 1972.

*The Economy.* The labor force is divided this way: subsistence agriculture and fishing, 30 percent, and industry, chiefly oil, 70 percent.

In comparatively recent times, Qatar's economy was based on fishing, pearl diving and some nomadic herding. Qatar has been a center of the pearl trade since the eighth century. The collapse of the pearl trade in the 1930s had a devastating effect on Qatar's economy, which recovered only with the discovery of oil in the 1930s, bringing newfound prosperity based on oil and natural gas. The export of oil began in 1949. In the early 1980s, it was estimated that the known oil reserves should last at least 35 years, while the offshore North Field contains what is probably one of the world's largest natural gas deposits.

Major industries include cement, fertilizers, iron and steel, petrochemicals and petroleum. Virtually all heavy industry projects that have been initiated so far rely on Qatar's petroleum reserve for fuel or feedstock.

# Saudi Arabia

*Official Name:* Kingdom of Saudi Arabia; *Capital:* Riyadh; *Government:* monarchy; *Subdivisions:* 14 districts; *Population:* 14,904,794 (July 1987); *Density:* 14.5 per square mile; *Currency:* riyal; *Official Language:* Arabic; *Literacy:* 52 percent.

*The Land.* Saudi Arabia is the twelfth largest country in the world. It is one-fourth the size of the United States and occupies four-fifths of the Arabian Peninsula. Its western coast extends for 1,094 miles along the Red Sea and its eastern coast runs for 350 miles along the Persian Gulf. The country shares these borders with its neighbors: 462 miles with Jordan, 556 miles with Iraq, 101 miles with Kuwait, 42 miles with Qatar, 364 with the United Arab Emirates, 420 miles with Oman, 516 with the People's Democratic Republic of Yemen and 390 miles with the Yemen Arab Republic. Its coastline is 1,560 miles long. The Arabian Peninsula tilts downwards to the north and east to the broad, oil-rich, al-Hasa plain on the Gulf. Water-bearing rocks underlie the plain; the underground water originates far to the west. The interior of Saudi Arabia contains varied desert scenery with rugged mountains in the west from which the land slopes gently eastward toward the Persian Gulf. It has no permanent rivers or bodies of water. Only about 20 percent of the land is habitable; the rest is covered by sand dunes. About 98 percent of the land is desert, waste or urban; 1 percent is agricultural; and 1 percent is forest.

*The People.* Nearly all of the people are Arabs, although some people of Negroid ancestry live in the Red Sea region. About 75 percent of the total labor force are foreign workers, mainly from Yemen, Egypt and Palestine. Other nationalities include Indians, Pakistanis, Koreans and Americans. The indigenous population is comprised of homogenous nomadic tribes.

Saudi Arabia is the only country in the Middle East where slavery is officially countenanced. Though slavery was officially abolished in 1962, demand for slaves is sufficient to enable slave traders to continue to operate profitably.

Life in Saudi Arabia is relaxed and slow paced. Saudis like to establish trust and confidence with the people they deal with before proceeding with any business. They are very conscious of personal and family honor and can be easily offended by any perceived insult of that honor. Next to Islam, the family is the strongest unifying force. An Arab is known by the family to which he or she belongs, and protecting the honor of the family is a paramount interest in life.

The Bedouins are a hardy, dignified, self-reliant tough people. They have long been known as "desert detectives." A Bedouin's word as to the weight, size and time of a man's footsteps in the desert sand is taken as evidence in Saudi courts. They can trace a lost man or animal—or jeep—with incredible speed. They have always been a keen, astute, alert people.

Nearly all manual labor is done by foreigners; manual labor carries a very low status. Nearly 100 percent of the residents are Muslim.

*A Brief History.* Saudi Arabia is ruled by the Saud family. The Kingdom was founded by the late King Ibn Saud who in 1932 gave it its present name.

Saudi Arabia, with its holy cities of Mecca and Medina, is the spiritual home of Islam, the birthplace of the religion. All Muslims who can are obliged to make the *hajj* or pilgrimage to Mecca, the birthplace of Muhammad, at least once. In the seventh century, it became the center of a huge empire that, by the A.D. 730s, extended from Spain to India. From 1517 Saudi Arabia was part of the Ottoman Empire, but the Turks were driven out by the Arab Revolt in World War I. Modern Saudi Arabia was founded by Ibn Saud who united the nation taking the title of King Hejaz in 1926. The name Saudi Arabia was adopted in 1932. After World War II, the vast oil reserves were opened and Abdulaziz began to use the oil revenue to speed the process of modernization, a process continued by succeeding Kings Saud, Faisal and Khalid.

*The Economy.* The labor force is divided this way: commerce, services and government, 45 percent; agriculture, 30 percent; construction, 15 percent; industry, 5 percent; and 5 percent, oil and mining.

Saudi Arabia is the world's leading oil exporter. The country also has the world's largest oil reserves (one-fourth of the world's supply). Oil was discovered in the 1930s, but large-scale production didn't begin until after World War II. Today oil accounts for 99 percent of the country's exports; as a result it has one of the strongest economies in the world. ARAMCO (Arab American Oil Company) is the major energy-producing organization and came completely under Saudi control in 1980. Because of the inhospitable climate and terrain, the nation must import the majority of its food, but dates, grains and livestock are produced.

Each work day is broken up by a two- or three-hour lunch period as well as breaks for prayer. The minimum age of employment is 10. Labor unions and strikes are banned.

Major industries include building materials, gasoline, petrochemicals and petroleum. Major commercial centers and infrastructural developments have been greatly modernized since oil was discovered in Saudi Arabia in 1938. In the decades since World War II, the Saudis have invested billions of dollars in building new roads, schools, hospitals and airports. A national telephone system has recently been installed by Canadian Bell. Large cities like Jubail, Yenbo and Khamis Mushayt are being built. By the year 2000, each is expected to have a population of tens of thousands of people. In ancient trading centers like Jidda, buildings of concrete and steel are edging out those of mud brick. Today, there are modern international hotels, television stations, air conditioning, and telex machines.

*Organizational Communication.* In Saudi Arabia, the protocol is to use the first meeting for social acquaintance, warm-up, or trust-building and not as a time to conduct serious business. It is impolite to point at Saudi Arabians or to signal them with the hand.

Religion and family are extremely important. In business, Saudis are tough, shrewd and cautious. Saudis typically are meticulous in manners and hospitality. Islamic law is the basis of all commercial and social law.

It has been said: "If you are in a hurry in the Middle East, don't bother." The Arab phrase is "Haste comes from the Devil."

Business cards are essential in Saudi Arabia because they provide data you may not find anywhere else. Arabs often have unlisted telephone numbers and private addresses. Your file of business cards becomes your private business directory.

Paperwork is considered routine and is therefore left to imported workers. Saudis, in their greatly underpopulated land, are the elite. Their job is to mastermind, to make contacts, make decisions, but then to bow out when it gets to details.

Both class and rank are quite important to Arabs despite the Muslim concept of all being equal before God. This becomes rather clear at doorways as they sort themselves out by status, the senior man going through first, being followed by the next and then the next in hierarchy.

Queuing up or standing in line is unheard of; whoever gets to a watering hole first – or a taxi – wins. The same is true of conversations, interrupting is not considered offensive.

If you think of how hard it has always been to wash one's hands in the waterless desert, you will easily understand how the famous Arab sensitivity to the left hand has become so deeply ingrained.

## Syria

*Official Name:* Syrian Arab Republic; *Capital:* Damascus; *Government:* socialist republic; *Subdivisions:* 13 provinces and 1 capital district; *Population:* 11,147,763 (July 1987); *Density:* 142.7 per square mile; *Currency:* pound; *Official Language;* Arabic; *Literacy:* 50 percent.

*The Land.* About the size of North Dakota, Syria is located in southwest Asia on the east coast of the Mediterranean Sea. The country is divided into a coastal zone with a narrow double mountain belt and a large eastern region that includes various mountain ranges and large desert regions. Behind the narrow Mediterranean coastal plain is the Ansariya range which rises to about

1500 meters. East of the range is the Orontes River valley. Syria's chief highlands are the Anti-Lebanon Mountains which reach 2,814 meters at Mount Hermon on the Lebanese border in the southwest. East of the Orontes basin and the Anti-Lebanon Mountains are broad plateaux that descend in the northeast to the Euphrates River basin.

Syria shares a border of 525 miles with Turkey to the north; 370 miles with Iraq to the east; 221 miles with Jordan to the south; 223 miles with Lebanon to the west; and 47 miles with Israel to the southwest.

The Euphrates flows through the country diagonally for 400 miles. Syria also has a Mediterranean coastline of 114 miles.

*The People.* About 90 percent of the people are Arabs. Minorities include the Kurds in the north, Armenians, Turks, Circassian Russians, Assyrians and Palestinian refugees. About 90 percent of the people are Muslims (74 percent Sunni Muslim; 16 percent Alawite, Druze and other Muslim sects). Most of the rest are Christians (Syrians were among the earliest Christians).

Although most residents are Arab, they do not constitute a unified or monolithic force because of internal divisions. Distinctions of language, religion, region and race cut across Syrian society and produce a large number of separate communities, each with its own system of shared values and loyalties.

Educated Syrians are cosmopolitan, traveled, multilingual and intellectually astute. They are also conservative, dignified and very proud of Syria.

The family is the basic unit of society and the center of an individual's life. All activities revolve around family members and family life, and any achievement by a family member advances the entire family. The father is the undisputed leader of the family.

*A Brief History.* The Arabs conquered Syria between A.D. 634 and 636 and under the Umayyad dynasty, Damascus because the center of a brilliant Arab empire stretching from the Atlantic Ocean to India. In 750, however, the empire's capital was moved to Iraq and Syria declined. From 1095 to 1291, Syria featured in Crusader wars and from 1516 Syria was part of the Ottoman Empire.

In 1920, following the breakup of the Ottoman Empire, France began to rule a Syrian region under a League of Nations mandate, and in 1925 a Syrian republic was administratively separated from Lebanon. An independent republic was proclaimed in 1941, although foreign troops remained in Syria until 1946.

*The Economy.* The labor force is divided this way: agriculture, 32 percent; industry, 32 percent; and miscellaneous services, 36 percent. About 5 percent of the work force is unionized.

Syria's economy has traditionally been based on agriculture and trading, but industry has recently played an increasingly important part. The country's resources include oil, the leading export since 1974, natural gas and phosphates. Arable land covers about 31 percent of the land, pasture of varying quality 45 percent and forest 2.5 percent.

Products manufactured include handicrafts such as leather goods,

brocades and inlaid metal work. It engages in oil refining, textiles, flour milling, cement, food processing, soap and glassware.

Major industries include cement, clothing, food processing, glass,
petroleum refining, soap and textiles.

Syria is one of the lower-middle-income countries with a centralized and
regulated socialist economy in which the public sector is dominant. Almost all
large businesses, industrial firms, banks and insurance companies come under
public control.

# ——————— Turkey ———————

*Official Name:* Republic of Turkey; *Capital:* Ankara; *Government:*
republic; *Subdivisions:* 67 provinces; *Population:* 52,987,778 (July
1987); *Density:* 167.5 per square mile; *Currency:* lira; *Official Language:*
Turkish; *Literacy:* 69 percent.

*The Land.* Turkey lies partly in Europe and partly in Asia. It occupies the
land mass of the Anatolian Peninsula in West Asia together with the city of
Istanbul and its Thracian hinterland. The Bosporus, the Sea of Marmara and
the Dardanelles, known collectively as the Turkish Straits, connect the Black
and Mediterranean seas. The coastal areas receive sufficient rainfall to support
intensive cultivation.

The greatest distance from north to south is 403 miles and from east to
west it is 993 miles. The total length of the Turkish coastline is 5,098 miles.

European Turkey is agricultural lands and is separated from Asiatic
Turkey by the Dardanelles. Anatolian Turkey is mostly a semiarid plateau surrounded by mountains and hills, with fertile lands and a long coast. It lies in
the approximate area of the ancient Asia Minor. It has two long coastlines: one
faces the Black Sea to the north and the other faces the Mediterranean and
Aegean seas to the south and west. Turkey is separated from the much larger
Asian portion of the country (Anatolia) by the Sea of Marmara, which has
outlets to the Black Sea and to the Aegean Sea through the Bosporus and the
Dardanelles, respectively.

Turkey shares these borders with its European neighbors: 167 miles with
Bulgaria and 132 miles with Greece. In Asia it faces the Soviet Union for 379
miles, Iran for 282 miles, Iraq for 205 miles and Syria for 545 miles.

As is usual with countries of this size, the topography is varied. The
western half tends to be hilly rather than mountainous and there are large areas
of fertile plains. In the east, the dominating feature is a mountain plateau.

*The People.* The 3 percent of the territory that is in Europe has 8 percent
of the population. Most people are identified as Turks on the basis of language
and their Islamic culture; there are a variety of physical characteristics and
many Turks look much like Europeans.

Turkey is often described as the link between East and West. The people
have incorporated many European and Asian features into their thinking and
lifestyle. Still, the people are fiercely nationalistic. The people are Turks, not

Arabs. They are not semitic, but are descendants of various indigenous peoples and of Turkish tribes who moved into Anatolia in the eleventh century.

*A Brief History.* The Muslim Seljuk Turks entered Asia Minor in the eleventh century and began the long process of Islamization and Turkization. In 1453, the successors of the Seljuks, the Ottoman Turks, captured Constantinople and went on to create a vast empire of their own which stretched beyond the bounds of the Byzantine Empire into the Balkans, the Middle East and North Africa. The Ottoman Empire survived until World War I when it allied itself with the Central Powers, upon whose defeat the empire was dismembered. Out of the ruins of the 600-year-old empire, Mustafa Kemal, a general in the Turkish army, fashioned the modern Republic of Turkey. Out of gratitude for Kemal's military and political genius, the Turkish parliament bestowed upon him the name Ataturk (Father Turk). The people rallied under his leadership, fought a bitter battle against the Greek forces and expelled them. Turkey became a republic. In 1952, Turkey joined NATO and has been a major base for American military and intelligence gathering.

*The Economy.* The labor force is divided this way: agriculture, 58.3 percent; services, 28.7 percent; industry and energy, 13 percent; and unemployed, about 20 percent. From 10 to 15 percent of the work force is unionized.

The public sector is important in Turkey's economy; state-owned or controlled enterprises account for about half of the aggregate industrial production. Turkey is the world's leading producer of chromium. It also mines iron ore, coal, zinc, lead and copper, has iron and steel works and cotton mills, and produces glass, cement and paper.

The country's economy is primarily based on agriculture, which employs around 65 percent of the labor force. Turkey is self-sufficient in foodstuffs and also exports many products, primarily to other Middle Eastern countries. Major agricultural products include cotton, tobacco, fruit, cereals, nuts and opium for medicine. Textile and clothing production are Turkey's largest manufacturing industries, followed by ceramics, steel and paper. The country produces a variety of mineral-based chemicals and metals. Turkey is one of the world's three largest producers of chromite. The country's new seaside resorts are attracting Western tourists for bargain vacations. More than three million foreigners spent $2 billion in Turkey in 1987, a 60 percent earnings increase over 1986. Turgot Ozal, Turkish Premier and a former World Bank official, has said that his country's export drive and free-market policies — including the privatization of state monopolies — brought growth of 7 percent last year that will enable Turkey's economy to "skip a century."[18]

In April 1987, Turkey — the only Islamic country among the five southern European nations — applied for membership in the European Economic Community. The country is making a bid to replace war-torn Lebanon as a banking center for the Middle East.

Major industries include cotton refining, engineering, fertilizers, food processing, sugar refining and textiles. From 10 to 15 percent of workers are unionized.

Turkey is a hierarchical society. Power flows from top to bottom. To accomplish more in less time, it is best to deal with the most powerful person in

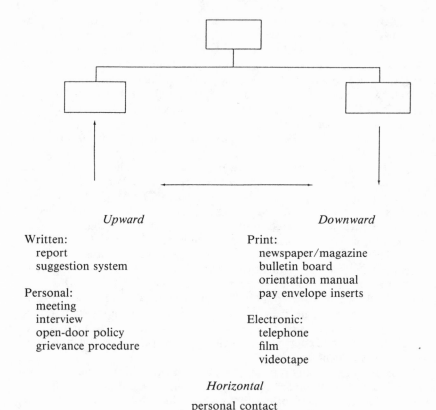

*Upward*

Written:
  report
  suggestion system

Personal:
  meeting
  interview
  open-door policy
  grievance procedure

*Downward*

Print:
  newspaper/magazine
  bulletin board
  orientation manual
  pay envelope inserts

Electronic:
  telephone
  film
  videotape

*Horizontal*

personal contact
meeting

**Figure 29. Communication system of Rabak Corporation.**

one's field. Dealing with lower personnel is often futile since they probably won't have the power to do what you need.

*Organizational Communication.* Initial letters may safely be written in English with the expectation of an answer.

The Turks will be punctual in meeting visitors at the agreed upon time and will shake hands with a firm grip. If more than one person is present when a visitor enters a room, he or she should greet each one, beginning with the eldest, and shake hands.

Business cards will be exchanged, and the foreigner's need not be translated into Turkish on one side. Cards should be presented to the receptionist and to the host of a meeting.

Extended small talk will precede any discussion of business, giving the Turk a chance to get to know the visitor, who will be asked about background and family. Turkish men like to discuss their families as well.

Older Turkish people use first names when addressing one another — followed by *bey* for man and *hanim* for women. The modern form is "Bay" followed by a man's last name or "Bayam" followed by a woman's last name.[19]

Nonverbal communication in Turkey, as in all Middle Eastern countries, is very important. Crossing one's arms communicates rudeness. Putting one's hands in pockets while speaking communicates disrespect. Crossing one's legs and showing the soles of the foot are offensive to the Turks. If an individual raises the chin, shuts the eye and tilts the head, the message is "no."

### CASE STUDY: RABAK

Privately owned and operated, Rabak was founded in 1957 with an initial annual capacity of 4,000 tons to refine blister copper and to produce copper and copper alloy products. Since then the company has experienced steady, rapid growth. Today it has 79 plants with five production lines in continuous operation. It is one of the world's leading copper, aluminum and steel wire producers with annual capacity of:

100 thousand tons of copper and copper alloys,

40 thousand tons of aluminum conductors,

20 thousand tons of aluminum billets, sheet ingots rolled products, and

35 thousand tons of high carbon steel wire products and at various levels for other products.

The company engages in joint ventures and has subsidiaries operating around the world. The Rabak communication system is shown in Figure 29.

## United Arab Emirates

*Official Name:* United Arab Emirates; *Capital:* Abu Dhabi; *Government:* federation of monarchies; *Subdivisions:* 7 emirates; *Population:* 1,846,373 (July 1987); *Density:* 37.2 per square mile; *Currency:* dirham; *Official Language:* Arabic; *Literacy:* 56.3 percent.

*The Land.* Located in the eastern sector of the Arabian Peninsula, the United Arab Emirates is a federation of seven sheikhdoms, which are, in order of size: Abu Dhabi, Dubai, Sharjah, Ras al-Khaimah, Fujairah, Umm al-Quwain and Ajman. The country is about the size of Maine.

The country has two coastlines. The one on the Persian Gulf is lined in places by coral reefs, island and small marshes, while the other, shorter coastline is on the eastern side of the Musandam peninsula which the UAE shares with Oman. The western interior is mostly flat and merges in the south into the Empty Quarter of Saudi Arabia, but uplands in the Musandam peninsula reach a height of 2,081 meters.

A barren, flat, island-dotted coast gradually gives way to rolling sand dunes that extend southward. The seven emirates are connected by good paved roads. The area in general is a hot, dry, inhospitable desert.

Neighbors include Oman, bordering for 319 miles to the northeast and southeast, Saudi Arabia for 364 miles in the south and west, and Qatar for 40 miles in the north. The Persian Gulf coastline is 483 miles long.

*The People.* Almost all citizens are indigenous Arabs. The foreign community includes numerous Arabs (Egyptian, Omanis and Palestinians) and large continents from India, Iran and Pakistan.

Of its total economically active population, only 2 percent are United Arab Emirates citizens. Specifically, these are the percentages: 19 percent Emirian; 23 percent other Arab; 50 percent South Asian; and 8 percent Westerners and East Asians. About 96 percent of these are Muslim; 4 percent are Christian, Hindu and other. New educational facilities have been established throughout the country since 1973, and citizens and temporary residents alike have taken advantage of them.

The majority of the native Arabs are of tribal background and are Muslims of the Sunni denomination.

*A Brief History.* From the early seventeenth century, Arab and European pirates were active in the area and what is now the UAE was known as the Pirate Coast. In 1820, Britain concluded a General Treaty for Peace with local rulers aimed at suppressing piracy and the slave trade. This was followed by the Perpetual Maritime Treaty of 1853, which ensured British protection against outside attack, and the Exclusive Agreement of 1892 whereby Britain assumed responsibility for the sheikhdoms' foreign affairs and defense while the rulers agreed not to cede territory or enter into treaties with any other foreign power.

Britain withdrew in 1971 and the UAE was formed on December 2. In the 1970s moves were made to unify services between the sheikhdoms and to combine the defense forces.

*The Economy.* The labor force is divided this way: industry and commerce, 85 percent; agriculture, 5 percent; services, 5 percent; and government, 5 percent.

Before 1960, this country was one of the poorest in the Arab world, the chief activities being fishing, oasis farming, nomadic pastoralism and trade in Dubai. Commercial production began in 1962 and by 1980 the UAE had the world's highest per capita GNP of US $30,070.

Major industries include aluminum smelting, foodstuffs, manufacturing, petroleum and steel. Industrial development of the country is concentrated on hydro projects.

## —— Yemen Arab Republic (North Yemen) ——

*Official Name:* Yemen Arab Republic; *Capital:* Sanaa; *Government:* republic; *Subdivisions:* 11 provinces; *Population:* 6,533,265 (July 1987); *Density:* 88 per square mile; *Currency:* rial; *Official Language:* Arabic; *Literacy:* 15 percent.

*The Land.* Smaller than South Dakota, North Yemen is in the southwestern corner of the Arabian Peninsula. Yemen is a surprisingly fertile region. The plain bordering the Red Sea is 30 to 80 kilometers wide. Inland are highlands that reach 3,760 meters above sea level. In the east the land slopes down toward Saudi Arabia.

The land is 79 percent desert, waste and urban; 20 percent agricultural; and 1 percent forest.

*The People.* About 90 percent of the population lives in rural areas. The inhabitants of the mountains tend to be short and olive-skinned. There is a heavy African mixture on the coast. They are 90 percent Arab and 10 percent Afro-Arab. They are also 100 percent Muslim.

Unlike other people of the Arabian Peninsula, who have historically been nomads or seminomads, the majority of people in this country have traditionally lived in small towns, villages or isolated clusters of houses and until recently loyalties were local, mainly to the family and clan. National patriotism is a rather new feeling.

One of the peculiarities of Yemen is the afternoon chewing of twigs from a shrub called qat which is cultivated in the terraced fields. Fresh twigs of this plant have a mildly narcotic juice which relaxes a person and gives him a sense of contentment. The cultivation and use of qat has some undesirable effects: it reduces ambition, it takes up land which could produce food crops, and the money spent on qat is needed for other purposes.

*A Brief History.* In classical times, the region was part of an important trading region called Arabia Felix by the Romans. The Ottoman Empire conquered the area in 1517. The country became an independent monarchy in 1918. In 1962 the monarchy was overthrown by army officers who proclaimed the country a republic. A civil war then ensued until 1969.

*The Economy.* The labor force is 30 percent expatriate laborers; the rest are almost entirely agricultural and herding. The country lacks minerals and has a lower per capita GNP than any other nation in the Arabian Peninsula. Farmland occupies 15 percent of the land, pasture is 36 percent, and forests 8 percent. Agriculture dominates the economy, employing 77 percent of the labor force. The chief crops are cereals, fruits, vegetables, cotton, dates, tobacco and coffee. Goats, sheep and cattle are raised. Textiles are the leading manufactures.

There are only 270 enterprises employing more than five workers. They engage in weaving, tanning, dyeing and traditional local handicrafts.

# People's Democratic Republic of Yemen (South Yemen)

*Official Name:* People's Democratic Republic of Yemen; *Capital:* Aden; *Government:* republic, ruled by Yemeni Socialist Party; *Subdivisions:* 6 governorates; *Population:* 2,351,131 (July 1987); *Density:* 15 per square mile; *Currency:* dinar; *Official Language:* Arabic; *Literacy:* 25 percent.

*The Land.* South Yemen is on the southern coast of the Arabian Peninsula facing the Gulf of Aden. The country stretches from the southwestern corner of the Arabian Peninsula for more than 752 miles eastward along the warm waters of the Gulf of Aden and Arabian Sea. The coastal areas are sandy and flat; the interior is mountainous, mainly rock. It consists of the former territories of Aden, Aden Protectorate and the 17 former sultanates and emirates that constituted the Federation of South Arabia. Behind the generally narrow coastal plain, most of Yemen is mountainous, occupying the up-tilted rim of the Arabian Peninsula.

*The People.* Almost all residents are Arabs; a few are Indians, Pakistanis, Somalis and Europeans. Most are also Sunni Muslims; some are Christian and Hindu.

*A Brief History.* Britain annexed Aden in 1839 and the port became important after the opening of the Suez Canal in 1869. In 1882–1914 Britain established the Aden Protectorate. After clashes between nationalist guerrillas and British troops, independence was achieved in 1967.

*The Economy.* Yemen lacks minerals and, outside the city of Aden, agriculture is the main activity, although farmland covers less than 1 percent of the country. The chief food crops are barley, millet, sesame, sorghum and wheat. Cotton is the chief cash crop. Goats, sheep and cattle are raised. Fish make up more than a third of the exports.

About 80 percent of industrial output comes from petroleum refining at Little Aden, nationalized in 1977. The government wants to nationalize all industry. Most people are subsistence farmers or nomadic herders.

Existing light industry consists of small factories providing cement, tiles and bricks, cloth goods, soft drinks and other consumer goods for local demand. There are 525 establishments employing over five workers.

# Notes

1. Mohamed Kamal, "Why Tar Arabs and Islam?" p. 4.
2. Michael W. Suleiman, "The Arabs and the West: Communication Gap," in Michael H. Prosser, ed., *The Cultural Dialogue,* p. 287.
3. Colonel Richard Norton, "The Sword of Islam," PBS program, Jan. 13, 1988, 10 p.m.
4. Neil Chesanow, *The World Class Executive,* p. 116.
5. Ibid., p. 113.
6. *Time,* August 20, 1956, as cited in Suleiman, p. 288.
7. Wilfred Cantwell Smith, *Islam in Modern History* (New York 1963), p. 47, as cited in Suleiman, p. 288.
8. Farid A. Muna, *The Arab Executive,* p. 26.
9. Jules R. Arbose, "How I Learned to Love the Middle East," pp. 26–7.
10. Ibid.
11. Ibid.
12. Muna, p. 29.
13. Jules R. Arbose, "The Generation Gap, Arab Style," pp. 84–5.
14. Elizabeth Warnock Fernea and Robert A. Fernea, *The Arab World,* p. 196.
15. Ibid., p. 199.
16. "Doing Business in the Arabian Peninsula," p. 3.
17. "Ghandour Is Envisioning Cooperation in the Air," p. 7.
18. Dennis Redmont, "Southern Stars Are Rising in European Constellation," p. D5.
19. Nancy L. Braganti and Elizabeth Devine, *The Traveler's Guide to European Customs and Manners,* p. 250.

# 6. Africa

## The Land

The second-largest continent in the world, Africa is four times larger than the United States, spans seven time zones, has vast untapped resources and huge, empty farmlands capable of producing enough to feed itself and Europe. Africa is just barely separated from Europe — just a 20-minute plane ride or an hour-long boat trip from Gibraltar — and from Asia at Suez, the opening of which in 1969 formed this artificial separation. In the Gulf of Guinea below the "bulge" of Africa, the Prime Meridian crosses the equator.

The northern and predominantly Arab countries of Africa are historically and culturally inseparable from the Middle East. Algeria, Morocco and Tunisia, along with the neighboring countries of Libya to the east and Mauritania to the west, form the Maghreb, the "Far West" of the Arab world. These countries share a common language with the Arab-speaking states, a common religion in Islam — about half of all Africans are Islamic, and common political aspirations within the Arab community. The coastal states of North Africa are African, Mediterranean, Islamic and Arab — all additionally influenced politically and economically by nearness to Europe. They are isolated from the rest of Africa by the Sahara Desert. So they are discussed here in their own section which could just as easily have been included in the previous chapter.

## The People

The roughly 2,000 black tribes in Africa, each with its own history, customs and culture, have been greatly influenced by the foreign powers which dominated them, to be described in discussions for each country. The African people have a triple heritage: indigenous cultures, the Islamic influences from the Middle East and North Africa, and Western forces — "fusing and recoiling, at once competitive and complementary."[1] Some think of Africa as having three zones: white-dominated Africa south of the Tropic of Capricorn, Arab-dominated Africa north of the Tropic of Cancer, and Black Africa between the two tropics.[2]

Another influence from the West has been the news media which, strangely, have taught Africa what it knows about itself as well as what separate countries and regions of this sprawling continent know about one another. African print and broadcast media subscribe to Western wire services, receiving data for their use from Western sources — even when that information concerns their own continent's affairs. One African described the continent this way:

> The African society is basically communalistic, highly structured and built around a deeply personalized set of relationships, in which individualism is suppressed. These set out a whole new complexion of outlook, attitudes and value-judgments which are bound to strike an outsider as well as the Westernized African as either primitive, uncivilized or even romantic but at best one step behind the needs of industrialization.[3]

Over a thousand languages are spoken in Africa, but Arabic, English and French are the most widely spoken languages on the African continent. Sixteen countries use English as a lingua franca. Hansa is the first language in West Africa and Swahili in East Africa for millions and a second language for millions more. Each has a literature dating back centuries.[4] Berber is still spoken by large minorities in Morocco and Algeria.

An extremely important part of African history and world history was the slave trade. By 1611, eleven years after the first settlement at Jamestown and two years before the *Mayflower* sailed, the first African slaves were introduced to Virginia.[5] By the time the United States Constitution was being written, a slave could be purchased along the West Coast of Africa for two pounds sterling and sold in America for over 30 times that amount.[6]

Polygamy is still practiced in Africa with the wives, and sometimes the husband too, living in separate houses with a well-delineated code of behavior. Divorce sometimes occurs because wives can't get along with other wives. On the other hand, some wives stay with impossible husbands because his other wives are congenial. In some African languages, the word for "co-wife" is from the same root as the word for "jealousy."[7] Many African countries are completely male dominated. A common greeting in Nigeria, for example, is "Good morning, madam. How is your master?"[8]

Descent groups or kinship group — either patrilineal or matrilineal — form the basis for most extrafamilial social organization in Africa. "They form political groups, religious congregations and even production and land-owning units."[9] They remain strong even among educated classes and show no signs of diminishing in importance in African society. Many Africans express concern that these kinship groups will weaken and maybe even perish because of industrialization.

In most of undeveloped Africa, no separation exists between occupational and domestic organization; most production of goods and services is in the home. Most homesteads produce what they consume and consume most of what they produce. The system affects social stratification relationships. "[W]hat is stratified is not a series of autonomous occupational categories and organizations, but rather a series of domestic and other kinship units whose economic functions are but one among a number of different characteristics on the basis of which their relative worth, in terms of cultural values, is judged."[10]

Industrialization, which separates occupational roles from domestic ones, will surely change a great deal about African life.

# A Brief History

The history of Africa is one of ancient beginnings, tribal living and migrations, colonization by several foreign powers and gradual return to independence, often with unsettling economic, social and political consequences.

The largest colonial area after India was Black Africa, divided into 55 artificial nations — whose boundaries ignored traditional tribal territories — which as independent states now constitute a third of the votes in the United Nations. Colonialism in Africa lasted for a far shorter time than the 300 years that Spain dominated Latin America. In most cases, a colony was founded around the turn of the century and ended in about the mid-twentieth century. During that period, however, most colonial powers paid little attention to developing the colony — to the economic infrastructure or to training programs for the population. Burundi did not have a single college graduate at the time of its independence in 1962.[11] Instead they followed policies designed to benefit the settlers and the homeland economically. Because the colony was viewed as an outlet for exports, manufacturing needed not be developed there. Western consumption patterns prevailed more than Western production techniques, so that colonists were successful in developing Western tastes but not much-needed Western skills.[12]

All African countries except South Africa belong to the Organization for African Unity (OAU), founded in 1963 to eradicate colonialism. Indescribable chaos replaced colonialism in many of the newly freed states — massacres, tyrannies, concentration camps, corruption, public thefts, genocide and starvation. In Burundi in 1972, the Watusi government massacred 200,000 members of the Hutu tribe. In Rwanda, the situation was reversed: the Hutu slaughtered 100,000 Watusi. The future can only be brighter than the past for Africa.

Meanwhile the present remains mostly bleak. The Population Crisis Committee ranked 130 countries by a "human suffering index" designed to show a correlation between rapid population growth and human problems emerging from it. The index was calculated from the sum of ten factors rated on a scale of zero to ten for their impact on human suffering. Seventy-four countries scored at or above 50; nine of the ten suffering the most were African: Mozambique, 95; Angola, 91; Afghanistan, 88; Chad, 88; Mali, 88; Ghana, 87; Somalia, 87; Niger, 85; Burkina Faso, 84; Central African Republic, 84; and Zaire, 84. Fifteen African countries in total scored over 80, along with Nepal, Cambodia and Bhutan. China scored 50 and India 61. (At the top of the list was Switzerland with an index of 4, followed by West Germany, 5; Luxembourg, 6; the Netherlands, 7; the United States, 8; Belgium, 9; Canada, 9; Austria, 9; Denmark, 9; and Japan, 11. Haiti, the poorest Latin American country, was rated at 74, while most Western Hemisphere countries ranged between Nicaragua's 67 and Trinidad and Tobago's 21. Brazil scored 50; Mexico, 47; Chile, 46; and Argentina, 38.)[13]

# The Economy

Excluding South Africa, Africa is the least industrialized continent of the Third World. African countries started industrializing later than Asian or Latin American undeveloped countries and have progressed more slowly despite the stimulus to industry of independence in the 1960s. Their economies remain largely at the Agricultural Age level, with much agriculture still at the traditional subsistence level. What industry they have is concentrated on the production of tropical agriculture or forest products for export — mostly in a raw state or barely processed — or in mining, including extracting concentrates or refining, also for export. Africa remains responsible for only about 1 percent of world Manufacturing Value Added (MVA) compared with 6.2 percent and 3.8 percent for Latin America and Asia respectively.

African manufacturing showed a rapid increase in the early 1960s as the newly independent governments encouraged import substitution industries. However, problems emerged from this policy in most countries — high cost protection, inelastic supply of raw materials, limited markets, and so on — and the rate of growth has declined since 1965.

Many of the countries of Africa are among the world's poorest and least developed. Thirteen countries had per capita income in 1976 of less than US $100, as expressed in constant 1970 values, and 23 others had per capita incomes of between $100 and $250.

The colonial past still influences the way African economies are integrated into the world order — usually along British, French or Belgian lines. The major categories of employers are the government, European and American multinationals, Third-World multinationals, other foreign businesses, large private indigenous firms and small indigenous firms.[14] All African countries suffer from a shortage of skilled manpower.

Most African organizations base their relationships with employees on contracts. Workers prefer to look beyond the legalities of the contracts toward more personal and intimate relationships with management. Reliance on the strict rules adds to the employees' resentment. African managers are constrained by the social distance between worker and manager; foreign managers add the element of race to that. All managers are frustrated by a lack of skilled labor and inadequate utility services with political instability thrown in. The unavoidable outcome is that managers have very little time to worry about workers' needs and they have little desire to use the time they do have in relating to people they really don't like.

Most employees have received the elementary education required in most of the continent and have begun work with a sense of lost opportunity. Many have had to move from villages to the city, more of a dislocation than a relocation. When workers do create a spirit of cooperation and community among themselves, it is often based on a shared feeling of injustice.

In most African countries, employees use European-style work councils or committees or joint consultation committees for dealing with management and participating in decision making.[15] Legislation in many countries has set up these bodies, which benefit employers also; Western managers assigned to

Africa often find they are unable to delegate even the most routine matters to their African employees. Decision making in middle management is almost totally centralized; delegation of authority is almost nonexistent; the style of management is very authoritarian—to avoid eroding a manager's authority through familiarity with employees. Much of this is based on past relationships in African life:

> In the traditional African setting, hired labour was often used especially in the planting and harvesting season. Usually the hired worker was made to feel like a "guest" who, apart from his wage, was often entertained with food and drink. The farm owner and his family worked with the hired man and showed him gratitude since, as far as the two parties were concerned, the hired man was working for the benefit of the owner. The agreed cash wage was thus only part of the unwritten bargain, gratitude and "return of favours" being an important part of a labourer's remuneration. In the modern setting, this attitude toward employers is prevalent. The African worker feels he is employed for the benefit of the employer who should show gratitude, a notion in conflict with the attitude that employment is contractual, based on a set of conditions of service. Such gratitude presupposes some amount of liking and respect which the manager has not got for the worker.
>
> There is a mutual lack of appreciation, between managers and workers, of the importance of the other's role.[16]

For the most part, however, applications of Western-style management methods have been unsuccessful. A better approach is to build a management style around the communalistic style of living that the Africans have created. "The community concept of management releases a whole new set of incentives, principles of organization, men-machine relationships and social relationships in business."[17]

That is not to say that communism is the answer to Africa's economic problems. In fact, in recent years that ideology has been the cause of many problems and is being abandoned by an increasing number of African countries. "Goodbye to Marxism" was the headline of an edition of the newspaper *Jeune Afrique* in the People's Republic of Benin, the latest country to convert to open markets. Tanzania has trimmed public payrolls. Angola is selling state companies to private entrepreneurs. Nigeria has abandoned exchange controls, a standard feature of centrally controlled economies. Another indication of the change is that 28 of Africa's 45 Subsaharan countries have taken the steps necessary for qualifying for loans from the World Bank's Special Facility for Africa, a $1.9 billion fund. To qualify, countries must adopt what the bank considers realistic exchange rates, pay farmers fair prices, cut government bureaucracies and sell unprofitable state industries. "Most African countries have gone through a period of setting prices and of setting up public corporations," said Kalu I Kalu, Nigeria's Planning Minister. "Now there is a need to recognize the role of efficiency, the role of prices for resource allocation."[18]

# Organizational Communication

A business enterprise coming to Africa must, above all, establish trust and confidence among its employees. No matter how long the intended stay, the visitor to Africa must get to know business associates prior to getting down to work. Personal relationships are more important than business matters. The small talk that always precedes a business meeting can go on for a long time.

Mail service throughout the continent, except South Africa, is unreliable. Letters frequently get lost. The telephone system is likewise poor. Telephone directories are out-of-date and inaccurate. It is often easier to make a phone call to another African nation through a European country, a legacy of the colonial system where communicating with the home office was more important than with the next community.

African business persons maintain a flexible view toward time rather than a rigid or segmented one. In Swahili, the first hour of the day is 6 a.m. Everywhere time is treated casually and punctuality is of little concern. People who rush are suspected of trying to cheat. Meetings that start late are the norm, though Africans try to adapt to foreigners' expectations about time.

Visitors should shake hands with all those present in a room, whether they are known or not. From that point on, a dignified approach will gain the best response. Africans respect age; to use first names, for example, with older persons would be highly offensive. The family unit is important and that includes the extended family and maybe even the tribe. In business, the tribal concept can cause preferential treatment in hiring and create obligations that force the African to seek more money. Successful tribal members are expected to send money home.

The community concept of management described above has implications for communication.

> In a community there is a free flow of information. Everyone has a right to know what is going on. The kind of society in which the African is brought up depends on this. Each member of the group is a custodian of its secrets. The African wants to know what is going on around him, and when he gets to know he wants to pass this on to those with him. He becomes suspicious, more curious and resentful when information is withheld. One cannot promote the community concept by withholding information and trying to manipulate acts.[19]

Many Westerners in Africa make the mistake of waiting for social invitations which never arrive. In Africa, you don't make appointments, but present yourself at a person's doorstep.

Africans listen differently than Westerners do; they often choose not to maintain eye contact while listening. A Westerner may misinterpret this to mean either dishonesty or a lack of attention. The employee, as a result, may receive a poor performance report which may even result in his dismissal. The outcome may be lawsuits for wrongful dismissal or damages under equal opportunity laws.

Africa provides an interesting study of gestures, many of which have different meanings than elsewhere. Patting a child's head or indicating the height of a plant or animal by a horizontal extension of the hand is considered in some societies to be an evil attempt to cast a spell upon the child, plant or animal so that growth will cease at the height indicated by the pat or the extension. Pointing to objects with the index finger in certain areas of Central Africa is considered crude and vulgar; the polite way to point is by sticking out the lower lip. Africans who have frequent contact with Europeans are often tolerant when outsiders violate their etiquette. An American sat with his legs crossed in front of the chief of an Ewe community in Ghana, a gesture showing disrespect; the chief indicated that he knew the impoliteness had been unintended.

The messages communicated by voluntary bodily movements are often intimately linked with extremely important values of the society. In particular there is a right and a wrong way to conduct one's body in order to demonstrate respect, but again the procedure varies and may be displayed in different social contexts:

Ashanti of Ghana — it is insulting to use the left rather than the right hand for gesticulation.

Chaga of Tanganyika — children receiving or giving something to an older person are expected to clasp their outstretched right hand with their left one; they must offer seats to old people who enter a hut.

Ganda of Uganda — inferior people receiving or giving something to a superior person must use both hands; if it is necessary to hold the object in one hand, then the free hand must touch the arm of the hand holding the object.

Luo of Kenya — while speaking, a man and his mother-in-law must turn their backs to each other.

Mende of Sierra Leone — anyone approaching a chief, including a young member of the chief's family, must bend his body, place his hands on his knees, and uncover his head.

Some, perhaps most, bodily movements convey information not only to others but also to the persons themselves. Zulu warriors about to go into battle chew a particular plant which they then spit out in the direction of the enemy, an action they feel would cause the enemy to make mistakes. When summoned to war, these warriors donned a special war dress and would leap about as if fighting, in order to get up steam.[20]

Among the Ashanti, the way to abuse or slander a paramount chief is to use certain stereotyped phrases (the child of a fool) or to invoke a special oath (May your ancestral spirits chew their own heads); such utterances were once punishable by death. The same abuse or slander may be conveyed by a simple gesture, which consists of closing the hands, placing the closed fists together, and holding up the thumbs. Among the Mossi, gratitude is expressed by saying, "My head is in the dirt." The words represent the custom of demonstrating gratitude by bowing so low that the head is actually pressed into the dirt, so humbled does one feel because of the graciousness of another.

Among the Amhara of Ethiopia, anger is shown by the wide opening of the eyes, by biting the lower lip or finger, by a knit brow, or by a furious, intent

### Table 25. Some Communication Practices of the African Firm

Many Africans:

1. Consider personal relationships more important than business matters.
2. Have a poor mail service.
3. Have an inadequate telephone system.
4. Have a relaxed attitude toward time.
5. Feel a rushed approach in doing business is a sign of an attempt to cheat.
6. Shake hands upon meeting.
7. Use first names except with older people.
8. Are still influenced by the culture of their former colonial power.
9. Listen differently than do Westerners.
10. Have a high-context culture.
11. Use time polychronically.

stare; melancholy by a wrinkled face; timidity and respect in the young by turning the eyes to the dust; impatience by rapidly shifting the glance; and greetings or acknowledgment of superordination by rhythmic handclapping. In commercial relations, a buyer and seller signify agreement by waving their right hands up and down and then touching each other's palms with the fingers stretched away. Master and servant sit differently: the master pushes his body way back as if to show that a special effort is required to rise; the servant, on the rare occasions when he is permitted to sit in the master's presence, must "sit lightly."

Table 25 lists some communication practices of the African firm.

# MUSLIM AFRICA

## ———————————— Algeria ————————————

*Official Name:* Democratic and Popular Republic of Algeria; *Capital:* Algiers; *Government:* socialist republic; *Subdivisions:* 31 departments; *Population:* 23,460,614 (July 1987); *Density:* 24.7 per square mile; *Currency:* dinar; *Official Language:* Arabic; *Literacy:* 45 percent.

*The Land.* Just over a quarter the size of the United States, Algeria is the largest nation in northwestern Africa and the second largest state in Africa. It has a Mediterranean coastline of 686 miles and shares these borders with its neighbors: Tunisia, 595 miles; Libya, 610 miles; Niger, 594 miles; Mali, 855 miles; Mauritania, 288 miles; and Morocco, 1,017 miles. Algeria is located midway along the Mediterranean littoral in the Maghreb region of North Africa and extends south to the heart of the Sahara.

Algeria is one of three countries in northwest Africa that comprise the Maghreb or the Arab West which lies between the Mediterranean and the Sahara Desert. The Tellian and Saharan Atlas Mountains cross the country from east to west, dividing the country into three zones. Between the northern (Tellian) range and Mediterranean is a narrow, fertile coastal plain. A high plateau lies between the mountain ranges with great rocky plains and deserts. South of the Saharan range is mostly desert. About 80 percent of the country is desert, steppes, wasteland and mountains. The Sahara covers the rest — 80 percent — of Algeria.

The land is divided this way: 80 percent desert, 16 percent pasture and meadows, 3 percent cultivated and 1 percent forest.

*The People.* In 1961–2, most of the one million European settlers left Algeria. Most people speak Arabic even though about 20 percent are of Berber origin. Nearly 60 percent of the population are under 20 years of age and about 91 percent of the population live along the Mediterranean on 12 percent of the land. About 84 percent of the population are Arab; the Berbers mainly inhabit the mountainous and desert areas of the country. Less than 1 percent is of French or European descent. Some 99 percent are Sunni Muslim and the rest are Christian and Jewish.

Algerians are a formal and traditional people, yet they are quite expressive and individualistic. One is expected to speak one's mind but do it inoffensively. Though Algerians greatly enjoy good conversation, being overly frank and direct in speech is considered very impolite. One never asks directly about another's private life or habits unless the other person brings up the subject. Expressiveness, courtesy, individualism and formality are key attributes of the Algerian personality. In this strongly male-dominated society, sex roles are clearly and rigidly defined. The Algerian family is a very important and private entity, often including three or more generations in the male line under one roof.

*A Brief History.* Since the pre–Christian era, the indigenous tribes of northern Africa (called Berbers by the Romans) have been pushed back from the coast by successive waves of invaders. The Berbers still account for a significant minority of the population. The greatest cultural impact came from the Arab invasions of the eighth and eleventh centuries A.D. which brought Islam and the Arabic language. From 1518 until 1830, Algeria was an integral part of the Ottoman Empire.

In 1830 the country became a French-controlled territory, and ultimately, a department of the French Republic. French colonization was bitterly resisted, although Algeria was proclaimed a French territory in 1848. Despite large-scale French colonization, a smoldering independence movement erupted into open warfare in 1954. After eight years of bitter fighting, Algeria was granted independence on July 1, 1962. Fearing for their lives, nearly one million French and other European colonists were evacuated when the French Army withdrew. During the 1960s and 1970s, Algeria went through a trying period of adjustment and internal change, emerging as a firm socialist republic.

*The Economy.* The labor force is divided this way: industry and commerce, 40 percent; agriculture 30, government 17, services 10, and unemployed, about 11 percent. From 16 to 19 percent of the labor force is unionized.

In 1980, Algeria had the highest GNP in North Africa. Although many people are engaged in agriculture, industry—particularly oil and natural gas extraction—dominates the economy. Algeria is Africa's top natural gas producer with some of the world's largest reserves, ranks third in oil production and is rich in other minerals including iron ore, lead, phosphates and zinc. Farmland, which covers only 3 percent of Algeria, grows cereals, fruit, olives, tobacco, vegetables and vines and raises sheep, goats and cattle. Forests cover 2 percent of the land and pasture about 15 percent. The government controls the economy. Almost everything, including agricultural land, has been nationalized to the extent of a controlling interest or a complete takeover. Algeria's economy is centrally planned and dominated by the public sector.

Once an exporter of food products, Algeria has been forced to import much of its food since becoming a socialist republic. Major exports include crude oil, petroleum products, natural gas and wine. Despite attempts at industrialization and major land reform, Algeria still faces widespread unemployment. Housing is one of Algeria's most pressing problems because of the high rate of population increase and the influx of people from rural areas to the cities.

Major industries are building materials, chemicals, clothing, engineering, food processing, natural gas and oil and textiles.

The government promotes self-management by workers in industrial establishments. Collective disputes must by law be handled through regional conciliation boards composed of employer and employment representation. Work councils, made up of elected employee representatives but chaired by management representatives, are obligatory in all enterprises employing over 50 workers.

*Organizational Communication.* Using the fingers to point at objects or people is generally considered impolite. As in all Moslem countries, separate use of the left hand should be avoided. When handing or receiving something from another person, use either both hands or the right hand only.

# Chad

*Official Name:* Republic of Chad; *Capital:* N'Djamena; *Government:* republic; *Subdivisions:* 14 prefectures; *Population:* 4,646,054 (July 1987); *Density:* 10 per square mile; *Currency:* franc; *Official Languages:* French and Arabic; *Literacy:* 20 percent.

*The Land.* Landlocked in north-central Africa, Chad consists of a sterile northern desert and a tropical southern region, but the central feature of Chad is the broad, shallow central bowl of Lake Chad in the southern and southwestern half of the country. The country is more than 1,500 miles from any seaport; it lies almost in the center of Africa and is one of the transitional nations between the desert to the north and the fertile southern area of the continent. About twice the size of France, Chad's population is 96 percent farmers or herders.

The land is divided this way: 35 percent is pasture, 17 percent is arable, 2 percent is forest and scrub, and 46 percent is other and waste. Chad shares borders with these neighbors: Libya in the north, 655 miles; Sudan in the east, 845 miles; Central African Republic in the south and southwest, 745 miles; Cameroon in the southwest, 651 miles; Nigeria in the west, 55 miles; and Niger in the west, 730 miles.

Chad has three topographical regions: the Chadian Sahara in the north is a dry desert rising to the Tibesti Mountains. Only 1 percent of the population resides here. The central portion is a semi-arid land of great treeless plains; this area traditionally has received enough rainfall to support cattle raising but is experiencing a drought. The green southern area supports 45 percent of the country's population who engage in cotton cultivation.

*The People.* Although some 200 ethnic groups compose Chad's population, it can be divided between Saharan and Arab Muslims in northern and central regions and Negroid peoples in the south. The latter group includes both those who have retained traditional animistic practices and those who have adopted Christianity. The people are 52 percent Muslim, 43 percent followers of indigenous beliefs, and 5 percent Christian. About 1,000 Europeans live in Chad.

*A Brief History.* As early as the eighth century, some Arabs may have entered Chad from the north across the Libyan desert bringing the Islamic faith which their descendants follow today.

Chad was a French colony from 1910 to 1960; it came to independence as one of the poorest and least developed countries on the continent. Not much is known of the early history of Chad. Various Semitic tribes and kingdoms were successively established during the western Dark Ages, including the powerful Oueddai Empire. This was a hunting ground for the early slave traders who transported their human cargo to Egypt and the East. Since independence, the country has had a series of governments.

*The Economy.* Some 85 percent of the population engages in subsistence farming, herding and fishing. About 20 percent of the wage-earning population is unionized.

One of the least industrialized countries in Africa, Chad is also one of the poorest of the world. It has a free-market economy with a dominant private sector. Poorly endowed in physical resources, the country's economy is dominated by small-scale subsistence agriculture. Chief commercial products include cotton, livestock and animal products.

Industries include agricultural and livestock processing plants (cotton textile mills, slaughterhouses and breweries). About 20 percent of the wage labor force is unionized.

# Djibouti

*Official Name:* Republic of Djibouti; *Capital:* Djibouti; *Government:* republic; *Subdivisions:* 5 cercles; *Population:* 312,405 (July 1987);

*Density:* 37 per square mile; *Currency:* franc; *Official Language:* French; *Literacy:* 17 percent.

*The Land.* Djibouti is located in northeast Africa on the strait of Bab al Mandab which links the Red Sea to the Gulf of Aden. Its area is part of the East African Rift Valley system. It contains high, uplifted blocks in the north and depressions and volcanic wastelands behind the narrow coastal plain.

The land is divided this way: 89 percent is desert waste; 10 percent is pasture; and 1 percent is forest. There are three main regions: a coastal plain, mountains and a plateau behind the mountains. The land is bare, dry and desolate, marked by sharp cliffs, deep ravines, burning sands and thorny shrubs. The entire country is sand and stone desert broken in places by lava streams and salt lakes.

The coastline on the Gulf of Aden and Gulf of Tadjoura is 196 miles. The Gulf of Tadjoura is 28 miles across and its entrance penetrates 36 miles inland. Djibouti shares a border with Ethiopia of 294 miles and with Somalia of 26 miles. The whole country is claimed by Somalia.

*The People.* The indigenous population is divided almost equally between two Hamitic groups — the Somalis in the south and the Afars in the north and west. The country also has a substantial number of foreigners. An estimated 47 percent of the people are Issas (a Somali clan), 37 percent are Afars, 8 percent are Europeans (mostly French) and 6 percent are Arabs. About 94 percent are Muslim and the rest are Christian.

Almost a third of the people live a nomadic life of bare subsistence in the rural hinterlands of the republic.

*A Brief History.* France grew interested in the area in 1859. The port of Djibouti was built in 1884, and in 1897–1917 French engineers built the railway to Addis Ababa. As French Somaliland, Djibouti became an overseas territory in 1946 but gained full independence on June 27, 1977.

*The Economy.* Djibouti has a small number of semiskilled workers at port and about 3,000 railway workers. It has a free-market economy with a dominant private sector. Mineral deposits are few; the arid soil is unproductive. The country has no industry. Services and commerce provide most of the gross domestic product. Major industries are transit, trade, port and railway services; live cattle and sheep exports; and secondary services to the French military.

Beyond near total lack of natural resources, two factors contribute to the poverty level: Practically all commodities are imported for consumption and prices of even basic staples are extraordinarily high. The high level of unemployment requires the working members of the family to be economically responsible for nonworking members.

# Egypt

*Official Name:* Arab Republic of Egypt; *Capital:* Cairo; *Government:* socialist republic; *Subdivisions:* 26 governorates; *Population:* 51,929,962 (July 1987); *Density:* 122.7 per square mile; *Currency:* pound; *Official Language:* Arabic; *Literacy:* 39 percent.

*The Land.* Although the country is the size of Texas and New Mexico combined, for all practical purposes, Egypt is the narrow strip of land that runs along the Nile. Located in the northeastern corner of Africa, it is more than 95 percent desert with irrigation only along the Nile. The Nile flows from south to north from 750 miles in a valley cut through the desert. It is strategically located at the junction between Africa and Asia, occupying the land route between Africa and Asia and commanding the sea route between the Mediterranean and Indian Ocean via the Suez Canal. Egypt is part of the wide band of desert that stretches from the Atlantic Coast of Africa into the Middle East. Egypt has four main land regions: The Sinai peninsula in the northeast is bounded by the Suez Canal and the Gulf of Aqaba in the east. In the north, a low plain borders the Mediterranean Sea. The land rises to the south where Egypt's highest peak is located. The eastern desert, east of the Nile valley, consists of rocky plateaus and a rugged mountain range overlooking the Red Sea. The western desert covers more than three-fifths of Egypt. This desert has several major oases. The fourth region, the Nile valley, contains the man-made Lake Nasser which is held back by the Aswan Dam in the south. Below Aswan, the valley is narrow, but it gradually broadens out in Middle Egypt.

Egypt shares borders with Israel in the west for 236 miles, with the Sudan in the south for 792 miles and with Libya in the west for 693 miles. Its Mediterranean coastline is 595 miles long; its coastline on the Gulf of Aqaba and Red Sea is 850 miles long. Its largest body of water is the man-made Lake Nasser, a reservoir behind the Aswan Dam. The land is 96.5 percent desert, waste or urban, 2.8 percent cultivated and 0.7 percent inland water.

*The People.* Egypt is the most populous country in the Arab world and the second most populous on the African continent. About 99 percent of the people live on about 4 percent of the land in about 35,000 square kilometers in the fertile, irrigated Nile valley in the cities of Cairo and Alexandria, elsewhere on the banks of the Nile River, in the Nile Delta, which fans out north of Cairo, and along the Suez Canal. These areas have a density of over 3,600 per square mile. There are also small communities throughout the desert around oases and along transportation routes. The area inhabited is about half the size of South Carolina.

Most people are Arabs, although there are small Berber minorities in the western desert and Nubian and Sudanese communities in the south. About 90 percent of the people are Muslim. The Copts form the largest religious minority. About 90 percent of the people are eastern Hamitic stock — native Egyptians. Small minorities include Nubians, Bedouin nomads, Greeks, Italians, Syro-Lebanese and Jews. About 94 percent of the people are Muslim; 6 percent follow Coptic Christian or other beliefs.

Egyptians enjoy a relaxed, unpressured life, characterized by the phrase *Ma'aleesh,* which roughly translated means "don't worry" or "never mind." Both their business and leisure activities are governed by the philosophy of *in-sha allah* (God willing) — which governs all aspects of Muslim life. They often have difficulty responding to the brisk, get-down-to-business attitude of many Americans. Because they identify with community groups, personal needs and desires often become secondary to those of the group. Egyptians are known throughout the Middle East for their marvelous sense of humor. They seem to endure difficult economic and living conditions with a great deal of composure.

*A Brief History.* Egypt is the oldest cohesive nation in the world, its history dating back to before 3000 B.C. It has endured as a unified state for over 5,000 years. Ancient Egypt was one of the world's greatest early civilizations. Islam was introduced during the Arab conquest of Egypt in A.D. 639–642. A process of Arabization and Islamization ensued. Although a Coptic Christian minority remained, Arab supplanted the indigenous Coptic tongue.

Egypt was part of the Ottoman Empire from 1517 to 1798, but the country's modern history began in 1805 when Mehemet Ali, a former Albanian officer, became governor and began to modernize Egypt. In 1881 Britain occupied the country and declared it a protectorate in 1914. Egypt became an independent monarchy in 1922, although British troops remained. The monarchy was overthrown in 1952 and General Muhammad Neguib became president in 1954. Colonel Abdul Nasser took over and Britain agreed to withdraw its forces in 1956. President Nasser nationalized the Suez Canal. Anglo-French and Israeli troops attacked Egypt but soon withdrew. Egypt was involved in wars with Israel in 1967 and again in 1973, by which time Muhammad Anwar as-Sadat had become President, Nasser having died in 1970. Sadat negotiated a peace treaty with Israel in 1979, but he was assassinated in 1981. His successor was Muhammad Hosni Mubarak. Under the peace treaty, the Sinai peninsula was returned to Egypt in 1982.

*The Economy.* The labor force is divided this way: agriculture, 40 percent; government, public-sector enterprises and armed forces, 35 percent; privately owned services and manufacturing enterprises, almost 20 percent; and unemployed, about 7 percent.

Egypt is Africa's second most industrialized nation, but it has a comparatively low per capita GNP. Its chief mineral resources include petroleum and natural gas, phosphates, iron ore, manganese and salt. Agriculture is the chief activity, although farmland covers only 3 percent of the land. The chief crop is cotton, and cotton goods are the leading exports. Cereals, fruits, rice, sugarcane, vegetables and fodder crops are also grown. Completion of the Aswan High Dam in 1970 increased the fertile land by one third.

Major industries include building materials, chemicals, fertilizers, food processing, iron and steel manufactures, petroleum and petroleum products and textiles.

The Aswan Dam has provided these benefits: more intensive farming on millions of acres of land made possible by improved irrigation; prevention of damage caused by periodic serious flooding; and production of billions of kilowatt-hours of electricity every year at very low cost.

Industry has played an increasingly important role in the economy in recent years. Textiles, food processing, chemicals, petroleum, construction, steel and cement are all chief industrial products. Other important sources of income are the Suez Canal and tourism.

In a series of nationalization measures begun in 1961, the government acquired control of over 90 percent of the basic means of industrial production. All high school graduates in the country are guaranteed a job, by law.

*Organization Communication.* Once you realize that it is often taken as a personal insult if you do business too quickly, it will be easier to slow your pace and allow enough time. The Egyptian likes to feel you think his business is worth consideration, deliberation, time. A quick, snap decision or what seems an "efficient" or "expeditious" handling of a job may seem demeaning to him. The implication of such speed is "my work was of no significance."

They want business but they want it on their terms, handled in their way. They will turn down a deal rather than be pushed. Take time; socialize; be available but not too urgent.

One needs to consciously provide more open expressions of courtesies, greetings, compliments and approval than are normal to most Americans. Take at least ten minutes in small talk to warm up before starting business. Don't be too personal, though. The mood in which business is done is important, as it is in all of the Arab world. Never lose your temper.

Shake hands with everyone present upon arriving and leaving. Use business cards. It is not unusual to interrupt a meeting with frequent telephone calls, visitors and unending cups of tea.

# The Gambia

*Official Name:* Republic of the Gambia; *Capital:* Banjul; *Government:* republic; *Subdivisions:* Banjul and 5 divisions; *Population:* 760,362 (July 1987); *Density:* 148 per square mile; *Currency:* dalasi; *Official Language:* English; *Literacy:* 15 percent.

*The Land.* Located on the bulge of West Africa and comprising a narrow strip of land at most 29 miles wide along the lower reaches of the Gambia River and 170 miles long, the ex–British territory of The Gambia extends along the banks of the winding Gambia River in West Africa. It extends inland for 292 miles from the Atlantic Ocean and except for the seacoast is surrounded by Senegal. Twice the size of Delaware, The Gambia has the smallest area of any independent nation in Africa. It is about four-fifths the size of Connecticut. Thick mangrove swamps border the lower half of the Gambia River. Its border with Senegal is 470 miles long.

The entire area is low-lying, never exceeding a height of 120 feet. Inland from the river is a region of swamps and river flats. About 55 percent of the land is upland cultivatable, built on and other; 25 percent is uncultivated savanna; 16 percent is swamp; and 4 percent is forest park. The climate is subtropical, with a marked hot, wet season (June through October) and a cooler, dry season (November through May). Rain falls only in the summer and amounts to up to 55 inches annually.

*The People.* Most groups are a mixture of West African Negro and Sudanic ancestry, including Mandingo (41 percent), Fulan (14 percent), Wolof (13 percent), Serahuli (10 percent), Jola (8 percent) and others (14 percent).

Their religions are Islam (90 percent) and traditional tribal beliefs and Christianity (10 percent).

About 99 percent of the people are African; the rest are non–Gambian. Almost all people live a rural, isolated life in which the family unit is primary. About 500 Europeans, mostly British, as well as Syrians and Lebanese, live in The Gambia.

*A Brief History.* The Gambia was once part of the Empire of Ghana and the Kingdom of the Songhais. Between the tenth and fifteenth centuries there was a migration of Hamitic-Sudanic people from the Nile River Valley westward. They arrived in The Gambia and Senegal, settled and intermingled with the West African Negro people already living there. The first Europeans to visit the country, about the same time Columbus reached the West Indies, were from Portugal. During this period, The Gambia was part of the Kingdom of Mali. By 1500 the lower river area had become a regular port of call for traders seeking slaves and gold. The Gambia was a British colony from 1816 to 1965. The Gambia elected to become a republic within the British Commonwealth in 1970 at which time Prime Minister David K. Jawara became president. Continued British aid makes it possible for The Gambia to function.

*The Economy.* The labor force is divided this way: agriculture, 75 percent; industry, commerce and services, 18.9 percent; and government, 6.1 percent. From 25 to 30 percent of the work force is unionized.

One of the least-developed countries in the world, The Gambia has a free-market economy in which the dominant sector is private. The Gambia's small export earnings come from peanuts, but it also exports rice and beeswax. Major industries include peanut processing, tourism, brewing, soft drinks, agricultural machinery assembly, small wood working and metal working, and clothing.

# Guinea

*Official Name:* Republic of Guinea; *Capital:* Conakry; *Government:* republic; *Subdivisions:* 33 provinces; *Population:* 6,737,760 (July 1987); *Density:* 57 per square mile; *Currency:* sylis; *Official Language:* French; *Literacy:* 20 percent.

*The Land.* Facing southwest on the Atlantic Ocean in the "bulge," the western extension of Africa, Guinea is about the size of Oregon. Guinea has an irregular but level coastline. There are four diverse topographical regions: a narrow coastal plain and foothill area rising eastward to central region of dissected plateaus; plateaus sloping on the east to a broad expanse of level savannah averaging about 1,000 feet above sea level; southern interior mainly of rounded mountains having general elevation of between 1,500 and 3,000 feet but peaks up to 5,000 feet including Mount Nimba, the country's highest point at 5,748 feet. Immediately inland there is a gently rolling area, covered with dense vegetation in the more southern coastal areas. Grassy plains, interspersed with trees, are found in the north coastal areas. Further inland the landscape slowly rises in a series of flat plains and table mountains.

Guinea shares these borders with its neighbors: 240 miles with Guinea-Bissau in the west, 205 miles with Senegal in the north, 579 miles with Mali in the north, 376 miles with the Ivory Coast in the east, 350 miles with Liberia in the southeast and 405 miles with Sierra Leone in the southeast. Its Atlantic coastline stretches for 219 miles.

About 10 percent of the land is forest; 15 percent is under cultivation; and from 60 to 70 percent is unused.

*The People.* Most people are a mixture of West African Negro and Hamitic-Sudanic ancestry, the most prominent groups being the Malinke, Fulani, Mandingo, Soussou and Kissi people. Each tribal group has its own language, customs and social organization. About 75 percent of residents are Muslim; 24 percent follow indigenous beliefs; and 1 percent are Christian.

More than 80 percent of the people in Guinea live a rural life on small farms. There are more than 16 distinct ethnic groups within the country.

*A Brief History.* Partial heir to the series of West African empires that before the arrival of the Europeans cast a degree of political and commercial influence over many ethnic groups from Guinea's Atlantic Coast to the southern edge of the Sahara, Guinea was dominated in early times from the tenth to the fifteenth centuries by the kingdoms of Ghana, Mali and Songhai, overlapping from neighboring countries. The vast empires of Ghana, Mali and Songhai successively occupied the country during the period. Earlier migrations of people to Guinea remained during the period of these kingdoms. The nomadic Fulani and the agricultural Mandingos, Malinkes and Soussous had become established in prehistory and today inhabit this area of West Africa.

French military penetration began in the mid–nineteenth century. Independence from France was realized in 1958.

*The Economy.* The work force is divided this way: agriculture, 82 percent; industry and commerce, 11; services, 5.4; and government 1.6 percent. Almost all workers are loosely affiliated with the National Confederation of Guinean Workers.

One of the least developed countries in the world, Guinea has a centrally planned economy using two basic forms of business organization: wholly government-owned, semi-autonomous state enterprises and mixed enterprises. When you think of Guinea, think of bauxite, the principal ore used for making aluminum. Guinea has from one-third to one-half of the world's known reserves. Other minerals are iron ore, gold and diamonds.

Major industries include bauxite mining, alumina, diamond mining and light manufacturing and processing industries.

# Guinea-Bissau

*Official Name:* Republic of Guinea-Bissau; *Capital:* Bissau; *Government:* republic; *Subdivisions:* 9 regions and 3 circumscriptions; *Popula-*

*tion:* 928,425 (July 1987); *Density:* 37.6 per square mile; *Currency:* peso; *Official Language:* Portuguese; *Literacy:* 9 percent.

*The Land.* The size of Connecticut and Massachusetts, Guinea-Bissau is a small enclave on the west coast of Africa. Its borders are with Senegal for 210 miles in the north and Guinea for 240 miles in the southeast. Most of the country is a swampy coastal lowland rising gradually to a savanna in the east. It also has about 60 small islands lying close to the shoreline. On its eastern and southern borders it is protected by the Foutah Djallon mountains. Its Atlantic coastline stretches for 247 miles.

*The People.* Ethnic background of 99 percent of the population is West African Negro; the rest are European and mulatto. About 65 percent follow indigenous beliefs; 30 percent are Muslim; and 5 percent are Christian. The population includes several diverse tribal groups, each with its own language, customs and social organization.

*A Brief History.* The Balante people are probably the oldest inhabitants of Guinea-Bissau, joined only during the last millennium by the Mandingo and pastoral Fulani people. Guinea-Bissau was a Portuguese colony from 1885 to 1974.

Nationalist guerrilla warfare was unevenly conducted from the dense interior jungles beginning in 1961; as a result, Portugal had to maintain up to 26,000 troops, half of whom were African, stationed within the country to oppose some 7,000 rebels.

*The Economy.* The labor force is divided this way: agriculture, 90 percent; industry, services and commerce, 5 percent; and government, 5 percent.

One of the least developed countries in the world, Guinea-Bissau has a centrally planned, socialist economy in which the dominant sector is public. Most people are farmers; manufacturing is the smallest economic sector. The Balantes live in a subsistence agricultural manner in the coastal lowlands; the Mandingos and Fulani people of the interior place greater emphasis on the ownership of livestock. Contact between the Portuguese and the Africans was minimal during the colonial period; almost no educational facilities were provided for the black people.

Portuguese investment in the country during the colonial period was minimal. There are known bauxite and other mineral deposits, but they have not been developed. Since independence, the country has asked for and received aid from Portugal and other sources. The main industries are agricultural processing, beer and soft drinks.

# Libya

*Official Name:* Socialist People's Libyan Arab Jamahiriya; *Capital:* Tripoli; *Government:* socialist republic; *Subdivisions:* 10 provinces; *Population:* 3,306,825 (July 1987); *Density:* 5.2 per square mile; *Currency:* dinar; *Official Language:* Arabic; *Literacy:* 50 percent.

*The Land.* One-fourth the size of the continental United States, Libya is Africa's fourth largest country. It is located on the central Mediterranean coast of North Africa. It extends 933 miles from the coast to the central highlands of the Sahara and 1,236 miles from the Egyptian border in the east to the Algerian border in the west. More than 90 percent of Libya is in the Sahara. The Sahara contains plateaus and vast depressions. In the north the desert extends along the Mediterranean Sea along the Gulf of Sidra, dividing the northern coastlands into two parts. The northwest contains a triangular lowland. This, Libya's most populous region, includes the capital Tripoli. The northeast contains a narrow coastal plain.

About 93 percent of the land is desert, waste or urban; 6 percent is agriculture; and 1 percent is forest. The coastline is about 1,110 miles long. Borders are with these neighbors: Egypt, 693 miles; Sudan, 238 miles; Chad, 655 miles; Niger, 220 miles; Algeria, 610 miles; and Tunisia, 285 miles.

*The People.* About 97 percent of Libyans are of Arab and Berber origin with some black stock. Three percent are Greeks, Maltese, Jews, Italians, Egyptians, Pakistanis, Turks, Indians and Tunisians. About 97 percent of them are Sunni Muslim.

Some 90 percent of the people live on 10 percent of the land; about 75 percent of them live within six miles of the sea.

*A Brief History.* The Arabs conquered Libya in 643 and most of the indigenous Berbers soon embraced Islam and the Arabic tongue and culture. From 1551 the north was part of the Ottoman Empire, but Italian rule began when Italy seized Tripoli in 1911 and made the country a colony. In 1934, Italy adopted the name "Libya" (used by the Greeks for all of North Africa except Egypt) as the official name. From 1943 Britain ruled the northern provinces of Tripolitania and Cyrenaica, while France governed the southwestern province of Fezzan.

The fully independent United Kingdom of Libya was established on December 24, 1951, under King Idris I. Libya was the first country to achieve independence through the United Nations. Significant oil reserves were discovered in 1959. In 1963 Libya became a unitary state and in 1969 the king was deposed and a republic was proclaimed. A Revolutionary Command Council headed by Colonel Muammar al-Gaddafi took control and the Senate and House of Representatives were abolished.

*The Economy.* The labor force is divided this way: industry, 31 percent; services, 27 percent; government, 24 percent; and agriculture, 18 percent.

Though a private, free-market economy, Libya's economy is experiencing increasing state intervention and participation in banking, insurance, public transport and petroleum industries. There are today 130 industrial units employing 20 or more workers.

Since 1960 oil has dominated the economy and Libya is now Africa's second largest producer. The chief oilfields are in the Sahara, principally south and southeast of the Gulf of Sidra. Natural gas is also produced and there are deposits of iron ore, gypsum, salt and sulphur. Although it contributes only 2 percent of the Gross Domestic Product (GDP), agriculture still employs 23 percent of the workforce. Farmland covers 1.5 percent of Libya, pasture 3.8

percent and woodland 0.3 percent. The chief crops are barley, dates, fruits, groundnuts, olives, vegetables and wheat.

Major industries are building materials, cement, chemicals, food processing, petroleum, textiles and tobacco.

# Mali

*Official Name:* Republic of Mali; *Capital:* Bamako; *Government:* republic; *Subdivisions:* 8 administrative regions; *Population:* 8,422,810 (July 1987); *Density:* 16 per square mile; *Currency:* franc; *Official Language:* French; *Literacy:* 10 percent.

*The Land.* More than four times the size of Nevada, Mali is a landlocked country located in the West African savanna region, a transition zone between the coastal rain and forest and the desert. The northern third of the country, north of Timbuktu, lies within the Sahara Desert and is sparsely settled. The terrain is flat throughout the country, although there are significant butte outcroppings in the west. Northern Mali is a flat, dry stretch of land which is part of the Sahara Desert. This empty land, inhabited by descendants of the Berber tribes, who live a nomadic, pastoral life, has virtually no rain. The otherwise flat terrain is broken occasionally by rocky hills. The country becomes more hospitable to the south of fabled Timbuktu, which lies along an ancient caravan route of Arab merchants. The Niger River, lifeblood of Mali, flows in an irregular pattern through lakes from Timbuktu to Bamako, the capital city. In a manner similar to the Nile, the Niger River overflows its banks each year, flooding the surrounding farmland, rendering it fertile.

The country shares these borders with its neighbors: 855 miles with Algeria in the northeast, 510 miles with Niger in the east and southeast, 747 miles with Burkina Faso in the south, 320 miles with the Ivory Coast in the south, 579 miles with Guinea in the south, 260 miles with Senegal in the southwest, and 1,390 miles with Mauritania in the north and northwest. About 75 percent of the land is sparse pasture or desert; 25 percent is arable.

*The People.* The population is fairly homogeneous. The population is Mandingo (Hamitic) with many subgroups; Moor and Tuareg (Berber), Peul (Fulani) and Sudanic. About 50 percent are Mande; 17 percent are Peul; 12 percent are Voltaic; 6 percent are Songhai; and 5 percent are Tuareg and Moor. Although each ethnic group speaks a separate language, nearly 80 percent of Malians can communicate in Bambara, the common market language. About 90 percent of the population is Muslim; 9 percent adhere to indigenous beliefs; and 1 percent is Christian.

The traditions of more than 80 percent of the people are derived from the Negro peoples of western Africa. Though of African Negro descent, these people are almost totally Islamic and have adopted many of the customs of the Arabs.

*A Brief History.* Mali is cultural heir to the succession of ancient African empires — Ghana, Malinke and Songhai — that occupied the West African savanna. It was from the Malinke Kingdom of Mali that the republic took its name. The known history of the Republic of Mali dates back to the eleventh century when a powerful Islamic king established his authority over the area about the same time William the Conqueror invaded Saxon England.

Known as French Soudan, Mali became part of the French Community in 1958, with almost complete internal autonomy. After achieving independence in 1960, the government withdrew from the French Community. At first the government pursued a socialist/communist course but it was unsuccessful. In recent years, it has turned to the West and efforts to unify the country are underway.

*The Economy.* The labor force is divided this way: agriculture, 80 percent; services, 19 percent; and industry and commerce, 1 percent.

One of the world's poorest and least-developed nations, the country is socialist; 26 companies are state run with only three or four making a profit. Only subsistence agriculture is normally possible in the southern regions, even though Mali has some of the best farmland in the country since it is nurtured by two major river systems — the Senegal and the Niger. Farmers are simply not paid enough by the government for their yields to make working hard worthwhile. Instead, there is more of an attitude of "I'll work just enough to feed my family." The traditional cash export has been peanuts, purchased mainly by France, and livestock raising has become a second source of income. Major industries engage in small local consumer goods and processing.

# Mauritania

*Official Name:* Islamic Republic of Mauritania; *Capital:* Novakchott; *Government:* republic; *Subdivisions:* 12 regions and a capital district; *Population:* 1,863,208 (July 1987); *Density:* 2.590 per square mile; *Currency:* ouguiya; *Official Languages:* French and Arabic; *Literacy:* 17 percent.

*The Land.* About the size of France and Spain combined, Mauritania is located in northwestern Africa, covered mostly by plains and low plateaus. The north is desert; the country acts as a link between the Arabic Maghreb and black West Africa. The country is bordered on the north by the Spanish Sahara and for 288 miles by Algeria, on the east and southeast for 1,390 miles by Mali, on the south for 505 miles by Senegal and on the west for 414 miles by the Atlantic Ocean. The country is geographically part of the vast Western Saharan "shield" of crystalline rocks, but these are overlaid in parts with sedimentary rocks and some 40 percent of the country has a superficial cover of unconsolidated sand. About 90 percent of the land is desert; the rest is pasture.

The Sahara zone, the northern two-thirds of the country, is mostly flat sandy desert occasionally broken by rocky plateaus. The Sahelian zone, a 100- to 200-mile wide belt south of the Sahara zone, running east to west, includes steppes and savanna grasslands. The Senegal River valley, a narrow belt on the north bank, is fertile land. The Coastal zone, extending inland about 20 miles the length of the coast, is mostly desert with little rainfall.

*The People.* About 75 percent of the people are Berber or Arab and 25 percent are Negroids who live in the south, but nearly all are Muslims.

Over 90 percent of the population live in the southern quarter of the country. Over 80 percent live in a seventh of the country's area. Mauritania has one of the largest nomadic populations in the world. The nomads constitute about 68 percent of the population as against an urban population of 23 percent and rural population of 9 percent.

The drought which began in the early 1980s forced many former nomads and oasis dwellers to migrate to urban areas, swelling the population. Some 20,000 Europeans, mainly French and Spaniards from the Canary Islands, live in Mauritania.

*A Brief History.* Mauritania became a French protectorate in 1903 and a colony in 1920. Independence was achieved on November 28, 1960. Mauritania became a one-party state in 1964; Arabic became an official language, with French, in 1968. Mauritania joined the Arab League in 1973.

*The Economy.* The labor force is divided this way: agriculture, 47 percent; services 29; industry and commerce 14; and government, 10 percent.

Mauritania is a free-market economy in which the private sector predominates. The traditional economy was based on nomadic pastoralism, crop growing in the south and fishing. But since 1963, iron ore mined at F'Derik has transformed the economy. Mauritania has other minerals, including copper. Arable land covers 0.2 percent of the land. The main products are dates, fruit, gum arabic, millet, sorghum and vegetables. Sheep, goats and camels are raised. The fishing industry is expanding but there is little manufacturing. Major industries include mining of iron ore and gypsum and fish processing.

# Morocco

*Official Name:* Kingdom of Morocco; *Capital:* Rabat; *Government:* constitutional monarchy; *Subdivisions:* 35 provinces and 2 prefectures; *Population:* 23,361,495 (July 1987); *Density:* 131.7 per square mile; *Currency:* dirhan; *Official Language:* Arabic; *Literacy:* 27 percent.

*The Land.* Located in the northeast corner of Africa, Morocco is a constitutional monarchy separated from Europe only by 18 miles of the Straits of Gibraltar. It has 1,200 miles of Mediterranean coast and Atlantic coast and contains some of the world's richest fisheries. It is sharply divided between open, agriculturally rich plains in the northwest and economically poor mountains and plateaus in the east and south. The country is dominated by four mountain chains and has the most extensive river system in North Africa. In 1979, Morocco absorbed Spanish Sahara. Neighboring countries are Algeria in the east and southeast and Mauritania in the south.

Morocco borders Algeria for 1,005 miles and Mauritania for 754 miles.

The country is 51 percent desert, waste or urban; 32 percent arable and grazing land; and 17 percent forest and esparto grass.

*The People.* Most people are Arabs but about 35 percent are Berbers who live mostly west of the Atlas Mountains which insulate the country from the Sahara Desert. Morocco is considered one of the least Arabized regions of the Maghreb. Compared to other North African nations, the population is spread over a large area. Over half of the population are under 20 years of age. About 98.7 percent of the population are Muslim; 1.1 percent are Christian; and 0.2 percent are Jewish.

*A Brief History.* In early times Morocco came under the influence of Phoenicians, Carthaginians and Romans. The Arabs took control of Morocco in the early 700s and in 711 Morocco was the starting point for the Muslim conquest of the Iberian peninsula. European interest in Morocco mounted in the nineteenth century and in 1912 the territory was divided between France and Spain with the International zone at Tangier. In 1956 French and Spanish Morocco became independent.

*The Economy.* The labor force is divided this way: agriculture, 50 percent; services, 26 percent; industry, 15 percent; other areas, 9 percent; and unemployed, 20 percent. About 5 percent of the labor force is unionized.

Morocco is rich in mineral resources though most are little exploited at present. The chief mineral is phosphate rock; Morocco possesses more than 60 percent of the world's proven phosphate deposits and is the world's largest phosphate exporter. Morocco is the third largest producer after the U.S. and U.S.S.R. Agriculture, forestry and fishing employ 55 percent of the people. The main crops include barley, citrus fruits, olives, vegetables and wheat. Sheep, goats and cattle are raised. Sea fishing for anchovies, mackerel and sardines is also important. Major industries are phosphate processing and oil refining. Other manufacturers include processed foods, cement, chemicals and plastics and vehicles. Others are carpets, ceramics, leatherwork and textiles.

A 1986 survey of world markets by the Business Environment Risk Information (BERI) group rated Morocco, along with Peru and Nigeria, the worst of 43 nations studied. Among other subjects, the study covered productivity and worker attitude.[21]

Major industries include canning, chemicals, food processing, phosphates, sugar refining, and tobacco production.

# Niger

*Official Name:* Republic of Niger; *Capital:* Niamey; *Government:* republic; *Subdivisions:* 7 departments; *Population:* 6,988,540 (July 1987); *Density:* 13 per square mile; *Currency:* franc; *Official Language:* French; *Literacy:* 10 percent.

*The Land.* Three times the size of California, Niger lies on the southern edge of the Sahara, 1,200 miles from the Mediterranean and nearly 1,000 miles inland from the South Atlantic. Niger covers an immense area in north central

Africa. A huge plateau, the country is desolate but diversified, sometimes rocky and sometimes sandy, furrowed in many places by fossilized beds of ancient Sahara rivers. Two-thirds of the country is desert. The remainder is savanna suitable mainly for livestock and limited agriculture. A narrow belt of territory in the south stretches along the entire width of the country and is the only fertile region. Little more than 2 percent of the land is under cultivation, most of which is gathered around the 185-mile-long portion of the Niger River within the country's borders.

This landlocked country is the largest in West Africa. It borders Algeria for 594 miles, Mali for 510 miles, Burkina Faso for 390 miles, Benin for 118 miles, Nigeria for 930 miles, Chad for 730 miles, and Libya for 220 miles. The Niger River flows through the southern part for 186 miles. It shares Lake Chad with Nigeria and Chad.

Niger is one of the hottest regions on the planet, with temperatures often rising to 122 degrees F. The intense heat makes rain evaporate before it reaches the ground.

The land is divided this way: 7.6 percent is permanent meadow and pasture; 2.6 percent is arable; 2.3 percent is forest and woodland; 0.02 percent is inland water; and 87 percent is other, mostly desert.

*The People.* Niger is one of the most thinly populated countries in Africa. Traditions and customs are derived from the ethnic groups of West African Negro origins with a mixture of Sudanic and Hamitic blood.

The population is divided into these tribes: 56 percent Hausa, 22 percent Djerma, 8.5 percent Fula, 8 percent Tuareg, 4.3 percent Beri Beri, and 1.2 percent Arab, Toubou and Gourmantche. About 80 percent are Muslim; the rest follow indigenous and Christian beliefs.

*A Brief History.* About 600,000 years ago, humans inhabited the area that has become the Sahara of northern Niger. An empire was established in Niger by the Songhai people in the seventh century. Not much is known of the life of the people in the centuries of the Dark Ages.

In the nineteenth century, contact with the West began. The country became a French colony and remained so until 1958. Niger was a member of the French Community from 1958 to 1960 but with independence withdrew. Since then the government has been trying to unite the country, which has suffered from a series of droughts in recent years. About 90 percent of the population lives along the Niger River.

*The Economy.* The labor force is divided this way: agriculture, 90 percent; industry and commerce, 6 percent; and government, 4 percent.

Niger is one of the least developed countries of the world. It has a free-market economy in which the dominant sector is private. Manufacturing is limited to processing of agricultural produce. In the 1980s, there were 56 manufacturing establishments of all types. Some 95 percent of the people have derived their income from agriculture and stock raising in the past. The peanut crop is raised in the narrow fertile belt of land adjoining Nigeria. Major industries include cement plants, brick factories, rice mills, small cotton gins, oil presses, and slaughterhouses.

# Senegal

*Official Name:* Republic of Senegal; *Capital:* Kakar; *Government:* republic; *Subdivisions:* 8 regions; *Population:* 7,064,025 (July 1987); *Density:* 85 persons per square mile; *Currency:* franc; *Official Language:* French; *Literacy:* 10 percent.

*The Land.* About the size of Nebraska, Senegal lies in the "bulge" of western Africa, bordered by Mauritania for 505 miles in the north, Mali for 260 miles in the east and Guinea-Bissau for 210 miles and Guinea for 205 miles in the south, and totally encircling The Gambia for 470 miles in the west. Its Atlantic coastline stretches for 277 miles. It and The Gambia are the westernmost countries in Africa and lie in the transitional zone between the steaming jungles of the Gold-Ivory Coast to the south and the endless, dry Sahara to the north.

The land is 40 percent agricultural, 13 percent forest, and 47 percent built up, waste or other. It is a flat, rolling plains country with characteristic grasslands and low tree vegetation. In the southwest there are marshy swamps interspersed with tropical rain forest and the coastline is often marsh and swampland. There are no high mountains but there are four rivers flowing in parallel courses from east to west.

*The People.* Six ethnic groups constitute 90 percent of the population. About 92 percent of the residents are Muslim, 6 percent follow traditional tribal beliefs and 2 percent are Christian, primarily Roman Catholic.

Ethnically, the population is divided this way: 36 percent Wolof, 17 percent Fulani, 17 percent Serer, 9 percent Toucouleur, 9 percent Diola, 9 percent Mandingo, and 1 percent European and Lebanese.

*A Brief History.* Senegal was inhabited in prehistoric times. There was a migration of Hamitic-Sudanic groups from the Sudan area of the Nile River but it is impossible to pinpoint the period of these migrations. These groups were well-established in approximately 20 distinct parts of the country at the time of the first European explorations.

In the thirteenth and fourteenth centuries, the area came under the influence of the great Mandingo empires to the east. During the nineteenth century, the French established control in the country. Independence came in 1958. For a brief period in 1959, Senegal and the former French Sudan were joined to form the Mali Federation which was ultimately dissolved when Senegal withdrew and proclaimed itself a republic.

*The Economy.* The labor force is divided this way: subsistence agricultural workers, 77 percent, and 175,000 wage earners — 40 percent in the private sector and 60 percent in government.

Senegal's economy has been totally dependent on the production of peanuts for the past three decades; production now exceeds well over one million tons a year. Manufacturing recovered from initial loss of markets and expanded rapidly, as did fishing. Dependence on France has declined since the mid-1960s but French ownership is still predominant in private business.

Senegal is a free-market economy in which the dominant sector is private. Major industries include fishing, agricultural processing plants, light manufacturing and mining.

# Somalia

*Official Name:* Somali Democratic Republic; *Capital:* Mogadishu; *Government:* republic; *Subdivisions:* 18 regions; *Population:* 7,741,859 (July 1987); *Density:* 23 per square mile; *Currency:* shilling; *Official Language:* Somali; *Literacy:* 60 percent.

*The Land.* Located on the east coast of Africa north of the equator in the area which with Ethiopia and Djibouti is referred to as the horn of Africa, Somalia has a narrow northern coastal plain bordering the Gulf of Aden behind which are highlands. The northern part of the country is hilly; the central and southern parts are flat. Somalia is the easternmost country in Africa. It has a 1700-mile coastline on the tropical waters of the Gulf of Aden and the Indian Ocean. Central and southern Somalia consist of vast plateaus and plains that slope generally southeastward to the dune-lined Indian Ocean coast. The south contains the country's only two permanent rivers.

Somalia has 650 miles of coastline on the Gulf of Aden and 1,350 miles on the Indian Ocean. Borders shared with neighbors are 424 miles with Kenya in the southwest, 1,022 miles with Ethiopia in the west, and 38 miles with Djibouti in the northwest. About 32 percent of the land is grazing; 14 percent is scrub and forest; 13 percent is arable; and 41 percent is desert, urban or other.

*The People.* Somalia has one of the most homogeneous populations in the world, with 85 percent belonging to Hamitic stock. Their ancestors came from Arabia. About 15 percent are Bantu. There are also some Arabs, Asians, Negroes, Europeans and Somali-speaking refugees from Ethiopia. By 1980, 30 percent of the people lived in or near urban areas and worked in agriculture, government, trades and fishing; the remainder were mostly nomadic herders who raised camels, sheep and goats. Life expectancy is 43 years, which is one of the lowest in the world.

*A Brief History.* In early times, Somalia was called the Land of Spices. Arab influence was strong from the tenth century and, between the thirteenth and sixteenth centuries, there was conflict between Ethiopian Christians and Somali Muslims. After the opening of the Suez Canal in 1869, Somalia became strategically important. The north became a British protectorate in 1884–86 and Italy took over the south between 1889 and 1905. Frontier settlements split Somalia into five countries.

In World War II Britain occupied Italian Somaliland, although Italian rule was restored in 1950 under a UN Trusteeship. In 1960 British Somaliland and Italian Somaliland became independent and they merged to form Somalia. In 1969 the armed forces seized control.

*The Economy.* The economy of Somalia is pastoral and agricultural, the main form of wealth being livestock — camels, cattle, sheep and goats. It is one of the least-developed countries in the world; its economy is centrally planned with the dominant sector being public. It was declared a socialist state in 1970.

The country has limited but unexploited mineral resources. Livestock dominate the economy. Farmland covers only 2 percent of the land. Crops include bananas, citrus fruits, cotton, maize, sesame, sorghum, sugarcane and vegetables. Fishing is increasing but manufacturing, 80 percent of which is government-owned, is small-scale, concerned with processing primary products and producing basic consumer goods.

The manufacturing sector is small, even by African standards, and consists of a few relatively large government-owned plants and about 255 small private establishments, each employing over five workers. Nearly 61 percent of all industrial workers are employed by the 14 state-owned corporations. Major industries include sugar refining, tuna, beef canning, textiles, iron rod plant, and petroleum refining.

# Sudan

*Official Name:* Democratic Republic of Sudan; *Capital:* Khartoum; *Government:* republic; *Subdivisions:* 9 regions; *Population:* 23,524,622 (July 1987); *Density:* 23 per square mile; *Currency:* pound; *Official Language:* Arabic; *Literacy:* 20 percent.

*The Land.* Africa's largest country, Sudan is covered by mostly flat plains. From south to north, the Sudan has tropical forests and savanna; vast swamplands, open semitropical savanna, and scrublands; and sandy, arid hills lying between the Red Sea and the Libyan and Sahara deserts. Highlands are in the west and northeast and mountains in the south. The vast Sahara Desert lies in the northern sector and is succeeded by a semi-arid plains country in the region of Khartoum, the capital city. This gently rolling territory is succeeded in the south by tropical plains land with more abundant rainfall; in the extreme south, the land becomes choked by dense jungle growth. The Nile River, the longest in the world, virtually divides the country and is the main route of north-south communication and travel between the Mediterranean Sea and the lower part of the African continent. The Sudan is about a third the size of the United States. Neighboring countries are Chad for 845 miles in the west, Libya for 238 miles in the northwest, Egypt in the east for 792 miles officially and another 222 miles, administratively (of non–Muslim areas granted limited autonomy in 1972); Ethiopia in the east for 1,408 miles; Kenya for 190 miles and Uganda for 270 miles in the southeast; and Zaire for 390 miles and Central African Republic for 725 miles in the southwest. The country has a coastline of 445 miles. About 37 percent of the land is arable; 33 percent is desert, waste or urban; 15 percent is grazing; and 15 percent is forest.

*The People.* Sudan is thinly populated. In the north, most people are of Arab origin, some of whom are mixed with Hamites and Negroes. Islam is the main religion. In the south live Nilotes, such as Anuak, Dinka, Nuer and Shilluk, Nilo-Hamites and Negroid people. Traditional religions and Christianity predominate in the south. Achieving an effective collaboration between the two poses one of the nation's principal internal problems. The cultural differences between north and south led to a civil war in 1964–72. About 115 languages are spoken in Sudan; Arabic is the official language. The Sudan is one of the least densely populated countries in the world. Half of the population lives on 15 percent of the land.

The people of the Sudan have gathered in many distinct groups; about 52 percent of the people are Black African; 39 percent are Arab; 6 percent are Beja; 2 percent are foreign; and 1 percent are other. About 70 percent are Sunni Muslim, 20 percent adhere to indigenous beliefs and 5 percent are Christian.

*A Brief History.* Nubia and Kush were important early civilizations in northern Sudan. Christianity was introduced into the Nile region in A.D. 543–569 and it survived there until the fourteenth century. In 1820 Egypt installed a governor at Khartoum and the Egyptian Khedive Ismail appointed the Briton General Gordon as governor-general in 1877–79. In 1881 Muhammad Ahmad began a rebellion against Egyptian rule. Gordon returned in 1884 as governor-general but he died when Khartoum fell to the Mahdi in 1885. The rebellion ended in 1888, and in 1889 Britain and Egypt agreed to rule Sudan jointly. Independence was achieved in 1956. A military coup in 1958 brought General Ibrahim Abboud to power, but civilian rule was restored in 1964. In 1969 a second military coup occurred and General Gaafar Mohammed Numeiry became President. In 1972 Numeiry ended the North-South civil war by granting the South regional autonomy.

*The Economy.* The labor force is divided this way: agriculture, 78.4 percent; industry and commerce, 9.8 percent; and government, 6 percent. Sudan is one of the Arab world's poorer nations, one of the world's least developed. Agriculture dominates the economy, although only 5 percent of the land is farmed. Cotton and cotton products make up more than half of the exports. Groundnuts, gum arabic and sesame are also important while sorghum is the staple food crop. Nomadic pastoralism is also important. Cattle, camels, sheep and goats are raised. Major industries include cotton ginning, textiles, brewery, cement, edible oils, soap, distilling, shoes and pharmaceuticals.

—————————————— **Tunisia** ——————————————

*Official Name:* Republic of Tunisia; *Capital:* Tunis; *Government:* republic; *Subdivisions:* 18 governorates; *Population:* 7,561,641 (July 1987); *Density:* 110.8 per square mile; *Currency:* dinar; *Official Language:* Arabic; *Literacy:* 61 percent.

*The Land.* Tunisia is the smallest and easternmost of the countries in North Africa, lying almost in the center of the Mediterranean Sea coastline. Tunisia lies about 90 miles across the Strait of Sicily from Italy. It is bordered by Libya for 285 miles in the east and southeast and Algeria for 595 miles in the west, and has a coastline on the Mediterranean a thousand miles long. Deserts are in the south and fertile wooded areas in the north. The land includes mountains in the north, steppes in the central region which slope eastward to the broad coastal plain, and in the south large salt lake depressions.

About 43 percent of the land is desert, waste or urban; 28 percent is arable and tree crop; 23 percent is range and esparto grass; and 6 percent is forest.

*The People.* Most people are Arabs although there are also some Berbers, most of whom live in the south. They are descendants of people who migrated to the area in the seventh century. About 99 percent are Muslim. The rest are Christian and Jewish.

The people of Tunisia are well-educated, modern and of predominantly Arab outlook, albeit with a strong European overtone. European customs have intruded into the lives of the people. French is widely spoken. Tunisia is the only Muslim country in which a woman can divorce her man.

*A Brief History.* Arabs conquered Tunisia in A.D. 647, founding the holy city of Kairouan in 670. Tunisia became part of the Ottoman Empire in 1574, but in 1881 France invaded the country and proclaimed it a protectorate. After World War II, mounting nationalist opposition to French rule was manifested in guerrilla warfare in the early 1950s. Tunisia achieved independence in 1956.

*The Economy.* The labor force is divided this way: agriculture, 33 percent; industry, 23 percent; miscellaneous services, 24 percent; and unemployed, 20 percent. About 20 percent of the work force is unionized.

Tunisia has a free-market economy in which the private sector predominates. Some 1,408 establishments employ more than five workers. Tunisia's most important resources are minerals, notably oil and phosphates. The country also produces natural gas, iron ore, lead, zinc and other minerals. Agriculture remains important, and farmland covers about 32 percent of the country, pasture 16 percent and forests 3 percent. The chief food crops are barley and wheat, while olive oil is the leading agricultural export; other cereals, various fruits and vegetables are also grown. The fishing industry employs more than 22,000 Tunisians, and crayfish, mackerel, sardine, tuna and sponges are major products. Traditional craft industries remain important, but oil refining, phosphate manufacturing and other industries based on minerals have been increasing.

Major industries include chemicals, fertilizers, food processing, petroleum refining, phosphates, pulp and paper products, and textiles.

# THE NON-MUSLIM NORTH

## Benin

*Official Name:* People's Republic of Benin; *Capital:* Porto-Novo; *Government:* Soviet-modeled civilian government; *Subdivisions:* 6 provinces; *Population:* 4,339,096 (July 1987); *Density:* 85 per square mile; *Currency:* franc; *Official Language:* French; *Literacy:* 20 percent.

*The Land.* Located on the south side of the West African geographic bulge, Benin (formerly Dahomey) is a long, narrow tropical land that is chiefly agricultural. Slightly larger than Tennessee, Benin lies in a small belt of land stretching from the warm waters of the Atlantic Ocean to a distance of 450 miles inland. The coastline on the Gulf of Guinea is 78 miles wide, but in the north the width of the country increases to over 200 miles. The coastal area is a region of picturesque lagoons and inlets. A narrow sandbar lies close to the entire coastline; the lagoons open to the sea in only two places. A series of clay plateaus extend further inland for a distance of about 50 miles terminating at the rocky foothills of the stretch of mountains which divide the north from the south.

Benin is bordered on the west for 385 miles by Togo, on the northwest for 168 miles by Burkina Faso, on the north for 118 miles by Niger and on the north and east for 466 miles by Nigeria. About 80 percent of Benin is arable land; 19 percent is forest and game preserves; 1 percent is nonarable.

*The People.* There are 42 distinct ethnic groups in Benin, all of West African heritage. The Fons, Adjas, Yorubas and Baribas are the largest, constituting more than half of the population. About 70 percent adhere to indigenous beliefs; 15 percent are Muslim; and 15 percent are Christian.

Traditional tribal religions are followed by 80 percent of the population; about 12 percent are Muslim and about 8 percent Christians. Education which prior to 1976 was largely in church schools was taken over by the state that year. The literacy rate is estimated to be 20 percent. The only newspaper printed in Benin is the semiofficial *Ehuzu,* a word meaning "all has changed."

*A Brief History.* Benin was a French protectorate from 1892 to 1960. The record of shifting tides of migrant people in Benin extends back to the sixteenth century. A group of people traveled west from the Mono River and settled near what is now the city of Allada, establishing a kingdom. After a war of succession to the throne in 1610, a young contender named Dacko went to Cana, near the present city of Abomey and founded the Kingdom of Abomey, becoming the first ruler. This monarchy expanded gradually; Dacko's son conquered the lands belonging to a neighboring king named Dan. Dan is reported to have said "If I don't surrender, you will go so far as to kill me and build over my corpse." Dan was beheaded, buried and a building erected over his body. The former name of the country, Dahomey, comes from the two words Dan Home which literally means "on the belly of Dan." The Abomey Kingdom quickly became paramount over all tribal rulers in the southern region. Their superior position continued for 350 years until the French abolished the monarchy.

Ghezo, ruler of the Abomey from 1818 to 1858, signed a treaty of friendship and commerce with the French in 1851. His son, Glele, ceded the commercial city of Cotonou to the French 17 years later. Since independence, the country has had a series of governments. Since the government veered toward Marxism, the lives of the people changed drastically. The state-run radio stations broadcasts a steady, tedious stream of propaganda which must be played loudly in each town square. Student unrest and strikes were met by stern orders to shoot strikers and vandals on sight. An atmosphere of tension prevails in what has become a police state.

*The Economy.* The labor force is divided this way: agriculture, 60 percent; transport, commerce and public services, 38 percent; and industry, 2 percent. About 75 percent of all wage earners are unionized. Benin is one of the least developed nations in the world. In November 1974, the government adopted a form of Marxism-Leninism as its guiding philosophy.

Benin's only exports are cotton, cacao and palm products, although chief commercial products include coffee, peanuts, kapok and tobacco. As a French colony, Benin (then Dahomey) developed over the years a proficient corps of civil servants who frequently were sought after by other French-speaking African nations. Following independence, France supplemented the economy with $8 million per year. The economy is now in utter disarray. The people of the north are starving because of drought and invasion of the Sahara desert into lands which once at least supported grazing, but now are filled with dust and sand.

## Burkina Faso

*Official Name:* Burkina Faso; *Capital:* Ouagadougou; *Government:* military; *Subdivisions:* 30 provinces; *Population:* 8,276,272 (July 1987); *Density:* 65 per square mile; *Currency:* franc; *Official Language:* French; *Literacy:* 7 percent.

*The Land.* Formerly Upper Volta, Burkina Faso is 50 percent pasture, 10 percent fallow, 10 percent cultivated, 9 percent forest and scrub, and 10 percent other. About the size of Colorado, the country is one vast plateau tilted toward the south.

Landlocked in West Africa, the country lies between the Sahara Desert and the Gulf of Guinea in the loop of the Niger River. The land is green in the south, with forests and fruit trees and desert in the north.

Borders with neighboring countries are these: 390 miles with Niger, 168 miles with Benin, 78 miles with Togo, 338 miles with Ghana, 330 miles with the Ivory Coast, and 747 miles with Mali.

*The People.* Among the more than 50 tribes in Burkina Faso, the Mossi is the principal one, making up two-thirds of the population. About 65 percent of the population adheres to indigenous beliefs; 25 percent are Muslim; and 10 percent are Christian. Most residents live in the south and center of the country.

*A Brief History.* Until the nineteenth century, the history of the country was dominated by empire-building Mossi, who are believed to have come from central or eastern Africa sometime in the eleventh century. For centuries the Mossi peasant was both farmer and soldier, and Mossi people defended their religious beliefs and social structure against forcible attempts to connect them to Islam. When the French arrived and claimed the area as Upper Volta in 1896, the Mossi resistance ended with the capture of their capital.

*The Economy.* The labor force is divided this way: agriculture, 90 percent, and industry, commerce, industry and government, 10 percent. Less than 1 percent of the work force is unionized.

One of the poorest countries in Africa and one of the ten poorest countries in the world, Burkina Faso has an agricultural economy highly vulnerable to rainfall. It has a free-market economy in which the dominant sector is private. Some 65 fairly large industrial establishments employ nearly 1,500 workers. Drought, lack of communications and other infrastructures, a low literacy rate, and a stagnant economy are all longstanding problems. The major industries include agricultural processing plants, brewing plants, bottling plants and brick plants.

## Ethiopia

*Official Name:* Socialist Ethiopia; *Capital:* Addis Ababa; *Government:* military rule and monarchy; *Subdivisions:* 14 provinces; *Population:* 46,706,229 (July 1987); *Density:* 77 per square mile; *Currency:* birr; *Official Language:* Amharic; *Literacy:* 35 percent.

*The Land.* Slightly smaller than Alaska, Ethiopia is a land of extreme variation. The western section is extremely rugged and mountainous. It is separated from the high plains and semi-desert regions of the east by the Great Rift Valley. The major portion of the easternmost African land mass known as the Horne, Ethiopia is bordered by Kenya for 488 miles in the southwest, Sudan for 1,408 miles in the west, and Somalia for 1,022 miles and Djibouti for 265 miles in the east and southeast.

About 55 percent of the land is meadow and natural pasture; 10 percent is crop and orchard; 6 percent is forest and wood; and 29 percent is wasteland, urban and other.

*The People.* The population of Ethiopia is represented by over 100 different ethnic groups. Although the great majority belong to the Semitic and Cushitic groups, cultural mixing over many millennia has produced great diversity. The dominant Amharic people of central Ethiopia and the related Tigre people in the north and west account for about 34 percent of this country's inhabitants. The Galla or Oromo (40 percent) and the Somali (6 percent) are important Cushitic peoples.

The population of Ethiopia follows these religions: 40 to 45 percent are Muslim; 35 to 40 percent are Ethiopian Orthodox Christian; 15 to 20 percent are animist; and 5 percent are other.

People tend to be somewhat complaisant and passive, enduring present adversity with a stoicism unknown in the Western world. They also tend to be quite formal in their dealings, with strangers and with each other. A strong sense of individualism pervades the Ethiopian personality.

*A Brief History.* Ethiopia is one of the oldest countries in the world and the oldest independent country in Africa. The most important period of consolidation was that of the Kingdom of Aksum (second to ninth centuries A.D.) during which the foundation of modern Ethiopia was laid. A strong monarchy was established which lasted from those early centuries until its eventual overthrow in 1974. Missionaries from Egypt and Syria introduced Christianity in the fourth century A.D. From then the majority of the population espoused Orthodox Christianity, which remains a major unifying cultural influence. Mussolini's army invaded and occupied Ethiopia from 1935 to 1941, when with the aid of the British army control of Ethiopia was returned to Emperor Haile Selassie, who had ruled since 1930. A revolution in 1974 overthrew the monarchy and a socialist state was established. The government turned away from the West and toward other socialist and communist countries.

*The Economy.* The labor force is divided this way: agriculture and animal husbandry, 90 percent, and government and military, 10 percent.

Ethiopia is one of the least developed countries in the world. It has a centrally planned socialist economy in which the dominant sector is public. Most major industrial firms and all commercial ones as well as urban and rural land were nationalized in 1975. Major industries include cement, sugar refining, cotton textiles, food processing, and oil refining.

Ethiopia's economy is almost entirely agricultural which contributes 48 percent to the country's GNP and 90 percent to exports. Coffee, teff (a native grain), wheat, millet, pulses and barley are the major crops. Coffee has been part of Ethiopian farming for so many centuries that some experts believe the word "coffee" derives from Kaffa, an agricultural region in the southwest. Ethiopia's main exports are coffee, hides and skins. Ethiopian agriculture has been plagued by periodic drought, soil erosion and relocation of farmers to the cities.

*Organizational Communication.* Like most Semitic peoples, the Amhara place great emphasis on formal but courteous greetings to both friends and strangers. Shaking hands with one or both hands, though more gentle than the Western handshake, is common between members of the same sex. Members of the opposite sex do not greet each other physically, but this rule does not usually apply to foreigners. Conversation should be positive and touch neither on highly personal topics nor on members of the opposite sex.

# Ghana

*Official Name:* Republic of Ghana; *Capital:* Accra; *Government:* republic; *Subdivisions:* 8 administrative regions and separate Greater Accra area; *Population:* 13,948,925 (July 1987); *Density:* 148 per square mile; *Currency:* cedis; *Official Language:* English; *Literacy:* 30 percent.

*The Land.* Ghana lies on the Gulf of Guinea coast of west Africa just north of the equator and is about the same size as Oregon. The country is entirely in the tropics. There are five geographic regions: low plains on the Gulf of Guinea, succeeded northward by highlands; a large central Volta River basin; and a dissected plateau in the north. On the east is a mountain range. The south is dominated by low-lying plains alternating between grass cover and mangrove. The west and southern interior are tropical-forest areas. The Volta River country is covered with savannah woodland and swamps. The dam on the Volta River has created the longest man-made lake in the world (Lake Volta). The north is primarily grassland. Ghana has a 328-mile-long shore washed by the warm waters of the Gulf of Guinea. The tropical rain forest belt, known as the "Ashanti," produces most of Ghana's cocoa, minerals and timber. About 60 percent of the land is forest and brush; 19 percent is agricultural; 21 percent is other.

Neighboring countries are the Ivory Coast for 415 miles in the west, Burkina Faso for 338 miles in the west and north and Togo for 545 miles in the east.

*The People.* About 99.8 percent of the population is black African; the rest are European and other. There are over 100 different ethnic groups, each with its own langauge and culture. Major groups are the Fante in the coastal area, the Asante in the south central area, the Ga and Ewe in the south, and the Hausa and Moshi-Dagomba in the north.

About 38 percent of the residents follow indigenous beliefs; 30 percent are Muslim; 24 percent are Christian; and 8 percent are other. Ghanians are proud of their diverse backgrounds. They are also proud of their position as the first sub–Saharan colony to gain independence from European powers.

Details of family structure vary from one ethnic group to another. Some groups have a matrilineal family organization, in which inheritance is passed down through the wife's family. In these groups, the chief responsibility for the family falls on the woman. Polygamy is also practiced by some Ghanians. The elderly members of the family are deeply respected and exert a great deal of influence in family decisions. Ghanians will normally sacrifice their own desires and ambitions for the sake of the family unit.

*A Brief History.* Ghana takes its name, though not its modern boundaries, from one of the great inland trading empires that flourished in West Africa from the fourth to the eleventh centuries A.D. The fabled university city of Timbuktu (now in Mali) was part of ancient Ghana. Because of the diversity of the ethnic groups, the history of the country is quite varied. The folklore of the people refers to migrations from the north and it is probable that these legends relate to the travels of Sudanese people from the Nile River in the tenth to fifteenth centuries. Modern history begins with contacts with Portuguese traders in 1470. They developed gold mining and slave trading in the area. The control of the "Gold Coast" (which became Ghana in 1957) fell into British hands in the nineteenth century, and after 74 years of battle with the Asantes of the interior, Britain gained control of the present area of Ghana in 1901. In 1957, Ghana became the first black African colony to gain independence from Britain. The Gold Coast was renamed "Ghana" because of speculation that the migrants moved south from the ancient kingdom of Ghana. A series of governments has ruled since then.

*The Economy.* The labor force is divided this way: agriculture and fishing, 54.7 percent; industry 18.7, sales and clerical 15.2, services, transportation and communication 7.7, and professional, 3.7 percent. About 13 percent of the work force is unionized.

Ghana has a free-market economy in which the dominant sector is private. It has a good natural-resource endowment, a relatively well-educated labor force, one of the best post-colonial administrations in Africa, and a fair physical infrastructure.

The Ghanian economy centers largely on agriculture. Cocoa accounts for about 70 percent of the country's exports. Other important agricultural products include root crops, corn, sorghum, millet and peanuts. Mining is also an important part of the economy. Ghana is the fifth largest producer of diamonds and the seventh largest producer of gold. Manganese, bauxite and aluminum are also important minerals. Important industries are lumbering, mining, light manufacturing, fishing and aluminum. Only one commercially exploitable oil field has been found.

*Organizational Communication.* Casual dress is the rule for most occasions, although a suit and tie or dress is required for more formal occasions. Western dress is the norm in urban areas, with officials often wearing the traditional *kente* cloth robes on ceremonial occasions. Men in rural areas wear the robes every day. The design of the cloth often reflects the status, purpose, and attitude of the wearer.

# Ivory Coast

*Official Name:* Republic of the Ivory Coast; *Capital:* Abidjan; *Government:* republic; *Subdivisions:* 34 prefectures; *Population:* 10,766,632 (July 1987); *Density:* 71.7 per square mile; *Currency:* franc; *Official Language:* French; *Literacy:* 24 percent.

*The Land.* Somewhat larger than New Mexico and roughly square in shape, the Ivory Coast is located on the south side of the West African bulge. It has a 315-mile coastline on the Gulf of Guinea. The Ivory Coast is bordered by Liberia for 445 miles and Guinea for 376 miles in the west; Mali for 320 miles and Burkina Faso for 330 miles in the north; and Ghana for 415 miles in the east.

The country is a vast plateau sloping southward with no major natural divisions or barriers. The country's dense forest in the western half of the territory extends to the sea, covering almost 40 percent of the land. From the border of Ghana for a distance of 185 miles to the west, it is flat and sandy with many inland lagoons. The country is almost entirely level. The land is 52 percent grazing, fallow and waste, 40 percent forest and wood, and 8 percent cultivated.

*The People.* About 60 ethnic groups, classified into 7 principal divisions, live in the Ivory Coast. No single tribe has more than 20 percent of the population. There is a heavy concentration of population in the south-central and southeast areas. Northeastern and southwestern portions are virtually uninhabited. The Ivory Coast is one of the few countries with no serious restrictions on immigration.

There are more than 60 distinct tribal groups, predominantly of West African Negro origin. Principal groupings include the Agnis-Ashantis-Baoules, Kroumen, Mandingo, Senoufo, Dans-Gouros and Koua. Religions include traditional tribal beliefs, 64 percent; Islam, 24 percent; and Christian, 12 percent.

*A Brief History.* Artifacts discovered in the Ivory Coast suggest that a Neolithic civilization flourished there in prehistoric time. Not much is known of the history of this country, however, before the fourteenth century.

At the time of the arrival of the first Europeans, there were three strong kingdoms: the Krinjabo and Bettie in the north and the Boundoukou in the east. There were also more than 50 other small tribal groups which had little contact with each other. The severity of the surf and the forbidding appearance of the land discouraged early European exploration. France made initial contact with the country in 1637.

When full independence was gained by the Ivory Coast in 1960, Felix Houphouet-Boigny became its president and remains so today. The Ivory Coast was a French colony from 1839 to 1960.

*The Economy.* The labor force is divided this way: agriculture, forestry, and livestock raising, 70.5 percent, and government, industry, commerce and the professions, 15.3 percent and 14.2 percent other. About 20 percent of wage earners are unionized.

Ivory Coast has a flourishing economy. An easy mixture of state-controlled enterprises blend with capitalism; the government follows a policy of economic liberalism based on private enterprise.

Major industries include food and lumber processing, oil refining, auto assembly plants, textiles, soap, flour mill, matches, three small shipyards, a fertilizer plant, and a battery factory.

---

# Liberia

*Official Name:* Republic of Liberia; *Capital:* Monrovia; *Government:* republic; *Subdivisions:* 13 countries; *Population:* 2,384,189 (July 1987); *Density:* 52 per square mile; *Currency:* dollar; *Official Language:* English; *Literacy:* 24 percent.

*The Land.* A little smaller than Pennsylvania, Liberia is located just a few degrees above the equator at the southwestern extremity of the Western bulge of Africa. It is bordered for 190 miles by Sierra Leone in the west, for 350 miles by Guinea in the north and for 445 miles by the Ivory Coast in the east and northeast. Its Atlantic coastline is 334 miles long. Liberia is located on the southern part of the west coast of Africa, facing the warm equatorial waters of the Gulf of Guinea. About 40 percent of the land is forest; 30 percent is jungles and swamp; 20 percent is in agriculture; and 10 percent is in other.

The coastal region is a belt of gently rolling plains 19 to 31 miles wide with tidal creeks, shallow lagoons and swamps. The plains rise slowly to a plateau. The eastern section of the country is rugged and covered with forest, while the far northern region is a densely forested mountainous terrain. From a narrow, level coastal trip dotted with lagoons, tidal creeks, and marshes, the rolling country rises in a series of plateaus. Low mountains are found intermittently throughout the country. The coastal area, receiving the most rainfall, is dotted with lagoons, tidal creeks and marshes. Farther inland the terrain rises slowly to 1000 feet in a series of plateaus obscured by the dense undergrowth. Low mountains rise occasionally throughout the country. Six rivers flow from the interior southwest to the Gulf of Guinea; they are not navigable for more than a few miles inland and are bounded by level and suitable for cultivation.

*The People.* There are some 17 ethnic categories: descendants of emancipated slaves from the Western Hemisphere (once known as Americo-Liberians) who had settled in Liberia in the nineteenth century and 16 "tribes" of indigenous Africans, including Kru, Mandingo and Gola. The descendants of freed slaves make up only 1 percent of the population but controlled the country for many years. Many forebears of present-day Liberians migrated to the area from the north and east between the twelfth and seventeenth centuries.

There is a basic divergence of cultural traditions in Liberia. The descendants of freed slaves living in the coastal regions are for the most part urban, Christian people. English is universally spoken by them, and the style of dress is American. They have particularly valued formal attire, including the use, until recently, of the top hat. The people of the interior lead a rural life based upon subsistence agriculture. They dress more in the style of the other nations of western Africa—colorful and flowing robes, and their heads are often covered with materials of brilliant colors.

There are more than 20 local languages and dialects. English is the official language of governmental affairs, formal education and the mass media. About half of the residents adhere to indigenous religious concepts; the remainder are about equally divided between Christian and Muslim faiths.

*A Brief History.* The Kru, Mandingo and Gola ethnic groups lived for countless centuries in Liberia prior to the arrival of an American settlement of freed slaves. Portuguese explorers visited Liberia's coast in 1461, and for the next 300 years, European merchants and local Africans engaged in trade. In 1816 the American Colonization Society, a private organization, was given a charter by the United States Congress to send free slaves to the west coast of Africa. The first settlers landed at the site of Monrovia in 1882. In 1847, Liberia became Africa's first independent republic with a constitution modeled after that of the United States. This country, easily reached by the slave traders' ships plying the Atlantic, was subjected to mass deportations of its native population into slavery. Sometimes the traders took only the men for heavy work.

About 75 percent of the population follow traditional indigenous beliefs; 15 percent are Muslim; and 10 percent are Christian.

*The Economy.* The labor force is divided this way: agriculture, 70.5 percent; services 10.8, industry and commerce 4.5, and other areas, 14.2 percent. About 2 percent of the labor force is unionized. Non-African foreigners hold about 95 percent of management and engineering jobs.

The private sector dominates Liberia's free-market economy. There is virtually no heavy industry, and manufacturing is limited to food processing. Chief commercial products are iron ore, rubber, diamonds, timber and cocoa.

Manufacturing consists mainly of small-scale operations having one to ten employees; a few larger enterprises (mostly foreign owned) produce import-substitution items. Major industries include rubber processing, food processing, construction materials, furniture, palm oil processing and mining of iron ore and diamonds.

---------------------------- **Nigeria** ----------------------------

*Official Name:* Federal Republic of Nigeria; *Capital:* Lagos; *Government:* republic; *Subdivisions:* 19 states and 1 capital territory; *Population:* 108,579,764 (July 1987); *Density:* 238.7 per square mile; *Currency:* naira; *Official Language:* English; *Literacy:* 28 percent.

*The Land.* The seventh largest country on the African continent, Nigeria is about the same size as California, Nevada and Utah combined. It lies facing the Gulf of Guinea on the southern coast of West Africa; its coastline on the Gulf stretches for 480 miles. The country is bordered for 480 miles by Benin on the west, for 930 miles by Niger and for 55 miles by Chad in the north, and for 1,050 miles by Cameroon in the east. About 24 percent of the land is arable, 35 percent is forests and 41 percent desert.

The country includes a coastal belt of mangrove swamps from 10 to 95 miles wide; a tropical rain forest of undulating plains and scattered hills from 50 to 100 miles wide; a high central plateau of open woodland and savanna from 2,000 to 6,000 feet in elevation; and semidesert in the extreme north. The country ranges from the grassy plains of the Jos plateau in the north to the sandy beaches and mangrove swamps on the coast. Park lands and tropical rain forests dominate the central region. Nigeria is divided into three segments by the Niger and Benue Rivers, which meet in the center of the country and flow together to the Gulf of Guinea. These three segments correspond roughly to the boundaries of the three major ethnic groups.

*The People.* Nigeria is the most populous nation in Africa. It is the world's largest black nation; one of every five Africans is a Nigerian. There are over 250 ethnic groups in Nigeria. They are of West African Negro and Sudanic-Hamitic origin. The Hausa and Fulani in the north, the Yorubas in the west, and the Ibos in the east together account for about 60 percent of the population. Each ethnic group has its own culture. Some 47 percent of the population are Islamic, 34 percent are Christian and 19 percent follow traditional tribal beliefs.

Individual Nigerians are proud of the unique cultural heritage of their particular ethnic group. There is some ethnic tension, but continuing efforts are gradually unifying the nation. Life in Nigeria moves at a relaxed pace which is in keeping with the Nigerian concept of time. English is the official language.

*A Brief History.* Nigeria, with its many ethnic groups, has a diverse history. The Hausa, located in the north, converted to Islam in the fourteenth century and established a feudal system that was solidified by the Fulani conquest in the nineteenth century. In the west, the Yoruba established the Kingdom of

Oyo and extended its influence as far as modern Togo. The Ibo, located in the east, remained isolated. At the end of the fifteenth century, European explorers declared the area around the city of Lagos to be a crown colony, outlawed the slave trade and annexed the remainder of the territory as a colony in 1914. When Nigeria became an independent republic in 1960, tension rose among the various ethnic groups. After two coups and much unrest, the Ibo-dominated eastern region seceded from the country and attempted to establish the Republic of Biafra. Two and a half years of civil war followed and the Ibos were forced back into the republic. In 1979, national elections were held and a representative civilian government was established. This government lasted only until late 1983, when a military coup left General Mohammed Buhari as military leader of the nation.

*The Economy.* The labor force is divided this way: agriculture, 54 percent; industry, commerce and services, 19 percent; and government, 15 percent.

Nigeria's is a free-market economy based on oil and dominated by the private sector. Nigeria's economy is one of the strongest in Africa. Agriculture employs about 70 percent of the people and is an important part of the economy. Nigeria is a major producer of peanuts, cotton, cocoa, yams, cassava, sorghum, corn and rice. The discovery of large petroleum deposits has reshaped Nigeria's economy. Nigeria is the second largest exporter of petroleum to the United States. It is the world's fifth largest exporter of petroleum and also produces a significant amount of rubber.

Major industries are cement, food processing, mining, petroleum, pulp and paper, rubber and textiles. The country has every conceivable natural resource, including crude oil.

A Nigerian industrialist who had worked in England was asked about the differences between managing companies in Europe versus managing companies in Africa and the Middle East:

> For me the biggest difference is that when working in Africa I get physically exhausted. The strain there is physical, not so much mental. In Europe, the physical demands are less because there is easy access to things. I don't have to go from London to Paris for a meeting, I can get my point clear over the telephone and get the same results as if I flew to Paris. In Europe I can run my companies from my desk in London. In Africa I have to travel everywhere.
>
> Another problem is middle management. We lack middle management in Africa and the Middle East. And because of this lack of middle management, every instruction you give you have to follow through. You have to spend a long time following it through and making sure it is done. You can't take anything for granted.[22]

*Organizational Communication.* Punctuality in an African organization is a strong point. Greetings in Nigeria are valued among the different ethnic groups. Refusing to do so is a sign of disrespect. Personal space between members of the same sex is much closer than it is in America. Nigeria is a multicultural nation and gestures differ from one ethnic group to another. Generally pushing the palm of the hand forward with the fingers spread is a vulgar gesture and should be avoided.

Business appointments generally have to be made by personal call or sending notes by hand, as the telephone and postal systems are unreliable and slow.

Nigerians expect open friendliness—do not hesitate to smile and start a conversation. Informal dress may be taken as disrespect; maintain proper professional appearances. Learn to tolerate the relaxed pace of business and be prepared to wait endlessly. Listen more than you talk. Personal space is very close; don't back away.

# Sierra Leone

*Official Name:* Republic of Sierra Leone; *Capital:* Freetown; *Government:* republic; *Subdivisions:* 3 provinces and the western area; *Population:* 3,754,088 (July 1987); *Density:* 130 per square mile; *Currency:* leone; *Official Language:* English; *Literacy:* 15 percent.

*The Land.* Slightly larger than West Virginia, Sierra Leone is circular in shape and located in the southwestern part of the great bulge of West Africa. It neighbors Guinea for 405 miles on the north and northwest and Liberia for 190 miles on the southeast. The country has a 210-mile coastline on the Atlantic Ocean.

Sierra Leone has a coastal belt of mangrove swamps 60 miles wide; stretches of wooded hill country; and an upland plateau, with mountains near the eastern frontier. The country is located on the Gold Coast of the immense portion of Africa that extends westward into the Atlantic above the equator. Stretches of wooded hill country rise from the coastal belt to gently rolling plateaus in the north. Mountains tower to heights of 6,000 feet in the southeast area near the Moa River.

About 65 percent of the country is arable; 27 percent is pasture; 4 percent is swamp; and 4 percent is forest.

*The People.* Mende and Temne live in the north; creole (descendants of freed slaves from almost every part of Africa) and 18 small groups reside elsewhere. About 70 percent of the population follow traditional tribal beliefs, 25 percent are Christian or mixed and 5 percent are Islamic.

*A Brief History.* Sierra Leone was thinly populated by the Mende and Temne people who date back to unknown times when the Portuguese explorer Pedro de Cintra visited the coastal area in 1460. It was he who gave the country its name of Sierra Leone meaning "lion mountains." European contacts with Sierra Leone were among the first in West Africa and Sierra Leone was one of the first West African British colonies. Following independence in 1961, the country had a series of governments.

*The Economy.* Most of the population engages in subsistence agriculture; only a small minority (about 65,000) earn wages.

Sierra Leone's is a free-market economy dominated by the private sector. The country relies on the mining sector in general and diamonds in particular for its economic base. Major industries include mining of diamonds, iron ore, bauxite and rutile; manufacturing of beverages, textiles, cigarettes and construction goods; and oil refining.

# Togo

*Official Name:* Republic of Togo; *Capital:* Lome; *Government:* republic; *Subdivisions:* 21 prefectures; *Population:* 3,228,635 (July 1987); *Density:* 130 per square mile; *Currency:* franc; *Official Language:* French; *Literacy:* 18 percent.

*The Land.* About the size of a half of Mississippi vertically, Togo is located on the West African coastline of the Gulf of Guinea. Its coastline is 31 miles long. Togo is bordered for 545 miles by Ghana in the west, for 78 miles by Burkina Faso in the north and for 385 miles by Benin in the east. Togo lies in the center of the Gold and Ivory Coasts. It is a long, narrow country stretching 360 miles from the Atlantic into the interior. The country is only 31 miles wide at the coast and 100 miles in width at its broadest point.

*The People.* Togo has about 37 ethnic groups. The major ones are the Ewe, Kabrais, Mina, Ghen, Konkomba, Bassari, Akposso, Bedere, Bobo-Ahlon and six other smaller groups of West African Negro and Sudanic origin. About 70 percent follow traditional tribal beliefs; 20 percent are Christian and 10 percent are Islamic.

The people of the populous southern coast area are better educated and economically better off than those of the sparsely settled north, a condition common to many countries in this area of Africa. The Ewe people have dominated the cultural life in Togo and extend beyond its borders well into Ghana to the west. Few communities lack educational facilities within the Ewe country. Although a few of this group continue the animist and pagan customs of their past, most are Christians, widely employed and leading modern, urban lives. In spite of this, Togo as a whole is only about 18 percent literate. The lives of the people farther inland are based on small family holdings of farmland, and they have little daily contact with the larger cities of the south.

*A Brief History.* Not much is known of the precolonial history of this region of Africa. It is certain that the majority of the population—of West African Negro origin—had lived there for countless centuries. A smaller group of Sudanic ancestry settled in northern Togo during the period of their migration in the tenth to the thirteenth centuries. For 200 years the coastal region was a major raiding center for Europeans in search of slaves, earning Togo and the region the name "The Slave Coast." Togo was Germany's only self-supporting colony from 1885 to 1916 and a French colony from 1916 to 1960. Since independence was granted it has had a series of governments.

*The Economy.* The labor force is divided this way: agriculture, 78 percent, and industry, 22 percent.

Togo's is a free-market economy dominated by the private sector. Subsistence farming is the dominant economic activity. Small family-type farms which grow cocoa and coffee are the basis of the predominantly agricultural economy of Togo. Phosphate exports constitute the number one source of income, but 90 percent of the people are employed in agriculture and stock raising. Major industries include phosphate mining, agricultural processing, cement, handicrafts, textiles and beverages.

# THE CENTRAL REGION

## Burundi

*Official Name:* Republic of Burundi; *Capital:* Bujumbura; *Government:* republic; *Subdivisions:* 15 provinces; *Population:* 5,005,504 (July 1987); *Density:* 465 per square mile; *Currency:* franc; *Official Languages:* Kirundi and French; *Literacy:* 25 percent.

*The Land.* Landlocked in the highlands of central Africa and slightly larger than Maryland, Burundi is bordered for 180 miles by Rwanda in the north, by Tanzania for 280 miles in the east and by Zaire for 145 miles in the west. Burundi is a high, rolling country that is part of the Great East African Plateau, forming the divide between two watersheds: the Nile and the Zaire basins. A cool, pleasant land of mountains and plateaus, Burundi was known as Urundi before its independence; it was the southern portion of Rwanda-Urundi. Fabled Lake Tanganyika, the longest fresh water lake in the world, separates Burundi and Zaire.

About 37 percent of the land is arable; 23 pasture, 10 scrub and forest, and 30 percent other.

*The People.* Burundi has one of the highest population densities in sub–Saharan Africa. Some 85 percent of the residents are Hutu (sometimes called Buhutu), 14 percent are Tutsi (sometimes called Watusi) and 1 percent are Twa or Pygmies. The Hutu are primarily farmers whose Bantu-speaking ancestors migrated into Burundi from 800 to 1,000 years ago.

The customs of the people of Burundi are unique and beautiful. The Tutsi reach heights of seven feet and possess a high degree of unity based on social order with the Ganwa traditionally at the top and the Bahima somewhat lower. About 60 percent of the people are Christian; 38 percent follow traditional tribal beliefs; and 2 percent are Islamic.

Since 1959, Burundi has experienced serious ethnic conflict between the numerically dominant Hutu and the socially and politically dominant Tutsi.

*A Brief History.* The old Kingdom of Burundi dates back to the fifteenth century; tradition indicates that the Twa (Pygmies) were the first inhabitants, a few of whom are found in the remotest parts of Burundi today. They were succeeded by the Hutu, a peaceful Bantu agricultural group, who in turn were subdued by the extremely tall Tutsi, who reduced the Hutu to serfdom. Before the Europeans arrived, Burundi was a kingdom with a highly stratified, feudal social structure. Rulers were drawn from princely dynastic families from whom a king was chosen.

Burundi was part of German East Africa from 1899 to 1917 and was occupied by Belgian troops in 1916. It was a Belgian trust territory under the League of Nations and United Nations from 1923 to 1962. After independence in 1962, inevitable rivalries made establishment of a workable government difficult.

*The Economy.* The labor force is divided this way: agricultural, 93 percent; government 4, industry and commerce 1.5, and services, 1.5 percent.

One of the world's poorest countries, Burundi has a free-market economy in which the dominant sector is private. Europeans own about 40 percent of industrial establishments, but they account for more than 98 percent of volume of business and 96 percent of industrial employment.

With an extremely dense population and a social system based on ownership of cattle, the economy of Burundi is difficult to find. In years of drought, thousands have died of famine. The government has programs underway to raise agricultural production, but resistance rooted in the traditions of the Tutsi has been met. Discovery of nickel deposits and the possibility of offshore drilling for oil in Lake Tanganyika give promise for improvement.

# Cameroon

*Official Name:* Republic of the Cameroon; *Capital:* Yaounde; *Government:* unitary republic; *Subdivisions:* 10 provinces; *Population:* 10,255,332 (July 1987); *Density:* 51 per square mile; *Currency:* franc; *Official Languages:* English and French; *Literacy:* 65 percent.

*The Land.* Located in the geographic and ethnic crossroads of Africa in the west-central area of the continent, Cameroon is often referred to as the "hinge" of Africa. It extends like an irregular wedge northeastward from the Gulf of Guinea to Lake Chad about midway between Senegal and South Africa. This land of contrasts, containing almost every species of flora and fauna of tropical Africa and numerous varieties of wild game, stretches north from the Atlantic in a "hinge" position between West and Central Africa. From the Polynesianlike beaches, there rise towering mountains which proceed directly north into West Cameroon. The southern part of Cameroon, extending eastward in a horizontal line, is characterized by a low coastal basin with equatorial jungles. In the more north-central part of the country there is a series of grassy plateaus.

About the size of California plus a quarter of Oregon, Cameroon shares borders of 1,050 miles with Nigeria in the northwest, of 550 miles with Chad in the northeast, of 490 miles with Central African Republic in the east, and of 385 miles with the Congo, 185 miles with Gabon and 100 miles with Equatorial Guinea in the south.

About 50 percent of the country is forest, 18 meadow, 13 fallow, 4 cultivated and 15 percent other.

*The People.* There are 200 ethnic groups in Cameroon, speaking over 80 major African languages, including the Cameroon Highlanders, 31 percent; Equatorial Bantu 19, Kirdi 11, Fulani 10, Northwestern Bantu 8, Eastern Sudanic 7, and other African, 13 percent. It is the only African country where both French and English have both been given official status.

About 51 percent of the population follow indigenous beliefs; 33 percent are Christian; and 16 percent are Muslim. By African standards, Cameroon's educational system is extensive. In 1961, the government established the University of Yaounde, the first African university to offer courses in both French and English.

The great majority of the people in Cameroon live in the simple, rural tribal life of their ancestors. There is a great diversity which is clarified by the religious grouping in the nation with Christians in the Southwest. Animists (half of the people) live in the central interior and a substantial community of Islamic people are located in the north. The many ethnic groups which make up the population each have a distinct heritage of art, music and folklore.

*A Brief History.* Originally populated by the pygmies, Cameroon was successively dominated by other native groups. The Bantus arrived in the fifteenth century, settling in the central plateau region. In 1472, Portuguese explorer Fernando do Poo arrived on the coast of what is now Cameroon. Cameroon was a German colony from 1884 to 1916, a British colony in West Cameroon from 1916 to 1961 and a French colony in East Cameroon from 1916 to 1960. The slave trade, while it lasted, was active along the Cameroon coast. Religious mission settlements appeared in the mid–1800s and have been active ever since. After France and Britain granted independence, the two Cameroons were reunited. The subsequent governments were many and unstable.

*The Economy.* The labor force is divided this way: agriculture, 74 percent; industry and transport, 11.4 percent; and other services, 14.2 percent. About 45 percent of the work force is unionized.

Cameroon has a liberal but planned economy; agriculture being the mainstay. It is a lower-middle income country with one of the most dynamic developing African economies because of a stable government, it follows a middle-of-the-road economic policy, has a prudent fiscal management, oil revenues, earned foreign investor confidence and low inflation and external debt.

The backbone of Cameroon's trade traditionally has been its cacao and coffee crops. When world prices dropped, there was a severe shock to the country. The government therefore began a "green revolution" in 1972, investing heavily in large farming operations for growing cotton, tobacco, tea and rubber. This diversification of crops is now paying off.

The industrial sector consists of a traditional, labor-intensive subsector, mainly small-scale artisan workshops, and a modern subsector engaged in the processing of raw materials and assembly of imported components.

—————————— **Central African Republic** ——————————

*Official Name:* Central African Republic; *Capital:* Bangui; *Government:* republic; *Subdivisions:* 14 prefectures; *Population:* 2,699,293 (July

1987); *Density:* 10.4 per square mile; *Currency:* franc; *Official Language:* French; *Literacy:* 33 percent.

*The Land.* Slightly smaller than Texas, the Central African Republic is located in almost the precise center of Africa, about 400 miles from the nearest ocean. It shares borders for 290 miles with the Congo and 980 miles with Zaire in the south, for 511 miles with Cameroon in the west, for 745 miles with Chad in the northwest and for 725 miles with the Sudan in the northeast and east. The Central African Republic is a vast, well-watered, rolling plateau. This sun-drenched land of agricultural and forest products found its original wealth in ivory from its once-large herds of massive elephants. There is a small area of jungle in the southwest which is rapidly succeeded by the rolling plateaus of the plains, rising gently to the mountains of the northeast.

From 80 to 85 percent of the land is meadow, fallow, vacant, arable, urban or waste; 10 to 15 percent is cultivated; and 5 percent is dense forest.

*The People.* More than 80 ethnic groups live in the Central African Republic, each with its own language. Important ethnic groups are the Banda, 47 percent, and Banda-Mandija, 27 percent. Religions are Christianity, 64 percent, and Islam, 24 percent. Traditional tribal beliefs are intermingled with the religious beliefs of the Christians.

Sangho, the language of a small group along the Oubangui River, is the national language spoken by the majority of Central Africans. Only a small minority have more than an elementary knowledge of French, the official language.

*A Brief History.* Little is known of the early history of this remote area of Africa. The country shared the various migrations of different ethnic groups, most of which are of Bantu origin. From 1894 to 1960, the Central African Republic was a French colony. Since then, the country has had difficulty establishing a stable government. In 1977 Jean-Bedel Bokassa crowned himself emperor at a cost of $22 million. In this land where the average per capita annual income was $120, many were outraged. Bokassa did not last long; on September 20, 1979, former President David Dacko led a successful, bloodless coup and restored republican government.

*The Economy.* The labor force is divided this way: agriculture, 85 percent; commerce and services, 8.9 percent; industry, 2.9 percent; and government, 3 percent. About 1 percent of the labor force is unionized.

The Central African Republic has a free-market economy in which the dominant sector is private. It is one of the least developed countries in the world. Agriculture, centered on the production of cotton and coffee, has traditionally dominated the economy — which has been in a shambles for several years. Nine out of ten people live in rural isolation, cultivating traditional subsistence crops on small farms, raising livestock and engaging in hunting and fishing.

# Congo

*Official Name:* People's Republic of the Congo; *Capital:* Brazzaville; *Government:* people's republic; *Subdivisions:* 9 regions; *Population:*

2,082,154 (July 1987); *Density:* 13 per square mile; *Currency:* franc; *Official Language:* French; *Literacy:* over 50 percent.

*The Land.* Located in West Africa, the Congo shares borders of 323 miles with Cameroon, 390 miles with the Central African Republic, 1,010 miles with Zaire, 125 miles with Angola, and 1,029 miles with Gabon. Its Atlantic coastline is 97 miles long.

This lush, green land of ancient tradition lies immediately to the north of the Zaire River. Formerly part of French Equatorial Africa, the country has the same general geographical features as Zaire to the south.

A low-lying treeless plain extends 40 miles from the coast to the interior, succeeded by a mountainous region parallel to the coastline known as the Mayombe Escarpment. This is a region of sharply rising mountain ridges covered with jungle and dense growth.

About 63 percent of the land is dense forest or wood; 31 percent is meadow; 4 percent is urban or waste; and 2 percent is cultivated.

*The People.* One of the least densely populated countries in central Africa, the Congo has about 50 identifiable subgroups of Bantu origin, with the following major groups: BaKongo, 48 percent, Songha 20, M'Bochi 12, and Teke, 17 percent. About 48 percent of the population follow animist beliefs; 47 percent are Christian; and 2 percent are Muslim.

*A Brief History.* As early as the fifteenth and sixteenth centuries, this land was part of the great native Kingdom of the Congo. Its present-day boundaries, as is so often the case in Africa, are based upon arbitrary determinations of the nineteenth century European powers rather than on cultural or physical reality.

As in the neighboring country of Zaire, legend in this region conveys the story of the Kingdom of the Congo, said to have been founded by Wene, also known as Nimi Loukemi, the first king, who reigned more than 400 years ago. From 1883 to 1910, the Congo was a French colony; from 1910 to 1960, it was part of French Equatorial Africa. After independence, the Congo established a socialist government and turned toward the Soviet bloc. A series of unstable governments has tried to survive.

*The Economy.* The labor force is divided this way: agriculture, 75 percent, and commerce, industry and government, 25 percent. About 20 percent of the labor force is unionized.

One of the most industrialized of African equatorial states, the Congo has industry oriented toward the production of consumer goods. However, most of the population engages in subsistence farming, producing corn, bananas, cassava, rice, peanuts, typical fruits, goats and chickens. Major industries include crude oil, cement, sawmills, breweries, cigarettes, sugar mills, and soap.

# Equatorial Guinea

*Official Name:* Republic of Equatorial Guinea; *Capital:* Malabo; *Government:* republic; *Subdivisions:* 6 provinces; *Population:* 340,434

(July 1987); *Density:* 36 per square mile; *Currency:* franc; *Official Language:* Spanish; *Literacy:* 55 percent.

*The Land.* Equatorial Guinea is located on the coast of west-central Africa and consists of a mainland province and five islands. Slightly larger than Vermont, Equatorial Guinea shares borders for 114 miles with Cameroon in the north and for 240 miles with Gabon in the east and south. The island portion of the country lies some 20 miles off the west coast of Cameroon. The sandy beach quickly gives way to the thick growth of interior jungle—immense ebony, mahogany and oak trees. Few roads penetrate into the interior, but the land is thick with streams which are the home of giant frogs.

The scenic island of Bioko is large and productive, the best source of cocoa in the world.

*The People.* The majority of people in Equatorial Guinea are Bantu; the largest tribe is the Fang, divided into about 50 clans. Another tribe is the Bubi (Bioko). Most people are nominally Roman Catholic; traditional tribal beliefs are intermingled with their Christian faith.

The people on the mainland live in rural solitude, surviving on limited forestry and primitive agriculture. Those on the more sophisticated island of Bioko have greater interest in contact with the outside.

*A Brief History.* Almost nothing is known about the precolonial period of this remote part of Africa. It was a Spanish colony—the island from 1778 to 1968 and the mainland from 1885 to 1968. The independent government fell into the hands of the mentally unbalanced Francisco Macias Nguema who wreaked havoc with the country. In August 1979, Lt. Col. Teodoro Obiang Nguema Mbasogo led a successful coup d'etat; Macias was executed after a trial attended by international observers.

*The Economy.* Most of the labor force is involved in subsistence agriculture. Cacao and coffee exports have been vital to the nation's economic survival, but since independence, production has dropped. Along with financial aid, the Spanish have sent an advisor for each cabinet officer.

Equatorial Guinea has a free-market economy in which the dominant sector is private. The economy is based on three products—cacao, wood and coffee. There is virtually no industry—other than a few sawmills and soap factories and there is no market for industrial products.

# Gabon

*Official Name:* Gabonese Republic; *Capital:* Libreville; *Government:* republic; *Subdivisions:* 9 provinces; *Population:* 1,093,006 (July 1987); *Density:* 10 per square mile; *Currency:* franc; *Official Language:* French; *Literacy:* 65 percent.

*The Land.* About the size of Colorado, Gabon straddles the equator along 550 miles of the west coast of Africa. It is surrounded for 240 miles by Equatorial Guinea in the northwest, for 188 miles by Cameroon in the north, and for 1,029 miles by the Congo in the south and east. Gabon is a land of hot and humid jungle. A series of plateaus rise further inland, spreading from the northeast to the southeast. They are densely packed with lush green vegetation. About 75 percent of the country is forest; 15 percent, savanna; 9 percent, urban and waste; and 1 percent, cultivated.

*The People.* Almost all Gaboneans are of Bantu origin, descendants of groups who came to the area from several directions in the past 700 years to escape enemies or find new land. There are 40 tribal groups, however. Some 60 percent of the people are Christians, their religion sometimes intermingled with traditional tribal beliefs. Some 1 percent is Muslim and the remaining people worship according to the tribal beliefs.

The majority of Gabon's people live in the cities and larger towns. The government claims a literacy rate of 80 percent but a more accurate rate would be 65 percent. The dress, language and customs of the people are as varied as the number of ethnic groups.

*A Brief History.* For countless generations, the Bantu tribes, divided into many distinct groups, lived undisturbed by explorers and adventurers. The first European visitors were the Portuguese merchants who arrived in the fifteenth century and named the country after the Portuguese word *gabao,* a coat with sleeve and hood resembling the shape of the Como River estuary. Gabon was a French colony from 1903 to 1960. After independence, the Gabon Democratic Party established itself as the ruling party.

*The Economy.* The labor force is divided this way: agriculture, 65 percent; industry and commerce, 30 percent; services, 2.5 percent; and government, 2.5 percent.

Gabon has a free-market economy in which the dominant sector is private. The country has the highest per capita Gross Domestic Product in black Africa. The heart of the economy is petroleum.

Gabon has one of the highest per capita incomes in Africa, based largely on its oil production as well as its exports of minerals and tropical woods. Manganese ore, with uranium and gold content, is an important resource; a deposit worth up to $2 billion remains to be mined. Wood products, principally Okoume, a moderately soft wood well suited for making plywood, is the largest non-oil export.

# Kenya

*Official Name:* Republic of Kenya; *Capital:* Nairobi; *Government:* republic; *Subdivisions:* 7 provinces and 1 capital district; *Population:* 22,377,802 (July 1987); *Density:* 89.8 per square mile; *Currency:* shilling; *Official Languages:* Swahili and English; *Literacy:* 47 percent.

*The Land.* Located on the equator immediately below the heart of Africa on the east coast between the Indian Ocean and Lake Victoria, Kenya is slightly smaller than Texas. Its Indian Ocean coastline is 325 miles long. The country borders the Sudan for 190 miles, Ethiopia for 484 miles, Somalia for 424 miles,

Tanzania for 478 miles, and Uganda for 480 miles. It is noted for its striking topographical and climatic variety. The northern three-fifths is arid, much of it semidesert, inhabited only by nomadic pastoralists. The climate is generally cool in the highland area of the south, but is hot and arid in the north and northeast. A coastal strip is 2 to 10 miles wide except in the valleys of the main rivers. Beyond the coastal plans, the country rises in well-defined steps. About 300 miles inland the plains give way in the Eastern Plateau region, including the Serengeti Plain. A vast Northern Plains land region, forming three-fifths of the country, stretches from Somalia in the east to Uganda in the west. The Western Plateau descends in a gentle slope to Lake Victoria.

There are seven geographical divisions encompassed in two macrodivisions consisting of the elevated southwestern one-third of the country and the outer two-thirds that form an arc of low plateaus and plains. The land rises westward from narrow coastal plain in a series of plateaus culminating in the highlands area, bisected north to south by the Rift Valley. Neighboring countries are Tanzania in the south and southwest, Uganda in the west, the Sudan in the northwest, Ethiopia in the north and the Somali Republic in the northeast. About 64 percent is mainly grassland; 21 percent is forest and wood; 17 percent is arable; and 13 percent is suitable for agriculture.

*The People.* The population is richly varied; between 30 and 40 indigenous ethnic groups live in Kenya, including traditional herders, Arab Muslims, and cosmopolitan residents of Nairobi. No ethnic group is numerically dominant. Social customs vary according to race, tribe and religion. The five largest — Kikuyu (21 percent), Luo (13), Luhya (14), Kamba (11), and Kalenjin (11 percent) — constitute 70 percent. The 32 major indigenous African groups constitute 98 percent of the population. The national language is Swahili but English is spoken widely, although the number of languages spoken, about 41, matches roughly the number of ethnic groups. The main religions are Christianity (66 percent), Islam (7 percent), and various traditional tribal religions (26 percent).

The southwestern quadrant of the country, just 10 percent of the land area, contains over 75 percent of the population. The standard of living in major cities is among the highest in sub–Sahara Africa. Most city workers retain close ties with rural extended families and may leave the city periodically to help work on the family farm. The country's national motto is *harambee,* "pull together." Every year, in the spirit of this slogan, Kenyan volunteers in hundreds of communities build schools, clinics and other needed facilities and collect funds to send students abroad.

The Kenyan people are generally warm, friendly and hospitable, and are cordial to Westerners. They are for the most part intensely loyal and place a great value on an oath or promise, regarded as semisacred obligations. Social systems are group oriented. The individual is expected to be willing to sacrifice personal interests for the interests of the group. The tradition in Kenya is that virility of the men in most societies is measured by the number of children they father. Further, the women and children of age do the vast majority of work in the fields. The men lead a rather leisurely existence debating and quarreling over little or nothing most of the day.

About 38 percent of the people are Protestant; 28 percent are Catholic; 26 percent follow indigenous beliefs; and 6 percent are Muslim.

*A Brief History.* Fossils found in East Africa suggest that protohumans roamed the area more than 20 million years ago. Recent anthropological finds near Kenya's Lake Turkana indicate that the *Homo* genus of humans lived in the area 2.6 million years ago. The first inhabitants of what is now Kenya were groups of hunting tribes (Dorobo, or Bushmen) who lived in the vast plains of the area. They mixed and married with groups of Bantu people from western Africa who had migrated to the same area. Other peoples from Arabia and North Africa also settled in this area and mixed with the indigenous people to produce a new race.

Kenya's proximity to Arabia invited colonization. Arab traders called on the coast of Kenya for an undetermined time, establishing a community in the eighth century A.D. which remains to this day. These people developed the Swahili language, a mixture of Bantu and Arabic; it became the lingua franca between the different peoples. By then Bantu and Nilotic people also had moved into the area. The Arabs were followed by the Portuguese in 1498, who established trading posts but were driven out by the Arabs, by Islamic control under the Iman of Oman in the 1600s, and by British influence in the nineteenth century. From 1740, Arabs ruled the Kenyan coast from a capital on the island of Zanzibar. In 1887, the British East Africa Company leased the Kenyan coast from the sultan of Zanzibar. Kenya became a British protectorate in 1895 and was organized as a crown colony in 1920. Kenya was officially made a British colony in 1920.

Kenya won independence on December 12, 1963, following a period of violent uprisings. On December 12, 1964, Kenya became a republic within the Commonwealth of Nations. Jomo Kenyatta, a nationalist leader, served as its first president until his death in 1978. Daniel Arap Moi, the current president, succeeded Kenyatta. Kenya is one of the most politically stable countries in Africa. It is ranked as the African country with the most freedom of the press.

*The Economy.* The labor force is divided this way: public sector, 50 percent, industry and commerce 18, agriculture 17, and services, 13 percent.

The private sector predominates in a free-market economy. In 1982, 506 industrial units employed 50 or more workers. Almost all economic activity — and 85 percent of the population — is located in the southern two-fifths of the country. Having meager mineral resources, Kenya's economy centers on agriculture, though only 12 percent of its land has a high agricultural potential. Tourism is also important. Kenya's major crops include corn, coffee, tea, pineapple, sugar cane, sisal (used to make rope), and pyrethrum (a daisy like flower used to make insecticide).

The adverse effects of preindependence strife have been largely overcome and increasing amounts of light industry are being located in Kenya. Major industries include consumer goods, food processing, paper, petroleum refining, rubber, textiles and tobacco.

*Organizational Communication.* Personal visits are warmly welcomed and generally regarded as the most efficient method of establishing new trade contracts. Punctuality is important to Kenyan business people and the business visitor should make every effort to be on time for appointments.

Most foreign business is conducted by the British and Indians. The British here are less formal than in Great Britain.

## CASE STUDY: EAST AFRICAN BREWERIES, INC.

The company is a holding company for the Group in which the public holds shares quoted on the Nairobi Stock Exchange and has around 30 employees. The Group Technical Services Division provides higher technology cover for the Group subsidiaries mostly to design, supervise construction and commission, extension and new installations for Group companies.

Ninety percent of the Group's profits come from Kenya Breweries Limited, the wholly owned subsidiary in Kenya which runs all Kenyan operations in the brewing and malting industries in the Kenya Republic. This includes breweries in Nairobi, Mombasa and Kisumu, the biggest maltings in Africa at Nairobi, an experimental barley farm, a barley syrup making plant, some 20 primary distribution depots and a fleet of 250 vehicles mostly for primary distribution, about half of which are ten-ton trucks and trailers. Secondary distribution is handled by agents and distributors since by law no manufacturing company in Kenya may distribute directly to licensees.

Kenya Breweries Limited also handles exports and earns Kenya foreign exchange outside of neighboring countries in Africa. Kenya Breweries Limited exports, among other things, some 150,000 cartons per year to the United States (marketed as Tusker Malt Lager) and 36,000 cartons a year to Great Britain.

The work force of Kenya Breweries Limited totals 4,000 persons. The trades union movement in Kenya is up-to-date and sophisticated and has learned much from the teething troubles of this movement in other countries. Virtually all industrial concerns in Kenya have direct relations and a recognition agreement with a trade union and such unions are virtually "closed shop." Kenya has benefitted from seeing troubles in countries like Britain in that the Kenyan government discourages the unions from involvement in national politics and they insist on one trade union covering the whole of a company's activities as opposed to different unions covering various trades in one company's activities.

The company uses many different communication methods (see Figure 30). Before any new communication systems are introduced the views of the union are sought. Annual staff parties and departmental get-togethers coupled with three monthly in-house magazines are opportunities for putting staff at all levels into the picture of company progress.

Most of the workers are shareholders in a small way, as from time to time special opportunities are arranged for them to buy East African Breweries Limited's shares. Also, the company says, "we use the surplus on bonus issues made on the basis of disregarding fractions as a source of including in long-service awards from 10 years and over to give free shares as part of the award. Thus many of our workers receive the Chairman's annual report and accounts

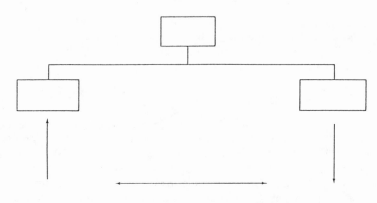

*Upward*

Written:
  memorandum
  report
  suggestion system
  question box
  newspaper/magazine

Personal:
  meeting
  interview
  open-door policy
  grievance procedure

*Downward*

Print:
  annual report
  annual report to employees
  newspaper/magazine
  bulletin board
  orientation manual
  letters
  pay envelope inserts
  manual
  handbook

Electronic:
  telephone
  film
  videotape

*Horizontal*

personal contact
memorandum
meeting

**Figure 30. Communication system of East African Breweries, Ltd., Kenya.**

each year and the minority of non-shareholders borrow this from their colleagues and copies are placed in their social halls."

One form of informal communication opportunity East African Breweries regards as vastly important is sports. "We have a very big budget for sporting facilities and a club for virtually every leading sport which is open to both management and unionizable staff. We find playing together and representing Brewery teams together is a wonderful cementer of cordial staff relations."

Seminars are also held on management/union interaction where both parties are present and encouraged to be very frank. The union has come to adopt the outlook that, except for annual negotiations on pay and the like, where it is recognized that both sides must try to look after their interests, it is vital that management and union work together as a team to maximize profits and promote the Company's public image, because the Company's success is essential to both parties for retaining jobs and producing ample funds to maximize benefits without the shareholders' having cause to complain.

Race relations in Kenya are among the best in the world and this causes no problems whatever these days. "We haven't had a strike in the last two decades and our consistently excellent results are in no small way due to the excellent working relations between our staff at all levels." (The chairman of the company, Mr. B.H. Hobson, provided this information.)

# Rwanda

*Official Name:* Republic of Rwanda; *Capital:* Kigali; *Government:* republic; *Subdivisions:* 10 prefectures; *Population:* 6,811,336 (July 1987); *Density:* 601 per square mile; *Currency:* franc; *Official Languages:* Kinyarwanda and French; *Literacy:* 37 percent.

*The Land.* A landlocked country located in east-central Africa and slightly smaller than Maryland, Rwanda is bordered for 135 miles by Zaire in the northwest, for 105 miles by Uganda in the northeast, for 135 miles by Tanzania in the east and for 180 miles by Burundi in the south. Often called "Africa's Switzerland," Rwanda is a land lying in the eastern lake region of Africa, composed for the most part of a gently rolling plateau land. Sharp volcanic peaks rise to towering heights in the west. Another mountain range lies to the northwest. Mainly grassy uplands and hills that extend southeast from a chain of volcanoes in the northwest, it is divided by the Congo and Nile drainage systems and has many lakes. Almost all of the land is arable. About 33 percent is cultivated; 33 percent is pasture; and 9 percent is forest.

*The People.* The population is relatively homogeneous. About 90 percent of the residents of Rwanda are Hutu; about 9 percent are Tutsi and 1 percent Twa or pygmy. Some 65 percent of residents are Catholic; 9 percent are Protestant; 1 percent are Muslim; and 25 percent follow traditional tribal beliefs.

The population density of Rwanda is the highest in sub–Sahara Africa and one of the most densely populated in all of Africa. More than 90 percent of the people of Rwanda are agricultural, rural folk, densely crowded on the large, grassy plateaus. It is a country almost without villages; nearly every family lives in a self-contained compound. Courtesy, respect and hospitality are important elements of their culture.

*A Brief History.* Like Burundi, Rwanda's first inhabitants were pygmies who seldom reached a height of more than five feet. The Twa were succeeded by the Hutu, an industrious people of hunters and farmers having Bantu ancestry. About four centuries ago, a warrior tribe of Hamitic origin, the Tutsi, sometimes called Watusi, invaded Rwanda from the north. The Hutu were unable to defend themselves against the Tutsi who were frequently more than six feet tall. The Hutu were reduced to serfdom, each choosing a Tutsi protector who gave them the use (but not ownership) of cattle, the most important status symbol and source of wealth among the Tutsi. Rwanda was part of German East Africa from 1899 to 1916 and occupied by Belgian troops in 1916. It became a Belgian trust territory under the League of Nations and the United Nations in 1923 and gained its independence in 1962. Afterwards strife was renewed internally among the various ethnic groups as well as between Rwanda and Zaire.

*The Economy.* The labor force is divided this way: agriculture, 91 percent; government, 7 percent; and industry and commerce, 2 percent.

Rwanda is one of the poorest and least-developed countries of the world. The economy is principally one of subsistence agriculture, conducted on almost four million acres of land. The export of coffee is the chief source of foreign exchange. Although there is exploitation of mineral resources, principally tin ore, this has yet to become a major part of the economy. The country has important hydroelectric potential, with several plants now in operation. Manufacturing is a relatively minor activity employing less than 2 percent of the labor force.

Major industries include mining of cassiterite (tin ore) and wolframite (tungsten ore), tin factory, cement factory, agriculture processing, and production of beer, soft drinks, soap, furniture, shoes, plastic goods, textiles and cigarettes.

———————————— **Tanzania** ————————————

*Official Name:* United Republic of Tanzania; *Capital:* Dar es Salaam; *Government:* republic; *Subdivisions:* 25 regions; *Population:* 23,502,472 (July 1987); *Density:* 62 per square mile; *Currency:* shilling; *Official Languages:* Swahili and English; *Literacy:* 79 percent.

*The Land.* Located in East Africa south of the equator, Tanzania consists of mainland Tanganyika and the islands of Zanzibar and Pemba. Tanganyika is located on the east coast of Africa between the great lakes of central Africa — Lake Victoria, Lake Tanganyika and Lake Nyasa — and the Indian Ocean. Zanzibar is located 20 miles off the coast, and Pemba lies 25 miles northwest of Zanzibar. Its coastline is 884 miles, of which Zanzibar's is 132 miles and Pemba's is 110 miles. About the size of Texas, it is a land of great variations. Tanzania contains the highest point in Africa (Mt. Kilimanjaro) and the lowest point (Lake Tanganyika). Zanzibar and Pemba are low coral islands, with a combined area about the size of Delaware. Neighboring countries are Mozambique for 470 miles in the southeast, Malawai for 280 miles and Zambia for 200 miles in the southwest, Zaire for 285 miles, Burundi for 280 miles and Rwanda for 135 miles in the west, Uganda for 260 miles in the northwest and Kenya for 478 miles in the northeast. It also has a 500-mile coastline on the Indian Ocean.

The land can be divided this way: 45 percent forest, 37 meadow and pasture, 6 inland water, 4 arable, 1 crop, and 7 percent other.

*The People.* About 99 percent of the people are native African in origin. There are about 130 ethnic groups, each with its own language; by far the largest percentage consists of 33 Bantu-speaking tribes. Swahili is the official language; English is a second official language. Tanzania ranks lowest in the world in urbanization; only 14.84 percent of the population live in towns. About a third of the population each follow Christian, Muslim and indigenous beliefs.

The Tanzanian social system is traditionally group-oriented. The individual is expected to put himself second to group welfare. Tanzanians are therefore extremely polite and generous people both in private and in public. It is considered very impolite to pass a person (except in large crowds) without showing some sign of recognition, be it only a smile.

*A Brief History.* Finds at Olduvai Gorge indicate that Tanzania has been inhabited for at least a million years. In the eighth century A.D. Arab traders from southern Arabia began to explore and settle the coast, founding the important city of Kilwa. Over many generations these foreign adventurers mixed with the Bantu population to produce both the Swahili language and the modern peoples of the coastal regions. From the 1400s to the 1700s, the Portuguese and Arabic overlords from Oman and Muscat developed a series of populous and powerful trading cities and sultanates — particularly on the islands of Zanzibar and Pemba. The Sultanate of Zanzibar controlled both the islands and the mainland with an iron hand until the mid–1800s. In 1886, Tanganyika became a German protectorate. Zanzibar retained independence, but lost some control to the British of Kenya. In 1920, Tanganyika fell under British rule. In 1961, it was granted independence followed in 1963 by a fully independent Zanzibar. In 1964 the two nations merged to form Tanzania, a successful union. The nation has become a socialist republic.

*The Economy.* The labor force is divided this way: agriculture, 90 percent, and industry and commerce, 10 percent. About 15 percent of the work force is unionized.

One of the least-developed countries of the world, Tanzania's economy is dominated by agriculture, employing about 90 percent of the labor force. Major exports include sisal, cloves, coffee, cotton and diamonds. Livestock production is limited because of the prevalence of the tsetse fly which, however, is gradually being eliminated by insecticides. Tanzania is the world's tenth largest producer of diamonds. The economy of Zanzibar is based primarily on cloves. Zanzibar and Pemba are the world's principal supplier of this spice. Industries include oil refining and textiles.

Major industries include diamond mining, oil refinery, shoes, cement, textiles, wood products and agricultural production of sugar, beer, cigarettes and sisal twine.

*Organizational Communication.* Westerners often think Tanzanians to be abrupt and occasionally impolite. This is largely because the words "please" and "thank you" are not native to the Bantu languages; the Swahili equivalents, *tafadhali* and *asante,* respectively, have been borrowed from Arabic. Requests

are often made without a "please" and help accepted without a "thank you."
This is not impolite, but simply a cultural habit.

# Uganda

*Official Name:* Republic of Uganda; *Capital:* Kampala; *Government:*
republic; *Subdivisions:* 10 provinces; *Population:* 15,908,896 (July 1987);
*Density:* 173 per square mile; *Currency:* shilling; *Official Language:*
English; *Literacy:* 52.3 percent.

*The Land.* This landlocked fertile expanse of highland lies astride the
equator in central East Africa between the Eastern and Western Rift formations. Most of the country is plateau. Uganda is dotted with lakes, including
the immense Lake Victoria. Neighboring countries are Rwanda for 105 miles
and Tanzania for 260 miles in the southwest, Zaire for 475 miles in the west,
the Sudan for 270 miles in the north and Kenya for 480 miles in the northeast.

About 45 percent of the country is forest, wood and grass; 21 inland water
and swamp; 21 cultivated; and 13 percent national park, forest and game
preserve.

Winston Churchill wrote of this country: "Uganda is a fairy tale. You
climb up a railway instead of a beanstalk, and at the top there is a wonderful
new world. The scenery is different, the vegetation is different, the climate is
different, and most of all the people are different from anywhere else in
Africa."[23]

*The People.* About 99 percent of the population are African; the remainder are European, Asian and Arab. Some 33 percent of them are Roman
Catholic; 33 percent are Protestant; 16 percent are Muslim; and 18 percent
follow indigenous beliefs.

The Ugandan people are traditionally an industrious, intelligent and lively
folk. There is little class distinction among the people within tribal divisions,
and there has been no antipathy between Europeans and African Ugandans.
Although a great majority lead a rural life, they are not provincial in the least.

*A Brief History.* It is difficult to trace the migrations of the Bantu people
whose descendants live in Uganda today. The last king of Buganda claimed to
be the 37th member of an uninterrupted line of monarchs. It is not possible to
determine the exact time that the Nilotic and Nilo-Hamitic groups came to
northern Uganda. The evidence indicates that there was a gradual migration
from the Nile Valley in the tenth to the thirteenth centuries. Uganda was a
British protectorate from 1894 to 1962. Years of political turmoil followed. A
coalition government led by Apollo Milton Obote was ousted in 1971 by Armed
Forces Commander Idi Amin Dada whose 8-year rule was marked by economic
decline, social disintegration and massive violations of human rights. Obote
was returned to power until 1985 when Lt. Gen. Basilio Olara-Okello installed
a military government.

*The Economy.* One of the least-developed countries in the world, Uganda
has a thriving agricultural economy. Coffee and cotton constituted 95 percent

of the value of exports in the past and were the basis of the economy. After World War II, the government used wealth produced from these to expand cultivation of sugar, tea and tobacco. Livestock production is limited by the ever-present tsetse fly. Major industries today are agricultural processing (textiles, sugar, coffee, plywood, beer), cement, copper smelting, corrugated iron sheet, shoes and fertilizer.

*Organizational Communication.* Drums, traditionally a widely used communication system, are used to spread news rapidly to remote areas. The official language is English but at least 40 tribal languages are spoken.

# THE SOUTHERN REGION

## Angola

*Official Name:* People's Republic of Angola; *Capital:* Luanda; *Government:* marxist people's republic; *Subdivisions:* 18 provinces; *Population:* 7,950,244 (July 1987); *Density:* 18.1 per square mile; *Currency:* kwanza; *Official Language:* Portuguese; *Literacy:* 20 percent.

*The Land.* Located on the west coast of southern Africa south of the equator and about four times the size of New Mexico, Angola is bordered by Zaire for 1,420 miles in the north, by Namibia for 855 miles in the south and by Zambia for 675 miles in the southeast. Its Atlantic Ocean coast is 891 miles long. Angola also includes the enclave of Cabinda, which lies on the seacoast northwest of Angola proper, and is bordered by the Congo, the Atlantic Ocean and the strip of Zaire that separates it from Angola. Most of the country is plateau, descending in the west to a coastal fringe of varying width, in the north gradually, farther south more precipitously. The eastern half of the country is mostly flat, open plateau of somewhat lower altitudes.

The land is divided this way: 44 percent is forest; 22 percent is meadow and pasture; 1 percent is cultivated; and 33 percent is other.

*The People.* The population is concentrated in the west, central highlands and north, primarily. The people are Bantu, primarily, with these groups: Ovimbundu, 38 percent; Kimbundu, 23 percent; Bakongo, 13 percent; and other, 24 percent. About 2 percent are mestizo (mixed black and European). About 68 percent of the population are Roman Catholic; 20 percent are Protestant; and 10 percent follow indigenous beliefs.

Angola was settled by the Portuguese in the fifteenth century and remained a Portuguese colony until 1975. Until 1974, there were two cultures in Angola — the approximately 300,000 Europeans, mostly Portuguese, who were the businessmen and farmers, and the original inhabitants of the land. The latter lived a marginal existence in the cities and in the hinterland, working as laborers in the factories and fields of Angola. Since independence all of this has changed. Most Portuguese left, although a few returned to offer their managerial skills.

*A Brief History.* Parts of the coastal region were a colony of Portugal since the fifteenth century. De jure control over the entire territory was awarded at the Berlin Conference of 1884–85. De facto control was not achieved until the 1920s. Angola was a Portuguese colony until November 11, 1975. A shaky transitional government soon collapsed and fighting broke out among the Popular Movement for the Liberation of Angola (MPLA), the National Front for the Liberation of Angola (FNLA) and the National Union for the Total Independence of Angola (UNITA). Support to these factions from outsiders—the Soviet Union, Cuba, the United States and South Africa—prolonged the Civil War to the date of this writing.

*The Economy.* The labor force is divided this way: agriculture, 85 percent, and industry, 15 percent.

Angola has a centrally planned socialist economy in which the dominant sector is public. It is potentially one of the richest nations in sub-Saharan Africa, with extensive petroleum potential, rich agricultural land and valuable mineral resources. Angola's economy prior to World War II was agricultural, centered mainly on coffee and sugar exports. This changed when the first oil deposits were discovered, resulting in tremendous growth of income. But the civil war has ravaged the economy.

Major industries include mining of oil and diamonds, fish processing, brewing, tobacco, sugar processing, textiles, cement, food processing plants, and building construction.

## Botswana

*Official Name:* Republic of Botswana; *Capital:* Gaborone; *Government:* parliamentary republic; *Subdivisions:* 10 administrative districts; *Population:* 1,149,141 (July 1987); *Density:* 5 persons per square mile; *Currency:* pula; *Official Language:* English; *Literacy:* 24 percent.

*The Land.* Slightly smaller than Texas, Botswana is a landlocked country that is a wide open tableland. The rolling sands and grassy areas of the Kalahari Desert cover the southwest. The country shares these borders: 1,105 miles with South Africa, 908 miles with Namibia, and 505 miles with Zimbabwe.

*The People.* Most people live in the eastern part of the country. Only 11 towns contain more than 10,000 people. About 95 percent of the population are members of the Botswana tribe. About 4 percent belong to the Kalanga, Basarwa and Kgalagadi tribes; about 1 percent is white. Half the population are Christian; the other half follow indigenous beliefs.

*A Brief History.* By the 1700s, the ancestors of today's African population had become self-sufficient herders and farmers or hunters. The first contact with Europeans was through missionaries in the early nineteenth century.

*The Economy.* Botswana has a free-market economy in which the dominant sector is private. More than 83 percent of the population live in the rural areas and are dependent on subsistence farming. Industry is limited to the processing of livestock products and the mining of diamonds, copper, nickel, coal, salt, soda ash and potash. Tourism is also important.

# Lesotho

*Official Name:* Kingdom of Lesotho; *Capital:* Maseru; *Government:* constitutional monarchy; *Subdivisions:* 10 administrative districts; *Population:* 1,621,932 (July 1987); *Density:* 125 per square mile; *Currency:* maloti; *Official Languages:* Sesotho and English; *Literacy:* 60 percent.

*The Land.* About the size of Maryland, Lesotho is completely surrounded by South Africa. The landlocked country is mountainous, with peaks reaching 11,000 feet; it also has plateaus and hills. About 10 percent of the land is arable, and 66 percent is meadow and pastures.

*The People.* Ethnic groups in Lesotho are 99.7 percent Sotho and small groups of Europeans and Asians. Some 80 percent are Christian; the remainder adhere to indigenous beliefs.

*A Brief History.* Once called Basutoland, Lesotho became a British protectorate in 1868 when Chief Moshesh sought protection against the Boers. Independence was granted on October 4, 1966. Elections, however, were suspended in 1970. An appointed Interim National Assembly was established in 1973, led by Prime Minister Leabua Jonathan.

*The Economy.* The labor force is 87.4 percent in subsistence agriculture, with the remainder in mining. Half of the male workers go to South Africa to find employment. Livestock raising is the chief industry; diamonds are the chief export.

# Malawi

*Official Name:* Republic of Malawi; *Capital:* Lilongwe; *Government:* republic; *Subdivisions:* 3 administrative regions and 24 districts; *Population:* 7,437,911 (July 1987); *Density:* 187 per square mile; *Currency:* kwacha; *Official Languages:* English and Chichewa; *Literacy:* 25 percent.

*The Land.* Malawi is about the size of Pennsylvania, stretching for 560 miles along Lake Malawi, most of which it owns. It is a narrow, high plateau with some rolling plains, rounded hills and mountains which line the Rift Valley for the length of the country.

*The People.* Ethnic divisions of the population include Chewa, Nyanja, Tumbuko, Yao, Lomwe, Sena, Tonga, Ngomi, Asian and European. Their religions are Protestant, 55 percent; Roman Catholic, 20 percent; and Muslim, 20 percent. Some people follow indigenous beliefs.

*A Brief History.* Bantus came to the area in the sixteenth century and Arab slavers in the nineteenth century. The region became the British protectorate Nyasaland in 1891. Independence was granted on July 6, 1964. Malawi maintains a pro–West foreign policy and cooperates with Zimbabwe and South Africa economically.

*The Economy.* The labor force is divided this way: agriculture, 52 percent; personal services 16, manufacturing 9, construction 7, commerce 6, miscellaneous services 4; and other areas, 6 percent. Major industries are agriculture, processing (tea, tobacco, sugar, coffee), sawmilling, cement and consumer goods.

# Mozambique

*Official Name:* People's Republic of Mozambique; *Capital:* Maputo; *Government:* people's republic; *Subdivisions:* 10 provinces; *Population:* 14,535,805 (July 1987); *Density:* 47 per square mile; *Currency:* meticais; *Official Language:* Portuguese; *Literacy:* 14 percent.

*The Land.* Located on the southeastern coast of Africa opposite the island of Madagascar, Mozambique has an Indian Ocean coastline of 1,556 miles. About the size of Texas and Indiana combined, Mozambique is bordered by Tanzania for 470 miles in the north, by Malawi for 930 miles and Zambia for 263 miles in the northwest, by Zimbabwe for 760 miles in the west and by South Africa for 305 miles and Swaziland for 47 miles in the southwest. The flat terrain of the coastline is filled with dense, tropical jungle in areas which are not cleared. It gives way gradually to a series of plateaus and highlands which gently rise toward high mountains in the part closest to the western borders. The country is divided by the Zambezi River into two halves. North of the Zambezi, a narrow coastline yields to hills and low plateaus and farther west to rugged highlands. South of the Zambezi, the littoral is broader, extending at spots almost the entire width of the country. About 56 percent of the land is wood and forest; 30 percent is arable; and 14 percent is waste and inland water.

*The People.* Mozambique has 10 major ethnic groups, each with a diverse language, dialects, culture and history. The most populous regions are the northern and southern coastal areas. About 90 percent of the population is rural. All of the many African groups of Mozambique are of Bantu ancestry; the Macoua, located in the coastal area, show traces of Arab and Indian blood. Religions are traditional tribal beliefs, 66 percent; Christianity, 22 percent; Islam, 10 percent; and other, 2 percent.

The European minority was located almost exclusively on the coastline and larger interior plantations of the country. Although most left before and after independence, about 30,000 Portuguese remain. The International Index of Human Suffering in 1987 named Mozambique as the place in the world where life is hardest.

About 60 percent of the population follow indigenous beliefs; 30 percent are Christian; and 10 percent are Muslim.

*A Brief History.* The first inhabitants of the country were hunters and gatherers. Between the first and fourth centuries A.D., waves of Bantu-speaking people swept down from the north. Prior to the arrival of European explorers, Arab traders had established active trading posts along the coast, dealing in the notorious slave trade, principally, and in commerce involving agriculture to a much lesser degree.

Portugal claimed Mozambique in 1498 as an integral part of Portugal and it remained so until September 7, 1974. Independence came a year later. Events since independence have been turbulent and radical.

*The Economy.* About 95 percent of the labor force is engaged in agriculture. Mozambique has a centrally planned economy in which the public sector dominates. The formerly thriving economy was based on agricultural production with only a small amount of light industry.

The exodus of the white population resulted in sharply reduced production. Nominally a client state of the communist bloc, Mozambique has tried to change this stance in order to attract aid and investment from Western nations. Industry is of some importance, but activities were seriously hampered by shortages of managerial, technical and labor skills after massive departure of the Portuguese between 1974 and 1977. By 1984, production had not yet regained 1973 base-year levels.

Major industries include food processing (sugar, tea, wheat, flour, cashew kernels), chemicals, petroleum products, beverages, textiles, nonmetallic mineral products, and tobacco.

*Organizational Communication.* There are numerous Bantu languages, each divided into several dialects, linked to an equal number of ethnic categories.

# Namibia

*Official Name:* Namibia; *Capital:* Windhoek; *Government:* South African colony; *Subdivisions:* 10 tribal homelands; *Population:* 1,273,263 (July 1987); *Density:* very sparse; *Currency:* rand; *Official Languages:* Afrikaans, German and English; *Literacy:* 100 percent for whites, 16 percent for blacks.

*The Land.* About twice the size of California, Namibia is surrounded by Angola in the north, South Africa in the south, Botswana in the east and Zambia in the northeast. Most of the land consists of a high plateau, a continuation of the main South African plateau. The narrow white beach of Namibia is quickly replaced by a 60-mile-wide stretch of red-colored Namib Desert which runs the entire length of the coastline. The barren Kalahari Desert stretches along the north and eastern borders of the territory, occasionally interrupted by harsh formations of gray rock and thin scrub vegetation. The central region is a vast plateau suited to pastoral raising of sheep and cattle.

*The People.* The population is 85.6 percent black, 7.5 percent white and 6.9 percent mixed. About 60 percent of the residents follow traditional tribal beliefs; some 39 percent are Christian and 1 percent are other. About 60 percent of the people speak Afrikaans; 33 percent speak German and 7 percent speak English.

A small minority of whites have enjoyed the wealth of Namibia and the vast majority (of blacks) have been living, for the most part, in backward poverty, engaging in herding livestock to support themselves.

*A Brief History.* In times past, the Bushmen began living in what is now Namibia, followed by several Bantu tribes. The inhospitable Namib Desert constituted a formidable barrier to European exploration until the late eighteenth century. The country became a German colony until independence after World War I.

South Africa has asserted control of the territory (as South-West Africa), claiming that a mandate under the League of Nations has continued since the formation of the United Nations. The United Nations passed a resolution in 1966 declaring South-West Africa to be under direct U.N. control and designated the area "Namibia" in 1968.

*The Economy.* The labor force is divided this way: agriculture, 60 percent; industry and commerce 19, services 8, government 7; and mining, 6 percent.

The economy of Namibia is a dual one—a modern market sector and a traditional subsistence sector. Exports of diamonds and metals provide most of Namibia's income. Karakul lamb pelts are the chief agricultural product and are higher priced since Iranian production dropped off. Boats operating out of Luderitz harvest tons of lobsters from the sea. Major industries are meat packing, fish processing, dairy products, copper, lead, zinc, diamonds and uranium mining.

# South Africa

*Official Name:* Republic of South Africa; *Capital:* Pretoria; *Government:* republic; *Subdivisions:* 4 provinces; *Population:* 34,313,356 (July 1987); *Density:* 68.2 per square mile; *Currency:* rand; *Official Languages:* Afrikaans and English; *Literacy:* 100 percent for whites and 50 percent for blacks.

*The Land.* Three times the size of California, South Africa lies at the southern tip of Africa, bordered by Namibia in the northwest, Botswana and Zimbabwe in the north and Mozambique and Swaziland in the northeast. Lesotho is enclosed in South Africa. Washed on the west by the South Atlantic and on the east by the Indian Ocean, the Republic of South Africa is the southernmost part of the continent, stretching from the Limpopo River in the north to Cape Agulhas in the south. Its coastline is 2,700 miles long. The government reserves 85 percent of the land for whites. The remaining 15 percent is designated as African "homelands." All black Africans belong to one of the homelands regardless of where they live.

*The People.* Ethnic groups include Bantu black Africans, with some Hamitic mixture, white, coloreds (mixed black, white and Asian), white, including descendants of Dutch, British, German, French, Portuguese, Greek and Italian, and Asian (primarily Indian). The Bantus and other black Africans outnumber the whites by five to one; combined with the coloreds and Indians, the figure is about six to one. About one-half of the population live in the cities. The people can be divided into four main groups. Black South

Africans constitute about 72 percent of the population. The blacks can be further classified into ten ethnic groups, each with a distinct culture, language, historical background and national identity. The Zulu nation is the largest black group, with a population of six million, and comprises over 200 tribes, each with its own chief. Next in size are the Xhosa and Sotho. The next largest ethnic group is the white South Africans, who constitute 16 percent of the population. They are divided between the English-speaking descendants of English, Irish and Scottish settlers and the Afrikaans-speaking descendants of Dutch, German, and French colonials. The coloreds, mixed descendants of whites, blacks and Asians, make up another distinct group (9 percent). Indians are the fourth group, comprising about 3 percent of the total population. Throughout most of South Africa, the four groups are segregated by law in employment, housing and education. White rule has been relinquished in the countries of Venda, Ciskei, Transkei and Bophuthatswana. However, these new nations are not recognized by any country other than South Africa.

The Boer people, ruling through their National Party, reason that because their ancestors were in some areas of South Africa prior to the arrival of the Bantu and Indian people, they are the rightful possessors of the exclusive control of the government. Conservative and clinging to their language and traditions, they have a strong desire to pass their way of life to their descendants. Apartheid (the "apartness" of the races) has controlled daily life in Africa for almost 30 years; historically its roots lie in the bitter conflicts between the Voortrekkers and the then savage Zulus, Sothos, Tswanas and Tongas during the eighteenth and nineteenth centuries. Interracial marriages and love affairs were strictly prohibited until 1985. The program to put all nonurbanized Africans in "black homelands" has been a "separate but equal" concept designed to enable the whites to continue their control, particularly over the wealth of South Africa; it simply has not worked.

South Africans consider themselves open-minded, sturdy, and independent. Hospitality is an old tradition. The moral standards in South Africa are generally high. South Africans are strongly nationalistic and may resent outright criticism, particularly of their racial policy.

The visitor may be distrusted by both whites, who tire of outsiders' disapproval, and by blacks who may think one is not doing enough to change the status quo. Black Americans face even harsher scrutiny and expectation. Some animosities exist between the white Afrikaners and the whites of British descent.

*A Brief History.* Hottentots, Bushmen and other Africans lived in southern Africa for thousands of years, although little is known of their history. The Cape of Good Hope was discovered by Portuguese adventurers in 1486. In 1652, the first permanent white settlers, led by Jan van Riebeeck, established a station for the ships of the Dutch East India Company at what is now Cape Town. This settlement was later expanded with the arrival of more Dutch immigrants as well as German and French Huguenot refugees. These people became known as Boers. At the beginning of the nineteenth century, Britain settled the Cape and later gained a foothold in Natal. Dissatisfied with British rule, many Boers migrated to the interior in the Great Trek of 1835–48.

Their migration led to war with the Zulus and other black African tribes. The Boers defeated the Zulus in 1838. After the discovery of gold and diamonds in the Boer territories in the late nineteenth century, Britain annexed parts of the area. Tension between the Boers and the British erupted into the Boer War (1899–1902) in which the Boers were defeated.

In 1910, the Transvaal, Orange Free State, Natal and Cape were united as the Union of South Africa and in 1934 the Union of South Africa became a sovereign nation in terms of the Statute of Westminster passed by the British Commonwealth of Nations. In 1960, the electorate voted in favor of a republican form of government and on May 31, 1961, the Republic of South Africa was proclaimed, with a state president as the nonexecutive head of state. Although South Africa remained a member of the sterling area until 1972, she withdrew from the British Commonwealth upon becoming a republic.

Since the 1960s, South Africa has been the scene of much political turmoil concerning its apartheid policies. In 1974, the United Nations suspended South Africa's voting privileges because of civil rights violations.

*The Economy.* The labor force is divided this way: services, 34 percent; agriculture, 30 percent; industry and commerce, 29 percent; and mining, 7 percent. About 17 percent of the labor force is unionized.

South Africa's economy is the strongest and most diversified on the African continent. Investment, output, employment and consumption have been constantly rising (with interruptions caused by anti-apartheid actions of foreign nations). Until about 1870, the economy was based almost entirely on agriculture. The discovery of diamonds in 1867 and gold in Witwatersrand in 1886, turned mining into the chief source of national income. By 1945, mining was overshadowed by manufacturing as the most important segment of the gross national product. The economy is more and more falling into line with that of highly developed Western nations. Boycotts by many nations of South African goods have only slightly affected the system because the country has most of the precious and other metals in constant demand on the world market, and is also the source of much of the food which is imported by surrounding black African nations.

Crops include corn, wool, wheat, sugarcane, tobacco, citrus fruits, and dairy products. South Africa is self-sufficient in foodstuffs. Industry is very important to the South African economy; the country has the most extensive and diversified manufacturing sector in Africa. Many valuable minerals are found in the vast areas of the country. South Africa is the largest gold producer in the world, producing nearly three-quarters of the world's total. It ranks second in uranium, and third in diamonds. Coal is also in plentiful supply. Important industries include automobile assembly, metalworking, machinery, textiles, iron and steel, chemicals and fertilizers.

Business customs in South Africa are generally similar to those in the United States and Western Europe. South African business people tend to dress conservatively, and sport jackets and slacks are rarely seen at work.

Be prepared for bureaucratic complexities and delays. Be self-motivating: some expatriates say the country's economic gravy train has caused management to be relaxed; people do not get much direction.

Labor unions, formerly compelled to be racially separated by law, are now allowed to integrate, and the labor movement is strong in South Africa.

*Organizational Communication.* Business cards should be simple, including only the basics such as name, address and business title. Punctuality is important to the South African business person, who generally makes every effort to be on time for appointments.

Although English and Afrikaans are South Africa's two official languages, English is the more frequently used commercially. Most firms in South Africa are able to correspond in either English or Afrikaans. There is some language sensitivity in South Africa, particularly among the Afrikaner population. Consequently, many firms print much of their literature, including annual statements, in both languages. Don't be too boisterous — both British and Afrikaners are reserved.

## CASE STUDY: BARLOW RAND LIMITED

The company is a conglomerate of 231,000 people divided into 10 separate divisions, operating in a decentralized management system. The company's house magazine, *Barlow's '86,* reveals a great deal about management's attitude about communication. The article "Getting to Know You" in issue No. 3 of 1986 described a trip by 14 employees to Golden Gate National Park — the first participants in the Company's People Interaction and Enrichment Programme. Figures 31 and 32 show the two parts of that programme, study and excursions. One topic covered during the seminars was "Intercultural Communication Skills." The magazine article commented on that subject:

> Cultural issues and communication issues are very often interrelated — especially in this country — and that interrelation comes through during the discussions, the role-playing and the presentation of life charts. Of course, the outdoor activities get people working and learning together in a different way.
>
> Communication is an acquired skill — therefore it can be improved upon. The mutual trust and respect that people develop on this course — as well as changes in personal attitudes — can be taken back into the workplace and beyond.

Another article in the company magazine discussed the communication programs at three subsidiaries.

*Middelburg Steel & Alloys.*

> Our man-to-man interface program revolves around every individual in certain categories being interviewed once every three months, says Middelburg Steel & Alloy's group manpower manager, Brian Wegerle.
>
> Generally the categories are from foreman down to laborer. Each person is interviewed privately and asked for his perceptions of the company and, at the same time, any grievances or personal problems are also discussed.
>
> We use this interview as an opportunity of giving the individual a structured company message. We try to get our workers to understand and identify with the company's objectives, philosophies, policies and regulations. So the message at a particular meeting could be related to pay policy,

Figures 31 and 32. Both outings and study are part of the new Barlow Rand Limited People Interaction Enhancement Programme. (Barlow Rand Limited, Sandton, South Africa.)

housing, safety, the company's business performance, or matters that the chairman wants to get across.

MS&A personnel officers (there is one to every 200 workers) conduct the interviews. Their assignment is to relay the same message to each employee within 12 weeks. Alan Tonkin, MS&A's group manpower executive, says,

> Clearly, not every company would have the manpower resources to adopt this system in exactly this way. However, our organizational structure facilitates it and MS&A has worked actively to develop interpersonal communications between workers and management. Our one-on-one interface program started nearly three years ago as a natural addition to the communication system already in operation. We were lucky when we started this program in that the right climate prevailed — people were willing to express their views without feeling apprehensive or intimidated.
>
> Our interface system builds on all our other communication vehicles. For example, we may put down a copy of a newsletter on the table during a man-to-man interface session. Then we will ask the employee whether he has read the chairman's message in the newsletter and what he thinks of it. We make sure during the interview that the message is fully understood.

The need to develop this system was sparked by attitude surveys which indicated that workers were fairly happy with existing communications but that there were still a few problem areas. A communication vehicle was needed to enforce MS&A's communications strategies — and it was found in the interface system.

> The organizational climate is an important variable [says Tonkin]. At MS&A the whole management approach is very participative — so much so that consensus on issues is sometimes reached after much debate. And that's not all. Perceptions and attitudes of workers are audited every month by surveys and questionnaires. This allows reliable feedback so that we can gauge the success of our communication program.
>
> In future, interviews will be conducted by individual supervisors instead of by personnel officers. We feel that it is beneficial for every worker to see his boss, rather than an outsider, as the communication vehicle.

It stands to reason that good communication leads to good industrial relations which in turn has an effect on productivity. An example of this can be seen in the fact that MS&A's alloys division is the lowest-cost producer of ferrochrome in the world and the stainless steel operations reject rate is lower than that of many mills in the United States, Europe and Japan. In addition, MS&A ranks as one of the 9 safest companies in South Africa. Proof enough of Tonkin's words, "For any company good communication is certainly an investment for the present and the future."

*Metal Box.* An alternative to the individual interviews of MS&A are briefing groups which are used internally by both Metal Box and Rand Mines. A carefully prepared written brief is given to managers at each level, who then convey the contents verbally to their immediate subordinates in their natural work teams.

At both companies management has committed itself to communicating with employees directly, whether or not there is a strong union presence.

Elected employee representatives or shop steward committees communicate with management on a regular basis, usually about negotiable issues. The briefing groups, by contrast, are designed to convey management decisions in as clear a way as possible to every level of employee from shop-floor workers upwards.

"The briefing group system was adopted for special reasons," says Peter Brown, personnel manager at Rosslyn plant.

We run 24 hours a day, 7 days a week, with 4 shift crews being on and off duty for 4 days at a time. Management works on a normal weekly cycle, so it may not have contact with workers in a particular shift for up to 16 days.

Prior to implementing our briefing groups, we used notice-boards, pamphlets and other conventional communication devices, but it was felt that these were inadequate on their own. So two and a half years ago our briefing group system was started.

We use these groups for induction purposes, to explain new policies, fringe benefits, health and safety procedures, required standards of performance and significant new appointments. The content of the brief is formulated by top management. This is then cascaded down to foreman level. At each level some specific information relevant to that crew only may be included — for example, how it is performing in terms of quality control.

Briefing groups at Metal Box are usually held once a month but occasionally special briefings will be organized to communicate matters such as negotiations with employee representative committees.

An audit and a situational analysis have been done since the briefing groups were implemented. From these it appears that the perceived authority and credibility of all levels of management — especially that of supervisors — has been strengthened.

"Supervisors have had to become knowledgeable on all important aspects relating to their staff. Managers have been forced into really managing people instead of rushing off to personnel wherever there is a problem," says Brown.

Doug Swanson, Metal Box's group personnel manager, maintains that briefing groups increase commitment to company objectives as they involve people directly and clear up misunderstandings. "People have an immediate opportunity to ask questions and learn the facts from the real authority — not along the grapevine," he says.

A regular feedback device has not been built in yet, but his will be part of the next phase of development. Swanson maintains that the briefing group system can easily be adapted for any company, provided that it gets full commitment at upper levels. "Management has to be prepared to be open and frank with employees, to communicate both good and bad news, to have its decision scrutinized and to enable briefing groups to meet during working hours." Attendance registers have to be kept and it is the foreman's responsibility to ensure that any absent members are properly briefed.

According to Swanson, "Apart from clarifying important information, 'down-the-line' briefing groups have made a major contribution towards team-building in our company and towards the development of a healthy sense of competition as far as performance standards are concerned."

*Rand Mines.* Employee populations ranging from 12,000 to 32,000, several different ethnic groups, a traditional autocratic climate with a linguistic and cultural gulf between workers and line management, differences between categories of workers, shafts and plants spread out over vast areas—this is the complex environment in which Rand Mines has established its briefing groups and its gold mines. According to Neville Richardson, gold and uranium division personnel consultant,

> Although briefing groups should ideally be based on the natural work groups—that is, each supervisor briefing his subordinates—environmental conditions underground may prevent this. Therefore briefing exercises often have to be conducted in the black hostels by trained personnel assistants, with line supervisors being informed of the nature of the brief so that they can reinforce it in the workplace.

The main objective of briefing groups at Rand Mines is not mainly team-building as in other companies, but ensuring that selected messages are actually received and understood. A variety of checking and monitoring procedures are followed after briefing sessions have taken place.

Briefing group leaders complete feedback cards which record questions and problems arising from the brief. These are collated and analyzed by the industrial relations (IR) departments which then report on the effectiveness of the brief to the general manager concerned.

IR officers attend as many briefing sessions as possible and report back on the speed at which the brief was handed down, the reaction to its content and how briefing group leaders handled the session. They also ensure that any outstanding answers are supplied as quickly as possible.

Regular formal audits of briefs are conducted by IR personnel among representative samples of employees. Once again, the reception and understanding of the brief are checked. Areas of misunderstanding are pinpointed and fed back to general managers, who then decide on whether or not a re-briefing should be held.

Major issues—such as a change in the remuneration package—are dealt with not only by the briefing groups but also during large-scale meetings held two to three days after the briefing. The meetings are manned by trained personnel who answer questions and clarify misunderstandings. Richardson says,

> Our briefing groups are not conducted in isolation. The brief is often reinforced by video programs, in-house journals and written notices. However, with more than 70,000 employees in the gold and uranium division, briefing sessions are our key communication vehicle. They are the only feasible device for structuring mass communications in a largely illiterate multilingual worker body.
>
> In the early 1970s industrial unrest often occurred as a result of sheer misunderstanding. Today we have a greater chance of preventing such situations by using our briefing groups to the benefit of both management and workers.

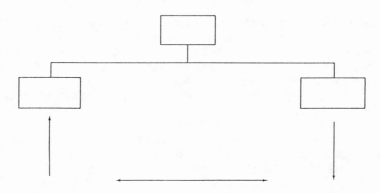

<table>
<tr><td>Upward</td><td>Downward</td></tr>
</table>

| *Upward* | *Downward* |
|---|---|
| Written:<br>  report<br>  newspaper/magazine<br><br>Personal:<br>  meeting<br>  open-door policy<br>  grievance procedure | Print:<br>  annual report<br>  newspaper/magazine<br>  bulletin board<br>  orientation manual<br>  letters<br>  pay envelope inserts<br><br>Electronic:<br>  telephone<br>  teleconference<br>  videotape<br><br>Personal:<br>  briefing groups<br>  staff meetings<br>  committee meetings at hostels for<br>    single employees |

*Horizontal*

personal contact
meetings

**Figure 33. Communication system of Sasol Limited, Johannesburg.**

## CASE STUDY: SASOL LIMITED

The company established an oil-from-coal operation in 1950 at Sasolburg, and the incorporation of the South African Coal, Oil and Gas Corporation Limited. During the sixties, Sasol diversified into the manufacture of petrochemicals and fertilizers, gas supply and crude oil refining. The company today is a strong divisional organization with decentralized responsibilities for coal mining, oil-from-coal production, oil refining, fuels marketing, chemicals, fertilizer production and marketing, as well as explosives production and marketing. Sasol Limited as the holding company of the group is listed on the Johannesburg Stock Exchange.

A letter from E.S. Kretschmer, group manpower manager, discussed the company's communication.

We do not have a formal communication policy although it is an established part of our culture that open communication forms the basis of our employee relations. This is also reflected in various practices and programs at our different divisions where briefing groups, liaison committees, management information bulletins, employee newsletters, staff meetings, etc., are common practice. . . . The briefing groups consist mainly of formalized communication meetings starting at the top as "need to know" information is defined that must be disseminated down into the organization, and the consequent cascading of this information through scheduled work team meetings right down to the shop floor level. Communication efficiency is monitored by spot checks.

Perhaps the only really unique element of our communication programs is related to our multilanguage and multicultural labor force which necessitates: (1) translation of most of our communication into a number of languages, (2) using translators when necessary, and (3) providing special language training, particularly on our mines, to facilitate communication.

The communication system of Sasol Limited is shown on Figure 33.

## Swaziland

*Official Name:* Kingdom of Swaziland; *Capital:* Mbabane; *Government:* monarchy, independent member of the British Commonwealth; *Subdivisions:* 4 administrative districts; *Population:* 715,160 (July 1987); *Density:* 96 per square mile; *Currency:* lilangeni; *Official Languages:* English and siSwati; *Literacy:* 65 percent.

*The Land.* About the size of Hawaii, Swaziland is landlocked, bordered for 67 miles by Mozambique in the northeast and by South Africa for 277 miles in the north, west and south. The land is part of the South African plateau; high plateaus with groups of forested mountains are found in the west. This gives way to lowlands in the east, and the Lubombo Mountains rise at the easternmost border.

*The People.* The population is mainly Swazi, with a small number of other Bantu ethnic groups, European and mulatto. Some 57 percent of the people are Christian; the rest follow traditional tribal beliefs. About 96 percent of the population are African; 3 percent are European; and 1 percent is mulatto.

Swazi customs completely dominate the cultural life of the people and are the source for a substantial quantity of the laws and court system. The Swazis are related to the Zulu and Xhosa people, have a highly developed warrior system and were historically regarded as a fierce enemy by the early white settlers and pioneers in South Africa.

*A Brief History.* People migrated south to this area before the sixteenth century. Swaziland was thinly inhabited by a variety of Bantu groups in the eighteenth century. The Swazis migrated to northern Zululand in about 1750. Unable to match the growing Zulu strength, the Swazi moved northward in the early 1800s to the modern Swaziland area. They consolidated their hold on the area under several leaders, most important among them Mswati, from whom the Swazis derive their name. The British-Boer competition in the last two decades of the nineteenth century resulted in Swaziland becoming a British protectorate. Swaziland was under South African protection from 1894 to 1906; from then until 1968, it was a British protectorate.

*The Economy.* The labor force is divided this way: agriculture and forestry, 36 percent; community and social services 20, manufacturing 14, construction 9; and other areas, 21 percent. About 15 percent of wage earners are unionized.

Swaziland is a free-market economy dominated by the private sector. Swaziland is modestly endowed with limited resources which provide a restricted level of prosperity. This has been made by substantial capital investment by Great Britain, some $100 million since World War II. In 1980, there were 113 establishments employing over 10 workers each. Sugar, wood pulp and fruit canning provide about 80 percent of their income.

# Zaire

*Official Name:* Republic of Zaire; *Capital:* Kinshasa; *Government:* republic; *Subdivisions:* 8 regions and a federal district; *Population:* 32,342,947 (July 1987); *Density:* 36 per square mile; *Currency:* zaire; *Official Language:* French; *Literacy:* 55 percent for males, 37 percent for females.

*The Land.* About the size of the entire portion of the United States east of the Mississippi, Zaire is a rectangle-shaped inland nation located in south-central Africa. It is situated almost entirely within the equatorial zone, with one-third of the country north of the equator and two-thirds south of the equator. While the Mitumba mountain range in the far east is part of the Great Rift system, the bulk of Zaire lies within the vast, low-lying Congo River basin. Most of the land is covered by lush tropical rain forest.

The country's only outlet to the Atlantic Ocean is a 25-mile strip of land on the north bank of the Zaire River. A vast, low-lying area is a basin-shaped plateau, sloping toward the west and covered by tropical rain forest. This area is surrounded by mountainous terraces in the west, plateaus merging into the savannas in the south and southwest and dense grasslands extending beyond the Zaire River in the north. High mountains are found in the extreme eastern region.

Neighboring countries are the Congo for 1,010 miles in the north and west, the Central African Republic for 980 miles and Sudan for 390 miles in the north, Uganda for 475 miles, Rwanda for 135 miles, Burundi for 145 miles and

Tanzania for 285 miles in the east and Zambia for 1,309 miles and Angola for 1,420 miles in the south. About 45 percent of the land is forest; 22 percent is agriculture; and 33 percent is other.

*The People.* There are as many as 250 distinct tribal groups, with Bantu peoples accounting for the majority of the population. Clan, tribal, and regional affiliations remain strong and important in all aspects of national life. With more than 700 different languages and dialects, Zaire has had to adopt a special language policy. Although French is the official language and is used in large business and administration, it is spoken by only about 10 percent of the population. The majority of local business and general daily communication occurs in one of four official regional languages (all Bantu): Lingala, Kikonga, Kiluba and Swahili. Most people speak their own tribal language as well as one or more of the regional languages. Approximately 90 percent of the population is nominally Christian but there has been a great deal of mixing between Christianity and traditional animistic religions. There is a small Moslem minority (1 percent). The remaining 9 percent practice native tribal religions.

The majority of Zairian people are members of one of the many Bantu tribal groups. The majority of Bantu peoples share a common cultural heritage and set of behavioral traits. Most characteristic, perhaps, is the general politeness and genuine concern for the welfare of others. This sometimes manifests itself as a gentle disposition and shyness with strangers, which visitors occasionally interpret as reticence. Although they seem shy, Zairians will reciprocate open and sincere friendliness. Another characteristic of Zairian Bantu groups is abruptness of speech ("please" and "thank you" are missing). Individualism is acceptable only if it does not interfere with group needs.

The family is the most important thing in life for the Zairian. Great emphasis is placed on group goals and family welfare. In western Zaire, families are mostly matriarchal with the mother's brother as the male with the greatest authority (not the husband). In other areas of the country, patriarchal, polygamous and combinations of these structures are common.

There are relatively sharp socioeconomic class distinctions in Zaire. The social ladder is largely unclimbable because one's social class is determined by birth.

*A Brief History.* Long ago, Bantu peoples from western Africa penetrated the Congo basin. The powerful Bakongo people were in firm control of much of present Zaire when the Portuguese appeared in the late 1400s. Little European intervention, however, took place until the 1800s, when Leopold II of Belgium formed an international trading company for purposes of exploiting the Congo region. The so-called Congo Free State became in effect a feudal estate. In 1908, the area became part of Belgium and was called the Belgian Congo. The harsh treatment of natives by Belgians led to an independent Democratic Republic of the Congo in 1960. Political unrest afterwards lasted for years.

*The Economy.* Zaire has no formal economic planning. Vast mineral deposits and other resources make Zaire potentially one of the richest nations in Africa, but this potential remains untapped. The country's main products are cassava, corn, palm oil, bananas, rice and timber. Coffee is the major export crop. Zaire is the world's principal supplier of cobalt and industrial diamonds and is a leading copper producer. Major industries are mining, mineral processing, consumer products (textiles, footwear, cigarettes), processed foods and beverages, and cement.

# Zambia

*Official Name:* Republic of Zambia; *Capital:* Lusaka; *Government:* 1-party state; *Subdivisions:* 9 provinces; *Population:* 7,281,738 (July 1987); *Density:* 23.3 per square mile; *Currency:* kwacha; *Official Language:* English; *Literacy:* 54 percent.

*The Land.* About the size of Texas, Zambia is located in south-central Africa, bordered by Angola for 675 miles in the west, Zaire for 1,309 miles in the northwest, Tanzania for 200 miles in the northeast, Malawi for 464 miles in the east, Mozambique for 263 miles in the southeast and Zimbabwe for 459 miles and Botswana for 109 miles in the south. Zambia stretches 750 miles west from the mountains of the great Western Rift. This is a high plateau country with an elevation of 3,000 to 5,000 feet above sea level. The gently rolling country alternates between the waving grasses of the plains and forests of widely spaced trees. The country is drained by two major river systems: the tributaries flowing north to the Congo River, and the Zambezi River, which flows southeast through Mozambique to the Indian Ocean. One of the greatest sheets of flowing water in the world is found at the incomparable Victoria Falls, near Livingstone in the south. The sparkling water of Lake Mweru and Lake Tanganyika are found in the north.

The land is divided this way: scattered wood and grass, 61 percent; dense forest 13, grazing 10, marsh 6; and arable and under cultivation, 5 percent.

*The People.* There are more than 70 Bantu-speaking tribes plus a European community in the copper mining area. The Africans constitute nearly 99 percent of the population, and the Europeans, about 1 percent; there are very few others. The majority are Christian; only about 1 percent are Muslim or Hindu. Twenty-four percent follow indigenous beliefs (sometimes along with Christianity). Zambia contains some of the most interesting ethnic groups of all Africa. The people are conservative and closely knit within their communities.

*A Brief History.* Like many adjacent countries, Zambia was probably inhabited in early times by primitive pygmies and other groups. The great wave of Bantu migration over several centuries virtually took over this country, and very few indications remain of earlier civilizations.

Zambia was under British South Africa Company administration from 1895 to 1923. From 1924 to 1964, it was a British colony. Northern Rhodesia became fully independent in 1964, taking the name "Zambia" from the great Zambezi River. Kenneth Kaunda was elected the first (and only) president in

1964. His most recent reelection was in 1983 by an overwhelming majority. Racial, religious and tribal frictions have been frequent since independence. Political repression has led to dissatisfaction among residents.

*The Economy.* The labor force is divided this way: agriculture, 85 percent; mining, manufacturing and construction, 6 percent; and transport and services, 9 percent.

Zambia has a free-market economy in which the dominant sector is public. The economy can be summed up in one word: copper. It has one quarter of the world's known reserves and has been the second largest producer since Chilean nationalization of copper production in 1971. Falling copper prices have created a financial crisis in the country.

Other major industries include transport, construction, foodstuffs, beverages, chemicals, textiles, and fertilizer. The work force is divided this way: 85 percent are in agriculture; 6 percent are in mining, manufacturing and construction; and 9 percent are in transport and services.

# Zimbabwe

*Official Name:* Republic of Zimbabwe; *Capital:* Harare; *Government:* parliamentary democracy; *Subdivisions:* 8 provinces; *Population:* 9,371,971 (July 1987); *Density:* 44 per square mile; *Currency:* dollar; *Official Language:* English; *Literacy:* 50 percent.

*The Land.* Zimbabwe is slightly larger than Montana. It is an inland country, but the interior rises in a series of fertile rolling plateaus called the veld. Zimbabwe is bordered for 452 miles by Zambia in the north, for 505 miles by Botswana in the southwest, for 140 miles by South Africa in the south and for 760 miles by Mozambique in the east.

Land usage is divided this way: 40 percent arable and 60 extensive grazing. About 48 percent of the land is worked commonly by Africans; 39 percent is owned by Europeans; 7 percent is national land and 6 percent is other.

*The People.* Some 96 percent of the residents are black — 77 percent Shona and 19 percent Ndebele. There are about 200,000 whites, 3.5 percent, including those of British descent and a small population of Greeks. There are also some small minorities, 0.5 percent, of coloreds and Asians. Only 19 percent live in urban areas. English is the official language, but in rural areas, most people do not speak English, preferring instead native languages. About 50 percent of the people are syncretic (part Christian and part indigenous beliefs); 25 percent are Christian; 24 percent follow indigenous beliefs; and there are a few Muslims.

The white and African populations lived apart for decades; independence has not changed this. The country has been in decline since the early 1980s as the government attempts to turn the country into a communist state.

*A Brief History.* There were successive waves of Bantu migration into Zimbabwe which may have started as early as about the fourth century A.D. The Zimbabwe ruins, the only pre–European remnant of architecture found below the Sahara in Africa, are attributed to people known as the Monoma and are dated sometime between the sixth and thirteenth centuries A.D. Between the ninth and thirteenth centuries A.D., a group of people who had established trading contacts with commercial centers on Africa's southeastern coast lived in this area. In the fifteenth century, the Karanga people (ancestors of the Shona) established a major trading center at Great Zimbabwe. That lasted until the end of the seventeenth century when it came under Portuguese domination. In 1830 the Ndebele people entered the area and conquered the Karanga. In the 1890s, white people began to trek north from South Africa hoping to discover gold fields. The countries of Matabeleland (home of the Ndebele) and Mashonaland (home of the Shona) were claimed by Cecil John Rhodes for England, under the terms of a Royal Charter from Queen Victoria, and became known as Rhodesia. In 1965 the white minority government issued a declaration of independence from the United Kingdom. After several years of civil war, independence was realized in 1980 and a government based on the black majority was set up.

*The Economy.* The labor force is divided this way: agriculture, 78 percent; mining, manufacturing and construction, 18 percent; and transport and services, 4 percent. About a third of European workers are unionized, but only a small minority of Africans belong to unions.

Zimbabwe's is a free-market economy in which the private sector is dominant. Before independence, Rhodesia was, along with South Africa, one of the most economically developed countries in sub–Sahara Africa. United Nations sanctions and the civil war took its toll. Today, agriculture, mining and manufacturing are the most important aspects of the economy. Less than 1 percent of the population is white, but they control more than 80 percent of the wealth, a situation tolerated because the black majority needs the white's expertise in running the country.

The principal crops are maize, sugar, wheat, cotton, tobacco (Zimbabwe is Africa's leading producer of tobacco), ground-nuts, sorghum, munga (cereal) and rapoko (cereal). Minerals mined are gold, asbestos, chrome, coal, copper and nickel. Manufacturing includes foodstuffs, textiles, clothing, footwear, furniture, paper, chemical and petroleum products, nonmetallic mineral products, metals and metal products.

*Organizational Communication.* Smartness in dress is more important here than it is in the United States. For men, a suit is the preferred attire for conducting business. Zimbabweans dislike sarcasm and loud, showy behavior.

## CASE STUDY: AFRICAN DISTILLERS LIMITED

Towards the end of World War II, a surplus of maize prompted the Southern Rhodesian government to build a small distillery at Umtali to make use of the excess in the production of alcohol. The scheme faltered. Meanwhile African Distillers was founded in 1944 to produce and market potable spirits. They purchased the government's equipment in 1946, the same year that Charter gin was introduced to the market followed by a widening range of

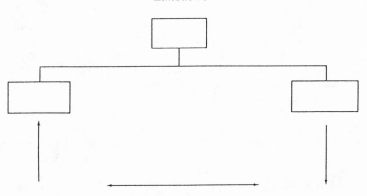

|  | Upward | | Downward |
|---|---|---|---|

| Upward | Downward |
|---|---|
| Written:<br>  memorandum<br>  report<br>  newspaper/magazine<br><br>Personal:<br>  meeting<br>  interview<br>  open-door policy<br>  grievance procedure | Print:<br>  annual report<br>  annual report to employees<br>  newspaper/magazine<br>  bulletin boards<br>  letters<br>  manual<br>  handbook<br><br>Electronic:<br>  telephone<br>  videotape |

*Horizontal*

personal contact
memorandum
meeting

**Figure 34. Communication system of African Distillers Limited, Harare, Zimbabwe.**

other liquor products using molasses instead of maize. In the following year the company began producing industrial spirits. By the late 1950s the company was established as the country's most progressive distillery and liquor distributor. Acquisitions and expansions over the years, both before and after Zimbabwe's independence in 1980, have made the company the largest wine and spirit producer in Zimbabwe, accounting for 92 percent of the potable spirits, 63 percent of the natural wines and 92 percent of the dessert wines on the national market. The company says this about communication:

> Effective communications are essential to the operation of any organization, and every effort is made to keep all staff informed of developments and happenings in the Company which may be of general interest, and policies which may have a direct influence on staff.

Information emanating from the top is normally passed down the line by department heads through personal contact, discussion groups, circulars, or through notices displayed on notice boards.

Staff are at liberty to approach their immediate senior in connection with any queries or problems they may have and may, if they so desire, after informing their department heads, discuss personal problems or queries with the personnel manager.

Issues requiring clarification should be openly dealt with and taken up through the correct channels. Department heads or the personnel manager will always endeavor to clear any misunderstandings and answer any reasonable question and, if they cannot provide an immediate answer, will indicate clearly when an answer may be expected.

While it is hoped that, once having joined, staff will stay with the Company, separations do naturally occur from time to time. On these occasions, staff are required to arrange to see the personnel manager before departure in order to have a final exit interview. It is hoped that frankness on departure will reveal shortcomings, so that the organization may learn through each individual's experience.

The communication system of African Distillers is presented in Figure 34.

## CASE STUDY: RIO TINTO

Rio Tinto Zimbabwe Limited (Riozim) is a member of the worldwide Rio Tinto organization headed by the Rio Tinto-Zinc Corporation PLC in London. Riozim carries out mining and allied operations in various parts of the country, producing gold and emerald, and custom refining nickel and copper. Riozim also has a subsidiary industrial company, Tinto Industries Limited. The head office of Riozim is in Harare.

Rio Tinto is a relatively large employer of labor in Zimbabwe, employing some 3,300 people, of whom 688 are engaged in the industrial division and the remainder in the mining, technical and administrative operations.

An article in *Profile,* the company newspaper, entitled "Never Underestimate the Importance of Good Communications," revealed much of the company's attitude toward that subject:

"I think management gets a far greater understanding of workers' problems and vice versa when you have an honest face to face relationship," stated Dave Ingram, executive director, operations. He was discussing the newly formed Mining Division Executive Works' Council, which he feels has gone a long way in assisting the exchange of ideas between management and workers.

The council consists of ten representatives of senior management, five of whom are chairmen of the location Works' Councils, and ten employee representatives comprising the chairman and secretaries of each of the location Workers' Committees of their alternates. Ingram is the Chairman.

The need to form such a council becomes apparent when one considers that Rio Tinto has several locations and, in trying to standardize various

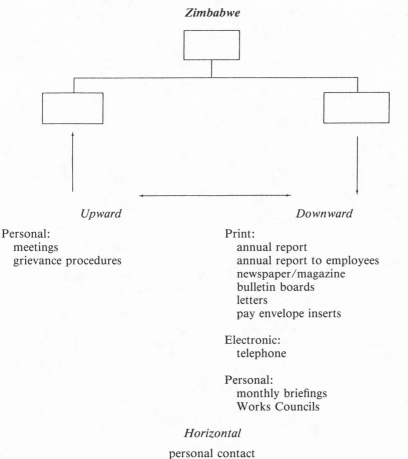

*Upward*

Personal:
  meetings
  grievance procedures

*Downward*

Print:
  annual report
  annual report to employees
  newspaper/magazine
  bulletin boards
  letters
  pay envelope inserts

Electronic:
  telephone

Personal:
  monthly briefings
  Works Councils

*Horizontal*

personal contact
meetings

**Figure 35. Communication system of the Rio Tinto Corporation.**

conditions such as housing and achieve a greater uniformity of industrial relations, realized it is important that one rather than several negotiating parties exist.

The Mining Division Executive Works' Council has been meeting three times a year at Eiffel Flats. About a month before the meeting, the Workers' Committees meet. This gives them the opportunity of visiting various operations and to date they have met at Eiffel Flats, Sandawana and Renco. At these meetings items for the Executive Works' Council agenda are put forward.

The items for discussion are wide ranging and the meetings are conducted in a cordial and constrictive atmosphere. Ingram feels that it is important that the parties negotiate in good faith. "We don't believe it is right when a request is received to give an off-hand answer; rather it should be fully investigated. Once something is agreed, it must be implemented swiftly."

Ingram went on to comment on the benefits which arise from the Executive

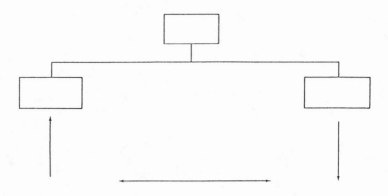

*Upward*                                          *Downward*

Written:                                          Print:
  memorandum                              annual report to employees
  reports                                  newspaper/magazine
  newspaper/magazine                       bulletin board
                                                    orientation manual
Personal:                                           letters
  meeting                                  pay envelope inserts
  interview                                manual
  open-door policy
  grievance procedure                    Electronic:
                                                    telephone
                                                    film
                                                    videotape

*Horizontal*

personal contact
memorandum
meeting

**Figure 36. Communication system of Zimbabwe Alloys Limited.**

Works' Council. He felt that one of the main advantages is that people with a group responsibility, for example, group personnel and public relations, Tom Williamson and the group industrial relations officer, Julius Munemo, get a "good feel as to how things are going at the locations. It is also of assistance to members of the location Works' Council who tend to get feedback as to how Head Office feel." Ingram makes a point of taking notes at the meeting and briefing the executive directors on the developments. In addition to it being an ideal opportunity of expressing the workers' view to the executive, it also enables Ingram to take the executive's views to the worker. "I don't think one can over stress the advantage of good communications at any level. If you cannot communicate you cannot understand one another."

Figure 35 shows the communication system at Rio Tinto.

## CASE STUDY: ZIMBABWE ALLOYS LIMITED

The Company was the first ferrochrome operation in Africa and was formed as an overseas investment of John Brown & Company, the British steelmaking and shipbuilding firm. Today, Zimbabwe Alloys has a mining operation supplying chrome ore from three mines and has greatly expanded production at the refinery from the original 9,000 tons a year to more than 70,000 tons a year, which is exported to 30 countries in North and South America, Europe and the Far East.

The company says this about communication in its Mission Statement:

Management believes that the above (responsibility to customers) can only be achieved through the commitment and dedication of our employees. We accept our responsibility to provide a safe and stable working environment; to develop potential and recognize individual contribution; to be honest and fair and to maintain high standards and integrity throughout the organization; to encourage communication and employee involvement in problem solving wherever possible.

The communication system of Zimbabwe Alloys appears in Figure 36.

# Notes

1. Ali A. Mazrui, *The Africans,* p. 20.
2. Ibid., p. 21.
3. C.C. Onyemelukwe, *Men and Management in Contemporary Africa,* p. 173.
4. Philip M. Allen and Aaron Segal, *The Traveler's Africa,* p. 60.
5. Sanford J. Ungar, *Africa,* p. 38.
6. Ibid., p. 125.
7. Paul Bohannan, "African Families," in Stanley Davis, ed., *Comparative Management,* pp. 67–8.
8. Roy Hill, "Coping with the Culture Shock of an Overseas Posting," p. 84.
9. Bohannan, loc. cit.
10. Lloyd A. Falles, "Social Stratification and Economic Processes," in Davis, p. 79.
11. Ungar, p. 425.
12. Ukandi G. Damachi and Hans Dieter Seibal, *Management Problems in Africa,* p. xii.
13. Don Irwin, "Places to Live, From Top to Bottom," *Daily Record,* March 16, 1987, p. A6.
14. Ukandi G. Damachi, "Industrial Relations: A Development Dilemma," in Damachi and Seibal, p. 133.
15. Onyemelukwe, pp. 115–6.
16. Ibid., p. 173.
17. Ibid., pp. 127–8.
18. "A New Economic Order Comes to Africa," *The New York Times,* July 19, 1987, p. 12.
19. Bohannan, pp. 72–5.
20. Leonard W. Doob, "Communications in Africa," in Haig A. Bosmajian, ed., *The Rhetoric of Nonverbal Communication,* p. 20.
21. Janine Perrett, "Survey Says Australian Workforce 'Difficult,'" n.p.
22. "Managing in Two Worlds," p. 36.
23. Allen and Segal, p. 321.

# 7. Asia and the Pacific

## The Land

A third of the world's land mass and 55 percent of its people are contained in Asia. One reason Asia has remained a bit backward for so long is its inhospitable topography. Great plateaus and ranges extend diagonally across the contents for 4,500 miles. Most of the people live in the lowlands near the big rivers and their tributaries.

## The People

East Asians speak radically different languages, but the Chinese, Japanese and Koreans share common physical characteristics, stemming from common ancestors who lived in Central Asia as recently as 15,000 years ago. They also share a written language, which the Japanese borrowed from the Chinese in about the fifth century A.D. and Korea borrowed several hundred years later. Finally the East Asians share a common heritage of agriculturally based family organization within a centralized state system. Strong family ties often extend to distant relatives.

East Asians consider equity more important than wealth, the group more important than the individual. Highly disciplined and motivated, they are very conservative in their spending habits, saving a large percentage of their earnings each month. Education is a means of earning prestige and economic security for the family. Citizens strive for harmony in everything, avoiding conflict whenever possible.

## A Brief History

Until well into the twentieth century, the fate of non–Soviet Asia was decided by Europeans and Americans, who dominated much of the continent physically and most of it economically. Since Japan began its expansion in the late 1930s, however, national consciousness has grown. Today the future of most Asians — whether living in the giant nations or the smaller ones — is largely in the hands of fellow Asians.

# The Economy

Everyone knows that the countries of East Asia have earned an enviable record for high economic performance under the leadership of Japan and the newly industrialized countries (NICs) such as South Korea, Hong Kong, Singapore and Taiwan. From 1980 through 1985 the trade deficit of the United States with the NICs increased 427 percent; with Japan it increased 202 percent, according to Commerce Department figures.[1] The NICs have been successful, economists say, because of their cheap labor and because they are masters at copying other peoples' technologies. Most of their exports are manufactured goods: electronic components, radios and televisions, telecommunications, tape recorders, toys and sporting goods, computer parts, calculators, clothing and textiles.

Some experts predict that world leadership in the twenty-first century will be from here. Already some signs point to that happening; for example, in 1985 three of five jumbo jetliners crossed the Atlantic; now three out of five cross the Pacific. "The center of gravity has already shifted in business, trade and investments," says Lloyd Vassey, president of the Honolulu-based Pacific Forum think tank. "It's where all the future action is going to be."[2]

The world recession of 1979 after the increase in petroleum prices caused performance problems in this region. Export prices fell and export volumes decreased sharply leading to slower growth and moderating inflation rates. The trends improved by 1983–84, following the upturn of the United States economy; increased demand in the United States creates demand for exports from East Asian countries.

The region will have to face the possibility of protectionism in the United States and Europe in the future, and the United States will have to find new ways to participate in the activity in addition to its present manufacturing operations in the region from which it exports to third parties. As Representative David R. Obey, chairman of the Joint Economic Committee of Congress said: "If we don't get aboard, the Asian-Pacific Express will leave without us."[3]

Western managers face an entirely different system of managing in working with East Asians. Hari Bedi, an Indian working for a large multinational company in Hong Kong, describes the difference this way:

> Asian internationals use the 5 C's of *continuity* (a sense of history and tradition), *commitment* (to the growth of the organization), *connections* (where social skills and social standing count), *compassion* (balancing scientific and political issues), and *cultural sensitivity* (a respect for other ways).... Western managers, according to Bedi, use the 5 E's: *expertize* (experience in managerial and technical theory), *ethos* (practical experience), *eagerness* (the enthusiasm of the entrepreneur), *esprit de corps* (a common identity), and *endorsement* (seeks unusual opportunities).[4]

The reader might feel challenged to add to the lists, for example camaraderie, courtesy and conservative approach for the East and efficiency, egalitarianism and extroverted nature for the West.

# PACIFIC-RIM COUNTRIES

Technically any country that has borders on the Pacific Ocean could be considered Pacific-rim countries, and 33 nations qualify, including Canada, the United States, Mexico, Peru and Chile. This section discusses, however, only those Asian countries of the greatest burgeoning economic activity in the world: Japan and the four NICs mentioned above (Hong Kong, Singapore, South Korea and Taiwan), and these developing countries: Indonesia, Malaysia, the Philippines and Thailand, all presented here in alphabetical order.

## ——————— Hong Kong ———————

*Official Name:* Hong Kong; *Capital:* Victoria; *Government:* British dependent territory, scheduled to revert to China in 1997; *Subdivisions:* Hong Kong, Kowloon and New Territories; *Population:* 5,608,610 (July 1987); *Density:* 13,366.3 per square mile; *Currency:* dollar; *Official Languages:* English and Cantonese; *Literacy:* 75 percent.

*The Land.* Hong Kong occupies a mere 400 square miles on the southeast coast of China, about 90 miles southeast of Canton and 40 miles east of the Portuguese province of Macau. The colony is comprised of the tip of the peninsula, the two large islands of Hong Kong and Lan Tao and 200 smaller islands. Its land mass, about equal to one-third the size of Rhode Island, is mountainous and short of fertile land and water. It consists of only 9.4 percent agricultural land. About 14 percent of the land is arable; 10 percent is forest; and 76 percent is other.

*The People.* Hong Kong is the most densely populated country in the world. More than 90 percent of the people live in the city, the third highest urbanization rate in the world. Hong Kong is a very ethnically homogeneous country; approximately 98 percent of the population are of Chinese descent. Of these, about 58 percent were born in Hong Kong. Most of the Chinese are Cantonese, with roots in nearby Kwangtung Province. About 90 percent of the population are an eclectic mixture of local religions; 10 percent are Christian.

These nationalities don't mix. Hong Kong is strongly segregated socially. Old-school Chinese live primarily in extended families with complex interfamily organization, responsibilities and support systems. About 43 percent are under age 20, and 60 percent are under age 30.

As a British colony, Hong Kong carries the overtones of a Western culture, but her roots are deeply embedded in Oriental soil. Living in Hong Kong enables one to experience two cultures at once. Hong Kong is referred to as the "Pearl of the Orient." It is a place of natural beauty, impressive modern structures and, most importantly, a place of resilient, adaptable and energetic people. The Confucian ethic of proper social and family relationships forms the foundation of Chinese society. The Chinese are very conscious of their social position in relation to the people they deal with. An individual's actions reflect upon the entire family. The Chinese are concerned with "saving face" by avoiding direct conflicts, and will try to allow a person to escape from an embarrassing situation with dignity. Therefore causing a person to lose face must be avoided. Business is respected, and wealth symbolizes success.

An American doing business in Hong Kong reported an incident in which a Chinese department assistant was offered the opportunity to fill in for his supervisor. The employee came to the American in a state of distress: "You Americans are always trying to get people to do your jobs." Some Asians, if they are happy with their jobs, are content to stay there and develop those skills thoroughly. This American also observed that when "persons of a different culture are conversing a common tongue it is no guarantee of mutual understanding. The Chinese, for example, tend to take things literally, which means that wisecracking American humor can sometimes have disastrous results."[5]

Certain attitudes among the Chinese are traditional. They are loyal to family and friends, they tend to be emotional, they love to gamble, they work hard, they love noisy parties, but they are rarely drunk. They live by a strict code of responsibility to mates, parents, children and close friends, but their lack of concern for those outside their immediate circle develops into the rude, aggressive behavior of pushing, slamming doors and uninhibited driving in public.

For years outsiders were referred to by the Chinese as *gwailos,* meaning literally "foreign devils." Perhaps a sign of toleration or partial acceptance of the international community is the use now of the term *sayan,* which just means "western foreigner." Blue and white are Chinese colors of mourning and should be avoided.

Chinese family members are bound by a strong tradition of loyalty, obedience and respect, reflected in the world's fifth lowest divorce rate. Family members are obligated to help each other in whatever ways they can. Harsh economic conditions and differences between traditional values and those exported from the West are among the sources of stress for many Hong Kong families. The Chinese do not usually display affection in public.

Children spend a great deal of school time in memorizing. They are not encouraged to form opinions of their own or to question and challenge what they are taught. This kind of education is reflected in office performance. Chinese office staff are often reluctant to take initiative or to make independent decisions. This reluctance also stems from the deeply rooted tradition which teaches respect for one's elders and one's superiors. Younger or "inferior" people simply do not mention errors they observe, make suggestions or discuss points with their superiors. They simply accept politely. You are likely to find that members of your office staff will feel more comfortable with a greater degree of formality in office relations than Americans are accustomed to.

While the British are loyal to their employers and consider job-hopping a sign of flightiness and unreliability, they do not get their identity from their association with a corporation or organization as Americans do. One's identity derives from values and image. Identification is first with family, then community, region and nation. A line is drawn between business acquaintances and personal friends, and formality and manners are important. It is wise to wait for your British host to use your first name before you call him by his. Titles are also extremely important, so if you are dealing with a "Sir," be sure to use his title.

*A Brief History.* Before the British occupation, Hong Kong was a small fishing village notorious for pirates. When Britain began trading with China, the harbor was a logical place to stop to replenish supplies. The ships were often full of opium, tea and silks on the return run to the West. This trade was important to Britain. Each side tolerated what they considered to be the "boorishness" of the other to maintain trade.

The Chinese placed severe restrictions on the British "barbarians." They could only trade through one port, Canton, and only at certain times. Families were not allowed and were left in Macau. It was illegal for a trader to learn Chinese.

In 1799 Emperor Tao Kuang declared opium illegal in China, but this did not stop the lucrative trade. The British continued to bring it in from India; it just went underground. By 1830 over $15 million in opium was being smuggled into China each year. In 1839 the British colony in Canton was barricaded until the supplies of opium, "foreign mud," were handed over. The affront to British sovereignty brought on the first Opium War (1840–42), still referred to as the Anglo-Chinese wars in Britain. When the parties negotiated a cease-fire, Britain acquired Hong Kong Island in perpetuity. Hong Kong's status was confirmed by the Treaty of Nanking (1842), and five other ports were opened by China for trade. The strategic and economic importance of the Island was soon evident.

Kowloon (Nine Dragons), the top of the peninsula directly north of Hong Kong Island, became part of the colony in 1860 under terms of the Convention of Peking. In 1898 China leased the New Territories, extending from Kowloon to the Chinese border, to Britain for 99 years. This lease is due to expire in 1997.

In December 1984, Britain and China signed an agreement returning all of Hong Kong to China upon the expiration of the lease on the New Territories at midnight on June 30, 1997. The territory will be set up as a Special Administrative Region of the People's Republic of China under these provisions:

- The free enterprise system, free trade policies and the free port will continue.
- The economic and financial systems will, in all essential respects, remain for 50 years after 1997.
- Hong Kong will enjoy a high degree of autonomy.
- Hong Kong will decide its own economic and trade policies in the light of its own needs and will be able to negotiate agreements and participate in international organizations such as GATT.
- Hong Kong will retain the authority to conduct its own external affairs in economic, trade, financial, monetary and shipping matters.
- There will be no exchange controls and the Hong Kong dollar will remain freely convertible.
- Existing lease and land rights will continue after 1997.
- Hong Kong will continue to enjoy its existing rights and freedoms including those in economic matters.

- Free movements to and from Hong Kong will continue.
- Hong Kong will maintain its own familiar system of law.

*The Economy.* The labor force is divided this way: manufacturing, 36.3 percent, commerce 22.1, services 18.4, construction 7.6, transportation and communication 7.6, finance, insurance and real estate 6.8, agriculture, fishing, mining and quarrying 1.2, and unemployed, 3 percent. About 15.2 percent of the work force is unionized.

The economy in Hong Kong is probably the freest capitalistic system in the world, largely untouched by government regulations. Only 9.4 percent of Hong Kong's small land mass is arable, and natural resources are scarce. Because of this, shipping, commerce and industry have become vital to its survival. "Hong Kong" means "Fragrant Harbor," and the 23-square-mile harbor with its parade of freighters and junks is the key to business. It is a free port; no duties are levied on imports or exports. No other country has a higher percentage of people engaged in manufacturing. Chief among the products of Hong Kong's light industries are textiles and clothing, plastics, electronics and toys. Tourism is also a significant source of income. Only 4 percent of the people are employed in agriculture, the fourth smallest percentage in the world. Hong Kong is dependent on outside sources, primarily China, for over 80 percent of its food.

Hong Kong is without any natural resources other than its strategic location, a fine natural harbor and an industrious and enterprising population. Its manufacturing industries with nearly 47,000 establishments, export about 95 percent of their total output. The colony is now among the world's top exporters of toys, clothing, watches and clocks and electronics.

Hong Kong's success as a manufacturing complex and major commercial center in Asia can be largely attributed to its economic policy of free enterprise, free trade, sophisticated commercial infrastructure, a conveniently located airport of international standards and excellent worldwide communications.

A strong work ethic prevails throughout the colony and at every level the will to work, the desire to make money and succeed, is very apparent. Absenteeism among workers is negligible; strikes and industrial disputes are practically unknown. Most want only to be allowed to work and to attain a higher standard of living. They are flexible and adapt well to almost any kind of employment. Trade and labor unions have developed with the government's encouragement but there is little local interest in such organized associations. Hong Kong's port has become the second busiest in the world, after Rotterdam. Per capita income is $6,300, following Japan and Singapore as the region's third wealthiest entity.

Any westerner doing business in Hong Kong must never forget the importance of *fung shui,* literally "wind water." The *fung shui* expert determines the most propitious circumstances for starting any project and for appeasing evil spirits. If proper deference is not paid to these spiritual laws, bad *joss* (luck) will be the result.

Although Hong Kong was shaken when the planned return to China was announced in 1982, business confidence has rebounded and experienced new growth. American companies are now "'licking their chops' at the prospect of

Hong Kong's becoming a gateway to China," says Ernest R. Astin, director of Hong Kong's Securities and Exchange Commission.[6] Gordon Leung, Hong Kong's acting commissioner of banking, says that dozens of United States banks, advertising firms, architectural consultants and other smaller and medium-sized firms are setting up in Hong Kong, eager to market to one billion Chinese.[7] Some 900 United States firms now do business in Hong Kong with an investment of $6 billion.

*Organizational Communication.* The key word for doing business with the Chinese anywhere in Asia is politeness. The Chinese, as a rule, are an extremely courteous people, to the extent that they will often give an answer which they believe a visitor wants to hear, rather than the true answer. In the Chinese culture the rules of courtesy dictate the avoidance of explicit disagreement; courtesy has a higher priority than accuracy. Raising your voice in anger will achieve an effect opposite to the one you wish. Firm, pleasant persistence will yield better results.

Appointments should be made well in advance—two to three months, if possible. Nothing is improvised in China, so a visitor should never just drop in to discuss business. For best results, a visitor should arrange an introduction before arrival. Trade associations or commercial organizations can help locate someone to write a letter of introduction. The representative of American businesses should be 50 years of age or older in deference to the Chinese respect for age.

Also for best results, visitors should send their proposals ahead of time to give the Chinese a chance to study them. During the meeting proposals should be explained thoroughly.

When appointments are made, a half-hour courtesy time is allowed for most people; however, punctuality is expected and business persons are generally on time. When sitting down, visitors should place their hands in their lap and keep their feet on the floor. Blinking the eyes at someone is impolite. The open hand, rather than the index finger, should be used for pointing. Beckoning is done with the palm down.

British influence of formality still dominates much of Hong Kong business culture. Virtually every business introduction starts with the immediate exchange of business cards. The business card in Hong Kong is an essential tool to identify and remember your business contacts. Small talk is exchanged over coffee or tea to give the parties an opportunity to get to know one another.

As in other parts of Asia, "face" and the loss of it are serious concerns to the Chinese. Always provide an avenue of honorable retreat for Chinese who may have been in error, or who may not be able to answer you or provide you with the assistance you need. Talk around a point so that your meaning is clear but no one has been challenged; always give the other person face-saving opportunities if there is disagreement. In an office situation, for example, you would not ask your secretary, "Did you telephone Mr. Tong as I requested?" Instead you might ask, "Have you been able to reach Mr. Tong?" This serves both as a question and as a reminder if the person has, in fact, forgotten. Office staff should never be criticized in front of anyone else.

Most Asians dislike being rushed. They like to deliberate, get a "reading"

**Table 26. Some Communication Practices in the Hong Kong Corporation**

Hong Kong Residents:

1. Expect business to be conducted in a courteous manner.

2. Often give answers they feel visitors want to hear rather than accurate information.

3. Want appointments to be made as early as possible.

4. Expect punctuality.

5. Are influenced by the British culture.

6. Exchange business cards.

7. Get to know visitors through small talk over hot tea.

8. Dislike loss of "face."

9. Like to have time for lengthy deliberation.

10. Consider telephones too impersonal for conducting business.

11. Have a high-context culture.

12. Use time polychronically.

on you through several encounters before they know whether or not they trust and want to work with you, especially on an important matter. They mistrust those who press them for quick decisions. In many parts of Asia people do not like to do business over meals and convey nothing important by telephone unless they know you well. Telephones seem too impersonal and too rushed. (Japanese and Filipinos are exceptions in using phones; the Chinese are exceptions as to doing business over meals.)

It is considered rude to shake your finger at people or beckon by crooking your finger. Americans laugh mostly to express amusement; for the Chinese laughter also serves to express feelings of distress.

Typically the Chinese businessman will not entertain you at his home. Functions are held in public restaurants or clubs. As in Japan, wives are seldom invited unless the host is very Westernized.

The Chinese practice reserve and modesty in dealing with others, and feel aggressive behavior is offensive. Humility or self-demeaning comments are normal in describing one's self or accomplishments. Sincere compliments are given and appreciated, but the Chinese way is to deny praise. Polite conversation usually includes inquiries about one's health, business affairs or school activities.

Hong Kong maintains two official languages: Chinese and English. Policemen with red patches on their shoulders speak English. Much of the discussion about the British in the United Kingdom section of this book applies here.

Table 26 lists some communication practices of the Hong Kong firm.

# Indonesia

*Official Name:* Republic of Indonesia; *Capital:* Jakarta; *Government:* republic; *Subdivisions:* 27 provinces; *Population:* 180,425,534 (July 1987); *Density:* 225 per square mile; *Currency:* rupiah; *Official Languages:* Bahasa-Indonesian, Malay-Polynesian, English, Dutch; *Literacy:* 63 percent.

*The Land.* The name "Indonesia" combines the Greek words, *Indos,* meaning "East Indian," and *nesos,* meaning "islands."

About the size of Alaska and California combined, Indonesia is an archipelago, largest in the world, in the eastern Indian Ocean between Malaysia and the Philippines to the north and Australia to the south. It includes the five main islands of Java, Sumatra, Kalimantan, Sulawesi and Irian Java, and about 30 smaller archipelagoes totalling 13,667 islands, of which about 6,000 are inhabited. The islands form an arc along the equator from the mainland of Southeast Asia to Australia with the greatest distance from east to west 3,275 miles (about one and a half times as wide as Europe). From north to south the greatest distance is 1,373 miles. The archipelago forms a natural barrier between the Indian and Pacific oceans. Indonesia's territory is together about a fifth the size of the United States. It includes low plains, dense forests, jungles, sandy beaches and mountains. Indonesia is the most volcanic region of the world with over 100 active volcanoes. The country is surrounded by the South China Sea, the Indian Ocean and the Pacific Ocean.

About 64 percent of the land is forest; 24 percent is inland water, waste and urban; and 12 percent is small holdings and estates.

*The People.* Indonesia's population is the fifth largest in the world. The island of Java is one of the most densely populated places in the world with 100 million people living in an area the size of New York State. Indonesia has more than 60 ethnic groups, each having its own customs, culture and language. Approximately 45 percent of the people are Javanese; 14 percent are Sudanese; 7.5 percent are Madurese; 7.5 percent coastal Malays; and the remaining 26 percent belong to various other ethnic groups. Nearly two-thirds of the population live on Java. About half the population is under the age of 20.

Bahasa-Indonesian (the official national language — an advanced form of Malay) is the language of all written communications, education, government and business; however, only 39 percent of the people understand it. More than 200 languages and dialects are spoken. Education is free and compulsory for all children between the ages of 6 and 12, but only 90 percent of eligible children are enrolled in primary school. Literacy among the 6-to-16 age group is 75 percent.

The Chinese in Indonesia remain a distinct and somewhat suspect ethnic group. Everyone knows who is and isn't Chinese; the Chinese are not fully accepted as Indonesians. Indonesians tend to be xenophobic; western influence is not fully welcomed.

Religious freedom has been granted only for the five religions recognized by the state: Islam, Protestantism, Catholicism, Buddhism and Hinduism. Islam was introduced in the twelfth century and gradually replaced Hinduism in most of the principal islands; those who didn't convert fled to Bali which is the only island today in which the majority of residents follow the Hindu religion. About 88 percent of the people are Muslim; 6 percent are Protestant; 3 percent Roman Catholic; 2 percent Hindu; and 1 percent are other.

Indonesian culture is based on honor and respect. Indonesians value loyalty to family and friends more than individual advancement. They rarely disagree in public, seldom say no (but rather say *belum,* "not yet"), and always have time for others. Punctuality is never emphasized at the expense of personal relations. Indonesians often view Westerners as too quick to anger, too serious about themselves and too committed to the idea that "time is money."

*A Brief History.* The Muslim religion was introduced to Indonesia by traders from Persia and the west coast of India in the twelfth century. The religion rapidly gained prominence among the people, first in coastal regions and then in the interior of the islands.

The first Dutch traders arrived toward the end of the sixteenth century. During the next 300 years, the Dutch progressively brought the Indonesian archipelago under their control, as the Netherlands East Indies. The early twentieth century saw the emergence of popular nationalist independence movements. During the Japanese occupation from 1942 to 1945, major nationalist objectives were achieved. On August 17, 1945, two days after the surrender of the Japanese, a unilateral declaration of independence was made. In December 1949, the Netherlands government unconditionally recognized the sovereignty of the new republic with Sukarno as president. During the early 1960s, President Sukarno moved rapidly to impose an authoritarian regime under the label of "Guided Democracy." (Attempts by the communists to gain control in 1965 were thwarted and the party is presently illegal in Indonesia. Although there are free elections in theory, issues and candidates are carefully screened by the ruling party.) Suharto was elected president in 1973 and again in 1978 and 1983. Parliamentary elections of 1982 gave a majority to GOLKAR, a federation of groups which operate as a government political party.

When Christopher Columbus discovered America, he was looking for the East Indies and access to the rich spice trade. Most of those islands are a part of present-day Indonesia.

*The Economy.* The labor force is divided this way: agriculture, 55 percent; manufacturing 10, construction 4, and transport and communication, 3 percent. About 5 percent of the work force is unionized.

Indonesia has a free-market economy which is dominated by the private sector. Indonesia is rich in natural resources, much of which remain undeveloped. Agriculture employs 64 percent of the people and accounts for 53 percent of production. Indonesia is the world's second largest producer of rubber and is third in rice. It ranks fifth in soybean and timber production. Other agricultural products are copra and tea. Industry is playing an increasingly important role in the economy and currently employs about 7 percent of the people. Petroleum, textiles, mining (copper and nickel), cement and chemical fertilizers are all important industries.

Employees do not consider it polite to question their employers. This means that employers need to be especially careful about explaining things clearly. Don't expect workers to let you know they have not understood. Watch their eyes and expressions. If you think they may not have understood what you said, repeat it quickly, but in some other form so as not to hurt their feelings. They will not want to imply by questioning you that what you said was not clear, lest you lose face.

Organizational decisions flow from the top down, and thus authority is seldom delegated. Lower levels rarely expect to initiate actions, and superiors demand accountability. However, the legalistic, Islam-inspired strictness in adhering to rules and decisions is balanced by the characteristic tolerance and relativism of the Indonesian culture.

At first it can be difficult for Westerners to adapt to Indonesia's more autocratic, centralized system. In the West, rules, procedures and systems are designed to simplify and make daily operations predictable. They apply and remain in force only as long as they are effective or until new ones have been agreed upon. In Indonesia procedures and systems may be retained to suit those in authority, even if they are not effective.

Major industries include cement, fertilizers, food processing, petroleum refining, textiles, timber processing and mining.

*Organizational Communication.* One rule is constant about doing business in Indonesia: personal interaction is dominant. Letters begin with *Dengan hormat* ("with respect"). Respect should always be remembered when addressing others.

Visitors need not make appointments at all except with the largest Indonesian companies. Even top managers receive drop-ins with no objection. Attitudes toward time are relaxed so that when you do have an appointment, the host may be late. Exchanging small gifts is common. Exchange business cards immediately. Ornate cards are acceptable here with degrees included for the Indonesians' examination. The atmosphere at meetings is always informal. Although hand-shaking is common, other physical contact is avoided.

Typical meetings, though, are conducted properly. Respect is paid to those conducting meetings. Indonesians greatly value a quiet voice, an unassuming attitude and agreement by consent. The worst possible insult is to embarrass another, so necessary disagreement and criticism should be handled privately. Laughing at another's mistakes is very offensive.

Avoid using the left hand and pointing with the finger or toe. Try, also, to avoid turning the back when leaving. Never say "no" to Indonesian hosts; they will do likewise to you, preferring a more evasive response. Expect business transaction to take time; nothing is settled quickly. Patience is the key; never show impatience or temper.

## CASE STUDY: PERTAMINA

The company was organized in 1968 as a merger between two state-owned companies, PN. Pertamin and PN. Permina, to engage in the exploration, exploitation, refining, transportation and marketing of oil and gas. Pertamina is directed and managed by a board of directors, headed by a president director appointed by the President of the Republic of Indonesia. The board of

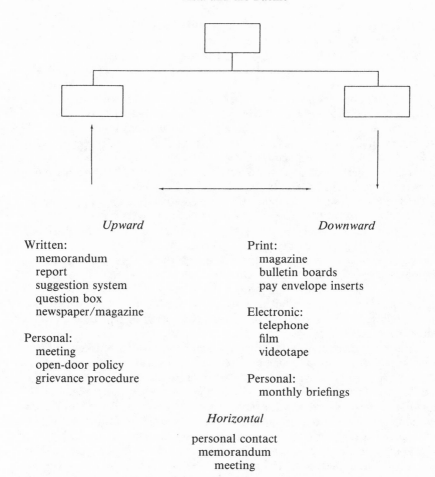

*Upward*

Written:
  memorandum
  report
  suggestion system
  question box
  newspaper/magazine

Personal:
  meeting
  open-door policy
  grievance procedure

*Downward*

Print:
  magazine
  bulletin boards
  pay envelope inserts

Electronic:
  telephone
  film
  videotape

Personal:
  monthly briefings

*Horizontal*

personal contact
memorandum
meeting

**Figure 37. Communication system of Pertamina, Jakarta, Indonesia.**

directors is made up of the president director and six directors, respectively, of exploration and production, processing, domestic supply, shipping and telecommunications, finance and general affairs. Since 1962, Pertamina has been a member of OPEC.

The company does have a communication policy as part of a compendium containing the rights and obligations of employees. A question one might ask is how does the fact that Pertamina is a state-owned company affect communication. The company representative who completed my questionnaire answered that in reply to the question of how the company might be able to improve its communication system: "You would understand that Pertamina is a state-owned oil and gas mining company. Therefore, the government's meddlement remains dominant, so that the overall policy and decision concerning management for Pertamina much depends on and should be approved by the

Government." Pertamina's communication system, shown in Figure 37, is a combination used in the Government and modern oil corporations.

# Japan

*Official Name:* Japan; *Capital:* Tokyo; *Government:* constitutional monarchy; *Subdivisions:* 47 prefectures; *Population:* 122,124,293 (July 1987); *Density:* 843.3 per square mile; *Currency:* yen; *Official Language:* Japanese; *Literacy:* 99 percent.

*The Land.* Japan consists of four main islands and about 3,900 smaller ones and is about the size of California. Japan is separated from the Asian mainland by 120 miles of choppy water. About 80 percent of Japan's land is mountainous; the remaining 20 percent is arable. Numerous hot springs, volcanoes, rivers and lakes enhance the scenic beauty of the land.

The land is about 69 percent forest; 16 percent arable and cultivated land; 12 percent urban and waste; and 3 percent grass.

*The People.* The Japanese of today emerged from the mixing of several ethnic groups. Predominantly they are of Mongoloid stock drawn in prehistoric times from the eastern fringes of the Asian mainland. Proto-Malayan and Polynesian strains migrated from the south by way of the Ryuku Islands. The earliest people of Japan were hunters and farmers. Living in small villages, these prehistoric Japanese cultivated rice paddies and irrigated fields. They had no writing system, and worshipped family ancestors and nature gods.

Japan's population is equal to about half that of the United States but they live on only 4 percent of the U.S. land area. Japan is the third most densely populated country in the world (after Hong Kong and Singapore). Nearly 80 percent of the population lives in urban areas; about 45 percent of the people are concentrated in the three largest metropolitan areas: Tokyo, Osaka and Nagoya. Japan's population is 99.5 percent homogeneous, with only a small number (0.5 percent) of Koreans, Chinese, native Ainu, and others.

Most Japanese observe both the Shinto and Buddhist rites; 16 percent belong to other faiths, including 0.8 percent who are Christian.

Conformity even in appearance is one of the distinct characteristics of Japanese people. The general rule is to act in a manner similar to, or in harmony with, the crowd. Men wear suits and ties in public. Avoid colors that are conspicuous.

Practicality, hard work and devotion to economic progress characterize the modern Japanese. Society is group oriented and people identify strongly with their group. Loyalty to the group and to one's superiors is essential and takes precedence over personal feelings. Businesses provide the Japanese with prestige and benefits. Employees usually remain with a company for life. To be fired is considered a disgrace to self and family. The family system is strongly evident in many areas of society. Group unity is strong and leaders seek consensus on most decisions.

To the Japanese there are two kinds of people—those who exist and those who don't; more clearly stated—those with whom one has some form of relationship and those without any relationships. Where there is a relationship there are clearly defined guidelines, but for those who "do not exist" anything goes.

Caught in a sudden and frightening experience, the American is likely to think "What will I do next?" Caught in the same position, the Japanese is more likely to think, "What am I expected to do next?" An individual Japanese is terribly sensitive to what others think or expect of him. This awareness of other people's opinions and expectations, this concern for "face," is the one major aspect of Japanese behavior.

Adjusting to its new position in the world economy, the Japanese have begun to try to "internationalize" themselves. That means different things to different people. To many, as determined in a poll, it means learning more about the United States, Europe and Australia rather than their Asian neighbors, and that requires fluency in English. One manager complained, however, that "I feel less Japanese as I become more fluent in English." The Ministry of International Trade and Industry and the Economic Planning Agency have outlined a broad series of steps to accomplish this broader perspective:

- The Ministry of Education has set guidelines for reforming the education system "to encourage development of an international perspective . . . and promote education in a way conducive to Japan's contribution to the international community."
- The ministry announced plans to increase to 1,000—four times the current number—the number of native English speakers hired to teach English in junior and senior high school next year and then triple that number within 10 years. The ministry also plans to increase the number of foreign students in Japan to 100,000 by the year 2000; there are now 15,000.
- Prefectural (state) governments, which once resisted foreign investments, are now trying to attract them.
- Even the Construction Ministry has gotten into the act, by announcing plans to modify more than 400,000 road signs throughout the country to help foreign drivers who cannot read Japanese.
- The business community is joining in, and large corporations are beginning to hire foreigners to work at their headquarters in Japan. "Internationalization training," aimed at changing the attitudes of Japanese employees, has been undertaken by department stores and trading and manufacturing firms. Even IBM Japan, a company that one would think would be international by definition, has such a program.
- Safety and product standards enforced by a variety of government ministries are being revised to bring them into line with international norms.[8]

To the Matsushita Electric Company, internationalization has meant a reexamination of the Japanese character. A team of middle-level executives polled workers and neighbors and produced an unusually frank list of the strong and weak points in ordinary Japanese:

*The strong points:* diligence, self-sacrifice, obedience, intelligence, love of country, etiquette and flexibility.

*The weak points:* exclusivity and insularity, one-dimensional, self-centered thinking, observing others before forming one's own opinion, lack of philosophy, making a fuss over small things, ability to act only in groups.[9]

*A Brief History.* Japan is known historically as the Land of the Rising Sun. Founded some 2,000 years ago, Japan's line of emperors has, according to tradition, continued to the present.

Japanese society was consolidated politically by the beginning of the fourth century. This ancient society was ruled by an imperial family and related nobility. From the twelfth to the nineteenth centuries, feudal lords or shoguns held political control. The emperor Hirohito reigned from 1926 until 1989; upon his death his son, Akihito, became emperor.

In 1895, the Japanese defeated China in a war fought over the right to rule Korea. Japan was also victorious in the Russo-Japanese War (ending in 1905), which led to widespread recognition as a world power. Involvement in World War I brought enhanced world influence and, at Versailles, Japan was one of the "big five." The postwar years brought great prosperity to a rapidly changing nation. Japan soon began to exercise considerable influence in Asia.

Manchuria and much of Asia were subsequently invaded in an attempt to create an Asian co-prosperity sphere, with Japan at its head. On December 7, 1941, Japan launched a successful attack on United States naval forces at Pearl Harbor. This enabled the Japanese military machine to encircle most of Southeast Asia. In 1943, the tide began to turn in favor of the allies. Complete collapse of the empire and surrender ensued. A military occupation by the United States lasted from 1945 to 1952. A new constitution was adopted in 1946 which renounced war and granted basic human rights.

*The Economy.* The labor force is divided this way: trade and services, 53 percent; manufacturing, mining and construction 33, agriculture, forestry and fishing 9, government 3, and unemployed, 2.68 percent. About 30 percent of the labor force is unionized.

Japan is one of the productive industrial nations in the world. The economy is the strongest in Asia. Japan has few natural resources. More than 65 percent of the land is forested. Arable land is intensively cultivated. Japan must import 30 percent of its food. Major agricultural products include rice, sugar, vegetables and fruits. Japan is the world's leading producer of fish and fourth in the production of eggs. Based on the promotion of manufacturing industries for the export market, Japan has achieved and maintained a very high rate of economic growth since 1945. This has been possible because of a reservoir of industrial leaders and technicians; an intelligent, industrious work force; high savings and investment rates; and an intensive promotion of industrial development and foreign trade. Japan is third in steel production.

Major industries include chemicals, electronics, iron and steel, machinery, motor vehicles, petrochemicals, shipbuilding and textiles.

Japanese management is quite different from that in most other countries. Recruiting by large companies is from among college graduates primarily and the new employee tends to stay with the same company for his whole career in what is usually called lifetime employment, although that is beginning to change. All employees move up the corporate ladder at about the same rate,

## Table 27. Japanese Management Trends of the 1990s

| Traditional Management | New Management |
|---|---|
| *Strategic Action* | *Strategic Action* |
| Operation-centered | Strategy-centered |
| Internal reserves | Use of external resources |
| Stress main lines of business | Diversification |
| Development research | Basic research |
| Efficiency-centered | Innovation-centered |
| *Organization* | *Organization* |
| Hierarchical pyramid | Horizontal division of labor |
| Power centralized | Power decentralized |
| Large head office | Small head office |
| Stable bureaucratic structure | Dynamic innovation structure |
| Bottom-up decision making | Top level decision making |
| Power in production department | Power in R&D department |
| *Systems/practices* | *Systems/practices* |
| Lifetime employment | No change |
| Seniority | Meritocracy |
| Total quality control | No change |
| Company labour union | *Raison d'etre* redefined |
| In-house education | No change |
| Welfare benefits | No change |
| *Human Resources* | *Human Resources* |
| Homogeneous talent | Heterogeneous talent |
| Collectivism/egalitarianism | Stress on individuality |
| Missionary-type leader | Revolutionary-type leader |
| *Behavior Mode* | *Behavior Mode* |
| Incremental | Entrepreneurial |

*(Source: Keizai Doyukai, as presented in "The Japanese Forge Ahead to Tackle Their World Problems," International Management, March 1987, p. 43.)*

based on seniority more than merit. Job rotation is common even to the point, in the early years, of college graduates working on the shop floor. Retirement is relatively early at 55 to 60 years of age, the retiree getting a lump sum payment in lieu of retirement benefits. Many of them, however, then begin to work for one of the company's subsidiaries. C. Itoh & Company attracted attention in 1987 by being the first Japanese company to appoint a foreigner — a Korean-American — to its board of directors. Table 27 shows how Japanese management is preparing for the changes and the challenges of the Information Age.

**Figure 38. Office arrangements like this at Nihon Chukuko Company, Ltd., of Tokyo allow easy interactions among all employees.**

Only highly placed Japanese executives have private offices. If the meeting takes place in a common office area, the visitor can discern his Japanese counterpart's status as follows: Senior managers sit near windows; junior personnel are crowded in the center. Figure 38 shows a typical office layout.

Quality-circle techniques, pioneered in Japan, have been adopted, in varying forms, all over the world. The quality circle is a work group which studies methods of improving anything about the company but primarily their own operations and then prepares both an oral and written presentation to management proposing changes.

*Organizational Communication.* Business cards are called *meishi.* They should be presented so that they can be read immediately by the recipient. The Japanese read from right to left and from top to bottom. A simple guide to facilitate correct presentation is to place the company logo or trademark in the top right corner of the Japanese side.

Communication is central to Japanese corporate life. Everyone does it constantly, from the chairman of the board to the rank and file. As one Japanese businessman said, "We could never achieve our high standards of quality or reach our current levels of productivity without good employee communication."[11]

The Japanese corporation collects and processes information more thoroughly than do companies in other countries. However, never is information gathering an end in itself. Vogel refers to it as "a group centered process closely linked to long-range organizational purposes, permitting an impressive range of information to be concentrated where and when the organization can best use it."[12] This access to information is undoubtedly one of the reasons Japan has become a great industrial power.

Communication, both formal and informal, moves in every conceivable direction in the Japanese company. The employee has a special need to know because of the collective form of decision making, according to Clark:

> Perhaps the best indication of a general awareness that decisions are made collectively is the very thorough dissemination of information that takes place in many Japanese companies. Dozens of documents seem to be in continuous circulation, so that company members know a great deal of what is going on, even if it scarcely concerns them. There are, of course, the *ringi,* the suggestions and proposals mentioned earlier, which usually start in one department and are passed to collateral departments to be seen by relatively junior managers before being shown to the directors. There are rules and directives in the name of the president, managing directors, or department heads. There are daily or weekly pep talks or discussion sessions, at which salesmen will be told of the operating ratios on the shop floor as well as the sales figures, and production line workers will be given details of the efforts being made to get new recruits. The effects of this generous flow of information are great and good. The knowledge that he is worth informing at all improves a man's morale, particularly if his prospects are limited and his self-esteem depends upon his giving the impression that he is always in the know. Understanding what is happening elsewhere in a company helps people to take a greater interest in their own work, which they can come to see as part of an estimable whole. And, of course, by distributing information so liberally, upper managements ensure that no one who really needs to know something is overlooked.[13]

Of pivotal importance in this system are middle managers, who, while considered to be the weak link in the communications of an American corporation, are largely responsible for the successful communication process within the Japanese company. Communication in the Japanese corporation, as with all others, starts with the first duties of the day. Japanese management makes it a chief goal to encourage the continual flow of information and communication between management and employees and among employees. Managers take an interest in each of their employees, and no message exchange takes place between them without some proof of that concern—an inquiry about family, health, hobbies and so on.

In a book designed to help foreign business persons succeed in Japan, the Japan External Trade Organization (JETRO) explains that communication in Japan is more than mere words:

> Communication is the most important and it's not a matter of a language barrier. You must establish understanding with the people you are dealing with, whether partners, staff or customers. For business to be done suc-

cessfully in Japan, you must know the social structure and hierarchical structure of the companies with whom you are dealing.[14]

The most important lesson a foreigner can learn about Japanese communication practices is that they frequently say "yes" when they mean "no." The story is told of Prime Minister Eisaku Sato who in 1969 visited Washington to appease angry feelings over a flood of Japanese textile products. President Richard M. Nixon said Japan had to exercise restraint in the area, to which Sato answered *Zensho shimasu* which the interpreter translated as "I'll do my best." What it really means is "No way." Nixon thought he had an agreement when in fact nothing was going to change.

"Japanese is a language that depends more on emotions and feelings," said Tatsuya Komatsu, president of Simul International, a translating service. "To be specific, to be concrete, is one of the weaknesses of the Japanese people." The Japanese believe they communicate without words in a system called *haragei* (belly language). Because of the country's cultural homogeneity, the Japanese say they convey intentions through penetrating stares, casual glances, occasional grunts and meaningful silences. Mr. Komatsu believes that foreigners are beyond such communication and that the younger Japanese generations are losing it.[15]

The emphasis in Japanese corporations is on personal, oral communication as opposed to written forms of communication. The formal communication system in the Japanese firm, diagrammed in Figure 39, is very similar to that in American corporations.

Literally dozens of documents are in continuous circulation to let employees know what is going on. For downward communication, there are print media: company magazines, newspapers and newsletters. There are also bulletin boards, called information boards in Japan, where they are used to communicate with employees much more extensively than they are in the United States.

Much more important to the Japanese corporation is upward communication. Meetings of all kinds are used to communicate information upward in the management chain. "Japan is today the land of meetings," Nakane observed, "and it is far from difficult to find a man who spends more time at meetings than at his desk. . . . Not only vital issues but those less pertinent are brought under consideration by a meeting."[16]

Meetings in Japan are longer and more frequent than in other countries because of the process of consensual decision making. They allow coordination of work by those on the same managerial level and communication between those on varying levels of the organization. "In the last analysis, they are the best known mechanism for efficient information sharing," state Pascale and Athos.[17]

The style of conducting meetings in the two countries differs, too. Americans invite open and honest confrontation at meetings. Japanese, as they are culturally trained to do, avoid open confrontation. Any subject likely to cause disagreement is discussed in advance of the meeting, and agreement is reached on a solution in a process called *nemawashii* — "binding the roots of a plant before pulling it out." During the meetings, then, everyone understands

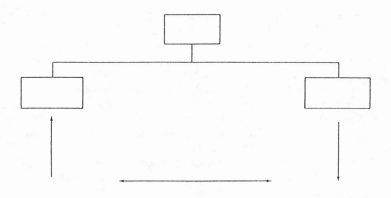

*Upward*

Written:
   memorandum
   report
   suggestion system
   *ringi*
   self-evaluation

Personal:
   personal contact
   meeting
   quality circle
   joint council
   *habatsu*
   interview
   open-door policy
   after-work socializing

Electronic:
   in-house broadcasting
   telex
   telefax

*Downward*

Print:
   newspaper/magazine
   bulletin board
   orientation manual
   letters
   manual
   handbook

Electronic:
   telephone

Personal:
   union activities

*Horizontal*

Personal:
   personal contact
   meeting
   *habatsu*

Written:
   memorandum
   *ringi*

Electronic:
   telephone
   telefax
   electronic mail

**Figure 39. The communication system of the Japanese corporation.**

how the issue will be settled, and no one disagrees or loses. In fact, the meeting can provide a formal approval of a decision reached during informal consultation.[18]

    When there is a problem to be settled at a meeting or alternative solutions to a problem, decisions are made through consensus. Each person at the meeting expresses his views for whatever length of time he wants. This process is known as *matamori*. Afterward, the leader of the group makes a decision based on the group's wishes, even when that is contrary to his own preference.

A requirement of the system is the sort of active listening that most Japanese can do and most Americans can't. Pascale and Athos say that Americans listen in an evaluative way, accepting or rejecting ideas presented, which leads to fatigue and listening shortcuts so that they actually absorb only about 30 percent of the message. The Japanese, the authors explain, practice "less-ego listening." "They hold 'principle' in abeyance, regard themselves as one among others in the situation, and thus achieve easy accommodation with the circumstances of the meeting.... This situational ethic enables the Japanese to air different views without falling into a duel of personalities."[19] This contrasts to the American push for a decision, which, as Pascale and Athos observe, "often prompts managers to choose prematurely, based on conceptual analysis and substantive merit, but without due regard for implementational feasibility."[20]

Another form of upward communication is a frequent survey of employee attitudes, usually administered by the personnel department and called by some the voluntary reporting system.[21] Annually and often more frequently, questionnaires are distributed to employees asking for their opinion on almost everything in their corporate lives, including satisfaction, office leadership, and personnel problems on the job, as well as much about their personal lives. The results become the basis for changes in the corporation and provide a profile of the morale of each office. It has been said that the system is needed because of the social distance between managers and employees.

The formal system of communication also includes letters, communications outside the company. Letter and memo writing and paperwork in general do not fit well into Japanese methods of corporate communication. Most business transactions take place through personal contact or over the telephone. International business is conducted by telex mainly. "Only the data in inquiries, estimates, offers, etc., are confirmed in writing, often in forms or form letters," state Saburo Haneda and Hirosuke Shima in an article in *The Journal of Business Communication*.[22] Letter writing in Japan is distinctive in its obligatory polite opening. Gibney explains:

> A reminder to pay a bill or an announcement that a new man has joined a bank's board of directors are equal occasions for the obligatory opening remarks about the rude necessity of imposing on one's time or the change of seasons. "Now that spring promises to come," the letter begins, "the first buds of the cherry blossoms can be descried climbing the far-off mountain. Although we hesitate to break in on your very busy schedule, troubled as you are with many worthy pursuits, it is time that necessity compels us to remind you that your firm's indebtedness...."[23]

The informal system of communication in the Japanese firm includes the grapevine, as it does in the American corporation; however, in Japan, the informal system is also comprised of *habatsu* or cliques.

**Table 28. Some Communication Practices in the Japanese Corporation**

The Japanese:

    1. Prefer oral to written communication.

    2. Expect an exchange of business cards, preferably printed in English and Japanese.

    3. Discuss a subject from every possible angle.

    4. Practice *haragei*—the art of the belly.

    5. Provide an "emotional massage."

    6. Frequently say "yes" but mean "no."

    7. Have a strong informal system of communication—the *habatsu*.

    8. Have a group-oriented system of decision making by consensus—*matamori, ringi* and *nemawashii.*

    9. Prefer compromise and conciliation to confrontation.

    10. Have a high-context culture.

    11. Use time polychronically.

Yoshino reports that because the traditional culture of Japan included no notions of the large organization, Japanese tended to feel uncomfortably isolated in them. In response, the Japanese created "narrow social groupings offering particularistic and emotional ties within the impersonal formal organization."[24]

Although a part of the informal system, *habatsu* are highly goal oriented—the major goal being to enhance their own power and influence in the organization. Membership in *habatsu* is not the result of random associations as it is in American informal groups. It is based on a specific common unchangeable tie, such as place of birth or school. Membership is also nonoverlapping, unlike the American system, which allows employees to belong to several informal groups. Members of a *habatsu* are drawn from various management levels, and the *habatsu* themselves are hierarchically organized.

*Habatsu* have their own highly effective network of communication. They can be very beneficial or deleterious to an organization's operations. They benefit by bypassing an occasional blockage in vertical communication. They also provide lateral communication with a high level of trust.[25]

On the other hand, their approval is required in extreme cases before a new policy can be implemented. Also, inter-*habatsu* rivalries develop; and the outcome may present a morale problem for those members of *habatsu* which are not dominant.

A favorite buzzword around Japanese businesses today is *kokusaika* (internationalism). Much as they may dislike the idea, they are moving into world markets and are having the usual intercultural communication problems. Ikuko Atsumi, founder of the New England Japanese Center in Stowe,

Massachusetts, said of Americans: "In this country, an employee is always thinking raise, raise, raise whenever he does something good for the company. For the Japanese management working in this country, this bothers them. In Japan, long-term recognition from above is enough."[26]

When the author toured the Nissan plant in Yokosuka City, Japan, in 1984, representatives of the Personnel Department explained how nonplussed they were when American women who are employed by their plants in the United States came to Japan for training. Not used to working closely with women, the Japanese explained how the women tried to assure them that they were to be treated "like one of the boys" in all of their relationships. The Japanese said they got over the uncomfortable feelings about the association.

Table 28 lists some communication practices in the Japanese firm.

## CASE STUDY: MAZDA MOTOR CORPORATION

Based in Hiroshima, Mazda started making automobiles in 1931 and has since then manufactured in excess of 17 million vehicles. Mazda products are now delivered to 120 countries. Now the third largest car manufacturer in Japan and the tenth largest in the world, Mazda employs 27,600 employees. On September 5, 1985, Mazda issued a press release with the headline: "Mazda Has Started to Introduce an International Communication System Between the United States and Japan":

Mazda Motor Corporation has started to construct an integrated communication system between its head office in Hiroshima, Mazda (North American), Inc., in Irvine, California, and the new manufacturing plant in Flat Rock, Michigan. This system has been developed to cope with the increase of information mainly caused by the new U.S. plant under construction, and to realize an efficient information transfer between the three places. This system connects the three places by both undersea cable and satellite. Therefore, there is always an alternate way in the event of line failure. With this network system positioned as a backbone of the "Mazda Network System," the company intends to expand the network to Europe and other parts of the world in the future.

The main features of this system are as follows:

1. By the adoption of the "Time Division Multiplexing System," three ways of communication—data transfer (computer data-base exchange), image transfer (facsimile), and voice transfer (telephone) are possible utilizing a single leased line.

2. As the data transfer by this system is done through the same architecture that is used for Mazda's current computer network, this system has access to Mazda's existing domestic marketing and manufacturing network.

3. The document (image) transfer by this system facilitates "electronic mailing." By using special terminals and personal computers at the three places, high-quality image transfer, confidential transfer, simultaneous transfer, reception confirmation or other electronic mailing functions can be carried out.

4. In the area of voice communication, simultaneous multiple phone calls

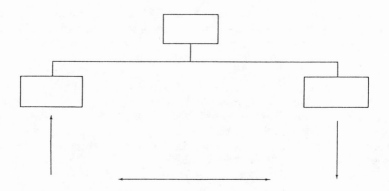

| Upward | Downward |
|---|---|
| Written:<br>  memorandum<br>  report<br>  suggestion system<br>  question box<br>  newspaper/magazine<br>  bulletin board<br>  letters | Print:<br>  newspaper/magazine<br>  bulletin board<br>  orientation manual<br>  letters<br>  pay envelope insert<br>  manual<br>  handbook |
| Personal:<br>  meeting<br>  interview<br>  open-door policy | Electronic:<br>  telephone<br>  film<br>  video<br>  electronic mail<br>  in-house broadcasting<br>  telex<br>  facsimile |
| Electronic:<br>  in-house broadcasting<br>  telephone<br>  film<br>  video<br>  electronic mail | |

*Horizontal*

| Personal:<br>  personal contact<br>  meeting | Written:<br>  memorandum<br>  bulletin board<br>    letters<br>    manual | Electronic:<br>  telephone<br>  electronic mail<br>  facsimile |
|---|---|---|

**Figure 40. Communication in Mazda Motor Corporation, Hiroshima, Japan.**

between the three places become possible by the adoption of the most-advanced digitizing technology.

Bunzo Suzuki, Senior Manager, International Public Relations, told the author in a letter that this international communication system has now been expanded to include Mazda's head office in Europe and its Parts Center in Brussels, Belgium. He reports that Mazda does not have a written communication policy, but that managers may use any of the methods for communicating to employees shown on Figure 40. "We have a fairly comprehensive in-house monthly magazine," Suzuki reports, "called *My Mazda* that reports on not only the progress and management policy of our company, but also gives lots of other information to keep every member of the company updated on various aspects of the company operations."

Suzuki continues: "Nonverbal communication such as a gesture is often used in our daily business operations, especially in noisy areas such as plants where we have a system of hand signals to communicate and give instructions, etc. Also Mazda members have a strong feeling of working together in harmony for commonly held goals. One result of this feeling of being 'in tune' with one another could be said to be that people understand each other at a deep level without always having to express their meaning in words."

Asked how the company would if it could improve its communication program, Suzuki stated: "As time goes by, new communication systems using sophisticated computers will be introduced into the market one after the other. We feel it to be necessary to update the computer systems we are currently using. From the standpoint of human communication, however, we should improve our ability to express our personally held opinions, an ability that is said to be a weak point of Japanese workers."

## Malaysia

*Official Name:* Malaysia; *Capital:* Kuala Lumpur; *Government:* constitutional monarchy; *Subdivisions:* 13 states; *Population:* 16,068,516 (July 1987); *Density:* 122 per square mile; *Currency:* ringgit; *Official Language:* Malay; *Literacy:* 69 percent.

*The Land.* Malaysia is a federation of 13 states that lies in the heart of Southeast Asia. The country has two different and distinct land regions: Peninsular Malaysia, about the size of Alabama, and the states of Sabah and Sarawak, about the size of Louisiana, located in the northwest region of the island of Borneo, about 400 miles east of Peninsular Malaysia across the South China Sea. Peninsular Malaysia lies at the southern tip of the Asian mainland and is bounded by Thailand in the north and linked by a causeway to Singapore in the south. Together, the land area is slightly larger than New Mexico. About 90 percent of the land is covered with dense forests. The country lies just north of the equator and has a coastline of 1,200 miles.

Peninsular Malaysia has long, narrow, steep mountain ranges in the center, coastal plains on the east and west; Sabah and Sarawak have flat coastal plains rising to mountainous mass in the center. About 70 percent of the country is covered by tropical rain forest. About 26 percent of the land is forest reserve; 20 is cultivated; and 54 percent is other. The mean monthly temperature throughout Malaysia is 80° F.

*The People.* The people of Malaysia are racially diverse and have many different cultural backgrounds. The Malays and other indigenous people (Bumiputras) are the largest ethnic group and comprise about 50 percent of the population. They are mainly rice farmers, civil servants or fishermen. About 36 percent of the population are Chinese; 10 percent are Indian; and 4 percent are other. Ties between these groups have developed through educational, social, sports and cultural organizations. The Malays are mostly Moslem, living in rural areas. Many people believe in animism and business activities will be affected by folk beliefs and customs. The Chinese are predominantly Buddhists; and the Indians are predominantly Hindu. The Chinese live mostly in the Malaysian tin and rubber belt (peninsular Malaysia). They also live mostly in urban areas and predominate in business. About 45 percent of the people are under 15 years of age.

A person's ancestral background is important to social status and future opportunities. Many people believe that success and opportunities are the result of fate which affects their attitudes toward work.

Traditionally the family system has been the most important social unit in Malaysia. It is common for two, three or more generations to live together in the same house. Cooperation, loyalty and unity are important in the family.

About 85 percent of the population speak Malay, the national language. English is used widely in government and business.

*A Brief History.* Indian traders brought Islam to Malaysia in the thirteenth century; today it is the national religion. Portuguese traders first arrived on the Malay peninsula in 1511. Britain first became interested in the area in 1786 when the British East India Company leased the island of Penang. By the early 1900s, Britain controlled all the Malay states as colonies or protectorates. In 1946, Penang and Malacca were united with nine Malay states and became the Federation of Malaya in 1948. In the same year, communist insurrections erupted and guerrilla terrorism spread throughout the countryside until it was finally quelled in 1959. On August 31, 1957, Malaysia was granted independence from Britain. Six years later, the Federation of Malaya and the former British colonies of Singapore, Sarawak and North Borneo (Sabah) united to become Malaysia in order to avoid a communist takeover in Singapore. However, tension mounted between the Malay-dominated government in Malaya and the Chinese-dominated government in Singapore, culminating in the creation of an independent Singapore in 1965.

*The Economy.* The labor force is divided this way: agriculture, trade, hotels and restaurants, 34.5 percent; manufacturing 15.6, government 14.9, construction 6.6, finance 5, transport and communications 4.9, mining 1.6, utilities 1.2, and unemployed, 7.6 percent. About 10 percent is unionized.

A free-market economy in which the private sector is dominant, Malaysia has one of the highest per capita incomes in Southeast Asia. About 42 percent of the people are employed in agriculture and about 32 percent in industry. Malaysia is one of the world's largest producers of rubber and exports large amounts around the world. Other major agricultural products include oil palm, rice, coconuts, timber and pepper. Industrially, Malaysia ranks as the world's largest producer of tin. Also, rubber and oil palm processing and

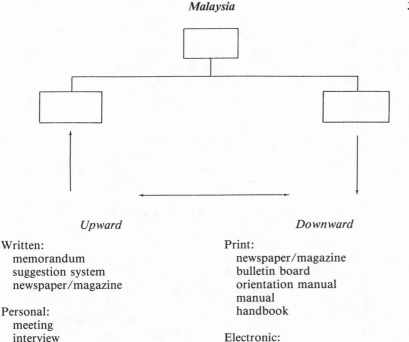

Figure 41. The communication system of Malaysian Airlines System, Kuala Lumpur, Malaysia.

manufacturing, electronics, logging and timber processing, and petroleum are important industries in the Malaysian economy. Malaysia has the third highest energy production growth rate in the world.

Major industries include electronics, fertilizers, petroleum processing, rubber, textiles and wood products. The Malaysian-made automobile, Proton Saga, produced by Perusahaan Otomobil Nasional, entered the U.S. market in 1988 at a price of $5,000 to $8,000. Most of the parts are shipped from Mitsubishi in Japan for assembly in Malaysia.

Malaysian management with whom the foreign visitor will be dealing is mainly Chinese. Much of what is covered for Hong Kong and Taiwan with regard to business associations thus also applies here.

*Organizational Communication.* Appointments should be made well in advance of a visit, and an introduction is best arranged beforehand. Send proposals beforehand to give the hosts a chance to review them. Someone 50 years of age or older should lead a delegation to Malaysia and they should show deference to persons they meet who are older than they are. The Malays are punctilious.

Men shake hands; close friends grasp with both hands. Business cards are exchanged immediately; the visitor's may be in English. Expect to provide a lot of information. Entertaining is an important part of business; follow important meetings with a dinner or lunch, and invite a number of people from the organization. Status is important.

### CASE STUDY: MALAYSIAN AIRLINE SYSTEM

The original Malayan Airways Ltd. was registered as a company in 1937, but it began flying operations in 1947. In 1963 the airline was renamed Malaysian Airways Ltd. when the Federation of Malaysia was formed and in 1965 Borneo Airways Ltd. was absorbed. The name was chosen because the acronym MAS in Bahasa-Malaysian means "gold," to symbolize the high quality service the airline must strive to achieve in all areas of its operations. One of the corporate objectives listed in the employee handbook that the company sent to the author is: "To contribute meaningfully to national aspirations and foster an organization which is in harmony with the multi-racial objectives of Malaysia." One of its goals in employee relations, stated in the same handbook, is: "To furnish each employee with adequate knowledge of the Company and what it is doing." The means that the company uses to accomplish that are shown in Figure 41.

# The Philippines

*Official Name:* Republic of the Philippines; *Capital:* Manila; *Government:* republic; *Subdivisions:* 72 provinces; *Population:* 61,524,761 (July 1987); *Density:* 471.9 per square mile; *Currency:* peso; *Official Languages:* Filipino (based on Tagalog) and English; *Literacy:* 88 percent.

*The Land.* The Philippines is comprised of some 7,100 islands; the 11 largest comprise about 95 percent of the total land area and population. Only 154 of the islands have areas of more than five square miles; only 700 are inhabited. The total land area is about equal to Arizona. The archipelago extends 1,100 miles north to south along the southeastern rim of Asia between Taiwan and Indonesia, forming a land chain between the Pacific Ocean on the east and the South China Sea on the west and separated from Vietnam and the People's Republic of China on the west by the south China Sea. The coastline, marked by bays, straits and inland seas, stretches for 10,000 miles twice the length of the U.S. coastline. About 53 percent of the land is covered with forests and mountains, 30 percent is arable; 5 percent is pasture; and 12 percent is other.

The islands offer great contrasts in terrain and climate. The rugged mountains of northern Luzon break down to form the tropical Central Plain, a comparatively dry and low northwestern coastal strip, and the Cagayan River Valley. The Visayan group includes islands with dense jungle, others with treeless, razor-backed ridges and rich, sugar-growing coastal plains.

*The People.* The people of the Philippines are predominantly of Malayan descent. Some 1.5 percent of the population are Chinese who have played an important part in commerce since the ninth century. Negritos, a short, dark-skinned people, inhabit the uplands of the islands around the Sulu Sea.

The Philippines is the only country in the Orient where Catholicism is the majority religion—about 83 percent of the population. Some 9 percent are Protestant; 5 percent, Muslim; and 3 percent, Buddhist or other.

Filipinos have been influenced by the Chinese, Malayan, Moslem, Spanish and American cultures. Sensitivity is considered an important character trait to Filipinos. Individualism is less important than loyalty to one's family, relatives and friends. Interdependence is more important than independence. A Filipino may even consider frankness and outspokenness to be rude and uncultured. Bringing shame to an individual reflects on his family and is avoided at all costs. Innovation, change and competition are often looked upon as gambles because failure would bring shame or upset the balance of social relationships. Fatalism is a common attitude toward life, characterized by the typical expression *Bahala na,* which roughly translated means "Accept what comes and bear it with hope and patience." Success may also be attributed to fate rather than effort.

The Philippines contains 55 ethnic groups, each with its own distinctive dialect, customs and traditions. The three major dialects are Ilocana (northern Luzon), Tagalog (central and southern Luzon) and Cebuano (southern islands). English has been and continues to be the unifying language, written and spoken. Table 29 compares the American and Filipino.

*A Brief History.* The history of the Philippines falls into four periods: the pre–Spanish period, the Spanish period (1521 to 1898), the American period (1898 to 1946), and the years since independence (1946 to present).

The first people to inhabit the Philippine Islands, the Negritos, are believed to have come from Borneo and Sumatra. Subsequently, people of Malay stock came from the south and settled in scattered communities. In the fourteenth century, Arabs arrived and introduced Islam.

The first Western contact made in the Philippines was made by Magellan in 1521, who claimed the area in the name of the king of Spain. China, Japan and other groups tried unsuccessfully to take over the Philippines, but Spain maintained its control for nearly 400 years. Jose Rizal, writer and patriot, helped inspire a revolt against Spain that began in 1896. War was declared between Spain and the United States in 1898, which resulted in Spain turning the islands over to the U.S. the following year. Internal strife continued until 1901, when American control formally began. In 1935, the Philippines became a self-governing Commonwealth. The Japanese invaded in 1941, and the Philippines

## Table 29. Comparison of Americans and Filipinos

| Americans | Filipinos |
|---|---|
| Encourage autonomy | Encourage dependence |
| See a dichotomy in work and play | Combine work and social life |
| Confront others face-to-face | Confront others through an intermediary |
| Stress the future | Stress the present and the past and live day-to-day |
| Perceive selves as individual human beings | Perceive selves in the context of the family |
| See human beings as evil but capable of change | See human beings as evil and beyond help |
| Believe time moves quickly | Believe time moves slowly |
| Stress measurement and concreteness | Stress qualitative feeling |
| Feel fulfilled from personal achievement | Feel fulfilled from smooth interpersonal relationships |
| Believe anything is possible | Feel life is determined by fate |
| Are informal and direct | Are formal and indirect |
| Divide duties among group members | Vest all duties in the leader |
| Make decisions as individuals | Allow authorities to make decisions |
| Value action and achievement | Emphasize "taking it easy" |

*(Source: Adapted from Edward C. Stewart,* American Cultural Patterns: A Cross Cultural Perspective, *"Dimensions of International Education," No. 3, The Regional Council for International Education, April 1971, as presented in Prosser,* The Cultural Dialogue: An Introduction to Intercultural Communication, *pp. 188–91.)*

fell under their control until the end of World War II. On July 4, 1946, the Philippines became an independent republic. In 1977, President Ferdinand Marcos declared the Philippines to be under martial law, and ruled by decree until 1986 when he was removed from power. In a peaceful transition of power, Corazon C. Aquino became the country's first woman president.

*The Economy.* The labor force is divided this way: agriculture, 47 percent; industry and commerce 20, services 13.5, government 10, other areas 9.5, and unemployed, 6.1 percent.

The Philippines has a free-market economy dominated by the private sector. Though the economy is still based on agriculture, lumber and fishing, the percentage of people employed in industry has climbed to nearly 50 percent in the past few years. The main agricultural products are sugar, rice, corn, coconut, bananas, abaca and tobacco. The Philippines is also a major world producer of minerals, including gold and copper. In the late 1980s, offshore oil exploration discovered some modest petroleum deposits.

Major industries include electronics, food processing, footwear, motor vehicle assembly, petroleum refining, pulp and paper manufacturing, textiles, tobacco, and wood processing.

The average Filipino businessman has evolved from the small, one-owner type business of pre–World War II days. He has grown with the company and been trained in-house.

*Organizational Communication.* Appointments should be made well in advance and kept punctually. If your company is not a well-known one, bring letters of introduction. Filipinos like to exchange business cards; it is acceptable for them to be printed only in English.

Business follows a period of small talk to give the hosts a chance to know the visitors. Toward the end, Filipinos don't hesitate to ask questions about family and background that may seem too personal to Americans. Visitors should appreciate Filipino hospitality and not let business judgment be misled by Filipino helpfulness.

A suit and tie are the appropriate dress for business, but afterwards dress is more casual than it is in the United States. A long-sleeved "Barong Tagalog," the national dress shirt, and black trousers are suitable for even the most formal occasions.

The Filipino businessman is proud and sensitive; he does not want to offend or to be offended. The slightest reluctance from your Philippine associates regarding work should be handled carefully. The message is slow down or wait, but he does not want to offend by saying so. Confrontations that in the United States are handled face-to-face in the Philippines are worked through intermediaries. With time you may get what you requested and your Filipino friend will still have kept face. Diplomacy is the keynote. Know when to back off, and always leave your friend an out.

Associates are extremely sensitive to and conscious of making a mistake, thus presenting problems in obtaining true opinions and feelings in matters of mutual concern.

## CASE STUDY: ATLANTIC, GULF AND PACIFIC COMPANY OF MANILA, INC.

An American, John G. McMahon, founded the company in 1900, when the Americans colonized the Philippines. McMahon set out to engage in public work projects that would serve as foundations for the economic and social development of the country. They developed and prospered until World War II when many of its facilities were destroyed. Reconstruction of the country meant new life and business for the company. Of the varied contributions that the company has made to the country's industrialization, the most significant were the design, fabrication and erection of structural steel for hundreds of industrial and commercial buildings as well as tanks of all kinds, towers and smokestacks. In 1970, a Filipino holding company took control of the company, and Roberto T. Villaneuva became the first Filipino chairman and chief executive officer. The company today is the largest of its kind in the Philip-

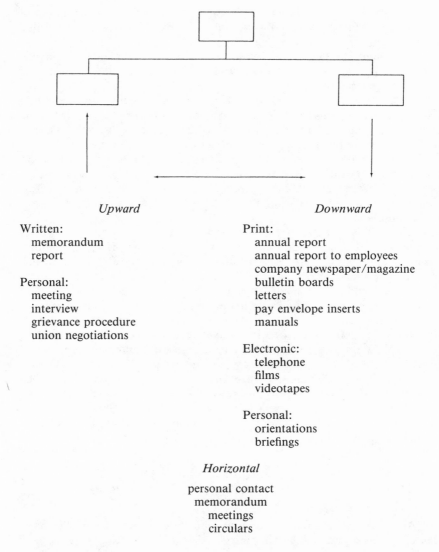

| *Upward* | *Downward* |
|---|---|

Written:
  memorandum
  report

Personal:
  meeting
  interview
  grievance procedure
  union negotiations

Print:
  annual report
  annual report to employees
  company newspaper/magazine
  bulletin boards
  letters
  pay envelope inserts
  manuals

Electronic:
  telephone
  films
  videotapes

Personal:
  orientations
  briefings

*Horizontal*

personal contact
memorandum
meetings
circulars

**Figure 42. The communication system of Atlantic, Gulf and Pacific Company of Manila, Inc.**

pines, doing business in ten countries. It employs 205 staff members, 475 managers, 1,836 regular employees and 6,989 project workers.

Part of the company's creed states its attitude toward these workers: "To treat our fellow workers with fairness and dignity, rewarding merit and hard work, and to afford them opportunities to develop their talent, skills and personalities...." Figure 42 presents the company's communication system.

# Singapore

*Official Name:* Republic of Singapore; *Capital:* Singapore; *Government:* republic; *Subdivisions:* none; *Population:* 2,616,236 (July 1987); *Density:* 11,466 per square mile; *Currency:* dollar; *Official Languages:* Malay, Chinese, Tamil and English; *Literacy:* 84.2 percent.

*The Land.* Lying at the southern extremity of Asia and separated from Malaysia by the Strait of Johore, Singapore consists of a main island and 57 smaller ones within its territorial waters. About 20 of the islands are inhabited.

The diamond-shaped main island is 26 miles at the broadest point from east to west and 14 miles from north to south. Most of it is flat lowland that formerly was swamp and jungle. Now it is urbanized and industrialized. It lies 85 miles north of the equator, at a narrow point of the Strait of Malacca off the southern tip of the Malay Peninsula to which it is linked by a causeway carrying a road, railway and a water pipeline. Singapore's topography is generally flat and low lying. Originally the island consisted of jungle, 85 percent of which has been cleared. Land-fill operations are enlarging the island by several feet per week. Singapore is about the size of the city of Chicago. Its total coastline is 120 miles. It is separated from Indonesia by the Strait of Malacca and Singapore Strait, among the busiest sea passages in the world. Singapore's climate is characterized by high temperatures and humidity and copious rainfall, even though there are no pronounced wet or dry seasons.

About 31 percent of the land is built on, roads, railroads or airfields; 22 percent is agriculture; and 47 percent is other.

*The People.* Singapore is the second most densely populated country in the world, after Hong Kong. Singapore is a multiracial, multilingual, culturally varied, secular state with complete tolerance toward all religions. It is predominantly (76 percent) Chinese, with 15 percent Malays, 7 percent Indians and 2 percent others. From the four official languages, English is the language of business. All of the people live in urban areas.

Lee Kuan Yew, prime minister of Singapore, said the toughest job in making Singapore a nation was building a common language. The city-state which got limited self-rule in 1959, joined the ill-fated federation of Malaysia in 1963 and became independent by itself two years later. "People wanted to keep their own languages," he said. "We speak at least five major languages. If you include the dialects, there will be about 20. So I had to knock a lot of heads to keep the language chauvinists in check." Though parents were given some choice, children will learn English in school "so that across the races, we will use English."[27]

The majority of Chinese are Buddhist or atheist; Malays are almost all Muslim; minorities of Christian, Hindus, Sikhs, Taoists and Confucianists also live here. The government aims to provide at least 10 years of education for every child. Although the overall literacy rate is 84 percent, for persons under 35 years of age it exceeds 90 percent.

"Face" is still important. There is some hostility between Malays and

Chinese. The society is very disciplined, with penalties for minor offenses (such as littering or jaywalking) or antisocial behavior (wearing hair too long or chewing gum). In some ways the past seems to do battle with the present and the future; business persons are seen, for example, to use the abacus to check on the results of a calculator.

*A Brief History.* Strategically located on the western edge of the Pacific Ocean, Singapore was a thriving port (Temasek) in the great fourteenth century Buddhist empire that ruled the area. It was notorious as a hideout for pirates until it came under British rule in 1824. Modern Singapore was founded in 1819 by Sir Stamford Raffles as a trading post for the East India Company. In 1867, the Straits Settlements of Singapore, Penang and Malacca became a separate crown colony of the United Kingdom. In 1945, after three years of Japanese occupation, a British Military Administration was established, but civil administration was restored in 1946 and Singapore became a Crown colony. In 1959, Singapore became an internally self-governing state with a fully elected government. In 1963, Singapore joined Malaya as one of the constituent states of a new Federation of Malaya, with virtual freedom from colonial rule. However, on August 9, 1965, Singapore again separated from Malaysia by mutual agreement and became a republic with a president at its head. With independence in 1965, Singapore assumed full sovereignty over its territory and full political, administrative and financial responsibility for public affairs.

*The Economy.* The labor force is divided this way: services, 30.2 percent; manufacturing 25.5, trade 23.5, transport and communication 10.1, construction 8.9, agriculture and fishing 0.7, and unemployed, 6.5 percent. About 17.5 percent of the labor force is unionized.

Singapore has a free-market economy in which the private sector is predominant. Although the smallest nation in Southeast Asia, Singapore has one of the most prosperous economies and offers the second highest standard of living in Asia, after Japan. It is rated politically and economically as safe as Switzerland. Singaporeans profit from a sharp sense of national purpose and entrepreneurial dynamism. Many Western business practices have been adopted but the Chinese ways predominate.

A 1986 survey of world markets by the Business Environment Risk Information (BERI) group rated Singapore's labor force the world's most productive for the fifth consecutive year, followed by those of Switzerland, Taiwan, Japan, South Korea and the Netherlands.[28]

Commerce is the foundation of the economy. Singapore is the fourth largest port in the world and has the fourth largest trade volume per capita. It imported more in 1986 than Hong Kong, Australia, Sweden, China and Taiwan, according to a study by the General Agreement on Tariffs and Trade. Much of the country's trade consists of receiving exports from other countries and then reexporting them. Petroleum refining is the largest industry in Singapore and the city has become the hub of petroleum exploration efforts in Southeast Asia. In recent years, the city has also become a financial and banking center for the region. Tourism also ranks high. Other industries include rubber production, electronics, and oil drilling equipment production.

Major industries include cigarettes, electronics, engineering, food and beverages processing, motor vehicles, petroleum refining and ship building and repairing.

*Organizational Communication.* Always be punctual. Business is generally straightforward. You can be very direct in money matters. Shake hands when meeting or leaving. Business cards are essential.

## CASE STUDY: FAR EASTERN LEVINGSTON SHIPBUILDING LTD.

Since 1967, the company has manufactured and fabricated a diversified range of products for local and overseas clients. As a heavy engineering contractor, the company has engaged in projects of steel fabrication, pressure vessel and boiler works, process piping, electrical and mechanical installations, instrumentations and controls.

Although the company has a communication policy, it is not written down. Choo Chiau Beng, managing director of the company, said this about communication in a letter responding to my survey:

> One of our most important means of communication is face-to-face communication on a one-to-one basis, at senior management weekly meetings, bi-monthly group meetings, project meetings, regular meetings with union officials and workers' representatives, work excellence committee meetings, Singapore national day address by the Managing Director, annual dinner and other social functions.
>
> Management adopts an open-door policy that any employee can have a personal interview with any manager including the Managing Director. There is a system of work excellence committees in which employees can bring forward suggestions about work. There is a grievance procedure through which employees can voice their grievances through it and through the Company house union to management.
>
> In communicating with one another, employees have the following means:
>
> 1. Personal contact in which all operations and administrative departments are under one roof which enables easier access;
>
> 2. There is a common lunch hour for all employees. Employees can therefore intermingle at the employees' canteen;
>
> 3. Through memoranda, one officer can also communicate with another but we discourage such communication as we feel a more personal contact is likely to be more effective and faster;
>
> 4. Work excellence committee meetings enable employees in different sections to discuss common problems; and
>
> 5. We also have a recreation club and cooperative society and through their activities employees socialize and foster team spirit.

An employee interviewed in the company magazine, *Feloship,* said this about communication, among other things:

> *Feloship:* How do you feel about the people in FELS?
>
> *Kian Guan* (Payroll Assistant): Ever since I joined the company 19 years ago, I have enjoyed the friendliness of colleagues and friends. I like the atmosphere and the environment here.

*Feloship:* How do you see our new office environment compared to the old one?

*Kian Guan:* It is certainly a cleaner environment to work. With all the departments under one roof, it is easier to coordinate our work. Communication has improved so we are more efficient.

*Feloship:* Do you find the present office management system more effective compared with the past?

*Kian Guan:* Yes, of course. This is especially true in certain areas where we are now fully computerized. In the past I had to count the monies manually every time I made a payment. Now with the computerization such inconveniences have been removed. It has made my job more pleasant.

## CASE STUDY: SINGAPORE AIRLINES

The Company completed 40 years in May 1987. Singapore is the progeny of Malaysia-Singapore Airlines which was jointly owned by the governments of Singapore and Malaysia. In 1972, Malaysia-Singapore Airlines separated into two entities, Malaysian Airlines System (MAS) and Singapore Airlines. From its beginnings with only 15 aircraft, the company has become one of the biggest in the world, ranked 14th in passenger miles and 12th in air freight. From links to 22 cities it has grown to cover 47 cities in 33 countries.

The company provided me this information about its communication program in response to my survey:

**Employee Communications Brief**

*I. Organizational Structure.*

The department, which was established in April 1983, has a staff strength of 17.

*II. What Is Employee Communications?*

Employee communications is the formal and informal process of sharing and interpreting business related information so that employees can make informed evaluations of issues and problems which can affect their jobs.

In using the term "employee communications," we do not differentiate between managers and general staff. All employees — regardless of their jobs — have the same basic need and desire for reliable communication which gives them a feeling that they are part of SIA and not merely faceless workers in the Company.

*III. The Role of the Department.*

The basic role of the Employee Communications Department is to provide the expertise and administrative services needed to develop and maintain channels through which management messages can be transmitted downward and through which employees' views can be sent upward to management.

Whilst the administrative responsibility for employee communication is delegated to the manager, Employee Communications, it is understood that the prime responsibility rests at departmental level.

*IV. Objectives.*

The employee communications objectives for SIA are:

1. To provide management with feedback on employee attitudes; and

2. To broaden the employee's job perspective, to create a "feeling of belonging," to integrate the employee with company purposes, to improve understanding of company policies.

*V. Communication Channels.*

An effective employee communications program requires a balanced use of written, oral and visual techniques. Most of the formal employee communications are in writing because this is a reliable way of reaching large groups of employees with a uniform message in a timely manner. However, oral communication must be a key ingredient in any communications program. Circumstances or the nature of the subject dictates the media or channels to be used.

1. Written Communication: (a) *Outlook,* the monthly publication for all employees (see Appendix I); (b) Divisional/regional publications; (c) Management briefs; (d) Management newsletters; (e) Let's Hear It; (f) Employee bulletins; (g) Notice boards; (h) Employee handbooks; (i) Management letters to employees.

2. Oral Communications: (a) Six-monthly business meetings; (b) Mini-business meetings—divisional level; (c) Staff meetings (frequency differs from division to division); (d) Senior staff get-togethers; (e) Weekly debriefings; (f) Lunches for AOs and senior managers.

3. Upward Communication: Upward communication occurs best when there are both formal and informal procedures for transmitting employee viewpoints, ideas and concerns. Effective use of it can head off potentially explosive issues by bringing problems to management's attention before a major confrontation occurs: (a) Staff ideas in action scheme; (b) Union meetings; (c) Exit interviews; (d) Staff appraisals; (e) Quality control circles/Worker's consultative committees.

*VI. Other Channels of Communication.*

There are other channels which can be used from time to time. These are posters, films, video, PA system, open house, exhibitions, retirement ceremony, long service awards ceremony, honesty awards scheme, community chest drive, and messages in payslips.

*Appendix I—Outlook*

*Outlook,* a 24-page monthly publication, is the anchor in-house newspaper which is circulated free of charge to all staff of SIA, including all our overseas stations, and shareholders. *Outlook* has one editor, two assistant editors, one senior editorial assistant and one editorial assistant. Clerical and administrative support for the section is provided by two secretaries and staff from Employee Communications. The aims of *Outlook* are:

i. To be the official source of information on the Company to all employees of the Group in Singapore and overseas. The newspaper attempts to pass on meaningful information on the operations, plans and progress made by the Company and the work of all employees with the aim of creating greater cohesion and esprit-de-corps.

ii. Outlook provides a channel of communication that links the divisions, overseas stations and the subsidiaries by keeping the employees updated on the activities and goings-on in the Company worldwide.

iii. To highlight employees and their achievements by featuring acts of courtesy, honesty and loyalty. Similarly, capturing staff on camera at a sports meet, carnival or during a voluntary visit to an old folk's home is one of the simplest yet highest form of recognition the Company can accord to its employees.
iv. To entertain staff with light articles, cartoons and photographs.
v. To provide an avenue for employee participation and creativity by welcoming contributions such as stories, articles and poems.

---

# South Korea

*Official Name:* Republic of Korea; *Capital:* Seoul; *Government:* republic; *Subdivisions:* 9 provinces; *Population:* 41,986,669 (July 1987); *Density:* 1,081.9 per square mile; *Currency:* won; *Official Language:* Korean; *Literacy:* 90 percent.

*The Land.* The name "Korea" means "high" (ko) and "clear" (ryu), giving one an idea of the country's basic beauty of towering mountains, light blue skies and clear, fast-running streams.

South Korea occupies the southern half of the mountainous peninsula that is about 600 miles long and 135 miles wide, projecting southeast from China and separating the Sea of Japan from the Yellow Sea. Its coastline is 819 miles long. Korea is slightly larger than Indiana; South Korea is about 45 percent of the whole. It is bordered by North Korea in the north and is only 123 miles from Japan to the east at the closest point. Nearly 70 percent of the land is covered by forests; only 23 percent of the land is arable. The predominantly mountainous peninsula of Korea is actually an extension of the mountains of southern Manchuria, from which it is separated by the Yalu and Tumen rivers. The spine of the mountains runs from northeast to southwest but remains close to the eastern coastline of Korea—east Korea is rugged, containing many scenic mountain peaks. The western coastal region contains most of the peninsula's level plains, interspersed with frequent rivers.

*The People.* Although there is a small Chinese minority, South Korea (along with North Korea) is the most ethnically and linguistically homogeneous country in the world. About 57 percent of the people live in urban areas. The population is almost wholly of Korean origin with no evidence of non–Mongoloid mixture.

Korea is known as the Land of the Morning Calm. Social stratification has been the rule for many centuries in Korea, making proper social relationships extremely important. Compliments are graciously denied. Success depends greatly on social contacts. Friendships are highly valued, and harmony in social interaction is important. Open criticism, abruptness and public disagreement are avoided because Koreans feel that no one has the right to upset the feelings or tarnish the self-esteem of another. It is usually considered much better to quietly accept an injustice to preserve the harmony than to assert one's individual rights. Koreans are proud of their country's cultural and economic achievements, which include the world's first movable metal-type printing, the first ironclad warship and the rain gauge.

The family is the foundation of society and is bound together by a strong sense of duty and obligation among its members. Koreans have about 200 surnames, but three of them—Lee, Park and Kim—are most common; in fact about half the population carries one of them. The surname comes first. The second name is that of a generation, shared by brothers, sisters and cousins. Last is the given or personal name.[29] When they marry, women do not change their names.

Korean culture, although distinct from that of Japan, resembles it in many respects. The people have the same ethnic heritage and have been exposed to repeated Chinese influences over many centuries.

*A Brief History.* First unified in the seventh century, Korea was a semi-independent state associated with China until the late nineteenth century. Silla kings united three warring tribes in A.D. 668. A new kingdom, Koryo, ruled the Korean peninsula from 935 to 1392, and from 1392 the Yi dynasty ruled. From 1637, Korea was a dynamic kingdom paying tribute to the Mongol rulers of China. In 1876, it was forced to open its ports to outside trade by Japan, ending a long period of isolation. In 1895, China and Japan fought a war on the peninsula. Ten years later, Russia's attempt to acquire Korea as a colony was halted by the Japanese. And in 1910, Korea was formally annexed by Japan as a colony, bringing an end to the 518-year reign of the Yi dynasty—one of the longest reigns in history.

At the end of World War II, Korea was liberated from Japan, but the Soviet Union entered the northern part of Korea and the United States entered the south. The two main powers agreed on an administrative division along the 38th parallel, and a separate pro–Western government was established in the south. In June of 1950 the North Korean army invaded the south, triggering a three-year war. The United States and United Nations supported the south and China backed the north. In July 1953, a cease fire was achieved. President Syngman Rhee resigned in 1960 under charges of election-rigging and political corruption. Although new elections were held the following year, General Park Chung Hee seized control of the government and was elected president two years later. He was assassinated in 1979 by the head of the Korean Central Intelligence Agency. Two military coups followed and Chun Doo Hwan emerged as the new president.

*The Economy.* The labor force is divided this way: services, 47 percent; agriculture, fishing and forestry, 30 percent; mining and manufacturing, 21 percent; and unemployed, 4 percent. About 10 percent of the work force is unionized.

South Korea has a free-market economy in which the dominant sector is private. Traditionally agriculture has been the most important sector of the economy, but today only 16 percent of the GNP comes from agriculture. Rice, barley and fish are the main products. Major industries include textiles and clothing, food processing, chemicals, steel, electronics and shipbuilding. South Korea has the best distribution of income in the world. Ten percent of the country's GNP goes to the poorest 20 percent of the people.

In one generation, South Korea has advanced from one of the world's poorest countries to full industrialization, while having to maintain one of the world's largest military establishments. Lacking natural resources, South Korea relies on its greatest asset, its industrious, literate people.

The long coastline and the nearness to some of the richest fishing grounds in the world have made the people, especially in the south, skilled fishermen and have led to frequent squabbles with individual Japanese and the Japanese government.

Business etiquette is conditioned largely by the strong Korean work ethic and the basically conservative nature of Korean business. This is reflected in an organizational and managerial approach which emphasizes harmony and structure over innovation and experimentation. This outlook can affect the style, pace, substance and results of negotiations.

Confucian ideology has left a deep imprint on business decision making. Both working and social lives are tied to groups and group structure. Paternalism and autocracy are ingrained; equality and participation are school subjects, not management principles. Group stability is desirable and the formal functioning of the group is seen as its optimal operating method. Loyalty is at its core. Offering loyalty leads to receiving similar support.

Practically all decisions come from top levels of the Korean enterprise; visitors should contact them, if possible, during business dealings. Lower-level executives are usually afraid to manage, feeling they lack both full information and clear authority. This state of affairs leaves the owner-manager or the chief executive and his top-level team as an overworked decision-making group, involved with both trivial and major deliberations. With an average of 54.4 hours, South Korea's manufacturing sector has the world's longest working week, according to the International Labor Organization.

*Organizational Communication.* Business persons succeed best in South Korea by contacting local representatives to serve as liaisons with the business community. Language is not a problem; most Korean business people communicate orally and in writing in English, which is good because Korean is one of three languages in the world which can't be simultaneously translated.

Large companies usually make available for foreign visitors a car and driver. If they don't, the visitor should be punctual for appointments as an early or late arrival may disrupt a normally full business schedule. Business meetings are commonly held in a hotel coffee shop. Koreans like to exchange business cards, regarded as an extension of the person, providing insight into the identity, position and potential of the presenter. It should be presented with right hand only, and, as in other foreign countries, the Koreans like it best when the card has been printed in their own language. Korean has been successfully transliterated into a phonetic spelling, called *Han'gul.* Meetings can generally be conducted in English which is spoken by most Korean business professionals. A medium-firm handshake should be part of a greeting; any Korean woman in the room should receive a nod instead.

It is proper to use the host's name in greeting him. In Korea the family name comes first, so that Kim Jung Soo is Mr. Kim. Never attempt to use other names.

## Table 30. Some Communication Practices
## in the South Korean Corporation

The South Koreans:

1. Work best with foreigners through local representatives.
2. Communicate in English.
3. Often make available a car and driver to visiting executives.
4. Expect punctuality.
5. Frequently hold meetings in coffee shops.
6. Exchange business cards.
7. Have had their language transliterated into a phonetic spelling.
8. Shake hands with a medium-firm grip.
9. Use only surnames in greeting others and that is their first name.
10. Maintain eye contact during conversations.
11. Ask personal questions to determine others' status.
12. Dislike loud demonstrations of any kind.
13. Have a high-context culture.
14. Use time polychronically.

The Korean host should be allowed to set the pace at initial meetings. Inquiries on the visitor's background may be raised to determine relative position and seniority (based on job position, rank and age) and to establish a personal basis for the business relationship which can prove crucial and can be reinforced over a lunch or dinner. It is proper to maintain eye contact during discussions, a sign of sincerity and friendship; without it you may be treated as a nonperson in South Korea.

Koreans dislike raucous laughter or behavior of any kind. Koreans may avoid saying yes or no; instead they will squint. If they are leaning forward on their elbows while listening to you, they will sit back in their chairs. They will crook their heads. But nothing may be said. These gestures indicate that you have reached an impasse. In effect, they skip a turn in the conversation and now it's your turn again to speak. Try to make some point from different perspectives. It may take several versions to clarify an issue.

Leaning back in one's chair is a neutral position; leaning forward, with arms on thighs, hands capping knees and eyes fixed on a document shows genuine interest. On sidewalks people bump and jostle others because they have no direct relationship with one another. Automobile drivers also will behave aggressively, showing disregard for others on the road.

Table 30 lists some communication practices of the Korean firm.

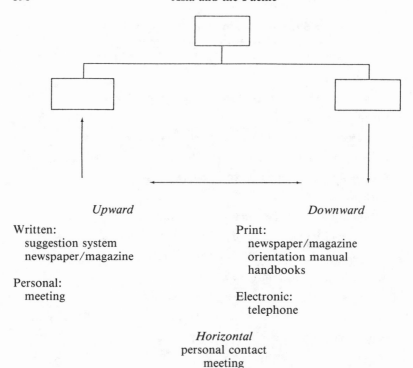

*Upward*
Written:
  suggestion system
  newspaper/magazine

Personal:
  meeting

*Downward*
Print:
  newspaper/magazine
  orientation manual
  handbooks

Electronic:
  telephone

*Horizontal*
personal contact
meeting

**Figure 43. The communication system of Daewoo Corporation, Seoul, Korea.**

## CASE STUDY: DAEWOO CORPORATION

Founded in 1967 as a small trading company, Daewoo has become one of Korea's largest business groups, ranked 49th on the *Fortune* International 500. It engages in worldwide trade through more than 65 offices, domestic and overseas construction and a diverse range of manufacturing and financial services. Korea Steel Chemical Company, Ltd., a Daewoo subsidiary, recently became the first company in the world to manufacture dioxin-free hesachloraphene, a germicide used in cosmetics.

Sung-Bong Lee, assistant manager, International Public Relations, stated his company's communication policies:

> In measuring international communication practices, one should be aware that Korean practices are very different from those of Western countries. Our attitude and way of thinking were influenced by Confucianism, which has dominated the country since the fourteenth century. In the meantime, with the development of various communication tools and a transportation system, our exposure to Western culture has been greatly increased, which consequently affected our Confucian idea, but not all. So we are somewhat in the middle of Western and pure Oriental thinking in the practice of communications.

Mr. Lee states that his company has no written communication policy:

It's rather a practice or custom than a policy. Our communication procedure has been developed quite naturally in the process of day-to-day business.

Mr. Lee states about his company's communication program:

We publish a monthly in-house magazine and distribute it to every employee. It contains corporate news, company goals, essays, theses, news analyses, etc.

Newly recruited college graduates take a 10-day orientation at our Training Center. They are given a manual that describes the developmental history of the company, how to prepare correspondence, work ethics, etc.

Though downward channels of communication have been developed rather efficiently, upward channels have not yet been so. Employees can communicate with management by meetings, suggestion systems and the in-house magazine.

The company's communication system is shown in Figure 43.

# Taiwan

*Official Name:* Taiwan (The Republic of China); *Capital:* Taipei; *Government:* republic; *Subdivisions:* 16 counties; *Population:* 19,768,035 (July 1987); *Density:* 1,381.5 per square mile; *Currency:* dollar; *Official Language:* Mandarin Chinese; *Literacy:* 94 percent.

*The Land.* About the size of Massachusetts and Connecticut combined, Taiwan is located in the western Pacific Ocean, 100 miles off the coast of China, 200 miles north of the Philippines and about 700 miles south of Japan. Taiwan is an island 240 miles long and 60 to 90 miles wide. It is surrounded by 77 small islands, many of which are not inhabited. The Pescadores Islands (Matsu and Quemoy), also controlled by Taiwan, are only two miles from the mainland and both are heavily fortified.

Rugged foothills and mountains cover two-thirds of the island, forming a backbone of the island. Forests stretch over half the island. Only a quarter of the land is arable. The land is divided this way: 55 percent is forest; 24 percent is cultivated; 6 percent is pasture; and 15 percent is other (urban, industrial, waste, water).

*The People.* Approximately 84 percent of the population are Taiwanese, 14 percent are mainland Chinese and 2 percent are aborigines. Over 60 percent of the people live in urban areas.

Frankness or abruptness, especially in offering criticism of any kind, should be avoided. People in Taiwan are generally reserved, quiet, refined and friendly. They respect a person who is friendly and who carefully avoids hurting the feelings of others. Loud, untactful or boisterous behavior is usually regarded as being in very poor taste. The Confucian ethic of proper social and family relationships forms the foundation of Chinese society. The schools and government foster the tradition of respect for and obedience to parents. Moral standards are very high. An individual's actions reflect upon his whole family.

The fundamental and lasting institutions of family life and farming completely dominated Chinese popular culture for thousands of years; this was certainly true throughout most of Asia, but these two foundations were developed to a higher level within China. The Chinese developed the first compass, printing and gunpowder. The value of work is a primary concern in Chinese society, along with the push for efficiency, punctuality and courtesy.

About 93 percent of the population are a mixture of Buddhist, Confucian and Taoist; 4.5 percent are Christian; and 2.5 percent are other.

*A Brief History.* Taiwan was first known to the West as Formosa, a name given by fifteenth century Portuguese sailors who declared the island *Ilha Formosa,* "Beautiful Island." In recent years, the Chinese name Taiwan, which literally means "Terraced Bay," has become increasingly popular.

The early Portuguese were not the only foreigners to be attracted to Taiwan. Since the seventeenth century, the island has been subject to a variety of outside influences, including those of the foreign nationalities who have occupied it in whole or in part: the Dutch, Spanish, French and Japanese. Culturally, economically and politically, however, Taiwan has remained predominantly Chinese since it became a protectorate of the Chinese Empire in 1206. In 1684, it was made a prefecture of the Fukien province and in 1887 it attained provincial status.

Chinese immigration to Taiwan began as early as the T'ang dynasty (618–907). In 1628, the Dutch took control of the island. In 1683, the Manchus of mainland China conquered the island and made Taiwan a province of China. The island was ceded to Japan following the Sino-Japanese War of 1895 and was under Japanese control until 1945. In 1949, the advancing communist forces of Mao Tse-tung forced President Chiang Kai-shek's Nationalist government and nearly two million soldiers to flee from the mainland to Taiwan. Since that time, the Nationalist government of Taiwan has considered itself to be the legal government of all China. The People's Republic of China's plans to invade the island were blocked in 1950 when President Truman sent the U.S. Seventh Fleet to patrol the Taiwan Strait. In 1955, the United States signed an agreement to protect Taiwan in case of attack from mainland China. In 1971, the People's Republic was admitted to the United Nations in Taiwan's place, despite U.S. objections. In 1979, the United States normalized relations with the People's Republic of China. As a result the 1955 mutual defense pact with Taiwan was terminated and official diplomatic relations between the U.S. and Taiwan were severed. However, relations continue on an unofficial basis through the American Institute.

*The Economy.* The labor force is divided this way: industry and commerce, 41 percent; services 32, agriculture 20, civil administration 7, and unemployed, 2.4 percent. About 18.4 percent of the work force is unionized.

There are many small business enterprises in Taiwan. The Chinese are natural entrepreneurs and prefer to work for themselves rather than seek lifetime employment with a big company. Companies in Taiwan encourage family members to go to work for the same company. Often a son will take his aging father's job as he would on the farm. Senior executives will often

**Figure 44. Communication is no problem for these young Chinese workers.**

"adopt" a junior manager from another department and act as a kind of mentor or godfather.

The Chinese corporation or partnership represents an extension of the traditional agricultural community. The Taiwanese corporation is an integral part of its employees' lives. Business people not only eat and work together, they spend many hours socializing with each other after work. The intent of the practice is to improve personal relationships in order to help everyone work together smoothly.

Chinese workers are well motivated by a social system that stresses responsibility to the employer. If a worker falls short of expectations, he "loses face." Economic motivation is also strong. A job is often referred to as a "rice bowl."

Taiwan's economy is one of the fastest growing economies in the world and one of the strongest in Asia. Major industries include electronics, textiles, chemicals, fertilizer, cement, plastics, aircraft, sugar milling, and shipbuilding. Major agricultural products include poultry, hogs, rice, sugarcane, tea, fruits and vegetables. Also forestry, mining and tourism are important. Even though arable land is limited, agriculture in Taiwan has been extremely efficient. Taiwan has most of the world's supply of camphor and camphor oil; it is the number two supplier of plywood to the United States and also sells a great deal of valuable hardwood. There are some minerals (gold, silver, copper, coal) and some natural gas.

Taiwan's goal is to be competitive with U.S. and Japanese markets and to establish major trade relations with South America and Africa.

The Confucian philosophy, with its foundation of hierarchy and obedience, is the precursor of contemporary decision-making modes, which are authoritarian. Indeed, authority in Taiwan is absolute. It is based on status, and status derives from age. Businessmen of Taiwan are not consensus or collective oriented. No group decision models exist, and the edicts of superiors are not questioned—at least not openly.

Many of Taiwan's enterprises are family-owned and controlled. Almost without exception the family unit governs and manages these companies. A patriarch is typically in charge; his eldest son is in the next highest power seat. It is common for major decisions to come before a whole body of relatives. Still, the outcome of deliberations will not rely on consensus, but on the wisdom and judgment of the senior member.

*Organizational Communication.* Politeness and etiquette are emphasized in all business exchanges in Taiwan. Personal contact is extremely important; serious business representatives should establish a good personal relationship in all meetings. Figure 44 shows some enterprising employees who have a unique opportunity for clear, continuous communicating. Business cards are exchanged, preferably with Mandarin printed on the opposite side.

It goes without saying that foreigners in Taiwan should reflect qualities important to the Chinese: dignity, reserve, patience, persistence and sensitivity toward and respect for local customs and temperament.

# Thailand

*Official Name:* Kingdom of Thailand; *Capital:* Bangkok; *Government:* constitutional monarchy; *Subdivisions:* 73 provinces; *Population:* 53,645,823 (July 1987); *Density:* 270.1 per square mile; *Currency:* baht; *Official Language:* Thai; *Literacy:* 84 percent.

*The Land.* Located in the heart of mainland Southeast Asia, Thailand is slightly larger than Texas. Laos, with a border of 1,090 miles, and Cambodia, 499 miles, lie to the east; Malaysia, 358 miles, to the south, and Burma, 1,118 miles, to the west and northwest. The Gulf of Thailand, which connects with the South China Sea, also touches the coast of southern Thailand. Its coastline on the Gulf of Thailand is 1,165 miles. The principal distinctive feature is a central plain dominated by the principal river, the Mae Nam Chao Phraya and its tributaries. It is the most fertile and productive area of the country. The north and northwest are more mountainous and are covered with jungles containing timber and mineral resources. Valuable teak wood is still brought from the jungle on the tusks of the Asian elephant. The northeast region is dominated by the arid Korat Plateau. The southern region consists of the narrow Kra Isthmus which is hot and oppressively humid on the coastal belt where quantities of rubber are produced by Thailand's Malay minority. Mountainous areas are chiefly in the northern portion of the country, but also run along the western border with Burma, and extend south into the narrow, largely rain forest covering the Malay Peninsula.

About 56 percent of the land is forest; 24 percent is farm land; and 20 percent is other.

*The People.* About 75 percent of the people are Thais, 14 percent are Chinese, and 11 percent belong to other minorities. Over 95 percent of the population are Buddhist; 4 percent are Muslim; less than 1 percent are other.

Thailand means "land of the free" and the Thais are proud of the fact that their country has never been under foreign rule. They now consider the communists in Laos, Cambodia and Vietnam to be their greatest threat. Wealth is looked on as a reflection of virtue. The Thais have much respect for those who unselfishly help others and who lead virtuous lives. Thais are a reserved people and usually consider criticism of others to be in bad taste. A sense of humor, laughter and a pleasant, smiling attitude are regarded highly. On the other hand, a lack of reserve such as speaking loudly or showing anger in public is offensive and may cause one to lose the Thais' respect.

Shortly after their arrival in Southeast Asia, the Thais were converted to the southern school of Buddhism, which came from the island of Ceylon. The numerous colorful festivals and the participating monks almost completely dominate the traditions of the people.

*A Brief History.* The migration of the Thai people from southwest China began as early as the seventh century A.D., resulting in recurring warfare with the Burmese, Khmers and later the Vietnamese. The Thais were able to solidify control of the area, and the Thais established the Kingdom of Sukothai in the 1200s. In the 1800s, King Mongkut was able to keep the Kingdom of Siam free from European domination. His son, King Chulalongkorn, abolished slavery and brought about many reforms. A bloodless coup in 1932 created a constitutional monarchy. Siam became Thailand in 1939. During World War II the Japanese occupied Thailand. The United States played a major role in keeping Thailand free after World War II. Recent history has been marked by a long series of military coups.

*The Economy.* The labor force is divided this way: agriculture, 73 percent; industry and commerce 11, services 10, government 6, and unemployed, 8 percent.

Thailand has a free-market economy in which the dominant sector is private. There is virtually no heavy industry. The most important industries are textiles, chemicals, food processing, iron and steel, mining, petroleum, refining, rubber tires and tourism.

Agriculture is the backbone of the nation's economy. About 76 percent of the people are employed in farming. Thailand is the third largest rubber producer and the fifth largest rice producer in the world. Other major agricultural products include sugar, corn and tapioca. Nine percent of the people are employed in the industrial sector. Agricultural processing, textiles, wood and wood products, cement and mining are important industries. Thailand is the world's second largest producer of tin and third largest producer of tungsten.

A system of promoting domestic and foreign investment includes tax incentives and favorable tariff treatment.

The overall societal emphasis on respectful vertical relations and submission to authority shows up again in the area of organizational structure. The subordinate is most concerned with complying with the wishes and orders of his superior, who behaves similarly toward his supervisor, and so on. Bold initiative is generally out of place, for it may tangle the delicately linked chain connecting one slot in the hierarchy to the next.

Assertively challenging the authority of one's superior is out of the question and he, in turn, is generally not interested in soliciting opinions from subordinates since the traditional view has been that one in authority is free to exercise his power without consulting his underlings. Even were he to give subordinates license to debate and criticize, other cultural factors and a tendency to mute differences of opinion would pretty well preclude a totally candid exchange.

If the concept of organization in terms of purposeful integration is the cornerstone of the American system, the corresponding Thai notion is *pen rabiab* — to be in good sequential order. The American pattern highlights horizontal consolidation; the Thai system, vertical protocol. In order for something to be *pen rabiab,* there must be an unbroken flow of documents and approvals. Correspondence, reports, purchase orders, and requests of various kinds must all, as the Thais would say, "pass many desks" until they arrive at the ultimate superior.

Adherence to protocol fulfills two important functions. It insures that power and authority will be concentrated in the top person, bearing out the truth of the adage that knowledge is power. The chief will know all or at least be in a position to refer to any matter should the need arise. To the Thais, this is of utmost importance, because should someone outside the section or department ask the chief about something for which he is responsible, he must be able to discuss it intelligently. If he could not, the situation would be *pralaad* ("strange" in the sense of being awkward), and his whole position as a superior and leader would be considerably undermined.

Thais, in attempting to keep things in good order *(pen rabiab),* mainly look up and down. Americans, in trying to make things well organized, often look sideways. Western managerial specialists have written critically of the Thai system, calling it duplicative, inefficient and disorganized, but these comments reveal ethnocentric bias. They miss the point that the Thai system is extraordinarily well-organized (or, again, perhaps better "well-ordered") to fulfill the demands of deep-seated cultural values. What has historically been important to the Thais has not been Western notions of productivity, efficiency and coordination but rather protocol, deference to rank, respect for authority and smooth interpersonal relationships. In stressing order over organization, *pen rabiab* over well-organized, the Thai system maximizes the values which society has long considered most important.

The Thai pattern of supervision involving deference, obedience and submission to authority tends to be autocratic and at least superficially formal. In describing an "ideal" supervisor, Thais put considerable emphasis on his personal qualities, particularly his capacity for empathizing with his *luuk nawng.* They say that he should *ruu cai* (literally "know the heart" in the sense of to

**Figure 45. A policy of Siam Cement Company, Limited, is to provide training to employees at all levels. (Siam Cement Company, Ltd., Bangkok, Thailand.)**

understand) or *ruu nisai* ("know the habits," characteristics, ways of doing things, preferences) of those he supervises. In off hours, he should be friend, elder brother, or respected relative depending upon the respective ages involved.

The traditional Thai pattern of decision-making has been more authoritarian and autocratic and although these terms have a negative connotation in the American context they clearly fit well with the strong vertical orientation of Thai society and the belief that a leader derives his power at least in part from past moral excellence. He is then the logical one to make decisions and bear the responsibility for their consequences. If he does call a meeting, it is often to issue orders or to have his subordinates substantiate his own predetermined point of view, decisions or policies.

*Organizational Communication.* Communication is an important part of the Thai firm's operation, as demonstrated in Figure 45; however, it operates differently than in other countries. The nerve center of this intricate system of protocol is what is called in Thai the *saraban* section. There really is no English equivalent of this term, but it involves elements of record keeping, office management and correspondence flow. The section sees that all documents flow smoothly from subordinates to superiors, that they circulate until they finally reach the top man. The *saraban* section also keeps detailed files which record this massive paper flow, so that someone wanting to see the step-by-step progression of a particular matter could do so by pulling out the appropriate folder from the *saraban* cabinet. There must be for every transaction that takes place in the office a *lakthaan* (a "basis" or "foundation") in the form of a written document of some kind, which eventually finds its way to the superior and is replicated in the *saraban* file.[30]

If a subordinate were to take independent action such as writing a letter to another firm or agency, without following the step-by-step procedure outlined above, it would be considered a personal matter on his part—outside the scope of his department's work. It would not pass the chief's desk for approval, it would be outside the *saraban* chain, and for all official purposes, it would be viewed as not having even taken place. This again is rooted in the idea that the superior must know everything about the work of his section so as to avoid the *pralaad* situation mentioned earlier where he would be asked about something of which he had no knowledge.

Given the vertical orientation of such a system, the idea of coordinating with other departments or agencies is not particularly appropriate. Each organizational entity has its own system of protocol and cross-linkages with outside departments could severely tangle these chains of protocol, causing the chiefs of the sections involved to lose tight rein on their own domains. Progressions from subordinate to superior would become extremely complicated if several parallel entities were involved.

Appointments should be made well in advance of any visit to Thailand. Business matters move smoothest when foreign business persons work through local representatives and also obtain letters of introduction. Everything takes time in the Thai organization. Documents flow through many management levels, the Thai deference to rank and authority.

# OTHER ASIAN COUNTRIES

## ———————— Bangladesh ————————

*Official Name:* People's Republic of Bangladesh; *Capital:* Dhaka; *Government:* republic; *Subdivisions:* 4 divisions; *Population:* 107,087,586 (July 1987); *Density:* 1,701 per square mile; *Currency:* taka; *Official Language:* Bangla; *Literacy:* 29 percent.

*The Land.* About the size of Wisconsin, Bangladesh is a low-lying riverine country located in South Asia on the northern littoral of the Bay of Bengal. Bangladesh is bordered on three sides by India for 1,605 miles and has a 145-mile border with Burma on the southeast. Its marshy coastline is 357 miles long.

Most of the land is flat, wet alluvial plain, formed over scores of centuries by three great river systems depositing silt as they near the Bay of Bengal. The small part of the country lying on the southeast in the hinterland of Chittagong has a different appearance. Possessing hills, valleys and forests, this is the only region where not all of the land is used for agriculture.

*The People.* The population of Bangladesh is more than a third that of the United States. About 98 percent of the people are Bengali, with tiny minorities of Bihari and tribal groups. About 83 percent are Islamic; 16 percent Hindu; and 1 percent are Buddhist, Christian or other. About 50 percent of the population are under age 15.

About 85 percent of the people are engaged in agriculture. The typical farmer lives with his large family in a simple hut of thatch and mud. The hut is on a low mound of earth so the monsoon rains cannot reach it. Because the land is very fertile, a very small plot can be one man's farm. He sells the produce from his little farm at one of the small towns located on the intersections of waterways. He can afford no modern luxuries; his main entertainment is sitting with his family and friends talking about the day's events and problems.

Despite Bangladesh's staggering population, it has only a handful of large cities, and in spite of the poverty of the country, about 20 percent of the population have some reading ability. The country's 65 million Muslims give it the second largest Islamic population next to Indonesia.

*A Brief History.* The territory of Bangladesh lies in a region which for many centuries bore the native name Bangla. This was taken into English as Bengal. British officials designated Bengal as a state in 1699, and it remained under British rule until 1947. When India gained independence in 1947, Bengal was bisected, with predominantly Hindu West Bengal incorporated into India and preponderantly Muslim East Bengal and the Sylhet District of Assam forming the eastern province of Pakistan. The territory then became East Pakistan. Although united by common religion, the Banalis of East Pakistan were not happy with the way they were treated by the Pakastani government dominated by men from West Pakistan. A civil war resulted and finally an invasion by India in support of Bengali secession at the end of 1971 achieved independence for Bangladesh—the Bengal Nation. After years of civil and political strife, Lt. Gen. Hussain Mohammed Ershad ousted the civilian government in a bloodless coup in 1982, dissolved parliament, suspended the constitution, banned political activity and declared martial law. In 1983, he proclaimed himself president while retaining his previous roles as commander in chief, chief martial law administrator and head of government.

*The Economy.* The labor force is divided this way: agriculture, 74 percent; services 15, industry and commerce 11, and unemployed and underemployed, 40 percent.

One of the least developed countries in the world, Bangladesh has a free-market economy dominated by the public sector. The country's main cash crop and export is jute, the tough plant fiber used in making burlap and rope. About half the jute export is in the raw state, the other half in jute manufactures. As industrial nations turn more and more to synthetic fibers, the demand for jute is declining, and the economy of Bangladesh is being affected by falling prices. Other export products are animal hides and good-quality tea.

Only about 300,000 people are employed in industry; many of these work in jute mills. The cotton industry has remained very small and other industries such as an iron plant and a few small chemical factories and oil refineries have no real economic significance. The only known mineral resources are some natural gas and coal; the coal is deep and cannot be mined economically at present. By any standard, Bangladesh is one of the poorest nations in the world.

# Burma

*Official Name:* Socialist Republic of the Union of Burma; *Capital:* Rangoon; *Government:* republic; *Subdivisions:* 7 divisions; *Population:* 38,822,484 (July 1987); *Density:* 150 per square mile; *Currency:* kyat; *Official Language:* Burmese; *Literacy:* 78 percent.

*The Land.* Largest country on the Southeast Asian mainland, Burma's environment consists of rich alluvial valleys and drier surrounding hills and high mountains which separate the county into strips of north-south ridges. The borders on the north, east and west are mainly mountainous, making access difficult and contributing to Burma's isolation from neighboring countries. The country extends 1,200 miles north to south and 575 miles east to west. Its total coastline is 1,414 miles. Burma's neighbors are China for 1,358 miles in the north and east, India for 872 miles and Bangladesh for 145 miles in the west, Laos for 148 miles in the east and Thailand for 1,118 miles in the east and south. The Irrawaddy River is the lifeline of the country, flowing through its entire length for about 1,350 miles.

About 62 percent of the land is forest; 28 percent is arable; and 10 percent is urban and other.

*The People.* Burma has over 100 indigenous ethnic groups and subgroups of Oriental Mongoloid mixtures. They divide this way: 72 percent Burman, 7 percent Karen, 6 Shan, 6 Indian, 3 Chinese, 2 Kachin, 2 Chin, and 2 percent other. About 85 percent of them are Buddhist; the rest follow indigenous beliefs, Christianity or other religions.

The population of Burma lives mainly near the rivers or in coastline communities. The Burmese government offers free education from primary through the university level. Although an estimated 88 percent of primary-age children attend school, only a small percentage of older children attend middle and high schools. In rural areas, traditional Buddhist temple schools provide basic-skills training for primary-school children.

Hinayana Buddhism pervades every aspect of Burmese culture. Monks are numerous and influential; most Burmese males spend some of their lives in monasteries. A strong attitude exists in Burma against the accumulation of wealth and that, along with a tendency to spend money for religious purposes and the fact that a Buddhist cannot make a valid will, all militate against the accumulation of capital required for developing industrial enterprises.

*A Brief History.* Burma was first unified during the eleventh century and remained independent until 1287 when Mongol hordes invaded the land. Two attempts to reestablish a dynasty failed. Burma was a British dependent from

1886 to 1947. During that period, many British, Indians and Chinese came to control the economy. Burma was separated from Britain in 1937 with a constitution that granted some self-government. The Japanese occupied the country during World War II, the Burmese suffering more devastation than any other Southeast Asian country. In 1948, the country finally achieved full independence from Britain. Some political and social instability have been experienced in Burma since then.

*The Economy.* The labor force is divided this way: agriculture, 66.1 percent; industry 12, government 10.6, trade 9.7, and other areas, 1.6 percent.

Since 1962, Burma has had a socialist, centrally planned economy in which the dominant sector is public. Rice, grown in the fertile river valleys, completely dominates the economy of Burma. Formerly the world's leading rice exporter, it fell to second mainly because of political unrest but has again begun to challenge Thailand for the leading position. The export of beautiful tropical hardwoods, of which Burma has varieties unknown in any other country, has been developed to only a fraction of what is possible. Major industries include agricultural processing, textiles, footwear, wood and wood products, petroleum refining and mining of copper, tin, tungsten and iron. Burma possesses substantial mineral resources, including lead, zinc, tin, tungsten and petroleum. The standard of living of Burma is one of the lowest in the world.

# India

*Official Name:* Republic of India; *Capital:* New Delhi; *Government:* republic; *Subdivisions:* 22 states and 9 union territories; *Population:* 800,325,817 (July 1987); *Density:* 601 per square mile; *Currency:* rupee; *Official Languages;* Hindi, English and 14 indigenous languages; *Literacy:* 36 percent.

*The Land.* India dominates the South Asian subcontinent; it extends 1,997 miles north to south and 1,822 miles east to west. Its coastline on the Bay of Bengal, the Arabian Sea and the Indian Ocean is 3,175 miles. Lying entirely in the Northern Hemisphere, India includes the Andaman and Nicobar islands in the Bay of Bengal and Lakshadweep in the Arabian Sea. It is the second largest country in Asia.

The country is adjoined in the north for 1,176 miles by China, for 937 miles by Nepal and for 356 miles by Bhutan; the Himalayas form India's northern border. To the east for 872 miles lies Burma, and for 1,605 miles Bangladesh, and in the northwest, for 1,260 miles Pakistan; a very small hook of Afghanistan also borders India.

The mainland comprises four well-defined regions: the great mountain zone in the north; the Indo-Gangetic Plains about 1,500 miles long and 150 to 200 miles wide; a small desert region in the west; and the southern peninsula, consisting of a fairly high plateau, mountains and coastal strips.

India is the seventh largest country in the world, roughly one-third the size of the United States. The Ganges plain below is fertile and densely populated.

Below that is the Deccan plateau. Approximately half the country is under cultivation; 22 percent is forest; 20 desert, waste or urban; 5 is permanent meadow and pasture; and 3 percent is inland water. The climate varies from tropical in the south to temperate in the north, with well-defined seasons throughout most of the country.

*The People.* Although India occupies only 2.4 percent of the world's land area, it supports nearly 15 percent of the population. Only China's population is larger. India is one of the most ethnically diverse countries in the world. Religion and language, however, separate the people more than race does. About 72 percent of the people are Indo-Aryan; 25 percent are Dravidian and the rest are of Mongoloid and other racial extractions. About 83.5 percent of the population are Hindu; 11 percent are Muslim; 2.6 percent are Christian; from 2 to 2.5 percent are Sikh; 0.7 percent are Buddhist; and 0.2 percent follow other beliefs. Some 24 languages are spoken by a million or more persons.

The population is still very much guided by the caste system. Caste was historically based on employment-related categories ranked in a theoretically defined hierarchy. Traditionally four classes were identified, plus a class of outcasts. It remains an important factor in Indian society.

Whistling is considered very impolite and, along with winking, unladylike. The Indian people are religious, family-oriented and philosophical and believe strongly in simple material comforts and rich spiritual accomplishments.

More than anything else, Hinduism has shaped the perception of time. The creator Brahma writes the fate of each man upon his forehead at birth. Acceptance of fate is each person's lot. Modern managers frequently will deny their relationship to old Hindu beliefs and traditions. However, they will discredit long-term planning because the Indian environment is uniquely unstable. Except in cases of natural calamity, the government will alter course haphazardly, forcing businessmen to cope with crisis after crisis.

*A Brief History.* About 3,500 years ago, Aryan tribes from Central Asia speaking Sanskrit merged with Dravidians (natives) to create the classical Indian society. Buddhism flourished in King Asoka's reign in the third century B.C., but declined afterward. Hinduism was adopted in the fifth century A.D. The Gupta Kingdom, from the fourth to the sixth centuries A.D., was a golden age of science, literature and the arts. Arab, Turk and Afghan Muslims ruled successively from the eighth to the eighteenth centuries. Islam was introduced in the eleventh century and by the thirteenth century Muslim rule governed most of the country. Later Portuguese, Dutch and French traders came, but the English eventually assumed political control of India. The British East India company was most successful in its rivalry with the other European powers. After World War I, the continuing nationalist movement was led by Mahatma Gandhi. He organized passive-resistance campaigns and advocated civil disobedience to British rule. In 1947, Gandhi's activities led to the partitioning of the peninsula into Hindu India and Muslim Pakistan. The partition brought about religious riots, killings and mass migrations. Gandhi was assassinated in 1948. In 1950, India became a republic in the British Commonwealth and Jawaharlal Nehru became prime minister.

*The Economy.* The labor force is divided this way: agriculture, 33 percent, industry 26.6, trade and services 34.2, and 6.2 percent unemployed and underemployed. About 5 percent of the work force is unionized.

India has a mixed economy in which the dominant sector is public; however, the Rajiv Gandhi government is supporting and seeking to expand the private sector. For the first time since independence in 1947, India has an economy of surpluses rather than shortages in such key areas as cement, synthetic textiles and electronics. The country is rich in natural resources and manpower. India ranks first in the world in the production of peanuts, second in rice and cheese, third in tobacco, fourth in wheat, cotton, milk and butter, and fifth in sugarcane and rubber. Other important crops include other cereals, oilseed, jute, tea and coffee. Important industries include textiles, food processing, steel, machinery, transportation equipment, cement and jute processing. Tourism is an increasingly important part of the economy. The country may now be described as a middle economic power in regard to production, which ranks about tenth in the world.

India is a paternalistic society and decisions are made at the top. Connections with the right families are very helpful.

Indian management has rested on the personal touch of the individual. Group functioning, open deliberation and consensus decision making have not generally worked because of status differences among the members. Committee work is rare because few, if any, natural peers exist.

Top management has not viewed lower ranks with confidence. Lower ranks have not been trained to function independently. Old patterns are thus reinforced. Decisions roll uphill, therefore, where an attitude exists that equates delegation with indecision. Another reinforcement for the concentration of power at top levels only is the prevailing paternalistic attitude of Indian managers. An executive shies away from delegation because he fears that he would unfairly and unduly burden lower level employees. In general, therefore, the foreign visitor must assume that the fate of his proposals rests up high.

A recent development in the Indian economy is the availability of a large number of technically trained workers, especially engineers and computer experts, and the availability of these low-cost people for international assignments. One estimate places India's pool of such workers as second in the English-speaking world only to that of the United States. "There's a tremendous intellectual manpower here," said M.R.S.N. Rao, general manager of the Karnataka State Industrial Investment and Development Corporation, a government agency. "We want to utilize this brainpower."[31] India's high-technology industries are still in their infancy, with low production and few exports; however, the country emphasizes its potential by citing the swift expansion in electronics industries. Since 1982, production rose at an annual average of 96 percent in computers, 55 percent in consumer electronics, 27 percent in components, and 19 percent in communications and broadcasting.[32]

Major industries include cement, chemicals, engineering, iron and steel, jute processing, mining, machinery, petroleum refining and sugar refining.

*Organizational Communication.* Telex is more reliable than mail. Men shake hands. When greeting a woman, do not shake hands. Make a *namaste* —

place palms together (as if in prayer) and bow slightly. Do not rush business. Several visits will be necessary to get business moving.

Business visitors are expected to be punctual. A short wait is normal, but even if it turns out to be as long as 15 minutes to 20 minutes, tardy callers will be perceived as unprofessional.

Use business cards. Shop talk can begin quite soon. The pace may be somewhat leisurely and consideration of human consequences may break the flow of technological data, but expertise will be present in the private and public sectors. The new elite of India is an astute, well trained cadre. To talk down to these professionals would be to offend them. Today's Indian executive understands the importance of time. He even judges others by their punctuality.

Space is less primary than social structure and interhuman arrangements. The sign of managerial perquisite may be a large office, but more commonly it is a servant crouching outside the office. Power over people indicates real status. Little body contact exists in business. In short, formality, ritual and distance go hand in hand.

# Pakistan

*Official Name:* Islamic Republic of Pakistan; *Capital:* Islamabad; *Government:* republic; *Subdivisions:* 4 provinces and 1 capital territory; *Population:* 104,600,799 (July 1987); *Density:* 326 per square mile; *Currency:* rupee; *Official Languages:* Urdu and English; *Literacy:* 24 percent.

*The Land.* The name of this country means "The Land of the Pure." Located in South Asia and extending 1,000 miles from the Arabian Sea northward across the Thar Desert and eastern plains to the Hindu Kush mountain ranges and the foothills of the Himalayan Mountains, Pakistan is about the size of Texas and Oklahoma combined. The country is generally flat and arid, with the exception of the slopes of the Himalayas in the north. The regions of Sind in the south and Baluchistan in the west are desert, while the forested regions lie in the north.

Bordering countries are India for 1,260 miles to the southeast, Iran for 516 miles to the west, Afghanistan for 1,532 miles to the north and China for 325 miles to the northeast. Pakistan has a coastline of 506 miles.

About 40 percent of the land is arable; 34 percent is mostly waste; 23 percent is unsuitable for cultivation; and 3 percent is forested.

*The People.* Communities are distinguished by language and religion, but these divisions do not correspond to physical features. More than half of the people are identified as Punjabis on the basis of language. Islam is practiced by 96 percent of the population.

Most Pakistanis live according to the philosophy that the will of God is evident in all things. The people feel deep pride in their own ethnic group. Many languages are spoken throughout Pakistan. Urdu is the official language of the government but is spoken by only 9 percent of the people. The provinces in Pakistan are free to use their own regional languages and dialects.

*A Brief History.* The history of modern Pakistan began with the arrival of Arab traders in the eighth century, who introduced the Islamic faith to the area. Muslim warriors conquered most of Pakistan in the 900s. By the sixteenth century, Muslim power had reached its peak under the Mogul Empire, a Muslim dynasty. Although many of the Indians were converted to Islam, the majority of the population remained Hindu. By the 1800s, the British East India Company had become the dominant power in the area and the last Mogul emperor was deposed in 1859. After the period of British control over the subcontinent, the people began to push for independence from the Crown. Muslim leaders, fearing they would be swallowed up by the Hindu majority, organized the All-India Muslim league. In June 1947, the British conceded the necessity of a Muslim and a Hindu state, and Pakistan was formed from the Punjab area in the west and the Bengal area in the east. West and East Pakistan were separated by 1,000 miles of Indian territory. Conflict with India flared several times over the disputed Kashmir area, where the Muslim majority were being ruled by a Hindu minority. This dispute erupted into war in 1948, and a peace agreement was not reached until early in 1966. Tension between East and West Pakistan reached a peak in 1971, when East Pakistan proclaimed its independence from Pakistan and called its nation Bangladesh. Aided by India, Bangladesh successfully revolted against Pakistani troops. In the vacuum of power created by the defeat, Zulfikar Ali Bhutto stepped in as leader, declared martial law, and strove to reestablish the confidence of the people. During a period of civil unrest in 1977, General Mohammed Zia ul-Haq, chief of staff of the army, seized control of the government and jailed Bhutto. Bhutto was convicted of murder and hanged in 1979. After General Zia was killed in a plane crash in 1988, Benazir Bhutto, daughter of Zulfikar Ali Bhutto, was elected president.

*The Economy.* The labor force is divided this way: agriculture, 53 percent; industry, 19 percent; and services, 29 percent. About 10 percent of the labor force is unionized.

Pakistan has a free-market economy in which the dominant sector is private. Pakistan is primarily an agricultural country; over half of the population is employed in agriculture. Pakistan's agriculture is supported by the irrigation of the Indus River valley, which runs through the center of the country. Chief products include wheat, rice, sugarcane, and cotton. At the time of its independence, Pakistan had very little industry. Recent efforts by the government have increased the industrial capacity immensely. Pakistan is a major producer of cotton fiber, which goes into the production of carpets, rugs and mats — Pakistan's chief exports. Other industries are food processing, cement, mining, metal manufacturing, paper, textiles, tobacco, engineering, chemicals and natural gas. Pakistan is a major exporter of labor to the oil-producing regions of the Gulf. These funds now represent the single largest source of foreign-exchange earnings, exceeding all other exports.

*Organizational Communication.* Appointments must be made well in advance of planned visits to Pakistan. Letters or telex messages will be answered.

During Ramzan (the Urdu word for Ramadan) business persons work only in the morning.

Pakistani businessmen are formal, reserved and deliberate in business matters. Women should not be sent to Pakistan because they will not be taken seriously in this male-dominated culture.

# Sri Lanka

*Official Name:* Democratic Socialist Republic of Sri Lanka; *Capital:* Colombo; *Government:* republic; *Subdivisions:* 9 provinces; *Population:* 16,406,576 (July 1987); *Density:* 647.5 per square mile; *Currency:* rupee; *Official Language:* Sinhala; *Literacy:* 87 percent.

*The Land.* A pear-shaped island in the Indian Ocean, Sri Lanka, formerly called Ceylon, is located about 500 miles north of the equator southeast of India from which it is separated at the closest point by only 18 miles. Its coastline is 748 miles long. The longest part of the island north to south is 270 miles; from east to west it is 140 miles. It is slightly larger in total land area than West Virginia. A plain only slightly above sea level makes up the northern half of the island and continues around the coast of the southern half. The south-central part is hilly and mountainous. About 25 percent of the land is under cultivation and 44 percent is covered by forests. The rest—31 percent—is waste, urban or other. The northern end of the island, inhabited by the Tamil minority, is flat and requires irrigation to cultivate crops. The southern and central regions are mountainous and inhabited by the Sinhalese majority. The coast of India is some 33 miles away across Palk Strait.

*The People.* About a fourth of the population live in urban areas. The main ethnic groups are the Sinhalese, descendants of the Indo-Aryan settlers of Sri Lanka (74 percent of the population); the Tamils, descendants of the Southern Indian settlers (18 percent); and the Islamic Moors (7 percent). About 69 percent of the population are Buddhist; 15 percent are Hindu; 8 percent are Christian; 8 percent are Muslim; and 0.1 percent follow other beliefs. Sri Lanka is not very different culturally or climatically from the regions of India nearest it, with which it is linked by ferry.

*A Brief History.* For 450 years (until 1948), Sri Lanka was under the influence of European powers—the Portuguese from 1505 to 1656, the Dutch from 1656 to 1766, and finally the British from 1766 to 1948. After the demise of Buddhism in India, Sri Lanka became the stronghold of Buddhism in South Asia. The island was named Ceylon by the British. In 1948, the island peacefully obtained freedom from British rule and since then a democratic government has been maintained. The name of the country was changed in 1972 to Sri Lanka, meaning "resplendent island."

*The Economy.* The labor force is divided this way: agricultural, 45.9 percent, mining and manufacturing 13.3, trade and transport 12.4, services 26.3, and unemployed, 19 percent. About 33 percent of the work force is unionized.

Sri Lanka has a free-market economy in which the dominant sector is private. Sri Lanka has few natural resources and only a small industrial capacity. Major products include rice, rubber, tea and coconuts. The processing of food products along with petroleum production are the main industries. Tourism plays an important role in raising income. A government-sponsored development program has begun to revitalize the economy.

*Organizational Communication.* Appointments must be made in advance; however, they can be arranged on relatively short notice. Initial meetings are often held over lunch in a restaurant or even in a home to allow the Sri Lankans a chance to get to know visitors. Business cards printed only in English are acceptable, and all collateral material can also safely be prepared in English. Women are fully accepted in business affairs.

# THE PACIFIC REGION

--------------------------------- **Australia** ---------------------------------

*Official Name:* Commonwealth of Australia; *Capital:* Canberra; *Government:* parliamentary state; *Subdivisions:* 6 states and 2 territories; *Population:* 16,072,986 (July 1987); *Density:* 5.2 per square mile; *Currency:* dollar; *Official Language:* English; *Literacy:* 98 percent.

*The Land.* The world's smallest continent but its largest island, Australia is the sixth largest country in the world, approximately the same size as the continental United States. It is the only country completely occupying a continent. The country lies southeast of Asia between the Indian Ocean on the west and the Pacific Ocean on the east, below the Southeast Asian archipelago. The continent includes the island of Tasmania. The driest continent in the world, Australia is mostly a low, irregular plateau. About a third of the land is desert and another third is composed of poor-quality land. A long mountain range follows the east coastline with fertile farmland between the Pacific coast and the Great Dividing Range. The western slopes and plains are the location of the great wheat-producing areas of Australia, with cattle stations reaching to the edge of the barren interior desert. The Great Barrier Reef, largest coral reef in the world, stretches 1,200 miles off the east coast of Queensland. Mountains lie roughly parallel to the east coast, in the center of the continent, and in the west.

*The People.* The Australian people are predominantly of British origin with a culture and origin similar to those of the United States. About 99 percent of the population are Caucasian, having migrated from many parts of Europe. Before World War II, 95 percent of the people were of Anglo-Celtic stock. Since the war, however, heavy immigration from other European countries has reduced that percentage to 60. Asians now account for about 1 percent of the population. A relatively small number of Aborigines also exist.

About 26 percent of the population are Anglican; another 26 percent are

Roman Catholic; 24 percent follow other Christian beliefs, and 24 percent are other.

Partly because of the White Australia Policy, the total non-European population of Australia is less than 1 percent. The social classes in Australia are also usually homogeneous. Most of the early immigrants to Australia were from a single class (the lower class), and the process of migration itself reduced distinctions between classes and reduced the traditional respect for social rank. The result has been the firm belief shared by most Australians that "Jack's as good as his master."

For Australians no shame or lower status is attached to performing manual labor. Because of their lack of class distinctions and social rank, one can approach most Australians no matter how high their position with the certainty of an attentive, cordial hearing.

Conditions confronting the first European settlers in Australia were very harsh. Consequently the settlers, most of them convicts, developed among themselves a sense of mutual independence. This sense was conveyed to subsequent generations and was nourished throughout Australian colonial history by similar circumstances and necessities. The people, for example, lacked doctors, hospitals and other facilities and had to rely upon each other. Although many of the circumstances have changed now, this pattern of interdependence has persisted.

Australians have traditionally expressed the priority they give to personal relationships in terms of "mateship." Through the loneliness, vast distances, and difficulties of existence experienced by the first Australians, men and women learned to help and trust each other. Australians still respect and share a genuine spirit of mateship, a sense that "we're in this thing together."

*A Brief History.* Aborigines were the only inhabitants when the Dutch discovered parts of the continent in 1623. Most of Australia was left undisturbed until 1770 when Captain James Cook took formal possession of the eastern coast for Britain. The British arrived in 1788 and penal colonies began in what has become modern-day Sydney, Hobart and Brisbane. Many of the early settlers of Australia were prisoners or soldiers. British convict settlements of various forms existed here until 1868, and more than 180,000 men and women were transported from England, most of them for minor crimes.

With the discovery of gold in 1851, immigration of free men increased rapidly. In 1868, the practice of transporting convicts was curtailed. In 1901, the six colonies agreed to federate and became the Commonwealth of Australia. It is still a member of the British Commonwealth, although a strong anti-royalist feeling has developed in recent years. The country celebrated its bicentenary in 1988 ("bicentennial" is an adjective and not a noun, the Australians said) with a worldwide television program in January and countrywide observances all year long—including World Expo '88 in Brisbane.

*The Economy.* The labor force is divided this way: manufacturing and industry, 26.9 percent, public and community services 22.4, wholesale and retail trade 20, finance and services 18.1, agriculture 6, and unemployed, 8.2 percent. About 62 percent of the work force is unionized.

Australia has one of the strongest economies in the world. Livestock is particularly important in Australia. The country is the world's leading producer of wool and the second largest producer of meat. It also ranks third in sheep production and fourth in cattle. Australia is also a major producer of sugarcane, wheat and oats. The country exports a wide range of minerals. It ranks third in the production of uranium and iron ore and fourth in salt. Silver, coal, gold and copper are other important minerals. Australia's manufacturing industry is geared largely to domestic demand with small numbers of a wide range of goods exported, particularly to countries of Asia and the Pacific. Major industries include chemicals, electrical equipment, food processing, iron and steel manufacturing, mining, motor vehicles, petroleum refining, pulp and paper, ships and textiles.

Decision making in Australia still tends to be concentrated at the top company echelon; however, Australians are also quite collaborative in their orientation. They believe quite strongly that decision-making procedures should be based on management's assumption that subordinates share equal interests, organizational goals and success; they should be consulted on major organizational decisions in order to reach a total organizational consensus.

A 1986 survey by the Business Environment Risk Information (BERI) group ranked Australia equal with the United Kingdom in the very "troublesome" category among world markets. A BERI spokesperson said of Australia, "The worst problem was relative productivity which was at the bottom of the scale. Worker attitude, which includes everything from days lost from disputes to absenteeism, was also extremely low." BERI did report, however, that Australia's performance had improved in the past five years.[33]

Like the rest of the world, Australia has begun to look to its Asian neighbors when it considers its future. "Our future and economic survival lie with the three billion people who live to the north of us," said Malcolm J. Bryce, the deputy premier of Western Australia.[34] Partly this has resulted from world events. Britain's entry to the Common Market closed their market to Australian agricultural products. Also, the manufacturing centers that use Australia's natural resources — coal, aluminum, oil and iron ore — moved from Europe to Asia. "Smokestack industries moved to Asia, and so our supplies to smokestack industries moved to Asia," said David S. Adam, a Melbourne businessman who retired at the end of 1986 as executive general manager of Broken Hill Proprietary Company, Australia's largest business concern.[35]

*Organizational Communication.* Australians are easygoing and amiable, except perhaps when religion and politics are discussed. Promptness is very important. Eye contact is important for showing real interest in a person. When conversing, Australians often gesture with their hands to emphasize and clarify.

The visitor must be punctual. A late arrival is likely to be seen as an indication of lax business methods. Business cards should be presented, even though the Australian businessman may not have one. Introductory conversation unrelated to business should be short; Australians adopt the use of first names as the method of addressing visitors very quickly, an indication of friendly informality. The visitor should reciprocate. Do not use social occasions to talk business; to Australians, recreation and eating are for relaxation, not business. Typical office attire is shorts, short-sleeved white shirt with tie, and white knee socks.

Hugh Mackay, Director of the Centre for Communication Studies, conducted a study on employees' attitudes toward the communication climate in Australian corporations. Among his findings were that:

> The quality and extent of personal contact between employees and their managers is, overwhelmingly, the most significant factor in determining employees' attitudes toward the communication climate in their organizations.... When employees feel themselves to be in close personal contact with their managers, other shortcomings in organizational communication may be overlooked.[36]

When employees lack such personal contact, the familiar "we versus them" attitude develops and all other forms of communicating are affected:

> Written messages which are transmitted without the support of a personal relationship tend to be regarded as "information" rather than "communication." ... Formal company publications for employees are no substitute for personal contact, and will generally be appreciated only when they are integrated into the personal flow of information and consultation. Employee publications are judged primarily on the basis of their relevance to each individual employee. Extremely local publications and those containing items of immediate interest, are most favourably received. The idea of Annual Report distribution is generally praised, though reactions to such Reports are sour where the communication climate is otherwise unhealthy.[37]

Mackay found that, paradoxically, the more an organization focuses on its systems of communication, the greater the risk of losing sight of a need for personal contact. In a sense, they thereby sabotage the whole communication program.

Rodney G. Miller, general manager of the Communication Centre at the Queensland Institute of Technology, described his study of cost/benefit analyses of communication in Australian corporations in a talk before the Society of Business Communicators of Australia. Among the benefits of such analyses is that they are able to:

> locate both broad trends, such as the degree of contact between groups of staff, as well as detail concerning the amount and quality of contact between particular staff. Broadly interesting information gathered about one organisation, for example, which had a well-developed forward plan and performance monitoring procedure, includes:
>
> 1. Relatively little written communication occurs between the directorate or senior management and middle managers or other staff;
>
> 2. Communication across formal work groups is generally restricted;
>
> 3. Lower level staff rarely initiate communication with the most senior staff;
>
> 4. Personnel and marketing areas tend to use communication more effectively than administration or production areas of the organisation;
>
> 5. People generally express satisfaction with the level of contact that they have with others, even where communication is far from optimal;

6. Significant proportions of all staff (26%) are unclear about their duties, even though many have sought out information on them;

7. Similar proportions of staff are unclear about organisational policy;

8. Up to 50% of staff claim to receive no formal information about the implications of senior managerial decisions on their own work and position, to the extent that similarly high proportions of staff claim that they are unable to perform their daily work efficiently;

9. Over 50% of staff receive no formal feedback on their performance and significant proportions of these claim that this lack of feedback reduces their ability to perform daily work efficiently.[38]

## Table 31. Some Communication Practices in the Australian Corporation

The Australians:

1. Expect punctuality.

2. Like to have business cards, though they sometimes fail to present one.

3. Spend very brief time on small talk.

4. Adopt usage of first names rapidly.

5. Separate business and social affairs.

6. Consider informal, personal communicating more important than formal, written methods.

7. Like to maintain eye contact when they converse.

8. Like to debate.

9. Have a low-context culture.

10. Use time monochronically.

George Renwick in *Australians and North Americans,* gives this advice to foreigners doing business with Australians:

> When talking with an Australian, take a definite position. Let him (or her) know where you stand, what you believe, what you feel. Show discernment, make judgments regarding people and events, express strong opinions (if, of course, they are genuine). Do this briefly and emphatically — and usually quietly. In other words, give the Australian a sense of who you are as a person. Give him something to react to.... Do not say something unless you mean it. An Australian will respect and respond to sincerity. Any hint of something phony, any pretense, will quickly turn him off.... Use few words, choose them carefully but say them casually. Practice conveying much of your meaning through your intonation, rather than simply adding more and more words.[39]

Table 31 lists some communication practices of the Australian firm.

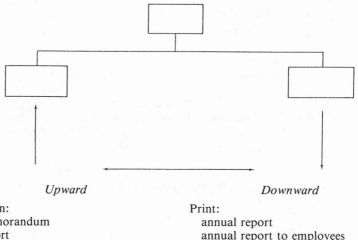

*Upward*

Written:
  memorandum
  report
  suggestion system
  question box
  newspaper/magazine

Personal:
  meeting
  interview
  open-door policy
  grievance procedure

*Downward*

Print:
  annual report
  annual report to employees
  newspaper/magaine
  bulletin board
  orientation manual
  letters
  pay envelope inserts
  manual
  handbook

Electronic:
  telephone
  film
  videotape

Personal:
  meetings
  seminars

*Horizontal*

personal contact
meetings
employee newsletters and publications

**Figure 46. Communication system of BHP Corporation, Melbourne, Australia.**

## CASE STUDY: BHP

The Broken Hill Proprietary Company Limited was incorporated in Melbourne in 1885 following a rich silver find by seven sheep-station-men-turned-prospectors. With 59,000 employees, BNP is Australia's largest company. Through joint ventures and shared investments, the company is linked with some of the world's largest corporations and ranks as Australia's major participation on the international business scene. J.S. Balderstone, Chairman of the Company, said this about communication:

Our Corporate Public Affairs Department presents an annual program for approval to the Board each year and the 1986 presentation summed up our current formal internal communications objectives:

*Strategic Objective (to 1990)*

To help improve the satisfaction of employees with the quality, frequency and credibility of the information they receive and thereby strengthen their job satisfaction, pride in working for their unit and pride in being part of BHP; to do this by helping support supervisors with the Company information they need for effective dialogue and to provide some corporate information direct to employees in a palatable and believable way; to measure progress in all this.

Figure 46 shows the communication system of BHP Corporation.

## CASE STUDY: CSR LIMITED

CSR was founded as a sugar refiner in 1855. It is one of Australia's largest companies, ranked 208th on Fortune's 1985 list of leading industrial corporations outside the U.S. Operations include: sugar milling, refining and the provision of marketing services to the Australian sugar industry; manufacture of building materials; quarrying and concrete; mining of gold, tin and bauxite; alumina refining and aluminum smelting; mining of steaming and coking coal; and the operation of coal loaders; production of oil and gas, and pipeline operation; shipping; and the production of ethanol and industrial chemicals.

The corporate representative says this about communication:

We favor a decentralised, site or activity based focus to our communications, with encouragement of person-to-person contact. We tend to like to give more information rather than less.

Accordingly, activity managers received this memorandum in March 1986:

*Keeping CSR People Informed*

As a company, we strongly believe we benefit significantly from having employees well informed about company matters of relevance to them. Most activities are now effectively achieving this aim, using a variety of techniques including meetings, publications and sometimes video.

In view of the extent of this communication, it is now opportune to change the CSR Group communications effort as follows:

We will replace the glossy CSR Report to Employees with a simple one sheet summary, covering key events and figures and carrying a short message from the CEO. It will be available in early June. It will complement local reports that most of you already issue.

We will continue to produce the CSR Group Plan (state of the business) publication for you to use as appropriate in your meetings to review operational plans.

The members of the executive general management group will visit activities more frequently. At least one of us will visit all major sites at least once a year.

Videos of the audiovisual prepared for the AGM will be available for you to show as you consider appropriate.

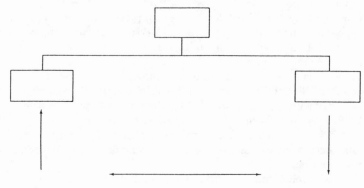

*Upward*

Personal:
 open-door policy
 performance appraisal interview
 union representation
 committees

*Downward*

Print:
 annual report
 annual report to employees (local)
 magazine
 bulletin boards
 orientation manuals (local)
 letters
 manuals
 handbooks

Electronic:
 telephone
 closed-circuit television
 teleconferencing
 videotape/audiotape
 electronic mail

Personal:
 personal contact
 meetings

*Horizontal*

personal contact
meetings
memorandum

**Figure 47. Communication system of CSR Limited, Sydney, Australia.**

We will produce videos, as needed, to explain major developments of importance to all employees.

I would strongly encourage those activities not already reporting their annual results and reviewing their operational plans with their employees to begin doing so.

If you wish to have a member of the executive general management group join your activity meeting which reviews your operational plan, we would be delighted to join you. If so, we would see our function as providing CSR Group perspective and answering company-wide questions.

The communication system of CSR Limited is presented in Figure 47.

# New Zealand

*Official Name:* New Zealand; *Capital:* Wellington; *Government:* parliamentary state; *Subdivisions:* 92 counties; *Population:* 3,307,239 (July 1987); *Density:* 30.9 per square mile; *Currency:* dollar; *Official Languages:* English and Maori; *Literacy:* 98 percent.

*The Land.* Located in the southwest Pacific, about 1,200 miles southeast of Australia and about midway between the equator and the South Pole, New Zealand is about the size of Colorado. The country consists of two main islands — North Island and South Island — separated by Cook Strait. It includes Steward Island to the south and various other small, coastal islands.

New Zealand is a mountainous island nation. Some 1,100 miles separate the farthest point south from the slim top of the north. No inland area is more than 70 miles from the sea. The more populous North Island has fertile agricultural land, the largest man-made forest in the southern hemisphere and a few isolated snowcapped volcanoes. The North Island also boasts of hot springs, mud pools and geysers in its thermal region. On the South Island, the Southern Alps provide magnificent scenery and opportunities for sports. There are many glaciers, lakes, rivers and fertile plains. On the southwest coast there are fjords rivaling those in Norway. Both islands have many sandy beaches. Other islands are Steward Island, off the southern tip of South Island, and the Chatham Islands, about 500 miles east of South Island. Nearly all of the fertile plains and most of the population and major cities are on the east coasts of the two main islands.

About half of the land is pasture; 16 percent is forest; 10 is park and reserve; 3 is cultivated; 1 is urban and 20 percent is waste, water and other.

*The People.* The people are principally of two cultural backgrounds: 87 percent are of European origin, primarily British; another 9 percent are Maori, or native New Zealanders; 2 percent are Pacific Islanders; and 2 percent are other.

About 81 percent of the population are Christian; 18 percent are atheists or unspecified; and 1 percent are Hindu, Confucian and other.

*A Brief History.* New Zealand was discovered and settled over 1,000 years ago by the Maori, a Polynesian race of the central Pacific, whose earlier origins are believed to lie in Asia. Although two main periods of settlement occurred, modern Maori history dates from the "Great Migration" during the thirteenth and fourteenth centuries.

The Dutch explorer Abel Tasman sighted the land in 1642 and named it Staten Landt which was later changed by Dutch geographers to Nieuw Zealand. In 1769, Captain James Cook of England landed in New Zealand. The Maoris ceded sovereignty to the British in 1840 in return for legal protection and rights to perpetual ownership of the Maori Islands. New Zealand made valiant contributions to both world wars. The country was made an independent, self-governing member of the British Commonwealth in 1947.

*The Economy.* The labor force is divided this way: services, 66.6 percent, manufacturing 21, primary production 11.8, and unemployed, 5 percent. About 41 percent of the work force is unionized.

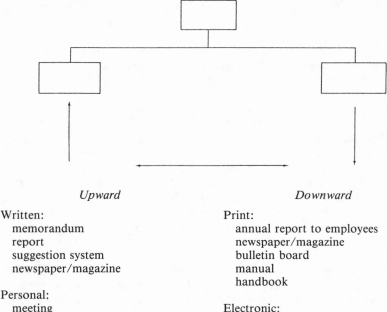

*Upward*                                              *Downward*

Written:                                              Print:
  memorandum                                 annual report to employees
  report                                      newspaper/magazine
  suggestion system                           bulletin board
  newspaper/magazine                          manual
                                            handbook

Personal:
  meeting                                   Electronic:
  interview                                   telephone
  open-door policy                            videotape
  grievance procedure                         electronic mail
  Joint Consultative Panel                    telex

*Horizontal*

personal contact
memorandum
meeting
telex

**Figure 48. Communication system of Air New Zealand.**

New Zealand has a modern industrialized economy comparable to some western European countries. Although only 13 percent of the population are employed in agriculture, it is an important sector of the economy. "In industralized countries, agriculture is kept as a sort of pet, a political indulgence to keep the votes," said Prime Minister David Lange. "In New Zealand it's not a pet. It's a working beast. It's the guts of our economy."[40] In fact, the country's 68.5 million sheep outnumber people in New Zealand almost 20 to one.

New Zealand's international trade depends heavily on exports of meat, wool, dairy products and forest products. These products are processed in highly efficient factories at relatively low cost. New Zealand is the largest exporter of lamb, mutton and butter. It also ranks second in sheep production and third in wool. New Zealand is also a major producer of meat and meat products. Important industries include cement, fertilizers, petroleum refining, food processing, textiles, machinery and wood and paper products.

Although the United Kingdom was formerly New Zealand's primary trading partner, trade between the two countries has been declining since the United Kingdom joined the European Economic Community.

*Organizational Communication.* Appointments must be made at least a month in advance for proper planning of a trip to New Zealand. Punctuality for appointments is important. Initial meetings often occur over lunch in a restaurant or hotel. Attitudes toward time are more relaxed than in the West, but business relationships are more conservative than they are in Australia.

## CASE STUDY: AIR NEW ZEALAND

Air New Zealand's history stems from two main sources—international services dating back to the formation of Tasman Empire Airways Ltd., (TEAL) in 1939, and the evolution of Union Airways into the domestic carrier, New Zealand National Airways Corporation (NAC) in 1947. In 1965, the company changed its name from TEAL to Air New Zealand and in 1978, it merged with NAC to form a company providing domestic and international services.

Concerning communication, a company representative stated in a letter to the author:

> We treat the communication issue as a live one, and it is not specific as such in any particular Company document. Our experience is that change is necessary to meet changing circumstances from time to time. Air New Zealand is dedicated to ensuring that matters of interest and importance to our staff members are communicated adequately, so that our staff are aware of the current environment in which the company trades, of future planned moves of the Company, and of problems which beset the organisation from time to time.

The communication system of Air New Zealand is shown in Figure 48.

## CASE STUDY: CABLE PRICE DOWNER LIMITED

The Company dates back to 1854 when the Lion Foundry was established in Wellington. Since then it has developed into one of New Zealand's largest and most diversified commercial enterprises. It comprises 13 major operating companies and numerous subsidiaries and associated companies, engaged in construction, engineering, manufacturing and merchandising activities.

Although the company did not return the questionnaire, the company Chairman, R.W. Steele, sent me a letter describing his communication policies:

> You set me some problems with your requests. I should, perhaps, explain to you that the Cable Price Downer Group is a relatively "loose knit" combination of companies, very diverse in activity, and none of which is of any great size. Whilst we have in total over 4,400 employees, the largest employer in the Group has only some 800. . . . The Group is not vertically oriented, but more horizontally so, and in fact I break every rule in the book by having some 14 general managers reporting directly to me. Nonetheless, I think it works.

Rather than reply to your questions seriatim, I think I should give a general overview of what communication policies are common within our Group. First, you must bear in mind that there is no great concentration of people at any one place. Probably 300 would be the maximum in any one plant or construction site, and the emphasis, except in extremis, is on informality. That is to say, the Company's Annual Report, a very formal document, is available to all employees as of right, but of course it is no substitute for the ordinary day-to-day, eye-to-eye, contact between management and the hourly paid worker. The larger companies within the Group regularly produce in-house magazines with the emphasis on informality, and a "family" approach. My own style of management is completely "open door" and I insist that my managers follow my example in this respect.

I guess if you want me to encapsulate management philosophy and style in one word, it would be "informality." The Group covers a country over 1,000 miles long, where you can never be more than 60 miles from the sea, and where there are only 3.2 million people. Regrettably, I see emphasis on MBA-style management styles which really, in my view, do not have a place in New Zealand. We can have drive without being driven, and we can have discipline without a plethora of orders.

# Notes

1. Jane Seabury, "East Asian Countries Pose Threat to U.S.," p. D8.
2. Roy Hofheinz, Jr., and Kent E. Calder, *The Eastasia Edge,* pages 42–3.
3. Darcy, Trick, "Why the Pacific Matters," p. 14.
4. Robert T. Moran, "Cross-Cultural Contact: The Composite of Qualities That Makes for the Best Internationalist," p. 65.
5. Anne B. Forrest, "The Continental Divide; Coping with Cultural Gaps," pp. 20–1.
6. Bob Rast, "Rapid Growth Spurs Hong Kong Concerns," p. 63.
7. Ibid.
8. "Many in Japan Beginning to Worry About Country's Internationalism," p. 46.
9. Ibid.
10. Myron Emmanuel, "Productivity Improvement—Japanese Style," p. 3.
11. Ibid.
12. Ezra Vogel, *Japan as Number 1,* p. 51.
13. Rodney Clark, *The Japanese Company,* p. 129.
14. Japan External Trade Organization, *How to Succeed in Japan,* p. 210.
15. Clyde Haberman, "Some Japanese (One) Urge Plain Speaking," p. 27.
16. Chie Nakane, *Japanese Society,* pp. 145–6.
17. Richard T. Pascale and Anthony G. Athos, *The Art of Japanese Management,* pp. 130–1.
18. Stephen Craig, "Functional and Dysfunctional Aspects of Government Bureaucracy," in *Modern Japanese Organization and Decision-Making,* ed. Vogel, p. 23.
19. Pascale and Athos, pp. 131–2.
20. Ibid., p. 112.
21. Friedrich Furstenberg, *Why the Japanese Have Been So Successful in Business,* p. 72.
22. Saburo Haneda and Hirosuke Shima, "Japanese Communication Behavior as Reflected in Letter Writing," p. 23.
23. Frank Gibney, *Japan,* p. 152.
24. M.Y. Yoshino, *Japan's Managerial System,* p. 208.

25. Craig, p. 14.

26. Katheryn Flournoy, "Japanese Firms Adapting to America," p. E1.

27. Barbara Crossette, "Western Influence Worries Singapore Chief," p. 16.

28. Janine Perrett, "Survey Says Australian Workforce 'Difficult,'" n.p.

29. Richard B. Rucci, *Living in Korea,* p. 23.

30. John Paul Fieg, *Thais and North Americans,* p. 53.

31. Richard Alm, "India's Intellect Is Latest High-Tech Discovery," p. D14.

32. Ibid.

33. Perrett, loc. cit.

34. Nicholas D. Kristof, "Australians Shift Their Sights to Asia," p. 17.

35. Ibid.

36. Hugh Mackay, *The Communication Climate of Australian Organizations,* p. 1.

37. Ibid., pp. 2-3.

38. George Renwick, *Australians and North Americans,* pp. 34-5.

39. Rodney G. Miller, "Effective Ways to Evaluate and Cut the Cost of Communications," p. 3.

40. Sid Moody, "The Unsung Heroes of New Zealand," p. A4.

# 8. Survey Results: Comparison and Discussion

## Introduction

For first-hand information on what corporations around the world use for internal communicating, the author conducted a survey. Questionnaires (see page 428 for a facsimile) were mailed to 475 companies from the Fortune International 500 list (those whose addresses were available) in December 1986 and January 1987 and to 100 companies of Third World countries with poor or no representation on that list. The results are shown in Table 32.

The 176 responses of the 575 letters and questionnaires sent out represent a response rate of 31 percent, slightly above average for a mailed survey. Only 111 of the responses, or 19 percent, were completed questionnaires, but this is a somewhat misleading figure because many respondents included in letters all of the information sought on the questionnaires—all without the formality of the completed questionnaire. The real response rate is somewhere in the middle of these two percentages.

The cover letter and envelope were addressed to the highest ranking officer of the company—either the chairman or president, whichever name was available. No return envelope was included because it was hoped that respondents would return more than the questionnaire—samples of their communication programs, for instance—and most did. An enclosed envelope might have discouraged such returns.

No reward for participating was offered other than a promise to send respondents a summary of the results which was done in December 1987. The questionnaires were in English only and not translated into the many languages represented by the Fortune International 500 list.

Initial survey questions were intended to learn whether these corporations base their programs on a communication policy and, if so, whether that policy is written down. As shown on Table 33, the majority of respondents (73 of 111, or 66 percent) said they do have a communication policy, but just less than half of those said it was written down. Some whose policy is written sent copies of the policies which were included in the preceding discussions of corporate communication.

The 29 percent (32 of 111 respondents) who have a written policy is well

427

Dear

You can be of considerable help to me in a study I am conducting of international business communication practices. I am writing to you as one of the 500 largest companies in the world as listed by Fortune magazine.

Specifically I am interested in knowing how your managers communicate with employees and how your employees communicate both with management and with one another.

1. Does your company have a communication policy?

2. If your company has a communication policy, is it written down? (If so, may I have a copy?)

3. In communicating with employees, do managers use any of these methods:

a. Print
  (1) annual report
  (2) annual report to employees
  (3) newspaper/magazine
  (4) bulletin board
  (5) orientation manual
  (6) letters
  (7) pay envelope inserts
  (8) manual
  (9) handbook

b. Electronic
  (1) telephone
  (2) closed-circuit television
  (3) teleconference
  (4) film
  (5) videotape
  (6) electronic mail

4. If management uses other methods for communicating with employees than those listed in 3, please describe them.

5. In communicating with management, do employees have available to them any of these methods:

a. Written
  (1) memorandum
  (2) report
  (3) suggestion system
  (4) question box
  (5) newspaper/magazine

b. Personal
  (1) meeting
  (2) interview
  (3) open-door policy
  (4) grievance procedure

6. If employees have available to them other means for communicating with management than those listed in 5, please describe them.

7. In communicating with one another, do employees have available to them any of the following:

  a. personal contact
  b. memorandum
  c. meeting

8. If employees have available to them other means for communicating with one another, please describe them.

9. Are any of the techniques that your company uses for communicating unique to your company or country? If so, please describe them.

10. How important is the informal system of communication (called the "grapevine" in the United States)?

11. How important is nonverbal communication?

12. If you could change your company's communication system, how would you do so?

The results of this study will be included in a book I am writing for Greenwood Press of Westport, Connecticut. I would like to include in the book case studies of organizations from throughout the world. For those, I need additional information about your company:

  1. Brief history.
  2. Management philosophy and style.
  3. Present status.
  4. Goals for the future.

Thank you very much for your participation in this work. I will send you a summary of the results of this study when it is completed.

              Sincerely,

## Table 32. Survey Results, by Region of the World

|  | Can. | EEC | non-EEC Eur. | Pac. Rim | Aus. & NZ | Lat. Am. | Mid-East | Afr. | Total |
|---|---|---|---|---|---|---|---|---|---|
| Total responses | 10 | 84 | 25 | 22 | 8 | 10 | 4 | 13 | 176 |
| Total questionnaires | 8 | 44 | 20 | 19 | 5 | 8 | 3 | 4 | 111 |

below the figure for the largest American corporations. A similar survey of the Fortune 500 corporations in 1981 found that nearly half of all American corporations have a written communication policy. One Canadian company said this:

> We do not have a communication policy in writing. However, we do have an extensive number of communications programs and four company communications departments to handle employee communications companywide. We believe that good internal communications help employees better perform their jobs by understanding the industry trends, the company's business plans and their place within those plans.

It was clear from the responses that companies everywhere consider communication important. Even companies who answered to explain their refusal to participate pointed this out. This comment was in one such letter: the chairman "regards your subject of communication to be a vital one but I regret to inform you that, due to other pressing business commitments, we will be unable to assist your research." Another letter, itself an exhibit of good, if specialized, corporate communication, read:

> Thank you for your letter dated December 27th asking for our participation in your survey of international business communication practices. Unfortunately, I must decline to participate in this study. We are so busy with a host of other projects and demands that with the best will in the world, I am afraid I cannot afford to burden ourselves with answering such examinations.
>
> I know that your work depends on the willingness of industry to participate in such studies; however, I cannot give you a more favorable answer at the present time.

Other companies replied that their companies were decentralized with each division free to choose its own system of communicating. It was impossible, they said, to answer the questions in a way that represented the whole company. A few companies reported a condition that seems a little worrisome:

> Unfortunately the information you seek is not readily available in a form where it can just be collated and issued. To do the necessary research would involve many hours of work for more than one department, and we just do not have the manpower these days to undertake this kind of detailed searching and collating.

Either this company and a few others which responded similarly misunderstood the scope of my study or their knowledge of their own communication programs is woefully lacking. Executives should be able to describe their company's program at a moment's notice in very general terms — regardless of the company's size. That is the sort of information being sought here.

Another person who misunderstood the scope of this study was the chief executive of an African Chamber of Commerce. He wrote, in response to one of many letters sent to such organizations around the world, without regard to avoiding offense:

> I am sure you must appreciate that if the Secretariat of this National Chamber were to attempt to answer your questions then we would have produced a very valuable thesis suitable for profitable publication in this country and elsewhere. The research work involved would be most interesting and a number of my staff would be delighted to do it if relieved of their normal duties.

> If of course a number of National Chambers carried out such work and privately sent to you the fruits of their labors you would have but a simple job to produce an even more valuable and authoritative text book on industrial and commercial communication.

> I regret, however, that neither myself or my staff could really afford the time to do this research for you.

# Formal Communication System

Responses to the survey show that regardless of the size of the company or its location, most business organizations use basically the same methods of communication internally.

Table 33 shows upward and horizontal communication for all countries, for EEC countries and for the Pacific-rim countries, respectively. More companies use more downward channels of communication than upward channels and more companies use personal means of communication up the chain of command than use electronic means.

Pacific-rim countries depend least on written means of communicating and most on personal methods. These countries also seem to emphasize upward communicating over downward communicating as shown by the channels that are made available to them. The reverse seems to be true of companies in European countries.

## Upward Communication

Asked whether employees have available to them other means for communicating with management than those listed, respondents emphasized formal activities planned and mostly executed by management. A few of their comments follow:

*Australia:* All sites are unionized. Employees can and do raise matters to be communicated to management through their unions. Some sites have

## Table 33. Communication Channels Used by Foreign Firms

| | UPWARD Written | | | | | Personal | | | | Print DOWNWARD | | | | | | | | | Electronic | | | | | | HORI-ZONTAL | | |
|---|---|---|---|---|---|---|---|---|---|---|---|---|---|---|---|---|---|---|---|---|---|---|---|---|---|---|---|
| | 1 | 2 | 3 | 4 | 5 | 1 | 2 | 3 | 4 | 1 | 2 | 3 | 4 | 5 | 6 | 7 | 8 | 9 | 1 | 2 | 3 | 4 | 5 | 6 | 1 | 2 | 3 |
| Canada | x | x | x | | | x | x | x | x | x | | x | x | x | x | | | | | x | x | | | x | x | x | x |
| EEC | x | x | x | | x | x | x | x | x | x | x | x | x | | x | | | | | x | x | | x | x | x | x | x |
| Non-EEC Europe | x | x | x | | x | x | x | x | x | x | | x | x | x | x | | x | | | x | | x | x | x | x | x | x |
| Pacific Rim | x | x | x | | | | x | x | x | x | | x | x | x | x | | x | x | x | | | | | x | x | x | x |
| Australia and New Zealand | x | x | x | | x | x | x | x | x | x | x | x | x | | x | x | x | x | x | x | | | x | x | x | x | x |
| Latin America | x | x | | | | x | x | x | x | x | | x | x | | x | x | | x | x | | | | | | x | | x |
| Middle East | x | x | x | x | | x | x | x | x | x | x | x | x | x | x | x | x | x | x | | x | x | x | | x | x | x |
| Africa | | x | | | | x | x | | x | x | x | x | x | x | | x | x | | | x | | | | x | x | x | x |
| | | | | | | | | | | | | | | | | | | | | | | | | | | | |
| France | x | x | x | x | | x | x | x | x | x | x | x | x | x | x | x | x | x | | x | x | x | | | x | x | x |
| Ireland | x | | x | | x | x | x | x | x | x | | x | x | | x | | | | | x | | x | x | | x | x | x |
| Italy | x | x | x | | x | x | x | x | x | x | x | x | | x | | x | x | x | x | | x | x | | x | x | x | x |
| The Netherlands | x | x | x | | x | x | x | x | x | x | | x | x | | x | | x | | x | | | x | x | | x | x | x |
| Great Britain | x | x | x | | x | x | x | x | x | x | x | x | x | | x | x | x | x | x | | | | x | x | x | x | x |
| West Germany | x | x | x | | | x | | x | | x | | x | x | x | | | | x | | | | | x | | x | x | x |
| | | | | | | | | | | | | | | | | | | | | | | | | | | | |
| Japan | x | x | x | | x | x | x | x | | | x | x | x | x | | x | x | x | | | | | | | x | x | x |
| Singapore | | | | | x | | x | | x | x | x | x | x | x | x | x | x | | | | | x | | | x | x | x |
| Australia | x | x | x | | x | x | x | x | x | x | x | x | x | | x | x | x | x | x | | | x | x | x | x | x | x |

UPWARD: Written—1. memorandum, 2. report, 3. suggestion system, 4. question box, 5. newspaper/magazine; Personal—1. meeting, 2. interview, 3. open-door policy.

DOWNWARD: Print—1. annual report, 2. annual report to employees, 3. newspaper/magazine; 4. bulletin board, 5. orientation manual, 6. letters, 7. pay envelope insert, 8. manual, 9. handbook; Electronic—1. telephone, 2. closed-circuit television, 3. teleconference, 4. film, 5. videotape, 6. electronic mail.

HORIZONTAL: 1. personal contact, 2. memorandum, 3. meeting.

various committees, e.g., safety, productivity, social, and these committees regularly meet with management to pass on comments, concerns and suggestions from employees.

*Canada:* As for other methods, I think that some of the special events we hold for employees could be deemed a communication of our corporate philosophies. These include our world-famous Christmas Party which 33,000 company employees and their families attend each year; Quarter Century Club dinners and presentations; new Profit Sharing Fund member breakfasts; dinners to recognize the completion of various apprenticeship and supervisory training courses and special dinners and golf tournaments for the company ladies and other groups.

*Denmark:* In almost all private and public companies in Denmark you will find so-called cooperation committees with 50:50 membership from management and labor. These joint committees serve an important role in the communication between management and the employees.

*Finland:* There is a fairly advanced form of employee participation in effect in this organization. Employees have a corporation-wide cooperation committee together with management and also they have a right to nominate representatives to the company's Supervisory Board.

*Great Britain:* In certain units (primarily manufacturing) managers above a certain level have an annual "grandfather interview," i.e., one hour with the boss's boss.

*Singapore:* Annual organizational health survey where employees rate all aspects of management and the company. Annual open performance appraisal system for management to review employee performance.

*South Africa:* We encourage informal functions as recognition for safety and other achievements and these also provide an excellent forum for horizontal and vertical communication. We have introduced a quality improvement process as an integral part of our corporate culture. The structure of this process provides an extensive communication forum at all levels. We have recently also introduced the use of attitude surveys which are inherently communication methods, in order to assist us in directing and evaluating our organization development activities.

*Sweden:* Reference groups — regular meetings with elected union groups.

*Sweden:* A common form of communication in Sweden is meetings. We have larger meetings where the management of a department, a division or if it's a smaller company a whole company meets for a presentation of current matters and for managers to answer questions. We also have different types of smaller meetings, often called work-place meetings, where a manager and his or her immediate subordinates meet once or twice a month.

*Switzerland:* Works councils with representatives elected by their co-workers. Regular meetings between local top management and works councils.

*West Germany:* According to the works constitution act in Germany there is a full system of communication in place with the works council and with ombudsmen/men of confidence. Specific committees are to handle the various concerns such as compensation committee, housing committee, vacation committee, etc.

*Zimbabwe:* Employees in the unskilled, semi-skilled and skilled categories can communicate with management via their representatives at Works Council meetings. At monthly briefing group meetings, any employee may ask a question which will be answered either immediately or in the next brief. Feedback cards are returned after briefing meetings so that management is aware of questions being asked and answers given or required.

## Horizontal Communication

Regarding horizontal communication, respondents were asked to indicate which channels are made available to employees for communicating with one another. They almost uniformly checked the three media listed: memoranda, meetings and personal contact, as Table 33 shows. In addition, respondents were asked what additional methods they use. These were the responses:

*Australia:* All employees are able to meet and talk among themselves and with their union representatives. There are a number of employee-promoted newsletters and publications that are freely circulated and in some instances company supported, which are available to employees and written and published free of management comment.
*Austria:* Letters, telephone, telex, employees' council, trade union.
*Canada:* Working together in teams or task forces from various areas or disciplines to complete projects.
*Denmark:* Sports organizations.
*Finland:* Bulletins, telephone, leisure activities.
*France:* Development of participation with management (task forces, quality circles, etc.), electronic mail, telephone.
*Great Britain:* Employees have available to them not only the 3 items listed by you but also the normal telephone networks within the work place. Outside the work place there are a number of sporting and welfare facilities available for the use of all employees where they can meet informally/ social.
*The Netherlands:* The Young Graduates Association organizes working parties, lectures, visits to company departments or plants, panel.
*Norway:* Small pause groups/coffee and lunchtime, telephone, intercom, electronic mail.
*Sweden:* To some extent electronic mail.
*Switzerland:* Different employee organizations, a rather large number of social clubs. Facsimile transmission, paging systems and data mail for quick information. Quality circle teams at certain locations. Team cooperation programs.
*Zimbabwe:* Social and informal interaction. This is particularly evident at our Stapleford factory where approximately 100 employees are housed in village conditions, with an inter-denominational church, general store, beergarden and an active social club.

## Downward Communication

Asked whether they use other methods of downward communication and, if so, what they are, the respondents provided these answers:

*Australia:* Much effort goes into face-to-face communication. Techniques vary from small group "toolbox talks" at mine sites, to mass site "tribal meetings," to "communication meetings" which usually involve managers from various areas and are normally followed by a drinks-and-nibbles gathering.

*Australia:* We encourage management to promote face-to-face communications whenever practicable. Our business managers appear from time to time on local radio and television, and we have recently introduced at our largest employment center (13,000 employees) a series of seminars where management, employees and union representatives get together in common-purpose seminars to discuss work practices, development of the plant and other items of mutual interest.

*Austria:* Information meetings — informal or according to Austrian labor constitution law, seminars, training.

*Bolivia:* Managers usually communicate in mass with employees through a conference. When they want to communicate with only one or a small group of employees they send a memorandum or have a personal interview.

*Canada:* We stress face-to-face communication, one-on-one meetings.

*Canada:* (1) Employees luncheons are held in local hotel function rooms on a quarterly (or so) basis. Every employee is to attend — from receptionist to CEO. At these luncheons there is an informative program of about one hour's duration, following dessert. (2) President's Luncheons are informal lunches held for five employees every six weeks in the President's office; he is host. (3) Any major event or appointment is communicated throughout the Corporation via a Communique to senior managers.

*Canada:* Our Recreation Park, which is established on 100 acres of property in Hamilton, includes an all-weather track, soccer/football field, five baseball diamonds, a double-pad ice skating arena, tennis courts and golf driving range and a mini putt. The various recreational programs which employees and their families participate in, certainly are a form of communicating and encouraging teamwork amongst our people.

*Denmark:* Interviews and meetings, a well-organized system of co-operation and an equally well-organized system of safety courses.

*Denmark:* All new employees participate in a 40-hour course introducing them to the industry and the company.

*Finland:* Computer network facilities.

*Great Britain:* Weekly ten-minute briefings in all areas of operation with general information, plus that relating to individual areas.

*Great Britain:* A further and most important system of communication which is specifically designed to detail business development is our system of "participation." This involves Site Committees at each of our UK sites whether these are factories, offices or research establishments, etc., where elected representatives of the employees meet with senior managers and where they are informed of the current state of the business and an outline of future plans. Managers are then open to questions and observations and Minutes are taken which are circulated to all employees. Representatives of these Site Committees also attend a Subsidiary Company Committee, where twice a year the progress of that Subsidiary Company Business is discussed in detail in much the same way as obtained at the Site Committee. Finally, elected representatives of the Subsidiary Company Committee meet with the Parent Board Directors at a Group Board Committee twice a year and a similar process of communication takes place covering the Group's worldwide operations.

*Great Britain:* The group managing director and operating unit general managers have serious management meetings the content of which get "cascaded" by attendees down through the organization.

*Great Britain:* Slide presentations on company's work by line managers.

*Great Britain:* On some of our sites we also have tannoy (public address) systems over which we can broadcast major items of interest.

*Greece:* Personal contact in branches and locations remote from the administrative offices.

*Indonesia:* Every year, management and employees have a meeting opportunity, i.e., Idul Fithri and New Year, monthly briefing every 17th day of the month.

*Ireland:* Press cuttings posted on bulletin boards and quarterly newsletters.

*Italy:* Training activities such as courses and seminars as well as the tools necessary to analyze the climate within the company (questionnaires, meetings, etc.) are also included in the communication practice and considered to be of great significance.

*Japan:* Various conferences and meetings, interviews, daily conversations, go out drinking after work, enjoy sports together on holidays.

*Japan:* Direct talks in off-time hours with drinks and eats.

*Japan:* Vocal tapes, computer communication system.

*The Netherlands:* Awards and internal competition on issues like quality, energy saving, pollution, etc.

*New Zealand:* We use a device which we describe as "Joint Consultative Panel." This involves regular (monthly) meetings between elected staff representatives and senior management personnel. This device gives staff the opportunity to raise issues of concern, or alternatively, to raise suggestions for implementation.

*Norway:* Corporate assembly, works committees.

*Singapore:* Management adopts an open-door policy that any employee can have a personal interview with any manager including the Managing Director. There is a system of work excellence committees in which employees can bring forward suggestions about work. There is a grievance procedure through which employees can voice their grievances through it and through the Company's house union to management.

*South Africa:* We use briefing groups and this concept is generally well-known in the literature. It consists mainly of formalized communication meetings starting at the top where "need to know" information is defined that must be disseminated down into the organization, and the consequent cascading of this information through scheduled work team meetings right down to the shop floor level. Communication efficiency is monitored by spot checks.

*Sweden:* The most used way to communicate with employees is in sound day-to-day contact between managers and employees.

*Switzerland:* Specialized noon-hour programs where members of management answer employees' questions concerning the business and behavior of the company.

*Switzerland:* Intensive use of teletype and telefax for real-time information of all subsidiaries worldwide.

*West Germany:* The German Works Constitution Act requires plant meetings (one every year) and reports on the economic situation of the enterprise (once a quarter).

*West Germany:* The general assembly of all employees twice a year; state of the company address of the CEO in front of senior and middle management twice a year.

*Zimbabwe:* The executives in charge of our three divisions hold monthly briefing group meetings for their senior managers at which information statements are issued. These statements cover changes in company policy or procedures, production, costs, sales, financial results, operational successes or problems, visitors, external appointments, industrial relations matters, etc. The senior managers then call briefing meetings for their heads of departments at which the brief is read and the process is repeated until every employee in the company has been briefed. Another means of communication is through Works Councils which meet regularly at all locations. A Works Council is composed of management representatives and Workers Committee representatives. Members of the Workers Committee are elected by, and represent, unskilled, semi-skilled and skilled employees. Discussion in Works Council meetings centers on industrial relations, domestic affairs and general grievances. Lastly, verbal announcements are made from time to time to Workers Committees and Trade Union representatives.

*Zimbabwe:* Works committees and departmental sub-committees play a vital role in facilitating upward communication.

## Unique Methods of Communicating

When asked whether any other methods that they use are unique to their company or country, respondents listed very few methods:

*Finland:* Internal real-time information system (mailbox type).
*Indonesia:* Religious gathering day.
*Japan:* Ideal for our communication is that we can intuitively understand

without saying or writing much. To achieve this, daily communication like personal contact in the small group activities has to be frequently conducted.

*The Netherlands:* "Octogons" are working parties of eight potential managers on important corporate issues. They make a report based on information gathered by interviewing top managers. This report is discussed by a panel including members of the board.

*The Netherlands:* As an international company, we have chosen the English language as our official company language.

*New Zealand:* We have two techniques which may not be commonly employed elsewhere: (1) A daily message is transmitted from the Managing Director to staff throughout our entire network. This is a means of acquainting staff with good achievements or bad, and of progress made with various projects and other matters. This message is transmitted by teleprinter/telex, and is made available on noticeboards, etc., usually by mid-morning each day. (2) We have a facility for staff to draw attention to breakdowns in procedure which could lead to adverse customer reaction. Any staff member is entitled to originate a teleprinter/telex message to our Head Office, briefly listing the details of an event or situation which has occurred during that day's operations. Matters raised may be deficiencies such as an overbooking, mechanical failure leading to a flight delay, or a potentially hazardous incident which could lead to a more serious event. This reporting system has become accepted throughout the company and where appropriate the originator of the report is given a reply either explaining the reasons for the incident or outlining what remedial action is being taken.

*South Africa:* Perhaps the only really unique element of our communication programs is related to our multi-lingual and multi-cultural labor force which necessitates: (1) translation of most of our communication into a number of languages, (2) using translators when necessary, and (3) providing a special language training, particularly in our mines, to facilitate communication.

*Sweden:* According to Swedish law, trade unions are entitled to appoint two ordinary and two alternate members of the Board of Directors.

*Switzerland:* We try to use all "state of the art" techniques as most Europeans do. We are somewhat behind with electronic mail and teleconferencing.

*Switzerland:* We make limited use of cartoons and graphs drawing attention to facts and figures concerning the nature of our business. They are put up in the elevators and get changed at regular intervals.

## The Grapevine

Next the questionnaire asked how important the informal system of communication (called the "grapevine" in the United States) is in the respondent's country. Answers to this question were three to one that the informal system is important:

*Australia:* It is both important and effective, although increasingly less so as a more participative and open approach to employee relations is adopted.

*Australia:* The "grapevine" exists. Its importance increases if morale is poor and decreases the more effective communication is. It also provides management with important feedback on feelings within the company.

*Australia:* The "grapevine," so our employee research indicates, remains probably the quickest means of communication, although not necessarily the most accurate. Our various communicators have to ensure that we combat "grapevine rumor" with a steady and quick flow of factual information. There are times when it is of value for the Company to "use" the grapevine to get certain information to a plant.

*Austria:* Informal communication is important due to the political situation (this is a state-owned enterprise and the two main political parties in the country have some influence); employees (sometimes in the third/fourth generation already) stay mostly till their retirement with the company and therefore the fluctuation rate is very low compared to other companies. So the informal communication via social benefits (such as company-owned dwellings, sport activities, company's holiday welfare facilities, social events, etc.) is very strong.

*Bolivia:* As in any human relations, the "grapevine" communication system has its importance in labor relations in Bolivia. Gossip at work affects management as well as workers. It has a negative incidence on general production, on work disposition and creates difficulties in team work.

*Canada:* Extremely important. Several active grapevines exist. Sometimes used by management to deliver information.

*Canada:* It's indigenous to the large organization. A force for good and evil in communication systems.

*Canada:* As with any large company, the grapevine is suspected to be active here and accurate most of the time. While efforts are made to ensure important and official news travels to the employee through the formal channels, invariably the grapevine continues to function.

*Canada:* It flourishes because of our family atmosphere. It is occasionally used by management to deliver information.

*Canada:* We would not rely on it to pass on information.

*Canada:* The grapevine is always important and useful.

*Canada:* Varies according to topic and location.

*Denmark:* The informal system of communication is extremely important and probably transfers more information than the formal system of communication. Some companies take this into account and facilitate means of informal communication. Other companies tend to believe that what is not transmitted through the formal system or communication is not known. This, however, seems to be a far too naive posture of the situation.

*France:* The informal system of communication exists in this company as well as in all other organizations. However, our company only acknowledges the communication practice through its institutional means.

*France:* Very important and part of our communication management system.

*Great Britain:* It is certainly evident in our company but it is a most unreliable method of communication since the "grapevine" often only has half the story or a very distorted and incorrect version.

*Great Britain:* The grapevine obviously exists and carries information on many things, sometimes accurate, sometimes not. It is management's job to supplement/replace the grapevine with regular, accurate information.

*Great Britain:* An important method, but it can be the conduit of completely false and sometimes vicious information. If there is a vacuum in a company's formal communication system, the "grapevine" will grow and prosper.

*Great Britain:* The "grapevine" system is not relied on or encouraged in any way in this company as it is thoroughly unreliable and open to misinterpretation and error.

*Great Britain:* The "grapevine" is an important channel of communication because it helps to supplement formal systems and often enables more honest views, comments and reaction to be expressed. A weakness of the grapevine is that misleading and inaccurate information may be transmitted.

*Italy:* The grapevine works parallel to the formal system.

*Japan:* We consider informal communication to be very important in our daily business operations. For example, every morning, the members of each division gather to hear and discuss the work schedule for the day. Also, circulars are distributed throughout the company, giving information on both work-related subjects and social activities.

*Japan:* The informal system of communication is very important in Japanese companies and it is sometimes considered almost obligatory. After work, employees of the same section or department often go out for a drink with their manager in order to frankly discuss their opinions and reveal their real intention. In Japan, it is considered impolite to speak plain, that is to say "no" or raise objection to proposals of their superior officials in a formal situation.

*The Netherlands:* As our company is very decentralized, with full profit responsibility for the product divisions, the "grapevine" is considered very important to get the right feeling what is going on in the company and also for getting things through, although we have rather elaborate authority schedules and directives.

*New Zealand:* We have to acknowledge that the "grapevine" is active in the Company, but it is not a communication method that we desire to perpetuate—it is too frequently wrong. However, since we are in part in the communication business, it is no surprise that conjecture and rumor are quickly spread throughout the network.

*The Philippines:* The informal system of communication is a very important means of communication. In fact, much of the information is sourced through the system.

*South Africa:* The grapevine is used extensively, often because a formal communication system is not well considered. Also, the socio-political environment in this country promotes this form of communication.

*Sweden:* The informal system is the most important. The formal system can never substitute for the day-to-day contact between managers and employees. It can only be a complement to the informal way to communicate.

*Switzerland:* In our communication concept, the manager should be the prime source of information for his employees. But the grapevine continues, of course, to exist and at times to flourish.

*Switzerland:* The grapevine mainly is there to sustain good friendly relationships.

*Switzerland:* Improvement of efficiency for all information techniques and channels decreases the importance of the "grapevine" more and more.

*Switzerland:* By anticipating future events and by informing rapidly, management wants to minimize the importance of the informal system of communication.

*West Germany:* In our opinion, the grapevine is as important as the formal communication system is to a company.

*West Germany:* Informal communication systems are without any doubt very important within our company, especially among employees on the same hierarchical level. Informal systems are used both for "official" and "private" matters.

*West Germany:* The informal system of communication is considered to be of high value; it contributes to communication between different functional levels.

*Zimbabwe:* In a small organization like ours, the "grapevine" is well developed. It is sometimes used to "leak" information deliberately. The informal social structure is a powerful force and particularly so in the post–Independence environment.

*Zimbabwe:* The "grapevine" is inevitable. For major issues, however, it is company policy to endeavor to forestall the "grapevine" by using more formal communication channels. The "grapevine" remains useful in indirect upward communication as a gauge of sentiment and as a possible early warning device.

*Zimbabwe:* The informal system of communication is very effective for both management and employees as the atmosphere created is informal and all parties feel free to air their views.

## Nonverbal Communication

Although many respondents interpreted "nonverbal" as "nonoral" and discussed the importance of their print media, others responded as follows:

*Australia:* Comparative to other cultures, Australians place less emphasis on nonverbal communication.

*Bolivia:* I understand nonverbal communications to mean gestures, which have little influence on labor relations.

*Canada:* Nonverbal communication, including body language, office set-up and arrangements, personnel policies and compensation packages all assist an employee to identify the Corporation's direction and his/her place in the overall scheme.

*Great Britain:* Nonverbal (nonoral) communication is important and effective in supplementing oral briefings and communicating standard practices and procedures.

*Great Britain:* You mean like segregated eating, etc.? I imagine it is fairly important – the sense it gives out, certain signals which employees presumably read.

*Japan:* Nonverbal communication is very important. Most frequently used method is eye contact. Facial expression and hand gestures are also used. When an executive says something improper, people working under him would not interrupt by words or outwardly express it. Instead they would show it through eye contact or give him a nudge with the elbow so that the other party would not become aware of it.

*The Netherlands:* Important in, for instance, the "telegenetic" radiation of the President in our video "Messages from the President."

*The Philippines:* Nonverbal communication is very important since Filipinos are very perceptive and sensitive to nonverbal communication.

*Sweden:* Nonverbal and verbal communication are equivalent. They complement each other.

*Switzerland:* Nonverbal communication is always underestimated.

*West Germany:* Nonverbal communication is of minor significance in our company.

*West Germany:* Nonverbal communication becomes more and more important. We know that it is used quite frequently but it is not consciously realized by managers or employees. So there will not be any consequences as to communication.

## Improving Corporate Communication

Finally and most importantly, respondents were asked to predict how they would change their company's communication program if they could do anything they wanted. Most respondents had definite ideas on how they hoped to improve their company's communications. In many cases this involved either providing opportunities for more face-to-face, informal communicating or increasing company use of electronic methods – particularly those involving the computer.

*Australia:* We would do the impossible and talk face-to-face with every employee. We would give the employees all the information first hand, rather than have them have to read about it or watch it on television. This, of course, is the impossible dream.

*Australia:* Establish a clearer, more consistent public image of the company that makes it easier for employees and others to identify with. This may mean a new corporate delivery and media advertising. Increase the frequency of meetings with the chief executive and employees at sites throughout the organization. Make greater use of video for internal communications. Reintroduce a company-wide newspaper to act as an idea-disseminator and as a means of providing recognition, incentives and commendation.

*Austria:* No changes of the present system are planned. The electronic possibilities are constantly being improved (better telephone system, personal computers are being made available to more and more employees, electronic quality control at machines, etc.).

*Canada:* The company reviews its communication efforts regularly by way of focus sessions, readership and attitude surveys, and external evaluations. When there is reason to affect changes to our programs, or introduce new ones, we do so. We believe in a strong, ongoing communication function that remains flexible to the current information needs of employees and delivers the information in the most timely media.

*Canada:* Get information up, down and lateral quickly, in such a way that all employees have the information they need when they need it.

*Canada:* Instill in first-line supervisors an appreciation for the verbal communication skills necessary to manage successfully.

*Canada:* Additional written means up and down.

*Colombia:* Intensive use of electronic communication.

*France:* We consider the communication system now existing within the company to be more than adequate. However, we will persist in our effort to improve both the technical tools and the quality of communication systems.

*France:* To keep it as humanized (direct contact) as possible but keeping in mind efficiency. It would be interesting to simplify the relations between manager and employees. It is a problem of attitude but also of training.

*Great Britain:* Continue to strive for improvement of cascading/briefing techniques.

*Great Britain:* Increase the level of face-to-face briefings and improve managerial communication skills.

*Great Britain:* Communicate even more frequently using the existing range of techniques. Continue to strive for improvement. Better use of briefing/cascading techniques.

*Great Britain:* System is flexible according to need and electronics are spreading the process. No fundamental change but increasing use of software to explain things better without paperwork, post, etc.

*Great Britain:* The most common criticism from our employees is that either the trade unions or the press can beat management to the draw.

*Great Britain:* It is not for this writer to say *how* the company's communications systems should change, but the individual feelings of different managers to employee communication certainly means that important company communications are not "broadcast" at the same time or with the same sincerity everywhere.

*Great Britain:* The company's communication system has and will change over time as the size of the Group gets bigger. Essentially we try at all times to ensure that employees are kept well informed by their most immediate managers.

*Greece:* Encourage more informal/social meetings for bringing employees closer in more frequent sequences. Also, I would like to introduce more modern electronic communication methods.

*Ireland:* We would like to add a worldwide teleconferencing facility. Difficulties: cost, varying international time zones.

*Italy:* I would like to give more support to functional and interfunctional staff meetings.

*Japan:* Introduction of electronic terminals to each desk if possible. Execution of enjoyable events temporarily, for example, sports game, drinking, picnic, etc., especially on some anniversary day and/or on the day when a project is completed.

*Japan:* At present we have no intention of altering our communication system, except that we are encouraging our management and employees to use upward and downward channels more effectively.

*Japan:* In order to change our company's communication system, it is best to make an aggressive movement such as organizing a voluntary project team.

*The Netherlands:* We constantly improve and intensify communication systems.

*New Zealand:* We would prefer to have less "grapevine" communication, because of its obvious limitations. Other than that, we are satisfied that our present systems work as well as can be expected, but we place importance on the subject as a whole, and are continually looking for methods of improvement.

*Sweden:* In the future, add electronic mail and use video more often. Personally addressed information to specific personnel.

*Sweden:* Communication can be provided in many ways. It must be concrete and based on results. Often it is the immediate superior who can best provide the information.

*Sweden:* A program has recently started in order to create regular management/personnel discussions within our "Customer Satisfaction Program."

*Sweden:* Seminars in human resources development for top and middle managers.

*Switzerland:* Improvement of all systems used is an ongoing process.

*Switzerland:* We do not think the company's communication system should be changed. However, the application of a direct, fast and uncomplicated style of communication needs continuous effort.

*Switzerland:* Invest even more time and money to train all managers to be efficient in communication and regularly judge also this aspect of their performance.

*West Germany:* If we wanted to change, we would have done so.

*West Germany:* The presently used communication means have proved to be effective. There are steady endeavors to improve the system or adjust it to modern techniques. Large enterprises need effective communication systems in order to remain competitive.

*West Germany:* If we could change our communication system, we would like to improve our electronic communication devices. We would like to use local networks in order to get an immediate access to existing data; as a result written communication will be reduced.

*Zimbabwe:* Films and increased access to video shows would be desirable. Improved implementation of existing systems and policies.

*Zimbabwe:* At this stage, the emphasis is on improved implementation of existing systems and policies.

## *Discussion*

Based on their responses to the lists of communication channels provided, we see preferences for certain channels of communication over others and we recognize them as varying by region. In downward communication Canadians chose the annual report and handbooks most often as the means for management to communicate with employees. The EEC countries selected the annual report and letters most often; non–EEC European countries picked newspapers/magazines first and tied annual reports and bulletin boards for second.

Among printed methods of communicating, the annual report, newspaper/magazine, bulletin board and letters got the most frequent mention. In the electronic media, the telephone and videotapes were used most. For upward communication, most respondents said that memoranda, reports and suggestion systems were commonly used as forms of written media and meetings, interviews and the open-door policy for personal methods.

One of the interesting aspects of conducting a survey like this one is the fact that the responses that companies make to it are in themselves manifestations of their interest in communicating. Some companies returned the questionnaire practically in the return mail with as many samples of their corporate communicating as they could possibly send. These will be useful for a long time to come.

Some of the materials sent me were astounding. Waterford Glass Group PLC of Ireland sent a beautifully bound and illustrated hard-cover book, nine by fourteen inches in size and priced at fifty dollars, called *Waterford: An Irish Art.* Others delayed responding for a while for unavoidable reasons but then sent everything they could find by international express mail. Some sent a thorough reply and then referred the author to their branch offices in the United States.

The best overall response came from the industrial giants: Canada, Great Britain, Japan, Sweden, Switzerland and West Germany. Usage of materials sent me has expanded their portions of this book beyond those of other countries.

It seems obvious that some responses were not forthcoming because of the language barrier (again, all questionnaires and correspondence were in English), which calls into question the idea that most businesses worldwide are capable of corresponding in English. Of course, one or another recipient may not have been willing to spend their valuable time or use their English facility on unimportant matters like academic surveys. Nevertheless, the materials that were received in this survey do provide an idea of corporate communication systems and practices around the world as described in previous chapters and compared here.

# 9. Communication *Is* the Organization — Worldwide

Despite variations on the theme, corporate communication programs around the world are remarkably similar in the channels that management chooses to communicate with employees and in the channels that management makes available to employees to communicate both with management and with one another. Whatever differences do exist can be traced to culture.

Corporate communication systems are designed to fit particular organizations and since organizations differ by country, systems of communication are also different. But why should organizational structures differ if all organizations strive to accomplish objectives as determined by their founders? The answer lies in the organizations' cultural setting.

Cultures that are highly structured such as those in northern Europe naturally produce organizations that are similarly structured. The people expect it and function best in such an environment an important part of which is the precise communication pattern that Hall has described as part of low-context cultures in which most of a message is put into words.

Other cultures place greater emphasis on interpersonal relationships and family life than on exact schedules and earned profit. As one would expect, organizations in these cultures are freer in form and function than those described above, and communication within these organizations is freer flowing and more informal. These cultures Hall referred to as high-context, meaning messages communicated include elements of the context along with the words being used.

To complicate matters, those countries that were colonies of foreign powers for extended periods have been eternally changed by that relationship. Also all nations of the world are influenced by the Western media, especially the electronic media beamed instantaneously and incessantly around the world. Ironically many countries use the Western media for information about themselves as well as about their neighbors on their own continents.

Understanding the corporate communication system of any organization requires study of both organizational structure and behavior as well as a thorough investigation of the culture in which the organization exists. The logical progression of such a study should be culture first, then organization and finally communication system.

The United States and Canada rely most on written channels of communication simply because such media provide the kind of efficiency and accuracy that these countries find essential for conducting business in their complex economies. Meetings and other interpersonal relating are on a low-context basis and time is used monochronically (that is, one event is attended to at a time) — all in tune with the overriding desire for efficiency and control.

Electronic communicating that is so popular in North America is being adopted more slowly than expected in the rest of the world. The ubiquitous telephone, of course, plays an important part of business in all countries, but its use as a part of conducting business varies. North Americans are willing to transact any type of business at any time for any length of time on the telephone. In some other cultures, telephone communication is acceptable for making appointments for personal meetings, and because of the uncertain reliability of the telephone system in some such places, even that may be impossible. North Americans must, therefore, change their approach from the very beginning in such situations. Writing letters is not a viable alternative for communicating with all but the very highest corporate levels in countries where the literacy rate is still on a very low level.

An initial personal visit is inevitable in some countries, if only to establish a working relationship with a liaison in the country where future business negotiations are desired. In that situation, the person one chooses will have everlasting repercussions. Often the personal, particularly family, connections of that individual are considered very important and success is surest when the individual has established his own long-term interrelationship with important segments of the business community.

Foreign visitors, especially those from North America and Northern Europe, will find upon arrival in Latin America, the Middle East and parts of Asia that the communicating patterns are diametrically opposite to what they are used to. These cultures are among the highest-context in the world, and use of time is almost totally polychronic (allowing several events to occur at once). The only option for the Westerner is to understand and adapt. Residents of these countries may have a far easier time communicating in one another's countries — cumulatively most of the world — than do North Americans and northern Europeans simply because their communication customs are so similar: high-context and polychronic time-users. North Americans and northern Europeans communicating in most of the rest of the world must overcome communication barriers, in addition to the usual ones, of a different contextual communication style with different time-use patterns.

Many business persons in other countries place people over business deals so that they attempt to know who they are dealing with through the exchange of largely personal information before they will address the business prospects which brought them face-to-face with strangers in the first place. This getting-to-know-you process may take days, weeks and even months before business will be discussed, to the frustration of Western visitors who, as we said, have efficiency on their minds.

The courtesies of shaking hands and exchanging business cards are very similar in most places, with only minor but important variations. Most non–English speakers expect the card to be translated or at least transliterated into their own language. The Japanese, for instance, use *romaji* for the writing of all foreign words, including names.

How the cards are presented is extremely important in some areas. As with anything else, the card should be presented only with the right hand in Arab countries. The left hand, the bathroom hand, is still considered unclean even though modern hygiene has removed the need for such precautions that were necessary in nomadic days. In these same countries, business cards become a directory of contacts because telephone directories are complex or out of date and usually both. Some cultures respect education so that one's academic degrees should be printed on business cards. In others, longevity is honored so that the founding date of very old companies should be included on business cards.

As for shaking hands, it may not be done at all, as in certain Oriental cultures, and the grip varies by area — from limp and loose to firm and pumping. The French have their own style of hand-shaking — a single, firm shake. In many regions, confronting more than one person in a room requires shaking hands with each one both upon arriving and departing and in a specific order, usually starting with the highest-ranking person present but sometimes beginning with the oldest person. Most people expect to maintain eye contact with visitors during the shaking of hands, as a sort of initial sizing-up period.

Many hosts extend visitors an invitation of refreshments before any discussion of business and it should not be refused. Over tea or coffee, the personal interrelating that many peoples of the world find so important begins. Without the refreshment, the excuse for informal conversation during which important information is exchanged is gone and probably the possibility for business transactions with it. Americans feel somewhat uncomfortable with this particular preliminary because they feel they are doing nothing. Their hosts, on the other hand, see it as very definitely doing something that is important.

During these conversations, certain subjects, usually religion and politics, should be avoided. The same common sense that governs such taboos anywhere should guide the visitor abroad.

The question of whose language to use in business relationships is a difficult one. For their own survival, most business firms have developed an English-language capability. That facility, however, tends to be limited to a few individuals so that materials should be translated whenever possible into the host's language for passing on to the company's decision-makers who aren't necessarily fluent in English.

Using interpreters or translators adds another dimension to difficult intercultural communicating. The interpreter should be briefed thoroughly in advance on the subject to be discussed and should be told how to translate — literally or meaning summaries only. Some languages, like Korean, are incapable of simultaneous translation. In some countries, like Japan, translators are given very low status, so visitors must be careful of the position and status granted to the interpreter, particularly in relation to the other members of the native culture present.

The messages, both verbal and nonverbal, exchanged during the interview period are very important. The visitor does best when the communicating customs are understood so that when a host says "yes" but means "maybe" that eventually will turn into a "no," the foreigner will know how to react to win instead a real "yes." Violating nonverbal rules such as not passing materials with the left hand or showing the soles of one's feet in Arab countries or failing to maintain the expected eye-contact in Northern European countries will not be viewed kindly, even though foreigners who might not know are often forgiven their infractions.

How does knowing a country's corporate communication system benefit the visiting business person? For one thing, it gives the visitor insights for approaching the business relationship long before the initial phone call, if that is appropriate, is made or the first letter is written. Knowing which of these is appropriate or which alternative means of communicating is expected comes from understanding a country first and then its organizations and finally the system of corporate communication in use.

Second, knowledge of the internal communication system allows the visitor to adapt collateral materials to fit the system. For example, if the usual procedure is for top management to meet with middle management to announce new programs with the expectation that the information will "cascade" down the organization in a series of subsequent meetings on progressively lower levels until everyone hears the message, then a visitor can present materials that can be used conveniently in that initial meeting with top managers and reproduced conveniently for use all along the way. If the company newspaper or magazine is the primary means of communicating with employees, materials can be presented for easy insertion into that publication. If the bulletin board is used most, announcements, shorter in length and larger in type, can be prepared for immediate posting.

If the corporate communication system depends on consultation committees or workers' councils for properly passing the word on in the organization, the suggestion can be made that the visitor meet with them to clarify a proposed change in procedure that the new business relationship will bring. Change, good or bad, is always disorienting, and any suggestions business persons can make to minimize its effect will be appreciated.

In certain regions of the world — mostly Latin America and the Middle East — most communicating is transmitted personally between the top manager who is usually also the owner and all of the employees through the open-door policy. These owners retain total authority for decision making with the result that practically everyone in the organization prefers to deal with that individual, sometimes by passing several layers of the chain of command to do so. Unity of command just doesn't exist. In these same organizations, employees place family concerns above business matters; managers succeed best who take a personal interest in employees' family lives. In those cases, the foreign business person does best to deal with that top individual personally.

In some cultures, the person sent to represent a foreign country or company is expected to comply with cultural expectations. That individual should be over 50 years of age, for example, in certain Asian countries in compliance with the hosts' feelings about age. In other cultures, again mainly Latin America and the Middle East, women as business people will just not be taken seriously.

Knowing the differences in corporate communicating customs can mean the difference between success or failure in business negotiations. Conducting this study has reminded the author of a panel discussion at Ehime University in Matsuyama, Japan, in the early sixties. A member of the audience wanted to know why, when 1962 Japanese society was so modern and Westernized, the American press so often emphasized the different and the unusual like the geisha. This speaker's response was that that was what Americans were interested in — not all of those ways that the two countries are similar but in the interesting ways they are different. Today it is even clearer that that is what foreign visitors *should* be interested in — the differences rather than the similarities between cultures. Being able to distinguish between them presupposes a thorough study of the foreign culture. That is necessary for an American person contemplating doing business in any foreign country.

This study has shown that although there are similarities among the corporate communication systems in the world — remarkable ones at that — differences do exist, and they are more important than the similarities. In most cases, the differences stem from organizational structures and management practices that vary from one country to another.

In highly structured societies of northern Europe with their complex organizations, a corporate communication system must be similarly structured. Direct communication between owner/manager and employees would be a worst-case scenario in Sweden, say, and the Swedish method of concentrating on the work that needs to be done in almost total disregard for personal matters would be a worst-case scenario for Latin America.

When the international business person studies communication in foreign cultures, nonverbal communication should be included. As discussed, a gesture as innocent to Americans as the "A-OK" signal of thumb and forefinger curved into a circle is viewed as obscene in other cultures. The safest policy is to refrain from using all nonverbal communicating until enough experience tells you what is acceptable and what is not acceptable in other areas of the world.

World studies like this one and like that recommended for international business persons can easily join two areas of the world into units connected by language and religion. The Middle East, with its Islamic and Arabic culture, and Spanish, Roman Catholic Latin America have common customs, though in both cases some exceptions exist. Other areas of the world — Europe, Asia, the Pacific area and Africa — have highly individualistic peoples in nearly each country and so each country here must be treated in a way more descriptive of its individuality instead of as part of a region.

Businesses, especially those in the United States, should train any employee who must deal in any way with foreign clients in the culture and customs of the foreign country and even as many foreign cultures as possible. An excellent textbook for starting this training is *Managing Cultural Differences* by Philip R. Harris and Robert T. Moran.

Colleges of business should introduce courses that try to accomplish the above objective and even teach a general course in communicating in the world market. Modern students will face eventually on an international level problems that students of previous generations prepared for only on a national scale.

# Appendix:
# General Motors Corporation
# Communications Policy

SUBJECT Employe Communications                              NO 1466

TO  General Managers of Divisions          DATE October 12, 1983
    General Operating Officers
    Group Executives
    Staff Executives
    Heads of Staff Sections

Effective two-way communication between management and employes is critical for success in our highly competitive worldwide business.

The need for employe understanding, involvement and cooperation has never been greater — and a broad base of information about the business is fundamental to the achievement of all these goals. More than that, GM has an obligation to keep its employes informed about important matters that affect the business and their own livelihood.

Two-way information-sharing can improve decision making and work performance by facilitating the making of decisions at the lowest possible levels by employes who know the most about getting the job done right. In turn, this increased participation can contribute to higher levels of employe satisfaction and quality of work life. We need ideas and suggestions from all employes about how to operate more efficiently — at every level of the business. Good communications also can promote better employe understanding and consequent support for the Corporation's positions on key public issues.

The best means of communicating is by regular face-to-face exchange of information. But employe publications, bulletin board postings, letters to employe homes and other media should be used to supplement management-employe meetings and other forms of face-to-face communications.

Although local news is of primary interest to employes, local communications must also include priority corporate information. Surveys of GM employes have shown a high degree of interest in many corporate activities, such as technological developments, new products, financial performance, government actions, worldwide competition and foreign affiliations, future plans and other key aspects of the business. Guidelines for optimum management/employe communications at each GM location are attached.

Effective employe communications are essential to General Motors and each of you is urged to give to this important activity your full support and cooperation.

/ *Signed* / R.B. Smith, Chairman

SUBJECT Guidelines for Management/Employe Communications

TO General Managers of Divisions
    Plant Managers
    General Operating Officers
    Group Executives
    Staff Executives
    Heads of Staff Sections

The Employe Communications Section of the Public Relations Staff is responsible for coordinating corporate-wide employe communication efforts. Included are development of corporate print information, audiovisual materials, and other services designed to help General Motors staffs, divisions, and plants maintain effective programs of information-sharing with all employes. These activities are developed in cooperation with the Industrial Relations and Personnel Administration and Development Staffs. This memorandum discusses recommended standards and outlines guidelines concerning priority subjects for employe-management communications.

## RECOMMENDED STANDARDS

To maintain a satisfactory level of employe communication throughout the Corporation, basic standards have been developed based on programs already in operation at many locations. The recommendations are that each location:

1. Establish a formal, organized program of regular communication with all employes involving key information about the business and its effect on employes.

2. Establish regular, frequent printed communications for all employes.

3. Encourage regular meetings between management and employes. At least twice a year, management should provide all employes with a review of the state of the business (from both corporate and local viewpoints), as well as discussion of management problems, goals and outlook, plus what is expected from employes. Employe questions should be encouraged, with answers ideally being given at the meetings or through other communication channels as soon as practical.

4. Make effective use of the supervisory structure to provide for two-way

communication. All supervisors should understand the importance of communicating key information to subordinate supervisors and to employes in their work groups. Top management at all GM locations should make sure that supervisors have a regular flow of information to discuss with their employes — weekly newsletters and regular meetings with all supervisors to exchange information are recommended. Also, supervisors have a responsibility to receive and transmit upward, through organizational channels pertinent employe opinions, problem areas, and ideas for improvement.

5. Conduct periodic surveys to evaluate the effectiveness of employe communications and to provide direction for continuing improvements.

## GENERAL GUIDELINES

* Managers and supervisors are the key communicators at GM locations. Without their active involvement, the communication system will be less effective. They should share as much information as possible with all employes. Only truly confidential information should be withheld.

* The professional employe communication coordinator or manager assures that the communication system is carrying the information smoothly and efficiently among all segments of the organization. They should have full support and cooperation from top management and timely access to essentially all management information of the types listed on the next page.

* Employe communication should serve the information needs of *both* management and employes. Special care should be given to maintaining a reasonable balance in coverage of hourly and salaried activities to demonstrate management's desire to communicate with *all* employes on an ongoing basis.

* It is good practice to communicate the bad news as well as the good news to avoid negative effects of rumors and misinformation and to maintain management credibility with employes. It also is good practice to respond promptly to rumors or negative information about the local organization or GM that would be of concern to employes.

* It is imperative that important information be communicated to employes prior to or simultaneously with its release to the news media.

* Make prompt and effective use of corporate information materials and special services made available by the Public Relations Staff. All of these materials are approved for release to employes and the public unless specifically restricted.

* Expand or rewrite Corporation information whenever possible to reflect local interests as a means of increasing its impact on local employes.

## PRIORITY CORPORATE INFORMATION

To help coordinate corporate-wide information-sharing, a list of priority subjects for employe communication is developed each year and made available to Employe Communications Coordinators. These cover a variety of subjects such as:

* Product quality.

- GM's worldwide competitive challenge.
- GM technological leadership.
- GM product leadership; selling GM products.
- Facts about GM's business – special emphasis on economic factors.
- Government actions affecting GM.
- GM's response to social, safety, and environmental problems.
- Benefits of being a GM employe.

## PRIORITY LOCAL INFORMATION

The corporate priorities provide a base for development of local priorities. In addition, special attention should be given to the exchange of local information with employes on other subjects, such as:

- Plans, goals, and problems of the local organization.
- Performance levels – production output, absenteeism, quality, reject rates, progress in meeting established goals.
- Work schedules.
- Reports on quality of work life and employe participation groups with emphasis on achievements through teamwork of employes, management, and unions.
- Other local projects involving joint efforts of management and unions.
- Competitive problems, such as: how local plant won or lost contracts for business.
- Expansion or modification of physical facilities, improvements of equipment – what these changes mean to employes.
- Action or events which require special employe understanding – layoffs, reduction in production levels, or changes in overtime needs.
- Plant safety – basic rules, reports on accidents and how employes can help.
- Personnel matters – benefit programs, job opportunities, training and development opportunities, employe levels.
- Role of the local unit in community relations – how its management and employes contribute.
- Significant, interesting news about employes at work.

## HANDLING OF CONFIDENTIAL
## OR SENSITIVE CORPORATE INFORMATION

While an open climate of information-sharing is desirable to satisfy both the needs of the business and of our employees, it is important to safeguard the security of certain types of confidential information. This would include information which, if available to competitors or to the general public, would be advantageous to competitors or detrimental to GM, its shareholders, or its employees.

Whenever there is a question concerning the release of information to employes, the matter should be reviewed with the appropriate plant, division, or corporation staff executives. The GM Public Relations Staff also is available to assist in the clearance of informational material.

William P. MacKinnon      John W. McNulty       Alfred S. Warren, Jr.
Vice President            Vice President        Vice President
Personnel Administration  Public Relations Staff  Industrial Relations Staff
and Development Staff

cc: Public Relations Directors
    Personnel Directors
    Employe Communications Coordinators (or managers)
    Employe Publication Editors

# Bibliography

## Books

Adams, Michael, ed. *Handbooks to the Modern World: The Middle East*. New York: Facts on File, 1988.

Adler, Nancy J. *International Dimensions of Organizational Behavior*. Boston: Kent, 1986.

Africano, Lillian. *The Businessman's Guide to the Middle East*. Harper & Row, 1977.

Agarwala, A.N. *The Emerging Dimensions of Indian Management*. New York: Asia Publishing House, 1970.

Aguilar, Luis E. *The World Today Series: Latin America*. Washington, D.C.: Skye Corporation, 1985.

Alexander, Robert J. *Labor Relations in Argentina, Brazil, and Chile*. New York: McGraw-Hill, 1962.

Allen, Philip M., and Aaron Segal. *The Traveler's Africa*. New York: Hopkinson & Blake, 1973.

Almaney, A.J., and Alwan, A.J. *Communicating with the Arabs: A Handbook for the Business Executive*. Prospect Heights, IL: Waveland, 1982.

Alsegg, Robert J. *Control Relationships Between American Corporations and Their European Subsidiaries*. New York: American Management Associations, 1971.

Ames, Walter L. *Police and Community in Japan*. Berkeley, CA: University of California Press, 1981.

Amsden, Alice Hoffenberg. *International Firms and Labor in Kenya: 1945–70*. London: Frank Cass & Company, Ltd., 1971.

Archer, Maurice. *An Introduction to Canadian Business*. New York: McGraw-Hill, 1967.

*Area Handbook* series, Washington, D.C.: U.S. Government Printing Office, various dates. Includes Argentina, Australia, Austria, Bangladesh, United Republic of Cameroon, Ceylon, Chad, Dominican Republic, Ecuador, El Salvador, Ghana, Greece, Guinea, Italy, Jordan, Lebanon, Mauritania, Portugal, Ivory Coast, Senegal, Sierra Leone, Singapore, Spain, Uganda, Venezuela.

Asante, Molefi Kete, Eileen Newmark and Cecil A. Blake, eds. *Handbook of Intercultural Communication*. Beverly Hills, CA: Sage, 1979.

Austin, Paul Britten. *The Swedes: How They Live and Work*. New York: Praeger, 1970.

Barnard, Chester. *The Functions of the Executive*. Cambridge: Harvard University Press, 1950.

Barnet, Richard J., and Ronald E. Muller. *Global Reach.* New York: Simon and Schuster, 1974.

Barry, Tom, and Deb Preusch. *The Central America Fact Book.* New York: Grove Press, 1986.

Bass, Barnard M., and Philip C. Burger. *Assessment of Managers: An International Comparison.* New York: Free Press, 1979.

Berlo, David. *The Process of Communication.* New York: Holt, Rinehart and Winston, 1960.

Berry, Eileen. *The African Family-Household—A Behavioral Model.* Worcester, MA: International Development Program, Clark University, 1985.

Birdwhistell, Ray. *Kinesics and Context.* Philadelphia: University of Pennsylvania Press, 1970.

Blough, Roy. *International Business: Environment and Adaptation.* New York: McGraw-Hill, 1966.

Bolweg, Joep F. *Job Design and Industrial Democracy.* Leiden, The Netherlands: H.E. Stenfert Kroese, 1976.

Bosmajian, Haig A., ed. *The Rhetoric of Nonverbal Communication.* Glenview, IL: Scott, Foresman, 1971.

Bradley, Patricia Hayes, and John E. Baird, Jr. *Communication for Business and the Professions.* Dubuque, IA: William C. Brown, 1983.

Braganti, Nancy L., and Elizabeth Devine. *The Travelers' Guide to European Customs and Manners.* New York: Meadowbrook, 1984.

Brislin, Richard W. *Cross-Cultural Encounters.* New York: Pergamon Press, 1986.

Bruyn, Severyn T. *The Social Economy.* New York: John Wiley, 1977.

Bryant, Andrew. *The Italians: How They Live and Work,* 3rd ed. New York: Holt, Rinehart and Winston, 1970.

*Businessman's Guide to Europe.* Boston: Cahners Books, 1973.

Calvert, Peter. *The Mexicans: How They Live and Work.* New York: Praeger, 1975.

Carew, Dorothy. *The Netherlands.* New York: Macmillan, 1965.

Carroll, Joseph T. *The French: How They Live and Work.* New York: Praeger, 1970.

Casse, Pierre, and Surinder Deol. *Managing Intercultural Negotiations.* Washington, D.C.: Setar International, 1985.

Cetron, Marvin. *The Future of American Business.* New York: McGraw-Hill, 1985.

Cherry, C. *World Communication: Threat or Promise.* New York: Wiley Interscience, 1971.

Chesanow, Neil. *The World Class Executive.* New York: Rawson Associates, 1985.

Child, John. *British Management Thought.* London: George Allen and Unwin, 1969.

Chorafas, Dimitris N. *The Communication Barriers in International Management.* New York: American Management Associations, 1969.

Chothia, F. *Other Cultures/Other Ways.* Denver: Center for Orientation of Americans Going Abroad, 1978.

Clark, Rodney. *The Japanese Company.* New Haven: Yale University Press, 1966.

Cleveland, Roy L. *The World Today Series: The Middle East and South Asia.* Washington, D.C.: Skye Corporation, 1985.

Cole, J.P. *Italy.* New York: Praeger, 1964.

Condon, John C. *Good Neighbors: Communicating with the Mexicans.* Yarmouth, ME: Intercultural Press, 1985.

————, and Mitsuko Saito. *Intercultural Encounters with Japan.* Tokyo: Simul Press, 1974.

_____, and Fathi Yousef. *An Introduction to Intercultural Communication.* Indianapolis, IN: Bobbs-Merrill, 1975.

_____. *With Respect to the Japanese.* Yarmouth, ME: Intercultural Press, 1984.

Connery, Donald S. *The Scandinavians.* New York: Simon and Schuster, 1966.

Copeland, L., and L. Griggs. *Going International: How to Make Friends and Deal Effectively in the Global Marketplace.* New York: Random House, 1985.

*Countries of the World and Their Leaders,* 2 vols. Detroit: Gale Research Company, 1987.

*A Country Study* series, Washington, D.C.: U.S. Government Printing Office, various dates. Includes: Angola, Belgium, Brazil, Burma, Chile, Costa Rica, Cyprus, Egypt, Ethiopia, Germany, Guatemala, Honduras, India, Indonesia, Iraq, Israel, Japan, Kenya, Liberia, Malaysia, Mexico, Morocco, Mozambique, Nicaragua, Nigeria, Oceania, Pakistan, Panama, Persian Gulf States, Peru, the Philippines, Saudi Arabia, Somalia, South Africa, South Korea, Sudan, Syria, Tanzania, Thailand, Tunisia, Turkey, Zaire, Zambia, Zimbabwe.

*Cutting Bureaucracy, Encouraging Enterprises.* Geneva, Switzerland: Business International S.A., 1986.

Czarniawska, Barbara. *Controlling Top Management in Large Organizations.* Hampshire, England: Gower, 1985.

Daigler, Geraldine M. *Living in the Philippines.* Manila: The American Chamber of Commerce in the Philippines, 1980.

Damachi, Ukandi G., and Hans Dieter Seibel, eds. *Management Problems in Africa.* New York: St. Martin's, 1986.

Daniels, John D., Ernest W. Ogram, Jr. and Lee H. Radebaugh. *International Business: Environments and Operations.* Reading, MA: Addison-Wesley, 1980.

Davis, Keith. *Human Behavior at Work.* New York: McGraw-Hill, 1981.

Davis, Stanley M., ed. *Comparative Management.* Englewood Cliffs, NJ: Prentice-Hall, 1971.

Dempsey, Michael. *Atlas of the Arab World.* New York: Facts on File, 1983.

Deutsch, Mitchell F. *Doing Business with the Japanese.* New York: New American Library, 1983.

de Villiers, Les, Jan Marais and Nic Wiehahn, eds. *Doing Business with South Africa.* New Canaan, CT: Business Books International, 1986.

Devine, Elizabeth, and Nancy L. Braganti. *The Traveler's Guide to Asian Customs and Manners.* New York: St. Martin's, 1986.

DeVos, George A., and Keiichi Mizushima. "Organization and Social Function of Japanese Gangs: Historical Development and Modern Parables" in *Socialization for Achievement.* George A. DeVos, ed., Berkeley: University of California Press, 1973, pp. 280–310.

Dicks, Brian. *The Israelis: How They Live and Work.* New York: Praeger, 1975.

*Doing Business in Hong Kong.* New York: Ernst & Whinney International, 1987.

Donavan, John. *The Businessman's International Travel Guide.* New York: Stein & Day, 1971.

Doran, Charles F., and John H. Sigler, eds. *Canada and the U.S.* Englewood Cliffs, NJ: Prentice-Hall, 1985.

*Do's and Taboos Around the World.* Elmsford, NY: Benjamin Company, Inc., for Parker Pen Company, 1985.

Dostert, Pierre Etienne. *The World Today Series: Africa.* Washington, D.C.: Skye Corporation, 1986.

Doubleday, Nelson, and C. Earl Cooley, eds. *Encyclopedia of World Travel,* 2nd ed. Garden City, NY: Doubleday, 1973.

Drysdale, Alasdair, and Gerald H. Blake. *The Middle East and North Africa.* New York: Oxford University Press, 1985.

Eells, Richard. *Global Corporations.* New York: Interbank, Inc., 1972.

Fernea, Elizabeth Warnock, and Robert A. Fernea. *The Arab World.* Garden City, NY: Anchor Press, 1985.

Fieg, John Paul. *Thais and North Americans.* Yarmouth, ME: Intercultural Press, 1980.

Fisher, Glen. *International Negotiation.* Yarmouth, ME: Intercultural Press, 1980.

Fryer, Donald W., and James C. Jackson. *Indonesia.* London: Ernest Benn Limited, 1977.

Furstenberg, Friedrich. *Why the Japanese Have Been So Successful in Business.* New York: Hippocrene Books, 1974.

Gibney, Frank. *Japan: The Fragile Superpower.* New York: Norton, 1979.

Globerman, Steven. *Fundamentals of International Business Management.* Englewood Cliffs, NJ: Prentice-Hall, 1986.

Glyn, Anthony. *The British: Portrait of a People.* New York: Putnam's, 1970.

Gootnick, David E., and Margaret M. Gootnick, eds. *The Standard Handbook of Business Communication.* New York: Free Press, 1984.

Gorden, Raymond L. *Living in Latin America.* Chicago: National Textbook Company, 1974.

Gorman, Liam, Garry Hynes, John McConnell and Tony Moynihan. *Irish Industry: How It's Managed.* Kildare: Irish Management Institute Task Print and Packaging, Ltd., 1975.

Grosset, Serge. *Management: European and American Styles.* Belmont, CA: Wadsworth, 1970.

Grunwald, Joseph, and Kenneth Flamm. *The Global Factory.* Washington, D.C.: The Brookings Institution, 1985.

Haire, Mason, Edwin E. Ghiselli and Lyman E. Porter. "Cultural Patterns in the Role of the Manager" in *Culture and Management,* Ross Webber, ed.

_____, _____ and _____. *Managerial Thinking: An International Study.* New York: Wiley, 1966.

Hall, Edward T. *Beyond Culture.* Garden City, NY: Doubleday, 1977.

_____. *The Hidden Dimension.* Garden City, NY: Doubleday, 1966.

_____. *The Silent Language.* Garden City, NY: Doubleday, 1973.

*Handbook of the Nations,* 7th ed. Detroit: Gale Research Company, 1987.

Harms, L.S. *Intercultural Communication.* New York: Harper & Row, 1973.

Harris, Philip R. *New World, New Ways, New Management.* New York: American Management Associations, 1983.

_____, and Robert T. Moran. *Managing Cultural Differences,* 4th ed. Houston: Gulf, 1987.

Harrison, Phyllis A. *Behaving Brazilian.* Cambridge: Newburg House, 1983.

Hartmann, Heinz. *Authority and Organization in German Management.* Westport, CT: Greenwood, 1959.

Hines, George H. *The New Zealand Manager.* Wellington: Hicks, Smith & Sons, 1973.

Hinton, Harold G. *The World Today Series: East Asia and the Western Pacific.* Washington, D.C.: Skye Corporation, 1984.

Hoffman, Ann. *The Dutch: How They Live and Work.* New York: Praeger, 1971.

Hofheinz, Roy, Jr., and Kent E. Calder. *The Eastasia Edge.* New York: Basic Books, 1982.

Hofstede, Geert. *Cultural Consequences: International Differences in Work-Related Values.* Beverly Hills, CA: Sage, 1984.

Hoopes, David. *Global Guide to International Business.* New York: Facts on File, 1983.

Irwin, John L. *The Finns and the Lapps: How They Live and Work.* New York: Praeger, 1973.

Jablin, Frederic M., Linda L. Putnam, Karlene H. Roberts and Lyman W. Porter, eds. *Handbook of Organizational Communication.* Beverly Hills, CA: Sage, 1987.

Jackson, Peter C. *Corporate Communication for Managers.* London: Pitman, 1987.

Jain, Sagar C. *Indian Manager.* Bombay: Somaiya Publications, 1971.

Japan External Trade Organization. *How to Succeed in Japan.* Tokyo: Mainichi Newspaper, 1974.

Johnston, R.J. *The New Zealanders: How They Live and Work.* New York: Praeger, 1976.

Kallas, Hillar, and Sylvie Nickels, eds. *Finland: Creation and Construction.* New York: Praeger, 1968.

Kaplan, Marion. *Focus Africa.* Garden City, NY: Doubleday, 1982.

Kay, Shirley. *The Egyptians: How They Live and Work.* New York: Praeger, 1975.
_____, and Malin Basil. *Saudi Arabia: Past and Present.* Garden Grove, CA: Inter-Crescent, 1979.

Kaynak, Erdener. *International Business in the Middle East.* New York: Walter de Gruyter, 1986.

Kennedy, Gavin. *Doing Business Abroad.* New York: Simon & Schuster, 1985.

Kepler, John Z., Phyllis J. Kepler, Orville D. Gaither and Margaret L. Gaither. *Americans Abroad.* New York: Praeger, 1984.

Kilbourne, William, ed. *Canada: A Guide to the Peaceable Kingdom.* New York: St. Martin's Press, 1970.

Kirkpatrick, C.H., N. Lee and F.I. Nixson. *Industrial Structure and Policy in Less Developed Countries.* London: George Allen & Unwin, 1984.

Kurian, George Thomas. *Encyclopedia of the Third World,* 3rd ed. New York: Facts on File, 1987.

Lauterbach, Albert. *Enterprise in Latin America.* Ithaca, NY: Cornell University Press, 1966.

Lawrence, Peter. *Managers and Management in West Germany.* New York: St. Martin's, 1980.

Learmonth, Nancy. *The Australians: How They Live and Work.* New York: Praeger, 1973.

Learned, Edward P., Francis J. Aguilar and Robert C.K. Valtz. *European Problems in General Management.* Homewood, IL: Irwin, 1963.

Lee, Eve. *The American in Saudi Arabia.* Chicago: Intercultural Press, 1980.

Leonhardt, Rudolf Walter. *This Germany.* Greenwich, CT: Graphic Society, 1954.

Leppert, Paul A. *How to Do Business with the Chinese: A Taiwan Handbook for Executives.* Chula Vista, CA: Patton Pacific Press, 1984.

Lightfoot, Keith. *The Philippines.* New York: Praeger, 1973.

Linton, Ralph, ed. *The Science of Man in the World Crises.* New York: Columbia University Press, 1945.

Long, Robert Emmet, ed. *Mexico.* New York: H.W. Wilson, 1986.

Lott, James E. *Practical Protocol.* Houston: Gulf, 1973.

Luce, Louise F., and Elise C. Smith, eds. *Toward Internationalism: Readings in Cross-Cultural Communications.* Reading, MA: Addison-Wesley, 1979.

Mackay, Hugh. *The Communication Climate in Australian Organizations.* Bathurst, NSW: Australian Institute of Management, NSW Division, 1980.

————. *The Management of Communication.* Bathurst, NSW: Mackay Research Pty, Ltd., 1984.

Martin, Judith N., ed. *Theories and Methods of Cross-Cultural Orientation.* New York: Pergamon, 1986.

Mason, R. Hal, and Robert S. Spich. *Management: An International Perspective.* Homewood, IL: Irwin, 1987.

Mayne, Richard, ed. *Handbooks to the Modern World: Europe.* New York: Facts on File, 1986.

Mazrui, Ali A. *The Africans.* Boston: Little, Brown, 1986.

Mehrabian, Albert. *Silent Messages,* 2nd ed. Belmont, CA: Wadsworth, 1981.

Moores, Alan, ed. *Living in Hong Kong.* Hong Kong: American Chamber of Commerce in Hong Kong, 1986.

Morris, Desmond, Peter Collett, Peter Marsh and Marie O'Shaughnessy. *Gestures.* New York: Stein & Day, 1980.

Morton, W. Scott. *The Japanese: How They Live and Work.* New York: Praeger, 1973.

*Multinational Executive Travel Companion,* 18th ed. Boston: Multinational Executive, Inc., 1987.

Muna, Farid A. *The Arab Executive.* Garden Grove, CA: Inter-Crescent, 1980.

Nakane, Chie. *Japanese Society.* Berkeley: University of California Press, 1970.

Negandhi, Anant R., and S. Benjamin Prasad. *Comparative Management.* New York: Appleton-Century-Crofts, 1971.

O'Hanlon, Thomas J. *The Irish.* New York: Harper & Row, 1975.

O'Keefe, Bernard J. *Shooting Ourselves in the Foot.* Boston: Houghton Mifflin, 1985.

Onyemelukwe, C.C. *Men and Management in Contemporary Africa.* London: Longman Group, Ltd., 1973.

Paden, John N., and Edward A. Soja. *The African Experience.* Evanston: Northwestern University Press, 1970.

Pascale, Richard Tanner, and Anthony G. Athos. *The Art of Japanese Management.* New York: Simon & Schuster, 1981.

Patai, Raphael. *The Arab Mind.* New York: Charles Scribner's Sons, 1975.

Peck, Reginald. *The West Germans.* New York: Praeger, 1969.

Perceval, Michael. *The Spaniards: How They Live and Work.* New York: Praeger, 1969.

Phillips-Martinsson, Jean. *Swedes As Others See Them.* Lund: Utbildningshuset, 1985.

Platt, Raye R., ed. *Finland and Its Geography.* New York: Duell, Sloan and Pearce, 1955.

Prosser, Michael H., ed. *The Cultural Dialogue: An Introduction to Intercultural Communication.* Boston: Houghton Mifflin, 1978.

————, ed. *Intercommunication Among Nations and People.* New York: Harper & Row, 1973.

Rangel, Charles. *The Latin Americans.* New York: Harcourt Brace Jovanovich, 1976.

Rehder, Robert R. *Latin American Management.* Reading, MA: Addison-Wesley, 1967.

Renwick, George W. *Australians and North Americans.* Yarmouth, ME: Intercultural Press, 1980.

Ricks, David A. *Big Business Blunders.* Homewood, IL: Dow Jones-Irwin, 1983.

_____, M.Y.C. Fu and J.S. Arpan. *International Business Blunders.* Columbus: Grid, 1974.

Robinson, Richard N. *International Business Management.* Hinsdale, IL: Dryden, 1978.

Robock, Stefan H., and Kenneth Simmonds. *International Business and Multinational Enterprise.* Homewood, IL: Irwin, 1983.

Rucci, Richard B., ed. *Living in Korea.* Seoul: American Chamber of Commerce in Korea, 1984.

Ruch, William V. *Corporate Communications: A Comparison of Japanese and American Practices.* Westport, CT: Greenwood, 1984.

_____, and Maurice L. Crawford. *Business Reports: Written and Oral.* Boston: Kent, 1988.

Ruhly, Sharon. *Orientations to Intercultural Communication.* Chicago: Science Research Associates, 1974.

Samovar, Larry A., and Richard E. Porter. *Intercultural Communication: A Reader.* Belmont, CA: Wadsworth, 1972.

_____, _____ and Nemi C. Jain. *Understanding Intercultural Communication.* Belmont, CA: Wadsworth, 1981.

Sarbaugh, C.E. *Intercultural Communication.* Rochelle Park, NJ: Hayden, 1979.

Schur, Norman W. *British English: A to Zed.* New York: Facts on File, 1987.

Shafer, Robert J. *Mexican Business Organizations: History and Analysis.* Syracuse: Syracuse University Press, 1973.

Shilling, Nancy A. *A Practical Guide to Living and Travel in the Arab World.* Garden Grove, CA: Inter-Crescent, 1978.

Skinner, Elliott P., ed. *Peoples and Cultures of Africa.* Garden City, NY: Doubleday, 1973.

*South Africa: An Appraisal,* 2nd ed. Johannesburg: Nedbank Group, 1983.

Spencer, Arthur. *The Norwegians: How They Live and Work.* New York: Praeger, 1974.

Stewart, Edward C. *American Cultural Patterns: A Cross-Cultural Perspective.* Yarmouth, ME: Intercultural Press, 1972.

Strode, Hudson. *Sweden: Model for a World.* New York: Harcourt, Brace, 1949.

Sullivan, Jeremiah. *Handbook of Accounting Communication.* Reading, MA: Addison-Wesley, 1983.

Sycholt, August, and Peter Schirmer. *This Is South Africa.* Capetown: C. Struik, 1985.

Tanaka, H. William, and Nobuyuki Takashima. *Doing Business with Japan.* New Canaan, CT: Business Books International, 1986.

Tatsuno, Sheridan. *The Technopolis Strategy.* New York: Prentice-Hall, 1986.

Terpstra, V., and K. David. *The Cultural Environment of International Business.* Cincinnati: South Western, 1985.

Thompson, Wayne C. *The World Today Series: Canada.* Washington, D.C.: Skye, 1985.

_____. *The World Today Series: Western Europe.* Washington, D.C.: Skye, 1985.

Thurow, Lester C. *The Zero-Sum Solution.* New York: Simon & Schuster, 1985.

Tregear, T.R. *The Chinese: How They Live and Work.* New York: Praeger, 1973.

Ungar, Sanford J. *Africa: The People and Politics of an Emerging Continent.* New York: Simon & Schuster, 1985.

Van Der Haas, H. *The Enterprise in Transition.* London: Tavistock, 1967.

Vogel, Ezra. *Japan as Number 1.* Cambridge: Harvard University Press, 1979.

————, ed. *Modern Japanese Organization and Decision-Making.* Berkeley: University of California Press, 1975.

Walker, J., and M. Ambrex, eds. *The Business Traveler's Handbook: A Guide to Africa.* New York: Facts on File, 1981.

————. *The Business Traveler's Handbook: A Guide to Europe.* New York: Facts on File, 1981.

————. *The Business Traveler's Handbook: A Guide to Latin America.* New York: Facts on File, 1981.

————. *The Business Traveler's Handbook: A Guide to Middle East.* New York: Facts on File, 1981.

Walter, Ingo, ed. *Handbook of International Business.* New York: Facts on File, 1981.

Watson, Jessie. *The Canadians: How They Live and Work.* Toronto: Griffin House, 1977.

Webber, Ross A. *Culture and Management.* Homewood, IL: Irwin, 1969.

Weinshall, Theodore D., and Brian C. Twiss. *Organizational Problems in European Manufacturer.* London: Longman Group, 1973.

Weir, David, ed. *Men and Work in Modern Britain.* Bungay, Suffolk: Richard Clay, 1973.

*World Labor Report,* 2 vols. Geneva: International Labor Office, 1984.

*World Traveler's Almanac,* Chicago: Rand McNally, 1975.

*Worldmark Encyclopedia of the Nations: Africa,* 2nd ed., vol. 2. New York: Wiley, 1984.

*Worldmark Encyclopedia of the Nations: Asia and Oceania,* 6th ed., vol. 4. New York: Wiley, 1984.

*Worldmark Encyclopedia of the Nations: Europe,* 6th ed., vol. 5. New York: Wiley, 1984.

Yoshino, M.Y. *Japan's Managerial System.* Cambridge: MIT Press, 1968.

Zeldin, Theodore. *The French.* New York: Pantheon, 1982.

Zimmerman, Mark. *How to Do Business with the Japanese.* New York: Random House, 1985.

# Periodicals

Adler, Nancy J., and Mariann Jelinek. "Is 'Organization Culture' Culture Bound?" *Human Resource Management,* vol. 25, no. 1, Spring 1986, pp. 73–90.

Anker, Richard, and Catherine Hein. "Why Third World Urban Employers Usually Prefer Men," *International Labour Review,* vol. 124, no. 1, January-February 1985, pp. 73–90.

Arbose, Jules R. "The Generation Gap, Arab Style," *International Management,* October 1983, pp. 84–7.

————. "How I Learned to Love the Middle East," *International Management,* December 1981, pp. 27–9.

————. "The Middle East Mirage," *International Management,* April 1979, pp. 20–4.

_____. "A Question of Attitudes," *International Management,* March 1980, pp. 40-3.

Bashleigh, Clive. "Confessions of a Far-Flung Communicator," *Communication World,* October 1986, pp. 14-5.

Bate, Paul. "The Impact to Organizational Culture on Approaches to Organizational Problem-Solving," *Organization Studies,* vol. 5, no. 1, 1984, pp. 43-66.

Beaty, David T., and Oren Harari. "South Africa: White Managers, Black Voices," *Harvard Business Review,* July-August 1987, pp. 98-105.

Berger, Michael. "The Japanese Force Ahead to Tackle Their World Problems," *International Management,* March 1987, pp. 43-7.

Bernier, Linda. "French Quality Circles Multiply, But With a Difference," *International Business,* December 1986, pp. 30-2.

Bernstein, Aaron. "Warning: The Standard of Living Is Slipping," *Business Week,* April 20, 1987, pp. 48-52.

Bottger, Preston C., Ingrid H. Hallein and Philip W. Yetton. "A Cross National Study of Leadership: Participation as a Function of Problem Structure and Leader Power," *Journal of Management Studies,* vol. 22, no. 4, July 1985, pp. 358-67.

Bruce, Leigh. "The Italians: the Best Europeans?" *International Management,* May 1987, pp. 24-31.

Chambers, Peter. "Encouraging an Open Corporate Atmosphere," *International Management,* August 1975, pp. 49-52.

Clutterbuck, David. "Breaking Through the Cultural Barrier," *International Management,* December 1980, pp. 41-2.

_____. "How Effective are Worker Directors?" *International Management,* February 1974, pp. 14-6.

_____. "Spanning the Communications Gap," *International Management,* October 1975, pp. 18-22.

_____. "A Tale of Great Pluck," *International Management,* July 1981, pp. 26-7.

"Communications Among Nations," *IPRA Review,* August 1983, pp. 42-4.

Copeland, Lennie. "The Art of International Selling," *Business America,* vol. 7, June 25, 1984, pp. 2-8.

"Culture Among the Nations," *Commentary,* vol. 74, November 1982, pp. 42-9.

Douglis, Carole. "The Beat Goes On," *Psychology Today,* vol. 21, no. 11, November 1987, pp. 37-39, 42.

Dowling, Peter J., and Trevor W. Nagel. "Nationality and Work Attitudes: A Study of Australian and American Business Majors," *Journal of Management,* vol. 12, no. 1, 1986, pp. 121-8.

Drucker, Peter. "The Coming of the New Organization," *Harvard Business Review,* January-February 1988, pp. 45-53.

_____. "What We Can Learn from the Japanese," *Harvard Business Review,* March-April 1971, pp. 110-22.

Emmanuel, Myron. "Productivity Improvement—Japanese Style," *Communication and Management,* January-February 1981, pp. 1-4, reprint furnished by author.

Flack, Michael J. "Communicable and Uncommunicable Aspects in Personal International Relations," *Journal of Communication,* vol. 16, 1966, pp. 283-90.

Forrest, Anne B. "The Continental Divide; Coping with Cultural Gaps," *Communication World,* June 1988, pp. 20-2.

Graham, John L., and Roy A. Herberger. "Negotiators Abroad — Don't Shoot from the Hip," *Harvard Business Review,* July-August 1983, pp. 160-8.

Gurdon, Michael A. "The Emergence of Co-determination in Australian Government and Employment," *International Labour Review,* vol. 124, no. 4, July-August 1985, pp. 465-77.

Haneda, Saburo, and Hirosuke Shima. "Japanese Communication Behavior as Reflected in Letter Writing," *The Journal of Business Communication,* Winter 1982, pp. 19-39.

"Harvard's Definitive Word on Globalization Trends," *International Management,* April 1987, p. 64.

Hawkins, Steve. "How to Understand Your Partner's Cultural Baggage," *International Management,* September 1983, pp. 48-51.

Hill, Roy. "Coping with the Culture Shock of an Overseas Posting," *International Management,* March 1983, pp. 81-5.

_____. "Once a Frenchman Always a Frenchman," *International Management,* June 1980, pp. 45-6.

_____. "The Ripening of Latin American Management," *International Management,* July 1982, pp. 24-6.

Hofstede, Geert. "Editorial: The Usefulness of the Organizational Culture Concept," *Journal of International Studies,* vol. 23, no. 3, May 1986, pp. 253-7.

_____. "The Interaction Between National and Organizational Value Systems," *Journal of Management Studies,* vol. 22, no. 4, July 1985, pp. 347-57.

_____. "National Cultures in Four Dimensions," *International Studies of Management,* vol. XIII, no. 1-2, 1983, pp. 46-74.

Holmes, Geoffrey. "How UK Companies Report to Their Employees," *Accountancy,* vol. 88, November 1977, pp. 64-6.

Housel, Thomas J., and Warren E. Davis. "The Reduction of Upward Communication Distortion," *Journal of Business Communication,* Summer 1977, pp. 49-55.

"International Communication," *Business Marketing,* vol. 68, September 1985, p. 100.

"The International 500," *Fortune,* August 4, 1986, pp. 181-201.

"International Language of Gestures," *Psychology Today,* May 1984, pp. 64-70.

Inzerilli, Giorgio, and Andre Laurent. "Managerial Views of Organization Structure in France and the USA," *International Studies of Management and Organizations,* vol. XIII, no. 102, Spring-Summer 1983, pp. 97-118.

Johnson, Michael. "The Soaring Demand for Global Training," *International Management,* May 1987, pp. 44-5.

Kanawaty, George. "Training for a Changing World: Some General Reflections," *International Labour Review,* vol. 124, no. 4, July-August 1985, pp. 401-9.

Laflamme, Gilles, Laurent Belanger and Michael Audet. "Workers' Participation and Personnel Policies in Canada: Some Hopeful Signs," *International Labour Review,* vol. 126, no. 2, March-April 1987, pp. 219-27.

Laurent, Andre. "The Cross-Cultural Puzzle of International Human Resource Management," *Human Resource Management,* vol. 25, no. 1, Spring 1986, pp. 91-102.

_____. "The Cultural Diversity of Western Conceptions of Management," *International Studies of Management and Organization,* vol. XIII, no. 1-2, Spring-Summer 1983, pp. 75-96.

Lebas, Michel, and Jane Weigenstein. "Management Control: The Roles of Rules, Markets and Cultures," *Journal of Management Studies,* May 1986, pp. 259-71.

Levinson, Mark. "Yanqui Come Back," *Across the Board,* October 1986, pp. 22–9.

"Making Yourself Understood Abroad," *Nation's Business,* July 1985, p. 66.

"Managing in Two Worlds," *International Management,* July 1981, pp. 35–6.

"Many Cultures, One Family," *America,* vol. 145, October 31, 1981, pp. 261–4.

Moran, Robert T. "Cross-Cultural Contact: The Composite of Qualities That Make for the Best Interculturist," *International Management,* March 1985, p. 65.

_____. "Cross-Cultural Contact: Handling Two Swords at the Same Time," *International Management,* July 1986, p. 58.

"Multilinguistics in the Global Economy," *Vital Speeches of the Day,* vol. 49, March 15, 1983, pp. 332–5.

"A New Era for Management," *Business Week,* April 25, 1983, pp. 50–3.

Piper, Allan. "Trend-setting Companies Elevate PR to the Level of Strategic Weapon," *International Management,* June 1985, pp. 50–5.

Psacharopoulos, George, and Ana Maria Arriagada. "The Educational Composition of the Labor Force: An International Comparison," *International Labour Review,* vol. 125, no. 5, September-October 1986, pp. 561–74.

Ratiu, Indrei. "Thinking Internationally," *International Studies of Management and Organization,* vol. XIII, no. 1–2, Spring-Summer 1983, pp. 139–50.

Ray, Carol Axtell. "Corporate Culture: The Last Frontier of Control," *Journal of Management Studies,* vol. 23, no. 3, May 1986, pp. 287–97.

Reynolds, Beatrice K. "A Cross-Cultural Study of Values of Germans and Americans," *International Journal of Intercultural Relations,* vol. 8, no. 3, 1984, pp. 269–278.

Roos, Poul. "Workers' Participation and Personnel Policy in Denmark," *International Labour Review,* vol. 125, no. 6, November-December 1986, pp. 703–13.

"The Rush to Communicate," *International Management,* June 1981, p. 43.

Sirota, David, and J. Michael Greenwood. "Understanding Your Overseas Work Force," *Harvard Business Review,* January/February 1971, pp. 53–60.

Sparrow, Paul R., and Andrew M. Pettigrew. "Britain's Training Programs: The Search for a Strategic Human Resources Management Approach," *Human Resources Management,* vol. 26, no. 1, Spring 1987, pp. 109–27.

"Taking Time to Communicate," *International Management,* December 1976, pp. 35–7.

Templeman, John. "Hands Across Europe: Deals That Could Redraw the Map," *Business Week,* May 18, 1987, pp. 64–5.

Thompson, Michael, and Aaron Wildavsky. "A Cultural Theory of Information Bias in Organizations," *Journal of Management Studies,* vol. 23, no. 3, May 1986, pp. 173–85.

Tokman, Viktor E. "Adjustment and Employment in Latin America: The Current Challenges," *International Labour Review,* vol. 125, no. 5, September-October 1986, pp. 533–43.

"Towards Communication Between Different Civilizations," *IPRA Review,* vol. 8, May 1984, pp. 29–31.

Treu, Tiziano, and Serafino Negrelli. "Workers' Participation and Personnel Management Policies in Italy," *International Labour Review,* vol. 126, no. 1, January-February 1987, pp. 81–94.

Wright, Peter. "Doing Business in Islamic Markets," *Harvard Business Review,* January-February 1981, pp. 34, 36, 38.

# Newspapers

Alm, Richard. "India's Intellect Is Latest High-Tech Discovery," *Daily Record* (Morristown, NJ), January 31, 1988, p. D14.

Burgwyn, Diana. "Dr. Dr. Dr. Dr., May I Call You Freddie?" *The New York Times,* May 22, 1988, p. 43.

"Canadian Premiers Sign Quebec 'Into the Fold,'" *Star-Ledger* (Newark, NJ), June 4, 1987, p. 2.

Crossett, Barbara. "Western Influence Worries Singapore Chief," *The New York Times,* January 4, 1987, p. 16.

"Economic Diversification," Special Supplement on Malaysia, *The Daily News* (New York), May 26, 1987, pp. 2–3.

Farnsworth, Clyde H. "Can Nations Set Aside Their Parochialism in Time?" *The New York Times,* November 1, 1987, section 4, p. 1.

Flournoy, Katheryn. "Japanese Firms Adapting to America," *Daily Record* (Morristown, NJ), July 28, 1985, p. E1.

"Foreigners Give the U.S. Mixed Reviews," *Daily Record* (Morristown, NJ), September 8, 1985, p. A12.

"Ghandour Is Envisioning Cooperation in the Air," *The Wall Street Journal,* May 20, 1988, p. 7.

Greenhouse, Steven. "The Global March to Free Markets," *The New York Times,* July 19, 1987, section 3, pp. 1 and 12.

————. "Making Europe a Mighty Market," *The New York Times,* May 22, 1988, pp. 1 and 6.

Haberman, Clyde. "Some Japanese (One) Urge Plain Speaking," *The New York Times,* March 27, 1988, p. 27.

House, Karen Elliott. "Rising Islamic Fervor Challenges the West, Every Moslem Ruler," *The Wall Street Journal,* August 7, 1987, pp. 1 and 4.

Irwin, Don. "Places to Live, from Top to Bottom," *Daily Record* (Morristown, NJ), March 16, 1987, p. A6.

Jones, Terril. "South Korean Steelmaker Prospers," *Daily Record* (Morristown, NJ), June 7, 1987, p. C4.

Kagay, Michael R. "Workers Want Their Employers to Listen to Them, Survey Shows," *The New York Times,* June 14, 1988, p. A25.

Kirk, Don. "Pacific Rim: Our Land of Opportunity," *USA Today,* April 23, 1985, pp. 1 and 2.

Kleimen, Carol. "Thank God It's Friday! Uh . . . Make That Monday," *The Daily News* (New York, NY), January 18, 1987, p. 19.

Kristof, Nicholas D. "Australians Shift Their Sights to Asia," *The New York Times,* January 11, 1987, p. 17.

————. "Tokyo Tacos: The Japanese Look to the West," *The New York Times,* September 27, 1987, p. 23.

Kurylko, Diana. "U.S. Firms Urged to Sell Overseas," *Daily Record* (Morristown, NJ), November 13, 1987, p. A14.

Lauerman, Connie. "Most Americans Flunk Foreign Language Test," *San Diego Union,* November 5, 1981, p. C3.

Lohr, Steve. "The Best of Times in British Business," *The New York Times,* April 5, 1987, Section 3, p. 1.

————. "Japan Training Global Experts," *The New York Times,* June 28, 1983, pp. 31 and 36.

"Many in Japan Beginning to Worry About Country's Internationalization," *Star-Ledger* (Newark, NJ), December 26, 1986, p. 46.

Merrill, Martha C. "Complex Philippines: A Study in Contrasts," *Daily Record,* June 14, 1987, p. C5.

Moody, Sid. "The Unsung Heroes of New Zealand," *Daily Record* (Morristown, NJ), July 19, 1987, p. A4.

"Mozambique Most Bleak," *The Daily News* (New York, NY), March 16, 1987, p. 2.

"A New Economic Order Comes to Africa," *New York Times,* July 19, 1987, section 3, p. 12.

O'Boyle, Thomas F. "U.S. Workers' Loyalty to Companies Wanes as Disillusion Mounts," *The Wall Street Journal,* July 12, 1985, pp. 1 and 10.

Perlman, Lisa. "From Desks to Office Dynamics," *Daily Record* (Morristown, NJ), June 13, 1988, p. B6.

Perone, Joseph R. "German Trade Fair Welcomes U.S. Firms," *Star-Ledger* (Newark, NJ), September 13, 1987, pp. 5 and 7.

Perrett, Janine. "Survey Says Australian Workforce 'Difficult,'" July 23, 1986, material provided by Australian Embassy.

Prokesch, Steven. "Stopping the High-Tech Giveaway," *The New York Times,* March 22, 1987, Section 3, pp. 1 and 8.

"Rapprochement in Canada," *Star-Ledger* (Newark, NJ), May 26, 1987, p. 41.

Rast, Bob. "Rapid Growth Spurs Hong Kong Concerns," *Star-Ledger* (Newark, NJ), May 28, 1987, pp. 55 and 63.

_____. "Singapore Fears Being Caught in Middle of Curbs," *Star-Ledger* (Newark, NJ), May 29, 1987, p. 39.

_____. "Times Are Changing for Americans," *Sunday Star-Ledger* (Newark, NJ), February 21, 1988, pp. 5 and 8.

Redmont, Dennis. "Southern Stars Are Rising in European Constellation," *Daily Record* (Morristown, NJ), May 15, 1988, pp. D4–D5.

Rockefeller, David. "Let's Not Write Off Latin America," *The New York Times,* July 5, 1987, p. 15.

Rohter, Larry. "Central American Plight Is People in Abundance," *The New York Times,* September 6, 1987, pp. 1 and 14.

Rosenblum, Mort. "European Population in Decline," *Daily Record* (Morristown, NJ), February 8, 1987, p. A10.

Samuelson, Paul A. "The Failure of the 'Swedish Miracle': Toting Up the Victories — and Problems," *The New York Times,* May 18, 1988, p. A5.

Schrage, Michael, and David Vise. "Launching Era of Global Television," *Daily Record* (Morristown, NJ), September 21, 1986, Section E, pp. E1–E4.

Seabury, Jane. "East Asian Countries Pose Threat to U.S.," *Daily Record* (Morristown, NJ), September 29, 1985, p. D8.

Sewell, John W. "Help the Third World Catch Up," *The New York Times,* May 22, 1988, p. 3.

Sharp, Daniel A. "America Is Running Out of Time," *The New York Times,* February 7, 1988, p. 3.

"Shultz to Seek Stronger Ties in Black Africa," *The New York Times,* January 4, 1987, p. 3.

Sieff, Martin. "W. German Banks Help Soviets as Part of 'Drive to East' Policy," *The Washington Times* (Washington, D.C.), May 11, 1988, p. A9.

Soler, Jose Antonio Martinez. "Spain Is Learning to Cope with Democracy and Progress," *The New York Times,* August 16, 1987, p. 3.

"Study Suggests U.S. Businessmen Take Comprehensive Look at Asia," *Star-Ledger,* August 24, 1986, p. 11.

Trick, Darcy. "Why the Pacific Matters," *USA Today,* April 23, 1985, p. 14.

Weisman, Steven R. "India's Tentative Turnaround," *The New York Times,* May 29, 1988, pp. 1 and 11.

Wilby, Peter. "Hard Work? It's Just Not Cricket," *The Sunday Times* (London), May 19, 1985, p. 64.

# Miscellaneous

"About New Zealand," Ministry of Foreign Affairs, Wellington, New Zealand, 1982.

Annual Report, 1984. Standard Telephone and Cable, London, England.

Bertran, Josep, Director of Industrial Products and Investments, Embassy of Spain, New York, NY, Interview, January 22, 1987.

Boyle, W. Philip. "On the Analysis of Organizational Culture in Development Project Planning," Institute for Development Anthropology, Binghampton, NY, 1984.

Bratt, Christian. "Employee Involvement in Sweden," Swedish Employers' Confederation, 1987.

"Building Bridges of Understanding," Series of Language and Intercultural Research Center, Brigham Young University, Provo, UT: Brazil, Europe, Hong Kong, Japan, Korea, Latin America, the Philippines, Samoa, Spain, Thailand.

"A Business Guide to the Near East and North Africa," U.S. Department of Commerce, Washington, DC, 1981.

"Businessmen's Guide to Saudi Arabia," Ministry of Commerce, Riyadh, n.d.

"Communication and the City: the Changing Environment," East-West Center, Honolulu, HI, 1978.

"The Communication of Information," 1984 Annual Report, British Petroleum Corporation, London.

"Communication of Information and Consultation," *Employee Involvement Arrangements in BP Companies Operating in the UK,* British Petroleum Corporation.

"Cooperation Agreement," Danish Employers' Confederation and Danish Federation of Trade Unions, June 9, 1986.

Cooperative Agreement on Settlement and Reserve Systems Analysis, Series: "The African Family-Household: A Behavioral Model," Eileen Berry, 1985. "Development Assistance: Revived Hopes and Great Expectations in Africa," Simon M. Fass, 1983. "Household Dynamics and the Organization of Production in Central Tunisia," Muneera Salem-Murdock, 1986. "Intermediate Cities' Role in Industrial Decentralization, Employment Generation and Economic Development in South Korea," Dennis A. Rondinelli, 1983. "Making Planning More Effective in Developing Countries: Lessons from Potosi, Bolivia," Hugh Evans and Douglas Siglin, 1983. "Southern Perimeter Road, Lesotho, Social Analysis and Environmental Assessment," Lee C. Wilken, 1983. "Urbanization and Outmigration in Somalia," Herbert S. Lewis, Carol Kerven and Nancy Southerland, 1983.

"Culturegram" series. David M. Kennedy Center for International Studies, Brigham Young University, Provo, UT, 1986: Algeria, Australia, Austria,

Belgium, Bolivia, Brazil, Canada, Chile, Colombia, Costa Rica, Denmark, Ecuador, Egypt, El Salvador, England, Ethiopia, Fiji, Finland, France, Germany, Ghana, Greece, Guatemala, Honduras, Hong Kong, Iceland, India, Indonesia, Ireland, Israel, Italy, Japan, Jordan, Kenya, Korea, Lebanon, Lesotho, Luxembourg, Malaysia, the Netherlands, New Zealand, Nicaragua, Nigeria, Norway, Pakistan, Panama, Paraguay, Peru, the Philippines, Portugal, Puerto Rico, Samoa, Saudi Arabia, Scotland, Singapore, South Africa, Spain, Sri Lanka, Sudan, Sweden, Switzerland, Syria, Tahiti, Taiwan, Tanzania, Thailand, Tonga, Turkey, Uruguay, Venezuela, Wales, Zaire, Zimbabwe.

Dekker, D.W., President, N.V. Philips Gloeilampenfabrieken. "Changes of Course in a Multinational," Transcript of speech to the Society of Young Graduates at Hotel Cocagne, Eindhoven, December 6, 1984.

"Doing Business in France," Imprimerie Nationale, Paris, 1985.

"Doing Business in Japan," Japan External Trade Organization, Tokyo, 1982.

"The Economy," Department of Economic Research, Toronto Dominion Bank, Toronto, Ontario, Canada, vol. 10, no. 3, Summer 1987.

"Employment Effects of Multinational Enterprises," series of International Labour Office, Geneva, Switzerland: Belgium, Brazil, Germany, India, Ireland, Kenya, Liberia, Ghana, Nigeria, the Philippines, Sierra Leone.

Eric Reports, U.S. Department of Education, Washington, DC. "Communication Popular: the Language of Liberation," Robert A. White, 1980. "Education— Key to the People's Republic of China's Industrial Power," Lawrence L. Kavich, 1982. "Family Policy in Canada: Some Theoretical Considerations and Practical Applications," H. Philip Hepworth, 1979. "The Values Learned in School: Policy and Practice in Industrialized Countries," Judith Torez-Ports and John Schnible, 1982.

Fairbairn, Teo I.J., and Thomas T.G. Parry. "Multinational Enterprises in the Developing South Pacific Region," East-West Center, Honolulu, HI, 1986.

"Finland as a Trading Partner," Finnish Foreign Trade Association, Helsinki, 1983.

Gershenberg, Irving. "Multinational Enterprises, Transfer of Managerial Knowledge, Technology Choice and Employment Effects: A Case Study of Kenya," International Labour Office, 1983.

Hancock, Mary Alison. "The Electronics Industry in New Zealand," East-West Center, Honolulu, HI, 1980.

"Honduras Welcomes You?" Ministry of the Economy, Tegucigalpa, n.d.

Hong Kong and Shanghai Banking Corporation. "Business Profile Series": Bahrain, Hong Kong, India, Indonesia, Jordan, Oman, Negara Brunei and Darussalam, Mauritius, Qatar, Saudi Arabia, Singapore, Sri Lanka, Taiwan, Thailand.

Honikman, Karen. "Problems, Processes and Politics: A South African Research Project in Organizational Communication," paper presented at International Communication Association, Chicago, May 1986.

*Industrial Relations Manual,* ARC, a member of the Gold Fields Group, London.

Kamal, Mohamed. "Why Tar Arabs and Islam?" In "Al Urdun, A Jordanian Newsletter," Embassy of the Hashemite Kingdom of Jordan, January–February 1987.

Kato, Hidetoshi. "Popular Images of America," East-West Center, Honolulu, HI, 1977.

"Labor Relations in Africa: English-Speaking Countries," Labor-Management Relations in Public Enterprises in Africa, 1983.

Lall, Sanjaya. "Technological Change, Employment Generation and Multinationals: A Caste Story of a Foreign Firm and a Local Multinational in India," International Labour Office, Geneva, Switzerland, 1983.

Leonard, David K. "The Political Realities of African Management," Institute for Development Anthropology, Binghampton, NY, 1984.

Lerner, David, ed. "Asian Communication: Research, Training and Planning," East-West Center, Honolulu, HI, 1976.

_____, and Jim Richstad, eds. "Communication in the Pacific," East-West Center, Honolulu, HI, 1976.

Lim, Youngil. "Industrialization, Trade and Employment in South Korea," East-West Center, Honolulu, HI, 1974.

"Malaysia in Brief," External Information Division, Ministry of Foreign Affairs, Kuala Lumpur, 1985.

Mead, Margaret. "New Lives to Old: The Effects of New Communication on Old Cultures in the Pacific," East-West Center, Honolulu, HI, 1976.

Miller, Matt. "Pssssst . . . Have You Heard the Latest?" *General-ly Speaking,* GenCorp, Akron, OH, May 1984, p. 2.

Miller, Rodney G. "Effective Ways to Evaluate and Cut the Cost of Communication," transcript of paper presented to Society of Business Communicators, Australian National Conference, Hilton Hotel, Melbourne, March 24, 1987.

_____. "Leadership Strategies to Identify Opportunities for Developing High Performance Organizations," transcript of paper presented to Society of Business Communicators, Australian National Conference, Hilton Hotel, Melbourne, March 22, 1987.

Naya, Seiji. "The Roles of Small-Scale and Labor-Intensive Industries: Employment and Exports," East-West Center, Honolulu, HI, 1985.

Noel, Emile. "The European Community: How It Works," The European Perspective Series, Brussels, 1979.

"An Outline of the Akzo Organization," Akzo Corporation, Arnhem, The Netherlands, May 1985.

Rahim, Syed A. "Communication and Rural Development in Bangladesh," East-West Center, Honolulu, HI, 1976.

Richstad, Jim, ed. "New Perspectives in International Communication," East-West Center, Honolulu, HI, 1978.

_____, and Jackie Bower, eds. "International Communication Policy and Flow," East-West Center, Honolulu, HI, 1976.

"Running Out of Time," Proceedings, 74th American Assembly, Columbia University, November 19–22, 1987, Arden House, Hamilton, NY.

Scharp, Anders. "Being Top Dog Is Fun When Everyone Is Pulling in the Same Direction," *X Magazine,* AB Electrolux Corporation, Stockholm, Sweden, No. 3, 1986, pp. 11–2.

"Setting Up in Finland," Ministry of Trade and Forestry, Helsinki, 1980.

SRI Business Intelligence Program, Menlo Park, CA, "Doing Business" series: Arabian Peninsula, Germany, Great Britain, India, Indonesia, Japan, Korea, Scandinavia, Spain, Taiwan, United States.

"The Sword of Islam," Public Broadcasting System program, January 13, 1988, 10 p.m.

*Teknologi, ledelse og samarbejde,* Publication of Danish Employers Confederation, Copenhagen.

"The Tower of Business Babel," Janesville, WI: Parker Pen Company, n.d.

"The Trade Union Movement in the European Community," Trade Union Information, European Community, Brussels, 1982: France, Germany, Ireland, the Netherlands.

"Update" Series, Intercultural Press, Yarmouth, ME: Britain, Egypt, France, Germany, Hong Kong, Indonesia, Japan, Kuwait, Mexico, Saudi Arabia, South Korea, Taiwan, Venezuela.

Varner, Iris I. "A Comparison of American and French Business Communication," speech presented at the Association for Business Communication International Convention, Atlanta, GA, October 1981.

_____. "A Comparison of American and German Business Communication," speech presented at the Association for Business Communication, Salt Lake City, UT, 1986.

"Will There Always Be an England?" transcript, *Frontline,* PBS Television Program, June 10, 1986.

"Workers' Rights in Industry," Commission of the European Communities, Brussels, Belgium, May 1984.

# Index

## A

Aalborg Portland (Denmark) 131-3
advertising 9
Africa 7, 11, 18, 36, 112, 117, 125, 134, 149, 150, 162, 273-353, 430; economy 276-7; history 275; land 273; organizational communication 278-80; people 60, 71, 78, 87, 88, 89, 90, 91, 94, 98, 105, 106, 273-5
African Distillers Limited (Zimbabwe) 348-50
Agricultural Age 7
Air New Zealand 423
*Aktiengesellschaft* (AG) 185
Akzo Corporation (the Netherlands) 158-9
Algeria 280-8; economy 281-2; history 281; land 280-1; organizational communication 282; people 281
Alia—the Royal Jordanian Airline 255-6
de Alvarado, Pedro 81
*ambiente* 162
America *see* United States
American Hoechst 188
Angola 329-30; economy 330; history 330; land 329; people 329
Arabic *see* language, Arabic
Arabs *see* Middle East
*Arbeitsfrieden* 186
ARC (United Kingdom) 176
Argentina 14, 59, 60, 69, 70, 95-6, 97, 100, 107, 108, 111; economy 96; history 96; land 95; organizational communication 96; people 60, 95-6, 108
Argyris, Chris 24
artifacts *see* nonverbal communication
Aruba 86, 94
Asia 18, 117, 355-425; economy 356; history 355; land 355; people 36, 40, 60, 355

Association for Business Communication 5
Atlantic Gulf and Pacific Company of Manila (the Philippines) 385-6
attire *see* dress
*Aufsichstrat* 185
aural communication 242, 243
Australia 413-20, 430, 433, 434, 438, 440, 441; economy 414-5; history 414; land 413; organizational communication 415-7; people 413-4
*Australians and North Americans* (Renwick) 417
Austria 120, 184, 196-9, 433, 434, 438, 442; economy 197-8; history 197; land 196; organizational communication 198; people 123, 150, 196-7
Austria Tabak 198-9

## B

*baella figura* 152
Bahamas 60, 92-93
Bahrain 243-5; economy 245; history 245; land 244; people 244-5
Bangladesh 404-6; economy 405-6; history 405; land 404-5; people 405
Barbados 86-7, 110; economy 87; history 87; land 87; people 87
Barlow Rand Limited (South Africa) 337-41
Barnard, Chester 19-20
barriers *see* communication, barriers to; intercultural communication, barriers
Bedi, Hari 356
behavioral model of communication 20-1
behavioral sciences 20
Belgian Congo (Zaire) 125
Belgium 14, 73, 121, 123-7, 133, 153,

154, 155, 184; economy 125, 154;
history 124-5; land 123, 171;
organizational communication 125-6,
127; people 123-4, 125
Belize 62, 70, 77-78, 81; economy 78;
history 78; land 77-8; people 78
Bell Laboratories 20
Benin 301-3; economy 303; history
302; land 302; people 302
Benkert, Rolf 117
Berlo, David 41
Bermuda 92, 93
de Bermudez, Juan 93
Bertlesmann (Germany) 9
Bertran, Josep 167
*Besehlstimme* 191
*Betriebsrat* 186
*Betriebsverfassungsgesetz* 186
*Beyond Culture* (Hall) 30
Birdwhistell, Ray 28
BMW (West Germany) 193-4
Bolivar, Simon 96, 103, 105, 113
Bolivia 59, 95, 96-97, 100, 107, 108,
109, 434, 438, 440; economy 63, 97;
history 97; land 96-97; organizational
communication 97; people 97
Bonaire 86, 94
*Book of World Rankings* 211
Bordaberry, Juan M. 112
Botswana 330; economy 330; history
330; land 330; people 330
Brazil 59, 60, 69, 95, 97, 98-100, 103,
106, 107, 108, 109, 110, 111; economy
99; history 98; land 98; organiza-
tional communication 99-100; people
98, 108
*Briefsteller* 189
Britain *see* United Kingdom
British Aerospace 179
British Honduras 62, 77, 78; *see also*
Belize
British North American Act 50
British Petroleum 176
British Telecom 170
Broken Hill Proprietary Company
Limited (Australia) 418-9
Brown Boveri (Switzerland) 218
Burkina Faso 303-4; economy 303-4;
history 303; land 303; people 303
Burma 406-7; economy 407; history
406-7; land 406; people 406
Burmah Oil Trading Ltd. (United
Kingdom) 179-80
Burundi 314-5; economy 315; history
314-5; land 314; people 314
business: cards 42, 66, 68, 76, 114, 119,
125, 127, 131, 138, 140, 144, 147, 152,
154, 156, 160, 161, 166, 174, 191, 192,
198, 201, 203, 204, 207, 208, 212, 213,
217, 218, 239, 264, 268, 287, 337,
361, 362, 365, 371, 376, 382, 389,
394, 395, 400, 409, 413, 415, 417,
446, 447; dinner 174, 178, 212, 213,
362, 382; lunch 53, 76, 113, 127, 139,
140, 147, 152, 155, 157, 174, 178, 198,
201, 207, 208, 212, 213, 382, 413, 423;
management *see* management;
representatives *see* representatives,
local business; secrecy in *see* privacy
Business Council for International Understanding 10

## C

Cable Price Downer Limited (New
Zealand) 423-4
Cadbury Schweppes (United Kingdom)
177-9
Cameroon 315-6; economy 316; history
316; land 315-6; people 316
Canada 10, 35, 48-58, 98, 203, 429,
432, 433, 434, 438, 440, 442, 444,
446; economy 51-2; history 50-1;
land 9, 48-9, 50, 51, 53, 56; language
*see* language, English, Canadian;
organizational communication 52-3,
54; people 40, 49-50, 51, 52
Cap Gemini Sogeti (United Kingdom)
172
de Carbon, Philippe Bourcier 117
Caribbean islands 59, 60, 86-94
*caudillo* 65
Celanese Corporation (United States) 188
Cement-Roadstone Holdings PLC
(Ireland) 148-9
Central African Republic 316-7;
economy 317; history 317; land 317;
people 317
Central America 35, 59, 62, 63, 72, 73,
77-86, 163
Central American Common Market 81,
84
Central American Federation 62, 77,
79, 81, 82, 83, 84
Central-European countries 18
Centre for Communication Studies
(Australia) 416

Chad 282–3; economy 283; history 283; land 282–3; people 283
Chandler, Sir Geoffrey 169
Chase Manhattan Bank 63
Chile 14, 59, 60, 95, 97, 98, 109; economy 63, 101–2; history 101; land 100–1; people 101
China 98, 107, 159; people 16, 36, 79, 89, 90, 91, 94, 106, 109, 110
Churchill, Winston 174
Ciba-Geigy (Switzerland) 219–20
Cie Luxembourgeoise de Télédiffusion (Luxembourg) 9
collateral materials 120, 152, 191, 413
Colombia 59, 62, 68–9, 77, 85, 102–4, 109, 442; economy 103–4; history 103; land 103; organizational communication 104; people 103
Colombian Manufacturers' Association 69
*comite d'entreprise* 136, 137
communication 2, 5–33, 122–3, 130–1, 234, 243; barriers to 10, 33; conflict 25–6; conflict, types of: conflict, methods of control: alterations 26, avoidance 26, bargaining 26, cooperative problem solving 26, dominance 26, third-party methods 26; conflict, types of: group 25, interpersonal 25, intrapersonal 25, organizational 25; definition of 19; *see also* organizational communication; intercultural communication
Communication Centre, Queensland Institute of Technology 416–7
*Communications: A Strategic Service* 156–8
communist countries 3, 69, 73, 86
Communist Party 101
*compadrazgo* 61
computerization 7
Condellis, J.E., S.A. (Greece) 144–5
*confianza* 73
Congo 317–8; economy 318; history 318; land 318; people 318
consultation 122–3
contextual model of communication 21
contracts 191, 192–3
co-operation agreements (Denmark) 128–31
corporate communication *see* communication; organizational communication
*Corporate Communication for*

*Managers* (Jackson) 177
Costa Rica 59, 62, 77, 78–80, 83, 85; economy 79; history 79; land 79; organizational communication 79–80; people 79
Cristaleria Peldar (Colombia) 67, 69
"A Cross Cultural Study of Values of Germans and Americans" (Reynolds) 184
CSR Limited (Australia) 419–20
Cuba 36, 59, 86, 87, 89
culture 3, 5, 12–9, 31, 32, 39, 445; and organizations 16–7; business management practices influenced by: attitudes toward work and achievement 17, decision-making patterns 17; definition of 12; other areas affected by: attitudes, beliefs and behavior 15, dress and appearance 16, food and eating habits 16, interpersonal relationships 15, sense of self and space 16, thinking and learning 15, time consciousness 16, universals 12–3
Curacao 86, 94
customers 126

**D**

Daewoo Corporation (South Korea) 396–7
Dahomey 89
Dalle, Francois 136
Danish Employers' Confederation 130
Danish Federation of Trade Unions 130
decision-making 17, 18–9, 23–4, 42, 45, 64, 65, 67, 68, 73–4, 108, 113, 137, 160, 164, 165, 170, 171, 188, 206, 212, 233, 234, 243, 267–8
de Gaulle, Charles 121, 135
*deleguees du personnel* 136
Denmark 14, 35, 73, 121, 127–33, 184, 197, 432, 433, 434, 438; economy 14, 128–33; history 128; land 126–7; organizational communication 130–1; people 126, 127–8, 169, 184
*dignidad* 61, 114
Djibouti 283–4; economy 284; history 284; land 284; people 284
Dofasco, Inc. (Canada) 53–5
Dominican Republic 86, 87–8; economy 88; history 88; land 87; people 88
*Drang nach Osten* 188

dress 16, 53, 76, 114, 120, 138, 152, 160, 161, 165, 166, 167, 172, 191, 217, 229, 238, 242, 307, 312, 348, 385, 416
Drucker, Peter 46
Dutch *see* the Netherlands

**E**

East African Breweries, Inc. (Kenya) 323-5
economy, global 9, 12, 41
Ecuador 59, 62, 85, 98, 103, 104-5, 109; economy 105; history 105; land 104-5; people 105
EEC *see* European Economic Community
Egypt 284-7; economy 286-7; history 286; land 285; organizational communication 287; people 285-6
Electrolux (Sweden) 213-4
electronic media 8, 121
*El Pais* 164
El Salvador 59, 62, 77, 79, 80-1, 83; economy 81; history 81; land 80; people 80
*empleado* 64, 73, 165
*enchufado* 167
England *see* United Kingdom
English language *see* language, English
Equatorial Guinea 318-9; economy 319; history 319; land 319; people 319
Esso Italiano (Italy) 152
Ethiopia 304-5; economy 305; history 304-5; land 304; organizational communication 305; people 304
Europe *see* Western Europe
European Common Market *see* European Economic Community
European Council of Ministers 154
European Court of Justice 154
European Economic Community 117, 121-3, 125, 135, 147, 150, 154, 160, 164, 168, 171, 197, 430, 444
European Free Trade Association (EFTA) 197
European Investment Bank 154
European School of Management 171
Europeans *see* Western Europe
eye contact *see* oculesics; nonverbal communication, oculesics

**F**

Far East 10, 150
Far Eastern Levingston Shipbuilding Ltd. (Singapore) 389-90
fax machines 42
Fearnley and Eger (Norway) 207
*Fingerspitzengefuhl* 188
Finland 131, 200-3, 432, 433, 434, 436; economy 201; history 200-1; land 200; language *see* language, Finnish; organizational communication 201-2; people 200
Flemings *see* Belgium
*Fortune* magazine 47; Fortune 500 list 429; International 500 list 2, 47, 427
France 14, 18, 50, 51, 89, 106, 110, 120, 121, 123, 127, 133-41, 150, 155, 159, 161, 168, 184, 197, 433, 438, 442, 447; culture 49; economy 136-7: decision-making 137, industries 135, managers 14, organizational structure 136-7, quality circles 137, social legislation 137; history 135; land 133; language *see* language, French; organizational communication 137-9, 140; people 36, 49, 50, 51, 59, 71, 72, 88, 89, 91, 93, 94, 95, 101, 106, 123, 124, 126, 133-5, 150, 153, 171, 185; revolution 135
*France Soir* 136
Franco, Francisco 163
French Antilles 93-4
French Guiana 105-6, 110; economy 106; history 106; land 106; people 106
French National Institute for Demographic Studies 117
"Frontline" 169
H.B. Fuller Japan Company 10
*The Functions of the Executive* (Barnard) 19-20
*fung shui* 360

**G**

Gabon 319-20; economy 320; history 320; land 319-20; people 320
Gaitan, Jorge 103
The Gambia 287-8; economy 288; history 288; land 287; people 287-8
GEC (Britain) 9
*Gemutlichkeit* 196
General Motors Corporation (U.S.) 43, 451-5

Germany *see* West Germany
*der Geschaftsfuhrer* 186
*Gesellschaft mit beschränkter Haftung* (GmbH) 185
gestures *see* kinesics; nonverbal communication, kinesics
getting acquainted time (at start of meetings) *see* meetings
Ghana 305-7; economy 306-7; history 306; land 305-6; organizational communication 307; people 306
Gilbert, Sir Humphrey 50
Giscard d'Estaing, Valery 135
Gold Coast 89
Great Atlantic and Pacific Tea Company (United States) 188
Great Britain *see* United Kingdom
Greece 120, 121, 141-5, 435, 443; economy 143; history 142-3; land 141-2; organizational communication 143-4; people 142, 150, 161, 184
Guatemala 59, 62, 70, 77, 78, 80, 81-2, 83; economy 82; history 82; land 81, 82; people 81
Guinea 288-9; economy 289; history 289; land 288-9; people 289
Guinea-Bissau 289-90; economy 290; history 290; land 290; people 290
Guyana 106-7, 110; economy 107; history 107; land 106; people 106-7
*gwailos* 358

**H**

*habatsu* 375-6
Haiti 36, 86, 87, 88-9; economy 89; history 89; land 88; people 89
Hall, Edward 30, 40
handshakes 42, 53, 66, 68, 76, 81, 115, 119, 125-6, 127, 131, 138, 140, 147, 152, 155, 157, 160, 161, 166, 167, 172, 178, 190, 191, 198, 201, 203, 204, 212, 213, 217, 239, 241, 268, 278, 280, 287, 305, 365, 389, 394, 395, 409, 446, 447
*haragei* 373, 376
Harris, Philip R. 449
*Hauptversammlung* 185
Hegira (Arab) calendar 228, 229
*The Hidden Dimension* (Hall) 40
high-context culture, definition of 30; *see also* intercultural communication
Hoechst AG (West Germany) 186, 187

Hofstede, Geert 17-8, 39
Holland *see* the Netherlands
Honduras 59, 62, 77, 80, 81, 82-3; economy 63, 83; history 83; land 82-3; people 83
Hong Kong 9, 357-62; economy 360-1; history 359-60; land 357; organizational communication 361-2; people 357-9
*hora ingles* 76

**I**

Iberia 63, 159, 161
Iceland 117, 126, 159, 161, 203-4; economy 204; history 204; land 203-4; organizational communication 204; people 204
*im Auftrag* 189
Inco Ltd. (Canada) 55-6
India 14, 18, 73, 91, 107, 407-10; economy 408-9; history 408; land 407-8; organizational communication 409-10; people 408
*individualismo* 162
Indochina 36
Indonesia 363-5, 435, 436; economy 364-5; history 364; land 363; organizational communication 365; people 363-4
Industrial Age 6, 7
Industrial Revolution 135, 169
information 8, 9, 122-3, 130-1
Information Age 5-9, 10, 41, 46
INSEAD/CEDEP 136, 151
Institute for Research on Intercultural Cooperation 17
intercultural communication 5, 29-33; barriers: differences in perception 31, 33, ethnocentrism 31, 33, lack of empathy 31, 33, nonverbal systems 31, 32-3, verbal systems 31; context in message: high-context 30, 68, 127, 140, 144, 152, 161, 167, 242, 280, 362, 376, 395, 446, low-context 30, 127, 131, 147, 157, 178, 192, 198, 203, 208, 213, 446; use of time: monochronic (M-time) 30, 127, 131, 147, 157, 178, 192, 198, 203, 208, 213, 446, polychronic (P-time) 30, 68, 75, 140, 144, 152, 161, 167, 240, 242, 280, 362, 376, 395, 446

Intermediate Nuclear Forces (INF)
Treaty 188
*International Management* 10, 104, 151
International Monetary Fund 41
interpersonal communication 21, 75,
99, 114, 242
interpreters 160, 447
intrapersonal communication 21
*in Vollmacht* 189
Iran 246–7; economy 247; history 246;
land 246; organizational communication 247; people 246
Iraq 247–8; economy 248; history 248;
land 247–8; people 248
Ireland 121, 145–9, 169, 435, 443;
economy 146–9; history 146; land
145–6; organizational communication
147; people 36, 49, 101, 146
Israel 164, 248–52; economy 250–1;
history 249–50; land 248–9; organizational communication 251–2; people
249
Israel Aircraft Industries, Inc. 251–2
"The Italians: the Best Europeans?" 151
Italy 14, 16, 120, 121, 133, 149–53, 196,
197, 435, 439, 443; economy 14,
150–1; history 150; land 149–50;
language *see* language, Italian;
organizational communication 151–3;
people 60, 95, 96, 98, 101, 107, 142,
150, 184
Ivory Coast 307–8; economy 308;
history 308; land 307; people 307–8

**J**

Jackson, Peter 177
Jaguar (United Kingdom) 180–2
Jamaica 78, 86, 89–90; economy 90;
history 90; land 89; people 89–90
Japan 12, 15, 27, 32, 39, 40, 159,
369–79, 435, 436, 439, 441, 443, 444,
447; economy 369–71; history 369;
land 367; managers 14; organizational
communication 371–7; people 1, 2, 5,
10, 14, 36, 71, 98, 108, 109, 198,
367–9
joint industrial committees (Denmark)
128
Jordan 252–6; economy 254–6; history
253–4; land 252; people 253
*joss* 360

**K**

Kenya 11, 320–5; economy 322; history
322; land 320–1; organizational communication 322–3; people 321–2
kinesics, definition of 28; *see also*
nonverbal communication
*Kinesics and Context* (Birdwhistell) 28
*kokusaika* 376
Korea *see* South Korea
Krupp (West Germany) 186, 194–5
Kuwait 256–8; economy 257–8; history
257; land 256; organizational communication 258; people 256–7

**L**

*lakthaan* 404
language 5, 8, 10, 29, 31, 32, 174;
Afrikaans 337, Arabic 162, 237,
Dutch 89, 125, English 66, 120, 121,
124, 131, 152, 165, 166, 337, 395, 444,
447; English, versions of: American
52, 120, 121, 124, 173, British 10, 11,
31, 32, 52, 77, 89, 93, 121, 124, 173,
178, Canadian 52; Finnish 200,
French 49, 125, 153, German 101, 125,
153, Hungarian 200, Italian 101, 151,
Kurdish 238, Letzeburghesch 153,
Persian 238, Portuguese 98, Scandinavian 200, Spanish 32, 62, 66, 70,
77, 81, 82, 87, 89, 92, 98, 114, 165,
166, Turkish 237
La Pergola, Antonio 122
*la raza* 60, 71
Latin America 3, 7, 11, 18, 35, 40,
59–69, 70, 71, 73, 77, 79, 80, 81, 83,
85, 97, 98, 99, 101, 109, 111, 112, 113,
448, 449; economy 63–5; history
61–3; land 59; organizational communication 65–8, 75; people 59–61,
62, 79, 94, 114
Latin American Demographic Center 61
Latin Europeans 119, 120, 121, 134, 184
Laurent, Andre 136
leadership 234
Lebanon 258–9; economy 259; history
259; land 258–9; people 94, 259
Lesotho 331; economy 331; history 331;
land 331; people 331
letters 41, 44, 66, 96, 99, 114, 126, 127,
131, 138, 140, 151, 152, 154, 155, 157,
160, 161, 165, 167, 174, 189, 192, 212,

213, 217, 238, 268, 278, 280, 312, 365, 375, 409, 411
Letzeburghesch (language) *see* language, Letzeburghesch
Liberia 308–10; economy 309–10; history 309; land 308–9; people 309
Libya 290–2; economy 291–2; history 291; land 291; people 291
Liechtenstein 196, 205; economy 205; history 205; land 205; organizational communication 205; people 205
listening 213, 278, 280, 375
local business representatives *see* representatives
longevity 120, 190, 218
low-context culture, definition of 30; *see also* intercultural communication
Luchterhand, Heinz 171
*luuk nawng* 402
Luxembourg 121, 123, 133, 153–4, 184; economy 153–4; history 153; land 153; language *see* language, Letzeburghesch; organizational communication 154; people 153

**M**

*machismo* 61, 84
Malawi 331–2; economy 331–2; history 331; land 331; people 331
Malaysia 379–82; economy 380–2; history 380; land 379; organizational communication 382; people 380
Malaysian Airlines System (Malaysia) 381, 382
Mali 292–3; economy 293; history 292–3; land 292; people 292
Malmed, Gerald 147
management 17–8, 233, 234, 243, 278
managers 10, 12, 14, 73–4
*Managing Cultural Differences* (Harris and Moran) 449
*maquiladora* 72
Maslow, Abraham 13
*matamori* 376
*The Mathematical Theory of Communication* (Shannon and Weaver) 20
Mauritania 293–4; economy 294; history 294; land 293–4; people 294
Mazda Motor Corporation (Japan) 377–9
Mediterranean: countries 18, 121; people 133, 143, 159, 162

meetings 18, 42, 66, 76, 100, 110, 112, 113, 114–5, 118, 119, 126, 127, 131, 137–8, 144, 152, 155, 157, 160, 165–6, 172, 178, 189, 190, 191, 192, 198, 201, 203, 207, 208, 212, 238, 239, 240, 241, 242, 264, 268, 278, 287, 312, 322, 361, 365, 373, 382, 385, 394, 395, 404, 411, 413, 423, 447; getting acquainted time (at start of meeting) 42, 66, 68, 76, 114–5, 119, 127, 137, 138, 140, 152, 166, 167, 172, 178, 190, 212, 213, 241, 268, 278, 287, 361, 385, 447
*meishi* 371
memos 114
Mexico 35, 59, 62, 71, 72, 77, 81, 82, 83; economy 72–4; history 71–2; land 59, 62, 69–70, 72; organizational communication 74–7; people 70–1
Middle East 3, 94, 117, 225–72, 448, 449; economy 232–7; history 231–2; land 225; organizational communication 237–43; people 27, 32, 36, 40, 42, 72, 101, 162, 164, 166, 225–31
Miller, Rodney G. 416
*Mitbestimmungsrecht* 186
MIT Commission on Industrial Productivity 41
Mitsubishi Company (Japan) 1
Mitterrand, Francois 135
Miyoshi, Yo 10, 12
Molson, John 56
Molson Companies, Ltd. (Canada) 56–8
monochronic time (M-time), definition of 30; *see also* intercultural communication
Moran, Robert T. 10–1, 449
Morocco 162, 164, 294–5; economy 295; history 295; land 294–5; people 295
motivation 212, 234
Mozambique 332–3; economy 333; history 332–3; land 332; organizational communication 333; people 332
Mulroney, Brian 51

**N**

names 66, 76, 80, 119, 126, 131, 160, 165, 167, 174, 178, 192, 201, 203, 204, 207, 208, 217, 268, 278, 280, 394, 395, 415, 417

*nameste* 409-10
Namibia 333-4; economy 334; history 334; land 333; people 333
NATO *see* North Atlantic Treaty Organization
*The Nature of Human Values* (Rokeach) 12
negotiating 126, 156, 166, 174, 191
*nemawashii* 373, 376
Nestle Group (Switzerland) 220-1
the Netherlands 17, 94, 110, 111, 121, 123, 124, 154-9, 184, 433, 435, 437, 439, 441, 443; economy 155; history 155; land 154; language *see* language, Dutch; organizational communication 155-8; people 36, 49, 59, 79, 91, 94, 95, 107, 110, 121, 123, 124, 154-5
New Jersey Bell Telephone Company 19
New Zealand 421-4, 435, 437, 439, 443; economy 421-3; history 421; land 421; organizational communication 423; people 421
Nicaragua 3, 59, 62, 77, 79, 83-4; economy 84; history 84; land 83-4; people 84
Nieswandt, Ferdinand 186
Niger 295-6; economy 296; history 296; land 295-6; people 296
Nigeria 12, 310-2; economy 311; history 310-1; land 310; organizational communication 311-2; people 310
Nixon, Richard 373
nonverbal communication 26-9, 32-3, 67, 68, 76-7, 100, 108, 155, 160, 269, 449; artifacts 28-9; definition of 26; kinesics 28, 53, 67, 76-7, 80, 82, 96, 97, 100, 108, 121, 138-9, 140, 143-4, 155-6, 160, 161, 166, 167, 191, 212, 213, 264, 269, 278, 279, 282, 311, 361, 362, 365, 395, 415; oculesics 28, 42, 80, 82, 96, 97, 100, 131, 138, 140, 155, 201, 213, 239, 241, 258, 415, 417; paralanguage 28; physical characteristics 28; proxemics 27, 66, 68, 80, 114, 121, 139, 140, 172, 178, 239, 242, 311, 312
Norsk Data (Norway) 208-10
Norske Shell AS (Norway) 207
North America 35-58, 62, 65, 77, 80, 85, 94, 128, 446; people 60, 67, 71, 75, 76, 82, 114
North American Aerospace Defense Command (NORAD) 51
North Atlantic Treaty Organization (NATO) 125, 185
North Yemen *see* Yemen Arab Republic
Northern Ireland 145, 146, 168
Norway 14, 73, 121, 126, 197, 203, 205-10, 433, 435; economy 206-7; history 206; land 205-6; organizational communication 207-8; people 206
Norwegian Centre for Organizational Learning 207-8
Norwegian Shipowners' Association 207-8

# O

*obrero* 64, 73, 165
oculesics, definition of 28; *see also* nonverbal communication
Oman 259-61; economy 260-1; history 260; land 260; people 260
oral presentations 120, 242, 243, 373
*Ordnung* 191
organizational communication 23-5, 41-7, 52-3, 65-8, 74-7, 79-80, 96, 97, 99-100, 104, 108, 112, 114-5, 118-21, 125-6, 127, 130-1, 137-9, 140, 143-4, 147, 151-3, 154, 155-8, 160-1, 165-8, 171-7, 188-93, 198, 201-2, 204, 205, 207-8, 212-3, 217-8, 237-43, 247, 251-2, 258, 264, 265, 266-7, 278-80, 282, 287, 305, 307, 311-2, 322-3, 327-8, 329, 333, 337, 348, 361-2, 365, 371-7, 382, 385, 389, 394-5, 400, 403-4, 409-10, 411-2, 413, 415-7, 423, 445-50; bypassing 64-5, 66, 75; channels 3, 44-6, 65, 430, 432-6, 446; formal system 3, 42-6, 47, 53, 54, 68, 74, 127, 132, 141, 145, 148, 158, 175, 178, 193, 199, 430; informal system 42, 46-7, 167, 375-6; open 25, 44, 74, 208; policy 43, 44, 152, 174, 178, 215-6, 427, 428, 451-5; survey of employee attitudes 375; variations: corporate climate 25, decision-making 23-4, management style 24, structure 23
organizations 5, 16, 136-7, 234, 243; definition of 5
Oy Wilh. Schauman Ab (Finland) 201-2

# P

Pacific region 413–24
Pacific-rim countries 357–413, 430
Pakistan 410–1; economy 411; history
411; land 410; organizational communication 411–2; people 410–1
Panama 35, 59, 62, 77, 79, 84–6, 103;
economy 85; history 85; land 77, 85,
103; people 85
Paraguay 59, 95, 97, 107–8; economy
108; history 108; land 107; organizational communication 108; people
107–8
paralanguage *see* nonverbal communication
Paribas (France) 137
*patron* system 65
*pen rabiab* 402
People's Democratic Republic of
Yemen (South Yemen) 271–2;
economy 272; history 272; land
271–2; people 272
Peron, Juan 96
*personalismo* 60, 114
Pertamina (Indonesia) 365–7
Peru 59, 100, 104, 108–10; economy
109–10; history 109; land 109; people
109
the Philippines 382–5, 439, 441;
economy 384–5; history 383–4; land
382–3; organizational communication
385; people 383
Philips International B.V. (the
Netherlands) 9, 156–8
physical characteristics *see* nonverbal
communication
Pinochet, Agusto 101
Plaza, Galo 104
Pollos Vencedor, Ltd. (Colombia) 104
polychronic time (P-time), definition of
30; *see also* intercultural communication
Pompidou, Georges 135
Portugal 1, 60, 98, 107, 120, 121,
159–61, 197; economy 160; history
159–60; land 159; language *see*
language, Portuguese; organizational
communication 160–1; people 36, 59,
95, 98, 111, 159
*pralaad* 402
privacy in business 172, 190, 192, 212,
230, 305
Procordia (Sweden) 215

proposals 120, 143, 172, 238, 361, 382
*pro procura* (ppa) 189
proxemics, definition of 27; *see also*
nonverbal communication
Puerto Rico 11, 35, 59, 66, 86, 87,
91–2, 94
punctuality 42, 76, 79–80, 82, 96, 100,
110, 112, 118, 126, 127, 131, 138, 140,
147, 152, 155, 157, 160, 165, 189, 192,
198, 201, 203, 204, 207, 208, 212, 213,
217, 268, 311, 323, 337, 361, 362, 382,
385, 389, 394, 395, 409, 415, 417, 423
Puritan work ethic 38

# Q

Qatar 261–2; economy 261–2; history
261; land 261; people 261
quality circles (France) 137, 140

# R

Rabak (Turkey) 269
Rank Xerox (United Kingdom) 182–3
Renault (France) 139–41
Renwick, George 417
reports 42, 120
representatives, local business 76, 165,
167, 238, 394, 395, 400, 404, 446
Republic of Gran Colombia 62, 85,
103, 105, 113
Restreto V., Gilberto E. 69
Reynolds, Beatrice K. 184
*ringi* 372, 376
Rio Tinto Zimbabwe Limited
(Zimbabwe) 350–2
Rockefeller, David 63
Rokeach, Milton 12
Royal Bank of Canada 40
Russia *see* Soviet Union
*ruu cai* 402
*ruu nisai* 403
Rwanda 325–6; economy 326; history
325–6; land 325; people 325

# S

Saba 86, 94
Saint-Gobain (France) 137
St. Maarten 86, 94
St. Martin 93, 94

Salazar, Dr. Antonio de Oliveira 159
Samuelson, Paul 211
*Sapphire* magazine 147
*Saraban* 403-4
Sasol Limited (South Africa) 342-3
Sato, Eisaku 373
Saudi Arabia 262-4; economy 263-4;
    history 263; land 262; organizational
    communication 264; people 262-3
sauna, doing business in the 200-1,
    203
*sayan* 358
Scandinavian: countries 14, 36, 117,
    127, 131; languages *see* language,
    Scandinavian; people 121, 127, 184
Scotland 145, 168; people 174
Senegal 89, 297; economy 297; history
    297; land 297; people 297
SGS (Italy) 9
shaking hands *see* handshakes
Shannon, Claude 20
Shannon-Weaver Model of Communi-
    cation 20
Shaw, George Bernard 174
Siemans (West Germany) 188
Sierra Leone 312-3; economy 312-3;
    history 312; land 312; people 312
siesta 113, 143, 162
Silva, Anabal Cavaco 122, 160
Singapore 387-9, 432, 435; economy
    388-9; history 388; land 387;
    organizational communication 389;
    people 387-8
Singapore Airlines 390-2
socialist countries 3
Societe Generale 137
Soler, Jose Antonio Martinez 164
Somalia 298-9; economy 298-9; history
    298; land 298; people 298
Somoza, Anastasio 84
Sony Corporation (Japan) 17
South Africa 334-43, 432, 435-6, 437,
    439; economy 336-7; history 335-6;
    land 334; organizational communica-
    tion 337; people 334-5
South America 59, 60, 85, 90, 94-115,
    155, 163; people 40
South Korea 73, 159, 392-7, 447;
    economy 393-4; history 393; land
    392; organizational communication
    394-5; people 36, 392-3
South Yemen *see* People's Democratic
    Republic of Yemen
Soviet Information Service 9

Soviet Union 7, 9, 48, 98, 117, 133,
    197, 200, 201
space, use of *see* proxemics; nonverbal
    communication, proxemics
Spain 1, 14, 33, 59, 60, 61, 62, 71, 72,
    73, 77, 79, 81, 83, 84, 88, 89, 90, 91,
    92, 94, 96, 97, 105, 108, 109, 113, 120,
    121, 124, 133, 151, 155, 159, 161-8;
    economy 164-5; history 163-4; land
    161-2; language *see* language,
    Spanish; organizational communica-
    tion 165-8; people 36, 71, 72, 79, 80,
    81, 83, 84, 85, 86, 88, 91, 92, 94, 95,
    97, 101, 103, 105, 108, 109, 112, 123,
    150, 162-3, 165
Spanish America 62, 103
speech 36, 52, 76
Sri Lanka 412-3; economy 412-3;
    history 412; land 412; organizational
    communication 413; people 412
Standard Telephone and Cable (United
    Kingdom) 176
stationery 120
*Statistical Abstracts of the United
    States* 41
Steelcase, Inc. (U.S.) 27
Stroessner, General Alfredo 108
de Sucre, General Antonio Jose 109
Sudan 89, 299-300; economy 300;
    history 300; land 299; people 299-300
Suriname 59, 95, 106, 110-1, 155;
    economy 110-1; history 110; land 110;
    people 110
survey 47-8, 427-44
Swaziland 343-4; economy 344; history
    344; land 343; people 343
Sweden 14, 73, 131, 197, 210-6, 432,
    433, 436, 437, 439-40, 441, 443, 444,
    449; economy 211-2; history 211; land
    210; organizational communication
    212-3; people 36, 210-1
Switzerland 133, 161, 184, 196, 216-21,
    432, 433, 436, 437, 440, 441, 443,
    444; economy 217; history 217; land
    216; organizational communication
    217-8; people 79, 216-7
Syria 264-6; economy 265-6; history
    265; land 264-5; organizational com-
    munication 265; people 265

## T

Taiwan 397-400; economy 398-400;

history 398; land 397; organizational communication 400; people 397–8
Tanzania 326–8; economy 327; history 327; land 326–7; organizational communication 327–8; people 327
teleconferencing 121
telegraphic communication 126
telephone 8, 42, 44, 52–3, 66, 67, 69, 75, 99, 114, 118, 126, 127, 138, 140, 189, 192, 212, 213, 238, 264, 278, 280, 287, 312, 362
telex 66, 127, 155, 157, 189, 192, 212, 213, 238, 409, 411
Tel-Plus Communication (United States) 188
Tengelman Group (West Germany) 188
Thailand 400–4; economy 401–3; history 401; land 400–1; organizational communication 403–4; people 401
Thomson (France) 9
time, use of 42, 75, 76, 80, 100, 110, 112, 113, 118–9, 127, 138, 160, 161, 165, 166, 167, 198, 230, 278, 280, 287, 361, 365, 423
titles 119, 120, 154, 155, 198
Togo 313–4; economy 313–4; history 313; land 313; people 313
touching 67, 68, 156, 157, 167, 172, 178, 203, 239, 242; *abrazo* 66, 76
Trinidad and Tobago 86, 90–1; economy 91; history 91; land 90–1; people 91
Trudeau, Pierre 50
Trujillo 88
Tunisia 300–1; economy 301; history 301; land 300–1; people 301
Turkey 117, 141, 143, 266–9; economy 267–8; history 267; land 266; organizational communication 268–9; people 142, 184, 197, 266–7

**U**

Uganda 328–9; economy 328–9; history 328; land 328; organizational communication 329; people 328
Unilever (United Kingdom) 183
United Arab Emirates 269–70; economy 270; history 270; land 269; people 270
United Kingdom 7, 14, 18, 30, 50, 51, 52, 90, 91, 96, 107, 110, 119, 121, 123, 124, 125, 128, 135, 145, 146, 151, 163, 168–77, 197, 432, 433, 434, 435, 438, 439, 441, 442, 444; economy 170–2; history 87, 91, 146, 169, 170; land 168, 169; language *see* language, English, British; organizational communication 171–77; people 12, 36, 49, 50, 51, 52, 62, 71, 78, 86, 87, 89, 90, 91, 92, 93, 94, 96, 101, 107, 110, 120, 128, 135, 169
United States 10, 14, 30, 32, 35–47, 49, 50, 51, 59, 60, 69, 70, 71, 72, 77, 82, 85, 86, 88, 90, 91, 92, 95, 98, 99, 103, 111, 119, 122, 124, 128, 197, 446; economy 9, 12, 14, 32, 40, 42, 46, 47, 51, 63, 125; history 51, 92, 128; land 35–6, 48, 91–2; language *see* language, English, American; organizational communication 41–7; people 1, 2, 10, 11, 16, 27, 31, 32, 33, 36–40, 52, 63, 70, 76, 118, 126, 184, 200
United States Bureau of Labor Statistics 39
Uruguay 59, 60, 95, 108, 111–2; economy 63, 112; history 111–2; land 111; organizational communication 112; people 111
U.S.S.R. *see* Soviet Union

**V**

Valmet (Finland) 201
Venezuela 59, 62, 85, 86, 90, 94, 103, 106, 112–5; economy 63, 113–4; history 113; land 112; organizational communication 114–5; people 112
VIAG (West Germany) 195–6
videotape 69
Vietnamese 36
Virgin Islands (American) 35, 86, 92
Virgin Islands (British) 86, 93
"!Viva yo!" 162
voice control 191
*Vorstrand* 185

**W**

Wales 146, 168, 169; people 174
Walloons *see* Belgium
wardrobe *see* dress
Waterford Glass Group PLC (Ireland) 149, 444

*Waterford, An Irish Art* 444
Weaver, Warren 20
West Germany 14, 16, 18, 27, 36, 49, 71, 79, 96, 121, 123, 127, 133, 135, 153, 154, 184–96, 432, 436, 440, 441, 443, 444; economy 14, 185–8; history 185; land 184; language *see* language, German; organizational communication 188–93; people 60, 98, 101, 107, 119, 120, 121, 123, 153, 169, 171, 184, 197
Western Europe 2, 7, 9, 10, 14, 16, 30, 52, 62, 76, 90, 95, 96, 111, 117–23, 446, 449; economy 118; history 118; land 117; organizational communication 118–21; people 60, 70, 71, 72, 78, 82, 84, 88, 91, 92, 97, 98, 99, 101, 106, 110, 111, 112, 117, 120
Western Hemisphere 59, 77, 80, 87, 88, 91, 93, 96, 112
Whorf, Benjamin L. 31
Wilkie & Paul, Ltd. (United Kingdom) 174
"Will There Always Be an England?" 169
"Workers' Rights in Industry" (EEC) 122–3
Wrigglesworth, Ian 170

**Y**

Yemen Arab Republic (North Yemen) 270–1; economy 271; history 271; land 270–1; people 271
Yugoslavia 101, 141, 196, 197; people 184

**Z**

Zahnradfabrik Friedrichshafen (West Germany) 190
Zaire 125, 344–5; economy 345–6; history 345; land 344–5; people 345
Zambia 171, 346–7; economy 347; history 346–7; land 346; people 346
Zimbabwe 347–8, 433, 436, 440, 444; economy 348; history 347–8; land 347; organizational communication 348; people 347
Zimbabwe Alloys Limited (Zimbabwe) 352–3